Sexuality in Premodern Europe

Sexuality in Premodern Europe

A Social and Cultural History from Antiquity to the Early Modern Age

Franz X. Eder

Translation: Jacob Watson

BLOOMSBURY ACADEMIC
LONDON • NEW YORK • OXFORD • NEW DELHI • SYDNEY

BLOOMSBURY ACADEMIC
Bloomsbury Publishing Plc
50 Bedford Square, London, WC1B 3DP, UK
1385 Broadway, New York, NY 10018, USA
29 Earlsfort Terrace, Dublin 2, Ireland

BLOOMSBURY, BLOOMSBURY ACADEMIC and the Diana logo are trademarks of Bloomsbury Publishing Plc

First published in Great Britain 2023

Copyright © Franz X. Eder, 2023

Franz X. Eder has asserted his right under the Copyright, Designs and Patents Act, 1988, to be identified as Author of this work.

Cover image: The Monk Sleeps With The Wife While The Husband Is Praying © Heritage Images / Getty S Capital Letter © bauhaus1000/istock

Bloomsbury Publishing Plc does not have any control over, or responsibility for, any third-party websites referred to or in this book. All internet addresses given in this book were correct at the time of going to press. The author and publisher regret any inconvenience caused if addresses have changed or sites have ceased to exist, but can accept no responsibility for any such changes.

Every effort has been made to trace the copyright holders and obtain permission to reproduce the copyright material. Please do get in touch with any enquiries or any information relating to such material or the rights holder. We would be pleased to rectify any omissions in subsequent editions of this publication should they be drawn to our attention.

A catalogue record for this book is available from the British Library.

A catalog record for this book is available from the Library of Congress.

ISBN: HB: 978-1-3503-4106-7
PB: 978-1-3503-4105-0
ePDF: 978-1-3503-4107-4
eBook: 978-1-3503-4108-1

Typeset by Deanta Global Publishing Services, Chennai, India

To find out more about our authors and books visit www.bloomsbury.com and sign up for our newsletters.

This book is dedicated to Erika and Anna-Lena

CONTENTS

List of Illustrations viii
Preface x

1 Introduction: Historical Research into Sexuality 1

2 Reign of the Phallus—Greek Antiquity 19

3 *Infamia* and *Pudicitia*—Roman Antiquity 61

4 How the Evil Thorn Pierced the Flesh—Judaism and Early Christianity 105

5 Contradictory Sexual Worlds in the Middle Ages 145

6 Reformation and Social Discipline— Fifteenth to Seventeenth Century 269

7 Coda 405

Bibliography 407
Index 507

ILLUSTRATIONS

1 Dionysus and Eros, second century CE 20

2 Zeus abducting Ganymede, Attic kylix, *c.* 470 BCE 30

3 Satyr and maenad, *Terracotta stamnos* (jar) red-figure, *c.* 350 BCE 40

4 Rites of initiation of a bride into the cult of Dionysus. Wall painting from Villa of the Mysteries, Pompeii, first century AD 62

5 Fresco from the Lupanar brothel in Pompeji, first century AD 90

6 Warren Cup, British Museum 102

7 Kissing couple on kline, terracotta, first century AD 118

8 Aphrodite Anadyomene (rising), marble statuette, first century AD 139

9 Walther von der Vogelweide (*c.* 1170–*c.* 1230). Illustration from the Codex Manesse, *c.* 1300 173

10 The Cosmic Spheres and Human Being, *c.* 1220–1230. Illustration from Hildegard von Bingen (*c.* 1098–1179), Liber Divinorum Operum 176

11 Bathhouse and brothel. Miniature from the French translation of Valerius Maximus "Faits et dits mémorables" (Memorable Facts and Sayings), fifteenth century 222

12 *Sheela-na-gig* figure at the Kilpeck church, Herefordshire, UK 239

13 The monk sleeps with the wife while the husband is praying. Miniature from the French translation of Giovanni Boccaccio, Decameron, *c.* 1450s 247

14 Artist follower of Albrecht Dürer, Women's Bath, *c.* 1505/1510 274

15 Title and woodcut of the *Constitutio Criminalis Carolina*, 1532 311

16 Albrecht Dürer (1471–1528), The Whore of Babylon, woodcut, *c.* 1497   332

17 Urs Graf (*c.* 1485–1528), Two mercenary soldiers, a prostitute and death, woodcut, 1524   346

18 Sandro Botticelli (1445–1510), Venus pudica, *c.* 1490   363

19 Jan van Eyck (*c.* 1390–1441), The Arnolfini wedding, 1434   365

20 Marcantonio Raimondi (*c.* 1475–*c.* 1534) engraving to Pietro Aretino's (1492–1556) Sonetti lussuriosi (I modi), 1524   370

21 Hans Baldung Grien (1484–1485), The witches' Sabbath, woodcut, 1510   372

PREFACE

Sexuality in our lives presents an itch, a rubbing sensation, a constant irritation. On the one hand, we are convinced the desire we feel is individual, our own sexual wants anchored in the depths of our bodies as genes and hormones and in the basic structures of our psyche. There is hardly anything we feel to be as real and to come from within as the sexual desire that involuntarily seizes us, makes us lust physically; and in our excitement and orgasm we experience two of the most intense feelings we are capable of. The absence of desire and aversion to certain sexual practices are also part of this authentic experience. And yet, we also know from our own intimacy with it that sexual desire can change in intensity, orientation, and object(ive) over the course of one's life. In terms of cultural and social history as well as over longer periods of time, sexuality proves to be a true chimera. People's sexual desire in earlier centuries, which persons or objects they lusted after, what practices they found to be natural, abnormal, or abhorrent and immoral in their sexual life, which behaviors they preferred, how they thought and spoke about the sexual, how they affixed it in images and regulated it with norms and controlled it with institutions—all these forms of sexual culture have changed dramatically over time.

However, even representatives of radical social constructivism will have to admit that it is not only the cultural, social, and political framework conditions that create and shape sexuality as an individual and social practice, as a desire and an emotion. The sexual comes from a force deep within, inherent to humankind—notwithstanding its different forms and manifestations—and which is perceived as pleasure or urge. How determinant this energy is, how it shapes our hetero-, homo-, bi-, trans-, etc., sexual orientation, how it manifests itself in the strength of our desire, how it defines our preferred objects of desire, and how it influences our sexual fantasies and appetites is as hidden in darkness as it has ever been. We have come no further in this respect than Sigmund Freud, who said: "Instincts are mythical entities, magnificent in their indefiniteness. In our work we cannot for a moment disregard them, yet we are never sure that we are seeing them clearly" (Freud 1964: 95).

Considering this mythically indefinable sexuality, this volume takes on the task of tracing the history of sexuality in Europe from a cultural and social perspective, from antiquity to the early modern era, while also taking into account the background economic and political conditions. This is based on the extreme proliferation of historical scientific literature in recent decades, in full recognition of the various controversial discussions and opinions that have arisen.

Many colleagues have enriched and influenced my work through discussions and debates at conferences, meetings, and workshops. Sven Tost, Christina Lutter, Andrea Pühringer, and Holger Th. Gräf have read and commented on individual parts of the manuscript, and the latter two have also edited much of the German version on which this translation is based. Jacob Watson translated it into English. I would like to thank them all very much for their suggestions and great help.

Compared to the first German-language publication of this volume under the title *Eros, Wollust, Sünde: Sexualität in Europa von der Antike bis in die Frühe Neuzeit* (*Eros, Lust, Sin: Sexuality in Europe from Antiquity to the Early Modern Period*, 2018), the content and literature have been updated for this English-language edition.

1

Introduction

Historical Research into Sexuality

Each of us, sliced in two like a flat fish, is but the half of a human—from one, two. And each is always looking for his other half. Now men who are a section of that double nature that was once called androgynous are lovers of women; adulterers are generally of this breed, and also adulterous women who lust after men. Women who are a section of the woman do not care for men, but are more inclined toward women: lesbians spring from this type. Finally, those are a section of the male pursue the male, and while they are young, being slices of the original man, they love men . . . When they reach manhood they are lovers of youth, and are not naturally inclined to marry or beget children. (Plato 2001: 231, 191d–2b)

> Call it not love, for love to heaven is fled,
> Since sweating lust on earth usurped his name;
> Under whose simple semblance he hath fed
> Upon fresh beauty, blotting it with blame;
> Which the hot tyrant stains, and soon bereaves,
> As caterpillars do the tender leaves.
>
> Love comforteth like sunshine after rain;
> But lust's effect is tempest after sun.
> Love's gentle spring doth always fresh remain;
> Lust's winter comes ere summer half be done.
> Love surfeits not; lust like a glutton dies.
> Love is all truth, lust full of forged lies.
>
> (Shakespeare 2005: 232, 793–804)

Plato and Shakespeare expressed poetically—one in the *Symposium* (380 BCE), the other in *Adonis and Venus* (1593)—what simultaneously fascinated and frightened people of earlier epochs about sexuality. As with the Plato citation, which he attributes to Aristophanes, they perceived the sexual as a force that drove people to reunite with their other halves so as to be with the desired person over time and to bring children into the world together. In doing so, they also fulfilled the social demands of marriage and wove the social fabric ever tighter. For others, it was primarily about the physical realization of desire and the pleasure of union—both in shifting constellations. According to Plato, Eros strived for another, higher goal—an aesthetic and ethical lifestyle (Soble 2009: 107ff.; Renaut 2017).

Shakespeare swapped the traditional gender roles and let Venus appear as a desiring lover and Adonis as the non-reciprocating object of desire. In the young man's death, however, the goddess—and thus also the reader—finds no fulfilment (Trapp 2003: 54ff.). The English playwright also made it clear that sexual contacts were often about power and impotence not only between the sexes and among members of the same sex, but also between social groups or, as we have here, between humans and gods (Hunter 2018). By juxtaposing love and lust—one tending toward moderation and truth, the other leading to insatiability and lies—he also pointed to the dark sides of the sexual. Without the influence of laws, norms, and discipline, marriage and family would be destroyed and the social and political order undermined.

Even more so than with other emotions, the people of earlier centuries also felt that they were not always "master of their own house" (Freud 1940–1955: 11) in view of sexual desire—be it because lust prevailed against rational thinking and free will, sexual escapades shattered the community, or the indomitable sexual urge even threatened the relationship with God or the gods. When poets, theologians, and philosophers thought about human sexuality, they encountered existential questions of life and death and its overcoming through reproduction. They encountered the transgression of one's own corporeality, the difference between oneself and the foreign/other, the impossible fusion of two people, the difference between love and sexuality, and much more. They had to deal with aggression and violence, with pain and suffering as well as with dependence and subjugation that are bound up in some sexual forms and relationships.

Irritations were also caused by sexual phenomena that deviated from the moral. While most contemporaries thought primarily of sexual relations between sexually mature women and men in their considerations of *eros* and lusty desire, they also knew that "carnal desire" could drive one toward same-sex and even more scandalous acts. In addition to vaginal penetration performed between a man and a woman through insertion of the penis, other body parts such as the anus, the hands, and the mouth came into sexual play. Although the ancient, medieval, and early modern societies were generally heteronormative, the limits of this paradigm were already evident back then. Not all people conformed to the norm of two polar sexes and a sexual desire that was directed only toward the other and which led at best to a lifelong coupling. Those who proved to be sexually ambiguous or deviated from the norm through non-heterosexual acts therefore found themselves caught in the clutches of apparatuses of persecution and punishment. Deviation also showed, however, that the moral and criminal evaluation of deviant sexual acts depended on who they were committed by, in what situation, and with/upon whom. The differences were just as great between men and women as between members of the various social strata (Traub 2008: 23f.). All of these were reasons why all the societies treated here more or less extensively regulated the sexual. They established guidelines for sanctioned and forbidden relationships and behaviors. Thus, the meaning and significance of sexual practices were deeply influenced, sexual fantasies and desires profoundly sculpted and shaped. None of these societies was exclusively pro- or anti-sexual. Instead, each tried to foster the productive, useful, and enjoyable aspects of sexuality and to keep in check that which they perceived to be dangerous, harmful, and frightening sexuality.

The Social Construction of Sexuality

Unlike today, sexual life in earlier European societies was not primarily understood as a private or personal relationship between two or more persons—not as one's sexual life—but as an elementary regulator of the social, political, and economic order (Weeks 2016: 33ff.). Marital coitus was the cumulation of the manifold demands on sexuality. With marriage, both sexes acquired the right to perform sexual intercourse, which served the procreation of descendants as well as the bond between the spouses. It must be noted, sexual life for men has always usually been tolerated also before marriage. Through sensual attention and regular coitus, intimacy, love, and trust were thought, and indeed ought, to develop and provide for a culture of mutual relationship of the body and the stability of marriage. Marital cohabitation was also the foundation of legitimate generational and inheritance succession, and thus it secured the claim to property and rights as well as care in one's old age. Functioning conjugal sexual relationships stabilized the socioeconomic structure. Political ends were often pursued through sexual relations in the higher social strata, such as dynastic succession, inheritance claims, and the passing on of birthright privileges. Marriage negotiations entailed customs and traditions, religious rites, legal provisions, and social institutions that guaranteed a marriage that conformed to regimented norms. Parents, peer groups, and the community were to prevent unwanted sexual contact before marriage, sanction offences, and at least disgrace deviants.

In all past European cultures, the sexual union of married couples had the elementary task of stabilizing the marriage and family ties, ensuring the fidelity of spouses and counteracting extramarital "fornication." Where love and affection arose even before marriage or were even decisive in the choice of future spouses, conjugal intercourse together with procreation formed one of the highlights of an honorable and righteous life praised by poets and thinkers. If marriages were entered into primarily for economic or political reasons and without prior positive (love) feelings, it was expected that the intimate bond would be established through coitus or at least that the man and woman would begin to feel a comradely bond between them (Wiesner-Hanks 2000: 256).

Sexual relationships should be based on gender characteristics. Until the final scientification of gender difference in the eighteenth century, however, the psychophysiological fixations of male and female characteristics proved to be relatively open (Flemming 2000; Fenster and Lees 2002; Farmer and Pasternack 2003; D'Ambra 2007; Surtees and Dyer 2020; Weikert and Woodacre 2021; Moore 2022). Humorism and its allocation of male and female characteristics based on bodily fluid and temperature balances maintained a link to the world of the individual, one's dietary habits, and the social and medical treatment of the body. In terms of the humors, then, the man should always act with more *ratio* (intellect and reason) in sexual matters, whereas the woman should let herself be determined by *sensualitas* (feeling and instinct). Christian moral theology supported such a gender-typical determination of man and associated it with the Fall of Man initiated by Eve. A somewhat pointed assessment of the sexuality of men and women could therefore be formulated as follows: Active men who were at the same time subject to their will and reason acted upon/toward—and not together with—their wives. The latter were the actual seducers and were imagined to be passive objects driven by their lust (Halperin 1990: 29ff; Karras 2003: 82; Myrne 2020: 31ff.).

However, the discourses and practices of sexuality in antiquity, the Middle Ages, and early modern times were more complex than the normative sources suggest. Many contemporary authors and a few female authors described ambiguous practices by both sexes or behavior that was even contrary to these polar images. We can thus assume that the reality corresponded with a great plurality of behaviors. If one considers the entire breadth of the surviving textual and pictorial sources, one comes across many men who could not control their sexual desires and women whose sexual lives had the civilizing part to play. Especially in early modern writings on marriage, the sexual domination and dominance of the man was not propagated; instead, what was insisted upon was mutual consideration and tolerance toward the weaknesses and strengths of the other (Schnell 2017: 329ff.).

Power and domination were also central categories in sexual relations between members of different social groups and strata. Wherever sexual contacts crossed those borders, factors such as status and possession, reputation and ancestry, gender and age of a person became matters of concern. Due to the accumulation of social, material, and cultural capital, men usually had much greater freedom in these matters. In the case of dependencies between sexual partners—be it between fathers and household members, husbands and wives, employers and servants, owners and slaves, victors and vanquished etc.—the probability increased for sexual overpowering, assaults, and rape. Sexual and sexualized violence against women, children, unfree persons, prisoners, etc. was one of the structural characteristics of societies in which power and domination were unequally distributed—and has been increasingly researched in recent years (Zanetti Domingues, Caravaggi and Paoletti 2021; Loetz 2021; Nolde 2020).

Marriage bans were another reason why some groups were excluded from legitimate sexual intercourse—such as apprentices, journeymen, and maids during their service, monks and nuns, foreigners and slaves. Due to the central social imperative, sexual relations and contacts from Greek antiquity through the early modern times were sanctioned primarily *only* within the institution of marriage. This did not mean, however, that there wasn't a legion of sexual constellations prior to, outside of, aside from, and intertwined with marriage. Some were tolerated and accepted, others were forbidden, persecuted, and punished by religious and secular authorities, or at least disavowed through defamation and dishonor. The numerous religious and secular bans and prohibitions, however, could not prevent men or women for that matter from entering into such short-term or long-term relationships. If the other was seen as a potential candidate for marriage or engagement, this was regarded as less serious.

Adultery, on the other hand, was usually considered a capital offence. It was severely punished, in particular, when the descent of a child fell into doubt or a marriage broke apart. Ambivalent sexual morals abound, however, as extramarital sexual contacts were differently sanctioned. Among the upper classes, quite a few men maintained regular contact with courtesans *hetairai* and mistresses or "kept women," that is, concubines. Such habits led to dishonor, abuse, and shame for men of the middle and lower classes—all the more so for women—or could even cost their means of subsistence or their very lives. Prostitutes were generally viewed poorly, but they were—under more or less legal circumstances—part of the usual sexual offer. Nevertheless, it was already a given in ancient times that they often represented the epicenters of venereal disease and moral decay.

In populations in which marriage was typical and occurred early and among whom contraception was low, women gave birth to around twelve children during their fertile years—the highest average number of children ever measured among American Hutterite families (Coale and Treadway 1986: 34; Alter and Clark 2010: 47f.). Such a large number of children was clearly too great even for groups dependent on family labor. Thus, pregnancy prevention practices were common in all societies studied here. This also applies to the reduction and cessation of sexual intercourse above a certain age. Avoiding pregnancy in premarital and extramarital relationships naturally played an existential role. By prohibiting abortion, former societies tried to bring the sexual behavior of their members into line with the prevailing social, economic, and political orders. The extent of the scope for social inclusion or exclusion can be demonstrated by the handling of non-heterosexual practices and forms of desire. Here, the palette ranged from singing the praises of *paiderastia* in ancient Greece to the burning of sodomites in the early modern period. The moral and legal sanctioning of the erotic body and pornographic imagery has proved equally controversial throughout the ages.

This historical longitudinal sectioning shows that the different sexual forms can only be understood in relation to each other (Lautmann 2002: 171ff.). Thus, for example, the acceptance and tolerance but also the persecution and punishment of same-sex sexual acts went hand in hand with the norms that formed the basis for "normal" heterosexuality between men and women. Such cross-sectioning has shown that homosexuality was essentialized (also by historians) for a long time as a minority and as an anti-category of heterosexuality, overlooking the fact that among "homosexuals" large differences existed according to gender, age, and social affiliation as well as sexual preferences and behavior (Sedgwick 1990). Conversely, the specifics and shifts of heterosexual culture can only be comprehended in relation to those sexual forms from which they were distinguished—that is, those variants that existed beyond the binary gender and sexual world, such as hermaphrodites, androgynes, "monsters," and people who coveted same sex.

In the Thicket of Terms

In the history of language, "sexuality" didn't exist until the turn of the nineteenth century, because the term itself had not yet been coined. And, as in most cases, the emergence of this new word also marked the emergence of a body of knowledge or an epistemic thing (an object of knowledge) that further fueled research and knowledge generation and subsequently colonized human self-perception and perceptions of the other (Rheinberger 2006: 27ff.). Thus, "sexuality" first saw the light of day around 1800 and since then has been a separate, delimited area of life with its associated phenomena, which were primarily elaborated and categorized by the human sciences (Davidson 2001; Eder 2009: 14; Sigusch 2008: 46ff.). From antiquity to the early modern period, however, words were in use that meant something other than the holistic modern connotations of "sexuality." Nouns and verbs such as *eros* (sexual love), *Venerem iungere* (connecting in the manner of Venus), *futuere* or *p(a)edicare* (penetrating, vaginally or anally), *ars amatoria* (art of love), *debitum conjugale* (conjugal duty or debt), *remedium concupiscentiae* (remedy of desire), and *libido* (sexual lust),

"lust," "sexual drive," "mating instinct," "coitus," "need," "witness," and "carnal knowledge" as well as other terms denote only one, from today's point of view, partial aspect of "sexuality."

Although this volume deals with the time before "sexuality" and there is justified criticism of the connotative and associative power associated with this term (Swancutt 2007: 13ff.), it is, nevertheless, what will be used here. In the cultural and social sciences, various definitions exist for this malleable and hollow *plastikwort* (plastiv word) sexuality (Swancutt 2007: 14ff.; Bromley and Stockton 2013; Schnell 2002: 79f.; Lautmann 2002: 19ff.). Underpinning all the variations are ultimately controversial concepts and theories (Horley and Clarke 2016; Sigusch 2013: 19ff.; Earp, Chambers and Watson 2022: 9ff.). Therefore, this volume takes a broad definition of sexuality: anthropologically speaking, sexuality is one of humankind's basic needs, but it goes beyond the natural necessity of reproduction and is not instinctively determined, as is the case with animals. Sexuality here is an umbrella for all phenomena related to sexual life or sexual desire—such as notions, ideas, knowledge, lusts, orientations, fantasies, experiences, and practices. Sexual actors make use of culturally predetermined categories, ideas, and forms of perception in order to experience and describe their psychophysiological state in terms of sexuality and to provide it with meaning and significance. In practice, sexuality is always constituted by performance and experience. The concept of sexuality used here includes desire, discourse, practice, experience, speaking, feelings/emotions, actions, body, and drive (Eder 2009: 15f.). It refers to both the discursive production of all that a time period would have connected with sexual life and the corresponding practice, which, of course, comprised non-discursive components. Sexual actors were/are subordinated to the sociocultural codes in their desire, speech, and actions, but they can rebel against such predetermined codes— for example, on the basis of differential experiences and ambiguous forms of knowledge. In view of such a definition, it would be almost obsolete to give credence to all those big categories that have been in force since the eighteenth and nineteenth centuries: essentialist categories such as "hetero-/ homo-/bisexuality," the attribution of identities such as "homosexual," the naturalization of "heterosexuality" and "heteronormality," the polarization of the body's "sex" and cultural "gender," or the attribution of universal and gender-specific concepts have been deconstructed by the history of science and knowledge in recent decades. Simply put, the biological beings of man, woman, and others have been called into question (Ingraham 2005; Schultz 2006b; Lochrie 2011: 37ff.; Traub 2016b: 13ff.).

The terms "lust" and "desire" are used synonymously in this volume. In cultural studies contexts, the former is usually used to bring to the fore the physical energy or driving force, the sexual drive or sexual urges. Desire, on the other hand, often refers to the process of cultural signification of erotic or sexual objects, be they people, images, or things. Both terms refer to fantasies and/or phantasies and the associated feelings, emotions, and affects that come from the body and the psyche together. The urge here comes from within the body and through its orifices between inside and outside, from its erogenous zones, from the vagina, vulva, clitoris, penis, nipples, anus, mouth, nose, eyes, ears, and skin (Verhaeghe 2003: 180). Orientation and objective as well as its objects and their pictorial, textual, and material representations result from cultural attribution (Walker 2017: 9f.). (Sexual) lust and desire express themselves as absence, shortage, and lack; the practice and quality as well as the direction and intensity of experience in the elimination of desire and lust are not inscribed within it. Temporal satisfaction is connected with the partial achievement of the desired objective or partial possession of the desired object. Its apparent realization is never ultimate, for complete realization of a phantasm never is. The urge fades for a certain time, only to swell again afterward. According to Jacques Lacan, human desire is based on a subject who, since his birth into the world and his separation from the mother's breast, feels that he is incomplete and wants to fill this deficiency with objects—without ever being able to restore the original state or achieve an actual fusion with what he desires. The other remains an object of ceaseless yearning and, at the same time, gives us the capacity for sexual desire and love (Widmer 1997: 87ff.). Lacan says that the desire between people—along with the erotic and sexual images they make of each other—encompasses an often underestimated social dimension: What he points out in his oft-cited statement "human desire is the desire of the other" is that the subject only desires and only can desire if it experiences the other, that is, the object, as desiring (Žižek 2008: 59ff.). Herein, we experience as Niklas Luhmann saw it: "In physical interplay one discovers that, beyond one's own desire and its fulfilment, one also desires the other's desire and thus learns that the other wishes to be desired" (Luhmann 1982: 33).

And like other forms of desire, sexual desire can wander from one object to the next. W.J.T. Mitchell has shown that it cannot be separated from the image question because the erotic and sexual urge generate material and mental images and vice versa—our desire finds those objects that the cultural sign system (language, images) makes available. In Ovid's myth of Pygmalion, this phantasm is fulfilled archetypically in both directions: Due to his bad experiences with women, the artist Pygmalion lives only for his sculpture. He creates an ideal-typical female ivory statue, with which he falls in love. He pleads to Venus, the goddess of love, for a woman who resembles the statue. When he later caresses the statue, her ivory lips warm and she comes to life. Pygmalion may thus take her as his wife (Mitchell 2008: 78ff.). Seen through Pygmalion's eyes, sexual fantasies and masturbatory gratification do not necessitate an actual other but rather only a desire that believes in its erotic or pornographic promises.

The aspect of the body's "sex" in terms of genitalia takes a backseat in the terms "eroticism" or "erotic"—both borrowed from French in the seventeenth century—without completely excluding it from the idea of sexuality. Rather, the focus for the erotic is on the imagined path to sexuality (gazing, wooing, swooning, longing). In addition, feelings of love and the emotional excitement for the desired body play a central role. Erotic attraction may be sensually directed at the body of another, sometimes one's own, without the objective of an immediate sexual realization. Platonic love relationships—whether same sex or opposite sex—may be driven by erotic desire, but in practice they are not necessarily realized in the sexual act involving genitals but rather through exciting and lustful touching of erogenous zones that are not directly genital (Andreadis 2008: 254ff.; Halperin 2017).

The attempt to realize sexual desire in sexual intercourse also shows that the phantasma of the desired body and the fusion with it can never be caught up in actual physical communication. The deception and disappointment of this experience of reality feed countless myths and narratives. For instance, take "bedtrick" tales in which a couple spend the night together and the next day one of them realizes that he or she has shared the bed with the wrong person, sometimes with the trickster! This plotline isn't merely about the question of intimate physical contact leading to recognition or even knowledge of the other; it's also about what is actually desirable about the other body, whether it is exchangeable, whether love or the flesh takes precedence, and whether sexual action is based on truth or lies. The transformation of the partner through sexual activity is one of the basic experiences that many people share. The religious historian Wendy Doniger formulated it as follows: "Sometimes we go to bed with an animal and wake up with a god; that is, we go to bed relatively indifferent and wake up enchanted by sexual magic" (Doniger 2000: 3).

Craving, longing, desire, lasciviousness, lust, excitement, orgasm, merging, satisfaction, fulfillment—these and other terms for sexual feelings and emotions can be drawn out by innumerable colloquial, poetic, and literary descriptions and innuendo that try to capture the experience before, during, and after sexual acts. Less extensive would probably be a list of all the terms that attribute negative sexual emotions. The history of sexuality is thus afloat in waters that have been deepened by a veritable flood in the last decades: the history of emotions (Frevert 2009; Schnell 2015; Liliequist 2016). Initially, the focus was on a less fruitful debate between universalism versus social constructivism. The former claims that our feelings are generated by neurochemical processes and thus remain largely unaffected by cultural significance. For example, intense physical pain is something we feel per se, no matter what words and images we use to express it. Social constructivists, on the other hand, assume that a breadth of emotions can be experienced in different manifestations and that the emotional categories as well as the emotional experience can be changed. The history of shame is often cited as an example, because it seems that the breaks in the culture of shame have shifted its meaning significantly from Greek–Roman antiquity to Christianity or from the nineteenth to the twentieth century (Bologne 2001;

Harper 2013). A bridge between the two directions has been established in recent years by neuroscience, which has shown that there is an interaction or feedback loop between the neuronal and physical basis of feelings on the one hand and their articulation on the other. Expressing one's own feelings/emotions and experiencing the emotional expressions of others, e.g., when watching a film, has an effect on the plastic brain structure and thus also transforms one's further emotional experience (Plamper 2012: 252ff.).

What is understood by "feeling" and "emotion" and how these terms are defined depend on the scientific discipline consulted. In most cases, *feelings* are understood as emotions experienced or the sensation caused by emotions, that is, consciously experienced mental states or psychic-subjective experience (Hartmann 2010: 31ff.; Schnell 2015: 31ff.). *Emotions* are usually defined as complex patterns of physical and mental changes in response to a situation perceived as significant. In addition to subjective experience, they are also made up of cognitive, action-related, psychophysiological, and expressive components (Mees 2006: 105ff.). Those who deal with emotions must thus consider felt inner states or psychological experiences, physical changes, behaviors and gestures, actions and social practices, linguistic and pictorial expressions as well as discourses.

Every form of naming and describing (sexual) feelings and emotions in the past and present is associated with a fundamental cognitive hurdle, for what a person feels may be articulated according to the discursive repertoire of the respective time—in its concepts, categories, and images—but his actual inner feeling cannot be communicated. Mental states are therefore conveyed through forms of expression, evaluations, representations, concepts, and norms—that is, cultural categories (Schnell 2015: 19ff.). This also applies to this book: What people in antiquity, the Middle Ages, and early modern times actually or really felt when they coveted carnally, when they practiced sexual intercourse with each other, or found an image erotic or sexually exciting, cannot be determined. Nor can this threshold be overcome when one is postulating a social construction of feelings. The qualitative impact of social and cultural framing on individual neuronal structures cannot be understood (at least not at present), nor can that of the social-cultural knowledge base and stock of imagery. Nor can the effects of brain structures altered by communication be known in terms of an individual's experience. Even if a differentiation of feeling and emotion seems necessary from the perspective of cultural studies, this cannot be redeemed in research practice in view of the inaccessibility of feelings.

Sexual feelings/emotions are *one* reason why people act sexually. In most cases, however, the frame of reference for their actions is much broader. Studies conducted from the 1970s through the 2010s in various social and cultural milieus have shown that individuals have multiple subjective reasons for their sexual activities: feelings of love; intimacy; mutual attractiveness; a physical trigger; the reduction of fear; boredom; the desire to be desired; duty; expectations of the role; the desire to belong to someone; the pressure of the peer group; to make a conquest; to transform a short-term alliance into a longer-term relationship; to prevent being abandoned by the partner; pure pleasure or pure lust; to gain prestige, status, and reputation; spiritual motivations; to give pleasure to the partner; out of gratitude; out of curiosity; for sexual variety; because the partner demands it; to improve sexual abilities; out of dominance or submission; to reduce stress and tension; out of revenge; out of financial motives; for the exchange of resources such as benefits, privileges, or professional opportunities. Extend this list to include motives mentioned in historical studies and the scope becomes even wider: marriage and the fulfillment of conjugal duties; the pursuit of beauty or virtue; fulfillment of family obligations; procreation of children; the demonstration of power; enjoyment of spoils of war; attainment of a higher status; obtainment of food or goods; fulfillment of a divine mission; appeasement of violent conquerors; and much more (Hatfield, Luckhursta and Rapsona 2012: 145ff.).

Also noteworthy is the list of reasons and motives that can deter people from engaging in sexual activities: because there is a risk of loss of social reputation; fear of severe punishment; in order not to commit a sin; the threat of sanctions from the peer group; in order not to risk the loss of social values; because one is not a whore or a lewd person; because of fear of infection with venereal and other diseases; because of physical rejection; because one is not in love; for fear of pregnancy; in order to avoid family difficulties; because of questions regarding the ancestry of potential offspring; for fear of pain; because one cannot feed another child; for fear of purgatory; because one does not want to surrender and lose control; because one is too young; because one has no available partner; for fear of failing or not living up to one's expectations; because one is not interested in sexual activities; because one lacks the spatial or temporal possibilities; for fear of negative emotions; and so on (*idem*). Enumerations like these show that in the past and in the present there has been and still is an almost indeterminable range of motivations and reasons for sexual activity and that it depends on the respective social and cultural background, age, gender, life situation, and many other factors for why someone decides for or against this activity.

The respective sociocultural framework is also relevant for the definition and delimitation of all those terms that are assigned to the traditional field of sexuality, such as prostitution, homosexuality, pornography, sexually transmitted diseases, contraception, and abortion. The following chapters show that the meaning of these categories has changed repeatedly throughout history, which is why their definition is discussed in more detail in the relevant sections. Indeed, terms such as "sexuality," "hetero-/homosexuality," "pornography," "prostitution," and other terms for historical sexual forms should therefore be marked with a graphic sign—such as an italicization or scare quotes—which draws attention to the fact that these words originate from modern linguistic usage and had no or a significantly different meaning in the period covered. In order not to overload the textual image, however, such optical markers have been omitted. It is up to the reader to keep this in mind.

Sexuality and Historiography

As a subject of historiography, sexuality has had a remarkable career (Weeks 2016: 23ff.). Interest in sexuality was first sparked within the historical study of life, customs, and morals—which primarily dealt with working-class mentality or the history of alcohol consumption—in the late nineteenth and early twentieth centuries. Authors of this time wanted to show that there had already existed a great variety of sexual phenomena in earlier centuries and that the past was by far not as bigoted and shamefaced as their own time. The often richly illustrated and almost culinary formulated works on topics such as prostitution, erotica, and feminine morality tread a fine line just this side of pornography—and therefore were hot sellers. If their spicy descriptions and frivolous pictures are to be believed, one would imagine that the medieval man could live out his sexual vices and lasciviousness despite the church or at least behind the back of its pastoral supervision.

With the spread of psychoanalysis in the interwar period and after the Second World War, historians adopted a Freudian perspective and assumed sequences of more or less "free" or "suppressed" sexuality in earlier epochs. Up through the 1970s, the master narrative of sexuality history was that most people in antiquity and the Middle Ages had lived quite liberally in terms of "sex" and that sexual oppression had only come into force with the Reformation, early modern social discipline, and, in particular, in the bourgeois society of the eighteenth and nineteenth centuries. In the course of the "sexual revolution" of the late 1960s and 1970s, the social shackles of *eros* would finally be removed again (Eder 2009: 10ff.).

In the late 1970s, however, the paradigm of repressed sexuality itself was radically challenged. Michel Foucault's *Histoire de la sexualité* in particular brought down that mental edifice. Volume one—published with the English title *The Will to Knowledge. Sexuality and Truth* (Foucault 1977)—immediately became one of the founding documents of the new history of sexuality (Martschukat and Stieglitz 2008: 177). Foucault called for the focus not to be on repression but on the production or social construction of sexuality through discourses and dispositives and their integration into non-hierarchical and decentralized power relations. Seen across the centuries, the silence about the sexual or its re-/suppression would not in the end take center stage; rather, ever more areas of life would be drawn into the spell of sexuality. Since the eighteenth century, even the search for human identity and truth has come under the reign of "king sex."

Foucault thus turned sexuality into a newly conceived research subject, which historians have been working ever since (Eder 2016; Taylor 2016; Downham Moore 2020). He also bound the history of sexuality with the promise that it could also be told as a complete history, a grand theory of Western civilization or at least in terms of big categories such as power, identity, and body (Cocks and Houlbrook 2006: 16). Through Foucault, the history of sexuality stepped out of the obscurity of a disreputable minority topic and entered the stage of academic historiography, which deals with questions of politics, society, and economy (Laqueur 2009: 434; Herzog 2009: 1291).

Following Foucault, historians as well as representatives of the gay and lesbian movement and feminism have greatly expanded the field of the history of sexuality (Smith-Rosenberg 1975; Weeks 1977, 2000: 53ff.; Walkowitz 1980). Formerly fixed categories such as hetero-, homo-, and bisexuality have been deconstructed and diversified, reflected in among other things the use of the plural—such as "homosexualities" (Eder 2014: 17ff.). According to Judith Butler, even the body's "sex" was to be produced by performative actions, particularly by acts of speech and naming (Butler 1991; Benhabib et al. 1993). This stream showed a total lack of stable relations between biological gender, social gender roles, and sexual desire. And this was often underpinned by a political claim: If the cultural and social sciences proved that discriminatory essentializations of gender and sexual categories were social constructs, new attributions, role models, identities, and subject positions could also be discovered (Weeks 2010: 12ff.).

Pursuing this line of thought, queer theory countered the established sexual categories and identity forms—especially hetero- and homonormativity—with the indeterminacy and change of gender and sexuality (McCann and Monaghan 2020). Queer studies thus also meant going to the margins of traditional categories and concepts. On the one hand, this led to research into liminal figures such as hermaphrodites, cross-dressers, and inter- and transsexuals, and, on the other, to consideration of sources who did not explicitly speak of sexual desire but metaphorically circumscribed it or addressed it only indirectly (Freccero 2006). To read queer would be, for instance, to find hidden erotic and sexual fantasies and practices in homosocial aesthetics and corporeality—thoughts and actions which furthermore remained unspoken in those times of silence and persecution of same-sex desire (Schnell 2013: 32ff.). The dissolution of essentialized or generalized categories of sexuality also resulted in the criticism and deconstruction of homonormative as well as heteronormative concepts. In the 1980s, one still spoke of gay and lesbian history or gay and lesbian studies, which were replaced by the comprehensive acronym LGBTQ, that is, lesbian, gay, bisexual, transgender, and queer.

Today, the historiography of sexuality embraces multiple perspectives and deals not only with discourses and dispositives but also with actors and actants, practices, scripts, and performances (Weeks 2016). It accounts for individual and collective contradictions as well as resistance to knowledge and sexual scripts (Simon and Gagnon 2003; Kimmel 2007). It should not be forgotten that social repression and the discipline of the sexual also represent another important aspect of the history of sexuality. Nevertheless, the "positive" production of sexuality is foregrounded generally, thus the question of which everyday sexual ideas and knowledge average women and men possessed and how they practiced their sexual lives—the same applies to persons without heteronormative gender classification (Traub 2016b: 4ff.). Particular attention is paid to the social and cultural framework in which desire in childhood, adolescence, and adulthood is enriched with meaning and significance, with images, objects, and narratives, and translated into action.

Ever since Foucault linked dispositives and discourses with the genesis of sexual identities, questions of identifying self-references and references to others in the context of sexuality have been part of the standard repertoire of the history of sexuality. Repeatedly, historical studies have been and continue to be concerned with whether people in premodern times perceived themselves to be gay or lesbian as sexual categories—even though these modern concepts and definitions did not yet exist. Similarly, it has been discussed at length whether women, men, and hermaphrodites/transgender persons who sold sexual services understood themselves as "prostitutes," that is, as subjects with their own sexual identity. The interaction of historical subjects or individual actors, on the one hand, and discourses, social practices, and things, on the other, is still one of the most exciting questions posed by a history of sexuality oriented toward cultural and social science (Reckwitz 2014; Latour 2010).

Objectives of This Volume

As far as it is possible to determine on the basis of existing sources and the state of research, human sexuality is to be understood in this volume as a thing that has come to be and thus is historical. As noted at the beginning, however, it should never be forgotten that we are dealing here with an indeterminate "mythical being" whose natural, genetic, hormonal, neuronal, and impulsive powers cloud clear vision (Freud 1982: 529).

The central concern of this study is to strengthen the socio-historical view of sexuality. By broadening the prevailing cultural-historical perspective, the social context in which sexual forms of desire and action evolved is given considerably more space. The economic and political aspects associated with this are taken into an intersectional account which also focuses on other differences and hierarchies, such as ethnicity, class, and religion (Buffington 2014; Traub 2016b: 29ff; Betancourt 2020: 14ff.). As already stated in the definition of sexuality, sexual action/behavior is understood as social practice—without falling short on sexual knowledge and the cultural framing of desire (Benkel 2012). Seen thusly, sexual subjectivation processes develop between somatic self-will, social mimesis, acquired and embodied experiences, and the associated body of knowledge (Villa and Alkemeyer 2010). From a praxeological perspective, the following chapters therefore deal with the function of the sexual in upbringing and socialization, its significance for the development men's and women's self-image and image of the other, its socialization in marriage initiation, and the significance of sexual life for marital relationships and concubinage.

Although we know little about the first-person perspective and the individual sexual experience or about the emotions of a large part of the population at that time, it is still possible to make statements about the significance of the sexual for differing social classes. The same applies to those social networks that were established through marriage and sexuality, because in this way families came together—through fruitful coitus, marriages became legally binding—and kinship was established, succession and the transfer of property were secured, and the goal of a productive and honorable life was achieved through marital status. A larger number of surviving children were also an economic factor for most population groups, including the future labor force, heirs, and care in old age. Access to legitimate sexual contacts was mainly regulated by the age of marriage and social marriage circles. This was done, for example, by setting a minimum age by law or tradition. Another way was by raising or lowering access thresholds through social and economic barriers. In guild trades, for example, the training period was subject to a marriage ban; apprentices and journeymen were subject to a period of abstinence until they were released, took over a master's position, founded their own household and a family—an ultimate unrealistic restriction.

As a social practice, deviant sexual forms such as prostitution, pornography, and same-sex acts are also addressed here. They might not have been welcome or were even forbidden in most societies, but there were niches in which they were practiced—an opening for many to gain sexual experiences before, besides, or beyond marriage. While research into the history of sexuality has so far dealt with such forms of the sexual primarily from the point of view of regulation and sanctioning, here they are understood as positive practices carried out to allow actors to understand their sexual desire and action as legitimate, accepted, or at least tolerated.

As is the case today, sexual life in earlier times was associated with certain things, places, and spaces, which are also addressed here. Whether it was obtaining and using contraceptives, having a separate bed for coitus, conducting intercourse in (semi-)public spaces, or going to districts of ill repute to visit prostitutes. In rare cases, we even resort to looking at the remains of buildings that say something about the spatial conditions of sexual activity. In the case of the *lupanar*, a brothel excavated in Pompeii, the size and furnishings of the chambers and the frescoes that have survived provide evidence of the sexual acts that took place there.

This study also shows that the new history of sexuality is based on diverse sources and sometimes ambiguous written, pictorial, and material artifacts. The results of such findings are differentiated accordingly. This differs markedly from the earlier historiography, which drew conclusions about the Early and High Middle Ages, for example, based primarily on textual and pictorial sources that came from the hands of ecclesiastical authors, many of them monastic. According to their *summae confessorum* (summae of penance) and *libri poenitentiales* (books of penance), the guidelines for the sexual life of the faithful looked rather bleak. Recent research in the fields of history and literary studies as well as art history have meanwhile expanded the sources and refined the methodological instruments of analysis and interpretation. State of the art today is to consider the discursive circumstances under which the respective genres emerged—be it texts, images, or things. Depending on the conditions of production, distribution, and consumption, even the utterances of a self-same author or artist could have greatly divergent meanings. Depending on whether a medieval text was written for a public or a private audience, in Latin or in the common vernacular, for men or women, for doctors, jurists, or theologians, and depending on the genre strategies employed, contradictory opinions about the sexual may be heard. Although the discourse strands of medicine, theology, and comedy, to name a few, did not usually touch, inter-discursive entanglements nevertheless occurred: Clerics referred to medical truths, for example, or the authors of farces and Shrovetide plays made fun of church dogma and the hardly chaste practices of clerics themselves. When it came to the sexual characteristics of the sexes, in particular, the statements in that sort of historiography could vary considerably depending on the respective source type. This is why research literature today broadly agrees that although dominant gender models did exist in antiquity, the Middle Ages, and early modern times, alternative ideas about the sexual nature of men and women were also offered throughout these periods and social practices were correspondingly colorful (Schnell 2002: 472ff.; Masterson, Rabinowitz and Robson 2014; Meade and Wiesner-Hanks 2021).

Despite our knowledge of the history of sexuality expanding considerably in recent decades, there are still some yawning gaps. We know very little about the sexual perspectives of most people, especially the lower and middle classes. We know as little about their sexual ideas, conceptions, and fantasies as we do about their everyday sexual practices. Due to their inability to write and lack of access to media deemed worthy of preservation, they remain voiceless throughout the epochs discussed here. Only the empirical sexual research of the twentieth century has been able to draw on a pool of contemporary interviews and first-person documents. Only since then have reasonably representative statements been possible about broader population groups. This source scarcity has often seduced historians of sexuality to blur the difference between discourse and practice and to (mis-)

understand the normative statements of some genres as an expression of the prevailing mentality and lived practice of the average population.

In comparison, we are much better informed about "sexuality at the margins" (Harris 2010). Due to the conditions under which the sources were created, we do have information about the regulation of premarital and extramarital sexual life through laws, orders, and court records. We can still view erotic paintings and frescoes that served to animate and satisfy the fantasies of the upper classes. And we continue to (re-)read comedies and caricatures about the "unnatural" practices of people who coveted same sex, for example. Archives, collections, and libraries still contain untapped text and image sources on deviant sexuality. On the other hand, everyday practices and the knowledge and imagination of the average population have not been reflected in this way. Nevertheless, we are not merely dependent on pure speculation when considering the "normal" sexual world of the masses. For one thing, we have access to sexual discourses whose producers shared their statements with others and are thus to be understood as collective stocks of knowledge that also seeped into broader social strata—for example, when clerics proselytized church-sanctioned sexual norms to the people. For another, speaking and writing about the sexual, including mediating images and traditional objects, never turned out to be a unanimous exercise. In theological and philosophical treatises, courtly romances, marriages, comedies, graffiti, and many other types of sources, there are differing opinions on sexual morality and practice—this too is an indication of the scope of sexual activity.

Studies on the history of sexuality usually deal with a period of one, two, or three centuries. Few handle an entire epoch. This temporal circumspection results above all from the epoch-specific and institutional division of the historical sciences and leads to a narrow view of each its own time. Historical sexual forms and especially sexual identities were consequently often postulated to be particularities, innovations, or even inventions of a certain period of time. In contrast, this volume pursues a *longue durée* of European sexual cultures, which is why the tradition and persistence of sexual phenomena and the tenacity of sexual norms and images are emphasized.

The individual regions of Europe have so far been treated differently by the history of sexuality. The focus has previously been on the sexual cultures of Southern, Central, and Western Europe. Eastern and Southeastern Europe, on the other hand, were rather neglected, with studies on Byzantium and the Ottoman Empire standing out (Peirce 2009; Messis and Nilsson 2018; Kallander 2021). Since Edward Said's groundbreaking research on Orientalism, we have known that the Western ideas of this region, especially of Islam, were shaped by the erotic harem images of the nineteenth century (Said 1978). Dipesh Chakrabarty has pointed out that the historical narrative about apparently peripheral regions also follows teleological tropes: According to this master narrative, developments first became apparent in

Europe, actually in Central and North/West Europe, and then traced back to or into other regions (Chakrabarty 2000). The new history of sexuality strives against both narratives and attempts to understand diachronic and synchronous sexual cultures side by side and in interaction. Studies that proceed in a comparative manner, for example, comparing Catholic and Protestant sexual cultures with Orthodox-Christian or Muslim culture(s), have proved quite productive (Traub 2008). Relatively little is known about large parts of Northern Europe during this period as well, which is due to the lack of autochthonous written sources over long periods (Riisøy 2009; Korpiola 2009: 347ff.; Liliequist 2017). Although this volume attempts to cover as many European sexual cultures as possible, it reflects this heterogeneous state of research. Some themes remain underexposed because they have not yet been studied systematically and over a long period of time by historians—such as sexuality in old age, masochistic and sadistic practices, fetishism, bestiality, and necrophilia.

In recent years, compact overviews and multivolume publications on the history of sexuality in Europe in general and on individual regions and territories have appeared, particularly in the Anglo-American region, and have significantly broadened our understanding (such as Karras 2006a; Crawford 2007; Classen 2008a; Stearns 2009; Peakman 2011; Phillips and Reay 2011; Fisher and Toulalan 2012; Angenendt 2015; Clark 2019; Mildenberger 2020; Wiesner-Hanks 2020). They offer a rich treasure for further reading. The numerous articles, essays, and books referred to in this volume also provide in-depth information on the topics addressed.

2

Reign of the Phallus—Greek Antiquity

Eros, Oîkos, and the Sexes

When we talk about ancient Greece (eighth to first centuries BCE), we subsume quite a wide variety of social and political systems thereunder. Because of this diversity, sometimes important differences did exist between the sexual culture of Athens—which we know about the most from sources—and Crete or Sparta. From the archaic period (eighth century to 500 BCE) to the classical period (500–336 BCE) to the Hellenistic period (336–30 BCE), striking changes can also be observed in sexual culture. Such regional and temporal variants are discussed again and again in the following, but the heterogeneity of the Greek culture(s) in all its rich detail can hardly be treated in full. Additionally, the history of sexuality for this epoch must be based on sources that are often disparate, contradictory, or at least open to interpretation (such as dramas and comedies, poems, legal texts, medical writings, graffiti, ceramic decoration, and sculptures). An overview of the historiographical literature on ancient sexuality reveals a clear intensification of the discussion in recent decades and thus also a pluralization of what was rather one-dimensional research through the 1970s. Pointing the way forward were the debates on Michel Foucault's self-constitution of the (sexual) subject, the feminist critique of genderless historiography, the inclusion of questions of power and hegemony, the radical critique of the heteronormality of male/female sexes, *queer studies'* evaluation of gender and sexuality, and the influences of theoretical and methodological debates on the various *cultural turns* (Richlin 1991; Skinner 2014).

Eros was of fundamental importance for the society and culture of the Greek city-states. Personified by the god of the same name, son of the goddess Aphrodite, *eros* stood in the largely agrarian and often warlike communities for the fertility of the soil, the reproduction of animals, and the reproduction of the *anthropos* and thus for a cosmic principle which promoted life and promised it a future (Kenaan 2020: 97). In humans, *eros* affected not only men and women but also had same-sex objectives. Integrated into the religious and social order, sexual strength not only provided for fertility and vitality but also contributed to the prosperity of culture, philosophy, and literature. *Eros* was clearly different from *philia*, familiar and friendly love, and from *agapê*, charity (Pechriggl 2009: 8) (Figure 1).

Eros possessed a dangerous, impetuous, not to say tyrannical side and was seen as a force of nature which could completely take hold of people and destroy social, political, and religious life (Winkler 1997: 129). The god Eros and his mother Aphrodite were able to fill people with sexual passion and love, but they could also lead them into madness and loss of self-control (Golden and Toohey 2011: 7). Even Zeus, the father of the gods, was at their mercy in Greek mythology. In view of his overpowering sexual desire, he gave his wife (and sister) Hera ceaseless grounds for jealousy because of his numerous affairs with earthly women (and not only). But Hera as well, the patroness of marriage, managed to seduce him with cunning and Aphrodite's help and triumph over him in the battle for Troy. According to

FIGURE 1 *Dionysus and Eros, second century CE.*

mythology, *eros* was usually at hand when the gods got into each other's affairs or even fell in love with mortals and subsequently physically enjoyed themselves. So, it is not surprising that the Greek communities tried to tame *eros* through laws, norms, and institutions, to civilize it through rites and cults, and to steer it in a productive direction (Thornton 1997: 139ff.).

The close connection between religion, ritual, and sexuality was also expressed in the Demeter and Persephone/Kore cult. The Thesmophoria festivals were dedicated to Demeter, the goddess of fertility, and celebrated by Greek women exclusively, that is, without the participation of the men, after the winter sowing had been ordered in the fall. For the fest, erect penises were carried in the form of pastries. The women paid homage to their fertility all the while making fun of these attributes of masculinity. This also led to a ritual union with the *choiroi* (piglets), a mythological stand-in for the female genitalia. The worship of the underworld and the fertility goddess Persephone/Kore had similar aims. Persephone's descent into Hades was an allegory for sexual intercourse and her annual return to the world above represented the change of seasons and the recurring fertility of plants, animals, and humans. At the *komos*, a ritual festival with processions in honor of Dionysus, phallus-bedecked poles were carried around and the god of joy and fertility was worshipped for his powers of stimulating growth (Vout 2013: 72). In the phallus cult, however, people didn't just pay homage to fertility; even more so they were in awe of the ambivalent potency of the male genitals—Dionysus didn't stand for ecstasy and madness for nothing. For one, the phallus was regarded as an instrument with which the man expressed his active sexual desire and his claims to power over others. Phallic symbols were secondly a reminder that the sexual could also act independently of the will of its owner and possibly deprive him of control over himself—a horrific image that made Greek men deeply doubt the attributes of their masculinity (Larson 2014: 214ff.).

In order to live ethically, the powerful lust of the *eros* had to be actively held at bay. In caring for oneself, special attention was paid to sexual pleasure and its creative direction (Foucault 1989a, 1989b; Nussbaum 2000a: 57ff.). In the *Symposium*, Plato (428/427–348/347 BCE) expounded on the superior nature of *eros*, indeed its heavenly as well as philosophical and artistic potential, while putting its common and crude powers in their place. According to Platonic duality, sexual desire isn't the only domain of love, instead it also drives the human need for beauty and virtue, even wisdom—whereby the aesthetic body (regardless of gender) offered a privileged surface for projection and expression (Detel 1998; 213ff.; Stähli 2006; Soble 2009: 107ff.; Grahn-Wilder 2018: 17ff.). The lesson of love presented in the *Symposium* calls for at best a ladder-like ascent through life:

> The correct order of going, or being led by another, to the things of love, is to begin from the beauties of earth and mount ever upwards for the

sake of that other beauty, using these as steps only, and from one going on to two, and from two to all beautiful bodes, and from beautiful bodies to beautiful practices, and from beautiful practices to beautiful notions, until from beautiful notions he arrives at the notion of absolute beauty, . . . in the contemplation of beauty absolute. (Plato 2001: 259, 211c)

The best way to tame *eros* and make him fruitful was in the *oíkos*, in the home or in the household, the center of which was a married couple. In addition to the family formed by ancestry and kinship, the *oíkos* also included slaves and free laborers connected to the household in a hierarchical order that was regarded as natural: man and woman, father and children, master and slave. The household community was led by a free citizen, the *kyrios*, who represented all members of the house to the outside world as head of the family. The *oíkos* belonging to the citizens of the *polis* also included agricultural land, plantations, livestock, buildings, tools, and household equipment. The Greek house was thus not only a social but also an economic unit, and sexual life within it played a decisive role in its survival and prosperity. The regulated and supervised sexual life of a household ensured that the ancestry and succession of the free citizens did not fall into dispute and that the children were indeed the physical descendants of the *kyrios*, an essential element of a slave-owning society. A well-functioning *oíkos* also demanded that free boys and girls received a moral education and married according to their status. Slaves, however, were considered unfree even in matters of sex. In the view of many historians, slaves were counted as objects whose bodies were both the economic and sexual property of their owners; other historians believe that house slaves were offered at least fundamental personal rights (Stahl 2003: 20ff.; Wrenhaven 2011: 71ff.; Cohen 2014; Espach 2017: 184f.; Porter 2021). The social image of the *kyrios* also depended on the reputation and honor of the household community, because he had the responsibility to protect its reputation externally. As a symbol for this, a column emblazoned with the head of Hermes and a *phallus* as a symbol for the energy and potency of Dionysus stood at the entrance of many Athenian houses (Dover 2002: 20; Simons 2011: 53).

Women were considered keeper of the inner *oíkos* and had to look after and organize it. Indeed, they remained subordinate within the *oíkos* and were denied the right to become *kyrios*, or *kyria* rather, themselves or to escape domestic dependence. As daughters and wives, they possessed no personal right of representation and remained submissive to the father or brother, with marriage to the husband (within his *oíkos*). If widowed, they were passed on to the next of kin, that is, a man in the paternal line of descent and authority—often this was an uncle—and only the son conceived with this man would become the next *kyrios*. The citizens' wives' lives were centered around the domestic. Yet, even though they were effectively sequestered within the household, they did emerge into the public eye from time to time, at religious celebrations, for example. For female members of the lower classes, on the other hand, extra domestic work and earning one's keep was part of everyday life (Robson 2013: 22; Cohen 1991: 150ff.; McClure 2019: 3.1).

The *kyrioi*, on the other hand, formed a social, political, and cultural alliance of free and equal men in the *polis* that extended far beyond the household community. This institution was the home of politics. Here was where war campaigns were debated. But it was also where sport and gymnastics were practiced and pleasure pursued. Here was where free and equal speech was held. One paid homage to the virile body, bowed before male energy and assertiveness. The free man of the Greek city-states took every opportunity to show that in sexual matters he was master of himself and conqueror of others. Greek sexual culture was thus structured along the lines of active and passive acts, penetration and receiving, as well as willful self and sexual subjection, whereby the *kyrioi* and their sexual partners followed clearly defined roles and accordingly knew their place (Cantarella 1992).

Humors of the Gendered Body

These attributions were mirrored and are represented in the gender-specific body images. According to ancient Greek humoralism, the *chymos* (juice or sap) and energy balance of the female body was moist and cool, that of the male body dry and warm. Both were in continuous exchange with the social and natural environment, such as the climate, lifestyle, and diet, and could maintain physical and mental balance through dietetic lifestyles. The psychophysiology of the sexes also functioned according to these principles. For example, the male body was best suited to produce seed and sexual desire during the winterly humid cold, but in the heat of summer this quickly led to exhaustion and fatigue. A sexually "hungry" woman then even posed a threat by consuming his *menos*, the vital fluid that gave the man willingness to act, steadfastness, and tenacity. Even though in the Hippocratic theory of humors the sexes' constitutions were diametrically arranged, the hot and dry qualities and temperaments of men ranked higher than those of women (Thommen 2007: 45; King 2005; Bonnard 2013).

The female body was of a special texture, more permeable and softer, absorbed more fluid from food and, since it could not process and consume enough, the female body needed release at regular intervals through menstruation or passed the fluids on to the fetus during pregnancy (Dean-Jones 1994: 184ff.). According to the Hippocratic concept, women also produced a generative seed of their own, although this was comparatively weak. For Aristotle (384–322 BCE), the female body lacked this capacity completely, contributing only the fertile ground for the generative juice and *spiritus* of the male, which itself carried the actual substrate of reproduction (King 2011: 111ff.; Sissa 2014: 269ff.; Deslauriers 2021: 24ff.). For *eros*, however, the female constitution was much more receptive; her sexual potential seemed almost insatiable and did not fluctuate cyclically as with men. Women were possessed by the internal procreative instinct from birth and were more or less at its mercy. The mythological priest of Zeus, Teiresias, who appeared in the form of both sexes, proclaimed that women could feel nine times more pleasure in coitus than men. For men, sexual pleasure would be triggered more by external stimuli, such as the sight of an attractive woman or a beautiful boy. *Eros* had the power to overcome men, too, like an infectious disease, and subsequently upset the social order (Winkler 1997: 126ff.). The male gender thus bore an innate sexual drive by nature—it's not for nothing the penis was also known as the necessity in ancient Greek. However, the male should (better) be able to control it and under no circumstances be controlled by it.

Pythagoras (around 570 to around 480 BCE) therefore admonished wild and uninspired sexual acts between married partners, negatively comparing such conjugal intercourse to the romping and rutting of animals. And even when practiced in a cultivated manner, coitus absolutely should be followed by ritual cleansing (Dover 2002: 20). Women's most important tasks included the rites of worship and sacrifice and were thus especially contaminated by extramarital sexual contacts (Hartmann 2007: 54ff.; Gaca 2003: 94ff.). According to general belief, their primary concern and duty in conjugal coitus was conception. Men, on the other hand—after their semen transfer—a shiny offspring beckoned, which guaranteed the sex of origin or the clan as well as provision in old age. For pleasure and sexual satisfaction, the (married) men would rather visit the *hetairai* and prostitutes, both available for money and gifts. Depictions of exciting sexual intercourse was, for this reason, supposedly always with paid women and not with wives in ancient Greek iconography on vases, for example (Reinsberg 1989: 77).

Yet, this polar image of women—the decent and passive wife, mother, guardian of the inner *oíkos*, and maker of offerings, who barely appeared in public versus the erotically, sexually active *hetairai* and prostitutes, who participated in *symposia* and banquets—has meanwhile been criticized by historiography as all too one-sided and has since been relativized accordingly (Garton 2004: 36ff.). Such a redefinition became possible, among other things, due to new facets arising in the interpretation of ancient sources such as erotic vase painting: Many of the illustrations don't just show sexual practices, and the women depicted were not just buyable love servants. The images apparently also served to eroticize married life and were integrated into wedding preparations or could be seen on normal toiletry items and hydria water jugs (Skinner 2005: 104ff.). According to Barbara Borg, some Greek comedies in which wives refused to sexually pacify men were unthinkable without the "prerequisite of a regular and joyful conjugal love life" (Borg 2001: 308). Many of the literary and medical texts written by men also described husbands who also expected pleasure and passion from their wives—not only from *hetairai* and concubines (Hanson 1990: 314ff.; Deslauriers 2021: 39f.).

There are also doubts about the classical definition of male sexuality and the all-dominant penetration model. According to this model, sexual intercourse was about phallic intrusion into a hierarchically subordinate and passive sexual object, whether it was a wife, a youth, a slave, or a *hetaera*. As research has shown, however, penetrative practices in ancient Greek culture not only focused on the act itself but also on the communicative process associated with it and its social significance and coding. Thus, the penetrated also profited from this transaction or exchange, for example, by absorbing energy (according to the above body image), securing their position in the household community, or receiving gifts and social participation. Courting a sexual partner, longing for emotional exchange and the social image associated with the sexual event, as well as the gifts made coitus appear not only (or not primarily) as an act of overpowering and domination. Seen in this light, social and economic criteria and values were the most important aspects in the choice of partners and spouses—whereby, modern, romantic individualizing love and sexual categories played little or no role whatsoever. All these facets should give credence to the idea that sexual activity between married couples would have led to the genesis of at least intimate relationships and possibly love (Schmitz 2007: 98f.). A rather skeptical assessment to the contrary states that upper-class men and women in ancient Greece mostly operated in separate life-worlds and therefore their emotional, intimate, and sexual contacts remained rather underdeveloped—and this was more the case with men due to the variety of extramarital sexual offers (Robson 2013: 24).

Lifelong sexual asceticism was not considered desirable for men or for women, except for virgin priestesses who were ordained to Apollo or Demeter. This does not mean that some philosophical currents were not skeptical of *eros*, such as the followers of Pythagoras or the representatives of Orphism, who from the sixth/fifth century followed the example of the mythical singer and poet Orpheus. They demanded not only the renunciation of animal flesh as food but also abstinence concerning "animalic" coitus—at least outside of marriage. Euripides (480 or 485/484–406 BCE) dramatically put down the Orphic ascetic problem into a tragedy called *The Crowned Hippolytus* (first performed by Dionysia in 428 BCE): In it, he had Phaidra, the mythical wife of Theseus, King of Athens, become overwhelmed by her love and sexual desire—implanted by Aphrodite—for her stepson Hippolytus. Even though Phaidra is depicted here as over-sexualized, we see in this play a (mythical) Greek woman who fights with her (forbidden incestuous) sexual lust as well as caring for herself—which according to Michel Foucault should only exist among Greek men. The male side of the story is represented by Hippolytus, who, instead of physical fulfillment, dreams of untouched spring meadows where he hopes to find true love (Hubbard and Doerfler 2014: 167ff.).

For the philosopher Zenon of Citium (around 334/332–262/261 BCE) and the Stoics, *eros* was also a two-faced figure that alternated between indifferent, charitable love and aggressive, possibly even cruel passion:

desire bestowed by the gods could be the source both of joy and pleasure and of kindness and affection, but it could also entail exactly the opposite emotions between and among the sexes (Grahn-Wilder 2018: 69ff.). In Greek ethics, king *eros* was given much more attention than other virtues and vices problematized in the rigorous control of oneself—for example in dietetics. In the Athens of the fifth and fourth centuries BCE, philosophers had already dealt intensively with the question of how the legitimate *eros* had to be molded so that its destructive potential could be channeled and harnessed for friendship and education (Nussbaum 2000a: 65). The philosopher Epicurus (around 341–271/270 BCE) and his followers, who were actually said to have a penchant for hedonism and exaggerated sensual lust, counted *eros* among those desires that had to be satisfied naturally, but not necessarily and perpetually; they also opted for a balance between desire and aversion (West 2005: 50ff.): For example, the wise man should avoid sexual contact with all women with whom it is unlawful. He was to marry, conceive children depending on their circumstances and thus counteract adultery, which triggered negative emotions and social consequences that hedonists absolutely wanted to avoid (Jope 2014: 423).

From a medical point of view, sexual acts could also have quite unpleasant consequences: In the *Corpus Hippocraticum* (between the fifth and early third century BCE), exhaustion and loss of self followed the sexual act for men. Prodicus (between 470/460 and after 399 BCE) claimed that coitus led to dulling of the mind and even madness. Plato lauded physical abstinence in order to save one's vital energy for higher, mental purposes and spiritual love. Pythagoras claimed that sexual intercourse undermined self-control and reduced mental strength (Suárez Müller 2004: 210ff.). For women, on the other hand, the outlook was more positive; they were not or hardly weakened by coitus, on the contrary, the male sperm warmed their blood and got the *menses* flowing. Additionally, the desire of the *hystera* (the uterus) or its readiness to receive was believed to be satisfied by sex, and thus it stayed at the right spot in the body and remained open. No physical union for long periods would mean the uterus threatened to dry out or wandered closer to more humid organs. This, in turn, resulted in the female psychophysics becoming unstable and falling into a latent state of illness and deficiency (Dean-Jones 1992b: 148ff.).

In the fourth century BCE, Aristotle offered an alternative to the Hippocratic body image: His version had the female reproductive organ (and with it the entire body) functioning not completely differently from the male's but in analogy to the latter, to which he also added a liquid ejaculation during the female orgasm, which, however, contained no seed (Connell 2000). As Aristotle would have it, the absence of coitus and the male seed had no serious consequences for the female body. His model even enabled women to exercise sexual self-control and relieved men a little of the responsibility of exercising sexual control over the female being (Dean-Jones 1992a; Skinner 2005: 154). Aristotle's body theory also had a biopolitical objective: by regulating their sexual lives, Greek men and women could also contribute to the welfare of the city-state by promoting the increase of its population and military strength through procreation and child rearing (Ojakangas 2016: 41). No matter whether woman or man, according to Greek doctors, coital concerns should first of all maintain the physical and thus also the mental balance and avoid any form of excess and exertion.

Segregated Lives of the Sexes

Similar considerations were given to the raising of children. Girls should grow up in the largely female world of the home and be socialized there. Sexual maturation and modesty would have to be the focus of attention. Respectable women should appear decent in public—the higher their status, the more this imperative applied. Appropriation held it necessary for them to lower or avert their eyes in front of a stranger, to avoid contact with unrelated men and, if necessary, to wear a veil. Women who showed themselves to be more open were suspected of having too strong a sexual and possibly promiscuous nature (Glazebrook 2011a: 161). Early sexual experiences and resulting pregnancies should be prevented at all costs (Just 1989: 105ff.). According to Soranus of Ephesus (around 98–138) it was necessary to maintain virginity until the onset of menstruation—until the age of about fourteen; this seemed to him to be the right time for defloration and first sexual intercourse (Read 2015: 10).

Before the wedding, the aristocratic girls of Athens underwent a rite of passage called *arkteia*. In a place of worship dedicated to Artemis, their sexual-erotic potential and fertility were honored and they were symbolically transformed into real women through dance, fertility rites, and competitions. One of the tasks of the goddess Aphrodite was to make the women appear particularly attractive and seductive during the bridal period; erotically charged wedding ceremonies also pursued this goal (Hartmann 2002: 90ff.). The Greek women in classical Athens aged fourteen to eighteen were married mostly by means of an arrangement between two houses—which did not mean, however, that the young women had no say in their choice of husband, who was often twice their age (Laes 2021: 320f.). The engagement agreement between the wife's guardian and the future spouse then included a dowry. In Athens, girls were often married within the patrilineal family and offered to a half-brother, uncle, or cousin as a bride (Robson 2013: 5f.). In Sparta, the average age difference was narrower, brides were on average eighteen years old at the wedding and grooms were twenty-five (Glazebrook and Olson 2014: 70). In any case, the low marriage age of women, which was widespread across the city-states, was to ensure that the brides entered into marriage as virgins and that their honor—and thus also the descent of the offspring—would not be cast into doubt (Abbott 2001: 23).

Many spouses hardly even met before the wedding. During the three-day wedding ceremony, the bride gave up her status as a child and was introduced to her new role as wife and housewife (Wasdin 2020). This crescendoed during the wedding night, which for girls was undoubtedly a drastic experience with, for the most part, a complete stranger. In marriage, the wife also moved into the *oíkos* of her significantly older husband, a gulf in age and experience that left no doubt about the patriarchal relationship between the spouses from the beginning. The mother-in-law was now responsible for familiarizing the new wife with household life and preparing her for motherhood. Offspring should then come as swiftly as possible, for only then was the marriage complete. If this didn't come to pass, divorce or separation wasn't much of an issue, legally. Xenophon (around 430 to around 354 BCE), a student of Socrates, distills the criteria by which many Greek men chose their wives in his *Memorabilia* (or *Recollections*): "[S]urely you don't suppose that human beings beget children on account of sex . . . It is visible that we examine also from what sort of women we might get the best offspring, and it is with these we come together to produce offspring" (Xenophon 1994: 43; Kössler 2012: 111ff.).

Boys and adolescents also grew up in a same-sex environment. In the classical period, they underwent physical and sports training as sons of the citizenry from the age of seven and received military training in Athens from the age of eighteen. From the fifth century BCE, private schools were established in which, in addition to gymnastics and sport, reading and writing as well as poetry, dance, and literature were on the curriculum. After their twentieth year, men took part in the life of the *polis* and worked their way into occupational fields, such as public office. Higher education in philosophy, medicine, literature, and rhetoric could be obtained in larger cities such as Alexandria, Athens, Ephesus, and Pergamon (Littlewood 2006: 251f.). *Andreia* (masculinity) was then exhibited by the adult man not only on the battlefield but also as an educated and loyal citizen who cared for the welfare of the community, protected his honor and that of his house, kept his desires and lusts under control, and let himself be guided by reason (Masterson 2014a: 20f.). Once having fulfilled this male agenda, free men were then allowed to marry at an average age of thirty years. They had to provide for their own offspring and paternal inheritance, but they were also responsible for the sexual protection of members of their *oíkos*.

Even before that, however, they were free to gain sexual experience with slaves and prostitutes. Young men who were very obviously interested in the daughters of free citizens too early, however, were considered menacing and immoral. Overflowing sexual lust and promiscuous actions were seen as problematic and unmanly, as one was at the mercy of overpowering desire. One of the most important characteristics of the citizen old enough to bear arms was just the opposite: steadfastness, the ability to resist in any situation (Dover 2002: 22ff.). Be that as it may, a free man should also be sexually potent. The dangers of impotency, for example through excessive masturbation, was therefore a recurring theme in Greek literature (Krenkel 2006: 173ff.). Moderately practiced, self-pleasure was considered unproblematic and quite common. It was even Hippocratically therapeutic for women to do so, as it was deemed effective in removing excess and accumulated seed. However, the positive effects of the male vital humors could never be achieved in this artificial way (King 2011: 113ff.). Diogenes of Sinope (aka Diogenes the Cynic) (412/403–324/321 BCE) pointed out that the sexual experience did not necessarily require a second person by (allegedly) masturbating in public. Other authors, on the other hand, demanded that married couples cultivate not only sexual relations but also communicate with each other and share at least some of their areas of life (Skinner 2005: 160).

The Social Regulation of *Eros*

Sexual acts that violated or undermined the legal interests and, in particular, the honor of the free citizen and his rule over the *oíkos* were considered a disgraceful violation of honor. *Moicheia*, a hardly translatable term, included various sexual acts against the *kyrios*, which were considered particularly dishonorable—in effect, these were committed by one man against another or his legal assets (Cohen 1993; Robson 2013: 91; Perry 2020: 68). For example, if a married Attic citizen caught his wife committing adultery, he was entitled to kill the perpetrator according to Draconian law (around 650 BCE); in most cases, however, a mere fine was imposed. Restoring the injured masculinity and honor was its purpose, as Lysias (around 445–380 BCE) puts it in an ideal-typical court oratory—in which he isn't using the example of a real-world trial but giving a moral plea—in the case of Euphiletus: This man caught his wife with a certain Eratosthenes, and rejected compensatory offers of money, opting instead to kill him. In the ensuing trial, Euphiletus was acquitted and considered justified because he had acted not only in the name of the law but also on behalf of all Athenian citizens threatened by such a form of dishonor among his *oíkos* (Fisher 1998: 79; Kapparis 2018a: 190ff.). A convicted adulteress, on the other hand, was cast out in divorce, was no longer allowed to participate in ritual celebrations, and was even denied burial in the holy place (Johnson and Ryan 2005: 5; Younger 2005: 66).

The seduction of an unmarried daughter, sister, or niece, even of the widowed mother of *kyrios*—that is, all those women who were under his protection—was an act of *moicheia* (Omitowoju 2002: 72ff.; Wolicki 2007). Such acts were popular literary motifs because they could destroy the paternal lineage and trigger a family and social tragedy. Ancient Greek legal understanding held that a woman had thus committed a form of *hybris*, a sexualized act with which she had shamed and humiliated herself in favor of pleasure, not only from the point of view of society but above all also in her own self-perception (Cohen 2004: 64ff.). Yet, the outrage was always committed by someone else against her, regardless of her consent (Eidinow 2011: 90f.). So, it is not surprising that dishonor, rape, and kidnapping as well as non-consensual seduction/deception/overpowering were popular dramatic motifs. The mythical gods and heroes were also committing a never-ending chain of such acts against the will or at least without their victims' freedom of choice: Hades steals Persephone, the beautiful Ganymede is kidnapped by Zeus, and the sea nymph Amphitrite, who wished to remain unmarried, submits to Poseidon in the guise of a dolphin, thereby taking her as his wife. Godfather Zeus heads the divine list as perpetrator of rape and abduction, representing male supremacy and phallic power (Lauriola 2022: 60ff.). Even the heavenly females do not shy away from such empowerment, as when Eos, the goddess of dawn, kidnaps the Trojan prince Tithonos and subsequently gives birth to Memnon (Golden and Toohey 2011: 68). War then pretty much entailed that the women and daughters of the defeated were raped on a massive scale by Greek warriors (Gaca 2014b: 306ff.) (Figure 2).

Sexual human rights in the modern sense were not considered goods worthy of protection in the Greek city-states, in the sense that a or every person could possess a general legal property in the form of sexual integrity or sexual freedom of decision. Even though ancient Greek lacked a word equivalent to the modern term "rape," sexual acts performed against the will of the person involved (using physical or psychological force) were a recurring theme (Koutsopetrou-Møller 2021; Deacy and Pierce 2002). Both within marriage and in relationships with slave women or *hetairai*, numerous

FIGURE 2 *Zeus abducting Ganymede, Attic kylix, c. 470 BCE.*

structural dependency relationships existed between men and women in which sexual supremacy and violence were inscribed. Sexual acts using violence were addressed in the sources often as forms of humiliation and shame on the female side. The historian Herodotus (around 485–424 BCE) speaks of women who killed themselves after such an act because of the loss of honor. In court, a distinction was made between those perpetrators whose assaults were directed against a woman's *kyrios* and those who did not intend to hurt *him*. And indeed, there is plenty of reason to think that such acts only seldom surfaced in public and most were hidden due to the massive shame that a rape would have meant for the victim (married or unmarried), for the insufficiency of the protective *kyrios* and the whole family or clan (Robson 2013: 102ff.). In any case, the protection of blood-kinship and descent was a central theme in the literature. From Dracon in the seventh century BCE to the Hellenistic period, legislation also dealt extensively with this problem (Ornitowoju 2002).

Wives were to be sexually available for the man of the house, meanwhile he was allowed to maintain contacts with prostitutes and *hetairai* as well. The social fetters of *eros* were thus primarily aimed at regulating and disciplining the behavior of women, but indirectly they also said something about the social relations between men. Thus, some magical practices—such as those for increasing *eros* in women and for controlling it in men—reveal that alongside patriarchal culture and male control of the supposedly lascivious and sexually controlled female being, there was also an alternative culture that subordinated men to the magical control of women, moderate and chaste by nature (Faraone 2001: ix). According to John J. Winkler, "behind the façade of public docility women had lives of their own and, arguably, a more comprehensive understanding of men than men had of women" (Winkler 1990: 209). The numerous marital conflicts that came to the theater stages in tragic and comedic form are also an indication that sexual relations were by no means confined to the male power structure. In the comedy *Lysistrata* (411 BCE) by Aristophanes (between 450/444 and around 380 BCE), for example, the women of Athens and Sparta refuse to be amorous with their war-minded men until they stop fighting each other—which they do after some comical twists and turns. This piece illustrated for the Greeks the power of the nuptial bed, that it must be seen as greater than the sword and that ancient Greek society only functioned because women cooperated in it, choosing not to deprive *phallós* of its power by withdrawing their love. Men, or patriarchal society, were threatened here not only with the suspension of sexual intercourse, but with the interruption of procreation and male martiality (Yalom 2001: 10; Tsoumpra 2020).

Pleasures of the Marriage Bed

While the primary aim of conjugal intercourse was to conceive children, Greek husbands had reasons to give their wives sexual pleasure. One was simply because, according to the Hippocratic model of the body, only a mutual orgasm could lead to ejaculation and conception. But coitus that is also satisfactory for the women would also promote mutual trust and emotional bonding, thus the wives would perhaps be more likely to remain faithful during the absence of the men—during wartime, for instance (Johnson and Ryan 2005: 3). Even though historiographical literature has characterized the (sexual) relationship of married couples primarily in terms of authority and force or at least a lack of decision-making ability and power on the part of the woman, there are sources that also attribute action potential to her. Lysias, for example, in the speech *Against Eratosthenes*, made a great distinction between women who consented to adultery and those who opposed it. Even in the case of seduction by the gods, women were better off who were taken by the higher powers through no fault of their own or those who resisted. In Xenophons' (between 430/425 and 355 BCE) *Lacedaemonion Politeia*, it is explicitly deemed socially advantageous for wives to be of a consenting mind.

How coitus should be performed is also a topic of these texts. Among the sexual positions mentioned in Aristophanes' comedy *Lysistrata*, penetration "a tergo" (from behind) in the "riding position" was preferred (the woman sits on the man who is lying on his back and also turns her back toward him). In the archaic and classical period (up to the fourth century BCE), the "missionary position" was regarded as rather unusual, even unnatural; only later was it rated more positively (Younger 2005: 123f.). This change of position suggests that the marital sexual act evolved from a rather anonymous, often violent or overwhelming act—in which the couples did not look into each other's faces or make eye contact—to a more face-to-face interaction and intimacy (Younger 2011: 71). In surviving fragments of manuals, a wide variety of positions during sexual intercourse were mentioned, in which the advantage of expressing the man's dominance prevailed as a basic principle (Shusterman 2021: 55f.). Anal penetration also seems to have been part of the sexual repertoire, older couples may have practiced it for contraception. Some were familiar with contraceptives and methods, such as (abortive) concoctions, sponges soaked in olive oil introduced into a woman's vagina, or through magical practices. Coitus interruptus, on the other hand, was considered a seed-wasting practice and long rejected for this reason (Younger 2005: 36; Salisbury 2001: 68f.; McInerney 2022: 296f.).

As a result of the political and social developments of the fourth century BCE—the emergence of the Macedonian Empire, the conquests of Alexander the Great and the subsequent division of his empire—Greek empires emerged in which the *poleis* played only subordinate roles. In Hellenistic times (336–30 BCE), a more individual concept of love spread, in which greater importance was also attached to spouses' mutual sense of pleasure. In art and literature, the pros and cons of such personal marital alliances were played out. One's relationship with one's wife in particular was clearly emotionalized and eroticized (Lape 2004). The art of seduction and sensual love was now also supposed to be increasingly practiced within marriage, pushing *hetairai* and prostitutes into the background (Borg 2001: 308; Kaimio 2002).

A Greek woman's wider social life also changed in the pre-Christian centuries. She was no longer to simply live in seclusion in the house but rather participate more in public life, in accordance with her social position, of course. Many Greek women had to work outside the household for economic reasons. Outside, they increasingly came into contact with more men. The ritualized sociability of the male *symposia* would now also become accessible to wives (Ihm 2004: 24ff.). The ambiguous public position of the new woman was also highlighted in the symbolic pictorial repertoire: Statues of Aphrodite hid her (half-)naked "private parts" in an ambiguous gesture, for example. The goddess of love, beauty, and sexual desire thus pointed to the sexual and reproductive power of the woman, as well as to her need for protection. This simultaneously reveals the still skewed gender relations and the greater vulnerability of women. For centuries, nude men (and male statues), who presented their genitals in a real and symbolic way to the public, had been part of the artistic and mythological inventory of Greek culture and everyday life in the *gymnasium* (from *gymnos*, naked), the training and education center of athletes (Salomon 1997: 208ff.).

Prostitutes in the *Polis*?

Even though there have been countless publications on the history of prostitution in general since the 1990s, on individual eras and countries including non-European cultures (Rodríguez García, Heerma van Voss and van Nederveen Meerkerk 2017; Kapparis 2018b; McGinn 2004; Ringdal 1997; Núnez 1995; White 1990; Bullough and Bullough 1987), the concept of prostitution itself remains positively muddled. Simon Goldhill has raised the irritating question of whether a history of prostitution makes any sense at all in historical comparison, since it includes highly diverse social phenomena and sexual relations (Goldhill 2014). Ultimately, the question amounts to what is meant by prostitution and how can such a definition be applied to different eras and cultures. First off, the term "sex work" should also be included, according to the *Encyclopedia of Prostitution and Sex Work* (Hope Ditmore 2006: XXVff.). This term has been used since the 1970s as a non-discriminatory term for sexual services, transactions, and business—among other things to avoid negatively connoted and stigmatizing terms such as prostitute, whore, or escort. "Prostitution" is understood here as sexual exchange for money, objects, or valuables. Ultimately, respective criminal codes (or even civil law) have determined whether this practice was defined as legal or prosecuted and punished, whether it was simply tolerated or recognized as a form of promiscuity, polygamy, or concubinage.

The delimitation of prostitution always proves to be precarious where such attributions and categorizations are just as absent as the corresponding criminal or policing provisions, as will be shown in the case of ancient Greece.

In the Greek *polis* there was no clear definition of prostitution, and the terms also remained vague (McGinn 2014: 6ff.). Heterogeneous groups of people—significantly more women than men—were available for sexual services or were forced into them. The offer ranged from cheap *pornai* (brothel slaves) to the legendary *hetairai*, prostitutes whose reputation went down in mythology and historiography, to *pallakai* (concubines) living in long-standing relationships. However, the list of relevant terms also includes *gephyris* (bridge-woman), *spodesilaura* (street-walker), and *megalomisthoi* (high earning courtesans) (Glazebrook 2011a: 147). In the Greek city-states, prostitution was generally not punished because it did not contradict either religious or secular principles. By law, however, it was regulated that free persons and minors incapable of giving consent should be protected from sexual exploitation (Kapparis 2018a: 190ff.). A *Eleuthera*, a free women, was seen as "a woman with a claim to sexual honor" and *sophrosyne*, sexual modesty, a slave did not possess these properties (Harper 2016: 111).

What all these women have in common is that they remain completely voiceless in historical transmission. Our knowledge of them is above all shaped by literature and by legal texts. As is so often the case in (sexual) history, however, these genres of texts were produced by the hands of men, many of them members of the upper social strata. The Greek poets, in particular, constructed primarily idealized, glorified, or even comedic figures. In decrees and legal texts, in turn, we come across rules and norms that were often irrelevant or circumvented in everyday practice and thus mostly did not correspond to reality. Recent research has tended to include quite diverse sources, such as findings from painting and vase art as well as archaeological objects, which show buyable love in a more differentiated light and thus also open up social, economic, and political aspects (Cohen 2006; Schuller 2008: 13ff.).

Hetairai and Pallakai—Companions for Money?

The *hetairai* undoubtedly received the most attention—a euphemistic term that was increasingly used from the end of the fifth century BCE and which referred to female companions (as counterparts to male friends or companions) (McClure 2003: 10f.; Davidson 1997: 135). The first historical evidence of them was found in the late archaic period (from the last quarter of the sixth century BCE) on vase paintings, which represented the *symposia* of the *polis* elite. The paintings depicted young women who accompanied the men, some engaged in the art of conversation, playing the flute or the lyre, singing or dancing (Kapparis 2018b: 47ff.). As the banquet progressed, some of them appeared scantily clothed or even naked and finally enjoyed themselves with one of the *symposium* participants. Many of the scenes were clearly aimed at the erotic and sexual excitement of the viewer. Others show constellations depicting an intimate emotional connection between men and women, with the two facing each other, eye to eye in the truest sense. The fact that these were not servants, "ordinary prostitutes," or one of the usual entertainers is evident from the almost equal placement of the figures, their posture and clothing, and sometimes also from inscriptions of their names, an honor and a sign of import (Schuller 2008: 35ff.; Budin 2021: 62ff.). *Hetairai* belonged to the classical pictorial and textual program of Greek art throughout the centuries. Athenaeus (end of the second/beginning of the third century) compiled a whole collection of anecdotes about them around 200 CE: they were standard figures in comedies and dramas, and they were indispensable for vases and drinking vessels (Reinsberg 1989: 86).

In the *hetairikoi dialogoi* (whore dialogues, around 160 CE) of Lucian of Samosata (around 120–180 CE), we can find a comic instruction of a *hetaera*. The widow Krobyle informs her daughter Korinna on how to become such a woman:

> Krobyle: First she takes good care of her appearance, then she is polite and pleasant with everyone, not giggling with everything, like you do, but smiling nicely and seductively, then behaving gracefully and not deceitfully when someone comes to her house or she goes to someone's place, never directly approaching a man first. If she is paid to attend a dinner party, she does not get drunk—for it is ridiculous and men dislike such women—nor does she fill up with delicacies in a vulgar manner, but barely touches it with the tips of her fingers, and puts it in her mouth quietly not stuffing it into both sides of her mouth, and she is drinking gently, not guzzling greedily but in a paced manner.
> Korinna: Even if she happens to be thirsty, mother?
> Krobyle: Especially then, Korinna. And she does not talk more than she should, nor mock anyone present, but only has eyes for the man who hired her, and for those reasons they love her. When bed-time comes, she should not do anything shameless or careless, but everything she does has a single purpose, how to seduce him and make him her lover; everyone is praising her for these things. If you learn these, we will be fortunate too. (Kapparis 2018b: 56f.)

Some *hetairai* rose quickly through society's ranks: Born as slaves and raised in the lower classes, many achieved prosperity and prestige through relationships with one or more rich and respected citizens (Weiler 2018). They were known not only for their beauty and erotic charisma, but also for their social skills and talent for entertaining. The term *hetaira* first appeared in Herodotus' mid-fifth century BCE account of Rhodopis, a ransomed slave from Thrace, who achieved fame and wealth through her extraordinary beauty and sexual services. From the beginning, it was one of the peculiarities of the *hetairai* that the men, who mostly belonged to the urban upper class, could not (or not simply) buy their services with money and gifts in kind but also had to strive for their favor. The playful seduction was considered a value in its own right, which Timocles summed up in one of his comedies by juxtaposing an "ordinary" whore and a *hetaira*, whom he calls a "lass": "What an enormous difference between spending the night with a free girl or with a prostitute. . . . The fact that everything is not too much ready for you, and you have to wrestle a little, and get slapped and punched by her soft hands. That's nice, by Zeus the greatest!" (Silver 2018: 96; Hartmann 2002: 167f.).

If she chose one of the candidates, nothing stood in the way of a more intensive relationship in which erotic and sexual components undoubtedly played a central role.

Hetairai thus also had the function of prestige objects, which one had to conquer and then defend by cultivating the bond of companionship and letting her participate in social life just as much as in one's own prosperity. The bestowal of gifts was a necessity. The man usually had to offer her an apartment or a house, too. Particularly desirable women also required clothing befitting such status, expenditures for beauty care and servant slaves, because this was the only way for a man to present his *hetaira* to the (male) public in all her splendor. Gifts of jewelry and money had the advantage that the beloved could invest in securing her old age, because as a former slave or foreigner she was excluded from house and land ownership. It was thus paramount for a *hetaira* to avoid the appearance of being for sale or quickly changing suitors. Due to the financial demands alone, only wealthy men could afford such a lover; if their market value declined, however, less wealthy admirers got their chance.

Whoever had such a relationship (and with whom) was the talk of the town, and the poets included well-known beauties such as Laïs, Aspasia, and Kyrene in their dramas and comedies. The shining pomp of the lives of the *hetairai* led many a young woman to opt for this life path, or were designated to do so by their guardians and owners. Another, much more pressing reason for choosing this path was that these women were able to buy their way out of slavery from the proceeds of their sexual and amorous services and—once free or liberated—to achieve a certain prosperity and prestige (Schuller 2008: 136ff.). Some of them achieved a respectable education and artistic abilities, which were also in demand among their lovers. Some *hetairai* in Athens were able to keep up with philosophical conversations, according to one of the participants of Athenaeus' (end of the second/beginning of the third century) *The Sophists' Dinner*. Athenaeus reports that the philosopher Stilpon had accused the *hetaira* Glycera about a century earlier of seducing youths. Her pithy and apt response was

> We incur the same blame, Stilpo. For they say that you corrupt all that need you by teaching them worthless, eristic sophistries, while I likewise

teach them erotic ones. It makes no difference, therefore, to people who are utterly destroyed and down on their luck, whether they live in the company of a philosopher or a courtesan (McClure 2003: 103).

Even though *hetairai* had the luxury of (co-)determining with whom they entered into a sexual and possibly also an emotional (love) relationship, they remained—due to competition from the beginning and evermore so with advancing age—in the clearly worse position compared to their male lovers. Companions could quickly devolve into prostitutes who had to sell their sexual services to changing clientele or, with increasing age, became intermediaries for others, that is, as matchmakers or madams (Davidson 1997: 140; Hartmann 2002: 183). At any rate, their birth, origin, and promiscuous lifestyle prevented them from ascending to the status of free citizens. The life story of the *hetaira* Neaira has many literary renditions that recount the ups and downs of such a career: Raised and trained as a slave in a Corinthian brothel in the fourth century BCE, she became the city's priciest prostitute as a teenager and was acquired by two former clients as a shared companion. She was finally able to buy her way out with the help of an Athenian citizen and make her own way in Megara. Another free citizen, Stephanus, helped her to return to Athens together with her children. Back in Athens, the pair lived from her activities and income. The details of her life course were thoroughly examined in the indictment and defense speeches of several trials. The arbitration dealt with the ownership of this (former) slave, about questions of the legitimate paternity of her children, and the intricacies of civil law. Above all, the dispute settled the marriage of this non-Attic and (former) prostitute with an Athenian citizen, which was forbidden according to the marriage law there. In the case of Neaira, the boundaries between (brothel) whore and *hetaira* were barely discernible or clearly laid down (Hamel 2003; Glazebrook 2022: 63ff.; Kapparis 2022: 34). Unlike an honorable wife, who also possessed (legal) protection through guardianship, an unfree prostitute or a concubine who had bought her freedom and worked independently could never achieve the same level of protection from a man (Sossau 2012: 22).

The hetaearian system also provided plenty of grounds for conflict within the families and the *oíkoi* of the clientele. In principle, there was nothing to prevent a single or married, younger or older man from keeping such a consort for sexual services and companionship if this was done in a limited "private" setting or relegated publicly to the *symposia*. However, if ever it impacted the family, inheritance, or households, the limitations of the *hetairai* institution quickly became visible. Animated by the emotional and erotic bonds to the *hetaira*—so goes the argument from plaintiff family members—some men spent enormous sums for their affection and services and stood up for their social recognition. Children who had been conceived with their beloved and for whom citizenship rights were demanded or claims to property and assets made proved to be a special point of contention.

When a Greek citizen entered into a long-term extramarital relationship with a freed or free-bought slave, this concubine was called a *pallake*. The *pallake* served the "daily needs of our bodies," according to Pseudo-Demosthenes. This was, however, a narrow view since often these relationships endangered citizens' marriages and thus represented a serious social misstep. Unlike *hetairai* and one-off prostitutes, who were both more or less paid for sex, the *pallake* was not paid or rewarded directly for her (sexual) services. Instead, she lived in a second household financed by her lover. Most city-states forbade concubines from residing within the wife's *oíkos* already in the classical period (500–336 BCE) (Ogden 1995: 226). From Solon (around 600 BCE), only children conceived with their wives were considered legitimate descendants and those descended from concubines went unrecognized as family members (Lape 2011: 21). In the year 451 BCE, Pericles (around 490–429 BCE) enacted a law according to which Attic citizens were only considered as such if both parents also possessed this status. Declarations such as these discriminated against non-citizen women who lived in cohabitation with Athenians and had children with them (Robson 2013: 3). It was also generally unacceptable that an adult man would live long term with a concubine and thus call into question the social and economic lineage of his parents' house, instead of marrying a respected citizen's daughter (Hartmann 2002: 211). Long-term cohabitations in the form of concubinage sometimes came about when widowed citizens, after the death of their wives, entered into a stable relationship with such freedwomen—sometimes even remaining in the family home and household. Often, it was a question of looking after the children from the previous marriage or escaping a remarriage that was not particularly well regarded (Hartmann 2002: 224). Even in this case, the *pallakai* remained excluded from property transfer, but their children born to the citizen were also born free, albeit without citizenship status.

Pornai, Brothels, and Their Clientele

Sexual services could also be purchased from *pornai*, most often slaves but also free-bought ex-slaves and foreigners living in the *polis* (Weiler 2018). As *pornoi*—the adjective *pornos* probably derived from the verb *pernemi* (to sell)—men could also offer sexual services (Younger 2005: 108; Golden and Toohey 2011: 13). Even some citizens of Athens offered sexual services, but they then also lost some of their rights: Men selling their bodies were not allowed to speak before assemblies, for example, while women forfeited the right to marry. The penal laws stipulated that the integrity of a citizen's body and those of his family must not be violated. It was therefore illegal to sell children of citizens to brothels. If a married woman prostituted herself, this was also considered a serious crime. In the case of men, furthermore, a citizen who had his body penetrated by another man was deeply mistrusted, since he had given up phallic control over himself (Halperin 1990: 97).

The wage of the *pornai* could vary considerably depending on the market and could sometimes cost nearly as much as a *hetaira* (Cohen 2015: 162ff.). On average, *pornai* demanded only a drachma or two, which corresponded roughly to the payment of a flute player (*auletris*)—some of whom could also be employed sexually for an extra charge. In comparison, a trained craftsman or an official of the *polis* earned about a drachma a day. In classical Athens, cheap sexual services could be purchased for as little as one to four *oboloi*—one *obol* being one sixth of a drachma, thus four were just over half a drachma. High-priced *pornai* could demand many times this amount (Robson 2013: 84f.). Even as slaves, prostitutes were (sometimes) allowed to keep part of their wages, a special incentive to save the amount needed to buy one's freedom (Younger 2005: 110; Cohen 2006: 106ff.). This shows the power and ownership relations inscribed into this form of prostitution (Cohen 2015; Porter 2021): Unfree *pornai* were sold by their owners (possibly via an intermediary) to third parties for services; the slaves had no say in this and were—as Aristotle put it—an "instrument" whose body could be used (Goldhill 2014: 185). Free prostitutes outside brothels usually had a better status and were even able to conclude contracts with their clients, which in turn protected the latter from a possible accusation of *hybris* or adultery, for the prostitute might potentially be married (McGinn 2014: 90ff.).

The clientele also came from nearly all social strata of Greek society. Prostitution took place in publicly accessible brothels or via procuresses and pimps in private quarters. It was this dependence that marked one of the reasons why prostitutes were not well regarded in ancient Greece. Despite sexual services for sale by slaves as well as free citizens, in the brothels, in taverns, and out on the streets (Glazebrook and Tsakirgis 2016; Kapparis 2018b: 284ff.), in all price categories and all manner of venues, the Greek city-states did not think highly of it. Clients ought not get too involved with prostitutes or surrender themselves to the likes of whores. Accusations thereof could destroy careers and were used quite deliberately for political disavowal. The lamp manufacturer and politician Hyperbolus (?–411 BCE), for instance, fell victim to this experience when accused of having had affairs with married and unmarried women, with prostitutes, even with an illegitimate daughter. He had thus proved himself to be excessive, a man at the mercy of his drives and thus a demagogue—for which he was banished from Athens for ten years in the process known as ostracism (Kistler 2012: 47). Vulgar words such as *mysachne* (filthy in the feminine form) and *pornoboskos* ("whore keeper/holder," i.e., pimps or often bawds, i.e., procuresses) testified to the negative opinion many Greeks had of the *pornai* and their environment (Glazebrook 2011a: 147). They were regarded as people driven by strong sexual desires, unable to control themselves, thus representing the opposite of the respectable Greek female and male citizenry. If the latter surrendered too much to (sexual) excess, they themselves violated elementary ethical values such as moderation and self-control. The use of violence during sexual intercourse with whores and slaves was also considered reprehensible—for example, in one case where a client had beaten a whore with sandals and scalded her with an oil lamp (Kilmer 1993: 108ff.).

As a rule, Greek men had access to a wide range of sexual services. Especially in the flourishing cities, the multitudes of enslaved young women and men ensured a never-ending supply. The mainstay of *pornai* (and courtesans) was obviously not Athens, however, but Corinth (Robson 2013: 67; Gilhuly 2017: 11ff.). Here, as in Athens, sexual services included vaginal and anal penetration, as well as manual and oral practices. Vase paintings depicted fellatio and cunnilingus mostly in the context of banquets or as actions of satyrs and sileni, mythical figures associated with Dionysus; therefore, they cannot necessarily be regarded as common sexual acts. It should also be borne in mind that men would be giving up their active and penetrative role in such acts—in the first case they remained passive, in the second they no longer stood at the center of the sexual act but subjected themselves to female lust. The mythological figure of the satyr, an animal–human mixed being with characteristics of horse, donkey, and goat as well as a permanently erect, mostly oversized penis, symbolized *hybris*, the exaggerated and overflowing male desire and energy. Here lurked also one of the threats of the *pornai*: if their erotic-sexual power enabled them to

FIGURE 3 *Satyr and maenad*, Terracotta stamnos *(jar) red-figure, c. 350 BCE.*

completely bind a man to themselves, he was only an appendage of his penis and turned into a kind of orgiastic satyr, dominated by his desires (Isler-Kerényi 2007: 195f.; McInerney 2022) (Figure 3).

Most brothels were a collection of enslaved and accordingly cheap whores (Davidson 1997: 83ff.; Weiler 2018). Other *porneia* (whore houses) were quite well furnished, offering customers not only fast pleasure but also attractive and comfortable interiors, such as mosaic-decorated baths, as well as exterior courtyards (Glazebrook 2016). *Porneia* were concentrated in regular red light districts, but commercial and residential areas also had them in close proximity. The comedy poet Xenarchus mocked the public visibility of Athenian prostitution in the fourth century BCE:

> Terrible, terrible, and utterly intolerable, are the practices of young men in our city—here, where there are, after all, very good-looking young things in the whore-houses, whom one can readily see basking in the sun, their breasts uncovered, stripped for action and drawn up in battle-formation by columns, from among whom one can select whatever sort one likes—thin, fat, squat, tall, shrivelled, young, old, middle-aged, fully-ripened—without setting up a ladder and stealthily entering [another man's house to seduce his women], or slipping through the smoke-hole in the roof, or getting oneself carried inside by trickery in a heap of chaff. For the girls themselves grab people and drag them in, naming those who are old men 'little father', those who are younger, 'little bro'.; And each of them can be had without fear, affordably, by day, towards evening, in every way you like. (Halperin 1990: 93; Reinsberg 1989: 126)

Athens then leveraged the economic success of such institutions for the city budget and levied a tax which not only the prostitutes but also the pimps, bawds, and brothel operators had to pay (Glazebrook 2011b: 36ff.; Kapparis 2018b: 271ff.). Owners and intermediaries were often former prostitutes themselves who had managed to buy their freedom or had been bought out of slavery by a client. The organizers of glamorous *symposia* went to these procuresses to rent girls and boys for the attendees. On such occasions, it became apparent that some entertainers had a second, sexual source of income.

For the slave owners, it was also a business to sell desirable female slaves across borders. Some were even shipped to India and sold in harems as *yavani* (Ionic Greek). Or they worked as courtesans, barmaids, and flute girls in the entertainment business of ancient Indian cities and courts (Hain 2020).

Abortion, Contraceptives, and Sexually Transmitted Diseases

Although abortion was the subject of many medical treatises, this practice seems to have been mainly reserved for prostitutes and slaves. Married women were likely to have an abortion primarily if they had committed *moicheia* and become pregnant. No provision in Athenian law forbade abortion, it was a matter that concerned only the *oîkos* and its head (Pepe 2014: 21; Kapparis 2018a: 300). The primary means was to induce uterine contractions and thus an abortion. Many abortifacients are listed, such as garlic, sea scorpions, Spanish flies, wine lees, sodium bicarbonate, and copper, in the *Corpus Hippocraticum* (fifth century to second century BCE). These were processed into suppositories and creams, and introduced into the vagina or uterus using wool tampons. Orally administered mixtures, tinctures, and infusions of herbs, plants, and soils, such as the leaves of monk's pepper dissolved in wine or a decoction of pine wood in sweet wine mixed with galbanum and myrtle, were also purported to have an abortive effect (McLaren 1990: 26ff.; Riddle 1992: 77ff.). An abortive plant called *silphium*, frequently mentioned in classical antiquity, may very well have gone extinct due to its great popularity. Many of these substances actually had an abortive effect, which is why they were still recommended by doctors such as Soranus of Ephesus and Pedanius Dioscorides in the first century.

Contraceptives appearing in Hippocratic literature can be grouped into three categories: laxatives and emetics, applications directly affecting the uterus, and mechanical measures such as abdominal compression and impact or bodily convulsions (Jütte 1993: 34; King 2018: 47ff.). Abiding by the Hippocratic Oath, which doctors vowed to follow, it was usually not they who prescribed or administered these drugs but rather midwives and learned women who passed on their knowledge. There was no clear separation between abortion and contraception, as there was disagreement about the moment of conception and the beginnings of life: According to Aristotle, fertilization took place within the first seven days, and Pythagoras agreed that life began then. Soranus of Ephesus, on the other hand, was of the opinion that the soul entered the body through the process of pregnancy; Diogenes and Plato claimed that this only occurred with birth (Kapparis 2002: 33ff.; Younger 2005: 1). Thus, it isn't surprising that doctors' advice on what measures had to be regarded as abortion or contraception varied greatly (King 1998: 145ff.). Whatever the medical and ethical reason for prostitutes avoiding or aborting pregnancies, it was a ceaseless issue affecting their livelihood.

Another difficulty was sexually transmitted diseases. The symptoms recorded in the sources are difficult to reconcile with current diagnostic categories, but gonorrhea, chancroid, and chlamydia may have been common bacterial infectious diseases with visible manifestations on the genital organs (and beyond); this also applied to ulcers and warts on the genitals as well as verruca on the anus (Younger 2005: 125; King 2011: 115; Flemming 2019). Genital herpes was also among the culprits (Grmek 1991: 142ff.). Wherever prostitutes frequented—this was the case among military troops in addition to red light districts—infections occurred on a massive scale. At birth, a mother's gonorrhea often also led to an eye infection in the child (known as the "eye ripper"), the cause of about one third of all cases of blindness. Many doctors were well aware of how the venereal infection occurred.

The Intersection of Prostitution

An overview of the manifold forms of prostitution in ancient Greece reveals that the cultural integration of this sexual activity can only be understood intersectionally, that is, within the framework of networked social, economic, and cultural factors. In the ancient prostitution regime, what mattered was the difference between slaves and the free, between citizens and non-citizens, between men and women; it touched the institution of marriage, the security of the house or household, the separation of public and private, the ability to act autonomously; it entailed not only pecuniary but also symbolic forms of exchange, the possibilities of social participation, and much more (Goldhill 2014: 192f.). It should also become clear that the existing historical (textual and pictorial) sources were marked by clearly contradictory discursive strategies. The statements made there about *hetairai*, *pallakai*, and *pornai* must therefore be seen in the light of the genre and the medium of transmission, the social status of the producer, the audience addressed, and the intended objectives. Most authors undoubtedly did not think of the sexual services that slaves had to provide to their masters as prostitution in the modern sense—if only because slave bodies had no sexual integrity and autonomy, rather they were classified as *andrápodon*, as an "object that walks upon human feet" (Thommen 2007: 40). Slaves belonged to their owners not only for exhaustive work but also for sexual exploitation. This meant, however, that slaves were under their protection; thus, offences of *hybris*, that is, sexual assaults committed by others, fell well within the master's responsibility and became a question of his own honor (Cohen 2014: 186ff.).

The ancient writers were rather divided about the social (return) service and individual options and abilities of *hetairai* and concubines. Most placed them—and thus also their sexual desire—in a nexus of physical attraction and emotional affection and financial as well as social capital, and related potential opportunities. Few were willing to state that *hetairai* and probably also many concubines were fettered in a rather one-sided power relation and trapped in its corresponding dependencies, which in no way would have allowed their sexual trade(-off) to be a voluntary and wanted form of communication. Modern human rights, which (should) guarantee autonomy and self-determination in sexual matters as well, cannot at any rate be transferred to ancient Greece and its patriarchal slave-owning society. It cannot be overlooked, however, that even then the sale of sexual services was a profitable business—and this was especially true for the *pornoboskoi*, the pimps, bawds, and slave owners, who took a large part of the income (Cohen 2015: 171ff.).

When Greek historians reported on "barbaric" cultures, the "strange" and "wild" sexual life was mostly seen as an indication of their backward, even animalistic stage of development. According to Herodotus' *Histories*, for example, the inhabitants of the Caucasus, India, and Libya practiced sexual acts in public and wife swapping. He had the Thracians allowing their daughters to sleep with all the men they desired before marriage. He somehow knew that the women of the Libyan Ginandes wore chains around their lower calves, one for each of their lovers, and the woman who possessed the most anklets was considered the most coveted. The Greek historian Theopompus of Chios (around 378/377–after 320 BCE) was an expert on how the Etruscans didn't even know who their biological fathers were because of their promiscuous behavior. Countless other tall tales were also used to characterize foreigners as sexually immoderate and uncontrollable—counter-images to Greek ethics and morality. Such accusations were aimed, in particular, at the sexual behavior of barbaric men. They were often characterized as effeminate, excessive, promiscuous, polygamous, incestuous, and on and on. These wayward acts of desire would, in the historians' tellings, ultimately lead to the downfall of peoples and countries. Read with an eye for the sexual, these narratives actually reveal the desires and fantasies of the Greek men or the poets and historians who formulated them, as well as their deep-seated fears and anxieties about all forms of love and sexuality that evaded the patriarchal control of the *kyrios* (Roisman 2014: 401ff.).

Male sexuality and the proper place of honorable Greek women stand at the center of the antipodal myth of the Amazon: These enemy warriors allegedly descended from the war god Ares and the nymph Harmonia. They lived in purely female societies somewhere out on the Black Sea, in the Persian Empire or with the Scythians in the Eurasian Steppe. According to the narratives, they hated men, although some of them were themselves castrated men. Amazons refused to marry and behaved either asexually or excessively promiscuously. This nomadic "female tribe" dressed in animal skins. Its members proved to be excellent, wild riders who trained their animals themselves. They were superb hunters and powerful archers. To better draw back their bows, they burned off their right breasts. From time to time, they would make use of a foreign man for reproduction. Any male babies were abandoned or crippled. According to Herodotus, there were only two ways to become their master: Amazons could be killed or they could be tamed by sexual intercourse, pacified through submissive sexual acts (Mayor 2014: 249ff.; Taube 2013). These mythological figures—whose historical narrative was informed by farther Eastern tribal societies in which women did indeed take part in cattle breeding and hunting—were almost the antithesis of the "domesticated" Greek woman, sequestered in procreation and the household. At the same time, these women were regarded as the epitome of the barbaric and uncultured life that threatened Greek civilization from the outside. The consequence of all this was that the Amazons inspired the fantasy of Greek authors over centuries and engendered much literature and pictorial memory (Blundell 2002: 31ff.; Tiersch 2013).

Temple or Ritual Prostitution?

Historians have conducted an extensive and rather unwieldy discussion on the question of temple prostitution and cult and sacred prostitution in ancient Greece (and beyond) (Budin 2008; Silver 2019; Waqas 2022). In any case, there are indications of such a practice: In the fifth century BCE, for example, Herodotus reported in the *Histories* that Cypriot women had to surrender to a stranger once in their lives in the places of worship of Palepaphos and Amathus against payment in honor of the goddess Aphrodite. Also, according to Pindar (522/518–446 BCE), Strabo (about 63 BCE–23 CE), and Athenaeus (end of the second/beginning of the third century), the prostitution of slaves flourished in the temple of Aphrodite in Corinth. Strabo claimed that the temple had about a thousand sacred prostitutes dedicated to Aphrodite. The fact that these and similar passages have been regarded as evidence of prostitution was probably also due to the scintillating meaning of the term *aphrodisiac*, which was often used in the sources. In general, this meant indulging in pleasure in a broader sense. Nevertheless, the word could also refer to the performance of the sexual act and the active penetration by the man, as well as convey the statement that sexual intercourse was a sacred act (Foucault 1989a: 62; Younger 2005: 109f.). The partially synonymous use of the terms "temple prostitution" and "ritual" or "sacral prostitution" also contributed to this assessment: The first case refers to paid sexual services offered on the premises of places of worship or in the temple district, organized by temple staff or even carried out with the active participation of priests and priestesses. Cult and sacred prostitution refer to paid or ritual sexual acts that were consecrated to a deity and regularly performed to worship her or him (Scheer 2009: 10ff.).

Today, it is largely certain that this myth of temple/cult prostitution—created by ancient Greek authors—has no evidence from the *real* ancient Greece to back it up; it can be regarded as extremely unlikely (Budin 2008; Salisbury 2001: 292f.). Again, there are opposing views that argue, like Morris Silver, that prostitution carried out under the management of a god's temple has to be seen as cultic/sacred prostitution (Silver 2019: 10). Prostitution in the temple would have been antithetical because sexual intercourse was basically regarded as an act of desecration, and for this reason alone remained excluded from cult and sacred spaces, even from those consecrated places that were dedicated to fertility gods (Dover 2002: 20f.). It cannot be denied, however, that gods or the places consecrated to them received gifts in the form of slaves and that the proceeds from their work—including prostitution, but not in the sacred place—were used for the rites, preservation, and operation of a temple. Or as Budin put it:

"Sacred prostitution is the sale of a person's body for sexual purposes where some portion (if not all) of the money or goods received for this transaction belongs to a deity. (. . .) In Greece, it is usually Aphrodite" (Budin 2008: 3). It should also be stressed that Greek authors who wrote about such forms of prostitution often had distant city-states or even other countries—such as Egypt and Persia—in their sights and wanted to brand those distant lands as backwaters, populated by brutes who practiced archaic temple prostitution.

Pornográphōs and *Ars Erotica*

The erotic imagery of ancient Greece was populated by *hetairai*, whores, Amazons, and *paiderastia* (see Chapter 3) (Shusterman 2021: 30ff.). The modern term "pornography" is based on the Greek words *pornos* and *gráphō* and means "writing about whores" or "drawing whores." However, the word *pornográphōs* was first used by Athenaeus only at the end of the second century/beginning of the third century BCE. It stood for painters who depicted prostitutes (Younger 2005: 103). In today's pictorial memory, the best-known images of sexual excess from this period are found on drinking vessels from the archaic and classical periods. The vessels carry all conceivable sexual practices: Younger and older men who actively penetrate or get penetrated, women in sexual games with men—a few even with representatives of their own sex—as well as a variety of oral, manual, and anal practices. Some are obviously happening under coercion and use violence as well with the help of "sex toys" such as artificial phalli or "sadistic" props such as sandals used for "flogging and whipping"—some of them used in real life and others only in erotic fantasy (Kilmer 1993; Stafford 2022). Every now and then, satyrs appear, which is why one could even accuse these pictures of "bestiality," a transgression of the human–animal–god barrier (Vout 2013: 181ff.). Some scenes also show voyeurs observing others having sex, which points to the idea that producers of these visual whore stories may have been primarily concerned with the sexual stimulation of viewers.

Thus, the important attributes of modern pornography were already coalescing in ancient "*ars erotica*": The focus was on sexually active persons whose aroused genitals were to be seen *in actu*, who were striving toward orgasm and who animated observers to do the same—be it in their imagination or in anticipatory practice. We should be skeptical, however, because the current conceptual field of "pornography" (as well as the term "pornographer") was first coined by the classical philologists and archaeologists of the early nineteenth century: What they were describing was the generally obscene, that is, indecent, mostly forbidden literature and illustrations that had been collected since the Renaissance by lovers and collectors of such art, and hidden away in the poison cabinets of libraries and museums (Sternke 2012: 328ff.). Even for the enlightened writers of the eighteenth century, pornography primarily encompassed the genre of whore stories (Clarke 2009: 12).

For the erotic art of antiquity, on the other hand, a view aimed at discipline, prohibition, and punishment is largely lacking. Visual and linguistic representations recorded in *pornographai* were part of a regime of thought and imagination that did not (primarily) prohibit or punish the sexual practices shown and described; rather, their production was positive, on the one hand. *Pornographai* were offered up for imitation and (re-)vivification. On the other hand, the thought regime problematized them and made them a reference for moral, political, and social debate—and sometimes also used them for humorous and satirical purposes. Seen in this light, the Greek *ars erotica* was one of the cultural techniques with which sexuality was (again and again) produced and established as truth and knowledge (Foucault 1977). For historians, this results in the task of perceiving such erotic images beyond today's viewing habits and investigating the conditions of production and consumption in their own time (Clarke 2013, 2014: 510ff.).

Even though the *pornographai* occasionally depicted sexual acts between men (rarely between women), heterosexual scenes dominated in which men appeared as actors and women receivers—and the latter were iconographically mostly marked as *hetairai* and *pornai*. Undoubtedly, these images must have served the purpose of sexual stimulation and were meant to provide the mood on appropriate occasions, e.g., during banquets. But they also had the potential to convey the opposite, in that some of these scenes referred—in Athenian culture of the sixth and fifth centuries BCE— to transgressions and violations of the honor of aristocratic men as a result of unrestrained satisfaction of desire. In Athenian democracy, such images could also pursue highly political goals. Members of the old elite were thusly accused of an excessive and uncontrolled lifestyle that was increasingly regarded as anti-democratic and damaging to the community. In the pictorial representations of *pornographai*, whores increasingly appeared as used/consumed women whose bodies proved that this activity was morally humiliating and ugly—and that they were partly to blame for the moral decline of the upper social classes (Kistler 2012: 43ff.; Sutton 1992: 12).

On drinking vessels in late archaic Athens, one could also admire naked women in the boudoir who used a dildo or a penis of independence. Here too, the ceramic painters obviously had *hetairai* and *pornai* in mind, which they knew from the spatial proximity of the red light and pottery districts in ancient Athens. The buyers of these objects would conveniently walk past their stalls on their way to the brothel. Such a staging was out of the question for honorable Attic women, even though scenes later spread in which respectable brides could be seen partially naked at the ritual wedding bath (Skinner 2005: 105). In the early Hellenistic period (late fourth century BCE), the erotic-pornographic representations on vases and vessels changed significantly: Instead of orgiastic scenes at the *symposium*, more and more man–woman couples were shown in bed, sometimes accompanied by *eros*, who made coitus appear as a divine gift (Clarke 2011: 173ff.). But even in these moderate images—just as in the corresponding sculptures of copulating couples—the subject was not conjugal sexual intercourse but rather that of a client and a prostitute (Parker 1992).

Greek comedies and satyr pieces also thrived on innuendo and outright sexual allusions, more or less explicit gestures and actions; at the center of the mocking form of entertainment was the demonically well-endowed goat-man and his uncultivated animal sexuality (Younger 2011: 76). Literate, upper-class Greek men were also able get their hands on manuals that provided sexual information and inspiration. The oldest probably came from the historian Timaeus of Tauromenium (about 350–260 BCE) and contained a catalogue of positions for heterosexual coitus as well as instructions for oral practices. The manual of Philaenis of Samos (around 370 BCE), unfortunately only survived in fragments, was appealing to ancient authors because it was allegedly written by a woman and revealed love positions and seduction strategies from a female perspective. More likely, however, is that this work was written by a male author named Polycrates, whose deception as actor constituted the actual erotic-pornographic kick. In Greek antiquity already, male *pornographai* were producing their works primarily for male consumers, their texts and images revealing their own sexual fantasies and desires as well as their fears and anxieties (Younger 2005: 120f.).

Erotics of Beautiful Bodies

The ideals of beauty and eroticism also differed according to gender (Shusterman 2021: 44ff.). In classical Athens, light and white skin represented youthful beauty and was characteristic of women of the upper classes who did not have to expose themselves to the sun—unlike whores whose business was out on the street, for example, and the majority of women working outside the home, who were thus also known for their tanned skin. The youthful female body was paid homage with attributes such as blossom-like soft skin and firm flesh, in correlation to the young marriage age of Greek women. At weddings and on public occasions, the female citizens' repertoire of good manners included reinforcing beauty ideals with cosmetics, for example by applying white lead cream to her face, using a red cheek tint made from the root of dyers' bugloss, and blackening their eyelids. Too much emphasis on the eyes, however, was regarded as obscene—typical of prostitutes, who inverted the gaze regime by not averting their eyes in front of a man but contrarily stared fixedly at possible clients (Glazebrook 2009: 236f.). If an honorable woman relied too much on cosmetics, the suspicion quickly arose that she did not take shame and morality all too seriously.

In vase painting, female beauty was also characterized by a well-groomed appearance, exquisite clothing, a slender figure, round breasts, a straight nose, and languid gestures (Robson 2013: 120ff.). Erotic women draped themselves in transparent fabrics and covered their breasts with only a narrow band. The free and sexualized gaze of the man upon the female breast played an important role in visual representation: Breasts that matched the erotic ideal ought not be too big, but round and firm, and they should be the focal point of the male's attention. The woman's buttocks also received disproportionate attention: Typically, copulating couples were usually depicted in positions in which the man penetrated the vagina from behind and thus the visual communication was aligned accordingly. On vase pictures also the female pubic hair appears quite clearly; it was either clearly visible or just behind a transparent cloth, depicted as a darker triangle. Prolific pubic hair was regarded as unpleasant, however, and was sometimes plucked or singed off by well-kept women. The loss of these attributes for older women meant that they also lost erotic-sexual attractiveness.

Male beauty images were also structured along age differences (Robson 2013: 130ff.). Adult men appear on vase pictures shaped according to athletic and martial models, but they still had to have slender and supple bodies. Even the growth and care of the beard—which was considered an indication of virility and sexual maturity—referred to a man's social status, morality, and character. According to Aristotle in his *Problemata*, men with excessive beard growth were characterized by an impetuous temperament and corresponding sexual drive (Descharmes 2015: 254ff.). Young people, on the other hand, were to have a beautiful, well-proportioned body, whose glistening, fine skin was especially distinguishing. The staging of such youthful male bodies is reminiscent of an erotic and attractive girl's body. Sculpted muscles were not youthful beauty imperatives; nevertheless, they ought still to be quite fit (Osborne 2011: 27ff.). Aristophanes set the standard for boys in his comedy *Clouds*, premiering in 423 BCE:

> I tell you this—if you carry out these things I mention, if you concentrate your mind on them, you'll always have a gleaming chest, bright skin, broad shoulders, tiny tongue, strong buttocks, and a little prick. But if you take up what's in fashion nowadays, you'll have, for starters, feeble shoulders, a pale skin, a narrow chest, huge tongue, a tiny bum, and a large skill in framing long decrees. (Aristophanes 2004: 113)

Youthful mouths and thighs were also among the erotic features—the first as a target of erotic kisses, the second as a place of intercrural or interfemoral intercourse, whereby the older partner rubbed his penis between the thighs of the adored young man. It is iconographically conspicuous that young people were usually depicted not only with small, immature penises but also with premature foreskin, which bespoke their sexual self-control and modesty. The young male's gaze could also be meaningful, tell-tale for same-sex flirtation, effeminate shamefulness, or resistance, triggering quite opposing connotations between the communication partners (Hubbard 2002).

A Heaven for Gays and Lesbians?

If it were up to the early representatives of the homosexual movement, we would have to imagine ancient Greece as a veritable Arcadia for same-sex love and sexuality. How else should one evaluate a culture in which *eros* also encompassed the erotic desires between men and youths and in which homosexual practices could be admired in more or less unequivocal depictions on vases, murals, and sculptures? Hadn't the Greek poetess Sappho (630/612 to around 570 BCE) sung the praises of desire between women on the island of Lesbos in the sixth century BCE? Even in the gods' own heaven, signs of same-sex acceptance abound. Even the most powerful gods enacted same-sex practices. Zeus, in the form of an eagle, seized the beautiful Ganymede. Apollo, who, after the death of his beloved Hyacinthus, created a flower whose calyx was modelled after his lamentation.

Nevertheless, such a romantic view of Greek mythology and history has been critically questioned in recent decades, proving instead to be an emancipatory ideal of a consummate or better gay and lesbian past (Blondell 2008: 117). The historical contextualization of ancient written and pictorial evidence has made it clear that ancient sources, especially when it comes to same-sex sexuality, are usually polyphonic and ambiguous (Butler 2019). Also, with regard to the topic of same-sex sexuality, we have a rather unbalanced stock of sources for the numerous cities and city-states—with a clear predominance of sources on Athens—which makes not only a comparative presentation, but also generalizations, more difficult.

Paiderastia as Educational *Eros*

The best known of all same-sex relationships is still *paiderastia*, a term consisting of *pais* (boy) and *eran* (love) that describes an erotic or sexual relationship between an older, mostly socially superior man and a youth or boy (Lear 2014: 102ff.). The first written references to the existence of *paiderastia* appear in poems of the seventh and sixth centuries BCE. This asymmetry of the (sexual) partners led Michel Foucault to his famous assessment of same-sex sexuality in ancient Greece: that "pederasty" should be seen in the light of the aesthetics of existence, in which the elderly person exercised (or ought to exercise) sexual restraint for the purpose of self-disciplining control and moderation, thereby saving the younger person from humiliating penetration. On the other side, the young man, in view of his future position as an upstanding citizen, would have had to rally massive resistance against a passive sexual position and, if sexual contact was made, must at least ought not to feel desire—both contradicted the canon of values of a free man and citizen (Foucault 1989a: 237ff.). Critics have pointed out that Foucault's assessment of aesthetic self-stylization at the interface of excess and moderation as well as activity and passivity was based on a rather selective body of sources. It has been shown that asymmetry between men was also at the center of social and other cultural—not only sexual and ethical-aesthetic—imperatives. Such a constellation damaged the male honor and reputation and exposed the young lover to the danger of also submitting physically and putting himself in an unmanly position. Free men in public, especially, when they injured their physical self-sufficiency, they brought dishonor not only upon themselves but also—as (social) bodies—upon the patriarchal system and the *polis* itself (Larmour, Miller and Platter 1998; Goldhill 1995; Cohen 1991; Detel 1998: 151ff.).

Classical *paiderastia* was widespread above all among the ruling social classes, that is, persons who held an elevated public-political or military-warrior function or who intended to enter those fields. One of the distinctive features of these citizens, in addition to their ethical lifestyle, was an exceptional body that was trained and exhibited in the *gymnasium* (a preferred place for same-sex eroticism) or during the hunt. In contrast to what was often imagined in later traditions, the coveted boys and adolescents therefore would not have sought to possess an effeminate or androgynous body, but rather a virile, trained one that corresponded to the masculine aesthetic ideal (Vattuone 2004: 43ff.; Spanakis 2022). After all, the older partner (*erastes*, the active lover) ought not to have coveted the adolescent (*eromenos*, the passive lover) for his aesthetic body alone, but rather because the youngling also knew to refuse and let himself only be won through much attention and gifts (Lear and Cantarella 2008: 38ff.). From Plato's *Phaedrus* of the fourth century BCE to Plutarch's (around 45-125) writings of the first century, seduction was mainly associated with the erotic gaze, whereby who the attacker is shifts over time. As Plato has it, the desire of the *erastes* is "moistened and warmed" by a beautiful boy and his eyes—the visual echo of the elder brings about his love and desire. With Plutarch, on the other side, the attack comes from the languishing gaze of the older man, whom the youth must resist and stand firm against (Rakoczy 1996: 197). Thus, on representations of the *paiderastia* (over 1,000 have survived) the juvenile *eromenos* is mostly depicted with a penis that is not erect. As an expression of his continuing resistance, he should not allow himself to get carried away sexually, should mingling come about (Lear and Cantarella 2008: 60ff.).

This form of pederasty was ritually practiced among social elites, and that is why the youth must be pursued publicly, at least in part, within the contexts of male association (Stähli 2001: 200). Seen in this light, the practice can be compared to rites of passage in tribal societies in which youths became men through similar means—for example, by symbolic or real insemination into the mouth or anus (Herdt 1991: 604ff.; Dynes and Donaldson 1992a; Wallace 2007). It is considered quite probable that the Greek *paiderastia* indeed developed from an initiation rite practiced in Crete in the seventh century BCE; youths were introduced to the arts of hunting and fighting in seclusion and, in this way, to male society, and erotic-sexual contacts were possibly also made (Verstraete and Provencal 2006: 3). By the end of the ritual, the young initiates who became men received combat equipment from their initiators, a bull was sacrificed, and from then on the two stood together in battle formation rows, known as a hoplite phalanx (Detel 1998: 156f.). Through Sparta, eroticized nude martial arts spread to the Greek city-states in the sixth and fifth centuries BCE, and with these came the pederastic gaze, which was directed at the naked youthful bodies in the *gymnasium* as well. Inscribed therein was the age relation between *erastes* and *eromenos* (Scanlon 2005). After their *paiderastia*, both partners were expected to marry (a woman)—the *erastes* after this pederastic relationship was over at the latest, the younger after he himself had acted as *erastes* (Younger 2005: 92). *Erastes* could be married and maintain sexual contacts with their wife and other people.

In his *Geography*, Strabo recounts a two-month pederastic initiation rite on the island of Crete. There, twelve-year-old boys were kidnapped by warriors and taken into the military elite troops during a period of transformation, in which they remained until marriage at the age of about thirty (Percy 1996: 64f.). The "Sacred Band" of Thebes, a troop of warriors consisting of 150 couples, most likely only existing in legend, was regarded as an extremely feared enemy due to the closeness of these fighting *erastai* and *eromenoi* (Leitao 2000; Ogden 2011: 41f.). Again, militaristic Sparta was known for its erotic mentoring relationships between older and younger warriors (Reinsberg 1989: 163). Contemporaries of the period used yet another term to describe these erotic-physical relationships: *lakonizo*—to live in the Spartan way. Spartan boys left their families behind to train under an honorable and successful soldier, to then enter the master-teacher role themselves when they reached the age of majority. The eroticized male relationship was also seen as the ideal basis for a soldierly life and mutual responsibility among Spartan comrades-in-arms—even if it mutated into *philia* (intimate friendship) in adulthood.

Whether or not the practice of educational *eros* also included sexual acts such as mutual masturbation, and intercrural, oral, and anal intercourse is still controversial—and will probably remain so due to the few substantial and often contradictory sources (Lear 2014: 121). As already mentioned, anal penetration does not seem to have been widely practiced, due to the violation of physical integrity (Reinsberg 1989: 191ff.; Thornton 1997: 205ff.; Younger 2005: 91ff.; Skinner 2005: 90; Clarke 2011: 172). In recent years, criticism of the sexualized view of *paiderastia* has grown considerably. On the other hand, its function within the ancient Greek educational system has garnered support, as has its status as potential rites of passage (when a young man was admitted to the circle of male *polis* citizens and warriors) and as part of the political system. It has also become clearer that historical sources primarily concerned with erotic desire among men focused on the practice of wooing a young man; whereas, the sexual practices which actually led to an act were treated marginally at best (Ludwig 2002; Percy 2006; Lear 2014: 122). The fact that discussion about *paiderastia* was ongoing from archaic through Hellenistic times can also be seen as an indication that the Greeks viewed this institution with some ambivalence and its erotic-sexual practice with hesitation (Garton 2004: 33ff.). For many ancient authors, such as Xenophon, Plato, and Aristotle, sexual assaults on free boys and young men were considered a reprehensible act, which is why they accepted *paiderastia* only as an asexual relationship. They also criticized that the balance of power between an older, established man and a younger, still inexperienced man would be based on an exchange of lust and benefit that contradicts the spiritual and ritual character of this rite of passage (Detel 1998: 173).

Pederastic closeness was clearly the topic of many written and pictorial sources (ranging from manual to anal acts), yet the young people, at least, mostly adopted an attitude that could be described as dispassionate or disdainful (Shusterman 2021: 44ff.). Nonetheless, they were drawn in these pictures as involved actors in this exchange and not as passive objects. The iconography also makes it clear that the erotic, possibly sexual desire and possible satisfaction of the adult *erastai* was the focus. The classic position depicted on vases and bowls was not anal but intercrural (Reinsberg 1989: 194ff.; Clarke 2011: 172), which would then have left the physical integrity of the youth intact and did not deprive him of his honor and social future. Furthermore, precarious, that is, completely passive, positions were avoided even in the imagery. In poetry, same-sex sexual acts and fantasies took a rather metaphorized form. Those most direct on the topic of ancient Greek same-sex sexuality were the comic poets, who painted it in rather crass, phallic terms. In interpreting these sources, though, too much attention seems to have been paid to the sexual components and short-term sexual contacts, neglecting the fact that affection and love among men—as well as among women—was also a theme for same-sex *eros* (Davidson 2007).

The sensitive balance between erotic-sexual desire and physical realization on the part of the *erastes* was also discussed in Plato's *Symposium*, where the drunken young Alcibiades reports on his experiences with the older Socrates and in so doing confuses the roles of wooer and wooee: Although Socrates was apparently interested in the beautiful young man and had chosen him from among his many admirers, Alcibiades did not succeed in inciting action from the philosopher through joint sport and intimate dinner. So, Alcibiades had to go "all in":

> When the lamp was put out and the slaves had gone away, I thought that I must be plain with him and have no more ambiguity. So I gave him a shake, and I said: "Socrates, are you asleep?" "No," he said. "Do you know what I am meditating?" "What are you meditating?" he said. "I think," I replied, "that of all the lovers whom I have ever had you are the only one who is worthy of me, and you appear to be too modest to speak. Now I feel that I should be a fool to refuse you this or any other favour, and therefore I come to lay at your feet all that I have and all that

my friends have, in the hope that you will assist me in the way of virtue, which I desire above all things, and in which I believe that you can help me better than anyone else. And I should certainly have more reason to be ashamed of what wise men would say if I were to refuse a favour to such as you, than of what the world, who are mostly fools, would say of me if I granted it." To these words he replied in the ironical manner which is so characteristic of him: "Alcibiades, my friend, you have indeed an elevated aim if what you say is true, and if there really is in me any power by which you may become better; truly you must see in me some rare beauty of a kind infinitely higher than any which I see in you. And therefore, if you mean to share with me and to exchange beauty for beauty, you will have greatly the advantage of me; you will gain true beauty in return for appearance—like Diomede, gold in exchange for brass. But look again, sweet friend, and see whether you are not deceived in me. The mind begins to grow critical when the bodily eye fails, and it will be a long time before you get old." Hearing this, I said: "I have told you my purpose, which is quite serious, and do you consider what you think best for you and me." "That is good," he said; "at some other time then we will consider and act as seems best about this and about other matters." Whereupon, I fancied that he was smitten, and that the words which I had uttered like arrows had wounded him, and so without waiting to hear more I got up, and throwing my coat about him crept under his threadbare cloak, as the time of year was winter, and there I lay during the whole night having this wonderful monster in my arms. This again, Socrates, will not be denied by you. And yet, notwithstanding all, he was so superior to my solicitations, so contemptuous and derisive and disdainful of my beauty—which really, as I fancied, had some attractions—hear, O judges; for judges you shall be of the haughty virtue of Socrates—nothing more happened, but in the morning when I awoke (let all the gods and goddesses be my witnesses) I arose as from the couch of a father or an elder brother. (Plato 2001: 269ff., 216c–223d; Dorion 2017)

This passage lays out not only the pedagogical rules of *paiderastia*, but also key is the nuanced sort of communication necessary to bring about sexual activity without going too far. A desirable young man who offered himself directly, like Alcibiades, would have quickly been suspected of being a *pornos*. Alcibiades as a figure of other comedies was typically reviled as unmanly—above all because he was still acting as a passive *eromenos* in adulthood, but did so in an aggressive way with which he not only courted his lovers but also tried to implement his political goals (Wohl 2002: 124ff.; Descharmes 2015: 271f.).

The differences between *paiderastia* and same-sex prostitution are the subject of the speech by Aeschines (around 390–320 BCE) against Timarchus, in which he tried to convince the Athenian judges that the latter had allowed himself to be used for money as a juvenile. The charge is that he had violated the ethical system and its legitimate *eros* among men. Aeschines reveals that although anal penetration was not prohibited, it was still viewed quite negatively, the debase act of a prostitute, that of an effeminate, passive partner. Yet, the worst thing was that Timarchus had *desired* anal intercourse and thus lost self-control. He had gone over to the disgraceful position of a slave. Aeschines presents himself, on the other hand, as a representative of the "old" honorable *erastai* and thus legitimizes the pederastic poetry he had previously written about the institution (Lear 2014: 115ff.; Kapparis 2022: 32ff.). Accusations and defenses like these prove that the erotic *paiderastia* in classical Athens was no longer considered a self-evident practice but rather a problematized one in the Foucauldian sense. The meaning and opinion of *paiderastia* shifted significantly between the sixth and fourth centuries BCE: Especially with the emergence of democracy, the aristocratic lifestyle and with it pederastic practices increasingly fell into disrepute. Some of this ignominy fell upon the youth, as accusations of prostitution spread in this period. Education and training underwent professionalization during this time, thus pedagogical *eros* saw competition from the honorable upbringing and socialization of aristocratic men (Robson 2013: 50). But in the following centuries, too, classical pederasty continued to be seen as an ethical form of same-sex love, aesthetics, and eroticism among men. It didn't take a truly new form until Roman influence took hold. For (upper-class) Greek men, boys and young adult males were virtually gods (Lear and Cantarella 2008), whom they adored in the original sense of the word, that is, to worship, admired them erotically and aesthetically and, if necessary, sexually seduced them—usually in a pedagogical teacher/master/student relationship. The *paiderastia* was—at least as portrayed in the discourse—regarded as a privilege and an ideal of free elite citizens and was supposed to be ritualized. Conversely, the educational argument would likely have been employed by older men to approach young men sexually (Laes 2010: 38).

Same-Sex Male Love and Prostitution

The range of same-sex sexual acts in practice was much broader than *paiderastia* and included contact between young non-citizens, slaves, and male prostitutes, the *pornoi* (Cantarella 1992: 98). In the hundreds of Greek city-states, same-sex relations undoubtedly existed between adult men as well as among young people of the same age—but of this there is little historical evidence. Based on the sources we do have, though, same-sex male sexual forms can in any case be regarded as a pan-Hellenic phenomenon—*eros* did not distinguish between heterosexual or homosexual categories (Dover 1978: 60ff.). Man or woman, desire could take the same aesthetic, erotic, and sexual shape. Both parallel and successive erotic-sexual relationships to one sex or the other were quite common (Parker 2011: 130). In any case, one thing is for certain, the adult man's role was that of an active and penetrating lover, no matter whether with boys, *hetairai*, slaves, or his wife

(Golden 1992: 163ff.). His reputation indeed benefited from his possessing a large number of (male or female) lovers, going from one conquest to the next.

Instead of educational mentorship, payments in money and kind determined the sexual relations to catamites (from the Latin *catamitus* for the corruption of Ganymedes, whom Zeus snatched up as an eagle, above). From about 500 BCE, one could see purses being presented to the young men on Attic imagery; thus, increasingly we see the transgression of prostitution and the dishonorable sale of the body. When a free citizen, whose calling was within the affairs of state or as a warrior, dared allow himself to be sullied for payment, he was suspected of lacking integrity—being for sale—in other matters as well, and lost the trust placed in him (Younger 2005: 3). To prevent such cases, Athens excluded male citizens who were prostitutes from public office by law (Hupperts 2007: 38; Kapparis 2022). Teachers and trainers were also forbidden to have sexual contact with their students, and relationships with boys under the age of twelve were considered a disgrace and punishable. Slaves were also not allowed to have a *pais* (boy servant/ youthful lover), as they were—no matter what age—themselves considered as such (Reinsberg 1989: 164; Johnson and Ryan 2005: 6; Matuszewski 2021). Anyone who exerted sexual violence against a free boy was liable to severe, even capital punishment (Cohen 1991: 177ff.). Same-sex contacts on their own were not generally prohibited by law, however. People seem to have practiced such acts without further ado in their "private" life. Even married men coveted boys as sexual objects. Contacts between low-ranking people of the same age—both boys and adult men—must not have raised all too many eyebrows either.

Paid sexual services were generally offered by unfree, foreign, or immigrated young men at free market prices roughly equal to those of their female counterparts (Cohen 2015: 166f.). In Athens, their activities were considered an independent trade, which—like female prostitutes—had to be registered for tax purposes. Most exchanges took place in *oikemata* (living quarters), rented chambers, which existed in the red light areas near the pottery district and in Piraeus, Athens' port (Posch 2012: 72ff.). But long-term paid relationships with catamites, similar to those with the *hetairai*, are also documented. One such case was that of Theodotus of Plataea (who was not a citizen), over whom two lovers fought in an episode passed down in a speech by Lysias (around 445 to around 380 BCE). Simon, one of the lovers, eventually gives him the stately sum of 300 drachmas, thereby making a sole claim on Theodotus. Here ran the thin line between educational *eros* à la *paiderastia* and sexual services for sale by a *hetairos* or *pornos*: The prior relationship followed the quite common rules of wooing the young lover with gifts and keeping him interested, but as soon as payment of money came into play the narrative changes. Then there was the accusation of being for sale and being a *hetairos* or *pornos*. This case is also unusual in that men normally did not live together in concubinage; such relationships exceeded the limits of the accepted, which is why the comedy poets poked fun at them (Dillon 2004: 112ff.; Hubbard 2014: 143).

The *kinaidos* (catamite), those who desired penetration—no matter the social context—were the target of great mockery and comedic distortion. Aristotle characterizes this figure in *Physiognomonica* as follows:

> He has drooping eyelids. He is knock-kneed. He inclines his head to the right side. He makes effeminate gestures with open hands. He has two varieties of the gait, one in which he wiggles his bottom, and one in which he keeps it still. He rolls his eyes around a great deal, Dionysius the sophist (Peakman 2013: 79).

The *kinaidos* was thus effeminate and therefore—as Aeschylus (525/524–456/5 BCE) put it:

"Man, woman—or some despicable thing halfway betwixt them both" (Laurin 2005: 105f.). Graffiti have survived that display insults to men, calling them *katapygon*, he who takes it in the ass, *euruproktos*, he of a wide anus, or *lakkoproktos*, a man with an ass like a cistern (Williams 2014: 499).

This figure turned up the heat on the historiographical discussion about the Greek gender model and sexual desire as well as the associated identity (Skinner 2005: 124ff.; Sapsford 2022: 8ff.): According to John J. Winkler, the *kinaidos* should not be regarded as a "modern homosexual," nor should he be seen as "just an ordinary guy who now and then decided to commit a kinaidic act" (Winkler 1990: 45). Rather, he was regarded as deviant by nature, a violation of the masculine and thus also as a special kind of person—not as someone who merely performed an act. But *kinaidos* also ranked within the male spectrum—between masculine and feminine men—not crossing the gender divide. He was a loser (by social standards) who desired domination, contradicting the masculine imperative to be the master of oneself and others in order to protect one's own honor and that of his *oíkos*. Aristotle diagnosed him with disorders of the humoral balance that prevented the flow of the humor necessary for active sexual desire (Younger 2005: 31). Such physical as well as psychological disorder brought him close to the *androgynoi*, whose gender seemed completely indeterminable (Garton 2004: 41f.).

The *kinaidos* was not a sexual subject in his own right but rather the appearance of deviance. David M. Halperin postulated that he had at least the morphology of a sexual type (Halperin 2000a: 29ff.). John Thorp went even further and attested him to have a lifelong preference for men, which additionally would have included men considered too close to his own age for *paiderastia* (Thorp 1992: 202). At any rate, there is agreement today that this figure can hardly be grasped with modern categories of heterosexuality and homosexuality. The *kinaidos* comprises a sexual figure *Before Sexuality*, as in the title of a groundbreaking publication on

Hellenistic sexuality in the 1990s (Halperin, Winkler and Zeitlin 1990). According to Marilyn B. Skinner, the *kinaidos* amounted to a pejorative bogeyman that historians should be particularly skeptical of, since it existed primarily in fictional and political literature—and possibly had little to do with reality (Skinner 2005: 128). Striking this same groove, Mark Masterson also pointed out that the *kinaidos* was depicted as the antithesis of a proper Greek man—the armored and weapon-bearing hoplite—in an over-sexualized form, namely by means of uncontrolled desire and passive anal penetration. In the everyday life of Greek men, polar categories, such as honor and shame, activity and passivity, penetrating and penetrated, were less strictly defined than some in today's research presume (Masterson 2014b: 23ff.). According to Tom Sapsford, the *kinaidos* was both worrisome and alluring to the ancients, because this figure could flip across boundaries: "His outrageous demeanor may mark him out as perverse, yet he is never banished outright from classical sites and texts" (Sapsford 2022: 198).

Little is known about sexual relations between young or older men of the same age. Such relationships have so far remained underexposed in research, eclipsed by the hot debates on age-differentiated same-sex relations. They do, however, abound in literary and pictorial sources, for example as a mutual erotic attraction of young people of the same age in gymnasiums and at competitions. Pindar (522/518–after 446 BCE) recounts in an ode that the young star athlete Hippokleas, who, after having won the games in Delphi, now had his choice among the young men of his age, older men, and girls or young women (Hubbard 2014: 129). The fact that sexual practices among peers didn't attract further attention from contemporaries (and historians) may also be due to the fact that such contacts were regarded as quite common, that is, there was little reason to address such relations. In any case, there is no evidence that they were prevented for educational, medical, or moral reasons. Also, *kynodesmē*—young athletes covering their penis, often wrongly referred to as "infibulation"—is not an indication of any such measure, e.g., to hide the male sexual organ from their peers specifically. This refers to the practice of tying a leather strap around the glans and foreskin to affix the penis to one side of the hip for tournaments. The idea was to keep the genitals from becoming erect during competition, preventing the tip from showing in public—a sign of shamelessness and dishonor for the youthful citizenry. It also supposedly helped athletes to throw a spear farther and run faster (Sansone 1988: 119ff.; Fisher 2014: 252).

Sapphic and *Hermaphrodite* Love as Taboo?

There are comparatively few meaningful sources on erotic and sexual relationships between women (Boehringer 2014). As John Addington

Symonds rightly stated in his classic study *A Problem in Greek Ethics* (Symonds 1901: 71), female same-sex acts were hardly recorded because they did not belong to any special social system (like the *paiderastia* to the educational and military system). This is the reason for the lack of legal sanctions in ancient Greece that would have otherwise left traces in the archives. The only remaining clue is the term *tribo* or *tribas* from *tribein* (to rub) that problematized erotic and sexual relationships between women (Krenkel 2006: 439; Lardinois 1991: 24). Aristophanes used the verb *lesbiazo* for the cunnilingus practiced on Lesbos (Younger 2005: 68). Plato spoke of *hetairistria* in the *Symposium*, referring to women who passively engaged in same sex; their counterpart was then the *hetairistai* (Younger 2005: 68).

The most intense voice on *eros* among women still comes from Sappho, whose poems were addressed to girls and appear to be quite complex according to recent readings (Snyder 1997; Laurin 2005: 122ff.). Sappho's poetry doesn't offer any explanations of sexual practices, but ambiguous sexual metaphors can be found in it (Hallett 1996: 130). She alludes to physical incentives as well as female figures who act as erotic subjects or represent their objects of desire (Winkler 1997: 273; Greene 2002: 82ff.). Ellen Greene goes so far as to assert that Sappho was an example of female desire beyond male dominance and submission in ancient Greece, that it was indeed practicable and based on mutual recognition of female sexual partners (Greene 1996: 234ff.). Generally, however, sexual relations between women were regarded as a social taboo, pointing to why even comedies largely steered away from this topic (Dover 1978: 172f.). It was not until Hellenistic times (336–30 BCE) that the silence on such same-sex acts broke, at which point these practices were imputed to be unnatural (Skinner 2005: 187).

For Sparta, there are indications that pederastic relationships also existed between older women from the social elite (as teachers or mentors) and girls under their authority (Lardinois 1991: 26ff.). The extent to which age-specific and social-relational criteria played a role in these relationships is nevertheless still under discussion, as is the question of whether the sources written almost exclusively by men are not (also) to be read as male projections that would then say little about the actually lived same-sex *eros* among women (Halperin 2000b: 250ff.; Brooten 1996: 16ff.). According to James Davidson, some of the erotic relationships between women were indeed formal and visibly public; such unions were commonplace on Lesbos (Davidson 2007: 408f.; Gilhuly 2015). Interpretations of the pictorial representation of female pairs on vessels also diverge greatly: Whereas some argue against a view modeled on *paiderastia* (Boehringer 2007), others see clear representations of female sexual relationships and female eroticism beyond male *paiderastia* (Rabinowitz 2002). A few depictions also show women using dildos, sometimes in a context without men at all. These pictures may, nevertheless, have been created by men for men, amounting to nothing more than pornographic scenes (Laurin 2005: 120f.). Chorus poetry from choral lyric poet Alcman from the seventh century BCE poses similar difficulties for the history of sexuality as it also presents odes to homoerotic feelings between young women (Ogden 2011: 44).

The figure of the *hermaphrodite* also gave rise to contemporary discussions as it stood in contrast to the order of things in which two sexes dominated, raising questions about sexual "orientation" as well as about the existence of a "third sex." In mythology, Hermaphroditus arose from the fusion of a young god—the son of Hermes and Aphrodite—with a nymph to form a new being that possessed both sexual characteristics (Brisson 2002: 42ff.). Hermaphroditus first appeared at the turn of the fourth century BCE and probably originated from an Attic cult, which was reacting to the epidemics and devastations of the years preceding the Peloponnesian War (Ajootian 2003: 228). Apparently, Hermaphroditus was initially outlined as a positive divine figure that sprang from the two sexes and led to a third who stood for fertility and healing. Later, especially under the influence of Roman authors, the negative side of the god's dual gender came to the fore as an affront to male dominance.

3

Infamia and *Pudicitia*—Roman Antiquity

Coitus as a Civic Duty

The sexual culture of the Imperium Romanum fed on genuinely Roman elements from Greek, Jewish, North African, and Asia Minor traditions, and was finally influenced and transformed by new Christian elements. From the sixth and fifth centuries BCE, Romans came into contact with and grew to appreciate Greek culture in particular and remained fascinated by it in the following period, so that one can rightly speak of a truly Greco-Roman culture. Beyond all their convolutions, forms of sexual culture unique to Romans did emerge. More recent historiography reveals this distinctly Roman sexuality to be quite different than previously thought; the idea that a polar pair of opposites between pagan and Christian sexuality dominated is being revised. In doing so, today's understanding fills in numerous gaps due to the consideration of an expanded source stock. This has become possible because literary, moral, philosophical, and legal (textual) sources are being interpreted now in connection with diverse artifacts of material and visual culture (Dixon 2003: 114ff.).

Marriage, the Seedbed of the State

The aforementioned advances have also led to a new picture of marital sexuality. Marriage was the social institution in which Roman citizens not only came together legitimately but—as Marcus Tullius Cicero (106–43 BCE) put it—also understood it as the "seedbed of the state." Marriage and bearing and raising children were among the primary duties of every citizen (Krenkel 2006: 381; Perry 2020). Although central values such as property, family cult, and citizenship were based on a legitimate succession of generations, marriage—unlike for later Christianity—had no sacramental character (Finley 2002: 150f.). The *familia* (household community) included the *pueri* (children) and *servi* (servants and slaves) in addition to the *pater familias* and the *mater familias*. Entering into a marriage was the right of a citizen, but it was also seen as a right for all those who were entitled to marry a citizen. The *conubium*, or marriage prerequisites, defined—with regard to non-citizens or persons who did not befit their status—whether a marriage was permissible. And the right to enter into such a legal marriage was not extended to non-citizens until 212 (Karras 2012b: 17; McClure 2019: 10.1; Perry 2020: 74f.) (Figure 4).

At marriage age, women were mostly between fifteen and eighteen years old, men between twenty-three and twenty-eight years—at least that is one opinion (Glazebrook and Olson 2014: 75). Others assume that the broader population of Roman men and women entered marriage later, the women at eighteen or nineteen, the men at twenty-five to twenty-seven (Hin 2013: 175ff.; Laes 2012: 30ff.; 2021: 321f.). In either case, the age gap was somewhat smaller than for the Greeks—except in the upper classes, where girls were usually married much earlier; the legal minimum age for girls was twelve. In Christian times, the average age of marriage rose to at least seventeen years for women and twenty-six years for men (Treggiari 1991: 397ff.; Scheidel 2007: 13). For marriage, men had to be of age, that is, achieving full citizenship, and women "viripotent" (*viripotens*) or able

FIGURE 4 *Rites of initiation of a bride into the cult of Dionysus. Wall painting from Villa of the Mysteries, Pompeii, first century AD.*

to bear children. If the couple intended for marriage was of legal age, they had to agree to the marriage; but if they were younger, the parents could decide (Eisenring 2002: 73ff.). According to the work *De sanitate tuenda* by Galen of Pergamon (around 129–200/215), young men between the ages of thirteen and fifteen reached sexual maturity, which meant that they had to abstain from sexual intercourse for several years before marriage or experience premarital escapades (Read 2015: 11).

Young brides—especially from the upper classes—underwent rites of passage that prepared them for marriage (Wasdin 2020: 31ff.). A woolen *tunica recta* was the ceremonial dress, which girls would weave themselves before marriage to demonstrate their household capabilities and thus their suitability as brides. The night before the wedding, women tied their hair back in homemade netting as a symbol of their ability to tame their sexual desire in marriage, a sign of pursuing a moral life (Olson 2012: 21f.). Parts of the bridal costume, such as the bridal belt with a Hercules knot and the floral crown, were supposed to refer to sexual virginity, fertility, and the marriage bond (Hersch 2010: 113). The bedroom decorated for the wedding night contained fertility symbols such as green branches, flowers, and fruits (Glazebrook and Olson 2014: 77). By ceremoniously exposing his wife's ritually braided six hair plaits, the groom made it clear to the assembled wedding party that this would soon happen to her virginity as well. After the sexual consummation of the marriage, the bride exited the sleeping chamber the next day as *matrona*, a woman. The fact that the marriage of Roman citizens was aimed at childbirth can be seen from the high marriage rates and the fact that young wives usually gave birth to their first child—into their neolocal household—within one year (Scheidel 2007: 13ff.).

Young male Roman citizens received a *toga virilis* between the ages of fourteen and eighteen and were thus admitted to the circle of men. This not only gave them the right to vote but also enabled them to serve in the military (Caldwell 2014: 137f.). In their late teenage years, they acquired the claim to male alliance activities, such as drinking and feasting together, with the onset of puberty, the emergence of pubic hair, the first beard growth, and shaving, which was publicly staged at the *ludi Iuvenales* introduced by Nero (37–68 CE). This transition also meant that they could discard their *bulla amulet* (together with the *toga praetexta*), a phallic symbol that was supposed to protect them from sexual attacks through childhood. Now they were allowed to explore sex, which in most cases they experienced with female prostitutes or slaves. Only by their mid-twenties did they achieve their full legal maturity and the right to assume public office and to enter the Senate. As free Roman citizens, they now also possessed *virtus*—a term that is difficult to translate, but described manhood, masculinity, including military aggression and thus virtue, and also included the ability to defend oneself against enemies (Ivleva 2020: 242ff.). This martial definition of masculinity dominated until the second pre-Christian century and was then supplemented by civil values such as integrity, honesty, and commitment to the family. For the men of the first and second centuries after Christ, rhetoric and the ability to hold public office were also virile attributes (Masterson 2014b: 22f.). Becoming a *vir*, they could finally find themselves a *univira*, a woman who has only one husband and remains faithful to him for life. In practice, however, the high mortality rates of both sexes resulted in frequent remarriages, which were not a major problem for Roman society—neither were divorces, in which the children remained with their father by law (Harlow and Laurence 2002: 73ff.; Bof and Leyser 2016: 158ff.).

The Roman husband took guardianship over his wife until the Late Republic period (133–30 BCE). Later, this paternalism was pushed back in favor of the wife; from the second century, women were then able to inherit personally after the death of spouses or children (Evans Grubbs 2002: 219). In comparison to their Greek contemporaries, the Romans practiced a more individualized form of finding partners and did not (only) follow the instructions of their parents or professional matchmakers. It would be misleading, however, to view Roman marriage as a prelude to the romantic ideal of love and marriage, as was propagated in the eighteenth and nineteenth centuries. In the Roman Empire, too, spouses were primarily chosen according to their status, possessions, and assets, as well as family and political relations—social stratification was much more pronounced and visible than in the Greek city-states. Marriage primarily took two paths: The older *coemptio* (purchase marriage) was one in which the wife came under the authority of the husband (*manus*), who from this time on owned and exercised the *patria potestas* over her. The other path, common since the Middle Republic (287–133 CE), marriage came about between the partners in a form that was "manus-less"—through the marital bond of the *affectio maritalis*. In the event of separation or divorce, any property transferred in marriage had to be returned to the spouse (Schuller 2008: 126f.). In the Late Republic, *concubinatus*, a form of cohabitation that was also long term, spread among the upper social strata in addition to legally binding marriage; another, shorter form, of still at least one year, was referred to as the *usus* (Younger 2005: 77). During these decades, marriage also became increasingly popular among the lower classes, especially among freed slaves and former soldiers. Slaves were able to come together in the *contubernium*; but while this did not have any legal consequences, it was nevertheless considered a marriage. Some slave couples lived together in relationships even without a titular form, with the advantage that their offspring increased the wealth of their owners and therefore was under control of the slaveholders—an assumption that is under some dispute (Cohen 2014: 192; Perry 2021: 254ff.). The complex rules show that the institutionalization of permanent cohabitation in ancient Rome was much more differentiated than in ancient Greece.

This includes the legal regulations: Thus, Emperor Augustus (63 BCE–14 CE) issued the *lex iulia de maritandis ordinibus* (18 BCE) and the *lex papia poppaea* (9 BCE), which required all free Roman citizens—the upper classes in particular—to enter into marriage by a certain age (Evans Grubbs 2002: 83ff.; Wheeler-Reed 2017: 4ff.). In the event of the death of a spouse, the husband had to remarry immediately, and the wife within a year. Failure to comply with these provisions could result in tax and inheritance penalties. The law also dictated the marriage and sexual pool: Senators, their children, grandchildren, and great-grandchildren were not allowed to marry freed slaves, prostitutes, adulteresses, or other dishonorable people, nor their children. The freeborn were forbidden to marry these population groups as well as slaves. The tax and institutional preference for large families and married couples were aimed at the promotion of child production. Ultimately, freed and free-bought slaves were given similar rights to the free in issues of marriage (Steenblock 2013: 24ff.; Meyer-Zwiffelhoffer 1995: 124).

Marital Duties and Pleasures

The differences between Greek and Roman culture were also revealed in the sexual attribution to the sexes. In a nutshell, sexuality in Greece aimed to secure the male status and legitimacy as well as the linear ancestry of the (present and future) *kyrios*. In Rome, alongside the male social prestige, the focus was increasingly on individual and public morality and prosperity (Lape 2011: 26ff.). A male regime that, by means of *patria potestas*, was able to keep the sexual desire of (married) women in check could also bring order to the state—a central imperative of Roman sexual ideology (Joshel 1997). For both sexes, it was a political and military duty to produce an adequate number of descendants. Infertility was therefore a valid reason to annul a marriage. Toward the end of the Republic, women were also allowed to apply for divorce, which promoted their independence (Bof and Leyser 2016: 158ff.). In view of low birth rates, the Augustan marriage laws even declared marital reproduction to be a civic duty—this was addressed above all to representatives of the senatorial and knightly classes, that is, the wealth class that could afford a horse in the early days of the city-state militia system (McGinn 1998: 70ff.).

A little later, Plutarch's (around 45–125) *Erotikos* esteemed the marital duties to be just as important as emotional affection between the spouses; legal measures furthermore aimed at promoting these duties. According to his *Praecepta coniugalia*, conjugal sexual intercourse should be valued highly, because married life would be better with it and many disputes would be reconciled through it (Schnell 2002: 261). Plutarch's love of women is evident in his focus on the man's love for a woman as he places it at the center of the virtuous *philia*, enhancing its virtue and capacity for companionship, although he did not condemn pederasty or male-male *eros*

(Pechriggl 2009: 52). Catullus (around 80–51 BCE) had already declared in a poem written on the occasion of a wedding in the first century BCE that (early) married life not only fulfilled the marital duties but also brought about joy and let the couple grow together:

> Close the door, bridesmaids.
> We've had our fun.
> Now, you fine pair, have a good life
> and go to it, make the most of your thrusting youth
> consummating your conjugal duties over and over again.

And to the bride he says:

> "Play—however you like your pleasure
> —and give him children soon."
>
> (Dixon 2003: 119)

On the other hand, a multitude of poems and satire pieces exist in which it is the husband who becomes sexually dependent on his wife. This form of unmanliness also included the feeling of burning jealousy and fear that their wives would put horns on them, that is, cheat on them, for insufficient or unsuccessful marital bliss. Young Seneca (around 1–65) warned Stoic men generally against the rigors awaiting them in the marriage bed:

> The beginnings of married love are honourable, but its excesses make it perverse. After all, it makes no difference how a disease is actually caught. (...) And indeed it is a disgraceful thing to feel any love for another man's wife, but also to feel too much for your own. The wise man ought to love his wife reasonably, not passionately. He controls the onset of erotic excitement and is not rushed headlong into sex: there is nothing more disgusting than making love to your wife as if she were your mistress.' (Dixon 2003: 123f.)

Behind this was the insight that the sexual attraction of the first months and years of marriage could be lost over time and that the husbands might turn to whores, courtesans, female or even male slaves. The marriage bond should therefore from the outset not primarily rely on erotic attraction but instead on companionship. In the case of demands such as these, it should be borne in mind that most of the texts handed down come from men and reflect their views. This, of course, counts for the world of images, too, in which *eros* was celebrated among married couples. In erotic art, more personal settings also emerged, in which one could see intimate and married couples in domestic surroundings and in emotional communication, and not only exciting and unusual sexual positions (Clarke 2009: 45ff.).

Gendered and Social Contexts of Sexuality

Despite the revaluation of emotional and sexual contacts in marriage, Roman men continued to enjoy great liberties in premarital and extramarital affairs with prostitutes and female slaves as well as male slaves who served their masters sexually. Their sexual possibilities were also reflected in the *Oneirocritica* (*The Interpretation of Dreams*) by Artemidorus of Daldis (second century CE), who listed and interpreted the following erotic situations: the penetration of socially inferior persons such as the wife, prostitutes of both sexes, market women, male and female slaves, or the wife of another man (Matuszewski 2021: 107). For him, these acts were among the usual or natural sexual dream acts. He therefore took it for granted that socially subordinate persons or persons without citizenship status were to be penetrated by others (slaves, strangers, or enemies); this also included active and passive masturbation. All forms of incest and oral-genital acts were socially unacceptable. But under acts against nature, he categorized necrophilia, sexual contact with gods, bestiality, self-penetration, and self-fellatio as well as sexual acts between women (Laes 2010: 35f.). This thus shows that sexual activity was structured along the social position (free/unfree, citizen/non-citizen, higher/lower social status), gender affiliation, degree of kinship, active–passive paradigm, penetrating/penetrated, and body part involved (Kamen and Levin-Richardson 2015). It must be emphasized that categorizations and evaluations such as these usually originated from the quill of an educated and probably successful middle- or upper-class man and primarily reflect his point of view.

The sexual status of slaves, on the other hand, was precarious on multiple levels. For the "use of desires" (Foucault 1989a), the slave body was considered *infamia*—without honor or shame—and could be penetrated by its owners, used for labor, and beaten at will (Osiek 2003: 256ff.). For the masters, the commodity character of these sexual objects already became apparent upon purchase, where they could examine the naked bodies for possible bodily defects and health deficits and check the female slaves' virginity. For exceptionally beautiful girls and boys, slave dealers demanded greater sums, which is why the possession of exceptional specimens could also raise one's social prestige (Harper 2011: 292ff.). The fact that slaves were praised in poetry as lascivious and—because they mostly came from foreign cultures—experienced in extraordinary practices contributed to the eroticization and sexualization of this human commodity. The previously frequently held opinion that slaves who had been released or bought free must continue to be sexually available to their former masters has, however, been proven false (Butrica 2006: 210ff.).

Roman wives were obliged to *pudicitia*, to behave according to the dictates of shame and virtue, including unconditional loyalty—which should not be confused with matrimonial chastity (Langlands 2006: 29ff.). Accordingly, great importance was attached to premarital virginity. To signal this, girls (probably) wore a *toga praetexta* framed with a purple stripe (Caldwell 2014: 57f.). The high cultural appreciation of virginity was also visible in the six vestal virgins. These priestesses of the goddess Vesta, the protector of the home and hearth, chaste guardians of the eternal holy fire, served in a temple at the Forum Romanum and stood at the center of a state religion. Were a vestal virgin to lose her innocence—a symbol standing for the impenetrable city walls of Rome—this signaled great disaster for the community. The fallen priestess was excluded from the priesthood and buried alive (Stahlmann 1997: 129ff.; Berkowitz 2012: 97ff.; Undheim 2018: 31ff., 153.).

Overall, Roman women possessed significantly more rights and freedoms than their Greek predecessors. They could acquire and sell property. Some of them ran businesses and divorced their husbands, for example, if the man dared to bring a lover into the house (Clark 2008: 27). From the second century BCE onward, the *matronae* of the citizenry took up an even stronger position at the center of the *domus*, above all because their husbands were away from home for long periods of time for military, business, or diplomatic-political reasons. Women also had public lives—but always in a role defined in relation to a male family member—and took part in cultic-religious life (Staples 2004: 4ff.). The political and military uncertainty from 90 to 30 BCE brought about an upheaval within the Roman upper class. Many marriages ended in divorce, and the separated or widowed women were able to significantly improve their social status. For the poet Martial (40 to between 102 and 104) this was one of the reasons why Roman men did not like to marry such independent women: "You all ask why I don't want to marry a rich wife? I don't want to be my wife's wife. The matron . . . should be below her husband. That's the only way man and woman can be equal" (Swancutt 2007: 36). Some contemporaries warned against such relations becoming widespread, which they believed would endanger the patriarchy (Johnson and Ryan 2005: 6ff.). In the first and second centuries, politically successful women or those who were deployed for political purposes, such as Julia (the daughter of Emperor Augustus), Valeria Messalina (the third wife of Emperor Claudius), Agrippina the Younger (the mother of Nero), and Poppaea Sabina (the second wife of Nero), were often disparaged as adulteresses and whores. The Romans also regarded older women as "perverted," in any case, those whose physical beauty had diminished but who nevertheless articulated sexual interest and put this desire into practice (Meyer-Zwiffelhoffer 1995: 98f.).

The Male and Female Body

Roman doctors largely adopted the gender-specific body images of their Greek colleagues: They ascribed to the theories of the Greek doctor Soranus (around 100 CE), inspired by Aristotle, who said that although women did not produce their own seed during orgasm, their sexual arousal led to the relaxation and receptiveness of the uterus. Other Roman physicians were intensely concerned with reproduction and wanted to promote fertility among the citizenry, seeking to produce it among couples who had failed to have offspring (Salisbury 2001: 144). Unlike in the Hippocratic body, however, most people no longer believed that regular sexual intercourse was a basic prerequisite for the health and balance of a woman and that she would otherwise be at the mercy of *eros*. The Greek physician Galenus or Galen (around 129–216) had a deep impact and lasting influence (Grahn-Wilder 2018: 45ff.; Flemming 2018). According to him, the female body did indeed produce its own procreative seed. Women would ejaculate it during orgasm from the ovaries into the uterus, where it met the male humor, and both fluids made an essential contribution to the conception. Mutual sexual arousal was thus necessary for conception. In court, however, this view sometimes produced fatal results: if a woman became pregnant after rape, this was an indication that she had felt pleasure and hence wanted it. According to Galen, the main difference between the female and male sexual organs was their inward and outward orientation. Seen this way, his gender model functioned not antithetically but homologously, and the differences between man and woman corresponded to their positioning on the temperature scale between colder and warmer bodies. Galen didn't advocate an exclusive and unidimensional "one-sex model," as Thomas W. Laqueur postulated, but instead distinguished the sexes in the flow of humors and in the specific bodily functions (Laqueur 1992; King 2011: 110f.; Voß 2010: 37ff.). In other medical texts, however, comparisons found that the two sexes were completely different in their bodies (King 2013: 38). But it was Galen's model that got passed down to Renaissance medicine by Byzantine and Arab doctors and remained authoritative until the early eighteenth century. His teaching of the four bodily fluids (blood, phlegm, and yellow and black bile) and the associated four bodily qualities (hot, cold, moist, and dry) assigned different physical and psychological characteristics to the sexes and demanded careful dietary observation as well as the maintenance of the fragile equilibrium.

For the Epicurean philosopher Lucretius (between 99 and 94 to around 55 BCE), the sexual desire of men was primarily determined by their psychophysiology. In his work *De rerum natura* (*On the Nature of Things*), he explains how the seed of a sexually mature man is stimulated not only by visual perception, but also by imagination, a beautiful female body and erotic clothing, and how it surges against the genitals, the carnal lust directed toward this object and strives toward its imminent fulfilment through ejaculation. For an Epicurean like him, however, this encounter under the sign of Venus also had an urgent, aggressive, and suffering-inducing side. For Lucretius, sexual desire was a given by nature but was not—like hunger and thirst—a vital desire, and therefore it was considered rather ambivalent: on the one hand, he saw in it a reliable source for the experience of joy, on the other, troublesome for peace of mind. It thus stood in the way of a stable and equanimous *joie de vivre*, which consisted not only in avoiding but ultimately overcoming stirring, negative emotions such as fear, pain, and urgent desires. For Lucretius, the female part to play was quite clear, because the task of the wives was to receive their husbands in a quiet and amicable (sexual) act and thus lead them over time into a marriage of companionship (Gordon 2002). Whether a follower of Lucretius or another philosophical or medical school, one affiliated physical-sexual love in Latin with the goddess Venus. Thus, sexual intercourse was called *Venerem* (or *uenerem*) *iungere* (or *committere*); those who had low sexual desire were *frigidus in Venerem*; and a *homo Venereus* possessed *uoluptates Venereae* in great measure (Stroh 2000: 13).

Penetrative Hegemony

In sexual matters, Roman men had to be active and virile due to their physical attributions and their social and cultural (pre-)dominance. Even though the majority of the population led an agrarian life in ancient Rome, a martial mentality dominated from the historically misty Royal Period (753–509 BCE) to the oligarchic Republic (509–27 BCE) to the imperial period (27 BCE–284 CE). Warlike values therefore also shaped the image of masculinity, although most income and taxes came from agriculture. Even in the early Christian period, gladiators were still regarded as models of virility—despite their being slaves for the most part. Penetration was for the *vir*, the freeborn male citizen, a direct form of subjugating power and dominance. It should be noted, however, that the binary model of Greco-Roman sexuality completely oriented around penetration versus being penetrated as represented by historiography in the late twentieth century has meanwhile become obsolete (Langlands 2006: 13). Activity and domination in sexual matters were also regarded as masculine traits, the opposite of which was feminine (Kamen and Levin-Richardson 2014: 449ff.). Moreover, the axis of virility and femininity did not merely run along the gender divide; for male *pueri*, *servi*, and *molles* (men who liked to be penetrated) were also considered feminine because they passively abandoned themselves and some wished to do so. Another axis spanned the three bodily orifices: the vagina, anus, and mouth, and specific verbs were used to describe their active penetration or passive reception. With *futuere*, for example, the penetrator actively penetrated the vagina with the penis; *p(a)edicare* was for anal penetration; and *irrumare* for oral (Parker 1997: 48ff.).

Anyone unable to protect themselves from penetrative and phallic or even priapic hegemony was considered unmanly or effeminate (Walters 1997; Williams 1999: 17ff.; Levin-Richardson 2020: 346ff.). Standard motifs in Roman literature dealt with deeply asymmetric power relations between and within the sexes. For example, it wasn't enough for a young bride-to-be merely virginal and demure on her wedding night, but she should also be (at least a little) afraid of the deflowering. Stories about first-time pain and violence surely instilled and reinforced such fears (Hersch 2010: 62f.). Moreover, Roman citizens were to show their claim to power by dominating their wives and ensuring that they were not betrayed. In late republican times (133–30 BCE), one seems to have been particularly sensitive to the dangers of adultery. The supposed moral decline of the empire was associated not just with a lack of religious reverence and military courage and commitment but also with the dubious sexual and moral steadfastness of (married) Roman women (Skinner 2005: 206). Affection and sexual pleasure between the spouses were now more appreciated. This could also be seen in praise of the coitus position (of *coeo*, coming together) in which man and woman looked each other in the face (later dubbed the "missionary position"). It was now regarded as the natural one, in contrast to the *a tergo* penetration that seemed typical of animals and all those who behaved like them (Younger 2005: 124).

But Lucretius seemed to disagree with that now widespread view and made an effort to distinguish between forms of coitus as more or less conducive to conception and further differentiated between appropriate positions for wives and for prostitutes:

> And in what modes the intercourse goes on, is likewise of very great moment; for women are commonly thought to conceive more readily after the manner of wild-beasts and quadrupeds, because the seeds in this way can find the proper spots, in consequence of the position of the body. Nor have wives the least use for effeminate motions: a woman hinders and stands in the way of her own conceiving, when thus she acts; for she drives the furrow out of the direct course and path of the share and turns away from the proper spots the stroke of the seed. And thus for their own ends harlots are wont to move, in order not to conceive and lie in child-bed frequently, and at the same time to render Venus more attractive to men. This our wives would seem to have no need for. (Lucretius 1864: 209, 1263–77; Meyer-Zwiffelhoffer 1995: 74)

In other words, wives shouldn't take a position that suits their own pleasure or even that of their husbands, nor should they move all too much so as not to prevent conception!

Contraception and Abortion

Contraceptive issues, if they came up at all, were seen, as in Greek sexual culture, primarily as a female matter. Women used preventive mixtures—which if at all effective had an abortive rather than a contraceptive effect—in the form of ointments or soaked plugs to close up the uterus or even the penis; they rinsed with vinegar or other strong essences after coitus or carefully counted their days of infertility, which were thought to be around the middle and toward the end of the menstrual cycle, according to

Hippocrates (Jütte 2008: 45). Medical doctors such as Soranus, the Greek doctor who worked in Rome around 100 BCE, advised the use of wool tampons which, soaked with olive oil, honey, or the sap of the balsam tree, were intended to reduce the uterus' readiness to conceive or to close it up. Another application was vaginal douching with sea water or an alum–wine mixture, thought to have a spermicidal effect. Some women also wore special amulets during coitus to prevent pregnancy (Keller 1988).

Coitus interruptus was apparently also practiced, whereby it can be assumed that the men learned about this method from prostitutes and then also used it with their wives (Ranke-Heinemann 1999: 208ff.). Some men supported their women in prolonging the intervals between births by pursuing ascetic ideals themselves and refraining from regular sexual intercourse for health reasons—and prolonging their abstinence beyond the occasionally quite long breastfeeding periods (McLaren 1990: 55ff.). Contraceptive practices were suddenly cast in a bad light altogether, however, with fears of population decline from the second century BCE. Nevertheless, it cannot be assumed that the upper classes in particular wanted an unlimited number of children, which could lead to inheritance problems; they potentially also tried to extend the intervals between births. With an average marriage duration of fifteen years and a birth rate of five children, still, typically only two or three survived (Hin 2013: 192ff.; McLaren 1990: 50ff.).

In ancient Roman culture, for jurists, physicians, and moralists, questions of abortion were primarily about reproduction, personal status, and gendered power. Roman law focused on ensuring family succession, which could be jeopardized by abortion. For physicians, questions arose in connection with the Hippocratic Oath, which led the physician Scribonius Largus to opine in his writings in the first century AD that one should not disseminate anything about abortifacients, nor should one give them to pregnant women. Soranus of Ephesus distinguished between contraceptive, abortifacient, and expulsive measures and said that it was better to prevent fertilization than to abort the fruit. For moralists, in addition to individual responsibility over death and life, the political issues were paramount. For them, abortion was considered a civic vice that prevented large families and the growth of the Roman population and Empire (Mistry 2015: 25ff.).

The Double Standard of Adultery

Adultery remained a private offence until the *lex Iulia de adulteriis coercendis* (18 BCE), issued under the first Roman Emperor Augustus. It became a crime in which public prosecution was brought in front of a divorce court (Steenblock 2013: 27f.; Perry 2020: 73f.). According to the law, in addition to the dissolution of one's marriage, the convicted faced loss of property, banishment, and being forced to wear the male *toga*, and not the honorable woman's *stola*. Wearing the *toga* was a shameful demarcation that equated the wearer to prostitutes.

If an adulteress was caught by her father in his house or in the act, he was allowed to kill his daughter and the lover without criminal consequences. A husband could do the same with his wife's lover, providing the perpetrator was of a lower class, but the fate of his wife was a matter for the court (Treggiari 1991: 282f.). Despite the strict prohibitions, however, there still seems to have been plenty of adultery cases that went to trial (Friedl 1996: 64; Edwards 2004: 39f.). Amy Richlin pointed out that judgments and penalties greatly differ from source to source. Tradition and source type often dictate the range of sanctions for the adulterer, from legal persecution, exile, and monetary fines to flogging, castration, ear and nose mutilation, to fellatiating the disgraced man, anal penetration, or death (Richlin 2006: 330).

It remains unclear whether the Augustan laws actually brought individual sexual behavior more into focus, thereby creating sexual (legal) subjects beyond the traditional family context, at least among the men of the Roman upper class (Habinek 1997: 29ff.; Lape 2011: 32ff.). In any case, the criminal consequences of the *lex Iulia* make it clear that the relationship between the sexes was marked by extremely blatant double standards. Although scholars still dispute the objectives behind the Augustan marriage laws, it seems certain that, in addition to population policy objectives, that is, stabilization of birth rates, they also aimed at moral reform. From this point of view, these represented early attempts by the state to gain power over reproduction and thus over the family and population through marital sexual behavior. The success of these laws was limited, however, which is why later emperors and administrations repeatedly had to deal with the jurisdiction of marriage and adultery over and again (Steenblock 2013: 28ff.).

The most pressing concern in Roman adultery cases was the *patria potestas* and ensuring an untainted social pedigree; in contrast to early Greece, they were less concerned with the mythical lineage of blood. Moreover, it was feared that female citizens, especially those of the (aristocratic) upper class, would be committing not only a sexual violation but also a social one. If, for example, were they to have an affair with a slave, which was quite possible in the barely gender-separated household communities, the hierarchy of free and unfree would be upended. Historical evidence for a larger number of such crimes, however, is largely lacking outside the literary tradition (Parker 2007). A *matrona* dishonored in an adulterous act, be it rape or otherwise, was not only seen as a victim; she bore some of the blame, accused of pleasure-seeking behavior (Skinner 2005: 197). If such a scandal came to pass, it brought scandal and shame to cuckolded husband, since it was then presumed that his children were not indeed his own. Adultery by the *matrona* invalidated the patriarchal power of the phallus in more ways than one. Priapus figures and mural phalli found on Roman houses and gardens attest to the widespread homage paid to this epitome of masculinity;

ostensibly to deter thieves, some of these phallic figures, of course, were also meant to amuse viewers (Richlin 1992).

Concubinatus and the Enforcement of Fertility

Imperial Rome (27 BCE—284 CE) seems to have seen an increase in *concubinatus*, institutionalized cohabitation of two persons who did not fulfil the legal requirements for a marriage and yet wanted to live together in a secure status—from *com* (with, together) and *cubare* (to lie down). Soldiers could only obtain citizenship and marry after their period of service, so concubinage offered at least a temporary alternative. Even if this way of life cannot be overestimated quantitatively, it represented a way of impeding the social rise of unwanted groups of people at least for a while (Friedl 1996: 271ff.). Concubines, often freed slaves or foreign women, were required to possess almost the same virtues and qualities as wives—thus *libertae* were not excluded from male dominance practices. However, the children from such a relationship were not subject to the *patria potestas*, and thus they were given the mother's name and, of course, were not entitled to inheritance from the father. Concubines and their children mostly remained reliant on gifts and other alimony payments. In any case, the increase in concubinage was seen as an indication that customs and marital ties had loosened. From today's point of view, it may seem rather unusual that these forms of living together and also intimate and sexual relationships were even documented on gravestones: In the *Corpus Inscriptionum Latinarum*, for example, there is an inscription from Rome in which Allius, the *patronus* (ex-owner) of the slave Allia Potestas, whom he shared with another man, had written about his companion and at the same time about his antique throuple: "As long as she lived, she treated her two lovers in such a way that they became like Pylades and Orestes. One house received them all, and a spirit joined them" (CIL VI 37965; Clarke 2009: 158).

Ritual practices were also employed to regulate sexual desire and promote fertility. The fertility festivities *Lupercalia*, held in February, took place until Christian times and were dedicated to the herder god Faunus—whose sobriquet *lupercus* meant protector against wolves. In this archaic rite, priests as well as young citizens, dressed only in the skins of sacrificed goats, ran around the palatine and with a leather strap would slap married women waiting along the roadside for them to bring fertility at the beginning of a new fertility cycle (Beard, North and Price 1998: 119ff.). The *ludi florae* (florals) were celebrated in May in honor of the flower goddess Flora and were also dedicated to spring and vegetal rebirth and fertility. This festival was rather obscene as it was performed by naked men and prostitutes. It stood in sharp contrast to the April *Cerealia*, the festivities for Ceres, goddess of the harvest, fertility, and marriage, which focused on abstinence and shame (Staples 2004: 84ff.).

Sexual Misconduct and Social Stigma

If it were up to some Latin poets and especially the satirists, Roman wives were hardly a prudish bunch, and by many tellings did not behave in accordance with proper respectability. These storied women showed themselves to be sexually free and seldom averse to adulterous offers. However, it must be emphasized that such erotic stories and the sexual escapades of the matrons appearing in them arose from the fantasy of their male creators and by no means from the average female world. The ambivalence of the Roman female figures was also expressed in the visions of Venus presented by Lucretius and Virgil (70–19 BCE); somewhere between amoral lover and protective mother of the Roman people, at the same time she expressed cosmic forces of order and destruction (Skinner 2005: 239). As the research on Venus figurines in Roman Britain revealed, her figuration could also be used to protect family members and to encourage fertility, meanings that came about through a syncretic process of Gaulish and Roman beliefs (Fittock 2020).

The Roman emperors of the first three centuries—at least according to contemporary observers, who peppered the sources extensively with false accusations, slander, and moral propaganda—often led quite excessive lives and pursued a multitude of debauchery. In his biographies of the Roman rulers, Suetonius (around 70–after 122) presented a characteristic picture of the famous general and politician of the outgoing Roman Republic, Gaius Julius Caesar, more than 150 years after his death:

> It is admitted by all that he was much addicted to women, as well as very expensive in his intrigues with them, and that he debauched many ladies of the highest quality; among whom were Posthumia, the wife of Servius Sulpicius; Lollia, the wife of Aulus Gabinius; Tertulla, the wife of Marcus Crassus; and Mucia, the wife of Cneius Pompey. (Suetonius 2009: 53, 1; Hartmann 2015: 229)

Statesmen like Caesar also used adultery as a demonstration of power against their opponents in order to humiliate and dishonor them. Some emperors then deliberately eroticized their own person, for example by means of statuary: a virile and attractive man like the emperor—so goes the obvious message—was also much more successful and potent in sexual matters than an average Roman *vir* and was thus predestined to lead the empire (Vout 2007: 4ff.). From the (alleged) moral depravity or the (alleged) promiscuity of the emperors, some historians have concluded that similar conditions existed in the Senate and in high offices.

Controlling One's Sexual Desire

In fact, quite a few Roman rulers referred to Stoicism and its teachings that one should strive for lifelong self-control through suppression and liberation from all passions. The Stoics, many of whom were Roman senators, endeavored of the self to remain rational and free, particularly in that sexual desire must be kept under control. A person thus fortified should prevent both his body and his mind from being penetrated, and instead maintain autonomy and self-direction. Stoics offered an image of masculinity that was quite acceptable to Roman men who were striving for integrity, as it represented an alternative to phallic-aggressive virility (Bartsch 2005: 80f.). Sexual issues were even raised in speeches to the people and in the Senate, where the immoral behavior of a political opponent was seen as an indication of his character and social attitudes. It was expected of a freeborn Roman, and even more of an aristocrat, that he would also behave in sexual matters in a fashion befitting his status. On the other hand, those who were guided by their (sexual) desires were deemed immoderate and unrestrained not only in their dealings with themselves but also in social relationships. Seen in this light, the microcosm of gender life functioned in a "strict analogy to the social and political order" (Meyer-Zwiffelhoffer 1995: 66f.).

According to Michel Foucault, concern for oneself in the first two centuries of our era was accompanied by an evolving art of existence and led to a radical reassessment of marital and sexual relations:

> [T]his is not just a greater preoccupation with the body; it is also a different way of thinking about sexual activity, and of fearing it because of its many connections with disease and with evil. With regard to wives and to the problematization of marriage, the modification mainly concerns the valorization of the conjugal bond and the dual relation that constitutes it; the husband's right conduct and the moderation he needs to enjoin on himself are not justified merely by considerations of status, but by the nature of the relationship, its universal form and the mutual obligations that derive from it. . . . On the one hand, a more active attention to sexual practice is required, an attention to its effects on the organism, to its place and function within marriage, to its value and its difficulties in the relationship with boys. But at the same time as one dwells on it, and as the interest that one brings to bear on it is intensified, it increasingly appears to be dangerous and capable of compromising the relation with oneself that one is trying to establish. It seems more and more necessary to distrust it, to confine it, insofar as possible, to marital relations—even at the cost of charging it with more intense meanings within that conjugal relationship. (Foucault 1986: 239f.; Detel 1998)

Foucault's pointed assessment of marriage and sexuality in the Roman culture of the first centuries was met with criticism, however, above all for his choice of sources and interpretation and his genderless perspective (Ormand 2014: 62ff.). He had neglected the fact that these were Greek authors writing about Roman circumstances. It was also argued that marital love and sexual relations between spouses were more positively evaluated even before the new epoch (Cohen and Saller 1994). Objections to Foucault's take also came from feminist historians who accused him of perpetuating the patriarchal view and gender bias of ancient sources (Richlin 1998). But, like some historians of antiquity before him, Foucault rightly pointed out the concerns and fears of the upper-class men of the imperial era (27–284 CE), for whom the pressure was mounting. Many noble families had simply died out; the balance of power in the imperial palace became increasingly opaque and could hardly be calculated, and even freed slaves could now take up important positions. In the face of fears about status and social descent, these men saw in their bodies, health and dietetic lifestyles an essential symbolic capital that continued to promise them extraordinary rank and required strict social demarcation.

Controlling one's sexual desire was thus considered an all-consuming problem. Galen's theory of fluids delivered some arguments according to which the body could easily lose its equilibrium due to external influences, bad behavior, and unregulated desires, thus endangering social rules and the gender hierarchy. Cupid's arrows, therefore, should be given the most urgent attention. The physician Rufus of Ephesus (*c.* 80–*c.* 150) had already concluded in his treatise *Peri aphrodision* (*On Sexual Intercourse*) that coitus should be carried out moderately, whereas sexual excess was harmful (Rousselle 1988: 12). Seneca the Younger, and other contemporary writers and philosophers, racked their brains over the supposedly rampant feminine weakness and impotence of men and even found a threat to virility posed by fashionable lavishness and outfit mania. The satirical literature poked fun at bogeymen who fit this bill: the *cinaedus*, a man who liked to be penetrated by another, and the *tribas*, a woman who reversed gender roles, acting phallically male. Enemies of virility like these were believed to be found at the fringes of the empire and in hostile territories: among the Greeks, Egyptians, Jews, and Syrians, the *perversitas* of the sexes must indeed run rampant and be seeping into the masculine Roman culture from without (Skinner 2005: 249ff.; Roisman 2014). The historian Diodorus had already classified the Gauls as particularly "perverse" in the first half of the first century BCE:

> Although their wives are comely, they have very little to do with them, but rage with lust, in outlandish fashion, for the embraces of males. It is their practice to sleep upon the ground on the skins of wild beasts and to tumble with a catamite on each side. And the most astonishing thing of all is that they feel no concern for their proper dignity, but prostitute to others without a qualm the flower of their bodies; nor do they consider this a disgraceful thing to do, but rather when anyone of them is thus approached and refuses the favour offered him, this they consider an act of dishonour. (Clark 2009: 42)

In facing off against that effeminate and feminized society, the Roman man was to show that he was master of and could defend his small empire (marriage, *domus*, and sexual relations) as a stand-in for the great Empire of Rome (Williams 1999: 132).

But contrary opinions were also to be heard, for instance from the philosopher Gaius Musonius Rufus (before 30 to before 101/102), a late representative of the Stoics, who sided with marriage companionship in which the partners stood by each other like "oxen yoked together" to confront the demands of life. Intercourse was among the things they must share exclusively (Grahn-Wilder 2018: 262f.). Musonius was against husbands consorting with courtesans or slaves, nor should wives sleep with slaves. Of course, he condemned pederasty as well as, for example, teachers who took advantage of their social position to have sexual intercourse with boys (Laes 2019: 128). For him, nature predetermined the coming together of sexes in conjugal coitus, and thus united the psychophysical difference into a new whole. The dimorphism of the sexes continued even in the bodies, which he conceived of symmetrically and (largely) without male preference. It seemed central to him that not only the women kept their desires in check and transformed them into serenity and peace of mind through self-control, but also the men. Nevertheless, Musonius also ultimately saw the husband as the head of the family and his supremacy legitimized in his greater power of judgment (Nussbaum 2000b: 298ff.).

Desecration, Rape, and Kidnapping

Cases in which men failed to defend their own sexual integrity and that of members of the *domus* were desecration, rape, and kidnapping. In pre-Augustan times, these acts destroyed *pudicitia*, a person's modesty and sexual virtue. Perpetrators were to be prosecuted and punished by the victim's family. There does not seem to have been any special statutory provisions for doing so, rather such infamy was regulated by cultural *mores*, manners, and customs. According to the *lex Iulia*, *stuprum* (desecration/rape) could only be committed against free women and ex-slaves who lived honorably, but not against prostitutes, slaves, and adulteresses, that is, these groups had no rights to recourse and thus effectively no protection. Any member of society, including slaves, could be considered a perpetrator of *stuprum*. The penalty should be demanded from the victim as well as their husband or father. If this did not happen within a certain period of time, any free citizen could bring charges—and the inactive husband or father was sanctioned as an accomplice (Fantham 2011: 116f.). The rape of a free-bought boy or girl or a single or married free Roman woman was classified as a capital crime (Eidinow 2011: 99). The consequence of the legal stipulation meant that the matter was no longer (only) the responsibility of the *pater familias*—and as such the representative of the *res publica*—but also of the public courts, raised as a *publicum crimen*. Here, too, large sections of the population came into the crosshairs of political legislation and governmental efforts: In times of stagnating demographic growth or even population decline, the public and the courts were thus to take responsibility for all those who were unable to protect the family and household members under their control (Meyer-Zwiffelhoffer 1995: 112ff.).

In the successive *lex Iulia de vi publica et privata*, the criteria of shame and honor were no longer differentiated for cases of rape, rather the groups addressed were plainly listed: *pueri* and *feminae* were now the victims of violent "seduction" (Mette-Dittmann 1991: 72). But, make no mistake, the concern was not (primarily) to protect the individual rights of the girls, women, and boys concerned, but rather to maintain public order and to discipline and punish the male perpetrators, who were threatened with the loss of civil rights and exile. Kidnapping a woman was now punished much more severely:

> Whoever hath abducted a single or married woman will be punished with the death penalty, and if the father, softened by pleas, does not persecute his injustice, then another (outside the family) will be able to accuse him (Stahlmann 1997: 66).

According to Livy's (Titus Livius) *Ab urbe condita* (about 59 BCE to about 17 CE), a multivolume work on Roman history, sexual violence in the form of defilement and rape was pretty much an everyday affair in the political and military realm of the early days of Rome. Military conflicts put captured and injured women, men, and children at immediate risk of sexual violence—whether it was on the Roman or other side (Gaca 2018: 306ff.; Vihervalli 2022: 11ff.). The moral of many myths indeed reveals that defilement and rape didn't always lead down the path of destruction but often to creation, to a new divine being or half-human demigod, thus in effect productive outcomes. This aspect of sexual violence, which is difficult to understand from today's perspective, can be regarded as representative of Rome's self-perception in the decades before the common era. According to the authors of the Augustan period, the Roman Empire succeeded in bringing together Mars and Venus—and thus the two antithetic great powers: violence and love. This was demonstrated by the many enemy countries and opposing religions conjoined to their great empire. From violence and acts of war would emerge a new future-oriented and harmonious order (Arieti 2002). It is significant that, during the republican period, the goddess Venus was also imbued with a warlike side, connoted by desecration and overempowerment: temptation in general and seduction in particular are the result of both traits, often bringing violence into play. Coupling in a narrow sense and unification (of the empire) in the broader sense were thus seen as a victory over the *other*, worthy of celebration. As the goddess of victory, Venus differed markedly from her Greek predecessor Aphrodite, whose sphere of activity was dedicated exclusively to sexuality and love (Bolder-Boos 2015: 114f.).

In no way, however, should it be assumed that violence—or rape, as an act against the explicit will of a person—was tolerated at a basic level, much less advocated in sexual relationships. To recognize this requires a double reading of classical sources, such as Ovid's (43–17 BCE) *Ars amatoria* (*Art of Love*). In these teaching poems from the year 1, written in three books, Ovid used realistic situations based on personal experience to describe how a Roman could get to know a girl, spark her fancy, and capture her as a partner through mutually satisfactory sexual practice. In the seduction scenes, coercion and violence are used. There is an abundance of allusions to martial acts, some of which, however, are meant ironically. The female figures are described as enemies to be conquered, even if most of them wanted to be taken and defeated. Ovid thus, according to one reading, does more than palliate the helplessness and suffering of the victims of male violence. He eroticizes the unequal balance of power between the sexual partners, trivializes the overempowerment, and encourages imitation. Read against the grain, however, not only the ironic and caricaturing style, but also the shocking violent scenes should be understood as a clear indication that rape is being painted as an unacceptable practice of sexual seduction. In other words, he was promoting a form of love equally far removed from non-physical companionship as it was from mere sexual satisfaction (Richlin 1992: 158 ff; Sharrock 2002; Skinner 2005: 226ff.).

Public Shame and *Ars Erotica*

Naked bodies, their staging within the erotic ambience achieved in countless wall frescoes, drinking vessels, oil lamps, and jewelry, also depended on the respective perspectives of their producers and consumers. In contrast to Greek art, whose language of form and motif was considered exemplary by the Romans (Shusterman 2021: 77ff.), sculptors and painters—some of whom themselves came from Greek regions—took a big step toward individualized representation, which was reflected in individual facial features and even body shape. The Greeks' worship of nudity in their art was also qualified: "The Greek practice is to leave the figure entirely nude, whereas it is a Roman and military thing to add a breastplate," according to Pliny the Elder (23/24–79) in his *Historia naturalis*, written in 77 CE—marking the difference between the Greek gymnasium culture and Roman militaristic attitudes (NH 34.18.; de Angelis 2008: 82; Thommen 2007: 98; de Angelis 2008: 82). Also touching on a similar vein, Cicero quotes the poet Ennius: "The beginning of shame is baring the body in public." In art, therefore, figures—not including the head and face—conformed to an ideal that was generally more covered up. Right down to the exercise of sport, Roman citizens shied away from the Greek gymnasium practices of showing off their genitals to the public. Having to exhibit oneself uncovered and unprotected was considered a characteristic of slaves, prostitutes, and other disgraceful peoples to whom Roman citizens refused to expose themselves (Blanshard 2010: 30ff.). By this time, even nudity at the public baths was a talking point. Bodily covering was required at least in mixed facilities from the imperial period on (Busch 1999: 463).

In craft and artistic works on the subject of sexual intercourse, however, nude scenes and sexual depictions were regarded as largely unproblematic, and it was usually clear what the producers had in mind: to direct the viewer's gaze, and probably also the female viewer's, to the genitals and the sometimes acrobatic acts carried out with them. As in Greece, the women depicted are mostly identified as prostitutes. However, the appearance of Cupid/Amor figures could also have been an indication that married couples were the consumers of such art, as used in the context of wedding celebrations and rituals, for example. Also, one should not underestimate the potential that painted whore stories had for humorous intent. The Imperium Romanum was full of sexual pictures and stories mixed with humor, and all sorts of goods, promises, stimuli, and arousal could be bought from various businesses for one's husband. Many of these items were mass-produced (e.g., in terracotta from Arezzo), so that members of the middle classes could afford such erotic household goods.

Wealthy Romans also, apparently, were great consumers of erotic depictions. Their painting galleries contained many sexual scenes alongside mythological works. Ovid wrote about the collection of Emperor Augustus around 10 CE:

> Surely in your houses, just as figures of great men of old shine—painted by artist's hand—so somewhere a small picture depicts the various forms of copulation and the sexual positions. Telamonian Ajax sulks in rage, barbarian Medea glares infanticide, but there's *Venus* as well—wringing her dripping hair dry with her hands—and barely covered by the waters that bore her. (Clarke 1998: 91)

In Villa Farnesina, excavated on the banks of the Tiber in Rome, two related murals show a couple before and during sex. The fine clothing of the woman involved suggests that this is apparently not a whore story but a married couple from the upper class. Erotic pictures like these hung in respectable houses in private and semi-public spaces (Skinner 2005: 263). Many of the pictures paid homage to the virile penetration imperative, others depicted softer sexual scenes between married couples. The murals that have survived and their functions are still a point of contentious interpretation: Was sexuality to be domesticated here or was it merely decorative painting within the framework of the iconography customary at the time? Were the images to entice visitors or for the pleasure of one's own wife or own self? Are they also representative of some of the same misogynist tendencies that have been recorded in the graffiti of Pompeii (Myerowitz 1992; Clarke 1998: 106ff.)?

Lucky charms in the form of exaggerated genitalia, such as erect penises, on clay bells and metal amulets would ward off spells. Such defensive magic charms were subsumed under the word *fascinum* (penis), which, according to one theory, came from *fas* (auspiciousness) and promised fertility and prosperity. As an aegis against misfortune, erect penises were also chiseled into road crossings or erected at corners as phalli to protect against accidents. In houses and courtyards, the apotropaic ornaments warded against the evil eye and unpopular gods who could penetrate the bodies of respectable landowners and cause harm. The abundant Priapus images and statues scared off humans and demons alike, because they feared the figure might use his club-like phallus as a weapon. But here, too, satire and ridicule were at play: the Romans considered a small penis to be the norm even for adults, a (overly) large penis to be ludicrous.

The unusual and morally precarious sexual practices found on erotic-pornographic representations were most likely not part of the sexual repertoire of respectable citizens and their wives and lovers, particularly fellatio, cunnilingus, anal penetration, and female sexual dominance. The first two actions would have been emasculating to a freeman, since his performance could hardly be considered active, and the later situations presented complete passivity. Projections such as these were intended to shock the viewer and warn against this behavior—even if the visualization had quite contrary, namely, stimulating effects. At the same time, again, the Romans had a fine sense of irony and parody that should not go unaccounted for: no reasonable citizen could be exposed to humiliations such as these, so the figures depicted obviously had to be slaves or other lowly persons who had found themselves in, shall we say, an awkward position. With a heavy dose of contempt, *tribades* scenes showed women rubbing against one another, one seemingly penetrating the other. John R. Clarke has pointed out an important task of this pornographic motif: warding off the evil eye through the laughter of the beholder (Clarke 2002).

Erotic and Obscene Texts

Erotic and sexual narratives also permeated literature and poetry. A popular figure was the god Amor, who was also called Cupid and corresponded to the Greek Eros. Amor's domain wasn't limited to love; he also acted as a driving force for the erotic desire that made a couple fall in love, desire sexually, and conceive children. While he was celebrated for this (re-)productive side, he also posed a threat, in his unwieldy autonomy, for the Romans: In Ovid's first book of *Metamorphoses* (around 8 CE), he wounds the human heart with golden arrows and forces it into unconditional love for a particular person, with all the out-of-control behavior and feeling that come with love. But when Amor uses his leaden arrows, it results in a total aversion to one person. The god thus acted at the very least with complicity to one's self-inflicted and self-restrained shame and chastity, which is why Ovid blamed him—albeit with tongue in cheek—for himself only writing simplistic love poetry and not producing any more respectable types of texts (Armstrong 2004: 530ff.).

The authors of erotic and obscene texts were stuck in a dilemma that was also repeated through later centuries. Their recipients wondered whether they reported on actions and emotions they had experienced themselves: Had they put opinions and attitudes into the mouths of their characters that were indeed their own? How great was the difference between autobiographical background and artistic fiction? Catullus responded to this predicament in a diatribe against two of his companions who had described his love poems as *molliculi* (soft, unmanly) and accused him of possessing this quality (*mollitia*) himself:

> I will bugger you and face-fuck you,
> Aurelius the pathic [*pathicus*], and Furius the sodomite [*cinaedus*],
> who deem that I, like my verses,
> am immodest and effeminate, like this one here.
> Decorum is befitting of the poet himself,
> his verses not necessarily so at all:
> verses which then have taste and charm,
> if they are delicate and sexy
> and can excite and cause an itch,
> don't speak to boys, but to hairy old men
> who can't move their stiff loins.
> You, who read all these thousand kisses,
> you think I'm not man enough?
> I will bugger you and face-fuck you.
>
> (trans. Jacob Watson; Winter 1973; Janan 1994: 45; Meyer-Zwiffelhoffer 1995: 49)

Here, Catullus not only distances himself from the content of his own verses but also insists on the poetic freedom to portray some of his characters as unmanly. He is emphasizing his own aggressive-active masculinity and threatens his opponents with oral and anal penetration (Kamen and Levin-Richardson 2014: 449f.). For Catullus, the poetic imagination's greatest success comes through arousal among his listeners and readers by bringing in close the erotic and sexual actions and the emotions associated with them. A trick that was already popular at the time was to tell the aphrodisiac narrative saturated with experience from the perspective of a (supposedly) real person. This was also a strategy for authors reporting on the *ars meretricia*, the whores' art, who in so doing supposedly had procuresses and courtesans give their say, often identifying them as the real authors of the texts. In the vast majority of cases, however, these were male authors who portrayed the sexual desires and horrors of their (male) contemporaries. Lucian's *hetairikoi dialogoi* (whore dialogues, around 160) deeply influenced erotic and pornographic literature of the Renaissance and Enlightenment. In ancient Athenian gutter slang, *hetaera* and their clients, lovers, pimps, and bawds from the Attic demimonde conversed about the joys of hetero- and homosexual intercourse, as well as the woes of their everyday existence at the low end of the social ladder (Hartmann 2006; Fountoulakis 2022).

Regardless of whether fictional or autobiographical, the texts raise the question: Were the sexual acts portrayed at all acceptable to the audience? And what linguistic register was used for this literary communication? Catullus had no qualms about directly addressing or naming living contemporaries and attacking them with crude formulations. This confrontational practice became unusual in later times, and protagonists were given made-up names, also the rough colloquial slang was eventually dropped entirely (Meyer-Zwiffelhoffer 1995: 59). In addition, the authors were accused in their own time of polluting their listeners' and readers' minds with whore stories. To avoid such immoral thoughts, they ought to refrain from describing such sexual acts and certainly from using such crass language. A particularly problematic concern was what if children and young people or honorable women were to be confronted with these stories and blinded by them. So, it is not surprising that the ancients even considered censoring erotic art. Young authors in particular, however, vehemently opposed such artistic restrictions and demanded free, creative possibilities of expression, which could not stop at *lascivia*, unbridled debauchery—giving us the English word "lasciviousness."

Obscaenus or *obscenus* was indeed the established term to describe indecent and unseemly vocabulary surrounding sexual organs and sexual behavior. One could circumvent such obscenities by speaking of *coire* (to come together), *amplecti* (to embrace), or *dormire cum* (to sleep with). The *Carmina Priapea* collection of poems sums up the problem with these formulations:

> I could have said obscurely: 'Cast about
> for what, through given freely, won't run out.
> Give to me now what you may later seek
> to give in vain, once fuzz invest your check;
> what Jove has savored when his aquiline
> abductee greets his lover with his wine;
> what timid virgins on their wedding night
> contribute as an alternate delight.'
> It is easier to say: 'I want your ass.'
> Well, what did you expect? My muse is crass.
>
> (Priapus Poems 1999: 48ff.; Höschele 2012; Stroh 2000: 17)

Catullus demonstrates another tactic for dealing with obscenities: using them for seduction. Thus, he wrote the following literary note to Ipsitilla, a "boring young maid" from the area:

> Please, Ipsitilla, my darling,
> my charm, demand my presence
> at noon. If you do (and if you please),

be sure the door's open, and
don't go out but stay home:
prepare for nine consecutive
fuckings [*fututiones*]. If you can,
call me now: I'm in bed
full, lying flat and
pitching a tent.

(Stroh 2000: 15f.)

In the Brothel and on the Street

Matronae, respectable Roman women, demonstrated their social status in public by means of clothing, among other things: They wore the *stola*, the long dress of a distinguished woman, a *palla*, a long, open robe, and a *vitta*, a hairband. This outfit was not permitted for prostitutes known to the city, according to the *lex Iulia de adulteriis coercendis* issued by Emperor Augustus in 18 BCE. The law explicitly forbade prostitutes from wearing the *stola* and forced them to wear a *toga* instead, the male garment that was thrown over the left shoulder and hung down to the feet, leaving one arm free. This public marking was so prevalent that prostituting women were also referred to as *togatae*, and adulteresses were forced to wear this "scarlet letter" (Olson 2006). Even before Augustus' law, "disgraceful" women could be recognized by their colorful, short robes, their hairstyle, and their eye-catching makeup. Honorable women avoided drawing attention to themselves with flashy clothing, jewelry, and makeup to better avoid potential admirers or solicitors (McGinn 2014; Olson 2012: 80ff.; Strong 2016: 18ff.). Although there was no written law prohibiting prostitution per se (except for provisions on married women and children of the citizenry), its overall social connotation was negative: prostitutes stood for darkness, filth, effeminacy, cunning, and death, all antitheses to those values which a true and strong Roman citizen should stand for and which he stands to lose by consorting with whores (Edwards 1996: 84).

The modern term "prostitute" derives from the Latin *prostare* for "to offer or sell" or from *pro* and *statuere* and the resulting composite *prostituere*, "to present/display oneself." There were over fifty different words for prostitutes in republican and imperial Rome. In the sources, above all *scrota* and *meretrix* are mentioned. The first term referred to the male scrotum as well as female genitalia and was derogatory for base prostitutes of both female and male sexes. *Meretrix* (from mereō "merit, deserve" + -trīx, literally "she who earns") was used as a euphemistic attribution in literature in the sense of a "working woman." Thus, terms fluctuated between an assumed emotional relationship and possibly regular contact between client and whore, on the one hand, and a clear wage-salary relationship, on the other (Glazebrook

2011a: 148f.). For the most part, however, these terms were more or less indistinguishable, their most important joint feature being that the women described were not respectable citizens but promiscuous persons, which also included adulteresses (McClure 2006: 7f.).

Infamous Women Selling Their Body

What was distinguished were intermittent sexual encounters with prostitutes from stable relationships with concubines. According to the jurist Domitius Ulpianus (d. 223/228), the *meretrix* was characterized by two peculiarities in particular: the profit motive (*pecunia accepta*) and indiscriminately changing partners (*sine dilectu*) (Hemmie 2007: 23). Wherever honorable women might come into contact with disgraceful women, attempts were made to prevent or avoid such misfortune. For example, prostitutes were excluded from all religious rites normally carried out by Roman citizens or in which they were involved. Thus, the dishonorable women had to hold their rites for Venus Erycina outside the city walls, while the honorable citizens performed their rites on the Capitol. According to Seneca the Elder (around 54 BCE—39 CE), dishonorable women could never act as priestesses either and were even shunned by the latter on the street because they feared spiritual desecration through passing contact (McGinn 1998: 24ff.).

The majority of prostitutes were recruited from slaves as well as from those who had been freed. Some had grown up as children of prostitutes or had come to the Roman cities as prisoners of war or had been abducted from their places of origin, kidnapped from their homes in the countryside or abroad. There they worked for pimps and in brothels, some also independently. By making their bodies publicly available for payment, they violated citizen values of dignity, honor, and reliability to which the upper classes in particular attached great importance—the reason for the marriage ban between free Roman citizens and prostitutes. Pimps and bawds, too, brought *infamia*. The whole profession's infamous public dishonesty led to a reduction of their legal status under Roman law, which in turn disqualified them from state and municipal offices as well as the ability to appear in court and testify (Edwards 1996: 67ff.). They also had no personal legal protection for their activities: for example, if a prostitute was beaten or raped by her pimp, she could not go to court (Berkowitz 2012: 104). For (free) Roman citizens it was a disgrace to actively participate in prostitution, be it as pimps—or even worse—as sexual service providers themselves (Williams 1999: 40).

Contraception was also a major issue for Rome's prostitutes. They availed themselves of the same methods and means known in the Greek world to avoid or terminate pregnancy (Stumpp 2001: 93ff.). Infanticide was also a method: In the sewage system of a bathhouse and brothel of the city of Ashkelon (in present-day Israel), which was conquered by the Romans in

37 BCE, the bones of more than 100 newborns were found from between the fourth and sixth centuries, who had apparently been killed after birth. Surprising was that, contrary to the typical gender-specific neonaticide, more boys than girls were killed at this site—the main reason probably being the need for female prostitutes for the next generation (Faerman et al. 1998).

Venereal disease was one of the real dangers lurking among prostitutes. Infections were epidemic. Pompeii's graffiti writers even recorded their plight on the house walls: "Here I've at last screwed a beautiful girl, praised by many, but inside there was mudhole." Or "Anyone who buggers the inflamed burns his organ" (Varone 2002: 119, 122). Juvenal, the satirist of the first and second centuries alluded to getting warts from anal intercourse with prostitutes. As the first Latin physician, Celsus (around 25 BCE to around 50 CE) dedicated an entire section to the diseases of the sexual apparatus in his work *De Medicina*. He describes diseases such as balanitis and urethritis, inflammations of the glans and the urethra (Gruber, Lipozenčić and Kehler 2015: 4f.). Galen uses the word *gonnorhoea* (from the Greek *gonos* for seed and *rhoia* for flow) for the first time. The symptoms he lists, however, did not refer to the modern gonorrhea caused and transmissible by gonococcus but to another form of spermatorrhea, namely the "thin, cold, colorless and infertile" seminal discharge without erection. Galen also describes genital warts and presumably a form of the soft chancre together with the corresponding medical treatments (Oriel 2013: 5f.).

Places, Pimps, Taxes, and Clients

Based on findings from the ruins of Pompeii, the city swallowed by the eruption of Vesuvius in 79 CE, sexual services were available both in brothels and the relevant quarters in all urban areas. There was an accumulation in poorer quarters and secluded alleys, but even in the better areas graffiti pointed the way to the nearest whore, sometimes listing her name and price (McGinn 2006). Many prostitutes worked under a *leno*, a (mostly male) pimp, who was also the owner in the case of a slave. They spent their time in brothels, out on the streets, and in taverns, looking for clients in amphitheaters and theaters as well (Glazebrook 2011a: 152; Cantarella 1999). After the separation of the sexes in public baths was abolished under Emperor Claudius (10 BCE–54 CE), these became popular marketplaces, too (Faerman et al. 1998: 864). Anyone who lived full time from this business had to register with the city's *aediles* (police office), stating their place of residence and place of work. Clients benefited from this registration practice in that it protected them from committing adultery—with a married prostitute—an offence that carried strict punishments.

According to Tacitus' (around 58–120) *Annals*, Emperor Tiberius (42 BCE–37 CE) forbade daughters from noble families (from the rank of *equites*, or knight) from entering themselves in the prostitution register—the following occasion had been one such case:

> In the same year severe measures were passed by the Senate for the repression of licentiousness among women, and the profession of a courtesan was prohibited to any woman whose grandfather, father, or husband was the rank of a Roman knight. The immediate cause of these measures was the conduct of a woman, belonging to a family of praetorian rank and named Vistilia, who had publicly notified to the aediles that she had become a prostitute; this being the custom which prevailed among our ancestors, who considered that women of loose character were sufficiently punished by the public avowal of their shame. (Tacitus 1906: 120; Stumpp 2001: 258)

The daily tax on prostitution was calculated at the price of one sexual act, which in Pompeii, for example, was between two and sixteen assēs. For comparison, at the time of Emperor Augustus one could get a simple meal for two assēs (McGinn 2004: 40ff. and 134ff.). In Pompeii, two or three assēs could buy fellatio from a slave; penetrative intercourse cost quite a bit more (Younger 2011: 110). The *Corpus Inscriptionum Latinarum* (IX 2689) documents a price comparison for the imperial period on a comedic grave inscription:

> Sir landlord, let us add up!
> - You have a Sextarius wine, bread around one as, side dishes: two assēs.
> - All right!
> - The girl—8 assēs.
> - That's fine too!
> - Hay for the mule—2 assēs.
> - That damn animal will be the death of me!
>
> (trans. Jacob Watson; Porter 2018; Bannert 2005: 212)

Latin offered a rather graded conceptual inventory to designate the desired acts: *futuo* (penetration of the vagina with penis), *paedico* (active penis in the anus), *irrumo* (active penis in the mouth), *fello* (passive penis in the mouth), and *lingo* (stimulation of the sexual organs with the tongue) (Adams 1982: 118ff.). *Fellatrices* were therefore also called women who took the penis into their mouths, although it was not always clear whether they did this passively as in penetration or were an active sucker. *Fututrices* were women/men who actively fucked using their penis, hand, tongue, etc. (Kamen and Levin-Richardson 2015: 238ff.).

For Lucretius, a prostitute was also characterized by the fact that she moved during coitus and was not passive like a respectable wife—which was also related to the latter's willingness to conceive and the former's contraceptive strategies:

> Lascivious movements (*molles . . . motus*) are of no use whatever to wives. For a woman forbids herself to conceive and fights against it, if in her delight she herself thrusts (*retractat*) against the man's penis with her buttocks (*clunibus*), making undulating movements (*ciet . . . fluctus*) with all her body limp; for she turns the share clean away from the furrow and makes the seed fail of its place. Whores indulge in such motions for their own purposes, so that they may not conceive and lie pregnant, and at the same time that their intercourse may be more pleasing to men; which our wives evidently have no need for. (Kamen and Levin-Richardson 2015: 247f.)

Pimping and the sale of whores brought considerable profits in Rome, especially if one was directly or indirectly involved as a slave owner. In the first century, however, slave owners were able to stipulate with the provision *ne serva prostituatur* that house or field slaves, for example, could not be used as prostitutes after the sale (Espach 2017: 191; Pesendorfer 2018). The primary concern was not (only) the protection of slaves; the original owner's economic interests were the more decisive factor. Slaves used for prostitution lost value, a degradation also expressed in Augustus' *lex Fabia*. It stipulated that the abduction and use of a slave who was prostituting herself or a slave who belonged to someone else was not to be regarded as theft, since the reason for the offence was to be seen in the desire and not in the deliberate theft of a foreign good (Perry 2014: 32f.). This makes it abundantly clear that slaves could not determine their own actions. They were at the mercy of their owners. Their sexual services were commodities that could be sold or rented and that promised returns—an essential reason why prostitution flourished in the Roman Empire over the centuries.

Today's most famous Roman *lupanar* (brothel; from *lupa* she-wolf) is found among the buildings excavated in Pompeii (Levin-Richardson 2019). Its two floors each had five cells. It served exclusively for prostitution and was located slightly off the beaten track. Each of the small rooms was equipped with a brick bed, including headboard, which would have been made more comfortable with a mattress. The walls were decorated with frescoes of men and women in various positions, some of which have been preserved (or reconstructed). Intimate emotional exchange was not the purpose of this small, dark building with its two entrances. The prostitutes were inexpensive *scrotum*, and the clientele would have come for a quickie. They were probably men from the lower classes and simple soldiers (Stumpp 2001: 143ff.). The erotic frescoes were intended to stimulate their imagination and make this "assembly line sex" a little more enjoyable; in view of the multilingual clientele, the illustrations probably also served the purpose of a menu, saving them from having to know the specialized vocabulary (Clarke 2009: 64). If nothing suited a potential client of the *lupanar*, he could always go around the corner to *cellae*—chambers accessible from the street—with a *publica* (in the open) *prostituta* (literally, streetwalker). Although numerous graffiti remain, giving written evidence of the relatively affordable prices of the prostitutes, the clients came from nearly all social backgrounds (Levin-Richardson 2019: 99ff.). This was not the place for a wealthy man and attached courtesans. They met with their lovers and clients in far finer houses, which they may have even owned. For members of the upper class, dark brothels and cheap whores were considered beneath their dignity and damaged their reputation, grounds to avoid the *lupanares* (McGinn 2004: 71ff.; Edwards 1996: 66ff.) (Figure 5).

In addition to the *lupanar*, other relevant establishments existed in Pompeii, most of which also fulfilled other functions, such as restaurants and taverns. They were also located in narrow alleys and away from the busy main streets and residential areas of the affluent classes. Finding such a place was easy, one simply followed the phalli engraved on the surrounding streets and walls as advertisements and signs (Laurence 2006: 83ff.). In Rome, prostitutes could thus be found in the *Subura* district, in whose alleys the majority of the poorer population lived. Prostitution took place there in the lively surroundings of restaurants, markets, and baths as well as near temples. In other Roman cities, the scene was also concentrated in certain areas, mostly away from the better residential areas, keeping prostitution out of sight of the respectable population, especially the *matrona* and children. Emperor Constantine the Great (around 275–337) established a brothel zone in the *Zeugma* district of Constantinople (allegedly) in furtherance of Christianity by spatially delimiting prostitution. In practice, however, streetwalkers continued to look for their customers where they found them: for example, in the vicinity of the port, near the holy shrines, and in the side streets of the busy zones (McGinn 2006: 165f.).

FIGURE 5 *Fresco from the Lupanar brothel in Pompeii, first century AD.*

Although prostitutes and their consorts did not enjoy a good reputation, their services were generally regarded as an everyday affair. Horace (65–8 BCE) pragmatically stated that it was better for men to go to brothels than harassing or seducing the wives of other Romans (Johnson and Ryan 2005: 95). He was speaking mainly of younger single men, especially those from the Roman middle and upper classes, who wed only in their mid- to late twenties. It was nearly impossible for them to meet and get to know women from their own class, much less encounter them in terms of potential sexual partners. And meeting in private was an even farther off pipedream. So, depending on their social origins and financial standing, they turned to prostitutes for their first experiences or, if they had the means, even had their own courtesan. Roman authors saw visits to prostitutes as a common step in male socialization and as a factor not to be underestimated for the stabilization of the patriarchal system and the maintenance of marriage and family (Langlands 2006: 205ff.).

For the Roman military, female prostitution was widespread during military campaigns and in the vicinity of barracks. It also functioned as a form of systemic reinforcement. Soldiers had a relatively high code of honor to fulfill: they faced dishonorable discharge for the crime of adultery, for example (McGinn 1998: 40). Augustus went so far as to exclude married men from military service, which increased the demand for paid sexual services, especially in the camps of distant legions. Thus, soldiers sometimes found their gratification in the form of female and male slaves and "barbaric" prisoners of war, whose persons were part of the sexual spoils of war (Leitao 2014: 231). Rape was tolerated when it occurred in enemy territories and cities. Homosexual contacts of common soldiers with male slaves and male prostitutes were also allowed, but strictly forbidden between soldiers—although little is known about such cases, since ancient authors tended to stay silent on the topic and about the everyday sexual life of common soldiers (Phang 2001: 229ff.).

Courtesans and Concubines

At the time of the comedic poet Plautus (around 254–184 BCE), but also still as Ovid wrote his first work *Amores* about 200 years later, the Romans were intensely occupied with the figure of the Greek *hetaera*, in Rome the elite *meretrices*. Successful concubines and courtesans could achieve influential social and even political positions and financial wealth (Strong 2016: 62ff.). The Romans were fascinated by these women's (alleged) independence. In Plautus' play *Asinaria*, the courtesans have relative autonomy in their own business, conclude long-term contracts with their lovers and clients, for example with year advance payments, and retain a certain degree of independence from them. All this deeply unsettled Roman men, at least in the comedy. As with the problematization of the *hetaera* in Greece, Roman plays were often about how to win over another *vir*'s courtesan and somehow keep the interests, desires, and especially the sexual lust of these women under control at the same time. Their independence proved to be the main problem (and source of laughs): Unlike slaves and whores, men could not simply dispose of the *puellae* or pay them by the hour for a particular service, and, unlike their wives, courtesans were not subject to *patria potestas* (James 2006: 238). These spoken-for women were thus kept away from official social occasions, banquets, and celebrations. If one met for celebrations among men, however, it seems they were brought along (Gazebrook 2011a: 154). According to Martial, the erotic qualities of the *puella* in comparison to the *uxor* (wife) couldn't be missed:

> While the wife prefers to play at love in the dark, [the husband] wants to see his lover in the light and show himself to her; the wife does not undress, but the lover is naked; the former only gives kisses like among relatives, the latter like a dove's eager pecking; the wife helps neither with movements nor voice, the lover sits astride him and unlike her the latter refuses her ass. (Meyer-Zwiffelhoffer 1995: 74f.)

Promiscuous behavior among women was generally suspected of being prostitution and led to dishonor. Concubines—whose way of life was considered scandalous and often came into the focus of law and politics—also contributed to this. Clodia (around 94 to after 44 BCE) was one such victim of slanderous character assassination based on sexual behavior. Cicero attacked her in a speech *Pro Caelio* (held 56 BCE) on behalf of one of her own lovers, whom she had accused of trying to poison her. As the daughter of a consul, Clodia had been married to her cousin, the statesman Quintus Caecilius Metellus Celer—not unusual for patrician families—and had not remarried after his death (59 BCE). According to Cicero, however, the widow had since had numerous affairs, even worked as a *meretrix* and committed incest with her brother Clodius. He also then accused her of killing her husband with poison. All of these shameful deeds were outed, however, in defense of her lover, the politician Marcus Caelius Rufus (about 88–48 BCE). Clodia also appears in Catullus' love poems, as "Lesbia" and is similarly accused of sexual offences, such as fellatio with common Roman men from the street (Strong 2007).

Some courtesans gained fame and fortune due to their contact with an influential man, using this connection to their advantage—at least that was the accusation of their contemporaries. Cicero dealt in slander like this to weaken his rivals, the praetor Gaius Verres (around 115–43 BCE) and the senator Gaius Cornelius Cethegus (? to 63 BCE): Chelidon (Greek for "Swallow"), the mistress of Verres, was to have persuaded Cethegus to move his seat of office to her house and to take his decisions based on her advice alone (Schuller 2008: 153ff.). Praecia, on the other hand, Cethegus' courtesan, was to have used her influence to promote the political ambitions of her friends (Auhagen 2009: 286). Especially in the late republican period (133–27 BCE), authors like Cicero and Sallust (86–35/34 BCE) accused courtesans of political involvement and conspiracy. For them, the shadowy red light districts with their cheap taverns and inns were a breeding ground for conspiracy; among the urban mob there, subversive groups were supposedly ripe for recruitment to destabilize the political system. For the Stoic moralist Seneca, at the beginning of our era, these represented the clear front between *voluptas* (sensual pleasures), for which the prostitutes stood, and *virtus* (male virtue), for which the upright citizen should stand up:

> Virtue (*virtus*) you will find in the temple, in the forum, in the senate house, standing before the city walls, dusty and sunburnt, her hands rough; pleasure (*voluptas*) you will most often find lurking around the baths and sweating rooms, and places that fear the police, in search of darkness, soft, effete, reeking of wine and perfume, pallid or else painted and made up with cosmetics like a corpse. (Edwards 1996: 84)

Prostitution is stigmatized here in ancient Rome as will be done again and again in later centuries: crime, corruption, and immorality thrived in their sphere of influence—ultimately communicable to the clientele as well (Rauh 2011: 200ff.).

Male Same-Sex Services

Male prostitutes could also be found relatively easily in Roman cities. According to Cicero, Rome itself had a "plague" of thousands. Caligula (12–41 CE) wanted to ban them from the city, but in the end only taxed them more (Younger 2011: 69). Same-sex services were mainly offered by young slaves, some of whom attracted attention through their clothing—a woman's *stola*—and effeminate behavior. Male brothels also existed, whether on a large scale or only occasionally is unclear. According to Tacitus, there were two groups of male prostitutes he called *sellarii* and *spintriae*. The former was derived from *sellarium*, for public toilets, and was an indication of where these boys sought and found their customers (Younger 2005: 108). By *spintriae* he meant male prostitutes who could be used for the sexual acts pictured on the coin-like *spintriae*, which were used as tokens for visiting brothels (Schmieder 2008). Cicero called male prostitutes *pueri meritorii*, boys who let themselves be hired and paid; he also had primarily young slaves in mind. Their fate was a common theme in Roman literature. Seneca the Younger (around 4 BCE–65 CE), for example, criticized how the youths seemed to be commodities, be it at festivals or in brothels:

> I pass over the flocks of luckless boys, whom other physical abuse of the bed chamber await after the banquet is over. I pass over the troop of

catamite (described according to nation and colour), who should all have the same smooth skin, the same degree of first down upon their cheeks and the same hair style, so that no boy with rather straight hair get mixed in with the[se] dear/poor little curly haired slave-boys. (Pollini 2003: 157; Krenkel 2006: 431)

The fact that the "pleasure boys" were part of Roman society was also demonstrated by the festival of the *pueri lenonii* (boys of pimps), which was celebrated on April 25 according to a calendar found in Lazio—two days after the festival of female prostitutes (Krenkel 2006: 436).

Freeborn boys and youths who prostituted themselves caused a sensation, for which their clients, however, were threatened with severe punishments. Their motivations were myriad: For some of the migrant rural youths (and their families), there was little in the way of work or income in the overcrowded cities, as was the case for the sons of impoverished urban strata. Financial incentives aside, there were also opportunities for social mobility in prostitution—with the right contacts. The consequences were, nevertheless, risky for those who prostituted themselves, as freeborn men were no longer allowed to enter the temples, could no longer make public speeches, and lost at least some rights as civilians. So, it is not surprising that accusations of prostitution were often raised to denounce one's political opponents. In court, a person's character was impugned by means of sexual *infamia*. The second *Philippic*, attributed to Cicero, for example, dealt with the (alleged) whorish behavior of the young Mark Antony (86/82–30 BCE):

> Shall we then examine your conduct from the time when you were a boy? (. . .) You assumed the manly gown, which you soon made a womanly one; at first a public prostitute, with a regular price for your wickedness, and that not a low one. But very soon Curio stepped in, who carried you off from your public trade, and, as if he had bestowed a matron's robe upon you, settled you in a steady and durable wedlock. No boy bought for the gratification of passion was ever so wholly in the power of his master as you were in Curio's. How often has his father turned you out of his house? How often has he placed guards to prevent you from entering? While you, with night for your accomplice, lust for your encourager, and wages for your compeller, were let down through the roof. That house could no longer endure your wickedness. (Cicero 2018: 361f.; Meyer-Zwiffelhoffer 1995: 64f.)

Several accusations cumulate here: First, Antony had sold himself sexually and allowed other men to use him; second, he had entered another's *potestas*, come under the authority of another man; and third, he had thus lost his status as an *ingenius* (freeborn Roman man). Rhetorically, such *infamia*—disgraceful (sexual) behavior—made a statement about one's personality and called into question a person's social and political trustworthiness and honor.

Tribas, *Cinaedus*, and Bisexuality

In search of the Greek traditions in Rome's sexual culture, historical research has dealt extensively with questions of same-sex sexuality (Hupperts 2007: 69ff.; Vout 2007; Krenkel 2006: 429ff.; Skinner 2005: 212ff.). *Tribas* and *cinaedus* were the same-sex figures who opposed the otherwise all-encompassing primacy of the phallus in ancient Rome and broke through the essential heteronormativity. Both stood in opposition to the virtue of manliness (*virtus*), which permeated and shaped the social power relations between master and servant, free and slave, victor and vanquished, active and passive, and the hierarchy between the sexes (Hubbard 2003: 6ff.). No wonder then, that their behavior is threatened with ever stricter sanctions (Swancutt 2007: 11). Sexual contacts between women may have seemed strange and bizarre to the Romans, but they did not categorize them as abnormal or all too degenerate, which is why there were no (at least not yet substantiated) social consequences or even legal threats of punishment (Butrica 2006: 238ff.).

Tribas, Hermaphroditus, and Eunuchs

The female *tribas* was considered to be beyond the gender norm above all because here a woman turned into a man during a sexual act and penetrated the female body—or that of a boy—thus caricaturing the phallus (Brooten 1996: 39ff.; Parker 1997: 59f.). It was performed—at least in fantasies of the male authors—by means of an *olisbos* (dildo) or an oversized clitoris, or else by means of manual or oral stimulation (Kamen and Levin-Richardson 2015: 243ff.; Thumiger 2022: 148ff.). Either way, the supremacy of the male penis and the male agency were sidelined. True to the phallic-penetrative fantasy, Seneca the Elder (around 55 BCE–40 CE) recounts a man catching his wife in bed with another woman, in his *Controversiae*. Before killing both, he checks whether the man was "natural or artificial" and realizes that the woman was using a strap-on dildo (Clarke 2009: 128). Some Roman authors doubted that such sexual intercourse between women was possible or intended by nature and therefore negated its very existence. Alternatively, it was presumed that these women were actually a man in a female body (Ogden 2011: 51f.). How else could a woman have the urge to penetrate another? The astrologer and geographer Claudius Ptolemy (around 100 to after 160 CE), who likely came from Alexandria, saw this as a kind of disease caused by odd planetary alignments, which led to disturbances in the balance of the female body and her performing male actions as *tribas* (Swancutt 2007: 60).

In historiography, love and sexual acts between women were interpreted not only as a rejection of the male sex but also as a hypostasis of the sexually insatiable woman (Mencacci 1999: 74). Martial warns of two such fictional types of women driven by aggressive and exuberant libido: Bassa lives mainly in a male environment, and she satisfies other women with a strap-on. The married woman Philaenis is described as very masculine; she performs acts on both male and female slaves and this in a frequency which exceeds even that of her quite active husband. The first figure uses a dildo, while the second prefers cunnilingus (Butrica 2006: 260). In doing so, they transgressed two central paradigms of Roman sexual culture and the gender polarity that accompanied it: (Proper) men penetrated and were sexually active, whereas women were penetrated and remained sexually passive. Same-sex desiring and acting women, on the other hand, not only appropriated the phallus, but were—at least some of them—sexually proactive and agents (Kamen and Levin-Richardson 2015). As women, the *tribas* behaved beyond the pale for an honorable Roman *matrona*, acting like a "she-man" who had switched sides and fought the men over the same terrain in a sort of betrayal of the normal order. In the first and second centuries, *tribas* were therefore accused of contributing to the decline of the Roman Empire from within.

It was only a small step from the *tribas* to hermaphroditus, a figure of divine origin, which the Romans took over from the Greeks in the third and second centuries BCE (Swancutt 2007: 22). Such sexually and gender ambiguous beings, especially from the common era onward, have been the subject of great fascination, oscillating between stirring fear and inciting mockery. Some did see in them—like the early Greeks—primarily lucky charms and fertility symbols. They were embodied by female statues that revealed an erect penis by lifting up their *stola*. The model for this was the *aphroditos*, a male variant of the goddess Aphrodite, who possessed a phallus on statues from the fifth and fourth centuries BCE in Crete and Athens. He represented a double transgression: For one, he exposed the secret parts of a woman in the public space. Secondly, he reversed the positions of male and female viewers (Vout 2013: 77f.). The same applied in the second century BCE to the figure of sleeping Hermaphroditus, who from one side represented a beautiful woman, from the other presented a penis (Clarke 2009: 107). Here, the sexual body was being physically inscribed with similarly bothersome associations that arose with the *tribas*: women with an enormous clitoris or penis (even if it is only artificial) who had occupied the phallic center of the Roman *vir*, even incorporated it.

For the Romans, "Greek gender-freaks" (Swancutt 2007: 13) like Hermaphroditus and *tribas* were also irritatingly problematic because they offered a means to imagine the options open to Roman *matrona* with them (at least in fantasy). Even honorable women could presumably become hybrid beings out of the East who caricatured the male privileges in the *cubiculum* (bedroom), in the *domus* (household), and in the *imperium*. In the first and second centuries, it was one of the common fears that such masculine women endangered the *vir*, feminized it, and then not only challenged his domestic supremacy but also his imperial future. The story of Polycritus, told by Phlegon of Tralles in the second century, made hermaphrodites appear as dually dangerous physical and political *monstra*: On the one hand, his dimorphic figure did not allow for clear man–woman assignment; on the other hand, he/she had two different ethnic roots due to the Aetolian and Locrian origins of his/her parents and thus threatened the pure Roman ethnicity (Swancutt 2007: 24ff.).

According to mythology, Hermaphroditus is the son of Aphrodite and Hermes. According to Ovid's *Metamorphoses*, he was a handsome young man who came across the water nymph Salmacis during a hike near Halicarnassus (today's Turkish Bodrum). She tried to seduce him, but he resisted. As he bathes afterward, unobserved—he thinks(!)—Salmacis embraces him, kisses him against his will, strokes his chest, and calls on the gods to never let the two be separated again. Her wish is fulfilled, and they merge into one being with the characteristics of both sexes. Whereby, in the transformation, Hermaphroditus must choose whether to be both genders or neither (Brisson 2002: 42ff.). Ovid gave special weight to Salmacis' effeminate behavior: The Roman man, threatened by a blurring of the gender borders, was offered two equally unpleasant possibilities—namely androgyny, that is, the destruction of the man–woman dichotomy, or hermaphroditism, which due to the equal footing given to the sexes in such a state analogously narrows one's expectations in sexual as well as political and social concerns. For the upstanding Roman man, who had been socialized since his youth to be active, dominant, and penetrative, both were atrocities that inevitably led to submission, feminization, and passivity. The grounds for concern were that, although the peculiarities of man and woman were predetermined by nature, their bodies were open to change due to life circumstances. So, if men allowed themselves to be surrounded by too many women-folk or even physically conquered or otherwise softened, they threatened to mutate into in-between beings (Walters 1997: 41; Swancutt 2007: 32f.).

The cult of Cybele, worshiped in central and western Anatolia, was sharply criticized at the beginning of the common era, revealing that fears of gender aberrations were intensifying. In mythology, Cybele, the "Great Mother," had undergone a rather complicated genesis. This began with the carelessness of the Greek father of the gods Zeus, who dropped his seed to the ground while sleeping on Mount Agdos in Phrygia, from which the hermaphroditic demon Agdistis arose. He was castrated by the gods because of his fearsome form and manner. From his two parts, Cybele emerged and (from the separated genital) the god Attis. The male god, in turn, castrated himself in a frenzy, died and was awakened to eternal life by the *magna mater*. Thus, the worship of Cybele began in Greek Phrygia (Asia Minor). "The Mother is far off: thus I command you, Romans, go seek the Mother," was how the *Sibylline Books*, three holy works consulted in times of crisis, prophesied a means to defeat Carthage during the Second Punic War (218–201 BCE) (Turcan 2001: 110). The reference was to this Phrygian belief, which was then brought to Rome in 205 BCE in the form of a meteorite (the circumstances surrounding the prophesy included a rain of stones). The Mother was integrated into a statue in Rome, and thus it was believed that only thanks to this deity were Hannibal's Carthaginians defeated four years later (Alvar 2008: 63ff.).

From then on, the Great Mother was worshipped on the palatine as part of the state religion, and homage paid to her in the *ludi megalenses*. Their priests, the *galli*, castrated themselves in prostration to Attis—and, due to their conspicuous appearance, their long, wavy hair, their feminine, yellow silk robes, thick makeup, and their wild ritual dances, they represented a drastic contrast to the other, rather restrained priests and Roman men as such (Beard 1994: 164ff.; Kuefler 2017: 178; Tougher 2021: 7ff.). These *galli* eunuchs, who by law were not Roman citizens but foreigners or slaves, sparked discussion around the first century on the harmful influences of genderless/-fluid Eastern or Greek beings and their effects on the virility of the Roman man and his function in the Roman Empire.

Cinaedus and *Puer* Want To Be Taken

The counterimage to the virile *tribas* was the feminine *cinaedus*, who as an adult (also free) Roman man deliberately and actively (not under coercion like a slave) blurred, or even reversed the sociosexual gender characteristics further still. It was believed that due to a physical disturbance or insatiable lust, he desired to be taken and penetrated like a woman and thus behaved contrary to the phallic orientation of the *vir*—best represented in Priapus, the god of fertility with his club-like penis (Williams 2014: 468). In the sources, the figure of the female man appears under telling names, for example as the *mollis* (which generally meant soft, effeminate men), as the *pathicus* (a man who could be used passively like a woman), and, of course, the *cinaedus* (which originally meant dancers and pantomimes who represented women or carried out female body movements; later, this was primarily used to designate men who enjoyed anal penetration) (Meyer-Zwiffelhoffer 1995: 88). In addition to effemination and penetration, non-penetrative practices also resonated within such terms, especially a passive position like fellatio. Other associations tied in to this behavior, e.g., disgust with body excretions and smells, as well as fear of diseases and a general defilement and contamination of the mouth (Clarke 2009: 118). In contrast to the martial male code of conduct, some of these men would also be noticeable by their effeminate behavior, such as by using cosmetics, curling their hair, using perfume, wearing jewelry, or having their hair depilated. They would also be identifiable by their clothing, for example, by wearing particularly light fabrics or having them in striking colors that were also used by whores (Olson 2017: 138ff.). Men who cross-dressed in public were also suspected of revealing a sexual preference through this behavior, which was accompanied by homosexual passivity (Campanile 2017: 53ff.).

The profligate sexual acts of the *cinaedus* revealed him not only as thoroughly corrupt but also (possibly) suffering from a physical or mental illness. To willfully desire penetration was a sure sign of public dishonesty (*infamia*) and led to reduced status under Roman law (Edwards 1996: 69). Roman cultural sensitivity to the *cinaedus*' dishonorable peculiarities is shown in the countervailing use of the term *pedicatus*—mostly appearing in defamatory graffiti—which referred to unwilling anal penetration; the point being that neither *pedicatus* nor *cinaedus* was accepted, but the former was more acceptable than the latter in Roman society (Kamen and Levin-Richardson 2014: 451f.).

Sexual relationships between adult free Roman men and slaves, male prostitutes, or non-Romans were, on the other hand, nevertheless possible and common. Such sexual relations also existed in the Roman military, where masters erected funerary monuments for their male slaves (Ivleva 2020: 254ff.). Above the age of twenty, however, this was frowned upon (Adams 1982: 123ff.; Richlin 2006: 349). In the *Epigrams* of Martial, sexual contacts between slave owners and their adolescent *pueri* appear to be quite commonplace in the first century (Obermayer 1998: 30ff.; Ogden 2011: 48). For married men, though, it was a *faux pas*, as the *pueri* would then be competing with *uxor*. Martial also addresses this:

> Knowing as you do that your husband is faithful,
> and that no female dints or rumples your bed,
> why do you excruciate irrelevantly
> as if your lads (whose passion is fugitive, brief)
> were concubines? I'll prove that the slave-boys
> avail you more than they do their master,
> contrive that you are the only woman for him:
> they give what his wife does not wish to give.
>
> "I give it, though, lest roving Love should stray
> from the conjugal bed." It's not the same thing!
> I want a prime fig, not common or garden piles.
> (What's prime? Well, yours is common or garden.)
> A woman and matron should know her limitations:
> concede their part to boys, make use of your own.
>
> (Martial 1987: 495; Meyer-Zwiffelhoffer 1995: 80)

For the comic poet Plautus, unfree boys were equal to other socially subordinate and lowly persons of both sexes, which is why he preferred slave boys and avoided a freeborn (Clarke 2009: 88). His credo therefore was: "Love whoever you want, as long as you abstain from married women, widows, virgins, youth and freeborn boys" (Laes 2019: 117).

According to the Roman concept of masculinity, penetrators were considered virile simply because their social and legal status enabled them to protect their own bodies from invasive attacks (Walters 1997: 30 et seq.; Skinner 2005: 198 et seq.). Free boys must therefore be protected by law against sexual assault and loss of honor through rape or being overpowered. This problem also arose in the Roman military, where soldiers penetrated female prisoners not only to demonstrate their masculinity but also as a form sexual dominance, that is, an expression of the triumph of the *imperium* (Ivleva 2020: 246). Conversely, it was considered a destruction of the male *pudicitia* when one soldier was sexually abused by another. In Plutarch's biography of General Gaius Marius (158/157–86 BCE), Trebonius, a young recruit, is tried for killing an officer who attempts to rape him. He is acquitted despite this capital violation of the military hierarchy because he was defending his *pudicitia* (Phang 2008: 93ff.). The historian Livius drew attention in the first century BCE to an initiation rite in the earlier (Greek) Bacchanalia cult. Allegedly, free boys were penetrated by men as part of the rite, which was about to be imported into Dionysian celebrations in Rome:

> Romans, do you think that young men [*iuvenes*] who are initiated by means of this ritual can be made into soldiers? . . . Can these [young men], covered by their own disgrace [*stupris*] and that of others, fight with the sword to protect their sexual integrity [*pudicitia*] of your wives and children? (Leitao 2014: 235).

Paiderastia and Boy Love under Criticism

The *paiderastia* was perceived to be a negative influence of Greek culture in Rome and never achieved the function of pedagogic-ritual *eros* which it had fulfilled in the Greek city-states. When Roman authors mentioned it, they expressed their disapproval or described it as a foreign custom, with neutral dismissal (Lear 2014: 117). This did not mean that it was out of the question. In fact, in the first centuries BCE and CE, it became fashionable in upper circles to live according to Greek culture, including sexual relations with free young men. Whether this was tolerated or condemned in practice is largely unclear. Long-term relationships with slave boys have in any case been proven to have existed. At the latest from the *lex Scantinia* (149 BCE), the *stuprum* of a (free) boy and the sexual passivity of an adult man were legally forbidden and (probably) fined (Johnson and Ryan 2005: 8). The *lex Iulia de adulteriis coercendis* (18 BCE) then laid down severe (bodily) punishments for those *"qui cum masculis infandum libidinem exercere audent,"* daring to satisfy their desire with a free young man (Krenkel 2006: 432; Hergemöller 1998: 37f.). The inviolability of free boys was made visible by their *toga praetexta*, a white toga edged with purple stripes, which together with the *bulla amulet* was worn to protect against sexual attacks (Caldwell 2014: 57f.).

A special piece of *paiderastia* imagery is the so-called *Warren Cup*, a silver chalice created around the start of the common era in the eastern Roman Empire (although some doubt its authenticity). On one side, a bearded man is seen anally penetrating a young man sitting on him, on the other, a beardless youth is doing the same to a boy (Grove 2015). The wealthy commissioner of the piece would thus have been familiar with the variants of and issues surrounding Greek *paiderastia*, and the adaptation has some special features: A fifth young man can be seen in the background, perhaps a slave, watching the action through a half-open door; the cozy interior, which locates the scenes in a private household, is also conspicuous. In the first scene, the penetrated youth does not give in passively, as an object, but is apparently an active participant. The intimate hand gestures indicate an emotional connection between the persons. If the cup had pictured a free Roman man together with a male slave, or unfree or free-bought prostitute, there would be no problem whatsoever. As a practice among free Roman men or in the case of young men of the same age who were not clearly of differing status in the social hierarchy, however, such acts were considered "unnatural" and punishable. The cup could be interpreted in different ways and was perhaps therefore particularly exciting for the mind's eye. Compared to their Greek predecessors, the Roman patrons of the arts and artists on the whole were quite reluctant to depict young naked men, a development that was probably related to the declining significance of male-male eroticism in Roman culture (Vout 2013: 50) (Figure 6).

Nevertheless, some high-ranking men did maintain such relationships despite public knowledge. It was known that Emperor Hadrian (76–138) lived according to Greek ideals, thereunder the *paiderastia*. He had an open and homoerotic relationship with Antinous (110/115–130), who died quite young. Hadrian had (presumably) got to know him while hunting and developed an intimate and deep relationship with him, which ended abruptly with his death during a stay in Egypt. His reaction to the loss of a lover was momentous. Hadrian began a veritable Antinous religion, declared his lover a hero and god, who was worshipped especially in the Greek, eastern part of the empire, but also in Italy. He had a vast number of statues dedicated to his beautiful Antinous. Here, it became apparent that the emperor's personal obsession with a youth could certainly be used as a propagandistic tool of power politics (Opper 2008: 168ff.). Another reason for the rapid adoption of the Antinous cult may have been as legitimation for the love of boys among philhellenes in the Roman upper class (Zanghellini 2015: 43ff.).

Legendary and even more widely known were the devious same-sex relations that Nero pursued. In his youth, he was in love with a dancer named Paris. The emperor also had a boy named Sporus castrated so as to hold onto his feminine charms, or rather to transform him into a female creature whom he could marry. Later, he also married his freed-man/men

FIGURE 6 *Warren Cup, British Museum.*

Pythagoras and Doryphorus in a ceremony in which he assumed the role of the bride, with all the trappings (Demandt 2007: 103; Williams 1999: 260). The controversial texts on Nero and Hadrian make it clear that the sexual and love life of rulers could be used in support of but also against them to promote or damage their apotheosis and divine claims to power—whether these stories corresponded to historical reality or can be interpreted as propaganda or satire can hardly be determined.

Were There Homosexuals in the Roman Empire?

In the 1980s and 1990s, the figure of the Roman *cinaedus* found itself at the center of a rather revealing historical debate: The question was whether there had already existed a concept of sexual types or even identities in ancient Rome and, therefore, whether terms such as "homosexual" or "gay" should be used—as John Boswell did in his groundbreaking work (Boswell 1980; Larmour and Miller 1998; Kuefler 2006, 2018). Also discussed was whether Roman emperors who put their same-sex desires into practice could be considered "homosexuals," as Lex Hermans postulated (Hermans 1995; Hekma 1998: 317). John R. Clarke stated that in ancient Rome there was indeed a social field for dealing with male sexuality and the men who practiced it (Clarke 2005). Accordingly, there would also have been clear notions of specific male and female sexual types that did not correspond to biological sex. As lifestyles these roles would have been available (Larmour, Miller and Platter 1998) and would have led to the rejection of the dominant heterosexual male role (Gleason 1995: 58). Amy Richlin postulates further that the (free) sexually passive man already possessed a social identification model and had to bear a formative burden that corresponded perfectly to the modern construction of the homosexual (Richlin 1993: 530). That such a role model existed would also fit with the intensive discussion about masculinity igniting in late antiquity and, so goes the argument, flowing into the male image of early Christianity. According to Mathew S. Kuefler, members of the Roman upper class or aristocracy in particular feared the stigma of unmanliness or a sexually passive reputation, or even suffering accusations of being a eunuch or a hermaphrodite, that is, a non-phallic man (Kuefler 2001: 31ff.). The modern term "lesbian," on the other hand, was discussed cautiously in this context by historians, since verbs such as *lesbiazein* were generally used in antiquity for fellatio (Brooten 1996: 22).

Around the *cinaedus*, on the other hand, the Roman cities would have developed their own subculture of bathhouses and brothels, in which men who loved to be penetrated found each other (Taylor 1997). Graig Williams emphasized that the *cinaedus* was characterized above all by effemination and sexual lasciviousness and—like all women according to the Roman gender image—had incorporated the passive sexual role (Williams 1999: 178). But, since the *cinaedus* could also have sexual contact with women, it is to be understood as a figure who possessed a gender identity rather than a sexual identity and therefore could hardly be grasped with the modern term of sexual "orientation." Thus, there has been predominantly wide disagreement about what it meant for sexual preference, orientation, and identity—if such categories are permissible at all for antiquity—to take the active or passive part in same-sex sexual intercourse and to be penetrated or to penetrate (Karras 2000). An analogous discussion developed around Kenneth J. Dover's thesis that the *pathicus* did not feel any desire at all during anal penetration (Dover 1978; Obermayer 1998: 145ff.).

Halperin has already noted, however, that here short circuits are often triggered between recent gender and sexual orders and historical schemata of meaning and behavior: Quite a few historians have projected their often emancipatory attitudes and categories onto antiquity and thought that "in the case of men, there is something *more homosexual* about getting fucked by one than fucking one [. . ., and] that there is something *more lesbian* about being butch than being femme" (Halperin 2000b: 257). Projections like these can hardly be avoided, especially for the sexuality history of antiquity and partly also for later times. We can hardly know whether the social guidelines, rules, and norms were reflected in the concrete actions, attitudes, and feelings of the historical actors or whether they acted against or even outside the traditional discursive orders.

The *mollis*, too, the female or effeminate man, belonged to Roman culture in the first centuries of the common era and is found throughout the sources. Meanwhile, Roman society came down on unmanly men who allowed themselves to be used sexually to an ever greater degree. From the middle of the fourth century, they faced ever harsher punishment, a measure connected with the establishment of Christianity after the Constantinian shift (Hupperts 2007: 55).

4

How the Evil Thorn Pierced the Flesh—Judaism and Early Christianity

Break or Continuities?

A fundamental break between the Greco-Roman and Jewish sexual cultures, on the one hand, and Christian, on the other, never really took place. The myth nevertheless persists that sexual guilt and shame, as well as fear and oppression, were introduced by Christianity, wiping out the supposedly permissive ancient world (Dover 2002: 20; Garton 2004: 51ff.). As shown in the previous chapters, Greek and Roman culture was by no means a sexual free for all, and even those who found a relatively open playing field for their sexual desires were bound in a complex web of knowledge, rules, norms, instructions, and prohibitions that guided and limited their desires and actions. A "pornotopia" for cultivating a hedonistic-dionysical lifestyle, Rome was not. But the Roman culture was fiercely disavowed by early Christian authors as debaucherous and used as a negative counterimage for their new sexual ideology (Blanshard 2010: 5ff.). Contrary to what these writers would have us believe, the Greeks and Romans were deeply concerned about sexual moderation and abstinence, about the practical implementation of moral concepts, and about the rules by which one could make *amor* productive for society and the empire and keep its destructive forces in check.

Christian sexual doctrine in many ways followed the same norms, attitudes, and knowledge of Greek and Roman culture—as laid out by Plato, the Stoics, or the Pythagoreans (Foucault 2018: pos. 296ff.). Early Christian authors also found models in Jewish culture for their reflections on the strict moral and divinely sanctioned sexual life (Ranke-Heinemann 1999: 19ff.). In the writings of the New Testament, this point of view was as much incorporated as it was in the spiritual-moral teachings of the Church Fathers. From Plato, they were able to borrow his remedy for the problem of *aphrodisia*—human pleasures in general—excessive eating and drinking, for example. Plato said that one should under no circumstances passively abandon oneself to the carnal pleasures—as this leads to excess—but should actively keep them under control by living a measured life. As he explains in the first book of his *Nomoi*, one should refrain from sexual intercourse, limit it to within marriage, and do without catamites and slaves altogether (Foucault 1989a: 60ff.). Early Christianity shared the Stoics' suspicion toward all passions and the carnality of man, which led not only to a real crisis of the body image (Belting 2001: 95) but also to the appreciation of the spirit as key for a moral life. The early Christian writers also drew on the teachings of the Pythagoreans, who saw sexual pleasure as the main reason for the physical and mental disharmony. The Christians likewise followed their model of vegetarianism and regular fasting, cultivating a simple lifestyle and leading a faithfully married life (Detel 1998: 128ff.). In Jewish sexual culture, the Christian authors found the theistic approach of moral doctrine that affirmed marriage and reproduction as an integral part of *creation itself* (not merely the *polis*) and demanded more sincere love between spouses (Farley 2006: 38).

Most early interlocuters were in favor of keeping carnal desires in check in the rather controversial discussions about the correct teachings, but they differed considerably in the degree of abstention or moderation required: Some demanded asceticism and a celibate life, others simply more moderate sexual practice for the average married believer (Gaca 2003: 1ff.). It would be misleading, however, to interpret Christian sexual morals merely as an intensified continuation of earlier Greek-Roman-Jewish knowledge sources, as postulated by John Boswell (Boswell 1994) and Bernadette J. Brooten (Brooten 1996) in particular, for same-sex sexuality. The differences in the image of man were too marked for that—in both the religious concepts and ultimately in the sexual morality aspired to and (at least partially) realized. Regardless of whether one understands the change from pagan and Jewish to Christian sexual morals as a cultural (radical) break or as a slow transformation, it is "the point at which the ancient world still touches ours directly" (Lane Fox 1987: 11).

For the first believers, the spiritual relationship with Christ was the main focus; they tried to find closeness with him on earth already in preparation for the afterlife. For the radical sectarians and hermits who fled from this world and withdrew into the deserts, the turn toward Christ and God seemed necessary for the very reason that they—like the Jewish eschatologists in the two centuries before Christ—expected that the apocalypse was imminent. Many believed in the fast approaching "Kingdom of Peace" and saw it to have begun with the Messiah's redemption, but was not yet consummate. The apocalypse (literally unveiling) was understood in the adoption of the Jewish view not as the end of the world but as a turn of time, as the end of the old world and the transition to a new one. Strict followers said they had to prepare themselves for the dawn of the Last Judgment through asceticism, flight from the world, and physical–sexual abstinence (Deschner 1989: 68ff.; Brown 1988: 40ff.). God-fearing people tried to quell their desires on this side or to extinguish them completely in order to be able to direct all their love toward the One. Some even gave up their marriages for a mystical spiritual bond with God and followed the example of the preachers and hermits. For others, the union of marriage was an expression of divine love—probably also an alignment with the contemporary appreciation of marital relationships in Roman culture and the traditional appreciation of love and sexuality in Jewish marriage. However, the Church Fathers considered celibacy, including sexual abstinence, to be a more spiritually worthy condition (Angenendt 2015: 3–30). Only through lifelong asceticism could one, whether man or woman, establish a true relationship with God. Both sexes thus came into conflict with the prevailing gender and social roles, which nevertheless defined marriage and reproduction as the central life task of women in particular.

The Sexual Model of Jewish Culture

In order to understand these early Christian attitudes to marriage and sexuality, it is necessary to take a detailed look at Jewish culture, the most important starting point for Christian authors (Rubin 2021: 197ff.). In the Jewish tradition and in the Hebrew Bible (written down in the ninth to fifth centuries BCE), fertility ranked high on the scale of values (Clark 2008: 35ff.). The reason was demographic in nature, because the Hebrew or Israelite people—few in number—had to assert themselves against the more populous surrounding tribes and peoples, time and again. Marriage and procreation represented the covenant that the chosen people had with *JHWH*, elementary goals in the lives of all Jews, men and women. This covenant was even physically inscribed among the men; the circumcised foreskin of the penis was the visible sign of this alliance. Significantly, the term "healing" was used for coitus (Berger 2003: 29).

Fruitful Marital Love and Joy

Sexual desire within marriage, if it served reproductive purposes, was positive. Even the religious duty of the *levirate* pursued this goal: After the husband's death, a woman who had not given birth to a son was to marry her brother-in-law (who may also have no children) to conceive a son with him. Male descendants entitled to inherit was a major concern for Mosaic law, but so was the topic of Jewish expansion. The situation was similar for mixed marriages with gentiles, a controversial situation to be sure, but a practice which did occur and also produced offspring (Launderville 2010: 77ff.; Fuchs 2020). The sexual behavior of foreign peoples and pagans, on the other hand, was classified as immoral and "impure" in the Old Testament; idolatry quite simply led to sexual excesses (Anderson 2020: 137ff.).

Rules existed for both exogamy and endogamy. In the Old Testament the sexual offence with close relatives was laid down as follows:

> None of you shall approach any one near of kin to him to uncover nakedness. I am the Lord.
>
> You shall not uncover the nakedness of your father, which is the nakedness of your mother; she is your mother, you shall not uncover her nakedness.
>
> You shall not uncover the nakedness of your father's wife; it is your father's nakedness. You shall not uncover the nakedness of your sister, the daughter of your father or the daughter of your mother, whether born at home or born abroad.
>
> You shall not uncover the nakedness of your son's daughter or of your daughter's daughter, for their nakedness is your own nakedness.
>
> You shall not uncover the nakedness of your father's wife's daughter, begotten by your father, since she is your sister.
>
> You shall not uncover the nakedness of your father's sister; she is your father's near kinswoman. (RSV: Lev. 18:6-12)

Among the relations listed thereafter in Leviticus, more are married into the clan than are blood relatives—which illustrates the original sexual background of these incest rules. Nieces and cousins were not listed because they were hardly to be found in the households—and thus permitted as marriage candidates in Judaism. Sons and heirs, in particular, tried to marry within the wider family (Mitterauer 2011: 9f.). There was little difference from Roman practices in sexual intercourse with (non-Hebrew) slaves, whose services included sexual availability to their owner. An important exception was same-sex use of (male) slaves, due to religious prohibitions (Osiek 2003: 265ff.).

God's covenant with the Israelites also had a family touch, as it was made fruitful spiritually through marriage. If, on the other hand, an Israelite worshipped a Canaanite deity, such as the popular fertility god Baal, he broke the divine covenant, a major transgression in the Old Testament (Stone 2001: 125f.). Childlessness was interpreted as God's punishment of the individual. Homosexual acts, bestiality, and coitus during menstruation also violated the commandment regarding reproduction, and in the case of incest and adultery, the offspring were considered illegitimate. In the erotic Song of Songs of the Old Testament, sexually active women actually got to play an active role and sought out their own partners—which, however, was regarded as another transgression of the covenant. Purity from evil desires was altogether applicable to spiritual relationships just as much as marital and sexual ones. Extramarital relations and promiscuous behavior were therefore mentioned in the same breath as polytheism. Monogamy, on the other hand, was regarded as a positive expression of monotheism (Biale 1992: 12ff. and 29ff.). It was also assumed that a woman would remain a virgin until marriage and, synonymously, in the care of her family of origin. The bride's father was expected to confirm her purity, and it would be inspected by an older relative of the groom before the wedding night. This also ensured that the future spouse did not seek any extramarital pleasures (Loader 2012: 10, 45). In the Deuteronomy and the Qumran texts, it was also ordered that the bride should be examined by a "reliable and knowledgeable" woman before the wedding night on her physiological sexual integrity and after the wedding night she also had to show the bloody sheet (Rosenberg 2018: 44ff.). In sum, the books of the Old Testament are pervaded by a conjugal and sexual command that God had already given to Adam: Marry, be of one flesh, be fruitful and do so in marital love and joy—including having (moderate) sexual intercourse.

Polygyny, in which a man married more than one woman, was, in the Jewish tradition, one of the prerogatives of all those who could afford such a way of life. Patriarchs and kings such as Abraham, Jacob, and Solomon had several wives. However, this situation often gave rise to arguments, disagreements, and even murder—and was therefore tolerated in scripture but not regarded as exemplary. Provisions on inheritance law and transfer of property were intended to prevent it, with the firstborn child usually being the preferred heir. One could not marry slaves, but concubinage between Israelites and slaves did exist. In view of the Greco-Roman influence, polygyny relations decreased significantly in the late Hellenistic and early Roman period, while monogamy and the possibilities for divorce increased. In Ashkenazi Judaism, polygamy was permitted until around the year 1000, in Sephardic Judaism and in the Eastern Mediterranean it existed until the twentieth century (Loader 2012: 53f.). Divorce was already a common practice in the Old Testament. However, it was the man who released his wife by means of a bill of divorce.

Prevent *Yetzer Hara*, the Surplus of Lust

The ambivalence toward sexuality typical of Judaism was found in their thoughts on the generative juices. Sperm and menstrual blood (being the female part of embryogenesis, according to Hebrew physicians) stood on the one hand for God-given fertility, but at the same time these juices sullied the spiritual, since vital forces were lost with them—which is why persons who performed ritual acts must avoid them (Brenner 1996: 122f.; Fonrobert 2000). One had to stay away from religious ceremonies or perform ritual ablutions for at least one day after having conjugal relations. Wives had to go through ritual cleansing after the end of the menstrual period and could only then have sexual intercourse with their husbands again. Sexual intercourse during menstruation was already forbidden in the Old Testament: "You shall not approach a woman to uncover her nakedness while she is in her menstrual uncleanness" (RSV: Lev. 18:19). This counted for sexual abstinence after a birth as well. Characteristically, it primarily was to avoid tainting the men—women could not sully each other with impure juices. In patriarchal society, ascetic requirements such as these served above all to keep men away from their wives for certain periods and to focus on their religious tasks. Conversely, the menstruating body of a woman was called *niddah* (Hebrew for moved or separated), itself an argument to exclude the female sex from religious practices (Baskin 2002: 29; Clancy-Smith 2004: 103ff.).

Sexual acts did represent the divine power associated with the procreation of new life, but they also stood for the animal nature of humankind. For Philo of Alexandria (around 15/10 BCE–after 40 CE), one of the main representatives of the Hellenistic Jewish culture, excessive sexual activity would turn people into animals. Couples should not use their sexual desire for pleasure, but for procreation (Wheeler-Reed 2017: 45ff.). Therefore, he forbade, for example, sexual intercourse during menstruation and with an infertile or sterile woman (Wheeler-Reed, Knust and Martin 2018: 390f.). Sexual "appetite" is indeed an innate, but guilt-ridden passion (Gaca 2003: 297). If one indulged moderately and for procreative purposes only, it served God's purpose. According to Philo, the energies cultivated in asceticism may be used to achieve a higher spiritual level. Similar Stoic views were also popular among the Jews of Palestine at the time of Christ. Early marriage and regular conjugal coitus could prevent an excess of sexual desire. For the Jews, *yetzer hara*, surplus lust that hadn't been dissipated, possessed a seductively sinful potential that made man susceptible to evil.

The small group of elites, the rabbis, discussed not only issues of impurity but also the need for abstinence and ascetic practices. Even if some of them remained unmarried and lived without, they did not see celibacy as a solution for the general Jewish populace. Even priests and scholars had a responsibility to fulfill their God-given power of procreation and beget souls for the (coming) kingdom of the Messiah (Koltun-Fromm 2010: 214ff.). The rabbis also paid a great deal of attention to sexual life in their religious-medical writings. In the Babylonian Talmud and in the Midrash, the written interpretations of the Bible, they dealt with it in detail. The scholars were also concerned about the health effects of different positions (Satlow 1995; Bickart 2016): coitus standing up could cause convulsions, and spasms in sitting. Important factors for sexual intercourse were the right time (at night), the right situation (unobserved), and the acceptable level of nudity (differs depending on the author). In marriage, both rabbis and laymen should exercise modesty and moderation. The rabbis never came around to complete sexual abstinence; in Judaism it was regarded as a completely anachronistic idea (Rubin 2021: 197ff.). Nevertheless, the Babylonian rabbis remained skeptical about sexual desire: on the one hand, they emphasized the great importance of the sexual for the success of the marital community and procreation; on the other hand, they were pessimistic about it, even if sexual intercourse occurred within the framework of a legitimate marital partnership (Kiel 2016: 31f.). Attitudes toward masturbation were also negative based on a similar rational: Avoiding procreation by wasting semen broke the reproductive commandment—a treasonous act against one's people (Richlin 2006: 246ff.). That kind of unproductive behavior was believed to be what brought about the sexual anarchy in the Roman Empire and caused its decline (Biale 1992: 51ff.).

Inspired by Greco-Roman medicine, some rabbis decided that women should feel pleasure during sexual intercourse as this would be the only way they could reach orgasm and conception. The rabbis were reasonably unanimous about the nature of female sexuality: It was in the nature of a woman, wielded great power over her, and was difficult to control. It is therefore the husband's task to guide female desire and prevent an excess of sexual surplus (Farley 2006: 36ff.). Even prostitutes who were repentant and married, thus submitting to the patriarchal regime, were granted the right to regular conjugal intercourse (Artman-Partock 2021: 18). Women who prostituted themselves came from the social margins or had been released from captivity or set free as slaves. In any case, they were despised, since they lived outside the patriarchal system and the roles intended for women there. In some biblical passages, fornication at all was equated with Israel's betrayal of God. Despite this negative assessment, prostitution was part of everyday life in Israelite society, both in the city and in the countryside (Baskin/Ruttenberg: 24ff.).

From a rabbinical point of view, both sexes possessed a body animated by the soul, inextricably so; while most Greco-Roman and early Christian authors understood the body more like a container for the soul—a distinction that remains disputed in the history of historiography and philosophy, however (Boyarin 1995: 5). According to the first, unitary concept, sexuality was regarded as an elementary, integrative, and undeniable component of the human being; according to the second, it was possible for the soul to rise above the body, for example, by controlling one's (sexual) desire or completely eliminating it.

The Sexual Cornerstones of Early Christianity

The Jewish, Greek, and Roman traditions, to which the early Christian authors tied in or from which they distinguished themselves, were diverse in their own right and sometimes contradictory. Christianity emerged at a time when Rome had reached the height of its political-military power and Greco-Roman culture was shaping the Mediterranean. Due to its sweeping imperial power then, Rome was received as a counter-model for early Christianity. Jesus the preacher and his followers instead based their new teachings on anti-Roman Judaism. Central Christian principles came from the ancient Jewish writings—such as the commandment to love one's neighbor or to care for the poor and oppressed (Crompton 2003: 111). And Jewish as well as Greco-Roman ways were models in matters of marriage. At the same time, a clear line was drawn. Thus, Christians adopted the monogamy of Roman marriage law, but without its possibilities for divorce. Also, the possibility of unilateral divorce by the man in the Jewish culture was not a model for Christians. Jewish polygyny was also rejected (Bof and Leyser 2016: 158ff.).

How to Channel the Carnal Desires?

The biblical stories about Jesus of Nazareth and his disciples (which were only written down decades later) contain, at first glance, rather confusing guidelines for marriage and sexual life. They depict an itinerant Jewish preacher who was neither married nor did he reproduce, but on the contrary called his followers to leave their *oíkos* or *familia* to follow him and join the spiritual family of God (Clark 1995). At the same time, he left no doubt about the holy state of marriage, because the Creator, as Matthew says, "that he who made them from the beginning made them male and female." Through marriage the sexes merged into "one flesh," and "What therefore God has joined together, let not man put asunder" (RSV: Mt. 19:4-6). The imperative of the *familia* had such a strong influence that early Christians saw in Jesus not only the announced Messiah but indeed the Son of God. Confusion notwithstanding, practices that went against marriage were clearly condemned in the New Testament writings, including adultery and divorce, promiscuity and fornication. Jesus also made it clear that "unrighteous," "neither the immoral, nor idolaters, nor adulterers, nor sexual perverts" "will not inherit the kingdom of God" (RSV: 1 Cor. 6:9). Anyone "who looks at a woman lustfully has already committed adultery with her in his heart" (RSV: Mt. 5:28). But sexual sinners should by no means be excluded from Christian charity. Jesus himself addressed whores and adulteresses just as much as the poor and the sick. However, many of the sexual biblical passages allow for divergent interpretations and have repeatedly been reinterpreted and adapted to the respective gender and sexual conceptions of the succeeding centuries (Jensen 2010: 16ff.).

What Jesus says about the eunuchs aims at the heart of Christianity: "For there are eunuchs who have been so from birth, and there are eunuchs who have been made eunuchs by men, and there are eunuchs who have made themselves eunuchs for the sake of the kingdom of heaven. He who is able to receive this, let him receive it" (RSV: Mt. 19:12). What Matthew understood by eunuchs has been interpreted quite broadly: During Christ's lifetime they belonged to the street scene of Roman cities and were active as sexually harmless house slaves for wealthy Roman women as well as priests for the *mater deum*, the goddess of fertility. Being the opposite of virile, they were not held in high esteem. For the early Christians, castration was regarded as a violent pagan practice which dishonored the body and made men behave like women (Kuefler 2001: 245ff.; Ranke-Heinemann 1999: 54ff.). At the same time, the eunuch was not too far removed from the passive image of masculinity embodied by Jesus and his apostles, which was radically different from the martial *vir* of the Romans. Christian men cultivated not domination over others—they were not to exercise greater power but submit to the higher power of the will of God and stand up for the oppressed, the poor, and the ostracized. From the Roman point of view, Christian men who left their ancestral home as head of the household and penetrator to join one of the Christian communities were castrating themselves (Moxnes 2003: 72ff.; Tougher 2021: 99ff.). However, the eunuch metaphor in Matthew can also be understood as an invitation to Jesus' followers, who have separated from their wives, to cut off what could possibly lead them back to them (Van Tine 2018).

By adopting soft masculinity, they separated the phallus from the penis, a symbolic emasculation that played an enormous role in early Christian texts (Boyarin 2003: 14ff.). To the Christians, this was a way to calm the drive of desire, but the disciples of Jesus also searched for a middle ground where the instinct could be kept in check without dismantling the predominant culture and completely giving up hegemonic masculinity. They could not overlook the fact that patriarchal order throughout the Mediterranean societies was linked to phallic strength and dominance. This form of virility was no longer available to Christian men, however. For some exegetes, the above passage in Matthew therefore dealt with celibate sectarians and hermits who wanted to renounce the physical altogether (Heid 1997: 22ff.). Some brethren even took the message literally and castrated themselves— an (apparently) frequent practice, which was so alarming it was therefore ultimately forbidden by the Council of Nicea (325). Already in the early Christian writings, it is evident that sexual desire was regarded as a basic problem: Since the Fall of Adam, it reminded man of the original apostasy from God and that he was born as a carnal-desiring mortal (Diem 2013: 33; Kuefler 2017: 180f.).

The ritual abstinence and purity commandments of Judaism played no special role for Jesus—at least according to the Bible texts (Brundage 1996: 33). He owed his own earthly existence to completely asexual circumstances, which can also be read about in Matthew. He had been conceived immaculately—untouched by impure body fluids and sexual acts:

> Now the birth of Jesus Christ took place in this way. When his mother Mary had been betrothed to Joseph, before they came together she was found to be with child of the Holy Spirit; and her husband Joseph, being a just man and unwilling to put her to shame, resolved to divorce her

quietly. But as he considered this, behold, an angel of the Lord appeared to him in a dream, saying, "Joseph, son of David, do not fear to take Mary your wife, for that which is conceived in her is of the Holy Spirit; she will bear a son, and you shall call his name Jesus, for he will save his people from their sins." All this took place to fulfil what the Lord had spoken by the prophet:

"Behold, a virgin shall conceive and bear a son,
and his name shall be called Emman'u-el"

(which means, God with us). When Joseph woke from sleep, he did as the angel of the Lord commanded him; he took his wife, but knew her not until she had borne a son; and he called his name Jesus. (RSV: Mt. 1:18-25)

According to scripture, Joseph and Mary renounced sexual intercourse until the birth of Jesus (and probably thereafter as well). Mary's immaculate conception—giving birth to Jesus as a virgin—was a testament to physical love's subordination to spiritual love in Christianity. The clergy puzzled for many centuries over how exactly this holy fecundation should be understood and how it differed from the divine siring of the Greek heroes, such as Zeus and Leda's offspring Polydeukes (Blank 2007: 162ff.; Shoemaker 2016).

The Bible only contains sporadic and mostly ambiguous remarks about any ascetic commandment for Christians. This was one of the reasons why apostles and wandering missionaries so intensively sought to clarify the degree to which their followers must practice sexual renunciation. Paul of Tarsus (? to around 60) held the opinion that a true Christian may only be near to God when the body receded into the background (Brown 1988: 44ff.). After his road to Damascus moment, Paul remained celibate and proclaimed its superiority, comparing the soul/body relationship to that of good and evil in his Epistle to the Romans.

> For I know that in me, that is, in my flesh, dwells no good thing. For desire is present with me, but I don't find it doing that which is good. For the good which I desire, I don't do; but the evil which I don't desire, that I practice. But if what I don't desire, that I do, it is no more I that do it, but sin which dwells in me. I find then the law that, while I desire to do good, evil is present. For I delight in God's law after the inward person, but I see a different law in my members, warring against the law of my mind, and bringing me into captivity under the law of sin which is in my members. What a wretched man I am! Who will deliver me out of the body of this death? I thank God through Jesus Christ, our Lord! So then with the mind, I myself serve God's law, but with the flesh, sin's law. (WEB: Rom. 7:18-25)

Carnal desire versus free will—that was a decision that, according to Paul, every human being had to make. For him, pagans were slaves to their lust, while Christians had to make themselves slaves of God (Knust 2006: 63). Sexual desire went hand in hand with sin and evil and was associated with the remoteness from God and the worship of other gods. With this, he laid the keystone for the Christian Church's ambivalent attitude toward sexuality (Clark 1999: 25ff.; Koltun-Fromm 2010: 77ff.).

Being a passionate missionary and familiar with Greek and Roman philosophy, Paul targeted the carnal sins of his pagan surroundings and warned adulterers, prostitutes, and catamites of the abuse they inflicted on their bodies (Wallace 2010: 35):

> Don't you know that your bodies are members of Christ? Shall I then take the members of Christ and make them members of a prostitute? May it never be! Or don't you know that he who is joined to a prostitute is one body? For, "The two", he says, "will become one flesh." But he who is joined to the Lord is one spirit. Flee sexual immorality! "Every sin that a man does is outside the body," but he who commits sexual immorality sins against his own body. (WEB: 1 Cor. 6:15-19)

Paul also had carnal reservations about the Jews and thus marked a separation which, in view of a common textual past in the Hebrew Bible and the Old Testament, was not at all easy to draw:

> Indeed you bear the name of a Jew, rest on the law, glory in God, know his will, and approve the things that are excellent, being instructed out of the law, and are confident that you yourself are a guide of the blind, a light to those who are in darkness, a corrector of the foolish, a teacher of babies, having in the law the form of knowledge and of the truth. You therefore who teach another, don't you teach yourself? You who preach that a man shouldn't steal, do you steal? You who say a man shouldn't commit adultery, do you commit adultery? You who abhor idols, do you rob temples? (WEB: Rom. 2:17-22)

In his opinion, the moral hypocrisy and presumption of the likewise monotheistic Jews was particularly evident in the case of theft and adultery. Later Christian pioneers such as Origen Adamantius (185–c. 254) and John Chrysostom (c. 349–407) also worked on the image of the sexually aggressive carnal Jew who harassed and seduced innocent Christian women (Drake 2013: 24ff.).

Paul also offered a way out for precarious masculinity. The sexes represented a hierarchical continuum of relative masculinity (and not a polarity of different beings), with men and women at different degrees (Swancutt 2006: 75ff.). Christ had no place on this continuum. He had his own, as it were androgynous existence. Before the Fall, man was also androgynous, only then did the sexual bodies develop (Martin 2006: 83ff.; Dunning 2009: 57ff.). The intimacy produced through the union with Christ in prayer and religious ecstasy, in his opinion, went far beyond the sexual act between a man and a woman and brought about a return to the paradisiacal state. "Love" and "knowing," these biblical terms also underscored an intimate relationship to God, and at the same time they stood for the community of spouses and the "knowing" of the other in coitus. For our understanding today, it is difficult to grasp that Jesus was able to appear as a bridegroom in the visual language of that time and take his congregation as his bride (Zimmermann 2001: 230ff.). Sexual fornication would thus outrage not just the relationship between bride and groom but the collective relationship between Christ and the Christian community (Gaca 2003: 180). The questions of virile masculinity and fertile femininity so central to the Roman surroundings were just as irrelevant in this context as physical or social eunuchism.

Celibacy and Chastity as Better Standing?

Those unwilling or unable to give themselves to the ideal of abstinence should marry, according to Paul, but steer their sexual desire into regulated channels. In a famous and infamous passage of his first Epistle to the Corinthians there is the much-quoted sentence: "It is good for a man not to touch a woman." However, this statement is immediately put into perspective:

> But, because of sexual immoralities, let each man have his own wife, and let each woman have her own husband. Let the husband give his wife the affection owed her, and likewise also the wife her husband. The wife doesn't have authority over her own body, but the husband. Likewise also the husband doesn't have authority over his own body, but the wife. Don't deprive one another, unless it is by consent for a season, that you may give yourselves to fasting and prayer, and may be together again, that Satan doesn't tempt you because of your lack of self-control. But this I say by way of concession, not of commandment. Yet I wish that all men were like me. However, each man has his own gift from God, one of this kind, and another of that kind. (WEB: 1 Cor. 7:1-7)

In Paul's view, young Christians were faced with the fundamental decision of whether to marry and conceive children or live in celibacy. Marriage and family brought them into good standing before God, but celibacy was considered to be better—especially for those who believed in the looming apocalypse. From this point of view, conjugal coitus was a double *debitum conjugale*: It served the purpose of reproduction and as *remedium concupiscentiae* (healing of sexual desire) and prevention of (extramarital) fornication (Harnisch 1994: 460ff.). Unlike the Greek and Roman Stoics, Paul spoke out completely against the political mandate of marriage to increase the imperial population. Rather, their task would lie in mutual responsibility and spiritual love, both of which the spouses should use for higher and not carnal marriage purposes—which did not mean that the spouses should nevertheless live together in harmony and fulfil their marital duties (Deming 2004: xixff.) For Paul, there was a close interweaving of relationships between the couple and the relationship with God (Zimmermann 2011: 375ff.). From a married bishop he also demanded in his letter to Timothy that he ought to be a good father and have "children in subjection with all reverence" (WEB: 1 Tim. 3:4).

Ideas about sexual life and marriage in the New Testament were mainly shaped by Christian groups in the cities of the Eastern Roman Empire. There, through their exceptional moral behavior, they distinguished themselves both from the pagan population groups and from competing Jewish and Hellenistic redemption movements. Their particularly pure sexual life was a way for them to distinguish themselves from the dishonorable and sinful ways of others and come closer to God. Paul summed up this goal in his first Epistle to the Thessalonians: "For this is the will of God: your sanctification, that you abstain from sexual immorality, that each one of you know how to control his own body in sanctification and honor, not in the passion of lust, even as the Gentiles who don't know God" (WEB: 1 Thess. 4:3-5) (Stumpp 2001: 246).

With this marriage-friendly attitude, he also distanced himself from the radicals and heretics, who saw asceticism and body hostility as the only path to salvation and generally rejected sexuality as a sin. Theirs led to the desert and hermitage, a solution that could not be expected of the average Christian convert (Diem 2013: 33).

In everyday Hellenistic-Roman life, converts often encountered unclear or precarious situations in which the question arose as to how to react chastely. Offering or receiving a kiss, for instance: The Roman poet Martial (40–102/104) provided a satirical interpretation of the lurking physical irritations in his epigrams:

> When you have just returned after fifteen years,
> Rome gives you as many kisses as Lesbia did not
> give Catullus. The entire neighborhood presses you:
> the hairy farmer with a goat-smelling kiss; from here
> the weaver assails you, there the fuller, from here the
> cobbler having just kissed his hide, there the owner
> of a dangerous chin . . . there one with inflamed
> eyes and a giver of fellatio and recently cunnilingus.
> Now, to return was not worth the price.
>
> (Penn 2005: 10)

Kisses came in all kinds in ancient Rome—erotic, family, friendly, military, magical, ritual, thankful, and many more. In Roman art, kissing was clearly coded—most instances were in erotic and sexual contexts, in which a man and a woman kissed each other on the mouth. Rarely were two men or two women pictured kissing. Genital kissing like fellatio and cunnilingus between and within the sexes are to be seen on some representations. The Christian authors were skeptical toward the erotic kiss and wanted to push its family use. Thus, kiss symbolism was built into the Christian community rite. The usual kiss of welcome mutated into a sign of a brother or sister's belonging to the Christian community. If a Christian didn't kiss you in greeting, he marked you as not belonging to the community. Kisses exchanged in chastity between priests and believers, as well as among the latter, soon became the trademark of Christians. The anti-Christian agitators, on the other hand, interpreted this practice as a reference to sexual, if not incestuous rituals which these conspicuous groups must surely practice in secret. Athenagoras of Athens, a Christian apologist of the second half of the second century, spoke against such accusations, emphasizing the pure intentions behind it:

> According to age, we call some sons and daughters and others we hold brothers and sisters and to the aged assign the honor of fathers and mothers. Therefore, it is of great importance to us that the bodies of our brothers and sisters and the others called the names of relatives, remain not insulted and undefiled. Again the word says to us: "If someone should kiss twice because it pleased him . . ." and it adds: "therefore it is necessary to be careful of the kiss, or the salutation, because if our thoughts are the least bit stirred by it, it places us out-side eternal life." (Penn 2005: 107)

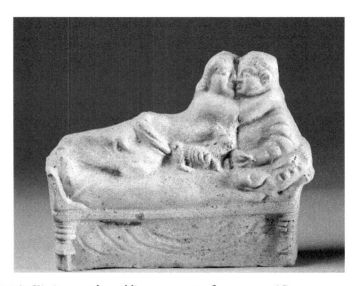

FIGURE 7 *Kissing couple on kline, terracotta, first century AD.*

Even if such concerns about the carnal demands of everyday life tormented the early Church Fathers, they mostly followed the Jewish models in the formulation of Christian sexual morals from the later first century and remained skeptical about radical celibacy and ascetic demands, such as those practiced by the all-male Essenes communities in the Judean desert (Figure 7). Like the rabbis, they placed emphasis on marriage, sexual intercourse, and reproduction, while at the same time opposing all premarital and extramarital contacts and all non-procreative practices such as masturbation, anal intercourse, and contraception (Foucault 2018: pos. 303ff.). They thus distanced themselves both from the socially hierarchical morality of the Romans and from the ascetic radicals from their own ranks and from the neighboring "sects." In distancing from the radical claims to virginity and asceticism, Christian marriage resulted in a more positive elevation of the effects of sexual intercourse for marriage and community (Burrus 2004: 3ff.).

The Holiness of Marriage versus Ascetic Life

The first Christian generations had to emphasize the holiness of marriage already because their marriage practice in the worst case could conflict with the supreme of all (Judeo-Christian) commandments: "You shall have no other gods before me. (. . .) you shall not bow yourself down to them, nor serve them, for I, Yahweh your God, am a jealous God, visiting the iniquity of the fathers on the children, on the third and on the fourth generation of those who hate me" (WEB: Exod. 20:3 and 5).

The success of the new teaching was dependent on marriage partners converting to the faith at the time of their union and that care was taken to not only raise the children as Christians but also that they not marry heretics in their turn. For women, the danger of temptation by polytheistic deities seemed particularly great as the Greco-Roman goddesses Aphrodite and Hera, for example, promised practical support in everyday life (in love/beauty and marital sexuality and childbirth, respectively). Pagans and unbelievers were regarded by Christians as another species, off limits in terms of the sexual because there was the threat of falling away from the one true God (Gaca 2014a: 553ff.). However, it could also prove very problematic to marry entirely within the *familia*, violating the endogamy and incest rules of Jewish and Hellenistic-Roman society. Marrying nieces and cousins was therefore adopted for priest dynasties from Judaism, which guaranteed the purity of the blood. The Roman legal tradition, on the other hand, had the effect of prohibiting marriage among other relatives up to the sixth degree, an extension that had been reduced in the imperial period (Mitterauer 2011: 11f.).

In the second and third centuries, discussions about the correct Christian sexual doctrine continued, but without resulting in a clear answer. Clement of Alexandria (approximately 150–215), who connected Christian-Jewish revelation with Greek philosophy, described conjugal coitus as a holy covenant between spouses and God. He oriented himself based on Plato and Pythagoras and wanted to create practicable rules of conduct with which one could reconcile reproduction and (periodic) chastity (Wheeler-Reed 2017: 89 ff.). According to Clement, married couples—once having fulfilled their obligation to multiply—ought to live together like siblings. He also allowed sexual contacts for preachers and clerics, but only until their ordination. Afterward, it is necessary that they live ascetically with their wives to fulfill the true gnosis. The vitae of the apostles served him as an example, since most of them had been married before the epiphany (Heid 1997: 58ff.; Foucault 2018: pos. 328ff.). By invoking the Christian gnosis, he simultaneously turned against the competitive doctrine of the same name, Gnosticism, which condemned everything here and now and especially the body as evil as it held the soul captive and blocked the path to spiritual perfection. An open view on marriage and sexuality was also held by Epiphanes (late first or early second century), whose work Clement was partly responsible for handing down. As a Christian Platonist, he advocated for a fulfilled marital love. Skeptical interpreters therefore accused his Christian communities based on justice and equality before God of sharing not only property but their women as well. Christians also endured such sexual insinuations from their persecutors, who suspected that their assemblies were actually promiscuous or even incestuous fertility cults (Harper 2013: 100). But the followers of the epiphany did not think of excess, but preached *agapê* (or *caritas*), a form of love that differed from *eros* and *philia* and found its highest expression in the Christian "love fest" (aka "*agapê* feast"). In the Eucharist, the congregation ate from one bread and thus—even if only symbolically—the body of Christ and thus became one flesh with the divine (Gaca 2003: 221ff.).

For the hermits and early recluse colonies, who had turned away from the world, such moderate views on marital love and sexuality went far too far. They wanted to silence the sexual drive by means of physical castration and dry up the source of continual temptation by the devil. Tatian, a Syrian apologist of the second century, even hoped for a marriage with the Holy Spirit through asceticism (Hunt 2003: 20ff.). In his opinion, the urge of desire first came into the world through Eve, who in turn had been tempted by the snake, aka Satan. Only through Eve did Adam succumb to the flesh. For Tatian, female sexuality embodied the low, animal side of being human. His teaching was practiced by the Encratites (the "abstainers"), a strict ascetic community. These Christians prohibited not only sexuality and marriage but also the consumption of meat and wine and strived for total spiritualization. For them, Roman moral chaos, secular matrimonial law, and prostitution were the work of the devil, which led the Roman Empire to ruin.

For the syncretistic Manicheans of the third century, who brought together Zoroastrian, Christian, and Buddhist elements, the physical world was fundamentally evil and detrimental to the spiritual. In fact, the Manichean worldview went even further. Followers of Zoroaster believed that the good, light, spiritual part of the world had been entrapped in evil, dark matter, and that procreation perpetuated this corruption. The epic battle between good and evil had already been lost and thus each new soul brought into a body was a further defeat. Therefore, they with the other ascetics condemned every form of sexuality, including marriage, which not only led them to suspect heresy but also made them opponents of the High Church (Salisbury 1992: 47). The followers of such ascetic groups were diametrically opposed to the Greek-Roman sexual world, which instead relied on the positive energies of the *eros*, engaging them fruitfully for marriage and procreation and equating virile potency with social supremacy. The anti-marital attitude also conflicted with Jewish culture, although it also condemned non-procreative acts (such as anal intercourse with boys) and extramarital sexual acts (such as prostitutes) as amoral and sinful.

The Christians of the late first and second centuries were convinced that Jesus had heralded the end of the age of demonic tyranny and that victory over the endless cycle of birth and death was imminent. Many of them, like the Manicheans, considered the urge of sexual life as proof that man had fallen into the bondage of the body and desperately tried to escape death through procreation (Brown 1988: 93). Ergo, those who renounced sexual intercourse could regain the lost freedom in the spirit of God. With their communities based on charity as well as the demand for purity and renunciation, they deliberately set themselves apart from the virile lust for power of Roman society (Clark 2008: 39). Prophets and preachers who vehemently stood up for their faith and were therefore persecuted and killed by Roman henchmen could enter the kingdom of heaven as martyrs. There was one other path of renunciation: deprivation and hermitage prepared the brothers and sisters of faith who went into the desert or to faraway places for the end of the old world (Clark 1999: 18ff.).

Christianity's Ambivalent Offer to Women

The Christian jurist and rhetorician Tertullian (around 150–230) opposed the idea that the body was merely a vessel for the soul and that carnal desires could be eliminated through spirituality and prayer. He saw the body and soul as one, human nature as immutable, and the sexual drive itself irremovable by castration (Kuefler 2001: 35). At the same time, he sympathized with the Montanists of Asia Minor, who also demanded asceticism, celibacy, or even separation from one's spouse as well as a willingness to martyrdom from their followers. In Tertullian's writings, women (from puberty) appear as sexualized beings who cannot escape their bodies despite lifelong virginity and asceticism. Through Eve, the sexual came into the world, which is why the female body was called the "Devil's gateway" in church dogma (Petrey 2016: 86ff.). The female existence was designed for temptation and she could not escape her fate even through baptism, prayer, or abstinence (Salisbury 1992: 13ff.). So that men are not permanently exposed to their sensual power, women must thus conceal themselves and their charms (Ranke-Heinemann 1999: 195). According to Tertullian, Christian virgins especially have to veil themselves, because the danger was great that they become prideful and represent a temptation for their brethren (Hubbard and Doerfler 2014: 175; Undheim 2018: 168). The role of marriage was thus to control and moderate the sexual force of nature that is woman. It was then a small mercy that lust and sexual energy diminish with age (Foskett 2002: 71). In this way, the spouses could then become brotherly servants of God and two in one flesh, thus achieving the best life (Schnell 2002: 201). Divorce or remarriage after the death of a partner should therefore be forbidden—a demand that was not implemented for a long period, but clearly deviated from Roman matrimonial law.

Christianity's ambivalent offer to women was most clearly expressed by Tertullian: On the one hand, this radical doctrine assured them a position beyond the patriarchal gender hierarchy. A virgin *sponsa Christi* (fiancée or "bride" of Christ) refused not only her sexual nature but also her marriage and thus the rule by her husband. Were she to become a hermit or nun, she also withdrew from the guardianship of her father or brother (Karras 2006: 73f.). Through chastity and prayer, she could become one flesh with Christ and thus escape the fate of the Roman and Jewish (married) woman, who lived to bear children. Spiritually, she then could stand on the same level as the man—a completely unthinkable presumption for other women. After the end of the world, or the transition into the new, gender hierarchies would indeed fall away and all the righteous would then together be "sons of God" (Lk. 20:36) (Boyarin 2003: 5ff.). Nevertheless, Tertullian also subordinated the woman to a certain patriarch, the (male) leader of the church. But he was ostensibly protecting women from sexual assaults by evil angels and demonic beings who lurked between God and man (Elliott 2008: 16ff.).

Consecrated virgins were considered prototypical believers for Christians of the second and third centuries as well as for their opponents—these women embodied the worldly consequences of Christian doctrine for the skeptics. In rejection of the common gender norms, they refused their traditional life tasks and submitted themselves to the protection of a community or a bishop. As brides of Christ they joined together to form pious circles of women (Shaw 1998: 182ff.). Such communes were considered not just a refuge of chastity but also an accumulation of the sexual dangers emanating from the female being. To their Christian contemporaries, on the other hand, the virgins appeared the purest of beings because they vehemently opposed the female sexual nature and thus embodied the direct descendants of Mary. They were inspired by Saint Thecla, a convert under Paul himself, who cut off her hair, dismissed feminine adornments, wore masculine attire, and led a virgin life (Tommasi 2017: 126). Disowned by her family and bridegroom, she miraculously escaped martyrdom and lived as a hermit in a cave for decades—where she had erotic experiences without physical penetration and wounding (Kotrosits 2018: 359ff.). Pure women like these possessed propagandistic potential and were stylized by the Church Fathers and bishops as the embodiment of the true faith. They became a standard component of processions and public staging.

Hagiographies, written in large numbers in the first centuries and found their way into the Christian scriptural corpus, were often conceived as erotic-sexual trials to be overcome. Regardless of gender, in their earlier secular lives, some of the later enlightened began as carnal sinners who had given themselves to the temptations of this worldly life. Resisting the diabolical temptations, however, they were ultimately able to develop a love for Jesus and since then abstained from worldly eroticism and sexual intercourse—which also meant separation from the social and family environment. Recent feminist research has shown that this physical self-denial was often accompanied by an intensification of desire and that the energies released were projected onto a divine, erotic joy, even a physical longing for Jesus. This was expressed above all in the practices of fasting and asceticism—hostile to the body indeed—which, however, also resulted in an intensification of the senses and perception as well as a spiritual sense of rapture and devotion. From the physical torment arose ecstasy and union with Christ. Renunciation seen this way by no means functioned as an anti-body practice. It was redirecting the erotic forces toward a new "love object" (Burrus 2004: 14ff.).

For Tertullian's contemporary Origen, the virginity (of woman and man) corresponded to the pure world before the Fall, when the body was still a temple of the Lord and the soul was not agitated by lust. Origen saw Christians therefore sullying themselves spiritually through intercourse and recommended to stay away from religious acts for some time and remain without the Eucharist (Phipps 2004: 87). Celibate clergymen, on the other hand, functioned as pure mediators between God and man. For them, the body also remained a permanent challenge; they must at all cost avoid desire and self-satisfaction. As they wrestled with desire, angels fought back the demonic powers that would tempt them. Origenes considered physical existence to be a transitional stage to be suffered until the entrance to the kingdom of heaven was thrown open—one reason why he had himself castrated as a young man to kill part of his physical urges (Isherwood 2006: 22ff.; Murray 2019: 99). Jewish authors criticized Origen's story and castration as such, seeing in them evidence of the fundamentally sex-hostile and thus life-denying attitude in Christianity. Conversely, in Judaism sexual activity would be understood as an elementary component of human life and thus an affirmative attitude toward vitality and life (Rubin 2021: 205f.).

The Sexual Division of Christendom

At the latest after Justin (around 100–165), Christian circles of study that had formed in the Mediterranean and the Middle East concerned themselves with defining true doctrine. In view of the diversity of voices, it became increasingly important what bishops and High Church members had to say or what they branded as heresy. As Peter Brown has shown in his groundbreaking study, the clergy tried to distinguish themselves from the broad constituency in physical and sexual matters and emphasized their privileged striving for virginity and asceticism (Brown 1988: 151ff.). Eusebius (around 260–340), bishop of Caesarea, referred to two different paths the Lord had planned for his church:

> Two ways of life were thus given by the Lord to His Church. The one is above nature, and beyond common human living; it admits not marriage, childbearing, property nor the possession of wealth. (. . .) Like some celestial beings, these gaze down upon human life, performing the duty of a priesthood to Almighty God for the whole race (. . .).

> And the more humble, more human way prompts men to join in pure nuptials, and to produce children, to undertake government, to give orders to soldiers fighting for right; it allows them to have minds for farming, for trade and for the other more secular interests as well as for religion. (Brown 1988: 205)

Now it is unmistakable that Christianity, by means of ascetic morality (at least that of the clergy), markedly set itself apart from the Hellenistic-Roman and Jewish traditions and drew a clear dividing line between itself and competing religions, sects, and cults—some historians even see in this demarcation the main reason for Christian aspirations to asceticism (Clark 1999: 18ff.).

In the third and fourth centuries, cenobitic monasticism established monastic communities of monks and nuns; within the ascetic life, the consecrated *virgo* (female and male gender) became quasi "professionalized" and thereafter embodied the highest rank under earthly conditions, because of its being closest to God (Diem 2005: 33ff.). The sexual division of Christendom into secular laymen on the one hand and the ordained as well as celibate clerics on the other hand proved to be groundbreaking for the further development of canonical sexual doctrine, because the decisive discourse contributions were now written to mirror the monastic ideal. The ordained were now not only concerned with practical norms of behavior, but they also thought about how they could stay pure in spirit and fight sexual fantasies at their roots. With the commandment of chastity in thoughts, words, and works, they committed themselves to a never-ending struggle against human nature. Spiritual success entailed the bodily efforts of fasting, sexual abstinence, and mortification. Monastery founders, in particular, saw it as an efficient means of purifying the soul and making room for the spiritual. If erotic fantasies and dreams continued to appear, they were seen as a sign that one had not yet freed oneself sufficiently from carnal impulses. According to the monastic ideal, obedient monastic servants should be guided by rules of conduct and thought formulated down to the last detail (Suárez Müller 2004: 322f.).

In order to do justice to these physical-psychological mechanics, some monks totally withdrew to remote areas or surrounded their monasteries with high walls to cut contact from the outside world and to protect themselves from any sensual temptation whatsoever. From the *Vita Antonii* (around 360), the life story of the Egyptian monk, ascetic, and hermit Antonius (around 251–356), one learns, however, that there is no escape from the demons and their carnal whispers even in total seclusion. All the more awe-inspiring therefore was the encounter with people who dedicated their lives entirely to virginity and emulated the purity of angels. By the late fifth century already sophisticated rules had been laid down for the guidance of the body and the senses for novices: At night, they were to tighten their belts fast around their garments so that they could not reach their genitals—humans, it seemed, were particularly susceptible to demonic influence through dreams. Since the aspirants were not yet morally established, they ought never look at the naked body of another brother or sister, let alone touch it. Nocturnal pollutions signaled that lust had not yet been defeated and that the chastity of angels had not yet been achieved (Elliott 1999: 14ff.; Salisbury 2008: 52).

However, even rigid Christian authors in the third and fourth centuries had to acknowledge that laymen were only able to partially adhere to the strict guidelines for members of the order and the higher clergy. Rules for the broader masses were more practical and beneath total virginity and asceticism. The necessity of such measured standards for the general Christian populace because otherwise interested parties were already deterred by the hard canon of the church; the spread of Christianity suffered at first as a result. In good Jewish tradition, married laypeople were therefore advised to devote their married life to reproduction and to behave with restraint and some chastity in sexual matters. Abstinence was reserved especially for church holidays, during Lent, and before taking the "Lord's Supper." Also the low clergy and the local priests lived according to these principles (still); for the most part they married and fulfilled their marital duties (Brown 1988: 255).

Consolidation of the Christian Sexual Doctrine

The tension between marital sexuality and spiritual asceticism subsequently permeated the Christian doctrine of marriage and sexuality

(Clark 1988: 631ff.). At the Synod of Elvira (now Granada), around 300/305, the bishops therefore dealt intensively with questions of marriage and adultery as well as the control over (married) women. The synod ruled out marriages with Jewish or pagan partners. With the *Codex Theodosianus* (of 428) this prohibition then applied throughout the empire—under threat of the death penalty (Hosang 2014: 96ff.; Humfress 2020). The decisions from Elvira also concerned the regulation of asceticism and the spiritual purity of the clergy (Metzler 2011: 101). Accordingly, bishops, priests, and deacons should abstain from conjugal intercourse. There remained disagreement as to whether this had to be permanent or only before liturgical acts after ordination (Heid 1997: 99ff.). Clerics were at least subject to a ritual celibacy of abstinence. Acceptance for such demands of general celibacy for these groups was yet far off, however. In 320, Emperor Constantine the Great, who himself had converted and under whose reign Christianity rose to a recognized and privileged religion in the empire, prohibited by law any behavior damaging to marriage and issued the death penalty for the abduction of virgins (also with their consent) (Albertson 2007: 99f.). He declared rape to be an official offence, making marriage a public institution under the protection of the state and the church (as rape here referred to married women or women of one's household). Nevertheless, victims of rape were suspected of having provoked or encouraged the aggressor even thereafter, and were subsequently also found to share the blame (Brundage 1987: 107).

In practice, divorce still existed under Constantine, and the clergy mostly agreed to remarry Christians through the following century (Wiesner-Hanks 2000: 32f.). At the Ecumenical Council of Nicaea (325), at which decisions of the whole church were made for the first time, bishops, priests, and deacons were forbidden to live together with a woman. Female household members beyond any sexual suspicion, like mother or sister, were excluded from the prohibition. That did not mean, however, that there were not still married and secular clergymen living with their concubines (Parish 2010: 46ff.). Under Constans (*c.* 320–350) and Constantius II (317–361), marrying one's niece was forbidden and punished by death as a particularly disgraceful act, a sanction that soon had to be eased in the Eastern Empire. The strict Roman and not the ambivalent Jewish incest rules were followed from the fourth century (Mitterauer 2011: 12).

John Chrysostom (*c.* 349–407), the Archbishop of Constantinople, questioned the reproductive commandment that had been elementary for the Roman Empire. In his opinion, it did not amount to a divine commandment that Christians must use their sexual energies for the benefit of the *polis* or the empire to bolster its population (Cooper 2007: 166ff.). The most important purpose of marriage was rather to channel fornication and to keep *eros* in check through moderate sexual intercourse. Marriage in paradise would, of course, be the best case scenario, as it was based on pure virginity—as opposed to earthly marriage (Neureiter 2010: 218ff.). But even in a woman living quite chastely, Eve's original sin continued to linger, issuing temptation from her for the man. The archbishop opposed all forms of adultery, regardless of gender, and included sexual contacts between husbands and slaves and prostitutes, by whom they were always surrounded. Thus, men would have to show their *ratio* and willful strength and resist temptation (Hartney 1999: 45f.). The basic evil of the Greek-Roman marriage lay for him in the fact that divorce was even a possibility and would in effect devalue the divine covenant, debasing it into temporary contract. In addition, he saw divorce in practice not ending well for women in particular (Harper 2013: 162f.). Chrysostom also condemned pagan fertility rites which were practiced in marriage initiation, including marriage among Christians that contained sexual allusions. During religious acts, lay people should best be separated by gender through the very division of the church space with a wall, thereby preventing sensual glances. In everyday life, the (exposed) body should be visible as little as possible; of course, men and women should also be separated in public bathhouses.

Following Chrysostom, clerics increasingly opposed archaic folk customs and condemned parishioners for moral lapses. Throughout the fourth and fifth centuries, they uncovered sensual scenes in Christian regions everywhere: in sport, while laboring and washing one's body, naked skin was revealed. At public games, one paid homage not only to the lust for cruelty, but allusions to sexual lust abound; brothels and courtesans continued to flourish, and even in prayer rooms and houses of God one came across fertility symbols. Suppression of the pagan cults and practices and the symbolic language associated with them rolled only very slowly. It took until the fifth century to ban the last remnant of the Old Roman cleansing and fertility festivals, the *lupercalia*, for its numerous sexual allusions (Markus 1997:131ff.).

Church Fathers: Virginity and Everyday Life

The branched paths of Christian sexual morality in the Eastern Mediterranean, Asia Minor, North Africa, and the Latin regions were first steered in a common direction by the three Late Antique Church Fathers of Latin Christianity: Ambrose (339–397), Jerome (Hieronymus) (347–420), and Augustine (354–430). According to Aurelius Ambrosius—Ambrose, the Archbishop of Milan—the human body carried the sexual stigma indelibly in itself. Only Christ had come into the world without this stigma. In virginity, he saw the highest possible integrity that man could achieve, and in Mary's body an *aula pudoris*, a hall of shame that remained closed forever. Her chaste example was to be followed by clerics of all levels: the marriage bed and its temptations should be avoided altogether (at the very latest upon becoming ordained). With the end of the bloody persecutions of the Christians—after the Edict of Milan in the year 313 and ultimately with the recognition of Christianity as state religion under Theodosius I (347–395) in the year 380—virginity received yet another religious connotation: a bloodless form of martyrdom. Instead of dying for the faith like their predecessors had done, one could now follow Mary's example through lifelong abstinence. Since Ambrose saw women determined by their sexual nature, he held them only partially at fault for their dependence. Men, on the other hand, he declared responsible not only for their own morality but also for that of women (Salisbury 1992: 23; Foucault 2018: Pos. 4080ff.).

Sophronius Eusebius Hieronymus, known as Jerome in the English-speaking world, was a hermit, priest, and founder of a monastery. He had lived with educated Christian women and had become acquainted with spiritual comradeship through their influence (Wheeler-Reed 2017: 100ff.). For him, too, the body belonged to the dark side of human existence, which is why it had to be controlled by dietary ethics and asceticism. Despite all precaution, the flesh continued to pose a threat not even married clerics could escape. Therefore, he proposed "spiritual marriages," in which the couples stayed in wedlock but refrained from intercourse. His own experience taught him that despite mortification, sexual desire could not be silenced (Hawkes 2004: 52). In his *Adversus Jovinianum*, a treatise against the teachings of Jovinian (fourth century to 405), which placed chaste and wed Christians on equal footing, Jerome squarely placed non-celibate clergy at a lower level of holiness and purity than their virgin peers (Hunter 2005: 127ff.): "I do not detract from wedlock when I set virginity before it. No one compares a bad thing with a good. Wedded women may congratulate themselves that they come next to virgins. (. . .) I praise wedlock, I praise marriage, but it is because they give me virgins" (Anderson and Bellenger 2003: 186).

The blessed state of (youthful) virginity—which in the ancient world had long been seen as a transitional stage before marriage—mutated into an ideal for him, a potentially universally applicable state of being. Even widowhood was regarded as its own *ordo* (state); widowed women were to repent of their earlier carnal sins and henceforth live ascetically.

Augustine, the Archbishop of Hippo, added yet another facet to the clerical view of sexual life: In his interpretation, sexual intercourse and procreation could have existed in paradise if not for the Fall, but it would have occurred without sinful lust and was entirely subject to human will. Total harmony was to have existed in paradise, between the soul and body as well as between will and desire (Clark 1986: 146; Thiel 2010: 74; Downham Moore 2020: 45ff.). Adam and Eve united in obedience and gratitude to their Creator. Only through prideful rebellion against God did the "*concupiscentia (carnis)*," the inclination to sin and evil so troubling to Paul and others, come into the world. Concupiscence is "a dark drive to control, to appropriate, and to turn to one's private ends, all the good things that had been created by God to be accepted with gratitude and shared with others" (Brown 1988: 418). Because of their arrogance, some thought Adam and Eve were punished with egoism, violence, greed, and other antisocial characteristics which made not only institutions such as marriage and family, but also political rule and legal regulations necessary for living together in society. Augustine held that while Eve was responsible for the Fall due to her weakness, Adam's positive social instinct to be with her brought him down as well—thus giving another, more nuanced reason for marriage. Sexual lust eludes, confounds, and balks at the will and intellect. For the early Christians, it became an ever-present reminder to man of his having turned away from God (Farley 2006: 40ff.). For Augustine, too, sexual intercourse provided a point of weakness for the carnal nature and *libido* of man to break out and gave no chance to enlightened thought, conscience, and morals (Foucault 2018: pos. 7212ff.; Angenendt 2015: 3–31). Even if man has free will in principle, it was bound by sexual desire. Involuntary or unintentional erections made this abundantly clear to mankind, as *eros* had done with the Greeks, but for the Christians this was man's inner nature—for all the talk of devilish temptation, this was not some form of temporary possession by a rambunctious god. Lust would therefore not only torture people from puberty to ripe adulthood, but for all of one's life and cannot be defeated by asceticism and bodily discipline. Augustine's doctrine of original sin holds that the evil thorn of sexual desire bit deep into Christian flesh and henceforth stood for the first and greatest of all sins, falling away from God.

Man's primary task was in consequence to fight against concupiscence and to use the sexual instinct righteously, namely only for the purpose of procreation. Augustine lauded the celibate "Josephite marriage" as being higher than a sacramental marriage that includes sex. Concubinage, in which he had lived for years before his own conversion and had fathered a child with his lover, ranked well below this. What made coitus acceptable to him were what he called the three *bona* (goods) of marriage, indeed the necessities of a sanctioned marriage: offspring, fidelity, and the sacramental bond—the indissolubility of the marriage covenant. When one of the spouses demanded sexual intercourse in order to satisfy the instinct, Augustine thought intercourse was good—as it also warded off fornication outside of the marriage bond (Ranke-Heinemann 1999: 145f.; Cooper 2007: 179f.). Regardless of which "good" coitus served at any one time, contraceptive measures in his view contradicted all three and were banned in the Christian Church (Jütte 2008: 26). Abortion, accordingly, was regarded as a most egregious sin—which applied when a fetus was formed (Riddle 1997: 84; Mistry 2015: 266ff.; Castuera 2017: 138ff.). Despite all his reservations and differentiations, Augustine defended marriage and its sexual functions and reinforced them against dualistic-Gnostic contemporaries who saw everything carnal as having been created by an evil deity.

Augustine made Christian marriage and sexual morals socially acceptable, so to speak. In contrast to the monastic ideals, which demanded completely unworldly behavior, he brought the whole church into harmony with the Christian-Roman social order: The Christian laity should accept social institutions and hierarchies, especially those between rulers and people, free and unfree, possessed and poor, parents and children, and between bishops or priests and believing people. The social order served to bring the chaos caused by the Fall under control and to master evil instincts. This goal was also pursued with the strict gender hierarchy. As the more sexual sex, women inherited original sin and passed it on from generation to generation and were thus less able to resist demonic attacks because of their inherent weakness. Men must therefore not only keep their own concupiscence in check but also resist the sinful seductions of the opposite sex. Ergo, they were born as the dominant half and thus responsible for their women (Sawyer 1995). Here, Augustine manifests, too, an imbalance in Christian sexual morality: Due to the fact that men faced a double sexual threat, one must accept that men are often less able to preserve their chastity than women (Schnell 1998: 319). So, according to Augustinian church doctrine, premarital coitus and adultery should be recognized as sins for both sexes and fittingly punished. But in everyday life such religious prohibitions did not prevent Christian men from cultivating pre- and extramarital relationships with (former) slaves, concubines, prostitutes, and married and single women (Lape 2011: 35).

It must be stressed, though, that Augustinian interpretation had a lasting impact on Christian sexual morality. The sexual was forever after classified in the Christian world as a fundamental evil of human existence and as an echo of original sin. In orgasm—the "little death"—everyone would experience the temporary extinction of the will and the delimitation of the ego and thus relive the Fall once again. More than the other carnal desires, lust was now basically regarded as unchaste and sinful, as a moral core where the virtue or sinfulness of a person was revealed (Brundage 1996: 35). The real problem was that sexual desire could not be overcome by the force of will. This seemed all the more precarious as sexual renunciation was still seen as the royal road to freedom of will and closeness to God. For the average Christian, conjugal sexual intercourse should in any case not be about satisfying pleasure but fulfilling the duties imposed by God. Since Augustine, however, there was no question that marriage and reproduction were God's will and part of the Christian way of life (Shaw 1998: 83ff.). Good Christians should succeed in transforming *eros*, the selfish love, into *philia* and *agapê* or *caritas*, forms of relationship and human love (Tracy 2005: 97ff.).

Sexual Desire versus Self-Care

Since then, Christian sexual morality has crossed three dividing lines: the separation of marital and non-marital sexual intercourse, the deliberate mastery of concupiscence or the failure thereof, and the distinction between natural and unnatural practices. One also referred to Augustine in order to legitimize the inferior position of women in the church and in society, because she would—as Uta Ranke-Heinemann pointedly formulated—"only be fit for reproduction" and was "not qualified for everything that has to do with spirit and intelligence" (Ranke-Heinemann 1999: 136). The contrary effects of such a rigid sexual ethic were also discernible with Augustine: precisely because the clergy placed sexuality within strict bounds, it was given an oversized meaning in the Christian universe. Since his time, sexual precepts and commands have not only led to meeting carnal desire with discipline; prohibition encouraged believers to pay greater attention to this area of life and to place it at the center of self-care and self-reflection.

Sexual violence against single and married women as well as slaves and prisoners came into focus as well. The moral shame of the pagan peoples was evident for early Christian authors in the way they treated the weakest among them. Prisoners of war, in particular, were enslaved and became a steady stream of prostitutes to quell the thirst of pagan lust (Stumpp 2001: 25). When Rome was plundered in the year 410 by predominantly Visigoth warriors under Alarich, and Christian-Roman wives, daughters, and nuns were raped, Augustine meditated on the sexual innocence and purity of these women in his *De civitate Dei* (*The City of God*, 413–426). Primarily thinking about raped holy women, he deemed the assault to have destroyed their physical virginity—but not their spiritual purity, leaving their chastity intact (Webb 2017; Vihervalli 2022: 5ff.). Here we see that the Christian authors ascribed excessive importance to the deliberate control of sexual pleasure and that in this respect men did not traditionally have a good showing. Who was to ensure their pacification? This fell to the women (Harper 2013: 172). The irony should not be lost that men were seen as responsible for women as guardians due to their weaknesses, while women were responsible to the men's vulnerability as a means of sexual solace or release—another echo of Greco-Roman thinking. With the condemnation of the mythological Lucretia, Augustine unintentionally created an opening for perpetrators of sexual violence at the same time. According to the historian Titus Livius (*c.* 59 BCE–*c.* 17 CE), Lucretia had been raped by the king's son Sextus Tarquinius and subsequently committed suicide. Her self-destruction, according to Augustine, is a reaction that should be interpreted as an admission of guilt, that is, Lucretia had probably encouraged her rapist to commit his crime (Staples 2004: 80ff.). The shame brought upon the households behind the Greco-Roman honor justifications becomes internalized in Augustine's version of guilty victimhood—the thorn cuts deep indeed.

Augustine and the Late Antique Church Fathers also offered a non-martial gender ideal to replace the ideal of masculinity held by the Roman upper classes up until then, which had become fragile in the face of a growing culture of justice before God. Whether baptized or not, many of these men worried about their virility in these politically and socially troubled times. By converting to Christianity, they could renounce the warlike image of men and incorporate a new masculinity which increasingly gained in esteem. Character traits traditionally regarded as feminine such as submission, humanity, and humility were now also exemplified by high-ranking personalities such as the emperor, some aristocrats, and bishops. They became the promising attributes of a new hegemonic masculinity. Real Christian men should no longer emulate the aggressive Roman warriors, but instead act as peaceful soldiers of Christ and faithful servants of God and the church (Kuefler 2001: 7). The heroic ideal of the fearless martyr also lost its splendor with the end of the persecution of Christians, as did its inglorious counterpart, the apostate, who cowardly turned away from the true faith in the face of torture and the threat of death (Cobb 2008: 86ff.). A strong Christian man now, it turns out, is the man who managed to take responsibility for and get his sexual lust under control successfully.

Sodomy—Acts against Nature and God

Questions of masculinity were the subject of a discussion in the early 1980s about the shift in same-sex sexuality in the first centuries of our era. John Boswell provided the provocative theses (Boswell 1980: 91 et seq., 1994): First, he claimed, Christianity arose in an atmosphere of relative tolerance toward same-sex eroticism in Roman culture—even if Roman morality and legislation proved to be quite ambivalent toward this sexual form even before the birth of Christ. Second, that the writings of the early Christian period did not yet contain any indications of a hostile attitude toward homosexual acts. Third, that there would not have been any real animosity toward same-sex in the Early Middle Ages (about 500–1050). Homophobia only developed in the twelfth and thirteenth centuries and from there it was projected back into early Christianity (Boswell 1980; Kuefler 2006: 2f., 2018).

Jewish and Roman Traditions

Many feet of library shelving have since been filled with discussions of Boswell's theses (Kuefler 2006: 10ff.; Rapp 2016: 40ff.). Today, there is a broad consensus that there was no marked break between the Hellenistic-Roman and Jewish sexual cultures on the one hand and the Christian ones on the other, but rather clear continuities in the attitude toward same-sex sexuality. As discussed in Chapter 3, the Romans' acceptance of same-sex sexuality was not all-encompassing and generally applicable; it was highly differentiated according to the social context, the persons involved, and their actions. Already in the two centuries before Christ's birth, criminal sanctions against same-sex practices were on the rise. In the imperial period and late antiquity, a general fear of unmanliness spread, which was taken up and perpetuated by Christianity (Kuefler 2001; Brinkschröder 2006: 7ff.). And it wasn't just men. According to Brooten, sexual relations between women were also seen negatively. In the Roman world, there never really came about a tolerance for female-female sexuality (nor for male *paiderastia*) because of the all-dominant phallic-patriarchal culture. Consequently, no significant break in terms of valuation or stigmatization could really have existed either (Brooten 1996).

Jewish influences on the early Christian view of same-sex sexual acts were also reassessed in reaction to Boswell. In Judaism, sexual contacts between members of the same-sex and the switching of gender roles in sex, as well as all unnatural sexual practices between man and woman (such as anal intercourse) were considered impure traits belonging to the Greeks, Romans, Persians, Egyptians, etc. (Crompton 2003: 113f.). The Christian interpreters could also find the story of Sodom in the Jewish writings of the Old Testament (Gen. 19:1-29): God rains down fire and brimstone on the city of Sodom because its wicked inhabitants want to "know" two male visitors (angels). They surround Lot's house and demand he send them out. Lot offers them his two virgin daughters instead—so as not to transgress Old Testament hospitality laws, these are after all God's messengers and the biblical law of hospitality actually demanded their better treatment (i.e., Lev. 19:34). But the men of Sodom refuse and attempt to break down the door. Lot and his two daughters are rescued by the angels, and God smites the sodomites (Walsh 2001: 28f.; Youssef 2017: 115ff.). The early Christian interpreters saw in this story a clear condemnation of same-sex desire (Jordan 2000: 30ff.). In an alternative reading, however, this episode was not (primarily) about punishing homosexual penetration but about condemning inhospitably, prideful behavior and ingratitude.

Further Old Testament passages in Leviticus (Lev. 18:22 and 20:13) were also concerned with men who "consorted," "slept," or "lie" with one another, as one did with a woman and thus put themselves in an unmanly, inferior position as well as ritually unclean (Walsh 2001: 205). In view of the abomination of their lustful deeds, again and again these laws require that transgressors "shall surely be put to death; their blood shall be upon them." In other words, they brought it on themselves with their desire. In addition to male-male practices, the violent overempowerment of one man by another and the associated dishonor and subjugation were also problematized here. Contemporary Jewish writings, such as those of Philo of Alexandria (around 15/10 BCE to after 40 CE), saw male-male behavior as an additional threat to the population of a small people, for here procreative seed was wasted. Participants also were seen as giving in to sexual desire in excess—alleged of the same dangers of alcohol-fueled banquets and fests. All this not only meant great shame, but also seduced and effeminated the man, making him passive and impotent—and thus the antipode of the Roman *vir*. For Philo, this was enough to demand the immediate execution of both actors (Loader 2012: 33; Swancutt 2007: 30f.).

Paul went so far as to declare same-sex the very epitome of corruption, which is why God's wrath came upon men. His Epistle to the Romans said:

> Therefore God also gave them up in the lusts of their hearts to uncleanness, that their bodies should be dishonored among themselves; who exchanged the truth of God for a lie, and worshiped and served the creature rather than the Creator, who is blessed forever. Amen. For this reason, God gave them up to vile passions. For their women changed the natural function into that which is against nature. Likewise also the men, leaving the natural function of the woman, burned in their lust toward one another, men doing what is inappropriate with men, and receiving in themselves the due penalty of their error. Even as they refused to have God in their knowledge, God gave them up to a reprobate mind, to do those things which are not fitting. (Rom. 1: 24-28)

Paul's message corresponded to the widespread rejection of same-sex acts in the Jewish world (Brooten 1996: 266). He took the Jewish concept and Greek tradition and fixed it upon a theological foundation (Ahern 2018: 218ff.). Whether it was Romans, the Roman Stoics (of whom it was said "preached water but drank wine"), or the common man, unnatural sexual intercourse was not just a shameful act—it was idolatry (Swancutt 2004). Caused by uncontrolled carnal desire, such men surrender to excess, be it in the form of anal penetration of one's wife, adultery or, finally, sexual intercourse with a man. Male-male acts were not only acts against (God-given) nature but against God himself. Those led astray to such passions disgraced not only themselves but also the Most High and would therefore have to reckon with the gravest punishments (Loader 2012: 306ff.; Winterer 2005). This also because of the threat of inversion of the sexes—Paul had, it seems, no polar man–woman model in mind, but rather a continuum of relative masculinity on which the sexes were located in different places (Swancutt 2006: 81). The ultimate punishment was that God's wrath would lead to the spread of theistic and non-procreative desires and the extinction of the affected groups in the near future (Gaca 2014a: 556). It is Paul who is "owed the credit" that no way of discussing same-sex actions in a positive manner has been possible within Christianity ever since. Now, only the category that existed was the sodomites, charged with guilt and sin, which carried out sexual acts between peers, between old and young, between lovers, and in prostitutive relationships.

Sexual relationships between women were not specifically addressed in the writings of the Old and New Testaments, but those of a woman (also a man) with an animal indeed were (Lev. 18:23) (Rogers 2009: 66ff.). In the later ecclesiastical reading of the above text, however, this epistle is also revealed to be concerned about sexual contacts among women—not only unnatural oral or anal practices between man and woman—which is why capital punishments seemed justified. All this should not obscure the fact that the first generations of Christians paid relatively little attention to same-sex desire and acts compared to other sexual issues and those of marital relations or asceticism. This also concerned the god Eros, who was less in the line of fire compared to Aphrodite and this although he was considered the patron of *paiderastia* (Gaca 2014a: 562).

Punish Them with Exquisite Penalties

In Paul's wake, the Church Fathers argued for an ever stricter handling of same-sex practices from the second century onward (Johansson and Percy 1996: 161ff.). In their reflections on asceticism, celibacy, and virginity, persons acting in this way were considered exemplary enemies of Christian life. At the Synods of Elvira (between 295 and 314), the *paiderastia* was only condemned for the time being, and rapists of boys were denied communion. By the Council of Ancyra (314), harsh punishments were demanded, and persons who had sexual intercourse with boys faced excommunication (Brinkschröder 2006: 11). From the late third century, the desert fathers and early monks—in the tradition of Platonism and Stoicism—advocated for a negative attitude toward sexuality generally. For these Christians living in renunciation and abstinence, however, erotic or sexual attractions within one sex represented a special temptation. Detailed rules of conduct for fraternal and sisterly relations were the result (Salisbury 2008). Already Pachomios the Elder (about 292/298–346), an Egyptian monk and monastery founder, laid down the following rules of conduct: "No one should speak to another after lights out. No one should sleep with another on a rush mat. No one should hold another's hand; but whether he stands, walks, or sits, let him be separated from another by one cubit" (Masterson 2006: 215).

Rules like these point to the fact that in monastic communities and first monasteries homophile relationships developed again and again and erotic as well as sexual acts took place. Provisions on the preservation of chastity in monastic institutions can also be found by Benedict of Nursia (480–547), the founder of Christian monasticism in the West, and have since shaped the basic sex phobic mood of the order's rules (Diem 2001). Late Antique texts about monastic cohabitation and the rules necessary for it were full of stories about brotherly feelings, which expressed themselves on different levels, as spiritual community, but also aesthetic attraction or even sexual desire between men. In practice, the spectrum probably ranged from homosocial to homoerotic to homosexual contacts and relationships (Rapp 2016: 138f.).

Augustine (354–430) issued a verdict which was to shape the attitude of the Christian Churches toward same-sexism until the twentieth century: All sexual acts not oriented toward reproduction were condemnable as they serve only the lust of this world and threaten the closeness to God in the afterlife (Brown 1988: 387ff.; Ahern 2018: 224ff.). He also rejected homoerotic relationships among women as against nature, but saw them primarily as a moral problem (Beukes 2021). In contrast, male-male sexual intercourse had been archetypically eradicated by God in Sodom. With John Chrysostom (around 349–407) and thereafter, the Sodom story increasingly dealt with the punishment of sexual acts among men and was ignored for other aspects. For him, these sinners possessed a morbid and excessive sexual desire which spun out of their control (Crompton 2003: 137ff.; Harper 2013: 147). At the latest by this point it was certain that the Christian clergy, in contrast to the Romans and Greeks, no longer distinguished between the sexual objects involved and their social status during penetration. Servant and master alike were condemned.

Already before this, corresponding provisions had been included in the church ordinances. In the *Apostolic Constitutions*, a multivolume collection of treatises on Christian doctrine and worship from the late fourth century, it was determined that: "Do not violate children, for contrary to nature is the evil born at Sodom, which was laid waste by the fire of God." Somewhat later in this context comes already the "sin of Sodom," going so far as to erase other terms from the record by refusing to list them: He that is guilty of sins "of unspeakable deeds, the *kinaidos*, and the debauched" should be "scrutinized" by the church and their moral conduct monitored before they could repent and confess. In the canonical letters of the Bishop and religious scholar Basilius of Caesarea, Saint Basil the Great (about 330–379), fifteen years of excommunication were foreseen for those who "committed shameless acts with men." Bishop Gregory of Nyssa (around 335/340 to after 394) increased the penance to eighteen years. Whereby those who confessed their guilt and sin themselves, should get a shorter penance imposed due to the repentance shown (Harper 2013: 144f.).

The Christian-Roman emperors had already taken penal measures (Bleibtreu-Ehrenberg 1978: 188ff.): According to an edict of the two sons of Constantine, Constans and Constantius, from the year 342, a man should be sentenced if he *nubit* another in the manner of a woman (Berkowitz 2012: 119):

> When a man "marries" [*cum vir nubit*] as a woman who offers herself to men, what does he wish, when sex has lost its significance; when the crime is one which it is not profitable to know; when Venus is changed into another form; when love is sought and not found? We order the statutes to arise, the laws to be armed with an avenging sword, that those infamous persons who are now, or who hereafter may be, guilty may be subjected to exquisite punishment [i.e., death]. (Crompton 2003: 132)

Boswell used this term, *nubit*, in his second influential work, *Same-Sex Unions* (1994), among other things as evidence that men in early Christianity could (still) enter into erotic love and couple relationships and even enter into marital relationships—which in turn was seen by him as an indication of reasonably accepted erotic and sexual relationships. In late antiquity and early medieval texts from Byzantium, he even elicited special ceremonies with which one could allegedly officially make an avowal to same-sex love and thus unions between two men (of the same age or of different ages) would have come into being. From a modern point of view, these *unions* could almost be understood as an early form of gay and lesbian weddings or marriages. Boswell famously cites one such couple, the martyrs Bacchus and Sergius, two Roman officers of the border troops who had died for their faith in the late third century. Unlike Boswell, however, with regard to such blessed couples of men and ceremonial brotherhoods, today the prevailing opinion is that these were not real marriages and that these communities in no way served the sexual purpose of marriage (Boswell 1980: 123; Neill 2009: 227f.; Younger 2005: 67; Masterson 2022). Sexual contacts between the male couples connected by such ceremonies should be avoided in general and were considered a great threat. Their friendship should be limited purely to the Christian covenant of souls (Kuefler 2006; Rapp 2016).

In the same edict, men who denied their masculinity and sought Venus where it could not be found were punished with an exquisite penalty. According to a later provision from the year 390, those who offered themselves passively (as *cinaedi*) were to be removed from the brothels of the city of Rome and, together with the pederasts, punished with the severest penalties—alternatively, they had to leave the city within two months. These sanctions were extended to all passive homosexual men in 438 by the Theodosian Code (Lauritsen 2003; Hupperts 2007: 55). This codex was extremely significant because it became the basis of early medieval law in the West. During the so-called Migration Period, however, the strict decrees of the Christian-Roman emperors remained more or less toothless (except in Visigoth Spain), since Germanic laws were widely applied in practice. In the latter, homosexual acts were hardly raised—which does not mean that Germanic legal customs did not provide harsh punishments for them (Lutterbach 1999; Johansson and Percy 1996: 165; Bleibtreu-Ehrenberg 1978: 231ff.).

Porneia—the Evil of Prostitution

While same-sex practices clearly saw greater condemnation and persecution, the attitude toward prostitution in early Christianity was ambivalent. Here, too, Christians were reacting to the Greek-Roman and Jewish environment. In the former cultural field, sexual contact with women other than one's own wife was not a major issue unless they belonged to another man or were under his protection—be it as a wife, slave, or prisoner. Such dishonorable women were out of the question as wives anyway. There are no direct prohibitions against prostitution in the Old Testament, but women who pursued this trade were considered dishonorable—for example in the book of Deuteronomy: "You shall not bring the hire of a prostitute, or the wages of a male prostitute, into the house of Yahweh your God for any vow; for both of these are an abomination to Yahweh your God" (Deut. 23:18) (Loader 2012: 13ff.). In Jewish culture at the beginning of the common era, it was not unheard of for men to have sexual relations with prostitutes or slaves before marriage in view of the advanced marriage age of twenty-five to thirty years for men and an age difference of more than ten years to the wives (Satlow 2001: 104). Adultery was prohibited by Jewish law, as was contact of a married man with a prostitute—both acts clouded family order and lineage. However, this did not mean that married Jewish men could not and did not use their slaves for sex. In Judaism, a double morality came to light here, which was to flow into Christianity (Raveh 2014: 100ff.)

Mary and Eve, the Virgin and the Seductress

With Mary and Eve, the Christian authors had two polarizing and sexualized images of women to offer: the perpetual virgin and the sinful seductress. The image of the latter was activated in particular when one got excited about premarital and extramarital sexual intercourse. The prostitute was considered the incarnation of the "fallen woman," she was a grievous sinner, her body also defiled her clients—according to Paul, sexual intercourse with a whore meant nothing else than to become one flesh with her and thus unclean (Brown 1988: 51f.; Koltun-Fromm 2010: 80ff.). In connection with prostitution, reference was often made to another female figure, Mary Magdalene. Glorious and damnable at once—she was regarded as the archetype of the sinful woman and the whore, on the one hand, yet this repentant sinner had turned to Jesus, threw herself down before him, and even washed his feet, on the other. It should not be forgotten that the negative attitude of early Christians toward prostitution was also influenced by the persecution of Christians, because the Romans had punished women and girls who converted to Christianity by locking them in whorehouses, according to Tertullian (McGinn 2006: 168).

What Christians thought of prostitutes was due to fundamental skepticism vis-à-vis the sexual. Although the authors of the New Testament and the Church Fathers argued about the share of sexual pleasure in marital unification, there was broad consensus that coitus should not be practiced for pleasure. The Greeks saw things quite differently, thanking the goddess Aphrodite for the sexual pleasures that sustained human life and not only for the purpose of reproduction. However, even in the Greek context one never forgot that lust had a dark side, which could lead to torments of love and excess. It is not surprising that Christians saw in the worship of Aphrodite and in its barely veiled statues and opulent temple cults a particularly hideous form of idolatry that could bring them to lustful thoughts (Gaca 2014a: 558ff.). According to Matthew, lechery started in the

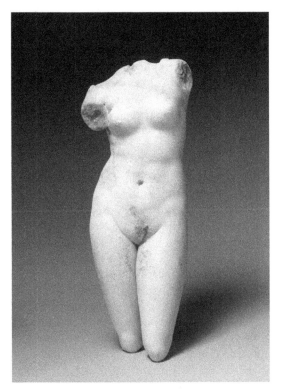

FIGURE 8 *Aphrodite Anadyomene (rising), marble statuette, first century AD.*

gaze and led directly to action and sin: "But I tell you that everyone who gazes at a woman to lust after her has committed adultery with her already in his heart" (Mt. 5:28). It was from there a small step indeed to women who publicly offered their bodies for sale along the path of visual enticement. Despite this iconic threat, it still took some time until the historian and Church Father Eusebius of Caesarea called for the destruction of the cult sites and statues of Aphrodite around 300 and demanded the banishment of their lustful aura from cultural memory (Figure 8).

Eusebius also reports that the prostitutes associated with Aphrodite were a thorn in the side of Constantine the Great (around 275–337). In the course of anti-pagan measures, he had several Aphrodite temples shut or Christian churches built in their immediate vicinity—with the intention of combating prostitution flourishing around those temples (Wallraff 2011: 13). The Christian reinterpretation of the goddess of love went one step further in the fifth century. The temple dedicated to her in *Aphrodisias* (in present-day Turkey) was transformed into a church by first enclosing it with a basilica, reappropriating the very columns of the Greek temple to support the massive naive, and then demolishing the original walls to be used elsewhere. The transformation turned the temple inside out, thereby recoding the practice surrounding this religion. On the spot where pagan priests once sacrificed animals, priests thereafter offered the sacrament of Christ. While worshippers of Aphrodite once gazed upon the cult image of the goddess when entering the temple, the Christians' gaze now focused on the altar and the image of Christ (Ebner 2012: 132).

Paul's recommendation to the Christian church in Corinth—virginity and chastity for some, monogamous marriage for others—also had to do with prostitution there:

> Don't deprive one another, unless it is by consent for a season, that you may give yourselves to fasting and prayer, and may be together again, that Satan doesn't tempt you because of your lack of self-control. (. . .) But I say to the unmarried and to widows, it is good for them if they remain even as I am. But if they don't have self-control, let them marry. For it's better to marry than to burn. (1 Cor. 7:5, 8-9)

Regular sexual intercourse in marriage was intended to protect against *porneia*, which offered Greek-Roman (married) men a way out of a sexually unsatisfactory marriage. In Christian linguistic usage this also meant sexual intercourse with a paid prostitute, not only with one's own slaves, but also with freed persons (Grieser 2018). The term also extended to all other sinful, non-marital, and non-procreative sexual acts and the actors involved. *Porneia* thus moved to the top of the catalogue of pagan vices (Stumpp 2001: 249f.; Glancy 2002: 57ff.).

For Cyprian (about 200/210–258), bishop of Carthage, there was a direct connection between prostitution, sinful behavior, and vices that were rampant in the social lower classes. In a letter about a follower of the opposing bishop Novatian (*c.* 200–258), he accused him of "having entered a brothel, the location of the sewer and the slimly black hole of the rabble, he has been befouled his own sanctified body, God's temple, with hateful filth" (McGinn 2006: 165). With this argument he could seamlessly invoke the Roman upper-class objection to polluting the social strata by mixing and mingling in brothels. It was also fitting that the Christian authors spoke out against abortion and contraception and, like Tertullian, established a connection to infanticide (in view of an already formed and fetus imbued with a soul)—all practices that were seen to be particularly widespread among the lower classes (Riddle 1997: 84; Mistry 2015: 38).

Bishop Basilius of Caesarea (*c.* 330–379) reflected on the whores' fundamental guilt and sinfulness in view of the prostitution that could not be overlooked in the cities of Cappadocia: "The difference is greater between those who commit sin and those who are righteous. For while the slave woman who was sold to a pimp is in sin out by necessity, she who happens to belong to a well-born mistress was raised with sexual modesty, and on this account the one is should show mercy, the other condemned" (Harper 2013: 181).

The bishop regarded prostitution as an imposed sin *par excellence*, against which the unfree could not defend themselves; free women, on the other hand, could deliberately determine their own sexual behavior. Under John Chrysostom (*c.* 349–407), voices against the moral double standards associated with prostitution grew louder. They derided the fact that Christian men could continue to enjoy the advantages of Roman culture, while women were obliged to premarital abstinence, monogamy, and fidelity. Even if adultery was forbidden in principle, Christian men continued to visit brothels and abuse their slaves (Harper 2013: 165ff.). That is why Chrysostom demanded: "The body of the *eleuthera* [free woman] and the body of the whore (porne) are the same" (Harper 2016: 119).

Back then already, the early Christian authors pointed to the connection between social need and prostitution and criticized that free Roman men exploited the precarious situation of poorer (free) women and forced them into the pleasure trade. Chrysostom therefore wondered to what extent the poor could protect their honor and purity and take control of their sexual existence. He also feared that the social imbalance could turn into envy and jealousy if the lower classes understood what profits prostitution were bringing in—many daughters of poor cooks, leather workers, and slaves growing up into prostitution. Some of them would think: "I am a free man and freeborn. I have chosen decent labor, but I couldn't dream of such luxury" (Harper 2011: 310f.). Since most prostitutes came from the lower classes, they were soon called "common women," a term that became widespread in the (Later) Middle Ages. As publicly accessible, purchasable whores, they belonged to a different category than the slaves, who were only available to their owners.

The Late Antique Church Father Jerome (Hieronymus) drew attention to the unbridgeable gap between the socially staggered sexual system of the Romans and the egalitarian morality of Christians:

> The laws of Caesar are one thing, the laws of Christ another. Their Papinian [a Roman jurist of the 2nd century] commanded something quite different than our Paul. Among them, the bridles of sexual restraint are unloosed for men. They condemn only *stuprum* (rape) and *adulterium* (adultery), letting lust run wild through whorehouses and slave-girls—as though social status determined what was an offense, and not sexual desire. (Harper 2011: 321)

Whores Impose Sin

Augustine also spoke out against the prevalence of prostitution in the Greco-Roman world: "What can be said to be baser, more worthless, more laden with humiliation and disgrace than prostitutes, pimps, and the other vermin of this type?" At the same time, he established an exception to the rule which was also used in the following centuries to legitimize prostitution: "Remove prostitutes from human society and you will throw everything into confusion through lusts. Confer on them the status of respectable women and you will only disgrace the latter through blot and humiliation" (Schuster 1992: 19). Whores were a necessary evil. To prevent worse things like extramarital intercourse and adultery (of men), society must resign to accepting them. Their social status secured by the service they provide in detouring the men's exuberance away from the *matrona*, the only thing left to do was segregate them and ostracize them.

For the patriarch Cyril of Alexandria (*c*. 375/80–444), there were two kinds of prostitutes in the early fifth century: "See how some wish to practice shameful pollution willingly and of their own volition while some are accustomed to impress it upon others as though by force" (Harper 2013: 182f.). In the year 428, the Eastern Roman Emperor Theodosius II (401–450) reacted to forced prostitution and enacted a law to prevent the sexual sale of slaves or daughters of poorer families. Pimps were also to be sentenced to forced labor and subsequent exile for turning women into whores against their will and bringing them to sin (Osiek 2003: 274). With this law, the Christian moral debates flowed for the first time into a secular law and thus reacted to a social grievance. A little more than a decade later, another provision followed, completely banning the trade of procuring prostitutes in Constantinople and threatening pimps with flogging and expulsion; the prostitutes remained unaffected.

With these laws at the latest, prostitution became a political matter pursuant to not just moral but also social policy. The measures remained largely ineffective, however, and prostitution in the Christian Empire remained an institution that supported the patriarchal, social, and gender order. The pleasure trade was not abolished because it was an important private sector factor from which the state profited through taxes (Stumpp 2001: 273f.). "Necessary" prostitution was derided with the never-ending sermon against the ineradicable, as it simultaneously created a narrative that separated good from bad Christians: The former followed premarital abstinence, lived in exclusive monogamy, and practiced chaste conjugal intercourse; the latter continued to have sexual relations with slaves and prostitutes—not only before but also during marriage.

For early Christians, there was a direct connection between prostitution and impure fantasies—expressed in images and stories that led to *porneia*. Their skepticism and fear of images resulted from the seductive power attributed to them in the Hellenistic-Roman world as a whole. Christian writers, too, only needed glance at an erotic image or idol to set its imaginative effect in motion, to arouse sexual desire, or at least to stimulate the imagination. The gaze animated the action and inevitably led to fornication and adultery (Vout 2013: 130). In Tertullian's *De Virginibus velandis*, there is a passage dedicated to the carnal evil in eye contact. In it, he deals with a conflict in the Church of Carthage in the second century about the veiling of consecrated virgins during mass. Some *virgines* had attended the celebration unveiled and argued that they were not subject to the Pauline veils because they were already obliged to sexual shame because of their vows of virginity and asceticism. Tertullian took this opportunity to reflect on the power of the sexualized gaze and chastity:

> For there is something that even the Gentiles fear and call 'evil eye', the unfortunate outcome of all too great praise and glory. We sometimes interpret as coming from the devil, because he hates good; then we again attribute it to God, because he judges pride by raising up the humble and oppressing the superior. A truly chaste virgin, therefore, will fear the enemy on the one hand because of the evil eye, and fear God on the other, as well as the envious being of the one, the eye of the other, and she will rejoice, confessing only herself and God. (Rakoczy 1996: 223)

When a consecrated virgin—even without sinful intentions—exposed herself to the lecherous gaze, she had to reckon with the judgmental eye of God. This applied to everything that attracted such a gaze and set *porneia* in motion—be it a shameless woman, a provocative whore, or even just an erotic picture or a racy story. For Christians the *pornographiae*, the whore stories, meant a first step to sin and were therefore regarded as a medium of the devil with which he infiltrated the imagination of believers.

In Augustine's *Confessiones* (c. 400), curiosity was added to the desirous gaze—the lust of the eyes—which led to:

> To this is added another form of temptation more manifoldly dangerous. For besides that concupiscence of the flesh which consisteth in the delight of all senses and pleasures, wherein it slaves, who go far from Thee, waste and perish, the soul hath, through the same senses of the body, a certain vain and curious desire, veiled under the title of knowledge and learning, not of delighting in the flesh, but of making experiments through the flesh. The seat whereof being in the appetite of knowledge, and sight being the sense chiefly used for attaining knowledge, it is in Divine language called The lust of the eyes. For to see, belongeth properly to the eyes; yet we use this word of the other senses also, when we employ them in seeking knowledge. For we do not say, hark how it flashes, or smell how it glows, or taste how it shines, or feel how it gleams; for all these are said to be seen. And yet we say not only, how it shineth, which the eyes alone can perceive; but also, see how it soundeth, see how it smelleth, see how it tasteth, see how hard it is. And so the general experience of the senses, as was said, is called The lust of the eyes, because the office of seeing, wherein the eyes hold the prerogative, the other senses by the way of similitude take to themselves when they make search after any knowledge. (Augustine 1909–14: 135)

In pagan Greece and in Rome the ethical-moral rules had been directed toward the avoidance of *impudicitia* and *infamia* (shameless vice and dishonorable behavior). Sexual shame was not regarded as an anthropological constant, rather it was distributed quite variably between the sexes and along social status lines and thus represented a deeply social category. Who had to feel how ashamed (or not) for what action was ultimately a question of social and cultural origins. The question differed if pondered by a man or a woman, a freeborn or a slave, a youth or an elder, etc. If a Roman citizen "took" his slave, *pudicitia* played no role because it ranked outside these categories. In early Christianity, sexual culture shifted from shame to sin (Harper 2013: 5ff.). The concept of sin contradicted such social-relativist morality (at least in theory). What was sinful in sexual matters had to be defined as the same for all people because otherwise the free will necessary for the sin–penance complex, including personal responsibility for thinking, feeling, and acting, would not work. Whether free or slave, man or woman, married or prostitute, the Christian catalogue of sins was one size fits all. With the absolute triumph of Christianity in late antiquity (284–476), the new sexual morality began to establish itself in the Western and Eastern Roman Empire and found its way into secular legislation. Local priests and (itinerant) preachers now saw it as their first task to inscribe the Christian register of sins and penance in the hearts and bodies of believers.

5

Contradictory Sexual Worlds in the Middle Ages

On the Ecclesiastical Path: Penitential Books and Erotic Riddles

Early Christian sexual debates were boisterous. They resonated well beyond clerical circles. The traces they left on the marriageable population and already married and how quickly they echoed across the social strata is still a controversial subject. What is certain is that many Greek-Roman traditions endured well after the establishment of Christianity and its elevation to the status of an imperial church in the fourth century. In view of the lack of institutional structures and possibilities for sanctions, the clergy had to more or less tolerate the sexual proclivities of the Christian laity (Garton 2004: 61). Non-marital and extramarital relationships continued to thrive around the Mediterranean, remarriage and sequential marriages (after the death of a partner) were the rule, not the exception. At the same time, however, legal concubinage was restricted and abolished as a legitimate alternative to marriage. Nonetheless, this did not mean that similar arrangements and extramarital relationships did not persevere (Karras 2012b: 6). Yet, big steps were made toward making marriage generally available. Emperor Justinian I (around 482–565) in particular lifted the marriage prohibitions for ex-prisoners, so that they no longer had to turn to a secondary institution but could be properly wed (Esmyol 2002: 40).

Slow Enforcement of Christian Practices

In the Christianized regions of Western, Northern, and Central Europe, betrothal, wedding, and marriage practices were accompanied by pagan fertility rituals, which the clergy adopted and adapted for their purposes, integrating them into Christian practices. Until the Late Middle Ages, phallic and cunnic figures could also be found on church portals; they continued to be employed for their fertility-promoting and demon-repelling effects. Nature worship and animistic forms of sexual magic and love magic originating from the Germanic and Slavic traditions remained rooted in popular piety and customs. In Ireland, for example, love charms and spells have been handed down since the sixth century (Borsje 2017). Fertility rites were used to establish a link between the fertility of animals and plants and that of humans. In reverse, it was believed that brides radiated a fertile aura that was transmitted not only to other people, but also to plants and the sowing of seeds. A crop, a stick, or a skewer could stand in for the male penis in fertility rituals and take over its fertilizing function (Ballhaus 2009: 137ff.). Conversely, many people met the childlessness of monks and nuns with skepticism and even avoided their sterile aura for fear of being rendered infertile themselves by the very presence of these asexual beings (Bohaumilitzky and Nägl 1989: 166ff.).

Strict monastic sexual morality penetrated only very slowly through late antiquity and into the Early Middle Ages (*c.* 500 to *c.* 1050) down to the clerics, monks, and nuns in a distilled form. It seems that they followed the laws and prohibitions propagated by the church with a host of reservations in their marital and even more in their pre- and extramarital practices. Wide differences of opinion exist among historians on this issue: James Brundage, for example, saw the demographic stagnation that took place between 500 and 1000 as an indication of the growing influence of the Christian orders of sins and penance on (conjugal) sexual behavior and thought that the low fertility may have been caused by a decrease of sexual intercourse and an increase of abstinence (Brundage 1987: 195ff.). More recent studies emphasize the opposite: that despite the strict church canon, mostly a quite positive, partly also sensual view of marital sexuality prevailed among the Christian laity (Karras 2005; Evans 2011). The hypothesis that the "barbarization" of the Roman Empire and the Germanic "superimposition" led to a widespread "lack of love in the emotions of the early Middle Ages" has itself been met with a cold reception (Dinzelbacher 1993: 79; van Houts 2019: 108ff.).

According to Foucault, the fact that Christian sexual morality was able to spread across large parts of Europe over the centuries was due to its specific mode of subjectivation. The faithful of late antiquity and the Early Middle Ages—at least the educated and literate among them—no longer took the philosophical-medical self-care of the Greeks and Romans as their model. Rather, they subjected themselves to the increasingly unified ecclesiastical rules, which unfolded their effective power by means of pastoral rituals (Foucault 2005a: 177ff.; Brieler 1998: 562ff.). The examination of conscience was one especially powerful ritual, with which they investigated their unchaste thoughts and inspirations. Confession and penance further proved to be particularly efficient techniques of (self-)control—even if this did not take effect across broad sections of the population until the High Middle Ages. The early Christians mainly used self-hermeneutics to purify their souls, but confession, while not obligatory at first, was one of the foundations for the Occident's logocenteric sexual culture. By means of interactive confession and avowal techniques, Christian men and women were to find out the truth about their sexual impulses and not leave any temptation unspoken (Suárez Müller 2004: 320f.). Oral-auricular confession was heard not only by priests. Monks also acted as confessors, being ascetic specialists who knew the insidious temptations of *concupiscentia* from their own world. Erotic-sexual desires and fantasies made it onto the checklist of this reflection on morality, alongside all the sexual acts actually carried out physically (Foucault 2005b: 989ff.). The Greek-Roman sexual regime had primarily been based on the prohibition of certain practices, namely those that were socially, sexually, and ethically as well as dietetically coded. Meanwhile, Christian morality traced the sexual into the very body and soul, and then provided efficient investigative techniques to root it out—as well as subsequent surveillance measures to maintain purity.

When Foucault offered his subjectivation thesis, he primarily had in mind the monks who, since the fourth and fifth centuries, had dealt extensively with sexual problems such as unwanted erections, nocturnal ejaculation, and masturbation (Boyarin and Castelli 2001: 362ff.; Clark 2017). Above all, the *manustupratio* was considered to be a flagrant weakness of will, as it left people with lust and fantasy. Reference to Onan of the Old Testament would have been misplaced as that story was not strictly about masturbation but rather the refusal to procreate in the Jewish levirate (in subsequent marriage to one's brother's widow) and thus about coitus interruptus. Rather, this solitary desire was an act against the plan of creation as it occurred outside the location intended by God and without any intention of reproduction. Canonists from the monastic class also listed other forms of sexual deviance (above all in their own ranks) and subjected them to differentiated casuistry. Sexual life featured prominently in the *libri poenitentiales* (penitential books), which were written between the sixth and twelfth centuries in continental Europe, but originated in Ireland. These registers of sins also contain assigned acts of repentance, ranging from strict fasting to prayers and almsgiving to corporal punishment (Payer 1984; Schwaibold 1988: 111; Lutterbach 1999). Although the penitential books never attained canonic validity, they influenced the further clerical view of sexual life due to their practical orientation. These prohibitions were then also elaborated in detail for the laity from the ninth and tenth centuries. Although priests knew that the layman's everyday life clearly deviated from the church ideal, the aim still was to record and regulate their sexual life—and, in particular, practices beyond the marriage bed (Brundage 1996 and 1987).

Into the High Middle Ages (*c.* 1050–*c.* 1250), private confession was also adapted to the needs of the sin-prone laity, which led to a differentiation of the confessional order. Their sinful sexual life became the center of confession after the Fourth Lateran Council (1215), when the Christian Church demanded from all believers at least once a year, namely at Easter, that they individually come to confess their guilt (Jerouschek 1990: 307). This form of searching for shame and repentance was to contribute significantly to the register of sins being recoded to account for many more inward transgressions and impure thoughts in the following centuries (Maasen 1998: 292ff.). It is impossible to gauge the extent to which the faithful actually complied with obligatory confession. In view of the often rather unchaste way of life of some clerics, they apparently recognized the occasion to confess and take responsibility for their own carnal sins (Haliczer 1996: 11ff.). In the repetitive remission of sins, confessors should in any case adhere to precise (sin) definitions of marital, premarital, and extramarital coitus. The *summae confessorum* (summae of penance), taken down from the twelfth century onward, compiled the older registers of sins, whereby even greater importance was attached to the contexts of the respective actions. The *summae*, in contrast to its predecessors, went into the (relatively) binding canonical legal codes. In so doing, monastic sexual morality ultimately became the guideline for the church's system of norms (Payer 1996: 5ff.).

Decretum and Penitentials of Sexual Acts

Since the middle of the twelfth century, clerics have thus been able to rely on a system of legitimate and illegitimate or chaste and sinful sexual acts. Around 1140, the textual basis was provided by the *Decretum Gratiani*, which aggregated Roman law, papal decrees, council and synodal resolutions, and older collections of laws. Two contributors were Burchard of Worms (around 965–1025) and Ivos of Chartres (around 1040–1115), who also had a lot to say about sexual issues. Until the Reformation the *Decretum* was to represent the church's legal interpretative corpus (Crawford 2007 68). The Camaldolese monk Gratian represented a two-stage model of marriage based on the consent of both spouses, the *matrimonium initiatum*, but was only completed and validated through the consummation of sexual intercourse: *matrimonium ratum et consummatum* (Karras 2012b: 54). Anyone who dared copulate for lust alone, and not to conceive children, were therefore not spouses, but fornicators (from Latin *fornix* "brothel") (Jacquart and Thomasset 1988: 90).

The following sexual offences and sins can be found in the *Decretum*, ranked according to gravity: unnatural acts (bestiality, same-sex acts, oral and anal intercourse, unnatural coitus positions, masturbation); incest; rape and abduction of a nun, a married woman, or a virgin; consensual acts with a spiritual person; dual or individual adultery by a man or a woman (if both partners or only one partner were married); defloration and seduction of a virgin; fornication; unchaste touches and unchaste kisses (Tentler 1977: 141f.). According to canonical law, sexual relations between Christians and non-Christians were not tolerated either. Any such sexual contact was considered heretical and also entailed a severe penitence.

The early and high medieval penitential manuals (Abraham 2017: 91ff.; 118ff.) as well as the decrees (the canons of the first phase) were more or less on the same page in questions of marital intercourse: a paradoxical sexual behavior norm was at the heart of a chaste marriage, according to canon law: "To give to the other that which they are not allowed to want" (Maasen 1998: 268). Coitus was primarily about conception and the fulfillment of marital duties—so the lust felt should remain a necessary, but venial sin. For this reason alone, conjugal intercourse and the associated mental impurity should not take place before Christmas and Easter, during Lent, before the reception of communion, and generally on church holidays (Brundage 1987: 154ff.; Hawkes 2004: 67f.). Detailed lists can also be found for coitus positions beyond the monk/missionary position, in which the spouses faced one another in a human fashion (as opposed to animalistically from behind). In the book of Theodorus of Tarsus (602–690), Archbishop of Canterbury, forty days of penance were doled out for intercourse from behind with the woman kneeling, seven years for oral stimulation of any kind, and ten years for anal penetration (Davies 1991: 90). According to penitential orders, all actions that primarily served pleasure were forbidden. The church authors therefore also considered sensual skin stimulation, uncovered unchaste body parts, and the use of aphrodisiacs to be sinful. For married couples, abstinence seemed to them above all to be an adequate penitential measure to restore the spiritual balance and the relationship with God. More serious sexual sins such as masturbation, conjugal intercourse during menstruation and pregnancy, and unnatural positions, on the other hand, resulted in several weeks or even several months of fasting and sexual asceticism. Several years of penance befell those who dared abort a child or practice prostitution or sodomy. The highest sentences punished the kidnapping of women, adultery, and fornication between relatives (Denzler 1988: 56). The latter incest regulations had already existed in the Frankish regions since the sixth/seventh centuries. These marriage prohibitions extended beyond blood relatives and included marriage relatives as well as spiritual relatives (such as marriages between godparents of the same child). The reasons for this were probably manifold and ranged from fear of mixing the sacred with the sexual, measures against clan alliances between kinship groups, and the long-term strengthening of the monogamous marital couple (Jussen 2014: 103f.).

The lists also envisioned alternative solutions for smaller sexual offences; penitents could obtain an indulgence by means of alms and gifts to the church. The penitential books also stipulated *debitum conjugale* (marital debt *or* duties) that spouses owed to one another and which were attributed as positive values for married life (Makowsky 1977: 99ff.; Persisanifi 2017). It should not be forgotten also that these ecclesiastical writings addressed the priests themselves, for many continued to marry until the twelfth century.

The cornerstones of Christian confession and penance were thus created under monastic leadership. The secrecy of confession ensured that sins could be confessed privately and repeatedly. Based on the sexual repression of the penitential books and lists, some historians have concluded that the medieval church maintained a fundamentally negative attitude toward sexuality. The same historians then projected this onto the sexual life and attitudes of all other Christians as well. As there are hardly any sources to back up the latter claim, it is all the more interesting to ask whether and how these ecclesiastical guidelines affected the average believer. From the sixth to the eighth century, the evangelization of large parts of Central and Western Europe progressed such that a large part of the population could be described as Christianized, and most people were members of a Christian community. But supplying these communities with priests was inconsistent at best. The believers, most of whom lived off the land, attended mass irregularly at best to rarely at all and interacted with the priest only when they needed something from him, for example, a ritual baptism, marriage, or funeral. For this reason alone, the behavioral norms and rules in the books of penance would only have reflected reality to a limited extent (Bitel 2002: 130ff.).

From the twelfth century, the church also claimed legal sovereignty over marriage and sexuality, which is why conjugal conflicts and sexual offences were mostly tried and punished in their courts (Karras 2011: 1011). At the latest with the Fourth Lateran Council (1215), the church also strengthened its pastoral efforts, taking aim at the sexual life of the faithful in doing so. But even in the High and Late Middle Ages (*c.* 1250–1500), the Christian canon affected marital sexuality to a lesser extent in practice than could be assumed on the basis of church sources (Evans 2011: 35). This is also due to the fact that people supplemented Christian rituals with pagan magic and fertility rites and their powerful sexual symbolism. Christianity had to compete with native practices until the early modern period. The few sources from which we can glean any information about these practices suggest that even the priests availed themselves of phallus rituals originating from the Scandinavian Cult of Freyr and Freyja, and indeed pagan conceptions of sin and law (Jones 2011: 140f.). Then there remains the basic fact that the broader population's primary goal in life was marriage and children; (conjugal) sexual intercourse was simply a part of the good life for the average person.

Medieval research has also shown that the monastic norms of sins and confession represent only one side of the church's sexual morality. Anti-sexual tendencies cannot and should not be interpreted as a general attitude of the church (Evans 2011). The church interpretation of the ideal of chastity itself was fluid: The longing for God, for example, became intertwined in clerical language with terms that (according to modern understanding) almost testify to an erotic-physical desire. And like the early Christians, the monks and nuns also described their love of Christ in terms of physical desire, even physical union with Him. As *mulieres fortes* (brave/strong women), nuns should await the arrival of their heavenly bridegroom Christ and, until then, let their carnal feelings succumb to spiritual ecstasy (Wiethaus 1991: 42ff.; Lutter 2008: 65ff.). Their erotic chastity was mostly intended to be spiritual and metaphorical, but could also become a "sexual identity" (Karras 2005: 63). The mystic Margareta Ebner (*c.* 1291–1351) actually kissed the statues and images of Christ she encountered, including a little Christ Child on a necklace which she wore between her breasts. She described the bodily sensations she felt as follows:

> But my desire and my lust are in suckling, that I may be purified by his pure humanity and be kindled out of him with his fervent love, and I may be poured through with his presence and with his sweet grace, that I may be drawn into the true enjoyment of his divine being with all the mincing souls who have lived in the truth. (Frenken 2002: 174)

The Dominican nun Mechthild von Waldeck (late thirteenth century) confessed that Christ wanted to "truely unite with me." He held her "with his divine arms," which for her amounted to: "it is nothing but that you caress me and I caress you and that we both caress each other" (Classen 2008a: 89f.; Dinzelbacher 2007). Especially for nuns, the spiritual love of Christ was to have offered a mystical, yet physical form of ecstasy and experience in some tellings (Bynum 1991: 181ff.). Some contradictory theories put forward the position that medieval clerics and especially monks were not merely desexualized by the church's moral debate but also demasculinized and degraded to a third gender. But monastic believers realized their specific masculinity precisely in that they resisted female seduction or same-sex lust (Karras 2008: 52ff.), which deeply undercuts the thesis.

Ambivalent Sources and Discourses

Most secular clergymen and (to a lesser extent) some of the monastic authors themselves were quite positive about a moderate, procreative, conjugal sexual life for the laity based in mutual love. As the more recent historiography has shown, the sources contain quite controversial statements, depending on the respective text and image genre. Thus, according to Rüdiger Schnell, the church's sexual discourse of the Middle Ages should be differentiated into three strands at least, namely into a dogmatic scholarly or moral theological discourse; a public pastoral and a private pastoral discourse; or, finally, a pastoral theological one (Schnell 2002: 151f.; Bein 2003: 25ff.; Haug 2004: 11ff.; Classen 2008a). In addition, there are types of texts such as literature for religious edification and hagiographies (biographies of saints) as well as general biblical texts and narratives on church history. Depending on whether the texts were written by monks or (a few) nuns, pastoral teachers, priests on site, or religious lay authors, they convey quite varied positions. Even in serious church texts, one does come across humorous and less shameful statements about sexual life. The *Exeter Book*, for example, is a collection of Old English literature written during the Benedictine reform in the tenth century. It features obscene riddles that one would not expect in such a context, but which certainly belonged to the idiom of that time. Riddle number 25 was probably easy to solve also for readers who were strict about their morals at the time:

> I am a marvelous creature, a joy to the ladies, a handy thing for neighbors. I harm no citizens save my slayer alone. My trunk is lofty; I stand up in bed. Down below there's hair—I can't say where. Once in a while, some man's very toothsome daughter, a haughty maid, plucks up her courage and takes me in her hand. She pounces on poor reddish me, seizes my head, and tucks me into a tight spot. Lickety-split, she'll feel the full force of my contact, the one who confines me, a woman with braided hair. That eye will be wet. (Murphy 2011: 221ff.; Davies 2006: 48)

The moral answer was: an onion.

In the tradition, however, the texts preserved primarily—and for a long time those preferred by historiography—originated from the monastic or high church, that is, rather strict milieus. For instance, one finds statements therein by Odo of Cluny (c. 878–942), the second abbot of the Benedictine abbey of the same name and initiator of the Cluniac monastic reforms. He spoke out against the human body in general and that of women in particular—he called the first *cadaver hominis* and the second a "a sack of pus." These statements have been repeatedly used as evidence for the hostility of the medieval church toward all things physical and sexual (Bredekamp 2011: 224). This is also the case with the statements by Francis of Assisi (1181/1182–1226). While he preached that the entire world was indeed God's creation and that the human body was also formed in his image, at the same time, he was plagued throughout his life by skepticism of the body and antagonism toward the sexual, which also found their way into his writings. Thus, he avoided looking directly at women so as not to be stirred by their bodies, and understood sexual asceticism as an earthly effort that brought him heavenly rewards. He even kept his distance from sisterly nuns, because: "The Lord has taken away our wives, but now the devil is providing us with sisters." To ward off overly powerful sexual temptations, he prescribed self-flagellation and baths in ice-cold water for his body, which he also called "brother ass" (Feld 2001: 50ff.).

Odo's and Francis' skeptical attitudes toward the body, women, and sexual acts was mainly due to their monastic environment. Many other statements appear in other clerical contexts that connect marital intercourse with *nullum peccatum* (no sin), and even premarital sex—if the couple had previously been engaged or were planning to marry—was seen as merely a venial sin. Alongside the prolifically loquacious and tradition-heavy rigid churchmen with the powerful weight of the texts they left behind, a complex range of opinions nevertheless did exist, and only extremely liberal doctrines were deemed heresy. It should also not be forgotten that the sexual culture(s) of Europe included others, mainly Germanic, Jewish, and (since the seventh century) Islamic traditions (which will be discussed later) in addition to the Christian discourse.

Sexual heterogeneity was expressed even more strongly in non-church sources and contributed to that shimmering and sometimes ambivalent picture we have of medieval love and sexual life. Unlike their clerical contemporaries, the authors of literary, legal, historical, and medical works often laid out a rather crude and sensuous scenario. Yet, these sources, too, must be questioned in so far as they reveal the moral, pedagogical, or satiric-parodist goals they pursued based on their clients and the audiences whom the writers had in mind. Obscene texts, for example, presented the urban and rural lower classes as a "sex-obsessed" folk who did not adhere to the strict moral standards preached by the elite. But this was not at all a realistic reflection of the medieval population's sexual behavior. These texts were meant either to be moralistic or—on the contrary—"pornographic" (Ziolkowski 1998). Many of the texts that have been handed down were oral traditions first and foremost, then copied over and over through the ages and thus constantly and subtly changed. One may search for a term corresponding to the modern concept of sexuality in medieval sources, but to do so would be in vain. The texts—as well as pictures and objects—brought up the sexual aspect above all when it was a matter of carnal desire and fornication, when virginity and chastity (or the opposite) were discussed, or when one's marital duty and reproduction were at issue (Karras 2001: 279; Burger 2018: 117). And, of course, sexuality is also mentioned in those sources that deal with love; although medieval ideas were far removed from modern or romantic ideals of love.

In the following discussion on medieval sexuality, the relatively long timeframe of this epoch (*c.* 500–1500) should not be forgotten. Over these ten centuries, both the nature and structure, but above all the number of sources changed dramatically, leaving historians an immensely rich tradition to explore: From the penitential books of the sixth century to the courtly *minnelyrics* and the *fabliaux* (French tales of frivolity) of the twelfth to the fourteenth century to the court records of the fifteenth and sixteenth centuries, not only did their textual expressions change but also their genres and their sociocultural context. In talking about medieval sexual forms, such large-scale shifts in sources must also be taken into consideration. For a long time, the dissemination and reception of texts were limited to a small ecclesiastical and elite secular class that could read and write—the same applies to the possession of the mostly quite expensive writings. What was hardly available for a very long time were autobiographical sources, such as letters, in which sexual experiences and personal ideas are reported— as we can infer from writings from later centuries—and which would provide insights into stronger first-person accounts (Karras 2005: 23ff.).

Like the Greco-Roman sources, the medieval texts and images prove to be polysemous: they drew from complex symbolic-narrative repertoires and iconological programs. All this makes them susceptible to controversial readings and interpretations, but also increases the allure of medieval sexual history.

The process of Christianity's ecclesiasticalization lasted until the eleventh and twelfth centuries, and it was associated with recurring economic, social, and ecological crises. The European climate from the eighth to the thirteenth century was fundamentally favorable and made innovative economic developments possible—such as the agricultural revolution of the three-field system in the Early Middle Ages and the expansion of grain production into pastures through the eleventh to the fourteenth century (Mitterauer 2003: 1ff.)—but large parts of Europe faced-off against invasions, especially by Arabs, Vikings, Magyars, and Mongols. In the twelfth century, these conflicts were less of a threat. Between 1095, the conquest of Jerusalem, and the thirteenth century, the crusaders were able to conquer back former Christian territory for the first time, and then there was the successful *Reconquista* on the Iberian Peninsula between the tenth and the middle of the thirteenth century. In view of this stabilization, the Roman Church and the nobles as well could increasingly deal with internal problems, including gender relations, love, and sexuality (Classen 2011a: 7f.). All this led to a real boom of relevant topics across low and high literature, in philosophical discourse, in medical writings, and in theological treatises.

Discourses on Marriage, Love, and Sexual Desire

According to Christian sexual norms, sexual intercourse should remain enclosed within marriage, serve for reproduction, and promote love between the spouses. Yet, in the choice of a spouse, affection and desire did not come first. Social and economic motives were the foremost concerns. Betrothals were usually arranged and sealed by parents and relatives—only in later centuries were they blessed by a priest. The spouses were tasked with maintaining or increasing property and possessions and continue the family traditions and lineage. When looking for a partner and initiating marriage, therefore, a multitude of social, economic, and sometimes also political factors came into play for the parties involved—the potential couple as well as the families, relatives, and community—to take into consideration (Signori 2011: 13ff.). In view of such diverse demands, the hope of offspring, indeed fulfilling the commandment to be fruitful, was always a feature of conjugal coitus for young couples. At an advanced age, however, unwanted pregnancies were a threat due to the lack of adequate and unsafe contraceptive methods. Unwanted illegitimate children, on the other hand, presented a Sword of Damocles hovering over premarital and extramarital liaisons. The connection between the sexual act and procreation weighed much more heavily for women than for men in view of the social guidelines, rules, and sanctions. Single mothers and their illegitimate children, who over the centuries were pushed ever farther to the edge of society, were particularly affected. Indeed, they were even (partly) also legally worse off.

Tribal, Roman, and Christian Marriage Laws and Practices

Before Christian sexual norms became established, a monotheistic belief had to establish itself among the clans and tribes that had immigrated and settled in Central, Western, and Northern Europe from the fourth to the sixth century. Subsequently, the empires of the Ostrogoths (in Italy and parts of the Balkans), the Visigoths (in Spain and southern/western France), the Franks (in large parts of France, Switzerland, and Germany), the Angles, Saxons, and Jutes (in Britain, northern Germany, and Denmark), and finally the Lombards (in Italy) emerged. Their orally handed down tribal laws merged with Roman legal norms (especially the *Codex Iustinianus* of 528) between the fifth and tenth centuries. Therein, numerous explications about the sexes, marriage, and family as well as sexual behavior can be found, which often do not in fact differ too much from the rules of the Roman *familia* and *patria postestas*. Here too, however, it should be remembered that the laws handed down didn't necessarily correspond to lived practices.

According to the tribal laws, the marriage covenant formed the center of the Germanic and subsequently Christianized or Romanized families and familial clans. Marriage initiation and formation were to be regulated by and through kinship. Some of the early medieval elites and upper classes, such as the Frankish rulers of the sixth to eighth centuries, however, had multiple marriages that corresponded to their customary rights (Friedl 1996: 35f.; Mohr 2009: 41ff.). What kind of marriage came into play or existed, nevertheless, can hardly be determined in view of the collection of sources influenced by Roman optics. For a long time, the so-called *Muntehe* (after *munt*, the bride's price or dowry) was seen as a possible form that marriage could take, in which guardianship over the wife was transferred to the husband, while the family of origin nevertheless continued to function as a protective association. This is only reasonably certain for the Lombard kingdom in Italy, however, which was strongly Roman in character and understood *munt* as analogous to *manus*, the power of the husband's control in Roman times. His patriarchal rights included the use of the female body and authority over the children they had in common. It was further assumed that the so-called *Friedelehe* (from the Middle High German *Friedel* for lovers' marriage) existed alongside the *Muntehe*. *Friedelehe* allegedly came about without a *munt* and was based more on consensus between the partners, legally offering the woman greater latitude. The *Kebsehe* referred to marriage to a slave. Here, too, there is a great deal of conceptual confusion, ranging from an analogy to the Roman distinction between *conubium* (cohabitation/ marriage among free citizens) and *contubernium* (marriage/bond between non-citizens or unfree) and the relatively free long-term relationships with a concubine. These forms of marriage constructed by historiography are, however, only documented for a rather limited geographical area (Lombard Italy) (Esmyol 2002: 6ff.; Karras 2006). On the basis of the current state of research, it can therefore only be said with certainty for early medieval marriage that a whole series of marital or marriage-like types existed and some of them were more strongly bound and had more rights for spouses and descendants than others, and could be dissolved with equally variable degrees of difficulty (Karras 2006: 130). The evolution toward a strong position of the married couple alongside a simultaneous weakening of male and female kinship influences can be observed for the Frankish culture since Roman times—with still dominant male lines of descent and strong kinship groups (Jussen 2014: 101ff.).

In the early medieval Germanic and Viking regions, girls were eligible for marriage from the age of about thirteen, boys one or two years later. Engagement or betrothal could take place much earlier, though. The aristocracy betrothed their children for political reasons, sometimes as early as five years of age. In practice, husbands of the upper class were usually eight to ten years older than their wives (Angenendt 1990: 195; van Houts 2019: 89f., Mueller-Vollmer and Wolf 2022: 14). The betrothal and marriage were to be performed by the bride's father, and the marriage covenant became a contract sealed by witnesses. The marriage was validated by a wedding ceremony, but not only: the husband then had to lead his wife home, successfully share the marriage bed with her, and present her with a morning gift. According to early medieval tribal laws, the purpose of marriage was twofold: marriage was intended to connect families and clans and thus possibly resolve conflicts (Magnúsdóttir 2008: 42ff.). In addition to marriage, these societies also practiced concubinage and polygamy. In the latter case, this led to a widening of the age gap between couples in later marriages. One consequence of this was that strong competition developed between men of higher social status and property for women, and those less well-off had fewer opportunities—aggression, coercion, and abduction were their common reactions to this (Raffield, Price and Collard 2017: 169ff.).

In addition, it was important to sire offspring, preferably sons. Love, individual affection, or sexual desire between the spouses was not considered a prerequisite—but it was certainly desired as a means to settle into married life. The bride's virginity was fundamental for assuring lawful descent of the firstborn. Failure to sire offspring meant that the husband could seek out another wife or it could even represent a reason to declare as heir any son from another non-marital relationship. It is not surprising that in the assessment of female characteristics, fertility ranked above beauty (Saar 2002: 100ff.). It should not be forgotten, however, that enslaved women who were captured and abducted during raids were not only considered merchandise, but also functioned as brides and concubines (Raffield, Price and Collard 2017: 182; Heebøll-Holm 2021). Even in later times, from the ninth to the fourteenth century, sexual violence was part of everyday life in the Old Norse world. In the face of Viking raids and warfare, the slave trade and rape of captured men and women was widespread in Northern Europe (Bell 2023).

The so-called spouse-centered family developed in Central and Western Europe—roughly west of the line from St Petersburg to Trieste—in the Early Middle Ages. It emerged from family forms in the *villication* system (from Lat. *villa*), which had established itself in the seventh century, especially in the Frankish Empire, and was widely used as a successful form of land rule in the ninth and tenth centuries. Around a *Fronhof* (estate villa) managed by the landlord there were several smaller farms (*Hufen*) or settlements. These were managed by "villein" (serf/peasant) farmers, their families, and additional workers. For land use, they had to pay a yield levy (*Zehent*, a tithe) and perform (forced) labor for the landlord (Slav. *robota*). In the High and Late Middle Ages, the personal *Hörigkeit* (bondage) of the peasants to the landlord was transferred to a rent-based system of rule, solely for pragmatic reasons. It was increasingly characteristic of spouse-centered families that only parent–child groups would live together in the same household, sometimes along with boy servants and maids as well as related and unrelated household members. Multigenerational or ancestral families, on the other hand, became rare, since the older peasant couple would hand over the management of the farm to the male heir (usually the eldest son), for example, when economic performance was declining or at the landlord's instigation. Then, with the takeover, he would marry, found his own family, and assume management of the household with his wife. From this point onward, the older peasants retreated from the main house to outlying hovels and were now considered to be merely fellow occupants. The consequence of this family system was that the inheriting sons were already relatively old by the time of marriage, and a not inconsiderable proportion of the (non-inheriting) descendants and all those who were unable to found their own estates remained single (Mitterauer 2003: 70ff.). Due to the success of this economic system, the spouse-centered family also prevailed in the newly founded cities. Even among craftsmen and tradesmen, first marriages came later, and a significant proportion of the populace remained single for a transitional period. In contrast to multigenerational clans, the ties of descent and the associated rites and traditions (such as blood revenge) were also eased in the spouse-centered families.

In Central and Western Europe, the parent–child family became that unit on which the Catholic Church could base its sexual teaching, or at least the non-celibate part of it. Late marriage meant that many people lived through a relatively long youth, which they spent partly as workers in another household or even further afield, wandering the countryside looking for work. After sexual maturity—according to the church guidelines—they should all live out these several years without sexual activity. It was not until marrying and taking over or founding one's own household that one may imagine a realization of sexual desire in marital pleasures. For some groups of the population, however, marriage remained a far distant prospect, which meant that wedded union rose considerably in stature as an overall life goal. From the twelfth century, the baptized considered matrimony to be concluded before and by God and therefore beyond dissolution—except when some obstacle such as a pre-existing marriage, sterility, or the impossibility of intercourse (of the man or the woman) or consanguinity (up to the fourth degree, since the Fourth Lateran Council in 1215) made annulment a possibility (Brundage 1996: 38; Rouillard 2020: 22f.). Discussions about companionship and a love-based foundation of lifelong marital relationships stemming from late antiquity once again intensified in the twelfth and thirteenth centuries (Schnell 2002: 165). In view of the high mortality rates (often of the wife in childbed), subsequent marriages also had to be taken into consideration, as the household economy forced the remaining spouses to remarry (Signori 2011: 52ff.).

What the Husband Can Do to His Wife

In the Christian Middle Ages, men were also regarded as playing the active part in sexual matters, and premarital and extramarital relationships were more likely to be tolerated for them, whereby socially higher-ranking persons were preferred. Women were assumed to have a rather passive-receptive attitude (Kane 2022: 42; Den Hartog 2021: 639f.). If they showed obvious sexual interest, they were soon suspected of being full of (sinful) lust. The art of a sensitive husband was to read from the body language of his wife whether or not she longed for him. Even if this may seem anachronistic at first, women were also considered the more sensual and sexual sex in this time period, as their constitution predestined them for reproduction. In source texts they are therefore described as fundamentally shameful, but nevertheless full of sensual attractiveness, even activity in the marriage bed. Sexual contacts before and during marriage should clearly be more strictly sanctioned for the female sex. Even if the sources differ depending on the genus and target audience, sexual acts were associated with specific expectations for both sexes—or as Ruth Mazo Karras puts it: Men and women imagined each "doing different things" (Karras 2005: 32). Medieval literature, which was mostly written by men, assumes that the man did something with the woman during coitus and that the woman in turn welcomed and wanted that which he was actively doing. He was expected to take the initiative—animated and enticed by his female counterpart—and act accordingly. Apparently contradictory things would come together in male behavior: Men should be sexually aggressive and engaging, but at the same time act moderately and in a controlled manner, following their own rationale and free will. Women were supposed to be the real seducers, driven by their sexual desire (Karras 2003: 82). In medieval terminology, sexual intercourse was referred to as "carnal knowledge," where the man actively knows his wife, and the woman passively is to be known. This gender-specific differentiation was found not only in religious literature, but also in late medieval court records such as the *Registre criminel du Châtelet de Paris* (Hutchison 2020: 134).

In the words of Étienne de Fougères (1168–1178), the Bishop of Rennes, the division of gender roles in the *Livre de manières* (Book of Customs) sounds like this:

> If a wife loves her husband, she sins neither against God nor man. Unworried, she speaks to him and turns to him with her longing.—By Holy Mary! No joy is as certain as that of husbands and wives, never will their joy be taken away from them.—They give each other as much pleasure as they both think good; they do not care who finds them together. Cursed be the joy that you hide, or for which you always tremble with fear.—What sin is in a young girl for the one who desires out of folly, the husband can do to his wife without too hard a penance. (Schnell 2002: 450)

Even if the roles and practices of marital sexuality were unequally distributed, the evaluation of pleasure and "satisfaction" did not necessarily have to be a burden on the female side. Ideas of sexual desire at that time were very different from those of today's Western societies: in the theological writings, it was attributed to *luxuria*, alternatively *libido*—one of the seven deadly sins that arose from the primary human vices (Niiranen 2015: 231). Both terms had to do with excessive lust, but not only sexuality was meant—other affects such as greed and ambition also belonged in this category. As with all desires, (sexual) lust was also about striking the right measure, a physical–emotional balance and the avoidance of excess (Lochrie 2011: 43). It should also be remembered that in ecclesiastical literature, at least since Gratian in the middle of the twelfth century, the marital debt was established and made it unmistakably clear that both spouses had the duty to perform sexual intercourse regularly (Persisanifi 2017: 511ff.).

In his writing *Dragmaticon Philosophiae*, the philosopher William of Conches (1080–1154) thought that it was necessary for successful fertilization that women also felt sexual pleasure and satisfaction during sexual intercourse. The text was written as a dialogue between a duke and philosopher and contained the following passage:

> Duke: I recall what you just said, that nothing is conceived without seed of the woman, but this is not plausible. For we see that raped women, who have suffered violence despite their protest and weeping, still have conceived. From this it is apparent that they had no pleasure from such an act. But without pleasure the sperm cannot be released.

Philosopher: Although raped women dislike the act in the beginning, in the end, however, from the weakness of the flesh, they like it. (Harris 2017: 134f.)

This argumentation, which is difficult for today's readers to understand, corresponded to the Hippocratic doctrine of semen, according to which women also ejaculated a semen during lustful coitus and this semen produced the new being together with the male counterpart.

Other medieval texts deal with the ways in which women could benefit from their marital duty or the sexual services to which they were entitled. For any emotional deficits it was the men who were blamed, as was the case for lack of intercourse or poor sexual performance (Elliott 1999: 35ff.). This was particularly striking in writings on widows. According to common belief, a widow's sexual drive had been ignited during the marriage and did not immediately die down after the death of her husband but continued to smolder (at least for a while) (Cadden 1993: 275). Sexually desirable widows therefore stood for independent female lust par excellence (McCarthy 2004: 11). Medieval literature also deals extensively with balanced sexual pleasure and satisfaction—a further indication that this field of life was under cultural tension in the Middle Ages and that there were a great many differences of opinion between religious, medical, social, and literary discourse. Whereas the debate on the consensual fulfilment of marital duties focused primarily on the salvation of the spouse's soul before the thirteenth century, this topic was eclipsed in later centuries by the routine fulfillment of everyday marital life, thereby also sexual duties (Schnell 2002: 216).

Sexual Desire in the Medieval Body Mechanics

Medieval doctors and scholars of the natural world also studied how men and women functioned sexually. Their psychophysiological concepts mostly had Greek roots and were later translated (from Greek and Arabic) into Latin. Since many of the medical authorities were at the same time educated theologians, they integrated the Christian worldview into their medical explanations. Beyond these similarities, there was little agreement in their writings on the functions of the male and female sexual body. Tension lines ran between classical—Hippocratic, Aristotelian, Soranic, and Galenic—theories of gender and reproduction for the most part and the resulting character consequences for men and women (Tasioulas 2011): Did animation at conception come solely through the male seed (according to Aristotle, 384–322 BCE) or did two equally potent *fluida* come together (according to Galen, *c.* 129–200/215)? If women did indeed produce procreative seed—and not only formed the fertile ground for the being produced by the man—did they have to experience an orgasm to release the juice, or did this happen involuntarily with penetration? The Arab-Greek physician Constantine the African (*c.* 1020–1087), for example, subscribed to the dual-seed theory and awarded women a double pleasure prize: their arousal would be fundamentally more powerful than a man's because during coitus they not only secreted their own seed but also received the male's seed (Cadden 1993: 57ff.).

There was also disagreement about the anatomical details and functions of the female reproductive organs, such as the clitoris and labia (Jacquart and Thomasset 1988: 44ff.). Two different ideas of the clitoris existed according to Greek-Roman medicine on the one hand and Arabic on the other: One held the clitoris to be a body part that could swell like a penis and then give women an active-penetrative potential. The other, expressed by Ibn Sina (Lat. Avicenna; 980–1037), who united Greek, Roman, and Persian medicine and whose canon remained one of the medical reference works until well into the early modern era, saw the clitoris to primarily serve sexual stimulation and pleasure. Considerate and experienced men should therefore rub it with their hands before penetration (Lochrie 2005: 76ff.). The majority of doctors, however, assumed that the male genitals were the basic standard, because they were more developed and directed outward due to the man's allegedly higher body temperature; the female genitals would thus be merely an inferior, underdeveloped version of the same (Downham Moore 2020). Because of his body heat, the man's urge for sexual acts would also be greater; he has to be more active in bed and can experience a more intense climax.

As in ancient times, the medieval body mechanics were determined by four humors (blood, phlegm, yellow and black bile) and the temperaments associated with them (sanguine, phlegmatic, choleric, melancholic). The male and female body produced these fluids differently, whereby the latter did not completely process the food taken in and was forced to excrete more (e.g., in the form of menstruation). Due to the heat deficit, so goes the thinking, female sexual organs were thus also located inside the body (Laqueur 1992: 80ff.). The followers of the Aristotelian tradition believed that the female body, due to its low temperature level, could not cook up the seed (from the blood) suitable for reproduction. Aristotelians also thought it would be against nature to oblige a woman to lifelong virginity, e.g., as nuns, for in order to maintain homeostasis the uterus must be used for its proper purpose. Vincent of Beauvais (1184/1194–c. 1264) set sexual maturity between the ages of twelve and fourteen in his encyclopedic work *Speculum maius*, in which he refers to the ancient authorities (Read 2015: 17). Because of their specific genitalia, he maintained that women would be the more sexual sex, but that they experienced less arousal peaks than men. The sexual aspect in them acted like a fire smoldering at low temperature and kept them permanently ready for reproduction (Cadden 1996: 57).

Women achieved greater pleasure from coitus, whereas men wanted it more. The uterus, and with it the female being as a whole, served as a *vas* (vessel) for the generative male seed (Le Goff and Troung 2007: 58ff.). This psychomechanical body image could have precarious consequences in the case of rape: If a woman became pregnant, this physical manifestation raised theological and moral questions in addition to legal and medical ones. Had she really remained pure or chaste in spirit or had she motivated the perpetrator to his actions or even tempted him? According to the Hippocratic-Galenic theory of humors, it was assumed that female ejaculation was necessary for conception and that this was associated with sexual arousal or orgasm. Therefore, women who became pregnant from a rape had gotten pleasure from it and thus lost their purity and chastity.

The Balance of Carnal Lust

Until early modern times, doctors advised sexual moderation and physical balance for health reasons alone. According to an *ars* manuscript (explanations of the three families of arts: *ars liberales*, *ars magicae*, and *ars mechanicae*) of the fifteenth century, *mynne* (coitus) had to be practiced regularly to ward off diseases. But intercourse with the *ehlich weip* (honorable wife) should only take place when one has *gute lust*. Men had to make sure that their bodies had digested all the food they'd eaten and that they had urinated properly and that the coitus did not consume all their physical strength. Prolonged build-up of seed was assumed to have negative effects, and some medieval doctors even advised therapeutic masturbation. Avicenna, for example, recommended manual seed extraction as part of a cure for female "hysteria" (Hawkes 2004: 79f.; Clark 2017: 465). The doctors' orders in these matters butted up against the limits of the Christian morality paradigm, which is why the most common therapy for seed congestion was a cooling diet rather than any of the abovementioned cures. In the case of male impotence, psychological and physical causes were not the only thing or even the first to come to mind—magic was often at hand. From the ninth to the fifteenth century, sources are found in which (married) women in particular are suspected of having been impotent and the men who brought the complaint usually sought annulment of the marriage bond (Rider 2006: 208, 2016).

In cases where the sexual system was out of balance, physicians could consult collections of medical prescriptions (Niiranen 2015). The Anglo-Saxon *Medicina de quadrupedibus* from the tenth/eleventh century offered potions against impotence, stimulants for sexual desire, remedies that promoted regular menstruation or even triggering it in the event of unwanted pregnancy (Van Arsdall 2002: 103). Preparations from animal and plant ingredients considered to be potent could be concocted to increase pleasure in women, as in the following recipe:

> For a woman's pleasure: mix the gall from a buck with frankincense and the seeds of a nettle. Grease the penis with this before intercourse. The woman will receive pleasure from the act of sex (Davies 1991: 90).

Bald's Leechbook, an Old English compilation of medical knowledge from the ninth century, contains a mix of Greek and Anglo-Saxon recipes that were supposed to help men with too much or too little sexual desire:

If a man be too salacious, boil water agrimony in foreign ale; let me drink thereof at night fasting. If a man be too slow *ad venerem*, boil the ilk wort in milk; then you will give him courage. Boil in ewe's milk, again, hindheel, alexanders, the wort which hight (called) Fornet's palm, then it will be with him as he would liefest [desire to] have it be. (Pigg 2017: 125)

In both cases, it was a matter of bringing men back into equilibrium whose carnal lust had knocked them off balance. Certain foods, spices, and drink to increase pleasure can also be found in pharmaceutical manuscripts such as the *Medicina Antiqua* from the first half of the thirteenth century. Take, for example, this rather expensive recipe for the treatment of impotence: The root of the herb *satirion* is to be rubbed with white pepper (at that time a luxury spice) and mixed with wine and honey, should be drunken for three days to restore one's sexual prowess (Bein 2003: 114). As in these cases, folk remedies and ancient medical tradition were in lively exchange throughout the Middle Ages with quite bit of cross-fertilization (Kieckhefer 1991).

From the middle of the thirteenth century and the boom in translations of Aristotle into Latin, single (male) seed theory gained increasing ground, and the procreative role of women was now mostly classified by medical experts as receiving and nourishing. The female body thus provided the incomplete substance for reproduction, the male seed revived it. Since no female sperm existed, according to this teaching, women did not necessarily have to reach sexual climax for conception—they did not even need to be emotionally involved. Some authors even thought about spiritual fertilization, for which no direct physical contact seemed necessary and the proximity of the male fluid alone was sufficient. Stories about pregnancies caused by bath water into which a man had masturbated did not lack a certain plausibility in the face of such theories. For Albertus Magnus (*c.* 1200–1280), the pioneer of Christian Aristotelianism, the fluids secreted by the female body during coitus also had no life-giving power whatsoever—this came from the man alone. He divided women into sexual types of different temperatures according to age and marital status, and classified their desire as dependent on seasonal variations and the constellation of the stars at birth. Men, too, displayed similar factors, giving rise to an individual "sexual profile" (Schnell 2002: 345). Black and dark-skinned women, for instance, would produce breast milk of a higher quality because of their special body heat and they would experience sexual acts more intensely (Biller 2005: 488).

For the practical implementation of the single seed model, physicians and theologians suggested a specific position for intercourse: The woman should lie on her back and stretch the pelvis toward the man kneeling above her with her legs spread wide apart. In this receptive posture, the generative vital juice of the man should be poured directly into the vessel of the female uterus, whereby any lusty arousal would remain minimal (Tasioulas 2011: 129). From the twelfth century, discussion about the sexual availability of women in treatises on marital duties grew, but analogous demands on men were approached with less verve (Lochrie 2011: 50). For one thing, if the (unfulfilled) erotic imagination became exaggerated in a woman, she would succumb to *amor hereos*, a lovesickness that Galen had already described and which medical doctors found difficult to cure (Haage 1990). Conversely, late medieval physicians also racked their brains over various male reproductive disorders. Ancient Greek and Arabic classics that had been translated into Latin in the late eleventh to thirteenth centuries sowed confusion. Questions revolved around a lack of seminal moisture and physical heat, which led to low spirits (related to distillation processes) and too little desire and energy for coitus and resulted in impotence and lack of or low seminal discharge (Rider 2016: 253ff.).

Medieval physicians busied themselves adapting ancient body concepts, of health or sickness alike, to the prevailing gender order and harmonizing the classical humoral theory and temperature (especially for women) with the Christian worldview. Their psychophysiological sexes and characteristics regularly collided with social reality in which the rigid juxtaposition of sexual types did not correspond to lived diversity. What physicians, natural philosophers, and especially theologians had to say about sexual conditions often differed clearly from what (married) couples practiced.

Fighting Concubinages and Sacralization of Marriage

For anyone living in long-term relationships not based on a Christian marriage the difference was evident. Social elites practiced concubinage throughout the Middle Ages (Rouillard 2020). Among the elites, polygyny was also common throughout Europe in the High Middle Ages (Rüdiger 2020). The second wives usually came from a lower strata and (together with their children) often had symbolic claims to the lover and his position, apart from financial ones (Wemple 1993: 229). With the Merovingians, for example, the oldest Frankish royal family (fifth to the mid-eighth century), concubines and mistresses came into play already among the princes, who were sometimes married at the age of fifteen. Theudebert II (585–612), who stemmed from a relationship between King Childebert II (570–596) and one of his concubines, was still able to become king (Esmyol 2002: 45ff.). Only in the eighth to the tenth century did concubinage and such alternatives to marriage recede. This did not mean that the social elites didn't continue to maintain longer extramarital or secondary relationships; concubines gradually became mistresses, courtesans, and lovers (Saar 2002: 219ff.). The Carolingian kings promoted the inheritability of kingship for the next generation. It was not important whether the heir to the throne came from the paternal or maternal lineage, but what his social status was, which is why sons of concubines were also eligible (McDougall 2017: 66ff.; Stofferahn 2017).

Not to be underestimated is also the *spread* of concubinage among the middle and lower classes. In Spain, the *unión de barraganía* (non-marital concubinage) was a legal form of cohabitation found in all secular laws. Until the second half of the thirteenth century, even clerics were allowed to live with an unmarried woman. Canon law, however, forbade such unions. But this did not prevent Catalonian clergy from doing so, of whom between 70 and over 90 percent lived in concubinage, for example, according to episcopal visitation reports in the first half of the fourteenth century (Armstrong-Partida 2013: 169f., 2019: 195ff.). Until the fifteenth century, unmarried couples who wanted to enter into this kind of life partnership had to make it known publicly before witnesses and only then were they allowed to live together officially. In most cases, these were temporary relationships that could be broken up just as quickly—unless there was a formal promise of marriage. The woman often drew the worst lot in such separations, because the *uniòns de barraganía* were not particularly respected, and the women were suspected of leading immoral lives. In the case of unofficial concubinage, she could also be accused of secret prostitution on top of fornication. Alonso Fernández de Madrigal (*c.* 1400/10–1455), the bishop of Ávila, said that "simple fornication with a prostitute, with a concubine or with a widow was the least sin of pleasure" (Lacarra Lanz 2002: 163). Even if the church considered such cohabitation to be fornication, it would have to continue to tolerate it. The social status of these couples living together in a non-marital union was furthermore subject to deep disparity: Men defined themselves through a variety of social and symbolic forms of capital, such as honor, social power, and control over the family household. For women, this depended primarily on their sexual reputation—and this, in turn, reflected their low social status, because otherwise (if they had been pure and chaste) someone would have married them (Karras 2012b: 68ff.).

Charlemagne (747/48–814) took a big step toward the ecclesiastical institutionalization of marriage by stipulating that it had to be announced by church proclamation—in order to prevent multiple marriages and remarriages (during a partner's lifetime). Pope Nicholas I (820–867) regarded mutual consent as a central prerequisite—that the future spouses agreed to their union and that this was not left up to the parents alone. If a priest was involved in the wedding, this served to further secure the marriage, but it wasn't yet foundational (Leppin 2012: 137f.). In the twelfth century, the church was able to assert itself at least to the extent that marriage before a priest was considered the only legitimate form and concubinage was forbidden by both secular and canon law. From the Second Lateran Council (1139), and confirmed by the Synod of Verona (1184), marriage was considered a sacrament. The wedding celebrations were now to take place on the church premises, with the spouses administering the sacrament of marriage to each other in front of the priest. In the twelfth and thirteenth centuries, the conflict between representatives of the consensus and copulation theory of marriage was also resolved.

The former had required the mutual agreement of the spouses, the latter had maintained that a marriage was not complete until intercourse was successfully undertaken. Pope Alexander III (*c.* 1100/5–1181) brought the two together in that he declared marriage must be anchored in spoken vows and completed with the physical act. (In exceptional cases, an engagement could be annulled if—before physical consummation and within a certain period of time—one of the spouses decided to enter a religious order to dedicate his or her life to religion.) This also meant that the priest endowed the actual sacrament, and the marriage—if both spouses agreed—could then also be carried out as a Josephite marriage, that is, without sexual union (Dannenberg 2008: 230ff.). In canon law, the following provisions for a Christian marriage were written down between 1150 and 1250: Marriage between man and woman was to be monogamous, it could only be concluded on the basis of the consent of both spouses at marriageable age, and it must be bestowed as a sacrament. Woman and man had to be able to perform conjugal coitus. A marriage existed as long as both spouses lived. In addition, there were a number of impediments to marriage: Close relatives (up to the fourth degree) were not allowed to marry, nor were already married persons; marriage to members of a non-Christian denomination was prohibited unless they converted (Donahue 2016: 33).

There is a controversial discussion on the question of whether priests also began to participate in the wedding ceremonies of families at this time—continuing a practice that was initiated by the bishops in the Early Middle Ages (Radle 2018). Part of their striving for supremacy in the ritual was to sprinkle the marriage bed with holy water and to cleanse the room with incense to drive out any lurking demons (Ariès 1992: 179). The church rituals adopted pagan symbolism and wedding customs among Jews and early Christians alike. In Sweden, the bride was brought to the groom's house in a wedding procession, and the celebrations that followed showed what marriage consummation should be about, for example, tossing grain at the couple and offering toasts. After the bridal couple were bedded by the most important wedding guests—a ceremonial practice that was also common in Germany, England, and France—the priest blessed the bridal chamber and bed and invoked the fertility of the new covenant (Korpiola 2009: 60ff.). Interventions with rites like these provide evidence for the clergy increasingly exercising spiritual sovereignty over marriage, turning it from a private affair between families into a public church act. The Fourth Lateran Council (1215) then confirmed that Christians had to announce marriage by means of an ecclesiastical banns and, moreover, priests were disallowed from taking part in a secret arrangement under any circumstances—both of which further consolidated clerical dominance in marriage matters.

Quite a few clergymen, as well as bishops, for their part continued to live in long-term relationships, thus snubbing their morally strict brothers and sisters in faith. Their domestic companions, however, increasingly faced harsh criticism, once insulted as "priest whores" (Moos 2005: 202). Priests continued to marry as before; in some places there were veritable priestly dynasties in which the parish was passed on from father to son along with the office. A famous sexual case concerned the clergyman and philosopher Peter Abelard (1079–1142), who used his position as educator to seduce his much younger pupil Heloise (c. 1095–c. 1164). They established a long-term relationship, he impregnated her and married her secretly. Heloise's family and especially her uncle and guardian Fulbert (around 1060–1142) could not come to terms with their behavior and eventually had Abelard castrated.

Purity and Celibacy for Priests and Bishops

From the ninth to the fourteenth century, popes and bishops tried to enforce celibacy with increasing vigor. By the eighth century already, the ritual position of priests at the celebration of mass changed and with it the claim to their moral and spiritual purity. The mass was meant to commemorate the sacrifice of Christ on the cross, and with that rite the priest took center stage as God's representative vis-à-vis the congregation. Priests were the only ones allowed to handle His (symbolic) body. The purity necessary to do so precluded any sexual intercourse beforehand. Boniface (around 673–754/5) reported to Pope Zacharias in 742 that he repeatedly encountered deacons who had lived in sin their whole lives and yet were ordained priests, wanted to intercede for the people and offer the holy sacrament. To him, this seemed incompatible (Leppin 2012: 87f.). In 1022, the Synod of Pavia decided, under threat of church punishments, that priests were no longer allowed to marry. Ritual purity was just one reason, the other being offices and property being passed on within the family. First off, descendants of priests' concubines should no longer be legally recognized (Wertheimer 2006: 393). The newly emerging dynasty threatened ecclesiastical centralism, especially among married higher dignitaries. If, on the other hand, the priests remained unmarried altogether, the bishops could fill the vacant posts at their discretion after the death of the previous officeholder and confiscate any inheritance. If the synods got their way, the priests' wives and children would even have been degraded to serfdom. However, since the practice of priest marriages and concubinages hardly changed, there was unrest. Shortly after the middle of the eleventh century in Milan, for instance, downright revolts against the "degenerate priesthood" broke out in northern Italy's most populous city (Goez 2008: 75f.). In the diocese of Braga in northern Portugal, a legate of Pope Gregory IX in 1228 discovered that a considerable number of priests were descended from non-marital relationships. This was a fundamental violation of canon law, which required a legitimate birth for this office and voted strictly against any priestly contact with the concubinate (McDougall 2019: 138f.). In Northern Europe, the establishment of priestly celibacy took much longer. In Norway, it was mentioned for the first time only in

1237, in Sweden in 1248; there priestly marriages held out for a long time indeed (Hemmie 2007: 93f.).

The tightening of celibacy regulations led to a decline in clergy marriages, but concubinage still increased. While priests were no longer marrying by the Late Middle Ages, they ought nevertheless to carry on modeling a moral life for the laity—a life in concubinage with illegitimate children was no proof of the ritual and moral purity and superiority of the clergy (Karras 2012b: 116ff.). It is not surprising that church authors also condemned concubinage and portrayed the clergymen in such relationships as victims of a women's power. Allegedly, the shameful companions regularly violated church property and promoted moral depravity among the lower churchmen (Tanner 2005: 125ff.). For the French canonist Jacques de Vitry (1160/70–1240), clerics who kept concubines were also reprehensible because they could no longer concentrate on their Eucharistic ministry:

> Truly unfortunate and insane arc those [priests] who rather strive to adorn the cadavers of concubines than the altars of Christ. More intricate and more glittering is the mantle of the whore than the altar cloth, and more intricate and precious is the nightgown of the whorish concubine than the surplice of the priest. Indeed they [the priests] spend so much on the clothes of their concubines that they are made paupers and are dressed in vile rags. In certain regions, moreover, priestesses of this kind are so abominated that the [lay parishioners] do not wish to give them the kiss of peace in church nor to receive it from them. (Elliott 1999: 121)

As in most European regions, concubinages of priests were common in northern Italy in the fourteenth century, with quite different forms of cohabitation in one house or separately, with or without children. Often, there was also a service relationship in which the woman provided for the priestly household and then willingly or under duress a sexual relationship grew out of it. As visitation records show, the concubine could be a lay woman as well as a nun. Even if the priests were threatened with sanctions, the concubines were the real vulnerable persons. Some of them never became part of the community and remained social outcasts, especially when there were children. This was also evident when a child was not born in the community, but the woman went to another place or a nearby town to do so. In the worst case, a court or the bishop could banish the woman from the village altogether. On the other hand, clerical concubines and their children were recognized in a parish and the priest and father cared for them beyond the end of his life, among other things by taking them into account in the inheritance (Cossar 2011: 112ff.).

The church reforms of the second half of the eleventh and the twelfth centuries were also aimed at bishops who had wed and had children. For

Bishop Peter Damiani (around 1006–1072), such behavior was tantamount to incest, which is why he admonished his fellow ministers:

> All the children of the church are undoubtedly your children. And it is also quite obvious that spiritual generation is something greater than carnal parenthood. Moreover, since you are the husband, the spouse of your church, symbolized by the ring of your betrothal and the staff of your mandate, all who are reborn in her by the sacrament of baptism must be ascribed to you as your children. Therefore, if you commit incest with your spiritual daughter, how in good conscience do you dare perform the mystery of the Lord's body? (McLaughlin 2010: 19f.)

The difficulty for some bishops to resist the bodily temptations of female (and male) parishioners and adhere to the strict ascetic or celibate guidelines was shown by Fulbert of Chartres (about 950 to about 1028), who wrote a teaching poem to approach perfect chastity in six stages:

> First, when you are awake, not to experience carnal pleasure;
> next, not to entertain lustful desires;
> then, when you see someone who is pretty, not to feel any craving;
> fourth, not to be physically aroused in any way;
> fifth, not to let the sound of love-making distract you;
> finally, when asleep not to dream of anything provocative.
>
> (McLaughlin 2010: 31)

Fulbert knew that the last stage could hardly be attained on one's own. One might only come within reach by the grace of Christ (and a responsible diet). Bishops should, in any case, lead chaste and celibate lives. They were the fathers of their communities, they had to be role models and remain pure for the sacraments. To demand appropriate moral conduct from the priests under their supervision and not live a proper life themselves would smack of hypocrisy. Therefore, in the High and Late Middle Ages, it became increasingly a central task for the bishops to prove themselves as an exemplary Christian through irreproachable sexual behavior or a virginal life, who could lead his flock (clergy and laity) like a saint (Harvey 2017).

Prohibition of Divorce, but Annulment of Marriage

By the High Middle Ages, the church also secured sovereignty over divorce. In the Early Middle Ages, divorce was possible without too much trouble (Bof and Leyser 2016: 157ff.), for example, when no heir was born and the fault was attributed to the wife—often divorce was granted in such cases because the husband had fathered a child out of wedlock. In 542, Justinian enacted a law limiting the grounds for divorce and promoting lifelong monogamy. Most significantly, he ended divorce by mutual consent of the spouses. With this, he took a big step toward the institutionalization of marriage and divorce, because now a couple wanting to divorce needed an external reason, such as the disturbance of the social order via adulterous acts. This also included the fact that a wife could now divorce her husband unilaterally if the latter kept another companion in his (own) house or frequently visited her in another household (Harper 2013: 171).

In the Carolingian Empire (800–888), marriage represented a central social formation, which is why the dissolution of marriage seemed almost unthinkable and the Augustinian position was implemented. The only possibility was to have a marriage declared invalid, thus giving the chance for remarriage. The reason *par excellence* for an annulment was to declare the marriage as not consummated (Bof and Leyser 2016: 157ff.). Between the ninth and twelfth centuries, divorce gradually fell victim to the sacred postulate of insolubility. Since the Fourth Lateran Council of 1215, consanguinity has been a good reason to end unsatisfactory marriages (Rouillard 2020: 24f.).

At the Second Lateran Council (1139), marriage was first mentioned as one of the sacraments endowed by God, thus taking divorce right out of the realm of possibility (Breitbach 1998: 22). Nevertheless, in higher circles and in corresponding political constellations reasons for divorce or arguments for a (canonical) legal annulment of certain marriages were found even thereafter (Goetz 2002: 43ff.). From the thirteenth century, it was common practice in the upper social class to obtain a papal dispensation for an unfulfilled marriage. Medical or anatomical reasons could play a role. For example, claims of a too large penis or a vagina too small, which prevented the exercise of conjugal intercourse, were sufficient grounds for annulment by bishops and in church courts (Elliott 1993: 145f.). In such cases, it also became apparent that the church was concerned with establishing a unique position in matters of matrimonial law and did not want competition from secular courts.

The (Re)discovery of Un/courtly Love?

In the course of the sacralization of the marriage covenant, in the eleventh and twelfth centuries more and more voices could be heard from church circles emphasizing the importance of the conjugal love bond and sexual intercourse (Karras 2006: 140). These clerics saw an important stabilizer of the marriage covenant in the physical–sexual union, as long as it was carried out with the appropriate modesty and chastity and in intimate conjugal love—an effective means against concupiscence and (extramarital) lust. In the opinion of some historians, the upper classes of this period experienced a true "(re)discovery of love," based on an individual and personal relationship between those who were seized by it (Dinzelbacher 1993: 79f.; Bein 2003: 11ff.). Depending on the genre of source and text, however, a wide range of love concepts and discourses were already to be found in earlier centuries: For example, as a passionate feeling that "erupts spontaneously and uncontrollably and robs the person of his or her reason" or as an "affection between spouses as the result of years of fellowship or a willing, reasonableness" (Schnell 2002: 19). Both true love and idealized love relationships between married couples could take various forms— e.g., caring love, brotherly-sisterly love, charity, and sexually desiring love (Schnell 2002: 34). In view of such sophisticated conceptions of love, the long-propagated binary between the premodern marriage of convenience versus the modern marriage of love simply cannot be defended.

Minnelyrik and the courtly romance were the two genres that put these feelings into literary form and fueled a discussion at the royal courts about the true nature of love—and thus the positions defended in these sources were often quite controversial. This poetry's authors joined the increasing criticism of aristocratic marriage contracts in the twelfth century— intertwining *höfische Liebe* (courtly love) into the Middle Latin poetry of the ninth to the eleventh centuries (Schnell 2015: 552ff.). They portrayed marriage among the nobility as coldly strategic—following dynastic and political objectives—which is indeed why sons and daughters were most often wed at a very early age, frequently as children or adolescents, and were, in fact, subject to marriage contracts without any say in the matter. Love and intimate sexual relations could nevertheless develop between the spouses, the authors encouraged, but were not a prerequisite for the true necessity of the union: procreation. For the men in these works, regular premarital and extramarital sexual contacts were not an obstacle to marriage but the rule. For women, on the other hand, both could have fatal consequences (Liebertz-Grün 2000: 67).

Tristam/Tristan and Isolde/Iseult represent prototypical lovers who were connected by true, genuine, and immortal longing, but only found fulfilment in a short, secret tryst and then had to suffer for it the rest of their lives. The courtly poets of the twelfth and thirteenth centuries conceived of the couple as lovers who held fast to their feelings, which were tailored to an individual person, even against political and social resistance and wanted to realize them in the marriage covenant. The texts therefore sang the praises of the wedding night as a night of love—for example Chrétien de Troyes (c. 1140–1190) in his courtly epic *Erec et Enide* (c. 1170):

> you shall hear of the joy and pleasure in the bridal chamber. Bishops and archbishops were there on the night when the bride and groom retired. ... The hunted stag which pants for thirst does not so long for the spring, nor does the hungry sparrow-hawk return so quickly when he is called, as did these two come to hold each other in close embrace. That night they had full compensation for their long delay. After the chamber had been cleared, they allow each sense to be gratified: the eyes, which are the entrance-way of love, and which carry messages to the heart, take

satisfaction in the glance, for they rejoice in all they see; after the message of the eyes comes the far surpassing sweetness of the kisses inviting love; both of them make trial of this sweetness, and let their hearts quaff so freely that hardly can they leave off. Thus, kissing was their first sport. (de Troyes 2006: 23f.; Schnell 2002: 430; van Houts 2019: 92)

The German minnesinger Walther von der Vogelweide (*c.* 1170–*c.* 1230), however, thought little of the unfulfilled high love in his song *Under der linden*, in which he has a noble dame recount her physical experience of the joys of love:

There he made
a bed
rich with flowers.
if anyone should come
by the same path and see it,
he would have an amused smile.
among the roses he can certainly,
tandaradei

see where my head lay.
That he lay by me,
if anyone knew it,
(God forbid!) then I would be ashamed.
what he did with me
no-one ever
will find out, only he and I,
and a little bird,
tandaradei,
and it will not betray me.

(Spearing 1993: 27; Müller 2007: 292)

The Songs of Neidhart in the first half of the thirteenth century were ambiguous, uncourtly, and courtly at once; although he called himself a knight, in his verse he mainly has the rural folk do the talking and thus he spoofs noble love from a (pseudo-)peasant perspective (Figure 9). For example, in one of his *Sommerlieder* (Summer Songs), in which a mother calls after her daughter, who is about to go off dancing with a knight:

Do you know how what happened
to your girlfriend Jüten, as her mother told me?
From this dance it happened that her tummy grew,
and she gained a child, which she called *Lempel* [a typical peasant name].
In this way her told her the *Gimpelgempel* [a onomatopoetic phrase
which may refer to a kind of bounce dance as well as sexual practices].

(Classen 2010: 10ff.; Fritz 2016: 41)

FIGURE 9 *Walther von der Vogelweide (c. 1170–c. 1230). Illustration from the Codex Manesse, c. 1300.*

Neidhart addresses the sexual conflicts between knights and rural peasant women, addressing desire as well as the lack of modesty and self-control on both sides. He criticized the use of violence and the empowerment of the higher nobility—wrapped up in mockery and humor (Classen 2010: 6ff.).

Violence and Romance in the *Frouwen Minne*

Sexual violence played a major role in court romance and in late medieval literature in general (Schnyder 2005; Kane 2022). Often, the violence amounted to several men fighting over a certain woman, which is why love and chivalry were only superficially the motive, actually the self-praise and the competition among men were the center of attention—the lyrics' real critical target. It was also about the poet's self-portrayal, the troubadour's own prowess in the expression of love and desire in lyrical form. The protagonists functioned as ideal-typical representatives of courtly society and the songs as an entertainment medium by which the audience could communicate about feigned feelings and actions (Schnell 2015: 550ff.).

Marital violence was also problematized in *Maerendichtung*, for example in Sibote's *Frauenzucht* (The breding of wives) from the middle of the thirteenth century. In it, a knight tames his newlywed wife. On the way home, he kills the horse he is riding for not following his commands, then he forces his bride to take its place:

And immediately
he saddled her and put the bridle in her mouth. . . .
I'll tell you the truth
about how far he rode the maid:
She took ill from the long journey,
he rode her three spear lengths.

The young wife, who is thus broken-in multiple times—three spear lengths can be interpreted as thrice-performed coitus, replies only:

I will tell you this in truth:
if we live a thousand years,
I will do as you please,
and be sure and certain of it.

(Kümper 2012: 457f.)

Whether or not the *minne* is more than just a literary production—rather a depiction of the lived practice between socially differently positioned persons—is itself a rather controversial thesis (Reddy 2012; Schnell 2015: 536ff.). Yet, the national literary forms of *amour courtois*, *cortezia*, and *frouwen minne* undoubtedly did contribute to channeling the seemingly unbridled power of *eros* in a controlled manner—in order to advance the "process of civilization" in courtly society (Elias 1976; Duerr 1988; Classen 2008b: 74ff.; Paul 2011). In addition to literary entertainment, the court romance also pursued educational goals and was intended to encourage the nobility to accept and adhere to the social mores and ethical ideals represented by the protagonists. Very often, this was about controlling aggressive and possessive male desire, which was acted out in the form of sexual violence against women (Classen 2011b: 12ff.). At most, a lyrical touch shared between the adoring (literary) couples was acceptable, but any physical touching represented a social transgression and was condemned in courtly love. Physicality would have been appropriation in which the desire passed into possession and this was neither wanted nor feasible between a lowly minstrel and a noble lady (*frouwe*) (Lechtermann 2005: 158ff.).

Sex-Skeptic and Sex-Friendly Directions

The new stock put into marital sexual duties in church literature must be seen in the context of contemporary heretical movements that accused the Roman Church of moral decline within its own ranks. These groups were skeptical about marriage and the sexual altogether. Among them were the Cathars or Albigensians, whose followers could be found in the south of France and parts of Spain, Italy, and Germany from the middle of the twelfth to the early fourteenth century. Like some early Church Fathers, they demanded sexual purity and asceticism from the laity, too, as well as vegetarianism, in order to completely avoid all forms of flesh created through procreation (Leppin 2012: 296). Following the Gnostic and Platonic tradition, they wanted to separate the pure spirit from the evil body through mystical-ecstatic experiences and thus remove the diabolic carnal thorn. The *Perfecti* and *Perfectae* (perfect) among them, who were also called "the good people," committed themselves to a chaste or ascetic life in poverty and fasting, because only by refusing to reproduce could they prevent even more angelic souls from coming into the world and being condemned to an existence in a sinful body (Deane 2010: 34). Nevertheless, the Roman Church accused them of sexualized rites, the revival of natural-religious cults, even downright orgies, and cast doubt over their spiritual undertaking (Dinzelbacher 2008).

This is one sexual history of the Cathars. The other narrative in recent years has come from a group of historians who have asked the skeptical question of whether this heretical faith group existed at all or was it an invention of the Roman Church and the Inquisition in particular (Sennis 2016). Given this change of perspective, it is also revealing that the church made a direct link between heresy and lewd sexual practices or those contrary to nature. One strategy was to attest to the Cathars' same-sex desires which allegedly prevailed among the Bulgars and thus heretics, whereby they behaved *contra naturam* and against the order of God (Biller 2016: 289f.). However, all other non-common sexual acts and positions were also understood by the inquisitors as contrary to nature—these were considered to be "Meaning embracing each other [that is, from the front] or from the side." This included everything where a man "shed his seed in whatever manner outside the due repository" (Théry-Astruc 2016: 105).

Many church affiliates loyal to Rome, such as the Benedictine Hildegard von Bingen (1098–1179), however, insisted that the human being was an inseparable body–soul unity and was also an *Opus Dei* in sexual matters. In her work on healing, *Causae et Curae*, we learn that the sexual act performed in love and mutual joy by spouses was a fulfilment of the will of the Creator (Schipperges 2001: 51ff.; Harris 2017: 133f.). The man's stronger sexual desire was the natural product of his constitution:

> A man's love [pleasure], distinguished by its burning heat, is like the fire of burning mountains compared with that of women, which is difficult to extinguish compared with wood fire, which is easy to extinguish. The love of women, compared to that of men, is like the sweet warmth radiating from the sun.

These differences were based on the gender-specific characteristics of the body:

When the tempest of lust rises in a man, it grinds within him like a mill. For his loins are like a blacksmith's forge that supplies the marrow fire. This blacksmith then pours the fire into the area of the male genital and makes it burn hot. But when the wind of longing arises in the woman's marrow, it falls into her uterus, which is connected to the navel, and touches the blood with longing. This wind spreads in her abdomen, because in the area around the woman's navel there is a large, so to speak open space in the womb. Therefore it burns more gently with longing, but more often because of its moist condition. Therefore, out of fear or shame, the woman is more easily able to suppress the longing within herself, which is why she pours out the foam of the seed less often than the man. (Classen 2011a: 87f.)

For the well-known Franciscan and penitential preacher Berthold of Regensburg (around 1210–1272), however, there was an *ungeordnet fride* (disorderly quietude) hidden in the flesh, which even in marriage could mean *sêle tôt* (death of the soul) (Classen 2008a: 2). From the early thirteenth century, the church discussion no longer revolved around asceticism and possible sins resulting from it; instead, it turned to the physical

FIGURE 10 *The Cosmic Spheres and Human Being*, c. 1220–1230. Illustration from Hildegard von Bingen (c. 1098–1179), Liber Divinorum Operum.

consummation of marriage and regular sexual intercourse (Maasen 1998: 273ff.). The church's attitude toward marital pleasures shifting as it did, casting a positive light on desire, was also in response to the epidemic in the middle of the fourteenth century. The Black Death cost the lives of around a third of the European population and left entire regions deserted (Ehmer 2011a: 142). In view of the shortage of labor and the lack of tax payments, many church princes (the Germanic *Fürsten* of the Holy Roman Empire) spoke out in favor of procreation (in wedlock, of course).

Scholastic Advocates of the *Debitum Conjugale*

The scholastic authors of the eleventh to the fourteenth century also supported the sex-friendly marriage doctrine, referring to the worldly truths of nature. In their opinion, conjugal coitus not only carried out the commandment expressed several times in the Bible to "be fruitful and multiply" but was also quite natural, that is, created by God and therefore fundamentally good (Boswell 1980: 215ff.). In contrast to Augustine, who spoke of an exception to be tolerated, the scholastics saw a divine *bonum* in marital intercourse, in which two created beings would unite in harmony (Signori 2011: 27ff.). They also posed the question of how a marriage became valid at all and whether a promise of marriage or consent given before God (and not necessarily before a priest) was sufficient validation. The majority believed that marriage was ultimately concluded and validated through sexual consummation. But the scholastics also pointed to the sinful potential of marital duties. They denounced non-procreative practices as harshly as they did non-marital forms. From the High Middle Ages, adultery was therefore no longer considered merely a sin—but rather an act against nature.

According to Thomas Aquinas (1225–1274), one of the main representatives of scholasticism, natural sexual acts fulfilled a purpose intended by God. A danger loomed, however, that people would take too much pleasure in the sexual and that lust could come to dominate their thinking and morals (Dreyer 2014: 58). If the intention was procreation, though, the spouses may come together without too much risk of sin. Even if Aquinas primarily had procreation in mind, the *debitum conjugale* ought also to be employed (or deployed) when the carnal desire of one of the spouses became overwhelming and the threat of a worse (extramarital) sin arose (Ranke-Heinemann 1999: 290f.). In his work *Summa contra gentiles* (*c.* 1269), he postulated, in defense of the indissolubility of marriage and following Aristotle's *Nicomachian Ethics* based on *ius naturae* (natural law), that sexual union contributed substantially to the intimate emotional bond between spouses (Schnell 2002: 246). Turning from Neo-Platonism to Aristotelianism, he declared the triad of marriage, procreation, and gender dichotomy based on natural law to be the guiding principle of scholarly discourse and Christian doctrine (Barnes 2010: 93ff.). The consistent implementation of natural law could well lead to serious legal and moral problems: According its logic, did a marriage actually have to be annulled if one of the spouses proved unable to copulate? Even more difficult was the question of what to do with couples who practiced intercourse but did not produce offspring. Conflicts also arose in the area of penal law: Must a rapist be prosecuted if he could get his victim to marry him? These and similar uncertainties regarding the formation and legitimation of marriage have occupied church and secular jurists over the centuries. The question of whether a man's extramarital sexual intercourse should be tolerated (by church law) was clearly negated (Schnell 1998: 343).

What Aquinas had to say about the sexual characteristics of women also found its way into broader Christian thinking (Leibbrand and Leibbrand 1972: 576ff.). On the one hand, the immaculate and chaste Virgin Mary, who had conceived Jesus through the Holy Spirit, radiated through his thinking. Neither the Blessed Mother nor her Son had come into contact with the male seed and original sin; moreover, Mary had never even felt any sexual desire throughout her life. With this postulate, Aquinas made a significant contribution to the Marian cult of the Middle Ages, for the asexual Madonna had transformed her motherliness into human love and now acted as an advocate of man in the hereafter. Since his writings, therefore, the topic of virginity primarily encompassed women. It was forgotten that—in contrast to early Christianity—physical and spiritual virginity was once also a virulent trait of men and especially monks (Kelly and Leslie 1999: 16ff.; Lynch 1999: 87). On the other hand, the *virgo* had her antithesis in the sexualized secular woman. Like Eve, the primordial mother, she could hardly resist sexual desire, was created for reproduction because of her anatomy, and drew men's attraction by her strong eroticism. In marriage, she had to be regarded as an equal in sexual matters. Both spouses were to develop their will to marry freely, had equal rights and duties regarding the performance of the *debitum conjugale*, and could not take a vow of chastity without the consent of the other (Plöchl 1962: 323). Premarital chastity imposed on both sexes had for Aquinas, as with many other medieval theologians and canonists, an advantage: due to the long latency period, the erotic desire was all the more intense and strengthened the marital bonds (Schnell 2015: 584). The sacrament of marriage then also constituted an affective contract that established the emotional and sexual bond between the couple (Burger 2018: 20f.).

Everyday Sexual Relations before, in, and outside Marriage

Even in the High and Late Middle Ages, everyday sexual relations between spouses were shaped by the respective family and social (power) relationships:

Men acted as head of the household and head of the family. They exercised guardianship over their wives (for the most part). The women were obliged to obey their husbands and fathers and were dependent on them in (most) legal matters, such as property rights, contracts, and inheritance rights. This dominance was already instilled in adolescents and young men—despite the social background and the virile upbringing and socialization of a knight, scholar, and craftsman differing quite significantly (Karras 2003).

Virgins for the Wedding Night

Patriarchal structures also included the husband (and his family of origin) confirming that the woman had entered marriage as a *virgo*, thus making paternity over the firstborn unquestionable. Not only the torn hymen and its bleeding provided proof but also the condition of the uterus, according to the Greek model. A midwife could allegedly determine a bride-to-be's purity by means of a urine test (Kelly 2000: 17ff.).

In (Christian) Spain of the tenth and eleventh centuries, the husband announced to the world with a morning gift that his bride had indeed been a virgin before their first nuptials. Also among the Germanic tribes of the Early Middle Ages, such gifts had served both as a substitute for the woman's lost virginity and as confirmation of the consummation and actual validity of the marriage. This then indicated that the man was now entitled to the sexual "usufruct" of his wife (from *usus* "a use" and *fructus* "enjoyment," also "fruit")—which also applied in reverse, however; usufructuary reciprocity left considerably fewer traces in the sources (Wettlaufer 1999: 87f.). The German vernacular summed this up with a succinct saying: "*Ist das Bett beschritten, so ist die Eh erstritten.*—If the bed's been tousled in, the marriage has been tussled over" (Epperlein 2003: 210).

The aristocratic "right of the first night" (also "right of the Lord's first night"), "*jus primae noctis*" or "*droit du seigneur*" is, on the contrary, a pure myth, one that is rather tenacious in popular historiography. Even if certain nobles did take young peasant women or forced female dependents to have intercourse with them, no such male right has been found in either customary law or in written law (Boureau 1996; Wettlaufer 1999).

As already mentioned, between the fifth and tenth centuries, the Germanic and Roman legal traditions mixed in the areas of Central and Western Europe. In both systems, a young woman remained legally subordinate to the family or her father or another male representative until marriage. Then, she passed into the guardianship of her husband in a marriage that was usually arranged. In the case of prenuptial sex, the penalty depended on the status of the woman involved: Was she an unmarried free woman or an already engaged one? Was she only a slave and under whose protection was she? Her punishment could thus fluctuate between moderate monetary fines to the death penalty. Rape of another's wife was considered a serious crime. In contrast, the use of sexual violence in the performance of marital duties was not sanctioned under penal law (Wemple 1993: 229ff.; Karras 2006: 177). In the collection of Bavarian laws, the *Lex Baiuariorum*, which was created between the sixth and eighth century, sexual offences with nuns—such as the abduction or theft of a spiritual woman and subsequent marriage to her— were punished with a much higher penalty than for laywomen. According to the Lombard legal code, the *Edictus Rothari*, which came into being in the seventh century, such *Entführung* (*raptus*, "carrying off, abduction, snatching away") of a woman was punished as long as the marriage covenant was not blessed by a priest. Ethnic origin was also important for such codes. If a Lombard man had sexual intercourse with the (also Lombard) maidservants of another lord, he faced a fine twice as great as he would have had he slept with a Romanic maid (Saar 2002: 250ff.; Wemple 1993: 240).

Epicurean Views on Sexuality and Shame

Town, rural, and village populations held rather Epicurean views on sexuality, as is the case with the fourteenth-century village of Montaillou in the French Pyrenees. Whatever gave pleasure to those involved in the sexual acts themselves—and did not lead to public attention—was seen by many as not too serious a sin or even merely a secular issue (Le Roy Ladurie 1980: 200ff.). The majority of people had direct access to sexual life simply because they lived with animals and experienced their mating behavior firsthand. The cramped living and sleeping conditions also made it impossible to not overhear and sometimes even to overlook what was happening in the surrounding beds.

We know little about the actual actions and behaviors, but in most cases conjugal coitus must have taken place in the dark for the most part— simply because wax and tallow were expensive, and daylight was used for work as much as possible. The many writings that spoke out against deviating from the monk/missionary position could be an indication that the opposite was indeed happening and that marriage beds were used for all manner of positions. This probably also included the woman's top position, which was criticized in the texts for its allegedly low chances of conception and the reversal of the gender hierarchy. In theological, medical, and literary sources from the Italian Renaissance, other reasons were given why women could not be "on top" during coitus: The deviation from the natural position is seen as a violation of the divinely (and naturally) ordained hierarchy, male health is threatened when female poisonous fluids fall into the penis, the woman gains the upper hand in this "battle" between the couple and the sexes, and finally the masculine identity can be damaged because the man has to feel ashamed and emasculated because of his inferior position (Den Hartog 2021: 639ff.). The "dog position," in which the man penetrated the woman vaginally from behind, was considered animalistic (Karras 2006: 170ff.).

There is much to suggest that the positive attitude toward carnal conjugal love found in folk and functional literature was also widespread among the population. In songs, lyrical poetry, and farces, at any rate, the subject was addressed very directly (Flandrin 1992; Wolf 1991). Fertility and intercourse were extremely important in times of high infant and child mortality and recurrent epidemics. Peasants and craftsmen saw a large number of children as a future labor force and their own old-age provision, while in the upper classes they thought of possible marriage contracts as political as well as economic advantages. In general, the sexual stood for the cyclically recurring fertility of nature, the reproduction and thriving of animals, fields, and gardens—all essential prerequisites for food security and survival. Whosoever would found an honorable Christian family was also subject to the divine mandate to procreate and maintain the community.

Intimacy and sexual longing were also expressed in letters. For example, in a letter that the Englishman Thomas Stonor sent from London in 1468 to his wife Jane, who had stayed at home, he called her "goode swete Lemman" and said "be ye myry and of goode comfort for to cumfort me when I cum." Due to a legal dispute, "I can not cum to youe as sone as I wuld." Even though the letter did not speak of romantic love and sexual desire, the two knew what to expect in terms of affective and physical marital exchange under longing for "comfort" (Kane 2022: 41).

Such a positive attitude did not mean, however, that sexual issues were everyday topics of conversation, discussed bluntly and without shame. On the contrary, sexually connoted (curse) words quickly led to disgrace and loss of honor for the titled persons and were connected with legal consequences for the denigrators—for example, when accusing a man of impotency or denying a woman's virginity. It was also serious and punishable to call a respectable woman a whore (without proof). Such accusations shook the foundations of the patriarchal and social order. Worst of all were those injuries which dealt with actions against nature: For example, when a man was accused of being a sodomite and of letting himself be penetrated. Here, it was enough to evoke the imagination with shameful words, which is why sodomitic sin was considered unspeakable (Puff 1998). Nevertheless, erotic-sexualized topics were addressed in closed circles, even if under the guise of innuendo, for example, in late medieval marriage treatises, which were written for a small, rather private and educated group and which presented marital pleasures in a rhetorically exaggerated, positive light. Latin was often used as a linguistic sanctuary in which more could be expressed than in the more accessible popular literature (Schnell 2002: 266ff.). The myriad salacious songs, farces, and poems, on the other hand, were almost all produced in the vernacular.

The shame regime could not be undermined even during the carnival period. Even in the topsy-turvy inverse world that medieval society used to reflect its other, unordered side, (sexual) obscenities in word and image were only suitable for the public to a limited extent. For example, in 1307 the Nuremberg Council banned a resident named Rosenlacher from the city because he had exposed his *virilia* on the market square to honorable citizens during carnival, a time that is associated with anything goes behavior. The pursemaker Ulrich received harsh punishment for unpacking his *geschirr* (tools) in front of Nuremberg's women in 1348 (Simon 1998: 201f.). Such unseemly actions were common during the carnival period because people dressed up for the occasion or at least painted their faces to make themselves unrecognizable. Black face paint had another connotation, though: under its protective spell, even diabolical attributes such as obscenity or excrement could be taken up during carnival and Shrovetide in the *civitas diaboli* (state of the devil), as Augustine (354–430) had called this period in his epoch-making work *De civitate Dei*.

Premarital Sexual Contacts

Premarital sexual contacts—even if they were prohibited by canonical and secular laws—did not pose too great a problem in most European regions (Metzler 2011: 108). Mild *fornicatio* was usually treated with leniency by the courts—in case it eventually led to marriage. Even in the thirteenth century, many people knew nothing of the sinfulness of *fornicatio*, and even clergymen did not always see it so strictly (Schnell 2015: 545). In Southern Europe there were greater reservations about it, and unmarried daughters were more strictly guarded around the Mediterranean. The loss of virginity led to acts of revenge and family feuds in southern Italy, for example. No matter where one lived in Europe, sexual contacts before marriage could, for the most part, be assuaged by an oral proposal or betrothal. If premarital pregnancy came about, a woman could demand marriage; such cases are abundant in court records. For men, prenuptial activities were justified by age difference at marriage and their longer waiting period. However, the age of marriage did shift: While in ancient times adolescent girls were married to significantly older men, the age difference in marriage between the Early Middle Ages and the twelfth century decreased and then increased again toward the end of the Middle Ages (Klapisch-Zuber 1992b: 163f.). Premarital sexual relations seem to have decreased accordingly. The legal framework conditions did not change, however: According to both Roman and canon law, boys had to be at least fourteen years old when they married and girls at least twelve (Hemmie 2007: 72).

During the Central Middle Ages in northwestern countries (England, France north of the Loire, the Low Countries, Germany), most women married in their mid- to late teens, their husband were some few years older. Renaissance Italy recorded a larger age gap, as men were about ten years older than their wives (van Houts 2019: 90f.). In the Late Middle Ages, women usually still married under the age of twenty and men only some years later. In the Central and Late Middle Ages, women from the nobility had the lowest marriage age with the age around fifteen (Kowaleski 1999:

41f., 326ff.). However, even in the (Late) Middle Ages, sons and daughters from poor families in particular—as in rural areas of England between 1250 and 1350—could have to wait until their mid or even late twenties to set up or take over their own household and to marry; the rate of people who never married was correspondingly high in these population groups (Bennett 2019).

In the case of premarital contacts between a socially higher-ranking man and a lower-ranking, usually younger woman, it was often hard to distinguish whether these were wanted by both sides or came about through coercion and pressure. The *pastourelles* was a French twelfth-century lyrical form about extremely sexually active aristocrats who, due to their social dominance, simply took young shepherdesses whose will was ignored (Gravdal 1991: 104ff.; Harris 2018: 106ff.). Stories of sexual violence against defenseless women run all through medieval literature. The protagonists were knights who overpowered maids along the roadside or warriors who defeated townships and regarded the local women as loot (Brunner 1998: 246ff.). One stark example is the saga of Grettir the Strong, written in the thirteenth and fourteenth centuries, which deals with the balance of power between the sexes and the social classes: As an outcast hero, the Viking Grettir hid away the night in a farmer's barn and was found asleep by the peasant's daughter and maid. When he awoke, the maid mocked him for his small penis, whereupon he raped her to demonstrate the functioning of his sexual organ (Karras 2006: 236). Here, sexual violence was practically a must for any hero whose sociosexual reputation was called into question. In many stories, the women of the peasant class were treated as prey, and medieval literature is full of such scenes of sexual violence (Rushton 2011: 97; Classen 2011b).

Alternatively, gifts were seen as an effective means to make a woman compliant. Verbal seduction alone should, in any case, make her distrustful. In the canon law of the thirteenth century, feigned marriage intentions were considered an illegal means of inducing sexual intercourse; instead, the woman's willful consent was required (Brundage 1982: 147). The legal and social consequences that such premarital contacts could have were distributed very unequally (Kane 2022: 42). If an unworthy mistress of a nobleman or a rich merchant bore a child, the child was excluded from any inheritance. Mother and child were usually dispatched with titles, land, or monetary payments. Flight and emigration were two ways in which the men from the lower classes were able to escape responsibility for an illegitimate child. For pregnant women and single mothers, however, there was hardly any alternative—and a great deal of social distain.

In the twelfth and thirteenth centuries, the social regulation and monitoring of marriage initiation was intensified in the rural world, too, ranging from erotic contacts to "trial nights" and marriage. Beginning with the *Kommnächte*, a suitor—usually accompanied by others—makes a first visit to the chamber of the beloved. This *Beilager* (nuptial) would apparently be carried out quite chastely and was limited to verbal intercourse. If the families and potential spouses agreed on the engagement and marriage, nothing more stood in the way of an announcement to the community and the marriage proposal was considered assured. Subsequent visits to the future wife—referred to in German by various terms: *Fensterln* (lit. "to climb through the window" in the manner of Romeo and Juliet), *Gassl gehen* (alley walking), Schnurren or *Kiltgang* (referring to a *kilt*, the type of couch one would meet upon)—could then also lead to sexual intercourse and tested, among other things, the ability of both partners to sexually fulfill their duties. In any case, premarital sexual contacts should never take place without social controls. Safeguarding against such behavior were well-worn customs for rebuking the perpetrators. Since the Late Middle Ages, there have been documented cases in which groups of boys and men took action against sexually deviant persons and handed them over for public disgrace and humiliation (Kaltenstadler 1999: 17). Since the church thought little of such customs and rejected premarital relationships on principle, it vehemently opposed these trial nights and rejected them wholeheartedly with total bans (Ballhaus 2009: 97ff.).

In Catalan cities, a different form of premarital sexual culture existed in the Late Middle Ages that was quite accepted. There, men from the patriciate and the upper middle classes lived with a woman for a long time before their formal marriage in their twenties, which meant that their illegitimate children later appeared in the sources. For these men, fathering children out of wedlock meant no shame; in fact, it represented a sign of manhood and procreative ability. The children could even become part of the subsequent formal family. In any case, it was assumed that the offspring would be financially supported and that the sons conceived out of wedlock would be brought to an appropriate professional career. For example, in the records of the *Dioces'a de Barcelona*, many successful dispensation requests must have been made because a legal birth was required for clerical candidates and this could not be proven for the sons from such concubinages (Armstrong-Partida 2019: 196ff.). Also in other regions of the Iberian Peninsula and in Italy, there was widespread practice of men from the social upper classes keeping a concubine before an official marriage (Karras 2012b: 72ff.).

At the same time, such premarital sexual relationships and concubinages were not very popular in England. There, it was assumed that young men of middle and higher status either refrained from living with a woman before marriage or ensured that there were no children from non-marital relationships. Respectable men who could not control their sexual appetites and their consequences were even considered not masculine and in any case not a moral example for a future father. Men were considered adults when they became husbands and fathers of legitimate offspring. In England, men from respectable families also paid for the bastards they fathered, but usually avoided any further contact with them (McSheffrey 2006: 189f.; Neal 2008: 69ff.; Armstrong-Partida 2019: 199f.). Even in the Holy Roman

Empire in the Late Middle Ages, it was still possible for the higher classes to obtain legitimation through an imperial rescript for children resulting from fornication or incestuous relations. Nevertheless, it became more difficult to find a good position for the "bastards" (Schmidt 2019: 23ff.).

In Sweden, the provincial laws from the thirteenth century onward contained divergent provisions on premarital sex, which reveal the underlying logic and everyday practice: According to the Västgöta laws, a man who had sexual intercourse with his betrothed had to pay financial compensation, a "friendship gift" to the marriage guardian, and thus become engaged to her. Other regional laws made no provision for this. In some codes, if a child resulted from premarital coitus, it was considered to be born in wedlock, and thus its inheritance status was determined. Christopher's law from the fourteenth century provided for a fine to be halved if the man married the woman. If the latter was a so-called "concubine child," the fine did not apply on marriage (Ekholst 2014: 159ff.).

Contraception and Abortion

Even once a marriage was consummated, it was nevertheless commonly believed that sexual life could still go against nature in one of two ways: The first was when a woman would not abide her submissive sexual role and wanted to be on top during coitus, for example, and thus violated both the social and divine order. The second was when a couple dared to have intercourse without the intention of procreation, anally or orally or during menstruation (Karras 2006: 45). It is difficult to estimate how widespread non-vaginal practices were among married couples, however, or indeed whether they were used as a contraceptive measure. Only the fact that doctors and theologians explicitly spoke out against such contraceptive methods may be taken as an indication that some couples deliberately practiced them. In the thirteenth century, Aquinas saw a grave sin in them. The theologian Jean Gerson (1363–1429) compared such measures with sodomy and therefore proscribed burning at the stake for such abuses (Kruse 1996: 169).

There was no clear boundary between prevention and abortion, since many of the potions, herbs, and baths used not only had a contraceptive effect but were also abortifacient (Jerouschek 1993; Riddle 1997: 87ff.; Biller 1998; Harris 2017: 150ff.). In medieval monastic medicine, for example, remedies were used which, in the event of a stagnation of a woman's monthly cleansing, were intended to (re)activate menstruation. As one recipe in the *Lorsch Pharmacopoeia* (around 800) shows, these potions had an abortive effect through ingredients such as fennel, celery seeds, and ginger. In view of these possibilities, some early medieval penitential books recommend suggestive lines of questioning. Priests would ask confessing women to elicit whether they had ever taken such a drink and wanted to prevent the carrying of a child (Riddle 1996: 262ff.). In the twelfth century,

Hildegard von Bingen mentioned in this context *hazelwort*, a poisonous plant that caused uterine bleeding. Among the natural remedies were savin juniper, rue aka herb-of-grace, parsley, saffron, pennyroyal, and ergot, which also had menses-stimulating effects (Kruse 1996: 169ff.).

As in antiquity, people relied on amulets and magical potions and spells for contraception, but they also employed pessaries and condoms made of animal skins, for example, which reeked of immorality, however. The knowledge of such *secreta mulierum* (secrets of women) seems to have been widespread. Due to the poor reading skills, though, such knowledge did not usually originate from the medical compendia written in the High Middle Ages but was passed on as oral tradition (Jütte 2008: 62ff.). The know-how behind coitus interruptus and its crucial timing must also have been passed on through the grapevine, so to speak (Jacquart and Thomasset 1988: 100ff.). Another form of birth control, which is underestimated today, was simply the numerous church holidays and fasting periods during which abstinence was the rule. In the High Middle Ages, observance was paramount, but later centuries were more lenient (Flandrin 1992). How many married couples actually renounced their marital duties on these days cannot be said. In any case, there appears to have been much complaint that the often excessive alcohol consumption on church holidays and feasts tended to promote sexual immorality, running counter to the abstinence regime. Also not to be underestimated is that older couples committed themselves to a second chastity, for which Augustine had already pleaded, and completely renounced coitus or the danger of (further) pregnancy (Cullum 2013).

Abortion was already a topic in early Germanic tribal law. The *Lex Visigothorum* (653/4) discriminated between the gender and status of the persons involved and calculated the value of the fetus from this:

> If anyone gives to a pregnant woman a drink for abortion or to kill a child, he will be killed; and a woman, who seeks a potion to have an abortion, if she is a slave-girl, will receive 200 lashes; if she is freeborn, she will lose her personal status and be handed over in slavery to whomever we decide. (. . .) A freewoman who induced an abortion in a slavegirl was to pay 20 *solidi* to her master. (. . .) A slave who induced an abortion in a freewoman was to receive 200 lashes in public and be transferred to the service of the woman. (. . .) A slave who induced an abortion in a slavegirl was to receive 200 lashes and his master had to pay 10 *solidi* to the slavegirl's master. (Mistry 2011: 89)

In the *Lex Salica* (507–511) a fine of 100 shillings was imposed for the killing of a child in the womb and a newborn (before it was christened). The *Lex Baiuvariorum* from the eighth century adopted the provisions of the *Lex Visigothorum*, but at the same time it differentiated according to the state of the animation of the aborted fetus—if the fetus had not yet been animated, 20 shillings had to be paid; if the fetus was already alive, 53 shillings were due. These sinners were particularly guilty of the fact that the (living) fetuses were abandoned to eternal damnation without the sacrament of baptism. Boniface (around 673–754/5), the most important church reformer of the Frankish Empire, associated abortion with the lewd lifestyle of some women:

> And it should be noted that beneath that crime [of fornication] lurks another immense outrage, namely murder. Because, when those whores (*meretrices*), nuns or otherwise, give birth to their offspring conceived in sins, they more often than not kill them; rather than filling the churches of Christ with adoptive children, they instead fill up tombs with bodies and hell with wretched souls. (Mistry 2011: 174)

Pagan rules, shaped by Roman law and Christianization, were counteracted and supplemented in the Early Middle Ages by the *libri penitentiales*, the penitentials (Mistry 2015: 126ff.). In these compendia, the abortion issue was largely based on the *Septuagint* (the older translation of the Hebrew-Aramaic Bible into everyday ancient Greek) and a kind of term regulation was established. The date of animation with a soul was set at the fortieth day of pregnancy and a penance period of one year. In late medieval penitentials, however, a whole series of mitigating and aggravating reasons could be found, such as the social status of the perpetrator, her office and property, the public attention her deed had caused, and the repentance shown (Jerouschek 1993: 57).

The canons also looked for a solution in the pregnancy's term. Between the twelfth and fifteenth centuries, their views found their way into secular penal law (Mistry 2015: 209ff.). According to the collection of the *Decretum Gratiani* (around 1140), murder could only be committed from the moment the spirit entered the fetus—this occurred successively and the punishment was to be correspondingly severe. In his glosses, Johannes Teutonicus (*c.* 1170–1245) agreed with Aristotle's *Historia animalium*, that the male soul was poured into the unborn child faster than that of the female soul, and therefore he set animation to have been the final forty days into pregnancy for a male child, and eighty days for a female. Before that, the fetus was to be considered *inanimatus* or *informatus* (inanimate or unformed), after that *animatus* or *formatus* (animated or formed). Clerics saw abortion during the latter stage as a sin and demanded a penance of months or years. After animation, abortion was an act of murder, punishable by excommunication and in secular law (sometimes) with the death penalty (Müller 2000: 16ff.). For Laurentius Hispanus (*c.* 1180–1248), the bishop of Orense, however, the punishment for offering an abortive potion depended on the social position, and he demanded

> that whosoever kills an already animate (fetus) must be punished with death; if he kills an uninitiated one instead, one must distinguish: If he is a nobleman, he will be banished and lose his goods; but if he is not noble, he will be condemned to the mines. (Müller 2000: 34)

From the end of the twelfth century onward, the princely and municipal authorities increasingly used ecclesiastical canons for jurisdiction in matters of abortion as well, which superseded customary law until the fifteenth and sixteenth centuries. With the *Constitutio Criminalis Carolina* of 1532, Emperor Charles V ordered that abortion was to be uniformly punished throughout the Holy Roman Empire:

> If any man can abort a living child of a wench by force, eating, drinking, whoever makes man or woman unfruitful, if such an evil, insidious, and evil-doing is done, shall the man with the sword be slain, and the woman, shall be struck down (. . .) or shall be punished to death. But if a child, which would not yet be alive, was aborted by a wench, the magistrates should (. . .) pass a sentence according to the [Carolina] order. (Jerouschek 1993: 66)

With all these sometimes harsh legal provisions on abortion, however, it should not be forgotten that there was often a wide gap with social reality. With their decrees and regulations, the medieval legislators endeavored to demonstrate themselves as Christian rulers. However, their guidelines provided the framework and were always adapted in reality to the circumstances and persons involved (Mistry 2015: 209ff.).

Adultery and Honor

In the Middle Ages, adultery was also considered a serious offence, and it, too, was sanctioned according to gender, even though the church insisted on equal treatment (Karras 2006: 252ff.). Early Anglo-Saxon laws from the time of the first Christian ruler of England, Æthelberht I of Kent (*c.* 552/560–616/618), show that this was primarily about male property rights over women. For example, adultery was punishable with the payment of a *wergeld* (paid to the family of the victim) by the adulterer according to social rank and sex—with which the cuckolded could pay the bride price for a new wife. According to the penitential sums of Theodorus, Archbishop of Canterbury, which remained valid for centuries, adulterers in the seventh century were supposed to repent for four to seven years, whereby the cheated-on husband could disown his unfaithful wife, but also had the option to forgive her (Davies 1991: 84ff.). For the Late Middle Ages, and particularly for London, Toulouse, and northern France in the fifteenth century, this male-female divide in the sanctioning of adultery was called into question, which is also due to the existence of corresponding sources for these regions. There, the courts acted with equal severity against male adulterers—their justification: an alignment of moral rules that was also demanded in the clerical writings (McDougall 2014: 207ff.).

In the opinion of these sources, most of which, again, were written by men, the wives had nonetheless committed the worse offence simply because they were damaging the honor of the husband and the family, and the illegitimate descent of a child could occur. The assessment of a man's extramarital contacts was less harsh, although he too must be held responsible for his actions. The relations of a married woman were considered an aggravating circumstance, because they affected the rights of another man; with unmarried persons and prostitutes, playing away was considered a minor offence. It was also argued that when the weaker sex took missteps, she was less able to defend herself against sexual pleasure. This monocular view of adulterers and adulteresses was also expressed in court, where it was mainly the latter who were condemned to shameful chastening, corporal punishment, and monetary payments. One of the sanctions handed down was that women were shorn bald and paraded naked through the village (Metzler 2011: 107). Even the suspicion of adultery led to reactions from the community, for example in the form of a skimmington or charivaris, in which the supposed adulterers (as well as unseemly remarriage or secret loves) were mocked with a discordant serenade. For the man, punishment often hinged on whether the tempted single woman was still a virgin or had already "fallen." In the *Speculum Virginum*, which was created around 1100 on the Middle Rhine, the seduction or desecration of a consecrated virgin was considered particularly bad, since in this case the covenant with Christ had also been broken and the entire body of the church had been desecrated (Ennen 1999: 115).

Sexual escapades probably occurred across all social classes, but their extent can hardly be determined. If the stories about men who wear the horns of the cuckold are to be believed, wives took advantage of the opportunity above all when their husbands were out of town for their trade or on nightwatch (Boiadjiev 2003: 337). One recurring crime scene, in addition to one's own home and the surrounding forests, was the church itself—which was also due to the moral impetus of the scriptures. In the High Middle Ages, together with adultery, unaccompanied public appearances made by both married and single women were the source of much speculation and a rich topic of discussion. However, it would have completely contradicted everyday practice—persons of both sexes could move about alone in public space (at least during the day). Still, the medieval thinking did not go as far as the ancient Greek city-states in advocating that noble and burgher women be sequestered at home and monitored at all times. In the Early Middle Ages, a cuckolded husband (still) had the right to kill his unfaithful wife, a sanction that was not tolerated in later centuries. Until the eleventh and twelfth centuries, however, he could certainly banish her from his house. With the indissolubility of marriage, this possibility ceased to exist and even a child could no longer be dispatched if it was (presumed) illegitimate; a new marriage was also inadmissible (Saar 2002: 307ff.). In the Late Middle Ages, an uncertain paternity as a result of adultery could still be an excuse for the violent acts of a betrayed husband. So it was in the case of William of Garton from Newsome in Rydale, England, who in 1348 beat his pregnant wife Ellen, killing both her and her unborn child. He then set out with his squire to kill the other man—the probable lover of his wife and presumed father of the child—and throw his body into the river. In court, he simply presented himself as the betrayed and thus was acquitted by the jury (Butler 2005: 22).

As a rule, however, both adulterers were punishable under late medieval penal laws, whereby milder penalties were usually provided for men. This inequality was clearly expressed in the Swedish regional laws: Adultery was categorized as a serious crime by the secular authorities. Children conceived in adultery also had no inheritance rights. Adultery was considered, first and foremost, an insult by a man on another man and the shame associated with it. The adulteress lost her right to the morning gift and all the rights she had as a married woman, especially her third of the common property. According to the Västgöta law, a husband could expel his unfaithful wife from the house. According to some regulations, she was led through the village in a disgraceful outfit, a ritual that could also affect the husband involved, who, however, usually did not have to pay a fine or give up property. Most provincial codes also provided for the right of revenge killings. According to this, the husband who was heard could kill the adulterer if he proved his guilt (Ekholst 2014: 173ff.). In later European laws—for example in the *Constitutio Criminalis Carolina* (1532) of the Holy Roman Empire—both sexes were threatened with the same severe punishment (Brundage 1987: 517ff.; Bardsley 2007: 144ff.).

The adultery of noble women is a particularly sensitive topic in high medieval courtly literature. It also represented a popular motif in popular farcical stories, which often figure women who are neglected and abused by their much older husbands and therefore seek a lover. Such literary texts are not proof, however, that adulteresses were more common in one social class or another. Especially in humorous episodes, satires, and farces, the circumstances were exaggerated; they were intended to entertain or even instruct. In many of these texts, despite the general rejection of adulterous behavior, a certain sympathy can be seen for women who sought a lover due to the neglect or even impotence of the husband (Schnell 2002: 218ff.).

In popular historiography, one still comes across an instrument in this context that was allegedly used in the Middle Ages by absent men to insure the marital fidelity of their wives: the chastity belt. Even though this mechanical device made of iron (and leather) was mentioned and illustrated, for example, in sources from Padua in the fourteenth century and in a writing on warfare and technology by Konrad Kyeser from Eichstätt (1366–*c*. 1405), it has meanwhile been proven that no such standard device was used by knights leaving for battle or merchants afield on business (Keyser 2008: 254f.). Due to hygienic and medical concerns alone, any such protective measure would have been quite impracticable, as urine and menstrual blood would have led to life-threatening infections. The chastity belt became a myth in the nineteenth century, when people debated their own sexual culture on the basis of this supposedly widespread device and dealt with questions of the development from a lower to a higher level of culture and morality—or vice versa. (Classen 2007).

Rape before Ecclesiastical and Secular Authorities

Sexual coercion and violence was a standard theme of high and late medieval literature and religious writing (Baechle, Harris and Strakhov 2022; Goldberg 2008; Classen 2011b; Saunders 2001). Contemporary chronicles, hagiographies, and sermons from northwestern Iberia from the tenth to the twelfth century can be cited here as an example. There, different constellations of male aggressors and sexually harassed or raped women become visible. If one believes these certainly morally colored texts, in many cases the perpetrator was a man from the victim's immediate kin, who was usually involved in or covered up the commission of the crime. Sexual assaults took place primarily under cover of night or after entering a house or apartment. In the texts studied, the perpetrators attempted to escape the threat of imprisonment or corporal punishment, as well as death, by agreeing to pay money or transfer property to the victim's family (Lorenzo-Rodríguez 2021: 122ff.). In the Iberian Peninsula, as in all of Europe, mass rapes during warlike conflicts were part of everyday life and were permitted, or at least not sanctioned, by military leaders. Even monasteries and nuns were not spared from such violent excesses. The fine line between seduction and rape was also problematized in the fourteenth-century Spanish *Libro de buen amor* of the Archpriest of Hita. There, the protagonist tries different courtship attempts, ranging from verbal approaches to the aggressive seduction of women who refuse but inwardly desire sexual intercourse, to "hunting," in which the aggressor's aim is to kill or succumb to the "game," including the use of force or drugs (Parodi 2020).

It is significant that the penal provisions for rape went hand in hand with the penalization of the abduction of an unmarried woman with or against her will. The template for this was provided by the story of the abducted Philomela from classical mythology. Chaucer (*c.* 1342–1400) adapted it to show that women were literally rendered speechless by male violence (Saunders 2002: 263). In both cases, what was at stake was that a proper marriage and thus the passing on of property and reputation was prevented. Rape narratives can be found in various literary genres, from "high" literature to pastourelle. They were used to deal with a wide variety of social conflicts, such as property claims, relationships between men, or acts of war. Only in some genres, such as the English pastourelle—a poetical confrontation between a man and a woman, which was about a knight or cleric inflicting sexual violence on a peasant girl or shepherdess in a rural setting—was the female side also discussed. Then, topics such as women's fear of sexual violence, the coercion exercised, and the possibilities of resistance also came up (Harris 2016: 264ff.).

In the twelfth and thirteenth centuries, clerical and secular penal law increasingly began to merge together, and jurisdiction in sexual matters was exercised by church and secular courts alike. From the second half of the thirteenth century onward, clerical courts dealt with sexual matters—such as extramarital sex and premarital sexual relations—in addition to their purview over marital problems and offences (Brundage 1996: 45; Karras 2006: 51f.). The majority of them handled quite everyday questions: for example, whether the degree of kinship of a couple allowed for marriage, whether a promise of marriage claimed by a pregnant woman was actually given, or whether consent to sexual intercourse was given voluntarily (Wiesner-Hanks 2000: 41f.). Secular courts usually came into play when, in addition to sin, a misdemeanor or crime was committed and social institutions or property rights were affected. Typical examples were accusations of adultery, (premarital) fornication, illegitimacy, and rape, which had far-reaching consequences for the individual, family, and community, and were therefore tried by a secular or mixed jurisdiction (Hull 1996: 16). The seriousness of the offence also determined whether a lower or higher court had jurisdiction. At all levels of the courts, it has been observed that the relatively severe penalties provided for in the law books were often converted into lower fines and forms of public shaming.

Legal discussions about rape often dealt with the use of physical violence and the question of whether the woman concerned had sexually stimulated or seduced the perpetrator and had herself felt pleasure. The loss of virginity, again, played a significant role as well, sometimes requiring an investigation into a woman's ante-assaulted purity. Since the thirteenth century, the question of whether or not the victim of rape had consented has been at the center of attention. Serious differences in status persisted; the sources hardly mention any violent crimes against slaves or maidservants. Conversely, men from the lower class who had sexually assaulted higher-ranking women were threatened with severe punishments. In England, the *Statute of Westminister* in 1275 made rape an official offence that must be prosecuted even if no charges were brought by the victim or her family. The penalties ranged from mutilation and the death penalty to financial compensation for the lost "legal property" (i.e., the woman's virginity and reduced chances of marriage). In legal practice, the statute brought a conflation between abduction and rape (Dunn 2013: 29). It appears that despite being enshrined in law, there was no significant increase in charges (Metzler 2011: 112). If such a case came to court, the sanctions depended on the social status and reputation of the woman. If she already had a bad reputation or, worse yet, earned her money as a prostitute, the path of the courts, ecclesiastical or secular, would have been quite in vain. In general, rape cases were rarely brought to court, rape convictions were rare, and penalties were light throughout Europe (Dean 2001: 82; Lansing 2021: 84).

In Swedish regional laws of the Late Middle Ages, the two crimes, abduction and rape, were closely related and on a continuum, but the fundamental difference was whether or not there was consent from the woman. Moreover, in the case of abduction, it was primarily the male relatives who were harmed, whereas rape was a crime directed at the woman. In the Västmanna law, the circumstances of rape, the evidence, and the punishment were clearly regulated:

> If a man takes a woman with force, and marks can be seen either on her or him [reflecting] what he did to her or she did to him, or if it is so close to a village or a road that cries and supplications can be heard. And if this is legally announced to witnesses, [then] a district jury shall find out the truth. If a man takes a woman with force and is caught in the act, and twelve men testify to it, then he shall be sentenced under sword. (Ekholst 2014: 190ff.)

In the law statutes of the fourteenth-century Serbian Empire—a mixture of traditional Serbian customary law and influences from the Rhomaian (Byzantine) Empire and the Orthodox Church—it was elementary whether the raped woman was a virgin or a wife. According to the provisions of the statute of the city of Kotor, if both actors were unmarried, the aggressor could escape punishment if he married the woman (without getting a dowry) and she and her family consented. If the woman was a slave, she and her master had to give consent. If no marriage took place, the rapist had to pay a fine depending on the social status of the woman. If he could not raise this, he was threatened with corporal punishment. Similar penalties applied to the rape of a married woman, but only if the last was honorable (Kršljanin 2021: 110ff.).

Rape was also a major theme in Byzantium and was found in ecclesiastical and secular sources over the centuries. For example, in the debates about Saint Mary's consent to the conception of Jesus. Had she consented to the conception when it was announced, or was it a case of overempowerment or even rape? In the discourse on rape, it was also a question of whether the victim had felt sexual pleasure when pregnancy occurred. In this case, it was believed that the woman had at least gained something from the event and that a distinction should be made between mental and sexual conception (Betancourt 2020: 19ff.).

The law *Ecloga* of Leo III and Constantine V from the year 741 was groundbreaking and the valid legal basis in Byzantium until the thirteenth century. There, a distinction was made between consensual "stuprum" and rape. In the first case, the virgin involved consented to coitus, but her parents did not, which included the refusal of permission to marry. If the man did not want to marry after the crime or if the parents still did not consent, he was threatened with money and property fines, and possible corporal punishment; the former went to the woman involved and not to the fisc. In the case of rape of a virgin, on the other hand, the aggressor faced splitting of the nose and (in a later law extension) also the loss of a third of his property. The most severe punishment was threatened for the rape of a girl under thirteen (i.e., under the legal age for marriage): In addition to the aforementioned corporal punishment, he was also to hand over half of his property to the victim's parents (Laiou 1993: 120ff.).

For Bologna, an unusually high number of rape trials have survived for some years of the thirteenth century, namely ninety-five from three years, 1286, 1287, and 1289. Most of them concerned urban poor, working women, who had little property or family support and were particularly vulnerable. Contrary to the usually low rate of reports by the women concerned and their families—there was fear of damage to their reputation—the rate was high here, because the procedure was easy to start and the chance was high that the aggressor would be forced to flee from justice and the city (Lansing 2021: 84ff.). In the *libri maleficiorum* (court records) of Bologna between 1396 and 1474, thirty-four rapes of women and eighty-one rapes of children (the same number of girls with an average age of ten as boys, on average 14.5 years old) were documented. It is striking that the perpetrators were charged with rape in the case of girls and sodomy in the case of boys. The former crime was punished with a fine, the latter by death. The perpetrators came from the marginal social groups, such as vagrants, servants, and domestic servants; the middle and upper urban classes were more or less absent, which also had to do with their possibilities to cover up such a crime (Lett 2017: 88ff.).

There are also surviving court cases from the Late Middle Ages in which sexual violence against children and adolescents are tried. For example, in 1364, Alice de Rouclif, who was not yet twelve years old, and eighteen-year-old John Marrays of Kennythorpe, near York, entered into a formal legal agreement to marry when both parties were of sufficient age. The promise of marriage was the reason why the man derived a right to sexual intercourse and one night he did it by force, although his bride-to-be wanted to wait until the wedding night. As the testimony of a witness located in the same room revealed, the girl reacted to the rape by the older and much stronger man by freezing instead of fighting back and screaming (Goldberg 2008: 26ff.). During the judicial hearing of rape cases against five- to seven-year-old girls in the Spanish cities of Lleida and Valencia in the years 1332–1398, midwives were used to provide an expert opinion on the physical condition of the victim. In the seven cases, this was done primarily to determine whether the girl was still a virgin and already anatomically developed enough for the perpetrator to actually penetrate her (Ferragud and Roca 2020: 326ff.). As here, it was often the social hierarchy between the sexes (especially age difference and social dependence) that led women and girls to endure this ordeal rather than actively resist rape.

Sexual violence and rape were also among the experiences that many girls and women had to endure when, for example, a town was captured and plundered in the course of military conflicts. Giovanni Sercambi (1348–1424), a chronicler from Lucca, described the events at the Sack of Arezzo in 1381 as follows:

> All the women were taken, Guelf and Ghibelline alike, in such a number that it was a pity, and they were shamed. And after some days, the aforementioned count Alberigo, who wished that the women should not lose their honor, proclaimed that all women should gather in the church of Santa Maria de' Servi, and many of them came, even if several of the young and beautiful ones remained hidden. And upon seeing such a multitude of women of every sort, it was granted to everyone to leave the city with not more than a loaf of bread. Then they were accompanied to the borders of Arezzo, but many of them returned saying: I do not know where to go. Or told a member of the company: this was my house, give your life up to me, and you can do to me whatever you like. And this is how the city was treated, and whoever saw that he cannot be so cruel not to feel pity for them; to see so many gentle youngsters, maidens, and nuns shamed, and many of them travelled the world as whores. (Bokody 2021: 584)

The Linkage of Marriage, Love, and Sexuality

Between the eleventh and fourteenth centuries, the triad of marriage, reproduction, and gender polarity—now also secured in natural law—was consolidated. It became the guiding principle of canonical teaching and penetrated the everyday life of all people. From the twelfth century, marriage was considered an indissoluble sacrament and all clergy—not only monks and nuns—were to observe celibacy (Crawford 2007: 64ff.). For women, monastic virginity offered an alternative to marriage and motherhood and the associated subordination in patriarchy. Despite often being quite different in practice, medieval Christianity had split the human person into a sexually procreative and an ascetic type. According to scholastic natural law, another dividing line ran through the high and late medieval sexual culture: Christians, both women and men, had to distinguish not only chaste from sinful behavior in their sexual lives but also God-given from unnatural acts. If, like the sodomites, one surrendered to unnatural practices, one was threatened not only with harsh but also capital punishment, and one placed oneself outside the divine order as a heretic. Nevertheless, walking the fringes of the Christian paths were couples in which the (married) woman was particularly active sexually or who consorted orally and anally.

Marriage, love, and sexuality were more closely linked in the High Middle Ages. This can be observed, for example, in the songs of the French and Catalan troubadours of the twelfth and thirteenth centuries, who based their poetry on Jewish-Arab motifs of love. They praised the worshipped by hiding their feelings or even singing about love as instantiation, imagining the woman or a certain woman as its embodiment (Clark 2008: 54f.). Even courtly love should no longer follow (primarily) pragmatic motives, but emotional forces, while remaining quite Platonic. Moreover, it was an appeal to the nobility not to practice the sexual act as physical overpowering (as with a subordinate), but to make it sensitive, in concert with one's wife. Some historians believe that courtly love was aimed less at a concrete person than at "aristophilia" in general (Schultz 2006a: 98). An example of the literarily exaggerated *ars amatoria* (art of love) was the *Roman de la rose* (*The Romance of the Rose*), a French verse romance written in the thirteenth century, in the first part of which noble courtship is presented as a moral achievement within the framework of the ideal of courtly love. In the second section, written by a town cleric, love appears as a natural urge and the (married) woman as a temptation that jeopardizes the man's morality and reason (Huot 2000). Here, too, male supremacy manifests itself in taking, for the protagonist Jaloux must ultimately pick the Rose (a virgin) by force:

> Pluck the rose by force and show that you are a man, when the place and time and season are right, for nothing could please them so well as that force, applied by one who understands it. For many people are accustomed to behave so strangely that they want to be forced to give something that they dare not give freely, and pretend that it has been stolen from them when they have allowed and wished it to be taken. (Desmond 2006: 80)

According to popular opinion, even common marriages should not be entered into for social and economic reasons alone; instead, marriage was considered to be a God-given *bonum* in which man and woman came together in love and good (sexual) togetherness. The marriage oath was now to insist on the free vow of both parties and, conversely, made infidelity not only a sin before God but also a breach of contract and a legal category (Illich 2006: 110ff.). The God-governed nature of Christian marriage was thus sealed. At the Council of Arles in 1275, sexual intercourse with non-Christians—for example, with a Jewess or "Saracen"—was therefore also classified as *contra naturam* and fell under those official offences that had to be reported to and/or taken up by the episcopal court (Schnitzler 2009: 260).

According to the discourses on marriage and love, men and women continued to have quite different ideas about marital duties and the expectations and hopes associated with them. Sexual acts were performed by a man as an actor with a woman and not both with each other. At the same time, one could read, for instance, in Walter of Mortagnes' (before 1100–1174), treatise on marriage, written around 1150, that married couples also came together for other reasons than those envisaged by theologians (procreation and servicing the marital *debitum*), namely because they desired each other carnally due to their mutual longing (Schnell 2002: 236). In late medieval literature, the tension between sexuality, love, and marriage formed a leitmotif, e.g., in Giovanni Boccaccio's (1313–1375) *Decameron* or Chaucer's (*c.* 1342/1343–1400) *Canterbury Tales*. On the basis of the successful and unsuccessful embedding of sexual desire in marital communication, they discuss how marriages thrive or lead to violence, aversion, and discord. However, literature could not offer a patent recipe for how this intimate exchange between the sexes should take place in a patriarchal society—which is why the tension-filled triad of marriage, sexuality, and gender relations remained on the agenda.

All this gives rise to skepticism about a simplistic view of medieval sexuality, which is still often encountered: Neither was it a permissive epoch, in which large parts of the population indulged in sexual pleasure— the church's sexual morals had seeped too far into individuals' minds and collectives' mores for that—and sexual order had become the foundation of the corporative-patriarchal society. Nor did people still live exclusively for their salvation and, therefore, try to silence sexual desire completely or give it totally negative connotations. Depending on the type of source, author, and addressee, divergent pro- and anti-sexual attitudes and lifestyles can be found. What monks, priests, peasants, merchants, craftsmen, nobles, and knights thought about the sexual and how they practiced it was probably as different and diverse as the everyday sexual lives of individual men and women, of single, married, or widowed. Even if the discourse on the pacification of concupiscence in marriage that had gone on for centuries left indelible traces, the numerous writings that made fun of lecherous clerics, vivacious virgins, and unfaithful husbands are a clear indication that, in reality, things often looked different than one imagined or wished in the scriptorium (Classen 2011a: 318ff.).

Byzantine, Christian-Orthodox, Muslim, Jewish, and Racial Sexual Cultures

Marriage and Celibacy in Byzantine and Slavic Orthodox Christianity

In the sexual culture of the Byzantine and Slavic regions, carnal desires in marriage also presented a struggle. There, the development was more strongly influenced by the local patriarch, however, and already between the fifth and eleventh centuries it significantly differed from the Roman-oriented world of Central and Western Europe. John Chrysostom (*c.* 349–407) was the most popular. He saw marriage as a means of channeling concupiscence but preferred the marriage in paradise. According to him, bodily shame and body covering should reduce sexual stimuli as much as possible even among married people.

Nevertheless, Chrysostom had quite a positive attitude toward marital intercourse and described the purity of the marital bed:

> How do they become one flesh? As if she were gold receiving the purest of gold, the woman receives the man's seed with rich pleasure, and within her it is nourished, cherished, and refined. I know that my words embarrass many of you, and the reason for your shame is your own wanton licentiousness. "Let marriage be held in honour among all, and let the marriage bed be undefiled." (Persisanifi 2017: 527)

In *Digenes Akritas* (twelfth century), the most famous of the Acritic songs, the power of erotic love is contrasted with other forms of love:

> And immediately I remind you about passion (eros), for this is established as the root and beginning of love (agape), from which affection (philia) is begotten, the desire (pathos) is born, which as it increases gradually bears such fruit as constant anxieties, worries and concerns and immediately brings abundant dangers and separation from parents. (Messis and Nilsson 2018: 162)

Eros was understood here as an extremely powerful emotion, which especially afflicts adolescents and young and adult men and virtually tyrannizes them. Girls and women were also seized by *eros* at the sight of them, whose energy could only be calmed by the sexual act (for a certain time).

The question of marital debt can be used as an example to illustrate the differences to the Occidental marriage and sexual system. In contrast to Western Europe, Byzantine sexual culture had no fixed marital obligations to perform regular sexual intercourse. In the West, the concept of *debitum* clearly referred to this and was recorded in ecclesiastical writings. This was not so in Byzantium; there was no duty to marital intercourse—even if it was expected of both spouses. Where Western writings of the twelfth to the fifteenth century spoke of a well-defined frequency of marital debt, Byzantine authors addressed marital fidelity and the safeguarding of household finances. They thus allowed for a more open and fluid interpretation of the frequency and commitment of sexual interaction between spouses. As a consequence, unlike in the West, the husbands in particular could not use legitimized force to compel coitus, but had to rely on negotiation with the partner. In the East, marital sex was accordingly not regarded as sinful in itself and did not need justification through the marital debt. In any case, there was no need to worry about whether sexual intercourse in marriage was a sin or whether refusing it might be a sin (Persisanifi 2017; Laiou 1993).

The (secular) legislation of Byzantium treated married men and women differently. In the case of adultery, for example, women were the primary focus of this offence. It was they who committed adulterous sexual intercourse. If, on the other hand, a man committed adultery with an unmarried woman, he merely indulged in fornication, which carried a considerably lesser penalty. But here, too, Christian influence in marriage law increased, for example, in the suppression of unilateral divorce or separation as such (Stolte 1999: 81ff.).

As in the Occident, clerical discussions in subsequent centuries remained quite contentious and contradictory. In spite of all its inherent asceticism, the vast majority of church and secular authorities advocated a rather positive attitude toward married sex. Throughout the Byzantine period, nuptial pleasures were seen as an important means of consolidating the marriage bond, although this was not to be an end in itself (Levin 1996: 333f.). A clear difference to Rome was cast in the Eastern celibacy regime: Married men were still allowed to be ordained priests in the Eastern Empire but were not allowed to remarry after the death of their wives, while bishops usually came from the monkhood and remained celibate for life. Yet, many monks and nuns entered a monastery only after marriage. Even eunuchs were admitted to the priesthood (Wiesner-Hanks 2000: 49f.). From the ninth century, marriage was supposed to be entered into in the presence of a priest, but in practice this was rarely the case. The rules for incest up to the third and fourth degree of kinship were also difficult to verify.

For Orthodox Slavs, virginity advanced to such an ideal status that it began to show a less positive light on the marital duties. Slavic clerics often oriented themselves toward the Bogomils, an ascetic community that came from the territory of present-day Bulgaria from the tenth century, and presumed that the flesh was a preferred dwelling place for demons (Versluis 2008: 53ff.). Since evil never sleeps, they broadened the grounds for divorce: Men could separate from their wives not only after the women had committed adultery but also if they stayed out at night unaccompanied, took part in a horse race, or went to the bathhouse alone. Unfaithful wives, then, should enter a cloister after dissolution of the marriage bond. Conversely, the husband's transgressions had to be much more serious and more frequent for a woman to seek separation. Slavic laws did not include provisions that considered non-consummation of a marriage as a reason for annulment—this would have contradicted the ideal of the Josephite marriage. Rather, even within marriage, a chaste life was of high value. The number of forbidden days increased and continued to rise into the Late Middle Ages: Sexual intercourse was not permitted during or around Communion, before ritual celebrations, on Fridays, Saturdays, and Sundays, during Lent, and during menstruation. This resulted in up to 300 days of abstinence per year for strict believers (Levin 1996: 339). The sexual separation of so-called blacks and whites was consolidated among clerics: The first class included celibate monks and nuns as well as the higher clergy. The white clergy, on the other hand, were made up of priests and deacons who could continue to marry, but who did not move up in the church hierarchy.

In Russia or in the dominions that emerged from the Kievan Rus' in the eleventh century, sexual rules followed the principles of Slavic Orthodox Christianity—about which surviving information is exclusively provided by church sources. According to these, one should mistrust sexuality even within marriage, because the devil is always at work even in procreative coitus between spouses. Here, as in other sexual issues, the Orthodox Church took a much more rigid position than the Roman Church. But church views and lay practices diverged also in morally strict Russia. Colloquial terms indicate that the population was quite positive about its sexual life (Levin 1993: 42ff.). In the land of the Rus, church canon mixed with popular belief, which is why in sexual matters people still trusted the pagan knowledge and the advice of wise women and consulted them, for example in the absence of a birth or the impotence of the husband, and sought herbal potions and other therapeutic remedies from them (Pushkareva 1997: 39). From today's point of view, it is difficult to understand the idea that the Virgin Mary had remained completely sexually pure not only during her marriage but also at the birth of her son; that is, she did not give birth to Jesus through her vagina or, rather, the birth canal (soiled as these were by original sin)—but rather out of her ear (Pushkareva 1991: 47). Spiritual impurity was also one of the reasons why women should abstain from worship for at least forty days after giving birth. As there were hardly any relations with the West during Mongol rule and after the consolidation of Russia under Ivan III (Ivan the Great) (1440–1505), the Renaissance and the Reformation passed more or less without leaving a trace on this territory, and such ideas persisted until the political and cultural opening of Russia under Tsar Peter the Great (1672–1725).

Al-Andalus between Muslim, Christian, and Jewish Cultures

On the Iberian Peninsula, between the first Muslim Arab-Berber conquest in 711 and the surrender of the last Muslim ruler in Al-Andalus in 1492, Muslim, Christian, and Jewish (sexual) cultures didn't only live in contention—there was also coexistence and interaction (Wilke 2016: 222ff.). Although the first Christian revolts against Muslim rule in Asturias broke out as early as 718, it took the Christian kings until the eleventh century to reconquer larger parts of the peninsula. But by no means did two uniform religious-worldly powers and cultural blocs meet here. In many cases there were also great political and social differences within the respective Muslim and Christian areas. Between Christians and Muslims, numerous social and economic interdependencies developed simultaneously, which led to acculturation and assimilation phenomena on both sides (Herbers 2006: 72ff.; Fernández-Morera 2015). The highly developed Arab culture exercised a great fascination on many Christians.

Even if they retained their own religions, they often adopted—at least in the early phase of relative tolerance in Al-Andalus—parts of the Muslim way of life and the cultural expressions associated with it (Schlicht 2006: 31 and 46ff.; Bossong 2010: 66ff.; Catlos 2014: 365ff.).

The *Reconquista* (reconquest) by Christian rulers was much more confrontational and resulted in Muslims being either killed, expelled, or forced to convert. Nobles and bishops campaigned massively for a *repoblación* (repopulation) of the conquered territories by Christians. After the defeat of Toledo (1085), the *Reconquista* also extended to the Muslim heartland of Al-Andalus, so that the remaining rulers called on the North African Berber dynasty of the Almoravids for help. In the High Middle Ages, ideological and military conflicts intensified between the defenders of Islam and the Sharia, on the one hand, and the "liberators" of Iberia, on the other, who understood their military actions as a "Holy War" of Christianity against infidels. Between the thirteenth and fifteenth centuries, the Christian kings conquered further cities and bastions. Finally, in 1492, the last ruler, the Emir of Granada, Muhammad XII (*c.* 1459–*c.* 1533) had to surrender. In the fifteenth and sixteenth centuries, Moors and Jews were forced to convert. Yet, these new Christians remained marginal figures in society and were then persecuted by the Inquisition.

During the centuries of coexistence, cooperation, and opposition between Christians, Muslims, and Jews, sexual and marital relations also came into the focus of religious and secular normative efforts. In this area of life, the hopes and fears associated with the crossing and mixing of boundaries between members of the different religions were clearly expressed. Concubinage and marriages between Muslim men (mostly from the elites) and Christian women were two ways in which relationships could be maintained in Muslim territories (Barton 2015: 76ff.). For a long time, the *muwallad* (descendants) of such concubines even rose to political leadership positions. On the other hand, legal scholars were less inclined to see connections between Christian men and Muslim or Jewish women in a positive light. Excluded from this were relationships of dependence, for example between a free Christian man and a slave or concubine of another faith. Penalties of shame and fines were frequently applied in Al-Andalus. In the re-Christianized areas, too, gender and status were decisive for the severity of the crime, in addition to religious criteria. According to the high medieval *Códido de las costumbres escritas de Tortosa*, a secular collection of laws, coitus between a Muslim or a Jew and a Christian woman ought to be punished particularly severely. The men faced torture and quartering—the women, immolation. In the thirteenth and fourteenth centuries, such capital punishments for sexual mixing between religions—and members of different *raza* (races)—were quite common practice in the courts (Nirenberg 1996: 132f.).

There is a long tradition of a bipolar image of Muslim sexual culture: on the one hand, it has been eroticized, on the other—as in recent decades—

it has been condemned as repressive (Heng 2018; Marín 2002: 3ff.). However, recent historiography has shown that neither one nor the other cliché of Muslim sexuality in the Middle Ages corresponds to the historical tradition. The sources available for Al-Andalusian society have been examined just as critically as the Christian and Jewish ones. Information about the early Muslim sexual culture on the Iberian Peninsula is mainly provided by religious and learned sources, which do not provide a representative view of the everyday sexual life of the population but rather a clerical or elitist one. Texts like the collection of the *Kitab Adab al-nisa'*, compiled by Ibn Habib in 853, for example, reflect the perspective of the urban upper classes and by no means that of average, everyday married life. In this sense, it represents a kind of marriage erotology, which was intended to teach men of this class "what a man has to do with his wife (. . .) on the night of consummation"—as one of the chapters was called. Other sections deal with questions of non-vaginal sexual intercourse, the frequency of coitus, and the condemnation of same-sex sexual contact among women (Marín 2002: 6f.). A larger collection of sources exists from the Late Middle Ages, including Inquisition documents, marriage contracts, and literary texts, which allow a more differentiated picture (Fuente 2009: 319ff.).

Muslim Men Should Lie to Their Wives

In the Muslim part of the Iberian Peninsula, it was the men's task to control their wives sexually and not to give them too much freedom in public, as when visiting *hammām* and the mosque. This was particularly so because it was believed that the female sex was dominated by a powerful sexual drive that was difficult to keep in check (Barnes-Karol and Spadaccini 2002: 233). Through their dominant behavior, Muslim men were also supposed to demonstrate their social supremacy and their religious superiority over other religious communities. During menstruation and pregnancy, women were considered spiritually unclean and were excluded from religious practices. They had to undergo ablutions to become ritually pure again (Fernández-Morera 2015: 90). They were also to be kept away from the eyes of strangers. Depending on the religious severity, this gaze regime included the wearing of the veil and other body coverings, from which only prostitutes and female slaves were exempt. In wealthy families, the free women rarely appeared outside the home. Slaves did the shopping and the necessary communication outside the domestic walls. The enclosed form of the buildings allowed family and household life to take place around the *patio* (inner courtyard). This served to keep female inhabitants invisible. Although the female family members were able to follow some of the events outside through covered windows and niches, they were not visible themselves. Joint visits to the bathhouses, separated according to gender, and religious events offered women of all classes some opportunities to escape domestic control. Members of poorer and rural families, on the other hand, had to appear outside the house more often; they also wore a veil less often and were therefore more vulnerable sexually.

Marriage was considered the norm for both sexes, and being single was at best a transitional period. This was because the Prophet had also spoken out in favor of marriage and its sexual practice. Asceticism and celibacy did not play a major role among clerics, and most imams were even married. Women ought to be wed at a young age so that sexual desire could not lead them astray. Men were allowed up to four marriages, women only one. Men had the right, as well as the duty, to sexually consummate their wives. Both of these—as well as the ownership relations between the spouses—were recorded in a marriage contract. Polygynous relations prevailed predominantly in wealthy families and opened up a tense network of relationships in which the sexual favors of the husband played a central role, and the wives literally fought for the position of favorite wife. After sexual acts, both sexes should cleanse themselves through ritual ablutions before prayer or even attending a celebration. As theologians and mystics repeatedly emphasized, it was not about the material *Ṭahāra* (purity) of the body, but about the purification of heart and mind (Heller and Mosbahi 1993: 106f.). In view of the spiritual impurity of sexual bodily fluids, masturbation also posed a particular problem and was considered a grave sin (Akashe-Böhme 2006: 33).

The Andalusian theologian, polymath, and writer Alí Ibn Ḥazm (994–1064), proponent and codifier of the Zahiri school of Islamic jurisprudence in the Caliphate of Córdoba, describes in *Ṭawq al-Ḥamāmah* (*The Ring of the Dove*, a treatise on the art of love) the struggle between two fundamental qualities that Allah has given to man: spirit, justice, and good, on the one hand, and the lust that led to evil and cruelty, on the other. One of his proverbs puts this conflict in a nutshell:

> He who is preserved from the evil of his clacker [his tongue], his rumbler [his belly] and his dangler [his penis], is saved from the evil of the whole sublunary world (Ibn Hazm 1994: 138).

His work was aimed at Muslim court society, where sexual relations with female slaves and erotic contacts between older and younger men were common. He himself had been given his first bride as a present, probably a slave, from his father's harem. But he, like the mystical Sufis, such as the Andalusian mystic and poet Abū al-Hasan al-Shushtarī (1212–1269), believed that asceticism made it easier to concentrate on Allah and that a wife was an obstacle to this (Álvarez 2005).

According to the *mālikī madhhab*, the dominant school of law in Al-Andalus, the *fiqh*, the Islamic legal doctrine from the Quran and the Sunna, Muslims were allowed to have sexual contacts with Christian and Jewish women and even to marry them. The offspring of such relations were considered Muslims. Muslim women, however, were strictly forbidden such relationships. Sexual acts with female slaves was a male privilege, as was (though less welcomed) contact with prostitutes. According to literature, young female slaves were considered particularly desirable and, if they had a child by their owner, were subject to the same rules as the wives. Male authors were also fascinated by those unfree women who knew how to enmesh a man, that is, her owner, with her erotic charms in such a way that the man became downright dependent and ignored other women. Female slaves were obliged to engage in sexual intercourse with their masters and, if necessary, were forced into compliance. It was the master's decision to have a slave woman circumcised. Especially during the reign of the Umayyads, there was a lively trade and distribution in Al-Andalus of young female sexual slaves and male children who were castrated to become eunuchs in the harems (Fernández-Morera 2015: 158ff.). A special attraction came from those female slaves (often Berbers imported from North Africa or Christians captured in war or bought at the market) who were chosen at Andalusian courts at a young age to become a *qiyan*, a singer, who then performed for entertainment or could also advance to a concubine or courtisane (Reynolds 2017).

Free women who were not under the protection of a husband, such as widows and divorced women, were easily suspected of *zina'*, which was understood as any form of fornication between those who were not married or living in a legal concubinage (such as between a free and an unfree woman) (Marín 2002: 16). Even if two unmarried persons signed a *Carta de compañía de mesa y cama* (deed of communion of bed and table) or a *Carta de amigamiento* (deed of friendship), the specter of *zina'* hung over them for a certain time. In 1481, for example, Anthon d'Aysa and María Martín agreed to a contract of this kind, in which it was stipulated that Anthon pay María 300 *sueldos* "on the condition that while she lived with me she would remain chaste, as a wife is to her husband." María agreed to have intercourse only with Anthon, otherwise she would forfeit any payment (Lacarra 2002: 159).

Women and Marital Obligations

In marriage, family, and household, the roles and tasks of wives, mothers, and daughters were clearly defined in Muslim society. This included religious and ritual acts at birth, marriage, and death. In marriage, women and men had the same right to sexual intercourse. Men were not obliged to perform coitus more than once a month, however—according to Islamic tradition—while the women must be available all the time. There were no such reservations about contraceptive measures, whether by coitus interruptus or other methods, as opposed to Christianity. The Galenic humor theory applied to the Eastern body image, as did its consequences for male and female sexuality (Pomata 2018: 197)—for example, the view that the female sexual body functioned in analogy to the male's and that the latter was regarded as a frame of reference. For Ibn Sina (Lat. Avicenna; 980–1037), the production or secretion of the female seed was connected with sexual desire and was therefore seen as necessary for procreation. He suggested that fertilization worked best when the woman and the man experienced orgasm simultaneously. And to get the woman in the mood, the man should stimulate the female breasts and clitoris—the latter also during penetration. Reproduction and female lust were thus causally connected in this medical discourse. In addition, sexual desire was seen as part of the (gender-specific) physiology of the body and considered natural, which is why younger and stronger people would also have a stronger sexual drive than older and weaker people (Dallai 2009: 403ff.).

The religious and legal scholar Muhammad al-Ghazzali (1058–1111) was not exclusively concerned with reproduction during sexual intercourse:

> The sexual appetite should surely not compel the begetting of children alone, but is also a wise arrangement in other respects. Desire and its associated gratification, which if it were everlasting would not be comparable with anything else, is surely a sign of the pleasures we are promised in paradise (Jütte 2008: 26).

In the case of coitus interruptus, which a man should only perform with the consent of his wives, Allah still determines whether a child is conceived anyway. In practice, older women in particular, and those in familial and economic straits, are likely to have used a wide range of means and measures to avoid becoming pregnant (again).

If a man failed to fulfil his marital obligations over several months, his wife could divorce him. If a man slept with an unmarried woman who was no longer a virgin, the sin was merely a minor one, if it counted at all (Karras 2006: 252). Divorce in court was relatively easy to achieve, for men; for women—without major financial losses—it was only possible under certain circumstances. These included disgusting diseases of the husband and impotence (Zomeño 2002: 114f.). Unchastity of a female member of the family and adultery were not infrequently the cause of injured honor between two families, resulting in acts of violence. Adultery by a Muslim woman was to be severely punished by law, if not with death, then at least with enslavement or publicly administered lashes and exile for a year (Nirenberg 2004: 133ff.; Fernández-Morera 2015: 144). Premarital coitus under Muslim law was also considered not only a sin but also a secular offence that endangered the legitimate descent of a child. Andalusian proverbs devoted much attention to this problem: The sexual pleasure of young women should be strictly monitored, otherwise it pollutes the future husband's "place" (Lachiri 2002: 43ff.). In the Muslim tradition, a child's secure line of descent was accorded the greatest importance. For this reason, even widows had to refrain from remarriage and sexual intercourse for a few months in order to ensure legal paternity in case of pregnancy. For a long time, the old Muslim tribal thinking also persisted in Al-Andalus, which meant that when a convert was adopted or married they not only changed immediate families but also their clan membership.

Marriage as a Contract in Jewish Law

The medieval sexual culture of the Iberian Peninsula is also remarkable because not only Muslims and Christians met there, but they also consorted with Jews (Catlos 2014). Sephardi, the Jewish population of Iberia, first lived under Muslim rule, then under Christian sovereignty after the successful *Reconquista*, and was thus used to reciprocal influence (Nirenberg 2004; Tartakoff 2015). As already mentioned, Jewish culture could draw on centuries-old discussions, reservations, and rules regarding sexual contacts with non-Jews. Especially among the diaspora, the rabbis paid keen attention to non-mixing with people of other faiths and to possible dangers that resulted from sexual relationships: acculturation and assimilation as well as, if necessary, conversion. Accordingly, the Talmudic provisions prohibiting mixed marriages were extended to a general prohibition of sexual contact with non-Jews. Also in the *halakhah*, the legal interpretations of the Torah, monogamy was insisted upon and polygyny was now made punishable for Jews. This did not mean the end of concubinage, however, which continued to be practiced well after the end of Muslim rule (Roth 1996: 313). Moses ben Nachman (1194–1270, known as Nachmanides), for example, voted for master–maid relationships: "A man may keep a concubine whom he has espoused (. . .) if she lives in his house, and is known to be exclusively his, her children bear his name, and the relationship is a licit one." One of the reasons for this attitude is probably to be found in the change in Spanish laws: these now punished visiting Christian prostitutes or soliciting Christian women on the street with the death penalty; sexual intercourse with maids offered a safe alternative (Wilke 2016: 204).

Under the Christian rulers, there were considerably more sexual contacts between the Jewish and Muslim populations than between either these two and Christians. Late medieval sources mainly deal with relationships between free Jewish men and Muslim women (most of them slaves), but there does not seem to have been any cases of the reverse. In the course of the conquest of the last Muslim territories, the Christian rulers began to enforce a strict ban on marriage and mixing with non-Christians. Many of the primarily urban Jewish subjects were much closer to the crown, due to their multilingualism and financial services, than the remaining Muslim population, which lived mainly in rural areas. In the thirteenth and fourteenth centuries, the Christian rulers and bishops intensified their legal discrimination against Jews—and "Saracens" as

Muslims in Europe were often called—and made sexual intercourse with Christians punishable for these peoples (Metzler 2011: 117). According to the provisions of the Fourth Lateran Council (1215), both groups were to wear a badge of their religious affiliation that was visible to all (Wilke 2016: 199). Pope Gregory IX (*c.* 1167–1241) proclaimed it had to be a circle of yellow felt or fabric attached to the back and front of clothing. Its purpose: to protect Christian women from the "guileful" and "lascivious" offers of Jewish men and to keep them from mixing the faiths (Resnick 2012: 80ff.).

In 1391, the bishop of Seville called on the Christian population to destroy the city's twenty-three synagogues, thus triggering a pogrom with thousands of deaths and a wave of conversions (Bossong 2008: 47f.; Tartakoff 2015: 730). In the middle of the fifteenth century, not only Christians but also Muslims were forbidden to convert to Judaism, which also made marriage and sexual interrelations more difficult. Antisemitism in Spain ran rampant during this period. The enactment of the Alhambra Edict of 1492 led to further pogroms as it essentially decried that Jews either convert or emigrate. The displacement led to cruel rapes and sexual violence against mostly unmarried girls (Wilke 2016: 215f.). In Portugal, the first heretic edict was issued in 1536. This mentioned "crypto-jews" alongside Lutherans, so that the Portuguese *marranos*—Jews who had been forcibly converted—were accused of secretly continuing to practice their faith and were thus persecuted by the Inquisition.

The similarities and differences between Jewish and Christian marriage were unmistakable by the twelfth century at the latest—not only on the Iberian Peninsula but throughout Europe. Under Jewish law, marriage was a contract (*ketubah*) for which there were clear moral, social, and economic provisions in the Talmud and rabbinical literature. Whereas previously concluded in private, by the High and Late Middle Ages it advanced to become a celebrated event in its own right, with specially designated wedding facilities. Couples got to know each other at a fairly young age—girls often at the age of twelve to thirteen, boys at fourteen to fifteen—through their families and were betrothed and wed. Socioeconomic factors played the major role, whereas (romantic) love between the bridal couple a rather minor one (Roth 2005: 43ff.). The—by medieval standards—very low age of marriage was due to large families; ten or more children were not uncommon. Households wanted to marry off their children as early as possible to ease the financial burden. Nevertheless, young couples usually spent a few more years living in one of the two parental households. Early marriage was also seen as a good opportunity to allow the budding sexual desire to flow directly into marital coitus. From the eighth century onwards, Jewish marriage was primarily monogamous in structure; additional wives were even precluded in some marriage contracts (Karras 2006: 131). However, this explicit mention is probably an indication that polygynous constellations and concubinages also existed here. By contrast, other forms of polygyny and concubinage—in the Muslim surroundings—were common alongside the main marriage. Legally speaking, though, first wives had to give their consent (Friedman 1989: 39). Another reason for early marriages was the increasing persecution from the thirteenth century onward; with it rose the pressure to transfer assets in good time (Baskin 2003: 426).

The medieval rabbis insisted there was to be no sexual contact before marriage. If it turned out that a bride had not entered the marriage as a virgin, she was threatened with fines in addition to annulment of the marriage contract. Marital sexual life continued to be seen as a positive matter, not only for procreation but also for the maintenance of the relationship between the spouses. Women were considered unclean during the monthly period and had to undergo a ritual washing in the *mikvah* before their next sexual intercourse. The following evening was usually scheduled for coitus. Depending on the type of source, however, other assessments of marital sexuality also existed. The Jewish moral literature written by clergymen was much less "sex-friendly" than the enshrined Jewish legal canon, the *halachic* texts. Both types of sources nevertheless insisted on the procreative commandment and the duty to engage in sexual intercourse (with the weight of obligation and responsibility falling to the men). Jewish culture did not offer an asexual way out, like the monastery for Christianity. The *ona* commandment (the sexual covenant) of the husband covered not only a woman's fertile days; the divine mandate stood throughout married life— also during (early) pregnancy and after menopause (Berger 2003: 25ff.). There were even rules for the frequency of conjugal sex, specified depending on social status, age, and health. Normally, weekly intercourse took place on the Sabbath, the day on which Christians were more likely to abstain (Stow 1992: 206).

(Married) Rabbis and Physical Desires

The rabbinical literature, on the other hand, was not very supportive of pro-sexual attitudes. Too much sexual intercourse leads to a waste of seed and energy in the man, and marital sanctification, as fulfilment of this aspect of the holy covenant was called, should therefore be carried out moderately, modestly, and only when there is a mutual high level of desire. The specific sexual acts should also remain within what was considered to please God. If the man did not fulfil his sexual duties, however, the rabbis regarded this as grounds for divorce—practiced across social classes. Jewish women often brought significant possessions into the marriage, which, in the event of separation, gave them (somewhat) more freedom of movement and made remarriage easier. According to Jewish law, women were also entitled to acquire their own property and run their own businesses during marriage.

It is conspicuous that despite the obligation to procreate, the Italian Talmudic scholar Isaiah di Trani (*c.* 1180–*c.* 1250), for example, permitted the use of contraceptives as a preventative measure in women's health

(Feldman 1974: 251ff.). In addition to herbs and potions, the *mokh*—already mentioned in the Talmud—was used for contraception: a woolen tampon immersed in a special liquid supposedly closed the cervix when inserted into the vagina (Klein 2000: 51ff.). The long periods of breastfeeding practiced by Jewish women—up to the age of two and over for boys and shorter by just a few months for girls—also represented a form of contraception, since breastfeeding can lead to lactational amenorrhea, a phase without ovulation (Karras 2006: 153). Male masturbation ran completely contrary to the God-given reproductive mission. It was roundly condemned and sanctioned in all Jewish codes. In biblical law already, punishment for adultery was precluded from the very persons concerned and their families, declared instead a matter for the congregation and the courts. In areas with Jewish self-administration and corresponding *halachic* courts, the nonetheless prescribed death penalty was usually commuted to corporal punishment and forced divorce due to the enormous burden of proof (Brundage 1987: 54ff.). In any case, one thing was beyond question over the centuries: there should be no carnal mixing between Jews and unbelievers, because it could lead to non-Jewish marriages and these in turn could weaken the Jewish community (Schnitzler 2009: 263).

From the twelfth century onward, Jewish scholars also took up Neoplatonic and Gnostic ideas and became more skeptical of physical desire writ large. The "sinister drive" was now regarded as the epitome of worldliness and as the antagonist of a more spiritual and religious attitude (Soble 2005, Vol. 1: 525ff.). Even in marital sexuality, one should therefore no longer merely pay heed to the actions themselves but also to the underlying purity of thought. Sexual intercourse should occur *le-schem shamajjim*, for "the sake of heaven" and under the sign of the divine. Sexual lust and physical pleasure, on the other hand, were forces of evil and impurity (Berger 2003: 52ff.). But sexuality was never considered so problematic that average rabbis would have refrained from it. On the contrary, they too were to marry a woman in order to fulfill the covenant. Some scholars did, however, call for men who devoted themselves entirely to the study of Torah to be sexually abstinent and not to marry, such as the authoritative philosopher and physician Moses Maimonides (around 1135–1204). His view for the general Jewish population was still to maintain marriages and carry on procreation (Biale 1992: 92). Even circumcision now received a new moral facet: the exposed glans would enable a man to reach orgasm more quickly and thus shorten conjugal pleasure (Karras 2006: 161). The representatives of Germanic Hasidism, a mystical movement of the twelfth and thirteenth centuries, pleaded in general for a turning away from the world and demanded more spiritual stoicism. But even they were mostly married and knew the worldly seductions from their own (bodily) experience (Baskin 2003: 427). Celibacy for the Christian mystics was, by contrast, unquestionable.

In the Late Middle Ages, therefore, the sexual differences between Jewish and Christian culture were obvious: in Judaism, men and women approached marital pleasures with fewer moralistic reservations. Nearly all of them, even the rabbis, married and were obliged by their faith to engage in sexual intercourse to fulfill their people's covenant. In Christianity (at least officially), first the monks and nuns, but later also increasingly the rest of the clergy were excluded from marriage and sexual acts. Asceticism and virginity applied to both sexes. The virgins in Christ, in particular, were offered an individual, marriage-like, ascetic-spiritual bond with the Lord in return for their abstinence—an option not available to Jewish contemporaries. As a contractual agreement, Jewish marriage could be dissolved for various reasons. Christian marriage, on the other hand, no longer provided for divorce under any circumstance; only in the event of (subsequently introduced) impediments to marriage could the bond be annulled—declared never to have existed. The rules of endogamy or incest also differed considerably: many Jews married within the fourth degree of kinship; Christians were forbidden to do so since the Fourth Lateran Council of 1215. Exceptions had to be obtained from the Pope, mediated by a bishop (Jørgensen 2008: 343ff.). Such a marriage dispensation could usually only be achieved with corresponding financial and political expenditure and was thus primarily a matter for the upper classes.

All in all, Jewish culture offered much greater scope for sexual activity within marriage, too. This was one of the reasons why some Christian authors of the High and Late Middle Ages claimed that Jews had a wicked sexual drive (Stow 1992: 207ff.). Converts were supposed to literally, physically feel it. Ostensibly, a change from a carnal to a more spiritual culture came with undergoing the *conversio* from Judaism to Christianity. However, many authors were skeptical that this transformation would succeed and that the sexual drive of the formerly Jewish body could actually be silenced. One way out was to radically take this step and, like Hermann of Cologne (*c.* 1107–*c.* 1181), son of rich Jewish parents, to enter a monastery—in this case joining the Premonstratensians—in hopes of killing the evil urge (Kruger 1997: 166f.).

In the Late Middle Ages, social conflicts were inevitable in sexual contacts across religious boundaries. Fornication offences of Jews with Christians that came to light were usually severely sanctioned. In 1470, for example, the Nördlingen Council Court pilloried a certain Mosse von Andernach for sexual misconduct with two Christian women and then had him driven out of town with burning screws. The women involved were also punished and expelled from the city for ten years (Schnitzler 2009: 253). In the late medieval sources there are often cases where young Jewish men had sexual contact with Christian prostitutes and were therefore punished or even attacked by urban groups of men protecting "their" women and denouncing the non-Christians. It is abundantly clear in the sources that it was mainly male members of the Jewish minority who were accused of having a (sometimes prolonged) sexual relationship with Christian women. The opposite case, however, is very rarely found in court records—which was due in large part to the selectivity bound up in the concept of honor and honor crimes as well as the gender-specific asymmetry of such relationships (Schnitzler 2009: 278).

The (Re)invention of Race and Sexuality

As the previous sections have shown, even in the Middle Ages there was a notion of different kinds or species of people and how they differed by physical and psychological characteristics. Therefore, in recent years, the term "race" has also been used to highlight such differentiation strategies more clearly—and has also become a category in the history of premodern sexuality (DiGangi 2020). According to Geraldine Heng, "race-making thus operates as specific historical occasions in which strategic essentialisms are posited and assigned through a variety of practices and pressures, so as to construct a hierarchy of peoples for differential treatment" (Heng 2018: 3). It was (and still is) often physical characteristics such as physiognomy or skin color that were used to postulate and carry out the racial categorization of people. In most cases, this was also done by attributing certain psychological characteristics to alleged types of people, such as greed, laziness, or deceitfulness. Frequently, in the ecclesiastical and secular discourses of the Middle Ages (as already in antiquity), sexual specifics were also attributed to racial groups. Since sexual desire was seen as a particularly strong human driving force deeply anchored in the body and its juice mechanics, sexual characteristics were seen as essentially formative and prototypical for the social or religious group labelled with them.

"Saracens" was a term used from the eleventh and twelfth centuries in Christian Europe for diverse peoples and populations, referring to their adherence to the Islamic religion. As enemies on the Iberian Peninsula and in the Balkans, the Saracens were considered particularly sexually threatening heretics. Their negative sexualization began with the image of Mohamed in European literature and religious writing. The Prophet was portrayed as a sexually greedy and promiscuous man who had twelve or more wives and also approved of polygyny among his followers (Heng 2018: 117ff.). This initial image of the oversexualized founder of the religion was also transferred to Muslim men who, because of their strong sexual desire, took pleasure in Christian girls and women or took them as concubines after the warlike conquest. In racial discourse, mixed-race sexual contacts were considered disastrous. An example is the Middle English romance *The King of Tars* (c. 1330), in which a Christian princess is forced to marry a black Muslim king. The mixed-race child from this relationship turns out to be a monstrous lump of flesh without blood, bones, or human face, who is only transformed into a beautiful white child through baptism (Heng 2018: 138ff.). Such narratives targeted interfaith concubinates between Muslim men and Christian women (often slaves) that were common practice in the

Iberian Peninsula (Barton 2015: 76ff.). In the *Travels of Sir John Mandeville*, a very popular travelogue circulating from the 1350s, one could read that the Saracens were so oversexualized because in the *Quran* they were promised not only an abundant life in the afterlife, but also new virgins who had daily sexual intercourse with them.

"For black women are hotter, and most of all dusky women, who are the sweetest to have sex with, so lechers say (. . .) because the mouth of their vulva is temperate and gently embraces the penis" (Biller 2005: 486; Heng 2018: 181). What Albertus Magnus had to say about black women in his *Quaestiones super de animalibus* (*c.* 1258) was also heard from other quarters about dark-skinned people. They were racialized by their skin color and stood for the opposite of white Christians. Women with dark skin or dark flesh were supposed to have a particularly soft physical consistency, their skin was extremely seductive, and the color black stood for sin, unchastity, and evil that was common in ancient and medieval religious discourses (Brakke 2001; Betancourt 2020: 161ff.). At the same time, the metaphor "black" was used to imagine a body that can be sexually possessed (Whitaker 2019: ch. 1). When black women (and men) were depicted in medieval art, they were generally naked or scantily clad, which also contributed to the image of a species driven by sexual desire (Strickland 2003: 44).

The "Ethiopians" were already imagined in late antiquity as a synthesis of heretics and race. Ethiopians were considered black, demon-possessed, and hypersexual. Their diabolical blackness represented the fears of same-gender desires and the homoeroticism of monastic life (Betancourt 2020: 180ff.). The image of the "Tatars" was also shaped by sexual specificities. Polygyny was common among them, as was sodomy with divination and idolatry, and they regularly committed all manner of atrocities. According to the discourse, they were sexually out of control and they also ignored the laws of consanguinity (Strickland 2003: 194ff.). Another example of sexual racialization and the inversion of the sexual norms of Christianity were the "Mongols." In the stories told by the Venetian merchant Marco Polo about East Asia at the end of the thirteenth century, Mongolian women behaved very differently from what was expected of European women. For example, Khutulun, the daughter of Kaidu (the grandson of Ugedey, Kublai's uncle), who only wanted to marry a man who defeated her in wrestling. Because she had defeated about 100 men in these fights for her virginity and received 100 horses from each, she became a rich woman. Even though other Mongolian women were described in a less martial way, they were also said to have a special morality and strength that was not part of the incarnated image of man in Christian women (Heng 2018: 338f.).

The bottom line is that the racial and sexual images of the Saracens, black/dark colored people, and certain ethnic groups served primarily to label non-Christian, heretical groups. Their counterimage was the idealized

Christian sexual life of lay people and clerics, which at the same time was fiercely debated and argued about throughout the Middle Ages.

Common Women and Municipal Brothels

Terms for Promiscuity and Selling the Body

Tolerance of sexual practices in the Middle Ages at its outer limits is on full display in the topic of prostitution. Women who were paid for sexual acts appear in the sources under various names, in Latin as *meretrix* (harlot), *meretrix publica* (public harlot), or *prostibilis* (women who offer themselves). Although these terms were also used for "fallen women" who had had sexual intercourse before or outside marriage or who lived loose lives. The boundaries were not always entirely clear. According to Thomas of Chobhams (*c.* 1160–1233/1236), *meretrix* denoted and connotated the following degrees of promiscuity: Firstly, this could mean a woman who practiced extramarital sex, secondly who had intercourse with multiple different men, and thirdly who generally did not refuse sexual advances (Hemmie 2007: 26). In the public statutes of Marseille, in the thirteenth century, "public" women were subsumed under the *meretrices* who received several men during the day and at night in their accommodations. This also included those who worked in a brothel (Rollo-Koster 2002: 110). A brothel was called a *lupanar* or *domus meretricum* in the Latin tradition or *prostibulum* in fourteenth-century Languedoc, which could designate not just a building but also an area or street where prostitutes worked (Otis-Cour 1985: 49).

In vernacular French, these buildings were called *bordels*, after the Latin *bordellum* or *hostal publique* or *maison publique* (Otis-Cour 1985: 49f.). In Middle High German, the women were called *huore* (whore), *gemeyn frouwe* (common woman), or *frie frouwe* (free woman) if they lived in a municipal *offen sunthaus*, *huorenhaus*, or *gemain frownhuß* as the brothels were called (Blaschitz 2008: 721f.). The *fahrenden frouwen* (vagabond women) and *soldiersen* (soldier's wives), on the other hand, were mobile. They followed the army troops, offered themselves at fairs and carnivals, or appeared at imperial diets and councils (Kühnel 1986: 40ff.). Wandering women who lived without a fixed family connection or domicile and wandered around with beggars, peddlers, gamblers, day laborers, scholars, mercenaries, and often also with a *cher homme* (dear man, as it was called in a Colmar ordinance) were also regarded as (potential) prostitutes (Schuster 1995: 37ff.). In the fourteenth and fifteenth centuries, then, it was common to speak of *gemeine* (from Old English *gemæne* "common, public, general, universal"), "public," "free," women and "whores" in the respective national languages. The social explosivity associated with such terms in everyday life could be set off by an insult. For example, in fifteenth-century Bologna, where accusations of such verbal abuse had a clearly gendered tendency: men were insulted by questioning their social position and the trust and honesty placed in them with terms like thieves, liars, or traitors—women by questioning their sexual life and decency with the term *puthana* (whore) (Dean 2004: 219).

For the church writers, what counted primarily was whether a woman had several lovers or suitors and briefly or notoriously practiced the immoral way of life as harlotry; the economic side of prostitution was more of an afterthought. The figure of the "hore" (from Proto-Germanic *hōran*, probably "one who desires"), and "harlot" (from Old French *herlot, arlot*, "vagabond, tramp, vagrant; rascal, scoundrel") or "strumpet" (either from Latin *stuprata* "have illicit sexual relations with") or Late Latin *strupum* (dishonor, violation) or Middle Dutch *strompe* (a stocking) or *strompen* (to stride, to stalk—as a prostitute might a customer) clearly expressed the contradiction in Christian sexual morals (Online Etymology Dictionary).

On the one hand, their promiscuity was considered unchaste and sinful, on the other, its function within urban life in particular was essential. At the same time, their actions and behavior were pushed to the edge of society and kept out of the public eye. Yet, they remained indispensable even to canonists and bishops, because they satisfied and pacified the sexual desires of unmarried men. In the Augustinian tradition, the *meretrix* was a "necessary evil" that ensured social order and domestic peace, thus keeping worse moral dangers out of the communities. Seen in this light, the whore functioned simultaneously as a social fringe figure and a central component of a moral economy by which the honor and morality of chaste women were also regulated and assured (Mummey 2011: 165f.). Even if they did not approve, the clergy thus had to come to terms with this necessary evil.

This resulted in unexpected commentary on their behalf. Thus, for example, in his early thirteenth-century *Summa Confessorum*, the theologian Thomas of Chobham argued that prostitutes had the right to demand an appropriate wage for their services and to receive it—after adequate performance. At the same time, he pleaded that they should not provide their services within the city walls, so as not to cause irreparable moral damage to the youth and the female population (Karras 2012a: 132). The church and secular authorities also publicly tolerated prostitution, with reference to Augustine no less. For example, in the fifteenth-century Nuremberg *Ordnung der gemeinen weiber in den frauenhäusern* (Order of common women in women's houses): "[F]or the sake of avoiding a greater evil in the Christian community, common women should be tolerated by the holy churches" (Mauf and Sladeczek 2012/2013: 337).

Contemporary commentators were aware that there were various reasons for prostitutes to put their bodies on the market, one being economic necessity to ensure bare survival. An example of this was women who had been abandoned because of an illegitimate child. Sometimes, young women were forced into prostitution by their parents for money or because they had been "seduced" by a man or they had to pay off a debt. Others worked independently on their own initiative or under the "protection" of a pimp. They viewed it as a form of making a living that seemed lucrative in comparison to other (possible) activities and the low earnings. Some mistresses, used to a modicum of prestige and prosperity, had no choice—if rejected by their lover—to venture into harlotry. It should not be forgotten that until well into the Middle Ages, prostitutes around the Mediterranean also came from the ranks of female slaves, who had to offer their sexual services and whose wages the slave owners collected. Female slaves were also available to their owners free of charge (Wyatt 2009: 397ff.). As an indication that the sheer numbers of women living in such conditions may not be underestimated, it has been shown that in Florence, for example, between 1385 and 1485 around 15 percent of the children living in orphanages were descendants of female slaves and had unknown fathers (Karras 2012b: 84).

Whores Have an "Ineradicable Inclination" to Sexuality?

The majority of ecclesiastical and secular sources, however, focus on the motives of the women concerned—less so on their clients' behavior. They problematize the morals associated with prostitution. Church officials were indignant that these women indiscriminately had sexual intercourse with multiple men, thus contradicting the model of the monogamous and faithful Christian (but also Muslim and Jewish) wife. For believers in the Bible, the strumpet was regarded as an obvious example of the Augustinian doctrine of original sin, according to which the indomitable sexual desire reminded man of the first of all sins, the falling away from God and the expulsion from paradise. Even though the evil thorn of sexual lust had been in both sexes ever since, it was Eve who had tempted Adam and was therefore condemned not only to painful childbirth but also to surrendering and subjugating lust. Skeptics were invited to read in the Old Testament:

> To the woman he said,
> "I will greatly multiply your pain in childbearing;
> in pain you shall bring forth children,
> yet your desire shall be for your husband,
> and he shall rule over you."
>
> (RSV Gen. 3:16)

Since Augustine, the prostitute had been considered a woman who practiced the "ineradicable inclination" to sexuality in an essential and unrestrained way and defiled suitors with her body. Hadn't Paul plainly written that sexual intercourse with a harlot led to becoming one flesh with her and thus unclean? But even the most morally strict Church Fathers believed that without prostitution the world would sink into lust, sodomy, and zoophilia. Augustine had created a powerful image to legitimize harlotry that held throughout the centuries: whores are comparable to the cesspits of a palace—without them the whole magnificent building would be sullied and begin to stink (Otis-Cour 1985: 12ff.; Richards 1990: 118ff.; Classen 2019: 13ff.).

What the clerics often overlooked, however, was that many of these women had come to this trade because of their unfortunate social and economic situation or even under duress. Yet, in the fifth century already, involuntary prostitution had been deemed one reason for the Eastern Roman Emperor Theodosius II (401–450) to pass laws against procuring and pimping (Osiek 2003: 274). Justinian I (*c.* 482–565) wanted to completely clear Constantinople of brothels and pimps and reintegrate repentant prostitutes into society in corresponding "penitential houses." As Procopius of Caesarea (*c.* 500–*c.* 562) notes in his *Historia Arcana* (Secret History), unwilling candidates were—under threat of violence—forced to enter these institutions and compelled to moral conversion (Brundage 1987: 120f.). With his decree from the year 535, Justinian was also reacting to the situation of many prostitutes, one characterized by dependency. In the preamble, we learn that pimps would roam the countryside, luring girls from the age of ten with promises of being taken to the city. Once there, they were forced to sell their bodies in wretched brothels (Harper 2013: 186f.). In any case, this legislation for cause and the institutional measures that followed show that the Christian rulers were willing to make sexual life—at least those forms that were publicly visible and concerned the social order—the subject of politics.

It was during this period that the legend of Mary Magdalene as a reformed prostitute was born and began to spread. Pope Gregory I (around 540–604) in 591 identified her as the anonymous sinner who washed Jesus' feet and was subsequently converted. From that moment, she became *the* role model for converted and penitent women. Around her rose up a true cult, which was reflected in numerous holy vows and church celebrations (Loewen and Waugh 2014: 2ff.). The figure of the repentant Mary Magdalene lasted well beyond the Middle Ages—as late as the nineteenth century she was synonymous with reformatories, the "Magdalene asylums" and "Magdalene laundries." Another conversion story of a "fallen woman" is the legend of Mary of Egypt, who became the patron saint of the repentant and penitent (Betancourt 2020: 19ff.; Cotter-Lynch 2020). Her vita goes back to the Greek Patriarch Sophronius of Jerusalem (560–638): Mary had lived promiscuously or as a prostitute in Alexandria. She converted during a pilgrimage to the Holy Cross in Jerusalem and then expiated her sins out in the desert for many years. In the eleventh century, the sexualized version of this story could already be found in English, Spanish, French, Portuguese, and German collections. Adgar's Anglo-Norman Marian legend (around

1300) recounts her lewd life: "She received everyone, and not for goods, but to fulfill her mad desire" (Karras 1990: 8). Later writers had many of the saints be the subjects of conversion stories themselves, having worked in brothels before their purification, brought into sin by their sexual bodies or their carnal weaknesses—and not by financial need. It was usual for (female) pride or other deadly sins to come into play.

Such converted sinners were supposed to illustrate that the female being was generally marked by sexuality and original sin. To put it pointedly, a potential prostitute slumbered in every woman. Only by the grace of their moral conduct could it be seen whether they had the capacity to defy their innermost character (Karras 1990: 32; Artman-Partock 2021: 19). It must also be noted that the woman, due to her nature as a bodily sin as such, was attributed with the (primary) guilt for the sexual sins of the man as well. Because of her moral weakness, she was simply less resistant to the seductions of the flesh. For Rabanus Maurus (around 780–856), the Archbishop of Mainz and former abbot of the monastery of Fulda, this was obvious:

> But because it is generally disputed what sins have been brought in by women and what sins have been brought in by men, it is good that it was not he but she who was tempted, for it is seen from this that the woman is the reason for his temptation and that this reason can in no way be reversed."

In view of this psychophysiological gender difference, Isidor (around 560–636), bishop of Seville and one of the most important medieval encyclopedists, drew the general conclusion: "The mind (of man) could not be tempted unless it was first tempted by the carnal weakness (of woman)" (Goetz 2016: 513f.).

Early Laws on Prostitution

In the Early Middle Ages, the legal provisions on prostitution were sometimes quite rigid—for example, when clashes occurred between Roman law, Christian doctrine, and the legal ideas of the immigrant gentile tribes. In the Visigoth and Burgundian Empire, harlotry was therefore prohibited and was even considered an official offence (to be pursued by royal officials) (Maier 2005: 120; Classen 2019: 12). However, it continued to exist simply because of slavery and the resulting offer of forced sexual services, which is why King Leovigild (*c.* 519–586), who ruled in Spain and southwest France, again took legal action against it (Nehlsen 2005: 36). According to a Visigothic codex of the seventh century, attributed to King Recesvinto (?–672), prostitutes should be punished to the same degree in both towns and villages:

> When a woman is a publicly known whore in the city, if it is proved that she received many times many men shamelessly, that woman must be

detained by the lord of the city and punished with 300 lashings in front of all the people, and afterwards should not be accused if she does not relapse. But if it is known that she relapses, she should be lashed again 300 times and given in servitude to a poor man and be banished from the city for ever. (Lacarra Lanz 2002: 171)

The Ostrogoths also continued the Roman slave system and thus the use and sale of unfree persons for their sexual desires. Louis the Pious (778–840), the Carolingian king of the Frankish Empire, tried to get a grip on venal love offerings in his kingdom and ordered that prostitutes and their clients be publicly flogged—a measure with which he (apparently) had little success (Brundage 1987: 147). The continuous repetition of such legal sanctions also makes it clear that there was simultaneously a wide range of sexual services available and that it was not possible to obtain them by legal means. In contrast to secular laws, the penitential books and early writings on canon law hardly mentioned prostitution. Up to the ninth century, for example, no such provisions were to be found in Irish, Anglo-Saxon, and Frankish penitential books.

During the Crusades (from 1095 onwards), people were confronted with the fact that, in addition to the female relatives who went along with them, there were also numerous unmarried women who did not dress and behave as one would expect of a respectable Christian. For the church commentators, it was enough for a single person to act outside the usual social framework for her to exhibit promiscuity and unchastity. Especially pilgrims and crusaders, who had lofty claims to spiritual purity, regarded such "beguiling" women as particularly threatening (Kostick 2008: 271ff.). At the beginning of the Third Crusade (1189), Emperor Frederick I Barbarossa (*c.* 1122–1190) ordered that around 500 prostitutes, thieves, and thugs be removed from the army camp in order to prevent these problems from arising in the first place (Ballhaus 2009: 175).

In the course of the church reforms of the eleventh and twelfth centuries, clerics changed their attitude toward prostitution: In the beginning, the opinion prevailed that the sale of sexual services should be subject to a severe penance of six years, as Burchard, bishop of Worms (*c.* 965–1025), called for in his *Decree* (1008–1012), a compilation of conciliar decisions, penitential books, and other canonical sources. About 100 years later, Bishop Ivo of Chartres (*c.* 1040–1115), referring to Roman law and the early Church Fathers, said that while prostitutes merit distain they should be offered spiritual support for their return to the moral life. Pimps and procurers in their midst, on the other hand, should receive no mercy. This change of opinion was a reaction to the increased visibility of prostitution in the budding towns and flourishing cities of the time and the problems involving the social order waxing within them. The rise of the figure of the repentant Mary (Magdalene) from the late tenth to the early twelfth centuries also fits into this picture (McLaughlin 2010: 39ff.).

Gratian (died before 1160), author of the *Decretum Gratiani*, a collection of medieval canon law written around 1140, saw promiscuous behavior as the decisive factor in classifying a woman as a prostitute. Once again, her intention to earn money seemed to be secondary to this. Fallen women should still be allowed to marry, according to him, because it offered them a path to reintegrate into society. However, there was a danger that they might get a new taste for infidelity in marriage. Gratian found it unacceptable that (male) pimps enriched themselves with the income from the unchaste trade, thereby prolonging prostitution. He deemed that prostitutes' offspring should not be burdened by the *infama* (evil reputation) and the sins of their mothers, but rather the descendants should be able to lead an honorable life (Brundage 1987: 248ff.). Other clerics also pleaded for the social reintegration of purified whores. Pope Innocent III (1160/1161–1216) thought that men who married a prostitute were even committing a pious act, since they thusly repented their own sins and brought the female sinners to their natural destiny as wives and mothers. A papal decree from the early thirteenth century thus allows Christian men to officially marry former prostitutes (Rossiaud 1984: 113). Thomas Aquinas (*c.* 1225–1274) even warned against abolishing harlotry completely, because of the threat of spreading sexual chaos in marriage and sodomy.

Institutionalization in Municipal and Private Brothels

Most of what is known about the spread, acceptance, and practice of medieval prostitution comes from sources dating from the twelfth century onward. The following developments can be traced from them: In the twelfth and thirteenth centuries, many European cities tolerated prostitution and, at the same time, sought to dissuade the fallen women from their immoral lifestyle. In the fourteenth and fifteenth centuries, there was increased regulation of city-bound harlotry up to and including institutionalization in public-municipal and private brothels (or stews) and religious houses for the social reintegration of penitents (Blaschitz 2008: 717; Mummey 2011: 168; Page 2022). In the sixteenth century, in the face of the Reformation, the confessional–political conflicts, and probably also the spread of the "French disease" (syphilis), people began to take a much harder line against all forms of prostitution. In many cities, brothels operated or regulated by the municipality were closed down. But in some, such as Italian cities, a few (municipal) facilities continued to exist.

There are several possible explanations for this change in dealing with prostitution (Page 2021: 9ff.): On the one hand, increasing urbanization brought immigration from rural areas, especially of apprentices, journeymen, farmhands, maids, day laborers, and merchants. As described above, this went hand in hand with a longer period of singlehood across broad swaths of both urban and rural society, that is, a corresponding explosion in the numbers of unmarried men and women. Even though there are reports of harlotry in the countryside, it was above all a phenomenon associated with the emergence and growth of urban spaces from the twelfth century onward. All of this made it necessary for the city authorities to become involved in the sexual life of the inhabitants and to show their political strength and autonomy—especially after the great plague in the middle of the fourteenth century, which killed about a third of Europe's population (Schuster 1992: 210).

David Wyatt has pointed out that the growing public interest and municipal administration of prostitution was accompanied by a reorganization of patriarchal surveillance of women. In England, the prostitution problem was used from the High Middle Ages to stabilize the gender order—and, at the same time, to channel the sexual energies of single men. Church and secular authorities did this by taking control of access to urban brothels—just as their early medieval predecessors had or wanted to control the sexual availability of female slaves. The whores of the High and Late Middle Ages seemed to have been much less threatening to the Christian marriage order than the (former) house slaves, who belonged to the inner sphere of the household and were thus at the mercy of the landlord and his sons (Wyatt 2009: 399ff.).

Before exhibiting broader toleration, they had wanted to expel prostitutes from the cities through legal and administrative regulation (Mazzi 2020: 67ff.). For example, in 1254, after his return from a failed crusade, the French King Louis IX (1214–1270) ordered that all *publice meretrices* had to leave the towns and villages and that their property be confiscated. Two years later, in view of the utterly failed implementation, their presence was limited to *within* the city walls and therein to certain areas. In 1266/7 and 1277, London tried to ban organized brothel prostitution, but had little success (Hausner 2016: 64). So, Edward II (1284–1327) once again instructed the London Council to abolish brothels in 1310 because they were a gathering place for thieves and murderers (Karras 1996: 14f). According to the Augsburg City Law of 1276, such women were only allowed to enter the city to go to market but not to pursue their own business (Schuster 1995: 44). An order of the city of York from 1301 sanctioned their activity with the loss of accommodation: "If any prostitute keeps a brothel and resides in the city, she is to be taken and imprisoned for a day and a night. The bailiff who takes her shall have the roof timber and the door of the building in which she is lodged" (Goldberg 1995: 210).

Some Italian cities, such as Bologna, Florence, and Venice, also enacted regulations in the early thirteenth century that forbade harlotry in their cities or restricted its occurrence to certain districts. In each case, whores were to stay far away from church buildings. Venetian tavern owners were forbidden to serve them drinks or rent them a bed. In the second half of the thirteenth century, the municipal magistrates in many parts of Europe began to tolerate the *ars libidinis* (art of lust) within the city walls, but to limit it to certain streets (Ghirardo 2001: 405ff.). Most of them were remote and disreputable districts. In the course of the fourteenth century, London decreed that they were only allowed to stay in a "red light district," Cocks Lane, and around the bathhouses in Southwark. In other cities, such as the Hanseatic and commercial city of Bruges or in northern Italian cities, they were also allowed in the business districts (Pullan 2016: 33ff.). In York, England, the following could be read in an ordinance in 1301: "No one shall keep pigs which go in the streets by day or night, nor shall any prostitute stay in the city"—which put the latter on a par with animals and expelled them from the city (Turner 2018: 129).

Brothels run by the magistrates themselves, licensed or publicly regulated by them, were found in the Late Middle Ages in (northern) French, Italian, Spanish, German, and some English towns. Smaller and medium-sized towns usually only allowed one whorehouse, the larger cities permitted several—again, limited to a certain district or a few streets. The reasons for such decisions were usually the same: the lesser of two evils. Only by accepting these institutions could worse sexual and moral transgressions by honorable men and women be prevented. For example, the brothel owners of the German city of Ulm had to swear that their business promoted piety in the city, averted harm to the residents, and offered adequate, pure, and healthy women—that is, regulated and supervised services of "common" women protected the honorable residents from sexual advances and assaults. In contrast to clandestine prostitution, customers of licensed brothels expected to find healthy women (i.e., not carrying venereal diseases) of suitable age and appearance (Roper 1985: 4f.). In Florence, the expressed aim of the *Signoria* was to keep young men away from sodomy and induce them to desire heterosexual sex (Mazzi 2020: 24). In German cities, the stated intention was to make the roads safer for moral wives and daughters (Karras 1996: 32). In sum, the municipal brothels of the fifteenth century served not only to maintain social order and peace in the community, but also to fold the prostitutes into the urban fabric (Schuster 1995: 186f.). Thus, these institutions helped to draw the public border between sinful and honorable women (Page 2019: 754).

Brothel Rules and Working Out of the Public Eye

In some places, brothels were housed in buildings belonging to the city, and their operation was managed or at least supervised by city officials. Often, the whorehouse was left to a landlady or pimp for a certain period of time and a corresponding share of the income was collected (Pullan 2016: 34). In some Italian and French cities, the right to run the municipal brothel was leased for a fixed amount per year—an apparently risky business, as the offer did not always find buyers (Ghirardo 2001: 913). Elsewhere, the city authorities did not intervene directly in the organization of prostitution but limited themselves, as in the large cities of London and Paris, to the definition of certain zones where the whores were allowed to work and where brothels were accepted. The number of privately owned brothels and dual-purpose bathhouses, however, fluctuated according to demand.

Many cities issued written brothel regulations, which laid down how the houses were to be run, who was to receive the revenues and taxes, and how the inmates were to behave (Karras 2012a: 134f.; Page 2022). Some commonalities can be found across these: They fixed a woman's bed fee for one night and the amount she got paid per customer, as well as the food she received, including any rations of beer and wine, and the times she was permitted to use the bathing establishment belonging to the brothel. What happened in the event of illness or unpaid debts was also strictly regulated. The prostitutes were given the right to freedom of movement and the opportunity to go to church. The rules also forbade them from refusing a client. The brothel owners' share of the income was also set—in Ulm this was one third the fee per woman (Roper 1995a:85). It was therefore a contract between the owner and the prostitute that regulated the employment relationship, payment, and care. The times when the brothel was to remain closed were also laid down in the contract (Rath 1986: 563ff.) (Figure 11).

FIGURE 11 *Bathhouse and brothel. Miniature from the French translation of Valerius Maximus "Faits et dits mémorables" (Memorable Facts and Sayings), fifteenth century.*

In Italian cities, the establishment of public brothels was combined with a ban on prostitutes loitering in the vicinity of churches and monasteries. The following (incomplete) list of Italian brothel foundational regulations gives an impression of their distribution on the Apennine Peninsula: Bologna and Lucca opened brothels in the 1340s, Perugia 1359, Venice 1360, Genoa 1363, Milan and Pavia 1390, Bergamo 1399, Florence 1403, and Pisa 1427. In 1412, Turin also considered setting up such an institution to provide for students. Amadeus VIII (1383–1451), Duke of Savoy and from 1418 also Prince of Piedmont, issued an instruction in 1430 that all towns in his territory should create a "common hidden place far from any respectable women, where all prostitutes lived." The owners and tenants of Italian brothels came, on the one hand, from the city's citizenship, on the other, many were strangers, both single persons and married couples (Pullan 2016: 34f.).

Late medieval towns also operated brothels in order to profit from rent payments and taxes. One ultimate effect was to push free prostitution out into the periphery. Among the brothel owners in fourteenth-century Avignon were respected citizens as well as church institutions, and thus, respectively, tax payers: Thomas Busaffi, a Florentine banker, for example, as well as the Convent of St Catherine's, and even a member of the Roman Curia—the latter, however, was forbidden from ownership by Pope Innocent VI in 1358 (Rollo-Koster 2002: 112). In many cases, the brothel business did not necessarily prove to be a goldmine, which is why the owners and tenants were recruited from the middle and lower classes. Often, the sale of food and alcohol provided an additional source of income, which meant that these places tended to be loud and boisterous (Roper 1995a: 3).

The buildings resembled typical inns and guesthouses. The brothel newly built in Frankfurt in 1451 had six rooms. The brothel in Nördlingen had a lounge (with a board game), a parlor (with a spinning wheel), a kitchen, and a bathing room, and above all three rooms for the women, which were equipped with a couch bed or a sack of straw. The *Frauenwirt* (madam, lady proprietor) lived on the upper floor, according to municipal archive documents from 1525 (Schuster 1995: 96f.). In medium-sized towns, the immodesty of these "houses of ill repute" ensured that respectable citizens did not want to be officially associated with them, and certainly not as owners (Lömker-Schlögell 1990: 69; Mummey 2011: 174). The primary goal of city authorities was that prostitution continued without problems and without much ado. One French alderman of the 15th century recommended the *prostibulum publicum* (public brothel) best be run as a "place of peaceful fornication" (Rossiaud 1984: 113). In some Italian cities—as in Bologna—this was the task of the *Ufficio delle bollette* (licensing office), whose employees now also supervised prostitution alongside foreigners, Jews, and innkeepers (Pullan 2016: 39).

Fornication was considered most peaceful when prostitutes were kept out of serious neighborhoods. In Prague, for instance, one inspection in

1379/80 located whorehouses and prostitutes along the Moldau, in the disreputable Hampays district next to the Jewish quarter in the old town, at the city wall on Venice Street, and on Krakow Street on the edge of the New Town district. Each of these were considered rather bad areas, known for their criminality (and prostitution) where respectable citizens tended not to linger (Mengel 2004: 412ff.). The city council in Castelnaudary in southern France also pursued regulatory policy objectives in 1445 when, in view of the high number of unmarried men and the lack of female candidates for marriage, it called for the establishment of a brothel outside the city, far away from respectable women (Otis-Cour 1985: 116). In Hamburg, Leipzig, and Vienna, the authorities decided to locate brothels at or outside the city walls. In Frankfurt and Constance, they were situated on the banks of the Main and Rhine (Schuster 1992: 44f.; Hammer 2019: 104ff.).

But there have been occasions, repeatedly, when prostitutes were deliberately brought into the public eye—if only to show that they were the objects of good municipal administration (Page 2022: 2ff.; Benito Julià 2018: 318). Thus, in 1438, the Vienna City Council had Albrecht II, who had just been crowned in Prague, ceremoniously greeted and received by the city's "free daughters." A few years earlier, he had velvet dresses made for inmates of the two Viennese brothels to prepare them for the visit of Emperor Sigismund (1368–1437) and his entourage. The Viennese whores also performed as a dance troupe for the solstice celebration. In carnival displays of the "topsy-turvy world turned upside down," they even held their own whores' procession in Leipzig (Ballhaus 2009: 169f.). In the lower Rhone valley, too, public presentations of prostitutes were common with a whores' race for the feast of St Mary Magdalene (Karras 199: 165). These *Dirnenläufe* are also known from Augsburg, St Gallen, Munich, and Vienna and were mainly for the amusement of the spectators. The women's prize: a handsome bolt of fustian cloth—an expensive and fine *accessoire*.

When business carried on without any major excitements, city authorities were rather reluctant to intervene. For example, prostitutes in Bruges were not forced to work in brothels or harassed with red light rules and dress codes. This is surprising, since prostitution flourished in the face of the many foreign traders and merchants visiting the city. Prostitutes were generally natives or from the surrounding regions. Court records show that in Bruges it was rather the environment of prostitution that was sanctioned. There was a focus on moral consequences and secondary criminal offences, which particularly affected innkeepers who let rooms to prostitutes and brothel and bathhouse owners. The number of brothels in Bruges increased from 25 to 140 whorehouses in the fourteenth century, only to level off at around 90—with a population of 35–40,000, which is a brothel for every 450 inhabitants. This was clearly connected to the increasing economic importance of the city as a center of the textile industry and trade-based capitalism. Both of these factors drew in merchants, young single journeymen, apprentices, and day laborers from the rural area. However, in the event of armed conflicts or as a result of epidemics, the high profits of brothel owners and accommodation providers could quickly collapse, as well as the income of the prostitutes themselves. The case of Bruges also demonstrates that women were involved in running brothels and bathhouses, even as proprietors. But most of the owners and innkeepers were men, and they probably also collected the majority of the profits. Bruges was able to innovate yet another special feature: due to active visits from foreign traders, the brothels were not located in the disreputable peripheral areas but where business flourished—in the city center (Murray 2004: 328ff.).

The Mediterranean port cities also had sufficient and changing clientele to offer in the fourteenth and fifteenth centuries, which led to an increased migration of prostitutes to Barcelona, Marseille, Valencia, and Palermo, for example. Quite a few women arrived on ships from other parts of the country or abroad, and then made their foreign origins their trademark. In Palermo, for example, Lisabetta Valenciana, Constancia Aragonisi, and Lisabetta Castillana were active in 1497. In Marseille, Caterina la Guasqua (the Gascon), Alareta Lombarda (the Lombard), and Margarida la Basqua (the Basque) worked and drew attention to themselves with their surnames. Significantly, the brothels in the abovementioned towns were located near the harbors and were regularly frequented by sailors and merchants. They were able to communicate and exchange information with them in their mother tongue or a pidgin lingua franca. Some of the women stayed permanently or for several years, others migrated on after some time (McDonough 2022: 404ff.). From Barcelona they went to Valencia, Mallorca, Naples, and Tarragona (Benito Julià 2018: 322).

Recruitment and Spread of Prostitution

In general, prostitutes were recruited primarily from the urban and rural lower classes and mostly came to this way of making a living for economic reasons (Paolella 2020: 215ff.). Indeed, the alternatives were few and dismal: In a trading and textile city like Lübeck, employment opportunities were limited to servant roles and auxiliary activities in the crafts, (hospitality) trade, and commerce. Typically, lower-class women were eligible for menial services and jobs in textile production, for example (Hemmie 2007: 55ff.). In England, registered women were described as seamstress, spinner, washerwoman, waitress, maid, hostess, and bath maid (Karras 1996: 54f.). Guilds usually had stricter regulations and criteria for women in the crafts. From the fifteenth century onward, they increasingly closed themselves off from female laborers, thus raising the bar for all who could prove neither an honorable Christian origin nor such a lifestyle. When the urban labor market dried up for them, prostitution offered a possible way out of destitution (Schuster 1995:195f.). The proportion of single women in the total female population should also be taken into account. In

Central, Western, and Northern Europe it was between 20 and 40 percent; in Mediterranean Europe it was significantly lower due to the early age of marriage (Kowaleski 1999: 46ff.).

Most prostitutes came into the business between the ages of fifteen and seventeen years. If they had migrated to the city, they often lacked family or social ties. Not infrequently, they were forced into prostitution, as was the case in the fifteenth century with a large proportion of women who moved to the French city of Dijon from the surrounding area to work as whores (Verdon 1996: 370). Others went to the city for job opportunities as maidservants to make ends meet until marriage. When the income and (former) fields of work for "clandestine" or "open" women were mentioned in court records, these were usually low-paid jobs such as a maid, day laborer, or seamstress (Schuster 1995: 196). Like domestic service, prostitution was potentially also a way to make ends meet in cases where the income from these activities was insufficient. Some young maidservants were even encouraged or forced to perform sexual services by their mistresses. Even parents, mostly from the poorest strata of society, encouraged their daughters to accept suitors and thus contribute to the family income (Paolella 2020: 216). The sources also hold cases where pimping is revealed through the man's other crimes. For example, in the fourteenth century, witnesses in a robbery trial against Francisco de Varea in Valencia declared that he lived off gambling and prostituting his wife (Mummey 2011: 178). Older casual prostitutes, on the other hand, mostly came from the city itself, some of them were married and, with the consent of the husband (and "cock bawd"), voluntarily pursued the profession. Mostly, however, prostitutes were (younger) women who had lost the protection of their families or husbands and now had to cope with life as single women.

In the town of Gradec in Slavonia (present-day northwestern Croatia), a part of the Kingdom of Hungary, prostitutes in the 15th century were mostly single or widowed, but some were married. They came from the lowest layer of society and appeared in court on another offence such as theft. They had migrated from the surroundings of the city and without their families. There they could not establish a stable working relationship, so they had to sell their bodies for sexual services, at least temporarily. In addition to these younger women, however, they also included widows from the lower craftsmen's classes who also needed an additional income. If married women prostituted themselves, they were threatened with harsh punishments, in the worst case with the death penalty; for single women, depending on the other offences committed, it was usually banishment from the city. On the whole, prostitution was not forbidden in Gradec; however, bringing a daughter into the business was proscribed (Karbić 2019).

In Manosque in the south of France, the influx of women who hired themselves out as whores in the fourteenth century depended heavily on the wars, famines, and epidemics in the region (Guénette 1987). Immigration from other regions and foreign women played no small role. The public brothels of Dijon were filled with women from the Netherlands and northern France in the fourteenth and fifteenth centuries, areas that had faced armed conflict repeatedly during this period. Many of them were victims of rape or were forced into prostitution (Rossiaud 1988: 32ff.). In the brothel quarters of Florence in 1490, 115 women came from the city and its surroundings, thirty-five came from France, Spain, Poland, Dalmatia, some from the Holy Roman Empire and the Netherlands (Trexler 1981: 985ff.). Of the twenty-five prostitutes recorded in notarial records in the 1330s and 1340s in Montpellier in the *Campus Polverel*, at least sixteen came from outside the city, namely from southwest France and Provence, some also from the surrounding area (Reyerson 2016: 131ff.).

Estimates of the actual number of prostitutes and brothels in late medieval cities vary widely. This stems not only from differences in the definition and coverage of professional women but also from the lack of accurate population censuses. For example, at the end of the fifteenth century, Lyon seems to have had seventy to eighty prostitutes for a population of 10,000, while in Paris, at the same time and with 150,000 inhabitants, the number was 5,000 to 6,000—ratios of 1:140 and 1:30, respectively. For Alsatian Strasbourg, it is estimated that in 1469 there were eighty-six whorehouses with one to six prostitutes out of a population of around 20,000. In the 15th century, Lübeck had around 25,000 inhabitants and, in addition to a public brothel, several smaller houses in which around forty prostitutes worked; although there are hardly any records of the little-regulated street prostitution there. In Bergen, Norway, with a population of 6,000–7,000 natives plus 1,000–2,000 male German counting house workers (who were in particularly high demand), between 150 and 280 whores were probably active in the late fifteenth century (Hemmie 2007: 115ff.)—a much slimmer ratio than even Paris.

Impossible to estimate is the proportion of unregistered casual prostitutes and clandestine prostitution. What is probable is that some of the prostitutes continued to work once they left the formal houses and sought clients on the street, in taverns, inns, and bathing establishments. Bathhouses were typical initiation spaces where the immoral intent was not immediately apparent and the women could act outside of municipal supervision, which is why the city councils repeatedly acted against whores frequenting the baths. In England, brothels were also called *stews*, alluding to the close connection with bathing establishments. The satirical German poem *Des Teufels Netz* from the 1410s also makes this connection:

> The barber surgeon and his servants
> Are ready whores and rogues.
> Thieves, liars and pimps
> And know all the foreign tales.
> Also they know just as well how to deal
> With lay-folk as with clerics.
>
> (Duerr 1988: 51ff.)

An often overlooked aspect of clandestine prostitution concerns female slaves who went whoring for their masters or were sold for prostitution purposes (Wyatt 2009: 397ff.). There is a well-known case from the Kingdom of Aragon, where King Pere IV had an inventory drawn up in 1374 of the slaves kept on the island of Mallorca, including those who worked in the brothels of the capital, Palma (Mummey and Reyerson 2011: 914). For the fifteenth and sixteenth centuries, there are documented cases from Spain in which Christian and Jewish slave owners took action against sexual assaults by strangers on their Muslim slave women. Conversely, Christian and Jewish women obviously had to tolerate that their husbands and sons used Muslim domestic slaves for sexual purposes (Green 2008: 113ff.). In Christian Valencia in the fifteenth century, the rule was that Muslim women who had sexual intercourse with a Christian were officially punished under Islamic law (with flogging and stoning), but in practice were enslaved. The new Christian owners then often resold them as prostitutes in brothels (Constable 2012: 493f.).

Marking Women Who Sell Their Body

The regulation of prostitution in the Late Middle Ages also meant making whores more visible through labeling, thereby distinguishing them from respectable female citizens (Mazzi 2020: 58ff.). Some cities tried to do this by making them wear a color-coded, monotone garment, as in Marseille and Toulon, or by requiring they wear a veil, as in Aix-en-Provence, and threatening fines and flogging for non-compliance (Rollo-Koster 2002: 112). In Paris, they were forbidden from wearing embroidered clothing, gold and silver buttons, jewelry, and fur collars (Geremek 1991: 222). Prostitutes in Merano in South Tyrol had to put a yellow flag on their clothes and were not allowed to wear luxurious clothing, furs, or valuable jewelry (Hammer 2018: 159). A Frankfurt order from 1488 commanded they dress in keeping with their lower moral worth (Schuster 1992: 146). In 1382, the city authorities of London stipulated that common women should wear striped bonnets (Amt 1993: 210). In fifteenth-century Vienna, they had to identify themselves by wearing a yellow shawl over the shoulder (Rath 1986: 562). In Venice a yellow collar was considered a sign, in Bergamo a saffron scarf, and in Bologna a yellow veil (Davidson 1994: 92; Clarke 2015: 427). The Cologne Order of 1339 expresses the intention behind all these measures: "In recent years, the common women wore red veils on their hips, so they may be detected before other women" (Rath 1986: 562). The color theory of the late medieval dress codes was thus clear: Yellow and red stood for carnal lust. Furthermore, prostitutes shared yellow with the Jewish population and its low social status, as well as with outlaws and women on the shameful side of life (Cady 2006: 300).

Color regimes and dress codes like these cloaked many a casual prostitute from identifying herself as a professional who belonged to the stigmatized urban fringe groups in a way that was perceptible to all. A casual and clandestine whore wore the camouflage of everyday dress. This was also the reason why in the Italian city of Ferrara in the middle of the fifteenth century, two women, Caterina "the Venetian" and Caterina "Schiava" (the slave), refused to identify themselves as *meretrices* by wearing the prescribed yellow clothing in public (Ghirardo 2001: 410). Distinguishability between "honorable" and "common" women is a recurring theme in the sources. In 1495, for example, the aldermen of the Spanish city of Murcia complained that the latest fashion made it impossible to tell them apart:

> [So] that all the women in town, those of great merit as well as those of lower strata, wear night and day hoods and cover their faces with their hands and headdresses [. . . and] it is known by experience and seems to be an ugly and dishonest thing, to give occasion to the public defamation of honorable and of honest women, because those who are dishonest and evil in their lives and customs dress to look like the honest ones [. . . we] order that all women of every condition and quality from now onwards do not cover their faces so that they can be recognized. (Lacarra Lanz 2002: 175)

The demarcation of prostitutes could also be an acoustic dilemma: In Barcelona, for example, in the first half of the fourteenth century, a church community complained about prostitutes loudly calling out to clients in the area. Their shouts were mingling with the congregation's prayers and songs, thus cacophonously intermingling the pious with the "abominable women." To avoid such contact with immorality, the authorities of the Catalan city of Girona went so far as to prohibit whores from even touching fresh fruit and vegetables at the market (Mummey and Reyerson 2011: 914f.).

In the Late Middle Ages, however, efforts were made to place repentant prostitutes in "penitent houses" where they were to renounce their way of life and begin a moral one. In the French city of Avignon, which was the Papal See from 1309 to 1378 and had a high demand due to the share of unmarried men, the city council initially regulated prostitution by registering the women and assigning them to appropriate red light zones; brothels also existed throughout the city and professional as well as temporary whores also appeared in taverns and bathing establishments. Later, attempts were made to morally reform women and to encourage them to marry and reintegrate, by offering charity and financial support. Finally, convents and Magdalene asylums were established, in which repentant women were to be integrated into the social order beyond the pressure of gainful employment through a monastic lifestyle (Rollo-Koster 2002: 110ff.). In Vienna in the 1380s, representatives of the trades and the city council set up an institution for the reintegration of the *poor freyen frawen*, the so-called *Haus der Büßerinnen* of St Hieronymus in the Singerstraße. To prevent recidivism after the penitential period, the inmates were to marry a well-behaved guild craftsman (Lutter 2021).

Besides the "marked" low prostitution organized in public brothels, another form of selling sexual services existed in the Late Middle Ages. On the "privatized" market of cities in the Southern Low Countries, there was a wide range of better-off women in stews. Other well-known private stews in Europe were the *Berlich* in Cologne, the *Casteletto* in Dubrovnik, the *Château Vert* in Toulouse, and the *Venice* in Prague (Haemers 2021: 20ff.). Some women there managed to advance to respectable "dames de femmes" or to become stew/brothel owners themselves. Bruges stews stood out from common brothels simply because these establishments also offered bathing, and some offered eating, drinking, and dancing; therefore, it was not clear that prostitution was also practiced there or if it was merely an entertainment venue. In London, such stews were operated in Southwark between the mid-thirteenth and mid-sixteenth centuries and had significant names such as the *Red Hart*, the *Bell and Cock*, and the *Unicorn* (Hausner 2016: 65f.).

Contraception, Abortion, and Physical Suffering

Contraception and abortion were also an explosive topic for prostitutes in the Middle Ages. As in ancient times, however, it is unclear to what extent they used contraceptive and abortive measures or whether their life circumstances and especially the widespread venereal diseases were the main reason for lower birth rates among them. The sources show that prostitutes, procuresses, and brothel keepers exchanged existing knowledge about contraceptives and abortion both by word of mouth and in writing among themselves. Some evidence suggests that common women not only knew about it but indeed were also deliberately employing abortion. For example, in 1471, Ursel von Constenz and other inmates of the Nördlingen brothels accused the landlady that she had given one of them, Els van Eystett, a drink made from evergreens, carrots, laurel, and cloves, thus causing a miscarriage in the twentieth week of pregnancy (Schuster 1992: 92). According to the balladeer François Villon (1431–c. 1463), prostitutes in brothels regularly used post-coital rinsing with herbal tinctures, using early forms of the bidet: "Anyone who does not recognize the small bath tubs, which are used in brothels has never visited a whore house" (Jütte 2008: 71f.).

Plant products and liquids were the most common (Riddle 1996). As Hildegard von Bingen before him, the theologian, physician, and botanist Otto Brunfels (1488–1534) described a purging agent extracted from hazel root and drew attention to its disgraceful use. The drink was actually only supposed to be used to repel a dead fetus:

> The women who are with children
> should not drink this water, as they drive to birth,

dead and alive. Which I would like to keep quiet about,
bad *schlepseck* [pimps]
who when they have such a piece of wisdom
drive out and kill the children in their mother's body
and put again a maiden's crants upon them. (Kruse 1996: 176)

Two preventive practices, namely coitus interruptus and non-vaginal penetration, appear in medieval medical texts and literature, if at all, only inimically. Augustine had already thought it better for men to realize their spoiled sexual desires not by these means with their own wives but rather in the typical fashion with a whore (Karras 2012a: 138). According to their contemporaries, there was yet another reason why whores so rarely got pregnant: As described in an important medical text from the twelfth century, the *Scuola Medica Salernitana*, these women would no longer have experienced sexual arousal due to frequent sexual intercourse—thus ceased two crucial prerequisites for conception according to the medical views outlined above, namely the woman's seed and its expulsion through orgasm (Tasioulas 2011: 124).

In addition to unwanted pregnancies, venereal diseases posed a constant threat to prostitutes as well as to their clients, lovers, and husbands. Since the High Middle Ages, translations of the Greek and Arabic classics have provided information about symptoms of illness and possible paths of infection. However, most people affected probably only learned about the diseases from firsthand experience or from the accounts of others. Still, the dangers were well known and widespread: In London, in 1161, a ban from working in Southwark's brothels was announced for all women who felt a burning sensation in their genitals (Morton 1977: 4). The physician and translator Michael Scotus (*c.* 1175–1234) formulated the path of infection in this way: "When a wench suffers from a flow and a man sleeps with her, his member shall spoil, as shown especially among young people" (Winkle 2005: 516ff., 538). According to Constantine the African (around 1020–1087), gonorrhea could be recognized by the "unusual seed flow," which also occurred without *concupiscentia*. As a preventive measure, Wilhelm von Saliceto (*c.* 1210–*c.* 1280) advised in his *Chirurgia* that men should clean their genitals with water or vinegar after having intercourse with an unclean woman or a prostitute (Gruber, Lipozenčić and Kehler 2015: 7).

Leprosy—a disease that was so feared in the Middle Ages that its sufferers were quarantined in leprosariums away from inhabited areas—counted among the sexually transmitted diseases according to contemporary ideas. The infection was supposed to occur through frequent sexual intercourse of infected men with a whore, in whom the vapors of the illness were to have settled in the uterus. From there, the fumes passed on to the next clients, who were particularly susceptible due to their excitement and heated genitals. For the infected women, there was supposedly a bright side, however: The noxious vapors could be released through menstruation, and they might not even suffer an outbreak of leprosy. Another theory was that coitus with a menstruating (but uninfected) woman could actually result in a leprous child. As the natural philosopher Wilhelm von Conches (*c.* 1080/1090– *c.* 1154) thought, this was again due to the different heat balance of the sexes: "Even the hottest woman is colder than the coldest man," which is why the vapors and fumes of venereal diseases nestle particularly well in the uterus and vagina and from there have an effect on penetrating men (Tasioulas 2011: 134f.). Physical suffering of this kinds was, therefore, one of the evils associated with prostitutes.

Women with a Prostitutive Identity/Subjectivity?

In view of the increasing debate about prostitutes in the High and Late Middle Ages, Ruth Mazo Karras has raised the question of whether they (already) had a specific sexual identity and whether these women also saw themselves as such. The ascriptions to this minority group certainly seem to say so; prostitutes were characterized as a certain *type* of woman who possessed a lustful soul. At the same time, however, they could always turn back, as the model of the repentant Mary Magdalene demonstrated. The urban prostitution regime contributed to the fact that these women were seen as a segregated and stigmatized group, that is, by marking them with clothing and badges, by assigning them to certain districts, through rigid regulations for brothel operations, and through surveillance by the urban authorities. In view of such indications, it can be assumed that some of them identified as "prostitutes" or as "whores" as a type, as characterized by their sexuality or their sexual behavior. At the very least, they had to wrestle with this identity ascription, which was most certainly on offer at the time (Karras 1999). From a historiographical point of view, however, the whore remains a social figure created from the outside. It is ultimately a figure that closes itself off to questions of identity, since there is no sufficient evidence for its self-image (Ferguson 2008: 7f.). This also applies to the significance of sexual attributions for subject construction. It is not known whether common women regarded their sexual lives and the social labels, practices, feelings, and fantasies associated with them as constitutive for their self-perception and social placement (van der Meer 1999: 179).

This is one side of historiographical opinions on identity formation and the subjectivity of (late) medieval prostitutes. The other side is represented by Jamie Page, among others, who argues that there are examples of how such women self-confidently negotiated and rejected illicit sexual behavior, for example, or took a resistant stance in cases of sexual violence and campaigned for better working conditions. It was precisely these negative experiences at the hands of clients, brothel operators, and the municipal administration that led them to such a subject position and allowed a self-awareness or at least a corresponding self-reflection as prostitutes to emerge. Or as Page put it: "Prostitution created subject positions which might facilitate and constrain agency in different measures (. . .), perhaps even of exploiting them. This is problematic whether one seeks to emphasize victimhood or agency in writing about prostitution" (Page 2021: 141).

This is also often visible when it comes to confusion surrounding the classification and objectivation of "lewd" prostitutes, e.g., in a cross-dressing case heard in the London city court in 1395. The accused was John Rykener, who prostituted himself dressed as a woman in London and other areas. He was picked up while having sexual intercourse with a man for money. Both defendants claimed to have plied his trade in a male-female constellation, since Rykener had pretended to be a woman named Eleanor and his client had believed him. Rykener confessed that he had had intercourse several times with other men and had learned "the vile fornication in the manner of a woman" from a (female) prostitute. Another prostitute/procuress had dressed him up as a whore and, along with herself and her daughter, he had sometimes done business as a threesome. In addition, Rykener had also blackmailed a client and threatened him that—as an allegedly married woman—he/she would tell his/her influential husband about the incident. In other situations, Rykener had acted as a man and had "taken" women, but had also let himself be taken as a woman by clerics. Regardless of whether Rykener's case was true or merely a good story, the explosive nature of the situation lay in the multiple crossing of boundaries and subject positions: between man and woman, between sexually active and passive, taking and being taken, and especially between normal or vaginal male-female prostitution and same-sex or anal sodomy between two men. In most of these constellations, Rykener acted as a sexual subject—and not as an object driven by the social circumstances. The court ultimately considered the transgression of the gender boundary together with same-sex sexual acts to be the main crime, while the fact that it also involved prostitution and blackmail remained secondary (Karras and Boyd 1996; Linkinen 2015: 62ff.).

Clients and Demand

The clients of the regulated and clandestine prostitutes came from all social classes: students, soldiers, apprentices, journeymen, merchants, nobles, clerics, and single and married men (Paolella 2020: 237ff.; Hammer 2019: 107ff.). In some cities, such as in Avignon during the time of the papal schism, demand arose due to the specific professional structure, in this case the increase of clerics. In trading cities, it was mobile merchants who were regarded as good clientele. In university cities such as Bologna, students frequented prostitutes, which meant that the city authorities could hardly distinguish the "professionals" from the "casual whores" or the concubines of the young men (Lansing 2003: 98). In a manuscript from the thirteenth century, the actual clientele was revealed as quite young:

> After surpassing fifteen years, they are already beginning to surrender to the excesses of the world. They run to the women's house and commit fornication and adultery and sometimes worse. Among a hundred of those who are fifteen years old, there can hardly be found one or two who have not lost their virginity (Schuster 1995: 237).

The municipal authorities had one group in particular in their sights: apprentices and journeymen who had to remain single during their training (Roper 1995a: 83). The students were also considered to be in a lusty life phase. For both groups, a visit to the whorehouse was part of the rituals of youth culture, with which they demonstrated their masculinity, sometimes by going to prostitutes together. The brothel regulations issued tried in any case to restrict the clientele to single men, but the large number of married visitors proved the infeasibility of the rules.

The numbers of prostitutes in late medieval cities thus rested on the respective demand structures (Hemmie 2007: 115ff.). In Augsburg, they were allowed to venture out of their places of business during visits from the rulers and their retinue to offer themselves throughout the city (Jankrift 2008: 165). Special occasions such as a council or an imperial diet attracted many whores in view of the many wealthy participants. During the Council of Constance (1414–1418), 700 public prostitutes and again as many clandestine prostitutes are said to have come to the city for the occasion. In comparison, there were probably 50,000 to 70,000 visitors to the Council (Irsigler 1996: 142; Page 2021: 1f.). The booming business also met with fierce criticism. For the merchant and chronicler Eberhard Windeck (*c.* 1380–1440/1441), this was worth a verse of its own in his song about the council, in which he criticized young local girls who also "gave themselves up" for money:

> Now new stories were heard throughout the land,
> since the Council came to Constance;
> the whores are frolicsome
> and blithesome and have grown quite rich (. . .).
> The Swabian maids, they have become nice and silly (. . .)
> (now) these strumpets want ducats, gold coins and crowns
> from their guests.
>
> (Schuster 1995: 44)

Prostitutes were not to accept all clients, no matter whom. Sometimes, however, men did not accept that they were rejected—for example, because of a visible disease such as leprosy—which could lead to coercion and violence (Turner 2018). Under no circumstances were they allowed to accept clerics as clientele, regardless of their office. The church penalty was rather negligible, however: According to a Mainz book of accounts from the beginning of the sixteenth century, a priest paid 16 groschen for a visit to a brothel in the accounting year 1519/20 and also had to give three masses. In comparison, clerics caught brawling cost them 22 groschen (Schuster 1995: 128f.). Prostitutes were also forbidden to have sexual relations with married men (Hammer 2018: 161). This rule was even more flexible than consorting with clergymen, as punishment from secular courts was handed down only if another offence, such as a violent act, was involved. The fact that adultery was also committed here was of little interest to the municipal administration until the early sixteenth century. It was only later that public shaming was implemented by secular courts, and marriage courts were first established during the Reformation.

There were also clear boundaries for non-Christian clients. In 1065, Bishop Petrus Damiani illustrated this prohibition with a story of faith: He praised three Christian prostitutes in Spain who had become martyrs. Allegedly, they had rejected the advances of Muslim men and were forced by a secular court under threat of the death penalty to freely accept all men, regardless of their faith. When they refused to perform this heretical act, they were put in prison and sentenced to execution. At the beheading, however, the executioner's axe was unable to even touch their skin, whereupon Christ appeared and presented them with the martyr's crown (Resnick 2012: 86ff.).

Although prostitutes represented a socially marginal group, as such they were not allowed to cross the border to heretics and contribute with their flesh to "the mixing." In the opinion of contemporaries, they must first and foremost heed the dress code: Like themselves, Jewish men had to wear a colored badge and were thus easily recognizable as off-limits clientele. From the Late Middle Ages, Spain also had secular penal provisions for intercourse between Christian prostitutes and Muslim or Jewish men. In contrast, sexual contacts of Christian men with Jewish or Muslim prostitutes were hardly ever sanctioned. Confessional and moral boundaries were also evident in one case in Daroca, Aragon, where Christian whores solicited along the path where Jewish women went to fetch water from the river. The fact that they sometimes were dressed the same way caused the Jewish women to complain to the council (Nirenberg 1996: 165f.).

Southern German court files from the fourteenth and fifteenth centuries, which dealt with sexual acts between Christians and Jews, mostly contain contacts between younger Jewish men and Christian prostitutes (Schnitzler 2009: 266). In 1359, the *Achtbuch* of the City of Augsburg recorded the case of a prostitute named Kathrin, licensed by the council, who had illicit sexual intercourse with a Jew. She had been caught with a Jew named Jecki in the house of the executioner, who supervised the registered prostitutes in the city brothel. She was banished from the city for a period of three years. Jecki, who did not belong to the Augsburg Jewish community but was a wandering merchant (a so-called "Shalant Jew"), was punished incomparably more severely and branded for the rest of his life, literally: both his cheeks were pierced with a red-hot iron, and he was expelled from the city forever (Jankrift 2008: 159).

Pornographiae—the Shameless Lust of the Eyes

Prostitutes were considered a permanent problem for Christian communities because, on the one hand, they both threatened and maintained the social order at once; on the other hand, they constantly reminded the morally upstanding believers that in their own flesh lurked concupiscence, too, which drove their sexual desire. The erotic and obscene depictions did the same, twisting the sexual thorn in the flesh. In late antiquity, Christian writers had vehemently opposed *pornographiae* (whore stories) and had demonized pagan idols, figures, and symbols that incited them to *porneia*—sinful acts due to their non-marital and non-procreative nature. The fear of such images resulted from the seductive, downright diabolical power they were said to have.

The Gaze Leads to Sexual Fantasies

In the Early and High Middle Ages, this topic remained on the agenda: known since Augustine, the "lust of the eyes" was connected with the curiosity about the carnal. Generations of clergymen racked their brains over whether just one look at the naked body or at erotic (art)works was enough to incite fornication and was therefore itself considered a sin. Or did the vice only begin with the fantasies and thoughts that arose from it?

The gaze also played a central role in the theory of love. Until the High Middle Ages, it was assumed that *Vrouw Minne* or Venus initiated love as an extra-personal power. In the literature of the twelfth and thirteenth centuries, this emotion was more often set in motion by visual sensory impressions and mental reflection. At least those who could read and write then understood such representations as *passio innata*, which came about through eye contact. Andreas Capellanus described the process in *De amore libri tres* in the twelfth century as follows:

> Love is an inner-born suffering [passion] (*passio*), which arises from the sight of and the excessive mental occupation (*cogitatio*) with the fine shape (*forma*) of the opposite sex, for which one desires above all else to obtain the embraces of the other and to see all the rules of love as desired by both fulfilled in the embrace of the other. (Sieber 2008: 27)

A curious look could lead to emotional excitement, which in turn could lead to erotic fantasies and sexual stimulation. Pictures, statues, and objects that triggered this should therefore be banned from the public sphere and withdrawn from eye contact. This did not mean, however, that artists and craftsmen ceased to produce nude and semi-naked figures in more or less unambiguous postures, among other things because they wanted to warn against sin and immorality. Therefore, depending on the context, the artistic representation of the naked female breast can have both a moral and an erotic function (Classen 2018a: 8ff.). However, small breasts in late medieval England also signaled that a woman had little sexual experience and thus a high moral reputation (Phillips 2018).

In contrast to today, moral norms in premodern societies were primarily communicated through face-to-face communication and in the presence of those involved. This exchange took place not only linguistically, but also above all through incarnated or embodied interactions, and these were inscribed in figurative and representational works. Medieval culture has thus rightly been described as one of visuality in which norms and morals as well as narratives and discourses were to a large extent visualized and communicated in a corporeal manner (Wenzel 2009).

One artistic strategy was to cleverly conceal the naked truth of the body, for example under translucent clothing, or to construct postures in such a way that the meaning of what was being portrayed becomes apparent. This is why artworks in Romanesque and Gothic churches include many works where the artist's deliberate use of a fine brush teases out the boundaries between moral norm and erotic allusion. Also, and especially in the Middle Ages, the border between shame and shamelessness was marked by a game of concealment and unveiling, which is difficult for today's viewers to even understand (Gvozdeva and Velten 2011: 6ff.). The "shameful shamelessness" that thus came about led to medieval art being treated almost like the stepmother in some of the erotic stories that seem to transcend time and culture, and the epoch being wrongly regarded as one of prudery (Salih 2011: 181f.; Döpp, Thomas and Charles 2012: 57). As the following examples demonstrate, the erotic spectrum—if you look at it with medieval eyes—was quite multifarious.

Anyone on the pilgrimage of Santiago de Compostela in northern Spain in the second half of the twelfth century who took a look at the overhanging roof of the church of San Pedro de Cervatos was confronted with a sequence of couples in various positions of copulation. What appears to today's viewers to be straightforward pornography was for the churchgoers of the time a way to show the pilgrims where and how the devil awaited them, always lurking with his temptations. At the same time, the viewers were exposed to the danger of stimulating their "lust of the eyes" through these scenes which brought them to unchaste thoughts—a test that the true pilgrim had to face and master. In addition, the pictorial program was probably also based on carnality so as to distinguish Christian art from the hitherto superior Muslim culture, which had dominated this region until the eleventh century: a public depiction of copulating bodies would hardly have been conceivable in contemporary Muslim art (Trinks 2013: 163ff.).

Even some biblical stories could not be easily translated into pictures, as they had a clear sexual message and warned against incest, sodomy, adultery, rape, and exposure. What at first glance seems to be harmless forms of nudity is found, for example, in the Genesis tale of Noah and his son Ham:

> Noah was the first tiller of the soil. He planted a vineyard; and he drank of the wine, and became drunk, and lay uncovered in his tent. And Ham, the father of Canaan, saw the nakedness of his father, and told his two brothers outside. Then Shem and Japheth took a garment, laid it upon both their shoulders, and walked backward and covered the nakedness of their father; their faces were turned away, and they did not see their father's nakedness. When Noah awoke from his wine and knew what his youngest son had done to him, he said,
> "Cursed be Canaan;
> a slave of slaves shall he be to his brothers." (RSV Gen. 9:20-25)

For medieval painters and sculptors, the exposure of Noah's genitals and the view of them formed an easily overcome hurdle in the representation. Between the eleventh and fourteenth centuries, some people circumvented this visual transgression by only depicting above the navel. Others dealt with the motif quite offensively and even revealed the genitals in churches— by having Noah's clothes slip or having his sons be eye-openers. In this way, not only church people (including monks) but also mere churchgoers were confronted with this shameless view. In some figurations, Noah's genitals could even be admired in a significantly enlarged stone version. Laymen thus not only learned about the Genesis story itself, but they also learned from their own perception how the sexual organ literally attracted the gaze and gave the viewer unclean thoughts. It's no wonder, therefore, that many of these stone and wooden figures fell victim to Protestant iconoclasm and were castrated (Caviness 2011: 107ff.).

A similarly ambivalent practice of pointing and simultaneously admonishing is illustrated on the tympanum of the south portal of the cathedral of Santiago de Compostela (end of the eleventh century). The relief there shows a seated woman with long open hair, dressed in a thin robe through which her breasts are clearly visible. In front of her belly, above her spread knees, she cradles a skull in her hands. In the pilgrim guide *Liber Sancti Jacobi* from the first half of the twelfth century you can read about:

> Nor must it be forgotten that a woman stands beside the temptation of the Lord; she holds in her hands the stinking head of her tempter, which was cut off by her own husband; twice a day she kisses that head, forced by her husband. Oh, what an admirable and just punishment for the adulterous woman (Bredekamp 2011: 224).

In the architrave above, a console figure shows a squatting woman with an oversized vulva protruding between her legs. Such *sheela-na-gig* figures—from the Irish *sighle na gcíoch* (old witch with breasts) or *síle ina giob* (old one on her bottom)—with disproportionately large sexual organs can also be found on churches in other Western European countries. Sometimes, they were in the company of figures with erect penises or lone phalli. These were not just warnings against sin and evil. With their apotropaic—demon expulsive, disaster averting—powers, these figures were also meant to ward off dark forces (Weir and Jerman 1986: 11ff.; Freitag 2004). Other interpretations, such as those of Irish *sheela-na-gig* figures, on the other hand, see them as pre-Christian fertility idols. They, among others, signified worship of the Nordic goddess of love Freya, from whom a blessing of reproduction was sought (McMahon and Roberts 2001). No matter how these figures were originally coded or what decoding the viewers could decipher, the carnal views and insights they offered did not fit at all into the picture and prohibitions of the gaze propagated by church authors (Figure 12).

Pagan fertility signs and idols remained in use, as the writings of their ecclesiastical critics testify. For example, the theologian and chancellor of

FIGURE 12 Sheela-na-gig *figure at the Kilpeck church, Herefordshire, UK.*

the Paris Sorbonne Jean le Charlier de Gerson (1363–1429) complained in 1402 that such pagan objects were to be seen daily in the streets of Paris:

> the most filthy corruption of boys and youths by shameful nude images [imaginibus], which are offered for sale in the very temples and on holy days, like idols of Belphegor, to which Christian children—o horrible shame—are introduced by impious mothers or sluttish maidservants, and the senseless laughter of damnable fathers, even to the most obscene songs, gestures and behaviours and to many other abominations, even in the churches, in holy places and on holy days. (Salih 2011: 184)

Ambiguous Worlds of Erotic Symbols

Erotic badges existed in different forms and meanings (Beutin 2004; Koldeweij 2004; Reiss 2017). They were mainly in circulation in the fourteenth and fifteenth centuries, but could be found also in the thirteenth century and until 1550. These figures preferably depicted genitals, with the torso and head formed by the vulva or an (erect) penis with testicles. The rest consisted of hands and feet that possessed either social attributes (such as a crown) or practiced human activities. Some of them bore animal characteristics, such as partial or completely furry bodies. Many represented dual beings, which illustrated that human existence comprised incompatible entities, such as the human and the animal or the moralistic and pleasurable, which were to be united in everyday life (Rasmussen 2014: 126f.). Some pieces depicted the male and female sexual organs in the act, upon a knife edge or carved into a ladder. On one pendant, a servant could be seen turning a skewer with a phallus on it and a woman drizzling sauce over it. Underneath, a vulva is attached as a grease trap; another male figure observes the scene. Another badge shows a woman in a field, caressing a phallus in the earth with her hand, a form of field work which she obviously likes because she smiles.

The function of such erotic badges included apotrophic as well as aphrodisiac purposes. They undoubtedly also served satirical irony and obscenity, for example when worn during carnival and thus caricaturing the frequently used religious amulets and badges. It was also conceivable to praise fertility by combining, as in the last example, the female procreational ability with the yield of fruits from the field, making the phallus a tool for sowing (Wolf 2004: 297ff.). It's quite characteristic of such a badge that in scenes where a penis figure comes into contact with a woman or vulva, the former loses its autonomy and is transformed into a passive object of fertilization. Ergo, late medieval badges also conveyed that women were the actual protagonists of reproduction and that male genitalia only served a perfunctory purpose (Rasmussen 2014: 134f.). One must not forget that these figurines—if they were shown at all—caused quite a stir, which could be an erotic invitation but also an insult. Since some of these obscene badges were carried during the pilgrimage and discarded at the end, they could also have a protective or symbolic use, such as promoting fertility or other religious significances (Reiss 2017: 166ff.). In any case, this play with gender roles and genitals makes it clear that although obscene pictures and pornography from the Renaissance onward were primarily aimed at men, there was no such clear addressee in the visual culture of shame(lessness) in the Middle Ages and both sexes were exposed to the lust of the eyes (Salih 2011: 211).

The fact that the visible genitals were considered problematic is also shown by the myriad erasures of erotic and sexual scenes from medieval manuscripts. An example is a page from a French psalter of the late thirteenth century, on which the Holy Family is seen fleeing to Egypt, being observed by an idol on a pedestal. Its pagan genitals had apparently been a thorn in the side of an observer, so he had eliminated them. Such erasures, on the other hand, indicate that the illustrators of the High and Late Middle Ages did not have too many reservations about depicting obscene scenes in the first place—among other things because they had not been aiming for sexual stimulation but moral reference points. In a manuscript of the *Roman de la rose* from the middle of the fourteenth century, it is humor that drives the eroticism: Jeanne de Montbaston, a Parisian book artist, drew a man led on a leash by a nun. The leash is attached to his testicles, which had also led to a near erasure from the page of the connecting organ. In the marginalia of this manuscript, one still comes across a tree with penis fruits and a monk presenting a penis to a dismayed nun. The latter images illustrate a passage, according to which "those who do not write with their styluses, by which mortals live forever, on the beautiful precious tablets that Nature did not prepare for them to leave idle" should lose them (the "styluses") (Blud 2017: 73). There is much to suggest that the iconoclasm of these book illustrations did not occur until the late fifteenth century or later and was accompanied by that wave of morality which led to the Reformation (Camille 1998: 146ff.).

Ambiguous worlds of symbols pervaded many medieval pictures and are often only recognizable for today's viewers at second glance or are misinterpreted—as in the countless illustrations of scenes in the chaste marriage bed. These depict couples who are usually clothed with a blanket up to the upper part of their bodies—often accompanied by Mary or an angel—in a situation which, at least from a modern perspective, sexual acts seem to be imminent. For the viewers of that time, however, a different message was in the foreground: even in the mutual fulfillment of sexual desire, husband and wife should never forget that in doing so they should moderate and control their feelings, remain shamefaced and pure, as the real aim was not to satisfy desire but to procreate a child. One of the most powerful depictions of such a scene is found as the frontispiece of a mystical treatise called *Soliloquium de quattuor mentalibus exertitiis* (*Soliloquium* of the four spiritual exercises) from the 1250s, which introduces the French translation from the 1480s. There, too, a couple can be seen lying next to each other, apparently naked under the blanket. However, the burgeoning erotic connotation of this arrangement is undermined by the context: at the upper left edge of the picture floats the Holy Trinity, sending the soul of a little child to the couple on a jet of air, thus underlining the true meaning (Wolfthal 2010: 21ff.).

Total or partial nudity occurred in medieval art in very different contexts: in biblical motifs with Adam and Eve, for example, as transcendental suffering bodies of saints of both sexes, as the lactating Virgin Mary, in bathing scenes, in the "Fountain of Youth" in illustrations for medical writings, as mythological figures such as Pygmalion or Venus, with demons and monsters, as anthropomorphic sexual organs in the form of a badge, or as lovers in the marriage bed, to name but a few. Accordingly, the naked body was also able to fulfill various iconographic tasks and, depending on the context, stood for purity, innocence, willingness to make sacrifices, shame, humiliation, punishment, sexual desire, and much more (Lindquist 2012: 1f.). The meaning of nudity also changes in the different types of pictures and texts depending on the objective, the situation, or a person's social status (Classen 2008b: 164, 2018a: 10ff.). In view of such complex statements, the more or less frequent depiction of the (partially or completely) naked body in medieval image and text sources can hardly be understood as an indication of an increase in feelings of shame or even "shame thresholds" (in the sense of Norbert Elias) and thus of a process of civilization from the Middle Ages to the early modern period progressing in a linear way (Elias 1976; Duerr 1988; Classen 2008b: 74ff.; Paul 2011).

Obscene *Fabliaux,* Farces, and Carnival Plays

Ben Reiss has rightly noted that "sexual images and stories were everywhere in the late Middle Ages, from manuscript margins and drinking glasses to the religious context of the Bible and churches" (Reiss 2017: 175). Literary texts brought eroticism into play in a number of ways. Their strategies ranged from the thematization of uncovered body parts to the, albeit often covert, description of sexual acts. Depending on the region, erotic texts have survived quite differently. In Norwegian runes, erotic and love-related themes make up between 3 and 5 percent of the corpus from the eleventh to the fourteenth century (Knirk 2017: 223). As explained above, erotic allusions can already be found in *Minnelyrik* and the courtly romances. Contrary to previous research, it can also be assumed that obscene texts were already widespread in the inhomogeneous, courtly cultures (at least in German texts) in the thirteenth century (Busch 2019). In the French *fabliaux* (fables of frivolity) of the twelfth to fourteenth centuries and the late medieval German *Maeren*, Christian and secular norms and moral concepts were thwarted not only by subtle hints but also by sometimes quite shameless words and scenes. The focus was usually also on the comical or serious negotiation of gender relations and the importance of love and sexuality in this context (Classen 2018b: 51ff.): It is also a characteristic of these literary genres that some of the themes and motifs (up to 20 percent) dealt with prostitution or the exchange of money for sexual acts (Page 2019: 742f.; Classen 2019). The surviving erotic texts are predominantly written by men and from a male perspective and thus deal—even if they are primarily about imagined sexual contacts with women—with male desire (Hopkins and Rushton 2007: 14). The most frequently used literary strategies were those of satire and humor, with which the authors could distance themselves from the erotic and obscene contents and, at the same time, raise the moral finger (Sidhu 2016: 6ff.).

One such ambiguous scene is found, for example, in the verse novel (*Spielmannsepos*) *Herzog Ernst* (of Bavaria), written around 1180 by a Rhenish poet. In it, the hero and his companions are stranded in a mysterious land called Grippîâ, where crane-people live, who are half bird, half human. After the victory of their king against the Indians, Ernst observes how the kidnapped princess, despite the physical differences, is to be married to the king, who stands out from his people by a swan neck and head. His violent attempts to consort with the beautiful young woman are described as follows:

> As often as he kissed her, he
> pushed his beak into her mouth.
> Such love was unknown to her as
> long as she had lived in India.
> She had to submit to such love in Grippîâ,
> among this foreign people.
>
> (Kasten 2002: 62)

What may appear to today's readers, informed by psychoanalysis, to be extremely modern phallic symbolism was already part of the unambiguous pictorial repertoire of the Middle Ages: swords, spears, knives, or beaks were also understood by contemporaries of the time in a sexualized context—in this poem as fellatio. Thus, such poets did not mince words. In the fifteenth-century carnival play, *Der kurz Hannentanz*, for example, a young woman very clearly animates a young man: "I am the sheath, you are the sword" (Jones 1994: 200).

Neidhart (first half of the thirteenth century) also left no doubt about the erotic ambiguity of sword and scabbard in one of his (so-called) *Summer Songs*:

> 1. (Once) a knight lost his scabbard.
> It grieved a lady deeply. She said:
> "My lord, I will lend you one that my wretched
> husband no longer wants. It's only newly that he

stopped caring for it. And if someone comes to
me now who needs it, how well I treat him
in this respect: I give it to him unblemished."

2. "Noble lady, tell me exactly whether it does not have
strong markings of use on the edge."
"No, by my soul and on my faithfulness!
I had given it to my husband all over again.
It is firm like a board, except at one point,
there on the hanging strap.
But it won't harm you or anyone else."

3. He now wanted to push his knife into the sheath.
But then the blade
bent back all the way to the handle.
But finally he pushed it in with all his strength.
He immediately pulled at it again.
"A black crow has lied!
This is unbelievable!"—"Go on, pull again:
the sauce has yet to be cooked!"

(Müller 1994: 175)

A frequent motif was women's concern about male potency—although in texts written almost exclusively by men. A historical work by Liudprand of Cremona (920–972) offers the following humorous episode, which is primarily about the description of sexual desires and the consequences of castration for women: In the war for Spoleto and Benevento, a woman—driven by her love—tries to prevent the emasculation of her captured husband by asking Tedbald, the Marquis of Spoleto, to let him go with the following plea:

> "What more cruel war, say you, can you wage against women, and what greater misfortune can you cause them than that of cutting off the gonads of their husbands, in which, after all, the revitalization of our bodies and, most importantly, the hope of the offspring that will be born is based? For when you unman these men, you are not depriving them of what is theirs but of what is ours." (. . .) As a result, all those present burst into laughter, and the goodwill of the people towards the woman grew so much that she was finally able to get back not only her husband unharmed but also all the livestock that had been taken from her. (Schnell 2015: 790)

Stories like these draw from centuries-old traditions of motifs and genres (here, the *Schwankliteratur* or the farce) and usually do not directly pursue a sexual objective. Rather, stories strove to convey a moral, to be instructive (for example, to show cunning as a female vice), and were intended to be entertaining and humorous (here, by naming the male sexual organ) or had a misogynous side (women are obsessed with sex). They were aimed at a male, mainly clerical readership that could read or understand Latin (Schnell 2015: 789ff.).

In the Iberian literature of the thirteenth/fourteenth century, erotic motifs and allusions are found again and again, especially in the corpus of the satyric *Cantiga de escarnio y maldezir*. For example, in an epistle of the Trobadour Fernando de Esquio, who sends the following text to a lady abbess, in which the following passage can be found: "I don't want to think about the cost, I just want to give this to you (. . .) four table dicks. (. . .) They will look great to you, if only because they wear cords (. . .) four ass-dicks, encrusted with coral so that you can get your bread" (Piquero 2020: 206). What was meant by "table dicks" was clear to informed readers: these were dildos that could be used for various purposes—in the text, the main purpose was "to ridicule and scorn libidinous nuns." However, the imagination was given free rein as to whether this should take the form of heterosexual or homosexual penetration or mutelle or solitary masturbation.

In German carnival theater pieces (*Fastnachtsspiele* or *Faschingstücke*) from the fifteenth century, one also encounters many carnal allusions and sexual conflicts between the sexes (Müller 1988). In *Der neu official*, for example, three women accuse their husbands of adultery because it also had consequences for them:

And must alone lie in that bed
And have no one to talk
to us and scold us and laugh
And then strum us like fiddles.

(Søndergaard 2002: 181)

Sexual incompatibility between spouses is addressed in the *Schaydung ains eevolks*: "She is too deep and he too short. That is a lack of both, thus she wants to leave him." In order to verify this claim, three midwives were commissioned to examine the man and woman's physical attributes. After they are certified as having incompatible genitalia, they are allowed to divorce and remarry. Mostly, however, the carnival plays are about the opposite: the initiation of marital and sexual relationships, for example, by encouraging young men to find a beloved, a marriage candidate and a sexual partner (in one person). *Di Vasnachl vom Maigtum Einsalzen* voiced this recommendation thusly:

The first speaker:
'Sir Keeper, I have come here,
Have ye not a maiden, that bears a heavy maidenhood [. . .]?'
Then the second speaker discovers a virgin among the guests and says:

"Sir Keeper, now hear my word!
You have a beautiful girl there,
who will get the prickly hunger [hunger for a penis]."

(Barton 2009: 180)

The (South) Tyrolean poet Oswald von Wolkenstein (1376/77–1445) gave the eroticized version of courtly love a personal, marital setting, here in a song in which he addressed the return of spring and sexual pleasures with his wife Margarethe von Schwangau in equal measure:

"Bring the bath tub,
let us have some fun:
Wash, my dear maid,
my head!"
"Rub, my dear young man, my tummy!
If you help me,
I might grab the little rat."

(trans. Watson and Eder; Classen 2008a: 45).

In another song, he longs for the absent Grete for shared joys of love, whom he is reminded of by his next awakening *Ratz* (the word "rat" for penis) (Lazda-Cazers 2008: 583):

In this way, dear Grete,
I shall pass the night until the morrow.
Your tender body fills my heart,
this I proclaim wholeheartedly,
come, finest treasure! I am startled by a rat with great ferocity,
by which I am oft awoken.
It bids me no rest, not by night, not by day;
Beloved, join in to (again) make the bed groan!
This joy I exalt on the highest throne,
when my heart awakes to
my beautiful beloved
tenderly and lovingly embraces me upon the morn.

(trans. Watson and Eder; Frey, Raitz and Seitz 1982: 95f.)

In the high and late medieval literature there is a variety of erotic to obscene texts, which today belong to world literature, like *Carmina Burana* (eleventh to thirteenth century), Giovanni Boccaccio's (1313–1375) *Decameron*, Chaucer's (c. 1342/1343–1400) *Canterbury Tales*, Juan Ruiz's (c. 1283–c. 1350) *Libro de buen amor*, or the songs of Oswald von Wolkenstein (1376/77–1445) (Classen 2008a: 90; Gust 2018). The manner and extent of these shameless passages depended on the respective literary genre as well as

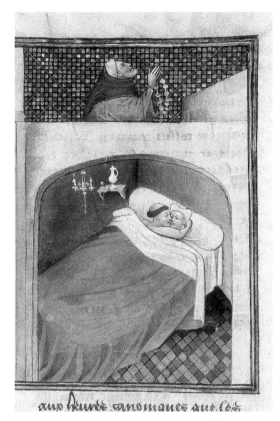

FIGURE 13 *The monk sleeps with the wife while the husband is praying.* Miniature from the French translation of Giovanni Boccaccio, *Decameron*, c. 1450s.

on the social context of those who commissioned its writing and the circle of addressees. Between *minne* songs, farces, and carnival plays, there was a wide range of literary options for approaching this sensitive thematic field: for example, through euphemisms, metaphors, and allegories, the game of erotic seduction in the guise of love, or by denouncing the immorality of contemporaries in order to expose their lewd fantasies, behaviors, and actions. However, literature omitted one subject area altogether: even though homosocial and even homoerotic constellations were staged across many scenes, the practice of same-sex love itself was omitted (Figure 13).

An example of this is the *Roman d'Eneas*, a romance of Medieval French literature, written anonymously in the twelfth century as a new translation of Virgil's *Aeneas*. In a passage that did not appear in the original Old French text, Queen Amata wants to prevent her daughter Lavinia from falling in love with Aeneas, the foreigner. The latter, she says, is a coward who does not care for women, but longs for male flesh and wants to embrace boys.

Moreover, he would have oriental tastes, expressed in a softness of manners and eccentricity of dress. The evoked images of male-male sexuality remain well within the bounds of heterosexual symbolism, but clearly stimulate the imagination of homosexual acts. For example, in the queen's question to her daughter: could Lavinia imagine letting a man ride on her who had previously done so on another man? (Babbi 2021: 228).

The Sin against Nature

On the Way to a Homophobic Christianity

The penitential books (*libri poenitentiales*) further laid out the Christian penalty for same-sex acts from the sixth century onward (Abraham 2017: 134ff.). As already described in detail, these works were written for priests and initially published mainly in Ireland and England. They contained rules for the sexual life of clerics and laity as well as concrete provisions for penance for individual offences (Hergemöller 2007: 57). The Book of Finnian (*c.* 590) provided a two-year penance for intercourse *a tergo* (from behind, by now referring to anal intercourse) with a boy, a three-year penance if with a man, and if it became a habit, even a seven-year penance (Brundage 1984: 82). The *libri poenitentiales* thus prove that the "homophobic phase" of Christianity had already begun in the Early Middle Ages (Payer 1984). The scriptures counted same-sex contacts among the worst of all sins. Punishments for female fornication were much milder, especially when committed by virgins and widows who could not find a place for heterosexual sex. With the penitential books, the clergy tried to influence the life of the faithful. Therefore, the *libri poenitentiales* say something about the prevailing homophobia and the stigmatization of homosexual acts not only among the clergy but also among the faithful.

It took some time before this Christian attitude became generally accepted, however. As with the Visigoths and Ostrogoths, Roman law combined with the gentile traditions and the Christian code of morals and sin (Valverde Castro 2020). What we do know about the weight and assessment of same-sex contacts among Germanic tribes is based on fragmentary, partly contradictory, and differently interpreted sources: On the one hand, according to Tacitus' (*c.* 58–*c.* 120) *Germania*, passive homosexual acts as well as effemininity and cowardice in combat seem to have been regarded as despicable characteristics and sanctioned with severe, sometimes fatal punishments (Bleibtreu-Ehrenberg 1978: 17ff.). It was enough to call a man a *ragr* (effeminate) to trigger sanctions. Yet, it has been shown that the frequently quoted passage did not refer to a sexual offence; Tacitus had military behavior in mind (Johansson and Percy 1990: 687ff.). Other historians such as Ammianus Marcellinus (*c.* 330–*c.* 395) reported in 380 about the Tayfals, who settled in present-day Romania, that they practiced a kind of pederastic relationship with boys similar to that of the Spartans. Pre-Christian gentile legal texts based on customary law did not contain penal provisions for male same-sex relationships. An Anglo-Saxon codex from the seventh century and the laws of Alfred the Great (848/49–899) contained no such provisions either (Crompton 2003: 151f.).

In Spain of the Visigoths, where Christianity had been established as an imperial religion since 589, homosexual acts were expressly prohibited. A revision of the law in 650 by King Khindaswinth (around 563–653) held out the prospect of castration, banishment, and excommunication for all men who deliberately performed active or passive sexual acts among their peers. Under the Visigoth King Egica (died 702), a council in Toledo came to the conclusion that men who lie together with other men not only committed an individual crime but also shamed the righteous life of the community and upended the social order, so that in addition to church penance, they should also be publicly shorn and whipped. Clerics experienced particularly harsh punishments: they were forbidden further contact with their Christian brethren, and preferably exterminated (Fone 2000: 119ff.; Valverde Castro 2020: 287ff.).

In the Byzantine East of Europe, the Archbishop of Constantinople, John Chrysostom (c. 349–407), also severely sanctioned male same-sex acts, namely with imprisonment, castration, or even death. Although there is little evidence that these punishments were implemented with any consistency (Wiesner-Hanks 2000: 51f.; Smythe 1999). Chrysostom was especially wary of same-sex sexual contacts in monastic contexts and criticized the seduction of young men by their teachers and mentors (Morris 2016: 9). Under Emperor Justinian I in 538, the death penalty was foreseen for both the passive and the active partner in "a sin against nature"; alternatively, castration would do, too. The bishops Isaiah of Rhodes and Alexander of Diospolis in Thrace were accused according to this law. The first was (probably) expelled from the country; the other castrated and publicly exposed (Allen 2006: 114). Justinian's decree came about in connection with a wave of persecutions by political opponents and, as was often the case in the Middle Ages, blamed the fornicating men for the occurrence of natural disasters. Their behavior was said to have had demonic effects, an opinion that would find resurgence later on (Crompton 2003: 147; Hergemöller 1998: 40). In the Slavic legal texts that emerged from Byzantine law, a distinction was made according to age, social origin, marital status, and the role in the sexual act. Whereby, the passive position was sometimes brought into consideration and the punishment mitigated. Meanwhile the—presumed to be coercive—feminization of another man sometimes played a role in exacerbating the penalty (Levin 1989: 199ff.).

Prohibition of *Liwāṭ* in the Muslim Territories

In Islam and the conquered territories in the Balkans and the Iberian Peninsula, on the other hand, the prohibition *liwāṭ*, from the seventh century onward, came to be based on the story of Lot and the people of Sodom in the Hebrew book of Genesis. In the *hadiths*, the sayings and actions attributed to Mohammed in the tradition, and the subsequent legal and moral discourses, not only was consorting between men punishable but also anal intercourse of a man with a woman as well as genital contact with animals. In the *Sunnah*, the Prophet's manners of acting, on the other hand, there are only statements about anal intercourse between men (El-Rouayheb 2005: 111ff.). Little was to be learned from the *hadiths* about *lūṭīya*, sexual contact among women, but a woman's assumption of the male gender would have been strictly forbidden in any case (Mills 2011: 61f.). Yet, none of the early Muslim traditions provided for the death penalty. The classical legal scholars of the tenth and eleventh centuries then began discussing—controversially—whether a capital penalty should be imposed (Schmitt 2001: 73ff.). In the end, the high bar of a fourfold testimony was required, and even then the imams only very rarely pronounced capital punishment, for example, by stoning.

In the Caliphate of Córdoba, which covered a majority of the Iberian Peninsula from 929 to 1031, the jurists and theologians also provided for a harsh penalty ranging from flogging to death. At the same time, the Islamic culture there was pervaded by a deep, romantic love of men, which entered literature as homosocial and homoerotic relationships, for example, in Ibn Hazm's (994–1064) and other poets' works. The Andalusian writer and judge Hazm can be representative of the ambivalence toward homoeroticism: on the one hand, he described same-sex love in his work "Ring of the Dove" quite kindly; on the other hand, he condemned it in his legal texts as sinful and to be reformed and stated that only a minor punishment of ten lashes was provided for it (in comparison, adultery was threatened with stoning) (Kotis 2020: 4ff.).

At the courts of the caliphs, for example under Abd ar-Rahman III (889–961), al-Hakam II (915–976), and Hisham II (966–1013), there seems to have even been a male harem. Under Badis Habbus (1038–1071), the ruler of Granada, there were male same-sex prostitutes who demanded more and serviced a better-off clientele than their female counterparts (Eisenberg 2003: 398). In contrast to the Christian regions, Al-Andalus continued to have a great number of male (and female) slaves who were also used for sexual purposes (Crompton 2003: 161ff.). This seemingly hypocritical facet of Spanish Muslim culture with regard to same-sex acts—on the one hand strict religious and legal sanctions, on the other, a high estimation of homosocial and erotic relationships, especially in the upper classes, as well as the sexual exploitation of slaves—was one reason why fears of (Muslim) homosexuality were mobilized for the *Reconquista* (Peña 2016: 43f.). The rape of Christian boys and men, even bishops, by Muslim warriors has also been part of the repertoire of Christian propaganda since the First Crusade (Karras 2020: 982f.).

Sodomia as Heresy and Sin against Nature

In the Holy Roman Empire, ruled by Charlemagne (747/48–814), bishops and priests promoted very strict Christianity. In the *Admonitio generalis* (general admonition) of 789, Charlemagne decreed that all monastics who sinned against nature, be it with animals or their own sex, be punished with the excommunication already demanded by the Council of Ancyra (314) (Reinle 2007: 186). In the *Paenitentiale Theodori*, dating from the eighth century, male-male sexual acts were for the first time associated with bestiality and thus labeled as unnatural sin (Wade 2020). In 829, the Council of Paris connected the sinful sexual contacts between men with the evils of the times, with Muslims (in 827 the Arabs conquered Sicily) and with famine and pestilence. Nevertheless, in the practice of monastic life in the Carolingian period, there were still voices that regarded sodomy as reprehensible, but at the same time as inevitable. Through strict discipline and control, however, it could certainly be kept under control (Diem 2016: 387ff.).

At the Council of Nablus (1120), decisions were directed against "sodomites," that is, men who actively or passively practiced *sodomia propria*, which (probably) meant anal acts similar to sexual intercourse. The penalty: "If any adult is proven to have defiled themself willingly with sodomitical depravity, both the active and the passive partner shall be burned" (Brundage 1987: 213; Karras 2020: 973). After the turn of the second millennium, Roman canon law quickly developed into a canon in which same-sex marriage was clearly condemned. According to the *Decretum Gratiani* (around 1140), pederasty and sodomy were counted among the gravest sins, especially because they were directed against divine nature (Crompton 2003: 172ff.). Here, a sexual categorization that had a strong influence on the entire Middle Ages was expressed: It was not the duality of active and passive or even hetero- and homosexual—in the sense of today's identifying and polar categories—that should determine human sexuality. It was whether the act followed or went against nature. Even the attribution of femininity and masculinity could be at odds with this: Not only men would therefore behave actively and penetratingly, but masculinized women could, too. Not only women but also effeminate men were passively receiving penetration (Lochrie 2011: 45). The "sin against nature" encompassed not only same-sex sexual forms (the real *sodomia*) but also (heterosexual) anal and oral intercourse, masturbation, and bestiality. With the *Decretales* of Pope Gregory IX (1234/1241), these writings were canonized and since then have determined the official canonical position toward (homo-)sexual sinners and perpetrators.

Texts such as the *Liber Gomorrhianus* (1049) by Peter Damiani (c. 1007–1072), a letter treatise to Pope Leo IX, extended the contra-natural sin with metaphorical appendages. The Italian monk also coined the (Latin) noun *sodomia* (Burgwinkle 2004: 203). In his charge against the allegedly prevailing sexual conditions among the male clergy, he presented the *sodomitae* (sodomites) as persons who were afflicted with some kind of disease, even a poison or a pestilence (the *pestilentissima sodomorum regina*, the plague-bringing Queen of Sodom) that festered a deadly wound in the *corpus ecclesie* (the body of the church). Moreover, he accused them of blurring the natural gender boundaries and becoming effeminate in their behavior (Mills 2015: 4f.; Rollo 2022: 1f.). In view of the spiritual impurity of the sodomitically defiled, God would no longer accept the Sacrifice of the Mass (Reinle 2007: 24ff.). Even if Damiani's desired campaign against the "sodomitic beast" failed to materialize, his moralizing and pathologizing statements fell on fertile ground among theologians following in his footsteps.

Arabic medical literature, which had been conveying ancient medicine to Europe since the eleventh and twelfth centuries, also left its mark. According to Ibn Sina (Lat. Avicenna; 980–1037), for example, a medical authority from Persia, male same-sex desire resulted from a deformed penis or malformed seed conduits (Jordan 1997b: 119ff.). Albertus Magnus (*c.* 1200–1280) then, without hesitation, called *sodomia* a contagious disease. His pupil, Thomas Aquinas (*c.* 1225–1274), characterized it as a *corruptio naturae*, which broke out as mental anguish caused by one's very constitution (Johansson and Percy 1996: 174f.; Puff 1994: 72ff.; Jacquart and Thomasset 1988: 155ff.). From Aquinas, the *vitium sodomiticum* (vice of sodomy), the *peccatum contra naturam* (sin against nature), and the *luxuria* (lust, unchastity) formed a triumvirate that stigmatized same-sex sexuality well into modern times (Jordan 1997a). In the twelfth and thirteenth centuries, the sodomite was already seen as a type that not only endangered itself but also poisoned the collective through its unnatural unchastity (Burgwinkle 2004: 21f.).

According to late medieval clergymen, not even the word *sodomia* was to be pronounced out loud or thought—for this alone was a sin and would tempt one to commit a perverse act, a reason for even the angels to flee from it (Puff 2003: 55). But there was also another reason why the monastics, in particular, were interested in preventing sexual contacts and possibly sexual assaults and coercion among clergies from becoming public. Already in a Carolinian advice for an abbot, one could read that a younger novice should not be punished in public if he had committed an offence against a younger one. The euphemism "the sin not fit to be named," introduced in the eleventh century, also served to conceal (pederast) scandals behind the monastery walls and, generally, sexual "relations between a sexually dominant adult and an often resistant child or adolescent" (Elliott 2020: 231). Given the church's efforts to ban marriage and concubinage for clergy, such a sin seemed less dramatic to some commentators.

Increasing stigmatization and religious-legal persecution were some of the reasons why some historians interpreted the high medieval sources that had been created around monasticism quite freely and equated passionate friendships between clerics with homosexual relationships. Boswell, for example, read "gay feelings" from the tenor of the letters that Anselm of Canterbury (*c.* 1033–1109) wrote to Gilbert Crispin (*c.* 1055–1117), the Abbot of Westminster, at the end of the eleventh century (Boswell 1980: 218; Haseldine 1999). It is now known that texts about feelings of love among men or about the beauty of the youthful male body followed a long literary, moral-ethical, and spiritual tradition. These must therefore be interpreted with caution. Instead of a sexual-erotic interpretation, more attention is then paid to aspects such as friendship in faith, the transience of the world, and the longing for an absent person (van Eickels 2003; Kraß 2016: 147ff.; Rapp 2016).

In vernacular courtly literature, the blunt depiction of sexual relations between men was also avoided and instead evoked through poetic displacement of marginalization, metaphorization, travesty, and mythologization (Kraß 2020). A similar situation applied to the Muslim societies of Europe, in which a rich poetics of the beauty of young people also spread, which however had nothing to do with the (present-day) concept of homosexuality or the deed of *liwāṭ* (Mills 2011: 70). Overall, a paradigm shift in the view of male homosociality can be observed in the twelfth and thirteenth centuries. While it had been the prototypical model of male alliance-building until then, it was now increasingly suspected of sodomy, which is why male friendships ought better to be cleansed of all sexual connotations (Kraß 2007). This was in keeping with the fact that the kiss between men—in addition to its many meanings, signaling feudal relationships, friendship, declarations of peace, greetings, and farewells—now also obtained an erotic-sexual connotation (van Eickels 2004: 26; Classen 2022).

The term "sodomy" now also included heresy and contained themes of gross carnality and barrenness that could be found in the discourse of ritualized heretical sex between men and women (Hergemöller 1998: 20; Barbezat 2016: 389). That the sexual life of disbelievers and non-believers ran against God's plan was something the early Christians had already blamed on the Greeks and Romans. This strategy was also applied to Muslims from the Iberian Peninsula. They were alleged to have sexually abused boys and men as well as clergymen after the conquest of the Holy Land (Reinle 2007: 29). Since the introduction of the Inquisition in the first half of the thirteenth century, unnatural fornication and idolatry were mentioned in the same breath; same-sex practices were subsumed under the worst of all sins. By the second half of that century, it was considered a crime punishable by death in secular law as well (such as in England and Flanders). Alfonso X (1221–1284), king of Castile, León, and Galicia, even stipulated in his code *Fuero Real* exactly how the execution should be carried out in public:

> We decree that whosoever they are who commit such a sin, that as soon as it is discovered, they both be castrated before the entire population, and afterwards, on the third day, that they be hanged by the feet until dead, and that they never be taken down (Hutcheson 2021: 195).

Sodomy could now also be leveraged for political disputes about the rule of the church—for example, in the fight against members of the Knights Templar and the Cathars, who were accused of anal penetration during the admission ritual (Karras 2020: 984; Roelens 2018: 241; Barbezat 2016). Christian authors also attributed unnatural fornication to the "Saracens," claiming the Prophet Mohammed himself had permitted them to do so (van Eickels 2007). There have also been reports on the spread of same-sex practices in Spanish Sephardic Judaism and among the Bogomils, other non-Roman Christian cultures that were sexualized in this way (Berger 2003: 80; Biller 2016: 289f.).

The connection between same-sex acts, heresy, and the Bogomils (a Christian neo-Gnostic group founded in the Bulgarian Empire) also led to the emergence of another term besides *sodomite* for men who practiced same-sex sexual acts: the late Latin *Bulgarus/bu(l)gerus* gave rise to *bougre* (French), *bugger* (English), *buzerant* (Czech), and *Buserant* (Austrian German), among others. The Bulgarians thereby stood for the Bogomils who fled to northern Italy and southern France during the Ottoman invasions of Bosnia (twelfth to fourteenth century) and who, according to the Roman clerics, brought same-sex sexual practices with them to Central and Western Europe (Trovesi 2020: 125ff.).

Secular institutions supported the church in its Inquisition with practical measures. Their task was above all to investigate, imprison, and punish sodomites (Given 2001: 205ff.). Clerics who were suspected of such a sin or crime nevertheless remained under church jurisdiction. Like aristocrats, they clearly had a better chance of escaping the stake. The accusation of heresy was inversely used by the English theologian and church reformer John Wyclif (1330–1384) to write against the papal church, whose representatives he accused of "spiritual sodomy" in the form of false preaching: "Just as in carnal sodomy contrary to nature the seed is lost by which an individual human being would be formed, so in this sodomy the seed of God's word is cast aside" (Linkinen 2015: 41f.).

Thus, with this example, one can see that sodomy was most powerful as a rhetorical tool in religious and political conflicts. This was also true for Jewish communities: there, same-sex sexual contacts between men that did not attract greater attention were treated roughly on a par with other sexual offences. In the case of sexual contacts between Jewish and Christian men, on the other hand, there was a transgression of essential boundaries, namely that between the religions and that to non-heterosexual sexual intercourse (Herzig 2017: 65). In the Christian culture this went so far that in the political tract literature or in the *Fürstenspiegel* compilations of the fourteenth and fifteenth centuries, effeminate officials faced complaints and were accused of sodomy right alongside simony (ecclesiastical sale of offices, etc.), bribery, and usury. In 1514, opponents of Cardinal Schiner of Valais accused him of not only allowing himself to be bribed by the Austrians, but that he had also "florenced" a boy, that he was an *arsbrutter* (arse buggerer) and a "mendacious man" (Groebner 2000: 27ff.).

Even in family and neighborly disputes and conflicts, the accusation of unnatural practices and thus of heresy was used. In Bruges, for example, in 1473/4, Katherine accused her husband, the merchant Jehan vanden Leene of sodomy with his servant. As she stated, this was done "out of malice, great hatred and envy, and because she wanted to destroy her husband totally." However, when the bailiff reminded her that this "le grant mal" could have serious consequences for the two men—and thus indirectly for her—she withdrew the accusation without penalty. In other cases, however, such serious, untenable sodomy accusations also had consequences for the initiators, for example, in that they themselves were sentenced to penalties of shame (Roelens 2018: 243f.).

But other voices were also heard in the discourses of the fourteenth and fifteenth centuries. In particular, natural philosophers wondered what explanations there could be for same-sex desire among men. The focus was on why some preferred their own sex, taking the passive or active sexual role. The answers went in two directions: Some claimed that bad habits had crept into these men that coincided with past experiences. Others argued that they were a specific type of men with anatomic characteristics present from birth. For the representatives of the latter direction, however, a fundamental logical problem arose: according to Aristotelian metaphysics, handed down by Galen and the Arab scholars, all natural phenomena (due to divine wisdom) had a certain purpose and nothing existed in vain. How then was "sin against nature," which was the very nature of the sodomite, compatible with the true nature of the individual human being? And could the natural then be shameful at all? The answers were controversial, but demonstrated that there were opposing voices to the ecclesiastical discourse and its postulate of an unnatural vice (Cadden 2013: 3ff.).

In the fourteenth and fifteenth centuries, voices could also be heard asking which behaviors and habits could lead to sodomy. At the top of the list was masturbation, which, as the French theologian Jean Gerson claimed, could have harmful effects from an early age. Some boys began this solitary vice at the age of three to five and soon became addicted to it. By continuing this with other boys and later with young men, they eventually ended up with full sodomy. Medical and ecclesiastical discourses were also able to add something to this thesis: Men who became accustomed to sexual pleasures at a young age soon lost volitional control over them, became effeminate and slipped into sexual excess and thus sodomy (Laqueur 2008: 175; Clark 2017: 460ff.; Zieman 2019: 67f.).

Identifying Sodomites and Male Same-Sex Prostitution

The accusation of heresy is also one of the reasons why in the Middle Ages, male same-sex prostitution was evaluated and treated fundamentally differently from sexual services between women and men. While the latter was tolerated and regulated by the municipalities, it was unthinkable for the authorities to allow any form of male prostitution. That there were, nevertheless, paid sexual services among sodomites is evident from the court records that have been handed down. However, it is usually difficult to determine which relationships actually existed because, as Bernd-Ulrich Hergemöller put it, "the boundaries between regular pay, voluntary gifts, hush money and ongoing financial support were quite fluid" (Hergemöller 1998: 67). In addition to monetary payments and gifts, there is evidence, for example in fifteenth-century Florence, that older lovers would take a boy into their home for several years, educate him, and, at the same time, use him sexually. The Franciscan Bernardino of Siena (1380–1444) accused parents of supporting such practices by not only dressing their boys "womanishly" but also hiring them out as sexual objects (Hergemöller 1998: 67). Bernhard also provided a psychophysiological explanation for sodomy: Those seized by it were branded by the image of a beautiful youth burned into their hearts, so that they would have had to obey this flame utterly (Zorach 2001: 202).

Italian cities and later other European cities issued directives against sodomites in the second half of the thirteenth century, such as Siena in 1262/70, Bologna in 1288, and Lucca in 1308 (Grassi 2007: 127). Some municipalities even set up their own "vice police" (such as Venice's *Collegium sodomitarum*) to conduct secret investigations and, if necessary, use torture to get defendants to confess to their acts contrary to nature. Fines and corporal punishments imposed by the courts were widespread, and in many cases the delinquents ended up on the stake (sometimes after castration). The first documented execution of a sodomite in the Holy Roman Empire took place in 1277 (Puff 2003: 17). It is not surprising that execution also prevailed in the Christian iconography of sodomitic sin: in Taddeo di Bartolo's (*c.* 1362–1422) fresco *The Last Judgement*, painted between 1393 and 1413 in the *Collegiata di Santa Maria Assunta* in San Gimignano, sodomites are impaled and immolated (Mills 2010: 196ff.). Because of the infamy of the act (or accusation), those who got off with lesser penalties had to expect loss of honor and social ostracism, which usually meant loss of their means of making a living. Across Europe, how fiercely sodomites were pursued and persecuted ranged significantly from place to place. Only around ninety executions took place in Bruges between 1385 and 1515 (or 1 percent of the execution cases and 15 percent of the corporal punishments in the city), whereas there were several thousand recorded suspects across northern Italian cities during the same time, most of whom escaped with fines and lighter corporal punishments (Dean 2017). At the Court of the bishop of London, for the period from 1420 to 1516 (among 21,000 accused), only one case of a man accused of sodomy and one of a defamed person are known so far (Boone 1996; Kelly 2003: 188; Puff 2007: 81ff.).

In addition to studies on Italian Renaissance cities, detailed studies are now also available for German and Swiss communities of the late fourteenth to sixteenth centuries that examine same-sex (sub)culture, existence in a fringe group, and homosexual networks (Puff 2007; Hergemöller 2007 and 1999: 74f.). Probably the most widely received study is by Michael Rocke on Florence. From a broad source base, he was able to show that homosexual relationships were an unavoidable factor in urban life despite intensive sanctions and persecution (Rocke 1996). Even if Florence certainly cannot be regarded as representative of European cities of the fourteenth and fifteenth centuries on average, its example can be used to illustrate the characteristics of the same-sex life of the time. The Renaissance metropolis was generally known as a city with a particularly dissolute (same-sex) culture. This was also expressed in the German verb *florentzen* (to florence someone), which was used to label the community as an El Dorado of sodomitic practices (Saslow 1999: 76). The humanist Antonio Beccadelli (1394–1471) published *Hermaphroditus* in Bologna in 1425, a Latin collection of obscene epigrams in which the Florentines (besides the Neapolitans) were described as particularly susceptible to pederasty (Parker 2010: IX). In his sermons, St Bernardine of Siena (1380–1444) reproached the community with an immoral way of life and emphasized the numerous crimes against nature. The city authorities took diagnoses like this very seriously, as there had been concerns for some time about the declining birth rate and the advanced age at which Florentine men married. In 1365, the death penalty for same-sex sexual intercourse was introduced to combat it, but there are no records of such executions. In the 1420s, the sentence was reduced again, and the number of convictions increased significantly. The *Ufficiali di notte* (officers of the night) were established in 1432 in order to better root out and punish the sodomitic circles (Burch 2019: 19ff.). By 1502—after only seventy years—these vice officers recorded in their lists some 17,000 people (out of a population of 40,000) on suspicion of sodomy, some 3,000 of whom were sentenced, most of them to fines.

The surviving *Ufficiali* records show that the suspicions and accusations were often based on anonymous tips and denunciations. These sources also provide information on the age and social background of the men involved and the nature of their sexual relationships. It seems that passive sexual partners were mostly adolescents between twelve and twenty years of age, while the active men were usually older than nineteen, with specific terminology to differentiate these roles (Rocke 1996: 45ff.). Sexual contacts among younger men are well documented, but those among older men do not appear in the records. Shifting from passive to active as a function of age was also quite common. At the age of about thirty, many of the men disappear from the *Ufficiali* lists, which might mean that they simply no longer had any contacts with adolescents. The records of the Florentine sodomites also reveal that the sexual acts took place in a homosocial culture in which male same-sex relationships were inscribed in the social power balance and mostly functioned as patron–client or master–disciple relations (Rocke 1996: 148ff.). Such homosocial relations also came to the fore in Renaissance theater, where friendship, love, and physical closeness were repeatedly propagated and practiced as the epitome of male same-sex relationships (Billing 2017: 449ff.).

The public presence of sodomy cases and homosocial culture as such also led urban administrations in the Late Middle Ages to see it as their duty to take an offensive stance against the "ineffable crime" and to take concrete measures. Therefore, the judicial sentencing of sodomites in the Kingdom of Castile was also about demonstrating good governance and underlining the authority of the municipal administration. Accusations of having committed the crime of sodomy thus functioned as a political instrument of urban governance and political conflicts between Castilian urban elites. As a by-product of this politicization, same-sex desire and action (between men) became a social threat—a stigma that has remained with them to the present day (Solórzano-Telechea 2022).

Homosocial and Homoerotic Relations and Networks

In contrast to the dominant active–passive structure in the Greco-Roman sexual culture, in which the active part was characterized by the (phallic) penetrator (whether in the vagina, anus, mouth, or between the thighs), he who activated the sexual activity also counts. Thus, he who performed fellatio on another was nevertheless considered the active partner as the initiator (even if he was then the one getting penetrated orally). This reflects the coercion—and thus the sin of temptation—that was always assumed to be at play. On the whole, even in Florence in the fifteenth and sixteenth century, it was mostly older men who played the active part, with 90 percent of them over the age of eighteen (on average twenty-seven). Likewise, 90 percent of the passive men were recorded as being significantly younger, namely between thirteen and twenty years of age (Rocke 2002: 153). As the court records of other Italian cities also show, the older active man was generally punished more severely, in view of their responsibility and their sinful temptation of younger people to commit unnatural fornication. In the incriminated age groups, many of the men recorded lived in a homosocial environment, which included eroticized dependency relationships. Compared with other European cities, arranged marriages with significantly younger women or girls predominated in Florence. Same-sex society thus flourished among men due to their advanced marriage age (Karras 2006: 294f.).

Often, larger groups of the urban upper class or the nobility were investigated over suspicions of same-sex impropriety. This happened in 1407, when thirty-three citizens of Venice were accused (Ruggiero 1985: 109ff.). Scandals such as this led to aggravated sentences or the death penalty—in which case, burning at the stake was practiced with great frequency. Younger, passive offenders could expect milder penalties, some even went unpunished. According to Venetian sources, the sodomites came from more or less all classes of the population; craftsmen and merchants were to be found among them, as well as servants and nobles.

Analyses of German, Dutch, and French cities in the fifteenth and sixteenth centuries also revealed a broad social spread of sodomy accusations (Puff 2007; Hergemöller 1998: 52ff.). Often, the men had only brief sexual contacts, which took place at certain urban meeting places such as inns, public bathrooms, and bathing establishments. In Augsburg, contacts were sometimes made outside the city and therefore beyond social control. The most frequent same-sex acts seem to have taken place within a domestic setting or household. Studies on other European cities showed that such contacts were often determined by hegemonic conditions, which in many ways is reminiscent of antiquity: sexual relations reflected the social position of the sexual partners—although the egalitarian connotation of this modern term is particularly inappropriate here. Alan Bray has shown that for England the contemporary specifics of same-sex relations had to remain secondary to the prevailing economic and social power relations between the participants (Bray 1982: 56). Social hierarchies and dependencies were also inscribed in the sodomitic relationships documented in 1440 during a visitation of the College of the Annunciation of St Mary in the Newarke, Leicester between a "canon of the place" and "choristers" (Zieman 2019).

This probably also applies to the stories about the English monarch King Edward II (1284–1327) and his lover, Piers Gaveston (1284–1312), which, in addition to the accusation of sodomy, centered on Edward's susceptibility to blackmail and the harmful political influences of his French-born favorite (Zanghellini 2015: 64ff.; Cornelius 2016; Kouamenan 2020). Sodomy as a political weapon was also wielded against King Juan II of Castile and Leon (1405–1454), the Swedish King Magnus VIII (1316–1374), Louis II, Count of Flanders (1330–1384), and Charles the Bold, Duke of Burgundy (1433–1477) (Roelens 2018: 241f.). The accusation of sodomy against the Swedish King Magnus IV (1316–1374) and his minions was not lessened by the fact that his wife, Queen Blanche of Namur (1320–1363) was also accused of political intrigue (Bagerius and Ekholst 2016: 105ff.).

Kings and rulers sponsored favorites, who were usually of much lower social status, generously showering them with titles and possessions—something that was unusual between men of such divergent origins. The extreme favoritism resulted in other courtiers losing access to the king. They suspected the regent had let himself be swept away by his erotic and sexual desires and the young men's enchantment, that he was no longer in control of himself, and that the natural order and hierarchy was endangered (Bagerius and Ekholst 2017). In any case, sources from different parts of Europe show that men regularly broke through such hierarchical relations with long-term love and sexual relationships. The (heterosexual) marriages they entered into often served as a cover or *had to be* consummated due to social status.

Homosocial groups such as those in the workshops of Renaissance painters and sculptors also reactivated the ancient practice of pederasty as well as the aesthetic worship of the classical youthful male body. Erotic friendship and mentoring relationships with catamites resulted. Whether there were long-term same-sex sexual constellations around Michelangelo, Leonardo, Botticelli, or others, especially those involving their pupils, or whether homoeroticism was primarily expressed in and limited to the works of art themselves, has been and continues to be the subject of historiographical discussions (Crompton 2003: 262ff.; Sternweiler 1993; Gerard and Hekma 1989; Saslow 1986, 2019).

Since the High Middle Ages, literature and poetry have also included praises of youthful love and the cult of friendship, as well as references to cross-dressing and role reversal. Such sources fuel the queer reading that hopes to reveal a subtext behind or below the text surface that says something about homoerotic or even homosexual passions and relationships (Kłosowska 2005: 5ff.; Schnell 2013). This also includes speculation that long-term forms of same-sex love and sexual relationships not only existed but were met with acceptance among contemporaries (Hergemöller 1999: 72f.). Whether the stories about the knights who lived together, noblemen who shared their beds, and men who rejected women, preferring *Ganymedes* (catamites) can also be understood as evidence of same-sex sexual acts, however, remains questionable (Karras 2006: 299ff.). Since the twelfth century, sodomy has been found as a literary motif in English and French literature, for example, where it served as an antithesis to the mostly heroically portrayed masculinity (Burgwinkle 2004). In German-language narrative texts of the thirteenth century, effemination was used to construct and problematize sexual relationships between men according to a heterosexual pattern. Speech in the form of separate, positive homoerotic praise was largely lacking (Moshövel 2009).

Homosexual and homoerotic motifs also became more frequent in the writings of humanism and in Renaissance art. However, their sexual interpretation is based less on the statements of the texts than on a rather loose interpretation by historians (Goldberg 1994 and 1992; Bredbeck 1991). Whether the "masculine love" traced by Joseph Cady in English Renaissance texts can be regarded as any indication of a "suppressed" homosexual orientation of men is more than controversial (Cady 1992: 12ff.). With such literary texts it must in any case be considered that criminal law and prosecution acted as a filter and may have led to self-censoring, and it therefore seems legitimate to interpret homosocial and homoerotic passages and allusions more openly (DiGangi 1997: 239). Recent queer research, therefore, also examines the economic constellations that were portrayed in Renaissance literature as homosocial male friendships (Garrison 2014).

Invisible Sexual Acts between Women?

"Doubly marginal and doubly invisible" is how Jacqueline Murray (1996) described the "lesbians" of the Middle Ages, referring not only to the lack of a specific contemporary term for same-sex forms of desire among women but also to their marginalization in research. This sexual form would have thus remained mostly hidden in medieval sources also because it contradicted the phallocratic and heteronormative sexual paradigm, leaving a historical blank in terms of non-penetrative female same-sex practices. In a secular French law of the thirteenth century, the *Livres de jostice et de plet*, written in the Orléans region, same-sex acts between women explicitly were designated as prohibited. As punishment the guilty should lose a "member," perhaps meaning rhinectomy, the removal of the nose (Karras 2020: 977f.). There are hardly any surviving legal provisions for other European cities and regions, and if there are, then for the late 15th century. In 1499, for example, the Portuguese King Manuel I issued an edict which later became part of his *Ordenações* in which he sentenced female sodomites to the stake and the scattering of their ashes. It also contained the justification for the harsh sanction for a woman who slept with another woman as if one of them were a man:

> She should be sentenced like a man who has committed the sin of sodomy in accordance with the Law. A gathering of lawyers who were present determined that the sentence should be the same as that of a man who commits such a sin with another man (. . .). This applies just as much to the active as to the passive woman. (Soyer 2012: 41)

Throughout medieval Europe, only twelve convictions for sexual acts between women have been found in court records (Linkinen 2015: 79). This figure must be supplemented by data from the southern Netherlands. There, for the period from 1400 to 1550, the files of twenty-five women accused of same-sex acts were analyzed (fifteen were executed), which corresponds to about 8 percent of the sodomites accused in this region. Jonas Roelens has attributed this to the relatively large public presence of women in Dutch cities, which meant that the crime against nature was prosecuted more frequently here than in other European regions. Even if the male penetration paradigm also applied here, a distinction was made in the proceedings between actual sodomy between women and "a certain kind of sodomy," and sentences were imposed accordingly (Roelens 2015: 9ff.).

Valerie Traub, for her part, believed that the late medieval debates on the impossibility/possibility of sexual contact between women primarily had the function of incorporating women into the paradigm of sodomy by also placing them under the "phallic paradigm" (Traub 2002, 2016a). In recent historiography, increased efforts have therefore been made to unearth the sexual and love lives of those women who lived "lesbian-like" existences

(Bennett 2000) and who can only be made visible in the archives with interdisciplinary or queer approaches (Kłosowska 2005).

This led to studies on same-sex desires in the writings of mystics, such as Margery Kempe (*c.* 1373–*c.* 1438), and in the *vitas* of the *beguines*, members of Christian communities who retreated to live a religious, non-married life in *beguinage*, which did not require them to take monastic vows or be cloistered. The same applies to the examination of the lives of cross-dressing women who acted in male roles and maintained intimate relationships with women (Amer 2008: 10f.; Sidhu 2016: 149ff.). Or an erotically inspired interpretation of the verse novel *L'Escoufle* (The Kite) by Jean Renart, written in the first half of the thirteenth century. In it, the relationship between Aenis, daughter of the Roman emperor, and Ysabel, a maid or slave, is described in a night they shared together, among other scenes. Ysabel "moves closer to her [bedfellow], she kisses her, embraces and hugs her" and promises "that she will accomplish completely her wish, whatever it is." The resulting relationship between the young women, who are socially incompatible indeed, is described in a language that allows for multiple readings and ranges from affection and love to physical–sexual feelings and actions (Amer 2008: 102).

As mentioned above, the penitential books of the sixth century already contained detailed statements on sexual sins among women. For example, mutual masturbation carried a penance of thirty-eight days of bread and water, which increased to forty days if the women had slept together—two years of penance for transgressions during menstruation (Peakman 2013: 113f.; Beukes 2020: 3f.). Characteristically, however, sentences were much more lenient than for male same-sex intercourse or adultery. The use of any artificial object or if the sexual acts took place among nuns, the period of penance increased significantly in the eighth century, as per the writings of the English abbot Venerable Bede (Karras 2006: 229). Married women also had to expect firmer penalties. The ambivalent view of female-female sexual practices came to light here, where penetration (with a dildo or a large clitoris) and masturbation were distinguished quite strictly as sins of differing gravity. In the case of married women, refusing to perform their *debitum conjugale* (marital duty) to their spouse was also a matter of grave consideration. Even for the philosopher Peter Abelard (1079–1142), who gave preference to reason over faith, sexual intercourse between women was described as *contra naturam*, that is, "against the order of nature, which created women's genitals for the use of men, and conversely, and not so women could cohabit with women" (Crompton 1981: 14).

Nonetheless, if phallic supremacy and gender hierarchy remained uncontested, sexual contacts between women do not seem to have been regarded as particularly serious offences. Yet, even if the punishments were less severe, mentions in confessional books, canon law, and theological treatises prove that these acts were also heavily sanctioned and considered unnatural fornication—same-sex sexual behavior among women was thus by no means subject to a general vow of silence, as some historical treatises have wished to show (Lochrie 1999: 196). The hypothesis that knowledge of the sexual qualities of the clitoris was lost in the Middle Ages and only rediscovered by the anatomists of the Renaissance (by way of Arabic detours) has also been proved incorrect (Lochrie 2005: 75ff.). The Muslim philosopher al-Kindi (c. 801–873) also gave a physiological justification for same-sex desire among women in the ninth century:

> Same-sex desire "is due to a vapor which, condensed, generates in the labia heat and an itch which only dissolve and become cold through friction and orgasm. When friction and orgasm take place, the heat turns into coldness because the liquid that a woman ejaculates in lesbian intercourse is cold whereas the same liquid that results from sexual union with men is hot. Heat, however, cannot be extinguished by heat; rather, it will increase since it needs to be treated by its opposite. As coldness is repelled by heat, so heat is also repelled by coldness." (Amer 2009: 216f.)

In view of ancient medical teachings, consideration was given in the High Middle Ages as to whether same-sex behavior between women was due to physical disorders or diseases—of the uterus, for example (Murray 1996: 200ff.). In a medical commentary of the tenth century, the first medieval mention of the term *lesbiai* is found, referring to the female inhabitants of the island of Lesbos, who were supposedly erotically interested in other women (Brooten 1996: 5). In French, the term does not appear until the sixteenth century (Amer 2008: 7). In the thirteenth century, same-sex contacts among women were, at least in theory, subsumed under sodomy. Yet, this did not mean that they were punished to the same extent and the delinquents condemned as harshly as male sodomites. An early case of a woman accused in Bologna in 1295 of sodomite use of a dildo ended merely with a hefty fine and banishment (Lansing 2005: 112). In the late fifteenth century, the *Malleus Maleficarum* (Witches' Hammer) of the Dominican Heinrich Kramer (Institoris) (c. 1430–1505) made it clear that the witch was also construed as a sexualized woman in opposition to phallic domination and cultivated not only contacts with the devil but also unnatural ties with her peers in a sexually inverted world (Zika 2003: 269ff.).

In court, it was part of the defense strategies that women stylized themselves as seduced and passive in the sexual constellation if possible. This was the case, for example, at the beginning of the fifteenth century with Jehanne and Laurence, two women who had worked together in the fields and had engaged in sexual acts on several occasions. According to a French royal register, both were condemned for this by a provincial court, against which Laurence filed an appeal for a royal pardon in 1405. There she argued that the other had behaved like a man: "She climbed on her as a man does on a woman, and the said Jehanne began to move her hips and do as a man does to a woman" (Cadden 1993: 224). Katharina Hetzeldorfer from

Speyer (1477) can be seen as an example of women who also aggressively sought sexual relations with other women. According to the court records, Hetzeldorfer had "deflowered a woman and loved her for about 2 years" and behaved like her married husband. For the urban authorities, the real scandal here was that a woman was behaving sexually like a man, acted like one by means of wood and leather dildos, and had a long-term relationship with her lover (Puff 1999).

The queering of religious and literary texts over the last two decades has indeed opened up alternatives to the heteronormative viewpoint. These have sought to break through the "confusing syntax of silence" at least somewhat (Sautman and Sheingorn 2001: 1; Phillips and Reay 2011: 88ff.). *Queer* constellations, forms of homoerotic sensibility, and same-sex attraction between women can be found in medieval literature, for example, among the writings of nuns, beguines, and mystics (Kłosowska 2005). *Thinking queer*, these texts can be seen as an attempt to create a homoerotic aesthetic of their own and to discover/create such practices—although it is not known to what extent the authors also transposed such ideas into sexual practice (Wiethaus 2003: 290; Klein 2021).

Virginity and chastity could also be interpreted as a queer space in which new possibilities for homosocial, homoerotic, and also homosexual relationships were opened up in rejection of the phallic-binary sexual and gender culture (Kelly and Leslie 1999). The same applies to texts that deal with the lifting or crossing of gender boundaries. In the Middle Ages and early modern times, cases of cross-dressing by women usually became public when they had assumed male work and social roles. There is no doubt, however, that gender role reversal also existed in real-life, long-term, erotic-sexual relationships among women (Losert 2001; Dekker and van de Pol 1990). In many cases, cross-dressing has also been classified as prostitutive-heterosexual behavior or the unnatural behavior of a witch.

Emergence of Homosexual Identities?

To what extent same-sex performing and desiring women—and men—perceived themselves as (self-)aware representatives and carriers of another sexuality in the Middle Ages is difficult to assess on the basis of the sources. In addition to questions of a sociocultural self-image of same-sex actors, the focus is on their ability to define themselves as part of a same-sex (sub)culture and/or social (fringe) group. Did forms of subjective sexual localization already exist among these people who desired same-sex and did they perceive themselves as a specific and distinct type of human being—as sodomites? Questions such as these were inspired by Foucault's reflections on the development of (homo-)sexual identities and the construction of same-sex desiring and acting persons as subjects belonging to this constructed type. There is a broad consensus today that the self-perceptions and self-identifications of women and men who had same-sex desires in the Middle Ages cannot be short-circuited with those of lesbians and gays in the present. What we do know about their social and cultural roles, their views of themselves and others lie beyond modern categories of self-conscious identity, "queer rebellion" against heterosocial norms, or an egalitarian-positive view of homoerotic and sexual lifestyles. Thus, the criticism seems justified that Foucault's dichotomy of action and identity has long made historical research blind to a multi-perspective view of same-sex sexual cultures in the past (Sautman and Sheingor 2001: 139).

This view also brings renewed focus to the sexual potential of homosocial environments, such as those prevailing in monasteries, artists' workshops, and similar constellations (Hergemöller 1998: 60f.). The urban environment and working contacts offered—it seems to men in particular—opportunities for sexual experiences, for example with male prostitutes, and meetings in certain pubs and pertinent places. In some cities, there even seems to have been nascent or early forms of same-sex subcultures. Yet, as shown above, since the High Middle Ages, ecclesiastical and secular penal provisions were formulated and tightened, and police and judicial prosecution also increased. Burning pyres were a widely visible sign of the stigmatization of same-sex sex/desire and a deterrent for all those who, because of their behavior, came under suspicion of such a capital crime. It can therefore be assumed that the persecution of sodomy and its discourse in various writings, literature, and art also found resonance among the "similarly affected" and that they perceived themselves as being under the sign of the law and God's punishment. Medieval theology not only described same-sex behavior as sinful, but it also stigmatized sodomites with characteristics which—like Mark D. Jordan has said—could result in a kind of identity template (Jordan 1997b: 161ff.; Dinshaw 1999: 195). Persecuted persons may have perceived themselves as members of a fringe group and subjected themselves to sociosexual self-attribution by others—but not to modern gay identity. From the Lateran Council of 1215, confession offered itself as a technique with which one was invited to speak and confess about sexual matters and encouraged to self-reflect under the sign of deviance (Salih 2002: 120).

As can be seen from court records and literature alike, the paradigm of sodomy has been thwarted and undermined over and over in practice. Some of the "silent sinners" accused of capital crimes and facing the severest penalties insisted on their natural lusts and desires, referred to a multitude of like-minded people, and challenged the prevailing sexual norm. In narratives and in poetry, there are homoerotic scenes and motifs in which passions and longings for one's own sex were expressed consciously and reflectively—even if the physical realization had to remain unspoken. In the Late Middle Ages, narratives came about with men and women who felt attracted exclusively to representatives of their own sex, but there was a clear differentiation between gender and sexual preferences. Accordingly, even a real man—and not merely a female—could desire and love his own kind. This should also apply to women-loving women. Thus, sodomites became deviant figures not because of their deviation from gender character but because they had certain sexual preferences that also influenced their social identity (Halperin 2000a: 34ff.; Ferguson 2008: 55ff.). Contradicting Foucault, it can thus be said that since the High Middle Ages, sodomy was already more than a "category of forbidden acts; their perpetrator [being] nothing more than the juridical subject of them" and that a sodomite was more than a "transgressor"—but not yet the representative of a "species" (Foucault 1977: 58).

It should also be borne in mind that the modern dichotomy of hetero- and homosexuality did not yet function as a template for thought and identity in the sexual economy of the Middle Ages. For the church, the dividing lines ran along procreative and non-procreative actions, those which (regardless of the sex of the sexual partners) were considered natural or contrary to nature and took place inside or outside the vow of marriage. Seen in this light, the question arose for the perception of oneself and others as to whether one complied with the imperative of marriage and reproduction and moved within this social framework. When the point was to marry and sire a child, whether one felt themselves to be "hetero-" or "homosexual" was secondary to irrelevant. For this reason, many same-sex desiring men seem to have satisfied the social requirements: they entered into marriages, fathered children, and had—as they had done as single men—further sexual contacts and relationships with sexual partners (Karras 2003: 166). The same can be assumed for women who desire women.

Assumptions like these point to the potential for ideological projection that medieval sexuality seems to offer. One's pre-existing ideas on the subject often served as a demarcation of, a foil for, or a reference to recent gender and sexual discourses. For the moralistic history of the 1900s, medieval sexuality provided eerily beautiful stories of sexual excess as the mirror opposite to the Victorian sexual morality of the time. For Freudian historiography, it was considered the uncivilized and uncontrolled counterpart of the (sexually) repressive bourgeois society of the eighteenth and nineteenth centuries. In the wake of Foucault, it was understood as an identity-less time of unsignified sexual pleasure before the emergence of modern hetero-/homosexual sexual subjects. Today's queer studies construct a medieval sexuality that lies beyond or before the concepts of modern bisexuality and hetero-/homosexuality, as a construction of the alternative: a medieval age of queer, hitherto largely unheard ancestors hidden in the subtexts of literature and art or found in court records at the deviant and marginalized margins. Functionalizing the Middle Ages thusly is often the result of a longing for the persistence of one's own history or, conversely, the postulate of a delimited modern and completely different sexuality, including the shell of its identity and form of subjectivation. As in earlier phases of the history of sexuality, however, such a projection influenced by the present hardly does justice to the diverse and ambivalent sexual forms of the time (Schnell 2013: 48ff.). At the same time, it can be said that many recent studies show the plurality of medieval sexual culture and accept its sometimes—by today's standards—contradictory character.

If one surveys the historical research of recent years and decades, it can be said that a variety of same-sex erotic possibilities existed in the Middle Ages. The palette ranged from homosocial and possibly also erotic as well as sexual companionships of monastics and knights. In literature, and especially in poems, worlds were imagined in which love and eroticism between women and between men were presented in the most beautiful colors and tones, even if they were usually packed with metaphors. In Muslim Spain, the poems of Hebrew poets, who were inspired by the Arabic tradition, were particularly varied and poetic in their depiction of these emotional and physical relationships. As shown in the previous sections, these possibilities were increasingly drowned out by phobic voices at the end of the Middle Ages. Now preachers expanded their warnings against sodomy into drastic images of hell. The persecution, judicial condemnation, and public execution of sodomites made it clear in many cities that this was a sin and heresy that could no longer be given a positive coloring even when dressed up in literature. The discourse of sodomy had arrived in social reality (Puff 2013: 379ff.).

Even regarding premarital, marital, and extramarital relationships between men and women, the late medieval sexual world was extremely heterogeneous and sometimes even contradictory. Attitudes and practices differed greatly between individual social groups, be they laymen, clerics, or monastics, as well as members of the major religions and the many religious fringe groups. It is not surprising that in the following centuries the moral reformers, as well as the church and secular rulers, increasingly took sexuality into consideration and wanted to shape, control, and discipline it according to their respective religious, social, and political ideas. This opened a path to narrowing the often considerable gap between religious ideals and norms, prevailing morals and lived practice.

6

Reformation and Social Discipline—Fifteenth to Seventeenth Century

Carnal Desire—Legal, Anatomical, and Philosophical

Vice Officers and Bastards

The *Ufficiali di Notte* policed morality and vice in the Italian Renaissance cities of the fourteenth and fifteenth centuries, primarily chasing down unchaste acts as fornication, adultery, and sodomy among the middle classes in order to preserve social order (Burch 2019: 19ff.). Deviant sexual behavior was considered threatening because it unsettled patriarchal rule and with it the social fabric—for example, a husband sexually surrendering to his wife (by taking a passive position) would be subordinate to her. Marriages entered into primarily on the basis of sexual attraction posed another major threat as these ignored differences in social status, or when couples separated on the basis of sexual disagreement. Fears of the like, which preoccupy many of the sources across genres—literature, clerical texts, and court records—are an indication that such "lapses of love" were not uncommon in practice and that physical attraction and sexual desire played an important role in marriage and conjugal conduct (Schnell 2002: 112). For noble rulers, strict bishops, and elected councils, however, these conditions were a sign of increasing disorder in and around marriage, which is why they wanted to shepherd (read control) parishioners in their bedrooms, too, everywhere in Europe. In the fifteenth century, marital issues were increasingly brought before the city authorities and courts. The codification of church law and the secular laws and orders influenced by such cases provided for sophisticated and varied forms of penalty (Karras 2006: 320). From the middle of the fifteenth century, major European cities tried by decree to prevent premarital contacts, adultery, and prostitution, and to punish such behavior accordingly (Günther 2000). This was followed in the early sixteenth century by legislators at the state and imperial level. The *Constitutio Criminalis Carolina* (1532) and the *Reichspoliceyordnungen* (Imperial Policy Orders) even had supra-territorial validity in the Holy Roman Empire and contained, in part, harsh punishments and measures for a number of sexual offences (Eder 2009a: 54ff.).

The Florentine morality laws from 1415 primarily concerned serious cases such as rape, adultery, incest, and procuration. Consensual acts with prostitutes and with women from the servant class, however, went unpunished. In France, attempts were made in the fourteenth and fifteenth centuries to limit the jurisdiction of the church courts over such offences in favor of the secular authorities; in England, on the other hand, these offences were tried directly before bishops and archdeacons (Kelly 2003: 177ff.). Nevertheless, the keepers of order, ecclesiastical and secular alike, were highly aware that the sexual life of communities and congregations usually obeyed their own set of rules and that, despite the canon of morals and criminal prosecution, the powers that be could do little to counteract social traditions and well-established practices. This applied not only to minor offences but also to cases of prostitution, (priestly) concubinage, and premarital sex. Although preachers and priests railed against such sins, secular courts, on the other hand, tended to be lenient in everyday life—unless the offences attracted greater public attention and important legal interests were violated. However, if one fell into the clutches of the Inquisition and were accused of heresy or acts against nature such as anal intercourse or even sodomy, the punishments could be extremely severe (Monter 1990: 113; Lavenia 2020).

In early modern times, municipal authorities and local courts acted not only as punitive authorities, but they also investigated deviant behavior. "Vice officers" and a specially established morality police force arose. Their task was, among other things, to trace hidden, illegitimate births and bring them to light. According to guild constitutions, such an offence led to exclusion from respectable trades or could result in demands from one's legitimate children. Therefore, the master craftsmen were required to pay close attention to the moral lives of their apprentices and journeymen and to report them to the authorities if necessary (Boes 2013: 348). The masters themselves could also come into conflict with the moral requirements of their guild if their wives gave birth to a child before the ninth month after marriage (Hull 1996: 43). Bastards were—if the fathers refused to recognize them—a burden on the community, which had to pay for their care. In contrast to Roman law, where illegitimate children had no claims whatsoever against their biological father and (legitimate) siblings, canon law argued more strongly in favor of (natural) positive law and the equity of their claims.

This rule applied to the 1–5 percent of all children born illegitimately. In the fifteenth and sixteenth centuries, their numbers increased somewhat, but then fewer illegitimate births were recorded in the seventeenth-century registers. The rates fluctuated quite markedly both regionally and according to the social background of the mothers; the numbers were also dependent on the sensitivity of the counting authorities (Bulst 1994: 27ff.). For example, in rural areas of Salzburg in the seventeenth century, the illegitimacy rates of first births were between 10 and 35 percent (Becker 1990: 241). In most cases, mothers were rural peasants or urban servants who had gotten involved with a servant or another man of equal rank or had been raped by their employer. A second group included younger women who had been abandoned by their fiancé.

A typical case concerned the Frankish maidservant Apollonia Vöglin, who, due to the repeated postponement of her marriage to her fiancé, had got involved with another man in 1577, who also promised her marriage and a future together. She became pregnant by him, hid her circumstances and killed the newborn. When this became known, she was arrested for infanticide and put on trial (Harrington 2009: 22). The social consequences of illegitimacy could be dramatic even when no killing was involved. One faced loss of honor, being publicly displayed as a delinquent (locked in the stocks) and shamed, or punishments, loss of employment, and little chance of finding a new job. As a rule, illegitimacy meant lifelong poverty (Fairchilds 2007: 88). Understandably, these women did everything possible to keep the pregnancy secret and to end it with abortive herbs, poisonous mixtures, or by other, often dangerous, even life-threatening means (Leibrock-Plehn 1992). Quite a few premarital pregnancies were also transformed into a legitimate birth through a hasty marriage. This becomes clear, for example, in Protestant England of the sixteenth and seventeenth centuries, where between a fifth and more than a third of brides approached the altar without a virgin's wreath (Adair 1996: 100). These figures are further evidence that couples already felt like a couple upon engagement and thus they had no reason to give up sexual intercourse. But it may also be an indication that many people who had sexual intercourse had to marry when pregnancy occurred.

On the basis of illegitimacy, it can also be shown that the strict canon law, in view of its massive social consequences, was in reality mostly executed with some leniency. Here, as with other sexual offences, the church and secular courts also considered the intention and the foreknowledge/conscience of the accused when determining the sentence. For example, in a case of incest it could be decisive whether the perpetrators knew about their degree of kinship and the legal prohibition against incest and would thus be fully or merely partially culpable. The self-regulation of sexual deviance and its toleration within the community should not be underestimated either. This is what happened in the case of Sebastian Stanghelin, who was accused in 1593 of having consorted with his daughter Mattia carnally, fathering and subsequently killing his own children over a period of five or six years in the Venetian town of Galliera Veneta. The investigation revealed that the incest relationship wasn't only the talk of the town but that the priest himself had known for a long while and had kept quiet about it. The close social and economic ties of the locals—based on mutual trust and multiple interdependencies—explain such behavior. In view of the threat posed by such relations, the disruption to such ties, sexual conspicuousness, and misdeeds were often swept under the table, rather than being brought before the authorities or—even worse—the Inquisition (Ferraro 2007: 445f.). The wall of silence was also the reason why historical sources seldom reported sexual violence within the family or among relatives.

(Un)Chastity Laws

But the church with their confessional practices and the secular institutions with their intensified investigative forces made huge efforts to expose local sexual practices and disseminate an official sexual canon and knowledge base. One method was for itinerant preachers to wander the land and spread word of the (allegedly) progressing decline of morals and the threat of God's retribution—by means of plagues, natural disasters, and epidemics. The pictures of doom they painted were quite vivid and thus popularized moral upstanding. It was mainly the Franciscans and Dominicans who stood out in this respect, in the wake of the church reforms of the thirteenth and fourteenth centuries. Their sermons to the people were held in the vernacular. They were able to package the causes and consequences of sexual impurity into rhetorical horror shows, clear to all (Wiesner-Hanks 2000: 42).

The secular penal system was also based on the canonical concept of unchastity. According to the *Spiegel des Sünders* (*Sinner's Mirror*), printed around 1475, the criminally relevant provisions included the following *Taten* (deeds or crimes) (Walter 1998: 60ff.): *fornicatio* (unchastity between single persons), *metricium* (harlotry as well as multiple or promiscuous premarital or extramarital unchastity and unchastity for the sake of money), *adulterium* (adultery), *stuprum* (coercion, deflowering, and weakening of a virgin), *sacrilegium* (unchastity in consecrated places and by clergy and with them), and *sodomia* (unchastity against nature, namely with oneself, with same-sex partners, and with animals). Finally, with the *incestum*, consanguinity and pregnancy fell under special protection of both church and secular law. While these provisions were aimed at both sexes, they applied much more frequently to women—partly because sexual acts led to a woman literally carrying the consequences. Social, economic, and sometimes political consequences were always to be expected in the wake of unchastity.

Public life ought therefore to pay much more heed to chastity—in the bathing establishments, for example. These facilities, many of which were sweat baths, usually on behalf of the community by a male or female barber, spread with the founding of towns in the twelfth and thirteenth centuries (Tuchen 2003: 23ff.). People met there not only for bodily cleansing, but also for hair and beard care, and cupping or bloodletting. The atmosphere has been described as quite convivial. Most bathhouses, as stated in the Paris Bathing Ordinance of 1268, were required to keep gender segregation, either with separate facilities or alternating male/female bathing times (Duerr 1988: 38ff.). In the Late Middle Ages, the righteous criticism of these faculties and the (im)moral intercourse between the sexes there increased significantly. Many cities sanctioned the violation of the bathing rules and punished morality violations particularly severely. Some bathing establishments were even suspected of being secret brothels—which was often true. Prostitutes were therefore forbidden to visit respectable bathhouses completely (Lömker-Schlögell 1990: 70).

However, historical research disagrees about the actual extent of (im)morality in the bathing establishments. Some historians see them as places where men and women could bathe together and naked, and thereby erotically intermingle (Ballhaus 2009: 145ff.). They refer to revealing depictions in which both sexes are sometimes seen naked or, as in Albrecht Dürer's (1471–1528) *Das Frauenbad* (1496), unclothed women being observed by men. The counter-faction believes that these were depictions of bathing brothels and that such images had voyeuristic and pornographic intentions. Some of these images were also intended to denounce the decline of morals instead of promoting them on the basis of bare facts. Another argument against a crude and carefree bathing culture among the general public is that in the morally impeccable establishments men and women had separate facilities and the bathers were served by personnel of their own sex. Anyone who did not follow the rules in these bathhouses was quickly suspected of unchaste intentions, had their reputation impugned, and risked being reported to the morality police. If bathing together was allowed, a chaste clothing or at least a chaste covering of the secret body parts was a must (Figure 14).

Objectionable clothing in general could quickly lead to a chastity issue. Those who could afford it showed not only which class they belonged to and how wealthy they were by their appearance, but also their advantageous physical attributes. Once again, the standard was different for men and women. In the Renaissance, aristocratic and wealthy townsmen emphasized the martial dimensions of their bodies. Their accessories imitated battle armor—even though the wearers themselves hardly (any longer) stood on the battlefield, but hired mercenaries to go in their stead. To emphasize the martial masculinity, the leggings were tight and puffed out at the top of the hose. A man's genitalia were accentuated with a codpiece (Talvacchia 2011: 23f.). In 1496, the Nuremberg Council clearly saw this practice as going too far and ordered that men should not unnecessarily enlarge this part of their hose/trousers and, above all, should not show it shamelessly at dances or in front of honorable women and girls (Simon 1998: 202). For the puritanical Reformers of the sixteenth century, these phallic protuberances were simply

FIGURE 14 *Artist follower of Albrecht Dürer, Women's Bath, c. 1505/1510.*

too much and they demanded a more chaste dress code altogether. This also applied to some badges worn during carnival, for example, depicting the penis and vulva and sometimes even the sexual act—leaving little to be desired, least in terms of sexual clarity (Rasmussen 2014. As already mentioned, these symbols were often ambiguous and served as suggestive stimuli and a moralistic wag of the finger at once (Stockhorst 2004).

In the female clothing, sexual connotations were rather muffled, going so far as to hide one's sexual characteristics. Laced up in a bodice, a woman's breasts and the neck did remain partially uncovered, but these were considered visible attributes of women's motherliness—while every defining bodily feature below was lost to flowing fabric (Hollander 1995: 80ff.). Clothing colors usually indicated marital status. For example, the Frankfurt dress code and police regulations stipulated that respectable young and single women should wear red, married women green and blue, while gray and black were reserved for the elderly. There were additional dress codes such as a hair ribbon to distinguish virgins. A woman's clothing should indicate whether they were still sexually available or out of bounds.

Prostitutes, therefore, had to wear clearly visible signs that distinguished them from respectable women (Boes 2013: 60).

Fashionable clothing, however, even back then could be quite *risqué* in terms of properly representing the sexual body: If a man oriented his appearance too much to the taste of the opposite sex—if he dressed too softly, for example—he was in danger of being ridiculed as effeminate and mocked, as was the case on the English stages of the sixteenth and early seventeenth centuries (Jones 2011: 38). Even worse and completely exposed to the scorn of the public were all who crossed the (allegedly) natural border between the sexes in their clothing choices. Cross-dressing was not prohibited in general, however. During the upside-down world of carnival it was quite popular to reverse roles. Figures appeared in the satirical to grotesque worlds of Giovanni Boccaccio (1313–1375), Geoffrey Chaucer (c. 1343–1400), and François Rabelais (c. 1494–1553) who no longer even knew whether they themselves were men or women and who indulged in sexual frenzy (Garton 2004: 71). One reason why people reacted so sensitively to such transgressions of the gender boundary was that it was possible to see and potentially also to sense what constituted the male and female sexual body and how the female experience could be shaped and changed by performative acts (Butler 1991).

The Secrets of Women—and Men

Cases like these show that in the Late Middle Ages and early modern period, social (dual) gender roles were difficult to reconcile with polar sexual bodies and a fixed attribution of different male and female sexualities—such as active/passive sexual behavior, more/less pleasure, greater/less satisfaction, etc.—was not always successful. The duration and intensity of the discourse on the male and female sexual body, as well as the attempts to physically underpin the psychological or mental sexual character, show that there was a fierce struggle over gender roles and scripts. Even back then—and not only starting in the eighteenth and nineteenth centuries, as some would have it—the hope was that the truths of anatomy and the body would finally clarify the gender characters. But well into the seventeenth century, newly minted natural scientists had to share the epistemological terrain with other sources of truth, especially theologians; only later did they secure scientific sovereignty over the psychophysiology of the sexes (Honegger 1991).

In the Late Middle Ages and early modern times, trained physicians and anatomists had even more competitors in questions of reproduction. Patients were able to draw on a fairly broad spectrum of opinions and therapies for ailments and diseases related to procreation and pregnancy. In addition to the learned doctors, there were also numerous barber-surgeons, wise women, midwives, pharmacists, herbalists, and various quacks who claimed to know the *secrets of generation* (Porter and Hall 1995: 36ff.), all offering advice, remedies, and cures for infertile couples, impotent men, and marital suffering (Crawford 2007: 125ff.; Thauvette 2016). In most cases, it was not possible to distinguish whether the therapies and medications were intended to arouse or improve sexual desire as aphrodisiacs or to enable sexual intercourse as therapies and improve the chances of conception and thus reproduction (Evans 2014: 87ff.).

It is not surprising that these problems also became the subject of obscene everyday jokes, such as those noted by the St Gallen linen merchant Johannes Rütiner (1501–1567) in his *Commentationes* notebooks (also *Diarum*) from 1529 to 1539. What was special about his notes was that he usually also recorded the social context in the Protestant Swiss town of around 4,000 to 5,000 inhabitants. Sexual and scatological humor were usually closely connected in these jokes, which were exchanged in inns and taverns as well as in the household environment. One of the jokes written down in 1535 read thus:

> "An old man married a young woman in Wittenberg. He came to an apothecary to have a strengthening [medicine] prepared. Meanwhile another man asked for a laxative. [The apothecary] made both, placed them at the window and left it to the maid to distribute them. She gave them the wrong way. The groom spent all night shitting. He wanted to kill the apothecary." Jakob Kuntz [heard it] from the publican in Leipzig, from where he came. (Roth 2017: 55)

Alongside impotence, cuckoldry was a dominant theme in sixteenth-century sexual humor. Jokes like these questioned the dichotomy between (male) aggressor and (female) victim and made fun of the inability and ignorance of men.

The great demand for practical sexual knowledge among both sexes becomes obvious in view of the often quite ambivalent tones that gender life was spoken about: a full pendulum's arc between shameful avoidance and obscene exaggeration. In the play, *The Antipodes* (1638) by the English playwright Richard Brome (c. 1590–1652), this lack of information is the topic of a dialogue between two women. Martha Joyless, a lady from the country who suffered the melancholy of a virgin as her husband had not consummated their marriage for the first three years. She discusses the causes of her illness in bed with her new London acquaintance Barbara Peregrine:

Martha:

> "A wanton mayd once lay with me, and kiss'd
> And clip't, and clapt me strangely, and then wish'd
> That I had beene a man to have got her with childe:
> What must I then ha' done, or (good now tell me)
> What has your husband done to you?"

Barbara (to the audience):

"Was ever
Such a poore peece of innocence, three yeeres married?"
(turns back to Martha)
"Does not your husband use to lye with you?"

Martha:

"Yes he do's use to lye with me, but he do's not
Lye with me to use me as she should I feare,
Nor doe I know to teach him, will you tell me,
Ile lye with you and practise if you please.
Pray take me for a night or two: or take
My husband and instruct him, But one night,
Our countrey folkes will say, you London wives
Doe not lye every night with your owne husbands."

(Traub 2016b: 104)

Beyond the humorous scenario and the erotic-sexual atmosphere between the two women, the innocence of the female sex and of some men is also on display here. This additionally reveals one of the ways in which women themselves—namely in experimenting with other women or through the exchange of know-how—might gain erotic and sexual knowledge (Gowing 2003: 84).

In the English medical, midwifery, and popular literature of the seventeenth century, one could even find out about the masturbation of women (and men). This was assessed and presented quite differently, namely as a pathological phenomenon, as a not so problematic habit, or as a practice that could be laughed at. According to these writings, the forms of self-stimulation in women were to include not only clitoral stimulation and the insertion of a dildo, but also breast arousal and sexual fantasies. There was nothing to be read about the actual spread of masturbatory practices in the various social classes and this will probably remain unexplored in the future (Donaghy 2020: 189ff.).

Anatomy of the Female Body

In the face of this competition for competence over the secrets of women, doctors were also forced to adopt a sex-friendly and procreative attitude and prescribed drugs and therapies that theologians strictly rejected (Astbury 2020). For men, this included erectile stimulants and measures that were not wholly undisputed. For example, the German doctor and professor of medicine at the University of Helmstedt, Johann Heinrich Meibom (1590–1655), in his *Tractus de usu flagrorum in re Medica & Veneria* (1639), stated that impotence could be cured by flogging oneself. According to other doctors, a woman's ability to conceive could be increased through penetration in special positions along with manual stimulation of the clitoris. In any case, both parties involved had to be physically mature enough to practice sexual intercourse and successfully carry out a conception. Both sexes, therefore, had to wait until the body possessed enough energy to cook up the seminal juice (especially from the blood) and thus be capable of reproduction. Helkiah Crooke (1576–1648), court physician to King James I of England, said in his anatomical writing *Microcosmographia, a Description of the Body of Man* (1615), written in English (and not in Latin) and therefore quite popular, that "children and decrepit old men do not yield seed, for that in these there is no ouerplus [of blood] left" (Toulalan 2012: 284f.). He added that for girls, according to contemporary knowledge, until the onset of menstruation their genitals are incapable of receiving the penis without pain and the use of force.

The humoral seed model was so widespread that it can even be found in the few instructions that fathers gave their sons in sexual matters. Karl Eusebius of Liechtenstein (1611–1684) instructed his son about the procedure of marital intercourse in an instruction written for him:

> When the man is quicker to seed than the woman, then nothing comes of it, and all coitus is in vain, then *ad=vel pro Conceptu*, both seeds of man and woman must come together equally in illo actu coitus and mix with each other. [The woman was] slower, thus a means to it must be sought (. . .), which the spouses must ask each other (. . .) thus must he *ante Congressum* excite his wife or she herself, that she burns with longing *pro actu*, when she is thus enflamed, *ad actum* to stride, such that as soon she experience the man, her uterus will open, and start to seed, (. . .) as he must also soon let his seed, as the conception shall happen, through the coming together of both seed at once.' (Flüchter 2008: 162f.)

Valescus de Taranta (*c*. 1350–1417), a member of the medical faculty of the University of Montpellier, pointed out a psychophysiological aspect of female sexual life that should not be underestimated: "God gave both sexes, especially women, the delightful feeling of lust for the act of reproduction as a kind of compensation for the troubles, burdens and pains of childbirth and breastfeeding and as an impetus to bring more children into the world despite these complaints" (Kruse 1999: 132). Unlike men, it should never be overlooked that the female sensation is overshadowed by the prospect of a burdensome pregnancy and dangerous labor, and that men therefore have to ensure a compensatory increase in desire and pleasure during coitus with their wives. For most anatomists, physicians, and practicing doctors, however, the female sexual and reproductive body remained a rather unknown and mysterious terrain in view of its inward physiology and the various contradictory theories floating around about procreation.

In England of the sixteenth and seventeenth centuries, the classical model was still used to determine the age of the menarche and was determined at twelve to fourteen years. If girls had their menses any earlier, it was to be interpreted as a sign of peculiar sexual development. If the first bleeding took longer, it could be considered the first symptom of an impending greensickness (iron-deficiency anemia) (Read 2015: 34). French doctors were also of the opinion that between the ages of twelve and fourteen the girl's body produced an abundance of blood for the first time and that it was drained off cyclically, according to the lunar theory (McClive 2015: 108). Halfway reliable figures on the actual age of menarche are available, above all, for privileged families with appropriate eating habits: Thus, in the second half of the fifteenth century, the girls of the Tucher family from Augsburg had their menses between the ages of fifteen and sixteen (Wunder 1992: 44; Seidel Menchi 2001: 66). According to a Tyrolean surveyist from 1610, girls in the countryside menstruated much later than in the city, namely first at the age of seventeen or eighteen—which was probably too high a figure—associated with living in poverty and their poor nutrition (Shorter 1997: 18f.). Bringing together the available figures, we would not be entirely wrong with an age at menarche of fourteen to fifteen years, with naturally occurring individual deviations up and down (Toulalan 2012: 283).

The female genitalia also remained in focus, because the debate about female seed and its role in the creation of new life continued to smolder. The physicians and biologists who espoused humanism primarily referred to the classical theories of Hippocrates, Aristotle, and Galen. However, they now traced the specific anatomy and functions of the female sexual and reproductive body much more precisely and above all by means of their own inspection to produce new visual material (partly with the help of skilled artists) (Petherbridge 1998; Park 2006). The Flemish anatomist Andreas Vesalius (1514–1564) became famous for his pioneering. He criticized Galen for dissecting animal carcasses and projecting their sexual functions onto humans. In his work *De humani corporis fabrica* (1543), he showed the uterus as a kind of inward-facing penis and depicted it heart shaped—probably also as an indication of the woman's role as a mother. The anatomist Prospero Borgarucci (1540–around 1590), who taught at the University of Padua, claimed in *Della contemplatione anatomica* (1564) that he had even observed the female seed with his own eyes and thus proved the vitalizing contribution of the woman at conception (Klestinec 2011: 118ff.).

Among the (re)discoveries of the Renaissance was the clitoris, thanks to bodily dissection and close observation of the body. This was due as much to the anatomists' craving for discovery as to the revival of the medical knowledge that Avicenna and other ancient doctors already possessed about the female pleasure organ, which had survived the Middle Ages in Arabic texts. According to Jacques Daléchamps' (1523–1588) *Chirurgie françoise* (1570), the place of Venus was more pronounced in some women than in others, and erection was correspondingly strong during sexual arousal. For him and others, the question was if a connection between this erogenous body part and conception indeed existed or whether it possibly only or primarily served pleasure. The explosiveness of this matter can be shown by a dispute in which Gabriele Falloppio (1523–1562) and Realdo Colombo (1516–1559) both claimed to have discovered the clitoris. One had allegedly described it in 1550, the other only in 1559. As in the Middle Ages, however, doctors and anatomists disagreed on its role and function. Some saw it as a pathological, even monstrous phenomenon; others declared it to be a normal component of the female body and praised its erotic and pleasureful potential (Park 1997: 174ff.; Lochrie 2005: 72f.).

Following Galen, the question of how the sex of a human being came about during procreation and maturation in the womb was also a major question. In the opinion of many anatomists, it was only in the uterus or in one of its chambers that one could know if a girl or a boy was growing from the seed. The uterus was thus divided according to the magic number seven—the number of mortal sins and virtues. Depending on which of the seven uterine chambers the little being lay in, it was exposed to different mixtures of temperature and humidity. Girls were born in one of the three left-hand areas near the cool spleen; the three right-hand areas near the warm, blood-boiling liver produced boys; and in between, hermaphrodites were born (Kruse 1999: 202f.). This humoral environment would also determine whether a person's physique and character were more masculine or feminine. Early guidebooks such as the *Secreta mulierum*, but also gynecological tracts and pharmacopoeias, gave instructions on how the flow of seed could be directed through a particular coitus position and thus influence the sex of the child. If the woman lay on the right side of the body during penetration, the juices flowed into the male chambers and a son was conceived—for girls one should take the opposite position. The multicameral theory also offered a physiological explanation for the different temperature and thus temperament typical of men and women. Sexual temperament within the sexes was also explained through this theory: The respective mixture of cold and warm as well as dry and moist *in utero* also decided whether a woman later tended toward lust or shame. In the case of men, the sexual course was also set in the womb, but due to the significantly higher energy level.

(Anti)Humanist Scholars and the Fulfillment of Love

Despite the Aristotelian-scholastic turn in theology, church thinkers remained skeptical about such concepts and their practical consequences. Nonetheless, an increasing number of clerics cited psychophysiology in their plea for deeper emotional relationships between the spouses. Feelings and affection, if they remained chaste and friendly, were an important prerequisite for later married life, even among engaged couples. The practice of premarital sexual intercourse was nevertheless an abomination for them. Positive emotions and love would only really come about through the fulfilment of intimate duties in marriage and thus contribute to a harmonious relationship. But sexual desire should never triumph over reason and religiousness. No stable marital union could be built on the basis of lust and sensual longing. However, the Carthusian monk and theologian Dionysius Cartusianus (c. 1402–1471) recommended in his marriage treatise *De laudabili vita conjugatorum* (c. 1450) that only those persons should marry who matched in age and beauty and not only in status and origin. If the bridal couple diverged too much from each other in these physical attributes, the door to adultery would crack open. The Italian humanist and canonist Lorenzo Valla (c. 1406–1457) believed that spouses should see marital intercourse not as a *debitum reddere* (duty)—a demand and task to be performed— but as a *debitum benevolentiam reddere*: as mutual affection and good will (Schnell 2002: 130 and 385ff.). But whether this also included physical intimacy, such as kissing or manual stimulation of the genitals, opinions differed widely. For theologians, it was a mortal sin if such conjugal acts were done for sexual pleasure alone, but downgraded to a venial sin when the purpose was procreation, avoidance of fornication, and fulfillment of marital duties.

With regard to the effects of the sexual on the individual and society, scholars in the fifteenth and sixteenth centuries tended to look to Italy, where the (supposedly) negative consequences of a sexualized community could be seen in Renaissance cities. In the opinion of Central and Northern European observers, the Italian clergy and secular upper classes indulged in total sexual debauchery. They apparently did nothing to combat the widespread immorality and fornication in the lower classes (Crawford 2010: 10ff.). In the city of Florence, prostitution and same-sex love was rumored to have spread like a plague, the basis of its bad reputation *par excellence*. Such a moral low road would lead inevitably to economic and political ruin, as was already becoming evident in the shift of trade and banking away from Italian towns across the Alps and into the righteous southern German commercial centers.

Those who appreciated Italian Renaissance culture but not its sexual excesses were guided by humanist scholars who criticized these conditions and offered alternatives. Girolamo Savonarola (1452–1498) was no such role model: The Italian Dominican and penitential preacher eloquently scourged prostitution and sodomy in Florence as well as the sinful lifestyle of the nobility and clergy. To remedy this, he would have burned everything that stood for moral depravity in a purgatory of vanities. He called for all persons who led an immoral lifestyle to be denounced and legally prosecuted (Weinstein 2011: 154ff.). Such a rigid moral authoritarianism did not (for the time being) seem worthy of imitation by the rest of the Catholic world. Instead, the Neoplatonic ideas that spread from Italy throughout Europe seemed more practicable. The central protagonist for the study of Plato and his ideas about love and sexual life was the humanist and physician Marsilio Ficino (1433–1499). According to his *Symposium* commentary *De amore*, published in 1469, the driving force of love was the pursuit of beauty. *Eros* aimed at the loftier—the spiritual beauty, wisdom, and virtue in approaching God—but on the way there he also realized himself in the earthly, physical beauty and the senses. The fulfillment of physical love was possible without man abandoning his relationship with God. Despite this fundamentally positive attitude, *amor profano* seemed to him to be a kind of (love)sickness, the *remedia* for which was sexual intercourse (Wurm 2008: 196ff.; Pechriggl 2009: 74f.; Webb 2018: 109ff.). But like other representatives of the theory of humors, Ficino believed that (marital) intercourse could lead to the depletion and waste of vital juices (Walter 1998: 346ff.). So, as a Christian thinker he differed from Plato in one basic aspect: Even if he advocated for homosocial relationships—higher spiritual and artistic beauty was, of course, ultimately realized between men—a man should under no circumstances allow himself to be drawn under the erotic spell of another man, for that is where the unnatural fornication lurked. The best way to prevent this is to avoid the impressive sight of a beautiful young man and not to expose oneself to his seductive gaze (Reeser 2016: 87ff.).

Ficino's heterosexual reinterpretation of Plato was gratefully received throughout Europe. In France, his adaptation ended up subordinating love to the male-female aesthetic in philosophical-medical debates, leaving (physical) homoeroticism out of the equation or rather, in the Christian doctrine, demoting it to mere friendship between men of mental or spiritual amity. In the spirit of Ficino, the Parisian poet and printer-bookseller Gilles Corrozet (1510–1568) warned in his writing *La Diffinition et Perfection d'Amour* (1542) of the anguish and despair that such fake love entailed. For him, love represented a desire for the pleasure of beauty and was manifested in the body as well as in the mind or in the harmony of the voice. However, those who chased only physical attraction were giving in to lower, animal, even slavish aberrations and not following the true, higher spiritual, indeed divine goals. It seemed irrefutable to him that attraction between man and woman through beauty led to them fulfilling their indispensable task of reproduction. However, due to their specific psychophysiology, the sexes each took two separate paths from physical to spiritual and divine beauty: Men, he maintained, possess reason and understanding and thus the possibility to resist base drives and gain the upper hand over them. With the female sex, however, the carnal nature comes to the fore: "If you love me not by habit, not for avarice, not for glory, but by the instinct of nature and by the similarity in complexion," that is "true love" (Crawford 2010: 133ff.).

The Neo-Platonists of the sixteenth century saw in heterosexual love, on the one hand, a natural and thus also God-given way to attain spiritual beauty. The aesthetic attraction of the female body is to be understood as the essential driving force of *eros*. On the other hand, they remained extremely skeptical about the *querelle des femmes* (controversy about women/gender) with regard to physical and carnal stimuli: female beauty being quite deceptive, a woman's body being prone to disorders, erotic love affairs leading to family and social disorder, the female being as marked by passion and horniness. Accordingly, men should treat their desires for the female body with the utmost caution. The homoerotic or even homosexual pleasures favored by Plato were only present in this program as intellectual friendship between men.

Love Marriages and Marriages of Convenience

The aforementioned early modern controversies about the meaning of love and desire before and in marriage were also reflected in the debates of historical scholarship. Questions here were not limited to the history of sexuality but were also about grand theories on the process of civilization, individualization, and the development of modernity. One example is a fierce dispute between historians in the 1970s and 1980s. The focus was on the question of whether marriage of convenience dominated in Europe at the turn from the Middle Ages to the early modern era *or* whether individual preferences, emotions, and sexual criteria already played an important role in the initiation of marriage. Lawrence Stone postulated for England that social and economic considerations were at the forefront of marriage settlement, especially when property, family, and power were to be maintained. Even in the landless and dispossessed classes, where such strategies were no longer used, the choice of partner was based more on rational calculation. On the whole, emotional aloofness and sexual violence would therefore have predominated in most marriages according to this theory. Because of the advanced age of marriage and early death, marriage was "a transient and temporary association" (Stone 1977: 55) between two people who ultimately remained strangers. Positive and intimate feelings would thus have hardly developed between the spouses or even between parents and children. Similar statements can be found in Edward Shorter's work on *The Making of the Modern Family* (Shorter 1975).

Alan Macfarlane and other medieval and early modern historians spoke out against this economic and functionalist determination of feelings in marriages of reason and a resulting lack of love and sexual affection. Referring to church and secular sources, literature, plays, autobiographical texts, and wills, they argued that positive feelings (of love) and sexual desire between candidates for marriage (regardless of social status) also played a role in the fourteenth to seventeenth centuries. Stone and Shorter (intentionally or unintentionally) drew a chilled picture of marriage and sexuality primarily because they wanted to accentuate modernity as a progressive epoch of emotionalization, individualization, and romantic love. In the meantime, numerous studies have shown that love and sexuality actually did have an important role in the initiation and management of marriage even before the alleged invention of romantic love in the late seventeenth and eighteenth centuries. Irrespective of whether the choice of partner was made by the parents or the future spouses themselves, in many cases the marriage candidates' wishes and ideas would be considered in the marriage settlement (Macfarlane 1979, 1986; Ingram 1987; Dean and Lowe 1998: 7ff.; Schnell 2002; Bauer, Hämmerle and Hauch 2005).

Even as early as the sixteenth and seventeenth centuries, autobiographical documents, such as letters and diaries, show that spouses corresponded or wrote about their partner in rather intimate tones. The language of love made use of tender, personal forms of address and affectionate words. However, it should also be borne in mind that a change occurred in this period whereby the writing and expression skills of women in particular grew and evolved—and this was accompanied by new genre specifications and knowledge (Ingram 2012: 318). In the letters that the Lady Lisle, for example, wrote to her husband Lord Lisle in the 1530s in England, she called him "mine own sweet heart" and he replied with "you bottom of my heart and beloved bedfellow." Each assured one another that they both had difficulties falling asleep without the other and longed to be together again. Sir Thomas Knyvett let his wife Katherine know in the first half of the seventeenth century that he is "wishing my selfe in bedde with thee" and "I wish my selfe hartely at home againe at little Thorpe in thy pretty little Armes." He concluded his letters with a long kiss (Wolfthal 2010: 68).

Intimate feelings and thoughts could go hand in hand with quite pragmatic considerations. Thus, on January 12, 1588, the English cleric Richard Rogers confided in his diary that he feared numerous inconveniences as a widower in view of possible complications during pregnancy and the imminent labor of his wife:

> First, the fear of marrying again, dangerous as 2 [sic] marriages are.
> Want of it in the mean while.
> Forgoing so fit a companion for religion, housewifery, and other comforts.
> Loss and decay in substance.
> Care of household matters cast on me.
> Neglect of study.
> Care and looking after children.
> Forgoing our boarders.
> Fear of losing friendship among her kindred.
>
> (Cowen 2000: 253)

By "want of it" he meant sexual intercourse, which was relatively high on the list, but only appeared to be one of several negative consequences of widowhood.

However, it should also be noted that in the (Late) Middle Ages and at the beginning of the modern era, love before and during marriage was not given the same weight that it later received in the modern partnership or romantic relationship and marriage—namely, it was predestined to be the social place where the intimacy and self-actualization of two individuals could be realized (Lochrie 2011: 51f.; Astbury 2020). Instead, it was advisable to have a *companionate marriage*, in which the focus fell upon the domestic marital peace and companionship between husband and wife as well as a common religious and spiritual orientation. Through marriage, both parties also gained their identity—if the concept of identity makes sense at all for these centuries—as husband and wife socially and personally. For both, marriage was *the* life goal *par excellence*, which drew the other important social attributes such as honor, breeding, and status in its wake (Roper 1995b: 55). Social and moral virtues in the choice of a partner therefore carried far more weight than physical-erotic virtues, across social classes and strata. However, the familial domestic space was to be created within the marital comradeship, shaped in "privacy" and through emotion. This space shared by the couple—at least according to the dominant marriage ideology—was fundamentally different from a marriage of status, which was primarily oriented toward social representation, socioeconomic capital, and sometimes also political calculation. Nevertheless, even in companionate marriage, it cannot be overlooked that women's subordination remained a fixed component of the very theory and practice of marriage (Traub 2002: 259ff.; Gil 2006: 1ff.).

Of Sinful Seed and Unclean Flesh— Reformatio Vitae

Celibacy as the Fundamental Evil of Church

The late medieval debates on the significance of love and sexuality in marriage also revealed that the clergy committed to asceticism and celibacy were not necessarily at their best in moral matters. Frederick of Heilo (late fourteenth century–1455) was one of those monks who railed against the moral decay of the clergy and his own confreres in his writings—and in doing so blamed the all too intimate knowledge of women of some confessors that would cause them to be more susceptible to temptation themselves:

> [The] defilement [of women] is washed away by the confessor, and like the filth from the sewer, he draws from them desire, and their emotion and passion penetrate the heart of the hearer. For just as a cloth, with which an unclean vessel is cleaned, absorbs all the filth of the cleaned vessel, so we ourselves, while we have cleaned them by confession and absolution, are often corrupted by what we have heard and other things. Therefore, the confessor should be very careful when he is called as a doctor to the fickle girls and women, lest, while he has to heal those wounds, he himself

should be wounded by the arrow of love, lest he should be pierced with the spear of desire, lest the flame should burn the flowers of chastity, lest he should give them advice for life, lest he should harm his own salvation. (Schlotheuber 2001: 74)

At the Councils of Constance (1414–1418) and Basel (1431–1449), the fight against priestly concubinage was a pressing agenda item. Although some bishops opposed celibacy, it was ultimately maintained (Karras 2012b: 123). But the reality that clerics lived together with a partner—despite a canonical ban—could be observed everywhere in Europe, and the fruits of their sexual relationships were abundant. Thus, between 1474 and 1495, for example, two thirds of all applications to the Castilian Crown for child legitimation came from churchmen (Lacarra Lanz 2002: 163). Also, the dubious morals of many a church prince and the partly arbitrary jurisdiction of the clerical courts in cases of unchastity and impropriety gave rise to complaints. The population tolerated and preferred clerics living officially and honorably with a concubine rather than pursuing their sexual desires by secret means. An episcopal investigation of the Augustinian mendicant friars in the western Hungarian town of Körmend in 1517/18 revealed that the inhabitants questioned condemned the morals of the conventual friars because they regularly frequented taverns, cultivated relations with wickedly slandered women, and even pursued upstanding single female citizens. The fact that local holy men lived with concubines and had children with them, however, was seen as a part of everyday life and wholly unobjectionable. In other monasteries of Transdanubia and present-day Slovakia, a visitation in 1508 revealed that the Benedictines kept concubines and were accepted for doing so. What was unacceptable was the contacts they maintained with multiple female companions and that they used their position (for example in confession) to seduce young women (Erdelyi 2009: 196).

The humanists—some of them clerics themselves—saw celibacy as a fundamental evil and, at the same time, pleaded for a re-evaluation of marriage. Erasmus of Rotterdam (c. 1467–1536), for instance, propagated a reform of the church's marriage laws in his *Matrimonii Encomium* (*In Praise of Marriage*, written c. 1498 and published in 1522). As a priest and Augustinian chorister himself, he criticized hypocritical men of the cloth who considered marriage inferior to celibacy while in practice they themselves drank wine instead of water and led a lively sexual life (Christ-von Wedel 2017: 131). In his opinion, celibacy was not provided for in the Holy Scriptures, but a later invention of the papal church—with extremely negative effects on the moral state of the clergy and even the priests' concubines. Although problems were to be expected in priestly marriage—such as the no longer guaranteed (sexual) immaculacy before Holy Communion and the financial costs of the church in providing for the potential widows and orphans—this seemed to him to be a superior solution to the tyranny of celibacy. In his 1503 *Manual of a Christian Knight*, he insisted on taking action against the unchastity of the clergy in any case:

> Thou art a priest, remember that thou art altogether consecrate to things pertaining unto God: what a mischievous deed, how ungoodly, how unmeet, and how unworthy it should be to touch the rotten and stinking flesh of an whore with that mouth wherewith thou receivest that precious body so greatly to be honoured, and to handle loathsome and abominable filth with the same hands wherewithal (even the angels ministering to thee and assisting thee) thou executest that ineffable and incomprehensible mystery. Now these things agree not, to be made one body and one spirit with God, and to be made one body with a whore. (Flüchter 2006: 69f.)

But Rome and the bishops' real foe in this regard turned out to be an Augustinian monk and professor of theology—Martin Luther (1483–1546) demanded not only a fundamental *reformatio doctrinae* but also a *reformatio vitae*, that is, a reform not only of the church doctrine but also of life practices. Luther signaled his radical break from the canon with a symbolic act: On December 10, 1520, the Reformer burned a collection of church laws in front of the Wittenberg Elster Gate, thus severing relations to the Pope and clerical marriage and sexual regulations. His return to the biblical text and the demand for a life reform fell on fertile ground. By the 1530s, the ideals of Reformation had gained acceptance in many European regions, especially in parts of Germany, France, Switzerland, Scandinavia, and England. Whereby the first and second Reformation of Lutherans, Calvinists, Zwinglians, Anglicans, Baptists, Anabaptists, etc., in the course of the sixteenth and early seventeenth century came up with quite divergent versions of a renewed marriage and sexual doctrine. The extent to which they actually affected people's lifeworld, sexual understanding, and lives has been the subject of research and debate for decades on social disciplining and the process of civilization. The same applies to the effects of the Roman countermeasures on the Catholic clergy and laity (Schilling 1994; Vocelka 1994: 31ff.; Wiesner-Hanks 2000: 255ff.). According to some historians, (re)confessionalization has led not only to new forms of church–secular discipline and regulation—and thus to intensified sexual repression—but also to counteracting effects, for example in the form of a sexualization of everyday life (Walter 1998: 488ff.; Eder 2009a: 20ff.).

Marriage Is a Necessary State (also for Clerics)

There is consensus today that the Evangelical or Protestant sexual concepts differed less clearly from Roman dogma and earlier debates on marriage and sexual life than was long assumed (Harrington 1995: 59ff.; Hull 1996: 17ff.; Wiesner-Hanks 2000: 60ff.; Puff 2017). In one point, however, the Reformers did radically break with tradition: Not celibacy but marriage was the "noblest state," and neither laymen nor priests should practice lifelong abstinence. For Luther, marriage represented "not only an honorable, but also a necessary state," which was already imposed on all people as a compulsory form of life in paradise and as a social institution (Arnórsdóttir 2018: 284). Without it man could not remain chaste:

> Unless she is in a high and unusual state of grace, a young woman can do without a man as little as she can do without eating, drinking, sleeping, or other natural requirements. Nor can a man do without a woman. The reason for this is that to conceive children is as deeply implanted in nature as eating and drinking are. The person who wants to prevent this and keep nature from doing what it wants to do and must do is simply preventing nature from being nature, fire from burning, water from wetting, and man from eating, drinking, or sleeping. (Trepp 2014: 305; DeRusha 2016)

Marriage and procreation had been laid out in the plan of creation and in nature by God himself. Barriers to marriage also represented a form of social injustice, which the wealthy had the power to remove by bribing the church people and the Pope:

> It is thanks to them that the Romans have become merchants today. What are they selling? Female vaginas and male members. Truly the most fitting commodity for these merchants, who, out of greed and godlessness, are worse than the filthiest and most licentious. For among the obstacles to marriage there is none today that cannot be turned into lawfulness with the help of money, so that it seems that these laws of men were created for no other purpose than to serve greedy people and predatory nimrods one day as money nets and pitfalls of souls, and to cause to arise in the Church of God in a holy place that abomination which publicly sells to people the private parts of both sexes. (Luther 1983: 101)

Even the "papal bunch," the bishops, priests, monks, and nuns, did not have the strength to remain chaste and therefore inevitably violated the sixth commandment in thoughts, words, and works (Luther 1995: 59ff.; Breul 2014: 33ff.). Contrary to what is laid down in the church dogma, marriage would also be a useful remedy against lust for them. Among reformed people there should, therefore, no longer be a sexual divide between clergy and laity. Luther himself set a good example and in 1525 married Katharina von Bora (1499–1552), a nun who had escaped from a Cistercian convent, and fathered six children with her (Roper 2016: 352ff.). Many other reformed priests also married, which is why within a few years the former "priest whores," who had been so shunned by Catholics, emerged as the wives and "co-regentesses" of the church people (Schorn-Schütte 1991). Reformed clerics could now at any rate rightly point out that they were married to respectable wives, while their Catholic counterparts lived in untidy concubinages or regularly visited whores (Karras 2012b: 125; Plummer 2014).

According to Luther, the faithful should build their marital bonds first and foremost on a spiritual and friendly relationship; Augustine and the Church Fathers served as his model. Once man and woman lived together in love and harmony, marital chastity would come about of its own accord. Love between spouses should above all be articulated in fidelity, consideration, and care. In contrast to the Catholic canon, marriage was not understood as a sacrament, but as a worldly thing that arose from the covenant between man and woman under the sign of divine grace (Donahue 2016: 40ff.). Luther had thus shaken one of the most important pillars of church power in the world: the priestly primacy over marriage. From the twelfth century already, marriage had been considered a sacrament within the church. At the Council of Florence (1439), Rome then succeeded in codifying marriage as the seventh sacrament. Now Luther was denying the clergy their legitimizing function and thus repositioning the marriage covenant closer to God and the spouses. But for him, too, the marriage foundation was not merely the result of the declaration of will between the spouses alone. Their will had to comply with the wishes of the parents and the community. Under no circumstances should the bond lead to social disorder, which is why he strictly opposed *Winkelehen* (secret marriages) (Burghartz 2016: 179f.). For both sexes, he provided a corresponding place in the marital union: I *Eheweiber* (wives) were supposed to be subservient and faithful to their husbands—failure to do so meant backsliding into whoredom.

In the matter of divorce, Luther also tried to draw a clear dividing line with Rome. The annulment of marriages, which was handled quite flexibly in the high and late medieval church—e.g., due to obstacles to marriage subsequently brought forth—should no longer be determined by the bishops and the Pope. In principle, the Reformers also insisted on the indissolubility of marriage. Under certain circumstances—including impotence and refusal of sexual intercourse—dissolution did seem legitimate, if only because it prevented extramarital fornication. Divorce of valid marriages should be possible for two reasons: Firstly, adultery would lead to the spiritual death of the guilty party, and secondly, there was the case of malicious desertion. The innocent spouse could then—in contrast to previous custom—marry again (Harrington 1995: 88). In practice, divorce rates remained very low even among the reformed population. Mostly men were granted this right. In Geneva, only three divorces were recorded between 1559 and 1569; in all of Norway there were eighteen between 1571 and 1596 (Crawford 2007: 78). The Anglican and Anglo-Irish churches maintained the indissolubility of marriage, which included living apart—the so-called separation of table and bed—but an act of parliament in 1670 cleared the way for civil divorce (Wiesner-Hanks 2000: 79).

The many polygamous forms of marriage and concubinage practiced by the nobility also proved problematic for Protestants (Heinig 2006:

12ff.). These included, in particular, morganatic double marriage. One such case directly affected Luther and his fellow proto-Reformer Melanchton (1497–1650): Philip I of Hessen (1504–1567), a promoter of the Protestant teaching, had married Christine of Saxony (1505–1549) in 1524, and in 1540 entered into a second morganatic marriage with his Saxon court mistress, Margarethe von der Saale (1522–1566). His first wife had even agreed in writing to the second marriage on the condition that the other wife and her children (fathered by Philip) were given an inferior position (Seidel Menchi 2016: 327f.). In all actuality, this form of bigamy was forbidden by canon law and was sanctioned with the death penalty in the *Carolina*. But despite such injunctions, this practice was considered common among the aristocracy. Its aim was to transform a sexual liaison into a semi-legitimate marriage relationship. But now concubines and mistresses were nevertheless blatantly called out as whores by the reformed. This did not mean that such legitimizing forms of relationships didn't hold up anyway. Some nobles, indeed, in addition to a politically motivated first marriage, maintained a second love and/or sexual relationship with another woman and possibly also married her morganatically, that is, without hereditary or dynastic rights (Burghartz 2016: 182ff.).

(Wol)Lust and the Moral Demands of Marriage

The Reformers not only accorded marriage a higher status for all believers, but they also increased the moral demands on this institution (Schnell 2002: 155ff.). Already for Luther, and even more so for the second, rigid wave of the Reformation, the moral handling of sexual desire was a central challenge before and during marriage (Puff 2017: 666f.). Bestowed by God, procreation was considered a fundamentally positive, physical, and spiritual drive of human life. Feeling sexual pleasure, this human ability should be understood as a benevolent gift from the Almighty. But even Luther believed that marital coitus could not be performed without sin, yet God forgave it:

> "All children are conceived, born and born in sin in the womb of their mother, for they are begotten of seed poisoned with sin, sin after sin cometh, which we inherit by birth; we are begotten of sinful seed and filthy flesh" (Leibbrand 1972, Vol. 2: 71ff.).

Sinfulness seemed omnipresent to him and also inscribed in all sexual expressions. Independent of the Pope, a bishop, or a priest, each individual must ask his personal God for mercy and forgiveness for his sinful existence (Ballhaus 2009: 264f.). In the opinion of the Reformers, sexuality was a powerful driving force and could only be subjected to the will to a limited extent. Luther saw sexual lust in man even before the Fall, and therefore it could only be directed into godly paths through marriage (Wunder 2016: 68f.). The fixation on the sinfulness of sexual desire also led to a change in the use of language. Thus, the term *lust* narrowed its meaning in Protestant England of the sixteenth century and here especially in the Bible translations into a term for sexual desire, away from its Germanic roots of being the word for general appetite, inclination, or pleasure. In the Late Middle Ages, however, the semantic field had still included various forms of desire (Lochrie 2011: 43). The German term *Wollust*, which for a long time did without any moral evaluation and generally meant joy and pleasure, experienced a similar contraction. Now it gained an increasingly (negative) sexual connotation.

Luther said that men clearly had the harder lot in dealing with *Wollust*, since they had to resist the sexual charisma of women (Wiesner-Hanks 2005). Excessive sexual passions endangered not only their bond with God but also the assumed natural hierarchy of the sexes and the society of estates as a whole. Men would therefore have to set themselves three central tasks: Firstly, as housefathers they had to watch over their wives, children, and servants; secondly, they had to take care of the upkeep of the household or house; and thirdly, they had to keep their own sexual desire and the seductive potential of their wives under control (Hendrix 2008: 71). He distrusted the female sex in sexual matters, as can be seen from one of his letters to some nuns in 1524: Among a thousand women not one could remain chaste, according to him, because "a woman has no control over herself" (Roper 2016: 353).

Marriage and social experiments that were attributed to radical reformist groups such as the Anabaptists (Mennonites, Amish, Hutterites)—directions that advocated a far-reaching separation of church and state as well as communities of property and goods and some of them for a lived brotherhood of the faithful including spiritual polygamy—were considered reprehensible to the mainstream of the Reformation and were discredited in propaganda terms and, in part, violently persecuted (Stayer 1980; Roper 1991: 309ff.). The reason for this was the exposure of ecstatic Anabaptist women in St Gallen or the spiritual second marriages of the *Träumer* movement in Franconia in the 1530s. More precisely, forms of sexual expression that caused a sensation among contemporaries usually had a religious background, for example the realization of a spiritual marriage with Jesus or end-time expectations that legitimized their deviant sexual behavior (Reinholdt 2012: 55ff.). The Catholic side, on the other hand, not only accused Anabaptists and other utopians of unchastity and bigamy, but suspected all Protestants of such sins.

Besides Luther, especially John Calvin (1509–1564) praised the God-given nature of marriage, but like other puritans was much more concerned about chastity and the right measure of marital joy. True Christians should first of all follow their individual conscience in matters of lust. He considered it important to strengthen preventive self-observation and monitoring as well as the constant examination of one's conscience (Schwanitz 1995: 179ff.). As an elementary moral regulator, conscience could distinguish between chaste and unchaste sexual acts and corresponding thoughts and words. In view of this internalization, practical and proven instructions for everyday chaste behavior did not seem necessary to him for the time being. The reformed confessional system was also intended to contribute to a self-referential morality, which is why, in addition to Calvin and Luther, Ulrich Zwingli (1484–1531) also strongly opposed secret and individual auricular confession. The penitential books and lists issued by the Roman Church for confessions lost their significance for the Reformers (Tentler 1977: 357). This did not mean, however, that Luther, for one, did not have a precise idea of what was to be confessed in view of the sixth commandment. Apart from the typical sins, he also considered lesser unchaste sins:

> That one has had the desire and will to shameful, lewd and unchaste words, songs, stories and paintings. That one has aroused or caused unchastity with lewd gestures, images, drawings or writings. That one has tempted oneself or others to unchastity with superfluous embellishments/ornamentation of clothes. That one has by overeating, over-drinking, idleness and other causes not avoided unchastity (Gutmann 1991: 147).

The confession of unchastity should now take place as an inner and direct communication with God—no longer mediated by the ministers of the (Catholic) church—and aim at a "future-oriented recapitulation of sinful conduct" (Maasen 1998: 334).

Condemnation and Persecution of Non-Marital Sexuality

The Protestant revaluation of marriage increasingly discredited non-marital sexual forms. On the one hand, this concerned prostitution, which was previously sanctioned by canon law, but more or less tolerated in everyday life. On the other hand, incest prohibitions were right at the top of the list for moral reformers, whereby the degree of kinship was more narrowly defined than in the Catholic canon. Mixing with blood relatives was considered bestial and should be punished as severely as unnatural fornication (Rublack 1995: 171ff.; Sabean 1998: 63ff.). In Frankfurt, Lutheran advocates demanded the death penalty for a father who had slept with his stepson's wife, and indeed he was executed by sword (Boes 2013: 48). Modest extramarital sexual contacts were also condemned, some reform supporters even demanded the death penalty for adultery.

Fornicatio, premarital sexual intercourse, was already mentioned as criminally relevant in German-speaking countries in a Zurich decree from 1534, but in practice it was (probably) not yet prosecuted. This changed in the second half of the sixteenth century. Penal practice followed and more and more cases of premarital frivolity ended up in court (Burghartz 2004: 88). In the reformed earldom of Lippe, the police regulations demanded a fine for premarital cohabitation. Delinquents that subsequently married were subject to reduced fines (Fleßenkämper 2014: 202). Luther had already associated *fornicatio* with social customs, church festivals, and holidays, and with visits to inns and dances, and had spoken out against these pleasures, which tended to lead to debauchery. In order to prevent viciousness, such as idleness, the reformed and Lutheran churches drastically reduced the number of holidays, so that only a few days remained free of labor besides Sundays—from upwards of 100 before the Reformation (Reinhard 2006: 474f.).

Reformers also set their sights on sexual intercourse between fiancées. In the Württemberg marriage regulations of 1534, premature coitus was declared lewd and inadmissible. Another order from 1553 then demanded a prison sentence of eight days for the man and four days for the woman for premarital sex. In Basel, accusations of sexual intercourse between engaged couples accounted for around 20 to 30 percent of all sexual offences (Burghartz 2016: 187f.). Such injunctions seem to have had little effect on the common practice of premarital sexual contacts between engaged couples, however. In Protestant cities such as Frankfurt, charges of sexual intercourse between single people thus increased significantly toward the end of the sixteenth century. If the illegitimate offspring had a right to the father's name, including inheritance claims until 1578, they were then passed on to the mother in their entirety. As in many places, the guild organizations were behind the change in the law, which excluded illegitimate candidates as guild members and competitors (Boes 2013: 16, 37).

In 1582, a Danish-Norwegian marriage order required an official engagement instead of a secret promise of marriage between those wishing to marry. At the same time, "weakened" women were granted the right to claim financial compensation from their fiancées in court if they did not keep their marriage vows (Johansen 2005: 27). In Reformation Norway, church discipline was undergirded by secular authorities and provided for public confession of guilt as punishment (Riisøy 2009: 125ff.). The Reformers also sanctioned sexual behavior not directly associated with marriage, but they didn't find it worthy of too much discussion either. Masturbation was to be found wherever marital duties were not performed in love and fidelity. In the case of young people, solitary lust should be preempted by wedding as early as possible, preferably between the ages of twelve and thirteen. Here, as in other issues of fornication, the Reformers largely followed the canonical guidelines and exaggerated them with moral verve and an oppressive burden of conscience. Where, as in England, Protestant enthusiasm fell on particularly fertile ground, by the middle of the sixteenth century at the latest, all non-procreative and non-marital forms of sexual life could no longer be removed from the penal and canonical indices (Dabhoiwala 2012: 13ff.).

In Sweden, the penal code was amended in 1608 and the range of punishments was increased for almost every conceivable type of sexual activity outside marriage. Similar tightening took place in the other Scandinavian countries. As part of state-building, the strict Lutherans of Sweden tried to achieve the most comprehensive control possible of pre- and extramarital sexuality, which also included public floggings and death sentences. However, a blind eye was always turned if the persons involved could credibly show that they really loved each other and that nothing stood in the way of marriage. This also included the recognition of the child by the father in the case of a premarital pregnancy (Österberg 2010: 166ff.). When fornication was tried before a court, it was of great importance, as in seventeenth-century Turku (then part of Sweden), how the families of the accused behaved toward the premarital affairs of the sons and daughters. The mothers and female heads of households were also responsible in court not only for the daughters and maidservants of the house, but somewhat to sons as well (Välimäki 2020: 32).

In moral matters, it seemed to the reformed communities that constantly examining one's conscience was absolutely necessary, but so was an external form of monitoring and discipline. With *Zuchtordnungen* (moral ordinances) they tried to achieve a form of marital cohabitation that was pleasing to God and, at the same time, adapted to the social conditions, and to sanction infringements with appropriate institutions. In cooperation with the secular authorities, matrimony courts and consistencies were created to implement and control moral standards—and punish delinquency. The first of these marital courts was established by Zwingli in Zurich in 1525 and was staffed with clerical judges. They dealt with broken marriage vows, secret marriages, but mainly with premarital and extramarital *Unzucht* (fornication/unchastity) and prostitution (Wiesner-Hanks 2000: 67ff.). The council in Basel followed in 1529 and set up a mixed secular and church marriage court which dealt with similar moral offences (Burghartz 1999: 107ff.). In the Schaffhausen Reformation Order from the same year, marriage disputes even became a matter for the municipal authorities:

> "And should married couples contrive to live together unkindly, quarrelsomely and reluctantly, or in open suspicion of adultery, let the marriage judges bring them in to warn (. . .) and tell them, if they do not desist, that they will be reported to the proper authorities" (Schnell 2002: 125).

Calvin then went so far with his Genevan church discipline in 1561 that he made the sexes equal in terms of marriage law and in the process also improved women's chances for divorce and remarriage (Ballhaus 2009: 272). Single women who had been raped and spouses abused by their husbands were also to now receive protection. Marriage was regarded as such an important societal and spiritual good that two years after Calvin's death in 1566 an order actually punished adultery with the death penalty (Kingdon 1995: 116f.)

As was the case with the earlier church courts, the reformed church discipline created numerous institutional interfaces between the religious-doctrinal discourse and the life and experiences of the faithful. Through the mediation of the church matrimonial judges, many of them laymen, the reformed communities also scrutinized the joys of marriage and extramarital pleasures and tried above all to uncover socially explosive acts—and in doing so usually came across accused persons who acknowledged their actions with silence and shame (Roper 1991, 1995a, 1995b; Dinges 1995). Since the simple sexual offences went mostly unreported, the institutions themselves carried out investigations. These concerned, for example, the missed notification of pregnancies. If no such announcement had been made and the child died unbaptized as a result of an abortion, a woman could be charged with infanticide. If instruction by the judge did not produce results, the courts also called in secular authorities who, if necessary, used embarrassing interrogation techniques. Sometimes it helped to interrogate local midwives and nurses to find out if women had secret pregnancies or if children had been born unannounced. Servants and maidservants fell under heightened suspicion (Wiesner-Hanks 2000: 84). Mostly, however, the church and mixed courts acted as mediators and only resorted to harsher measures in the case of repeated offences of morality or in those cases that caused public attention or endangered property rights. It was often the parishioners themselves who turned to the church courts in the event of moral conspicuousness among their neighbors. In London in the middle of the seventeenth century, sexual defamation, especially accusations of fornication between women, made up the majority of cases before the church court (Smith 2011: 110). The contribution of non-church social institutions to the spread of the new moral norms should not be underestimated—craft guilds and urban citizens, for instance, advocated church discipline in everyday life and a stricter approach to simple sexual offences (Rublack 2012: 46).

Ambivalent Reaction of the Papal Church

The papal church reacted to the *reformatio* with the Council of Trent (1545–1563) and, with the *Catechism Romanus* (1566), it presented the first official Catholic book of faith for priests and lay people. With lasting resolutions on marriage and sexual life, the Catholic Church was above all trying to fight the Protestant aberrations in this so important area of life (Denzler 1988: 700; Wiesner-Hanks 2000: 105ff.). Although celibacy proved a controversy at the council, too, the representatives of the ascetic direction ultimately prevailed. They held that priestly celibacy continued to be superior to marriage. In order to eliminate the pre-Reformation excesses within the priesthood, supervision of their way of life was to be the key. In some areas, this surveillance of the priesthood seems to have been successful. For example, during the council itself about half of the clergy in Würzburg (45 percent) were suspected of concubinage. In the years 1616 to 1631, only 4 percent practiced such cohabitation (allegedly) (Wiesner-Hanks 2000: 1228). In Valencia, Spain, the church was less successful, for a visitation there in 1481 found that about a third of the clergy lived openly in sin. A condition that hardly changed even after the Council of Trent, since the church did not take appropriate measures (Haliczer 1996: 11).

In the monasteries, the situation was hardly different. An episcopal visitation showed that in the monastery of Neuberg in Styria in 1575, among the five monks, three lived together with a concubine and had twelve children between them. By 1591, the situation had by no means improved, for each of the ten monks now had a concubine with him (Tanner 2005: 126). In addition, religious women, many of them of lower social rank, could hardly resist the sexual demands of priests and confessors. They were bound to obedience to men and superiors, plus the idealization of priests who controlled access to God and the fate of their eternal salvation. As cases from Spain after the Council of Trent show, this opened the door to sexual abuse (Rhodes 2020: 875).

In any case, it was clear to the Catholic Church leaders that the faithful could only be converted to a more moral (sexual) life if the priests and the monastics were also role models. If the confessors lived chastely, the laity's readiness to confess and repent of sexual sins—and (possibly) to make amends—also increased. In order to achieve this, monastic training intensified and monks' living environment was further walled off from all possible sexual stimuli. For example, male seminarians were no longer allowed to dress in front of each other, and Benedictine women were to keep their hands on the bedspread while sleeping. It is not surprising that the body parts thus concealed and stigmatized in the struggle for a virginal life behind monastery walls hardly dimmed in their minds, but became even more burningly interesting.

The exemplary virginity of Mary was also emphasized at the Council of Trent; her maternal traits grew stronger. Average women, on the other hand, were then generally even more prone to great sinfulness in carnal matters. In view of the Reformation's praise of marriage, its new regulation was postponed for quite a long time. The *Decretum Tametsi*, published in 1563, finally presented the following result: The sacrament of marriage was no longer to be administered (alone) by the spouses and (merely) before God—but instead required public blessing by a priest in front of at least two witnesses. This apodictically ruled out the possibility of a couple living together and having sexual intercourse legitimately after a mere mutual promise of marriage. The families were barred (in principle) from having an opinion on the matter, which is why the French king didn't allow the decree to come into force and punished marriages without the consent of the parents if the bride was younger than twenty-five and the groom younger than thirty-five (Ingram 2012: 315). In order to prevent clandestine marriages and bigamy, the engagement had to be officially announced by a priest and before the congregation; this was also required in earlier centuries, but now a non-public banns could lead to the invalidity of the marriage (Zarri 2001; Donahue 2016: 36). This was meant to draw a stark contrast to Protestant marriage, which was not considered a sacrament and (under certain circumstances) could be divorced.

In defining the marital tasks, the influence of Reformation ideas could not be overlooked. Whereas the procreation of offspring had previously been the primary goal, now above all the spouses were to provide mutual support. Furthermore, marriage should serve to avoid the (extramarital) sin of lust. The Catholic bishops emphasized that it, first and foremost, represented a pious and holy covenant between the spouses (Clark 2008: 83). Likewise, great attention was paid—here the Catholic Church was no different from the Lutherans, Calvinists, and other reformed churches—to avoiding interdenominational alliances. If these did come about, any children conceived had to be educated in the right confession. In practice, it turned out that the denomination of the children was mostly chosen according to the father's wishes and model.

Like the reformed clergy, Catholic bishops also railed against premarital sexual intercourse between engaged couples. Accordingly, they apodictically insisted on its prohibition or sinfulness. It usually took quite a while longer, however, until the Catholic cities equaled their Protestant role models in the criminal prosecution of premarital sexual relationships (Behrisch 2007: 63). The Catholics also shared a newfound skepticism toward the social amusement, dances, and wooing customs of young people. In order to limit these practices, Pope Urban VIII stipulated in 1642 that there should be only thirty-four Catholic holidays (besides Sundays) and that the attendance of Mass was obligatory on these days (Reinhard 2006: 474f.). He thus agreed with all the forms of reprimand common to the early modern congregations that flagged violations of standardized marriage initiation as well as broken marriages and other sexually unacceptable behavior. The unmarried members of fraternities, journeymen's associations, and guilds used reprimanding customs to point out internal and external sexual abuse, to bring it to light, and to undergo a purification process. The repertoire of accusing and mocking rituals ranged from *Katzenmusiken* (cat concerts), *Eselshochzeiten* (donkey nuptials), and jester's feasts to carnival games and demands of penalty payments. The true purpose of each embarrassing rite was to bring moral purification to those affected and to reintegrate them into the proper order (Haldemann 2015: 441ff.). In the premodern *face-to-face societies* this was carried out in a very sensual way by physically exposing denigrates or by smearing their house—and thus also the sexual honor of the person(s) living there—with excrement, decorating it with phallic symbols, or organizing spectacles in front of it (Cohen 1992: 618).

When it came to divorce, Catholic bishops could not make any concessions to the rival denominations (Brugger 2017). Although the practice of *Trennung von Tisch und Bett* (separation of table and bed) was intended to allow the spouses to live apart but keep their marriage intact—ruling out any chance of a new marriage, of course. A marriage could only be annulled for classic reasons such as impotence and refusal to have sex. Protecting marriage also meant that adultery should be more strictly prosecuted and sanctioned. Under Pope Sixtus V (1521–1590), Rome declared extramarital sexual intercourse to be a capital crime in 1586. Punishment was severe. As a rule, the (Catholic) courts did not exhaust the full criminal repertoire in cases of onetime adultery, but in most cases resorted to shorter prison sentences, shame sentences, and fines. Recidivism, however, meant much harsher penalties, in addition to corporal punishment and banishment, and could also include the execution of the adulterers (Rublack 1998: 311ff.).

However, according to the Council of Trent, bigamy was considered heresy and, like other matters of faith, was persecuted by the Inquisition and its local helpers. If they occurred, multiple marriages usually came about because marital conflicts could not be resolved and a table-and-bed separation proved impossible; as a result, one spouse, if he or she was not bound by the social network and livelihood, left the area and after some time entered into a new marriage in a different place. Sexual problems ranked high among the reasons that encouraged spouses to flee and remarry: In Italy, for example, women in the sixteenth and early seventeenth centuries would sometimes be forced into prostitution by their husbands. Many women rebelled and rejected their tormentor, or even ran away to find a new spouse. In other cases, extramarital sexual contacts and relationships had occurred during the first marriage, which led to the adulterers settling elsewhere and later getting married. Second marriages also came about in the post-Tridentine period because social pressure on persons who'd lived in concubinage increased. Frequently, they would remarry officially, hoping that nothing would come out about the first marriage (Siebenhüner 2006: 129ff.).

Catholic confession was also modified by the Council of Trent. Like their Protestant competitors, the Catholic faithful should now conduct an intensive examination of conscience, as well, and own up to the confessor not only sinful deeds but also unchaste thoughts, erotic desires, even sexual dreams (Pallaver 1987: 108ff.). The emphasis here—in contrast to the Calvinists' doctrine of predestination—was on free will and that anyone could therefore choose moral or sinful actions, not fateful determinism (Crawford 2007: 83f.). The dissemination of sexual knowledge, for example about contraception and abortion, was also fought tooth and nail: According to the *Effraenatam*—a papal bull issued in 1588, but remained in force for only two years—not only abortion was to be considered infanticide, but every other form of contraception was too (Riddle 1997: 211).

In sum, the post-Trentine Roman Church was thus committed to the preservation of the previous marriage and sexual dogma. At the same time, the Catholic bishops were fascinated by the regulatory and institutionalization potential of Protestant control and disciplinary measures and adopted some of them in their own church orders. For example, regular visitations were now ordered to the dioceses, which also monitored the moral state of the parish. In Italy, for example, bishops, priests, and confessors very quickly placed themselves at the service of the Tridentine program (Siebenhüner 2006: 18). The practicability and social manageability of the Protestant measures also convinced many Catholic princes and allowed reformed elements to flow into the secular orders, laws, and institutions. Ecclesiastical and secular authorities pursued three main goals: First, the conjugal partnership should be protected from destructive and socially disorderly forms of fornication, and potential threats such as brothels or excessive sensual pleasures should be eliminated. Secondly, all manifestations of lewd lust, such as adultery, concubinage, and premarital sex, were to be prosecuted under church and criminal law. Thirdly—and most importantly—existing marriages should be promoted and measures taken to combat the "marriage devil" and malicious abandonment (Harrington 1995: 217ff.).

Measures of Social Discipline

Apparently, the moral orders and measures of the old and new denominations were much more successful among social elites such as the urban citizens than among the urban lower classes and the rural population. For most people, even in the early modern era, the informal, small-scale control and regulatory mechanisms of family and community remained more significant and more realistic than the top-down orders and laws. Where the church and secular authorities with their regulations on sexual and married life did not orient themselves to the interests of the social groups, they had little chance of enforcement (Wiesner-Hanks 2000: 259ff.; Arnórsdóttir 2018: 286 ff.). It cannot be denied, however, that in the course of denominationalization and (social) disciplining, effective means of sexual self-reflection and the reflection of others were spread far and wide. Thus, the regular confession in the Catholic Church and the examination of conscience among the Protestant denominations compelled a lasting moral momentum of its own. Through institutions such as marriage courts, consistories, and denominational schools—and in some circles also thanks to the printing press—sexual norms came closer to broad sections of the population than was possible in earlier centuries (Muurling, Kamp and Schmidt 2021). Now, one could see what happened to those who did not adhere to the moral guidelines and were sanctioned and brought before the court—even in one's own congregation—with shame and corporal punishment or even excommunication. What was once the stuff of courtly tales was now an everyday occurrence; the moral of the story became the morality of the moment. Until after the public penance ordered by the church, offenders in any case had to refuse Communion in the reformed-Calvinist areas—signaling their own wrongdoing to their congregation.

The practices of social disciplining mentioned above, whether of Protestant and Catholic origin or initiated by secular institutions, led to a contouring of the Christian image of men (Hendrix 2008). Even more than before, men could see their social and cultural value in their position as the father of the house and as a married head of a Christian household. By providing for the honor, safety, and welfare of their wives and members of their families and households, and by maintaining moral order in their home, they proved themselves to be real men. Even in Spain, where there was a long tradition of macho-promiscuous masculinity, the Counter-Reformation attempted to pacify the image of men and propagated monogamy, respectability, and hard work as a new imperative (Behrend-Martínez 2012: 333ff.). Social, economic, and political participation (such as becoming a master craftsman or assuming public office) solidified as standard practice to begin the process of marrying and starting a household. Legitimate sexual intercourse including the procreation of descendants was the (often long desired) threshold of entry into this marital status and thus the fulfilment of a central stage in the Christian life. Those who could not or did not want to marry—like the Catholic priests and bishops—fell out of this (according to Luther) God-willed scale of values just as much as all lewd men who before or beside marriage gave themselves over to moral disorder (Wiesner-Hanks 2012: 36f.).

For women, church discipline, moral orders, and penal laws had even more far-reaching consequences in the sixteenth and seventeenth centuries: In the case of premarital sex, adultery, divorce, abortion, contraception, or prostitution, their sex was the first thing that came to mind and they tried to get a grip on the (allegedly) threatening excrescences of the female sexual body. Significantly, it was primarily women who were affected by the imposition of public shame penalties. The church courts and secular judges charged them much more frequently with sexual offences than their male counterparts. The social devaluation of frivolous single women and prostitutes made it clear that they were seen as a lewd irritation for the male members of the community—and that they were accordingly to be forced into marriage or (re-)integrated into patriarchal society (Wiesner-Hanks 2012: 36f.). As the example of Luther showed, the ambivalent attitude toward the sexual nature of women came to a head in the sixteenth and early seventeenth centuries. Because of their enticing bodies, on the one hand, they posed a constant sexual danger to men; on the other hand, they offered God's intended sexual healing for carnal desires. It is not surprising that theological and secular scholars agreed on who represented the "hornier" sex, namely the woman. According to the prevailing opinion, her entire physical, mental, and emotional being was marked by sexuality.

Jewish Skepticism toward Unregulated Sexual Desire

Not only in the Christian denominations did the skepticism toward unregulated sexual desire intensify. From the Late Middle Ages, corporeality had also been increasingly devalued in Jewish moral literature. Sexuality for the Jews was no longer primarily linked to life energy and reproduction by the early modern era, but instead blamed as an evil drive for man's sinfulness and impurity and his susceptibility to demonic forces. Marital intercourse should therefore be practiced exclusively for the sake of heaven and thus lead to the sanctification of desire and a godly attitude. Most rabbinical authors, at the same time, admitted that this goal could not be achieved entirely without sensual pleasures. It remained undisputed in European Judaism, however, that lifelong asceticism and celibacy (as with the Catholic clergy) was only possible for a small group of rabbis who devoted themselves entirely to studying the Torah—and even then it was less than ideal. The religious ideal continued to be marriage and procreation.

The practice of spilling seed was given special attention in Jewish moral literature in the sixteenth and seventeenth centuries. Until the fifteenth century, masturbation had been considered primarily as a ritual impurity and as a dissolute activity. Now "self-abuse" was not only a sinful behavior and selfish pleasure, it also caused tremendous damage to the holy covenant. Elijahu de Vidas' (1518–1592) work *Re`schit hokhma* provided the following justification in the second half of the sixteenth century, which was to last until the eighteenth century: The "artificial" ejaculation causes serious damage to body and soul due to the overheating of the entire body. What weighed even more heavily was that man thereby uncoupled himself from the "divine energy flow" and a "contamination" of the covenant took place. For de Vidas it was clear: "There is no sin that defiles man more than the vain spilling of seed" (Berger 2003: 64). Even involuntary pollutions now had serious consequences: weakened by masturbation, a man could not even defend himself at night against the attacks of the demons that defiled him in his dreams.

Split between Moral Policy and Everyday Life

For the representatives of the different denominations and religions, however, it also became clear in the sixteenth and seventeenth centuries that many forms of sexual misconduct could not be condemned strictly according to the law, but had to be handled flexibly and sensitively. The behavior of "commoners" was often far removed from the moral orders. The expression of a farmer who was caught having sexual intercourse with his mistress in Somerset, England, in the early seventeenth century and was threatened with punishment was significant. Entirely in keeping with everyday logic, he responded to the accusations: "Did you never seen a cow bulled before?" In the year 1632, a man from London put in a nutshell his view of the penalization in terms of church and criminal law even more clearly: "Fornication [premarital coitus] was not a sin at all if both parties are agreed" (Dabhoiwala 2012: 19). In view of the gulf between everyday practice, the law, and church punishments, the local judges had to act with great social sensitivity, handling warnings, fines, and light penalties and trying not to push the delinquents out of the social structure. The decision depended on the social position of the offenders and, here again, on gender, marital status, status, and the social consequences. The efforts of the authorities to maintain order often went so far that, for example, according to the Württemberg marriage code of 1553, officials were required to restore marriages that were separated or even divorced: "But while the spouses are divorced due to the [abovementioned] cause with the judgement, they may reconcile with one another again in Christianity and give each other every possible assistance, in which our officials should devote all possible diligence." (Eder 2009a: 64 and 58ff.)

What the Catholic as well as the Protestant institutions were striving for in matters of morality and mores was quite in line with the interests of the sovereign princes and secular authorities (Heiss 1989: 207). This led to the criminalization of sin or the Christianization of secular (sexual) criminal law from the local jurisdiction to the national and imperial level. At the same time, secular jurisdiction in matrimonial and moral matters increasingly developed into a competition with clerical judges. By the eighteenth century at the latest, the ecclesiastical courts had to hand over their power and function to the secular *policey* and the secular courts. In England this was already the case in 1641, even though the clerical courts (albeit with considerably weaker powers) were reinstated after the Stuart Restoration in 1660 to 1689 (Crawford 1994: 83ff.). In any case, with the divergence of everyday practice from the moral canon of church and secular law, it became increasingly difficult in the course of the early modern era to answer one central question satisfactorily: How was it to be justified that sexual acts by two consenting adults, which did not harm any third party, ought to be persecuted and punished simply because they contradicted the religious or moral canon? Catholic authorities referred in this context to the Tridentine decisions (right up until the twentieth century). The representatives of the Reformation insisted on their renewed moral policy. If necessary, both also referred to the broadly interpretable (natural) positive law. However, the Christian denominations could not bring themselves to undergo a fundamental renewal or reformation of their sexual dogma. This was also one of the reasons why the ecclesiastical canon increasingly came into conflict with a new enlightened worldview in the seventeenth and eighteenth centuries, which spread in philosophy, the natural sciences, and ultimately through jurisprudence as well. From the middle of the seventeenth century, doubts increasingly arose as to whether the religious or church norms were in accordance with the laws of nature—or whether nature itself should rather be used as the determining factor for human behavior (Davidson 2011: 106f.). The secular liberalization of criminal sexual law in the late eighteenth and early nineteenth centuries finally made it clear that Christian moral teachings on sin were behind the times.

Marriage Patterns, Premarital Contacts, Rape, and Adultery

European Marriage Pattern

While the clerics in the sixteenth and seventeenth centuries were busy arguing about marriage and sexuality, the marriage opportunities for large swaths of the population in Europe diminished. With that tendency, the chances of fulfilling Catholic as well as Protestant marriage norms faded considerably.

While women in the Late Middle Ages usually married under the age of twenty and men some years later, a new marriage pattern developed in Northern, Western, and Central Europe as a result of demographic, social, and economic change. The border between this Western and Eastern European marriage pattern and the different rates of singles and married couples can be roughly traced by the line between St Petersburg and Trieste first drawn by John Hajnal in 1965. Since then, there have been controversial debates about the chronological and regional differentiation and the economic, social, and cultural causes of this pattern. These include the spread of marriage based on consensus, an increase in human capital with lower fertility due to the greater agency of women, the development of labor markets for both sexes, especially for women, the increasing institutional possibilities for property transfer, lack of opportunities to marry due to poverty, and much more. Despite the necessary differentiations today, the specifics of marriage and sexual behavior in Europe can still be illustrated by this European marriage pattern (Foreman-Peck 2011; van Zanden, De Moor and Carmichael 2019; Perrin 2021; Bennett 2019).

During the sixteenth and seventeenth centuries in Northern, Western, and Central Europe, women were about or over twenty-five years old at the time of marriage, men even some years older (Kowaleski 1999: 326ff.). Both now had to go through a considerably longer period of single life than their medieval predecessors—and thus also a longer period in which they were supposed to practice premarital abstinence (Livi Bacci 1999: 141f.). Nuptiality changed partly quite slowly, partly erratically: For example, for Tuscan women, the minimum and maximum ages at first marriage were fourteen and nineteen years in the middle of the fourteenth century, then rose to seventeen and twenty-one years in the middle of the fifteenth century, seventeen and twenty-four years in the middle of the sixteenth century, and twenty and twenty-five years in the middle of the seventeenth century.

Florentine women entered into marriage with an average age of 17.6 years in 1427; their husbands were about ten years older. By 1480, the female age of marriage had risen to 20.8 years, the age difference to men decreasing slightly (Livi Bacci 1999: 140f.). Aristocratic and rich families continued to marry their daughters off very early: In Renaissance Florence, girls were already married before the menarche, while the men were often over thirty years old. Here, the marriage contracts were primarily understood as *mercatanzia*, as a trade in financial and dynastic capital (Jones 2011: 40f.). This did not rule out the possibility that even in the households of rich urban citizens and the wealthy aristocracy, daughters and sons opposed their parents' marriage plans and a consensus had to be sought between the generations (Dean and Lowe 1998: 10f.). William Shakespeare's romantic tragedy *Romeo and Juliet* (1597) can be understood as a dramatic escalation of this conflict of family interests (of hostile clans in Verona) and the individual desires of two lovers.

For the majority of the population, especially for land- and property-less groups, for urban and rural servants, for journeymen and students, but also for soldiers and vagabonds, access to marriage was made considerably more difficult in the sixteenth and seventeenth centuries. Only when a couple was economically independent *and* in a position to set up their own household *and* had received the blessing of their parents to establish a marriage could they wed. Such conditions were increasingly difficult to achieve for the groups mentioned and for the poorer population as a whole. As a dramatic consequence, their chances of marriage diminished and led to the typical European marriage patterns (Duhamelle and Schlumbohm 2003: 12ff.). In premodern societies, menarche often occurred later, depending on the living standard and diet of women aged twelve to seventeen. Women's menopause, however, generally began much earlier than today, namely in their early to mid-forties (Livi Bacci 1999: 132ff.; Ehmer 2011a: 146f.).

We have been well informed about these and other demographic conditions since the sixteenth century through parish registers and church books. These contain information on baptisms, marriages, and deaths that can be converted into demographic figures using family reconstructions and thus provide an insight into the social embeddedness of fertility. The analysis of these sources shows that the already short fertile lifespan of women (the time between marriage and menopause) in Northern, Western, and Central Europe was even further reduced by the death of one of the spouses in about 10–20 percent of marriages. On average, the marital reproduction timeframes thus did not last much longer than fifteen years (Pfister 1994: 33f.). The interval between births and, with it, the number of children, varied considerably depending on the family and household cycle, economic resources, and (in)secure time periods, and depended on several factors: The time between pregnancies was increased by prolonged breastfeeding as well as by postnatal abstinence. Crises in the food supply and the consequences of diseases and epidemics also reduced the chances of conception. In view of the often high mobility of the late medieval and early modern population, couples also often lived separately for long periods and thus often had no sexual contacts for quite lengthy stretches of time (Ehmer 2011b: 21f.).

Strategies of Birth and Family Planning

The fact that some couples also deliberately engaged in birth or family planning can be seen from the seasonal fluctuation and variable intervals between births. The former showed a typical distribution: Most children were born in the less labor-intensive winter months, during which women who had recently given birth in agricultural societies had more time to care for babies. And in the summer months, with their high workload, came the fewest offspring (Pfister 1994: 33). As in England and Spain in the sixteenth century, most children were thus conceived between April and July, the fewest between August and November (Schofield and Wrigley 1981: 286; Reher 1990: 102). Conception was also influenced by other things: For example, many married bricklayers and stone workers from the Italian Alpine valleys spent much of the year as migrant workers outside the country, returning to their wives only in winter. In the sixteenth and seventeenth centuries, a disproportionately high number of births and baptisms between September and November were registered there (Viazzo 1989: 132f.). Even nine months after Lent, the birth curve continued to fall (Le Goff and Truong 2007: 66). On average, birth intervals were two to three and a half years, with an increasing tendency for subsequent births. Due to this chronological sequence and the short fertile lifespan of the women, five to six children were the rule. However, due to the high infant and child mortality rate (about half of those born died before the age of fifteen), the number of offspring reaching adulthood was significantly lower, namely two or three children (Ehmer 2011b: 23). For this reason, the myth of the pre-industrial extended family and the high number of children in the early modern era was rightly put to bed decades ago (Mitterauer 1977)—which, however, does not prevent such notions from persisting to this day.

This relatively low number of surviving children also explains why fertility and legitimate offspring were among the fundamental values of premodern European society. In view of postponed marriage, the dramatic infant and child mortality, the high mortality of women at birth, through diseases, epidemics, wars, and accidents, and the consequences of famine and resource scarcity, family growth was by no means a given. Even if this is difficult to understand from today's perspective: Couples have always and perhaps even primarily been interested in sexual life in order to procreate a larger number of sons and daughters—a goal that has only shifted with increasing age and a house full of children. A corresponding number of children was also necessary and desirable because households and economies had to fulfil different roles according to gender. Descendants made it possible to maintain the division and organization of labor, to pass on the farms and estates; they guaranteed old-age provision, and vouched for the social status and reputation of a family. Children were a symbolic and real bartering commodity for social networking. And finally, offspring testified that a married couple had fulfilled the divine mandate of procreation and the reproduction of the social order.

Even if clerics did not like it, numerous traditions and practices in early modern European societies promoted marital fertility and—with this aim in mind—sexual desire. For example, the interiors of Italian wedding chests depicted lightly clad or naked beauties, which were intended to inspire the bridal couple, but also as they aged (Tinagli 1997: 26ff.). A large number of children was the reasoning behind magical rituals designed to keep evil away at birth, for example, by painting crosses on the front door or placing blessed herbs in the bed of those giving birth or who had recently done so (Labouvie 1999: 90). Not only medical advisors attached great importance to the physical "preparation" of the woman. Men should, for example, promote orgasmic ability and thus female ejaculation by "warming up" and stimulating their external genitalia. By means of special ointments and tinctures, one wanted to make the uterus ready for conception (Laqueur 1986). Even remarriage was aimed at increasing fertility. Due to the high infant mortality rate, subsequent marriages can be shown for most social classes, but are preferred by the wealthy and the affluent. According to French registers, half of all widows and widowers entered a second marriage in the seventeenth century (Wiesner 2000: 91). Men often remarried within a few months, thus ensuring that the gendered organization of work in the household was maintained and the number of children increased. Widowed older women took considerably longer to remarry (Eder 1990: 117ff.).

Premarital Sexual Contacts and Their Consequences

Members of the lower social strata often had to spend the premarital transition phase in service to another household. About 30 to 40 percent of women over fourteen years of age (and a similar number of men) had to spend time as servants, with some starting at the age of ten. During their service, maids were subject to the will of the man of the house and were not infrequently subjected to sexual assault by their employers and their employers' sons. The better-off groups of young women remained in their parents' household until marriage, were introduced to the tasks of housewife and mother, and, if necessary, even worked in production or business. Only very few entered a monastery at a young age (Harrington 2009: 23ff.). It should not be forgotten that a not inconsiderable proportion of the population (up to 20 percent) remained single for life because they were unable to meet the marriage criteria and thus had no official legitimation to copulate. In some regions, the number of female singles was even higher, as can be seen from English tax lists dating as far back as the late fourteenth century—albeit with great variation between urban and rural areas (Kowaleski 1999: 46). The number of illegitimate births shows that these women and men, who were temporarily or lifelong in waiting, by no means renounced sexual relations but rather practiced them under that particular Sword of Damocles, threatened by illegitimate pregnancy and attacks of moral frivolity (Breit 1991; Pfister 1994: 31; van der Heijden, Schmidt and Vermeesch 2021). In the case of fiancées who were waiting for a farm to be handed over or an inheritance, or who had to save up first, intimate contact was widely tolerated. If pregnancy did occur, the couple was hastily married before the birth or better still before the visible signs of pregnancy (Hardwick 2015: 649ff.). In the sixteenth and even more so in the seventeenth century, local poor relief and charitable institutions as well as foundling hospitals were created in many European cities, enabling women pregnant out-of-wedlock to bring their children into the world and thus opening up a space for them to agency (Muurling, Kamp and Schmidt 2021).

There were, in fact, sufficient opportunities for the initiation of premarital contacts and orientation on the marriage market in the early modern period. Young men were admitted, for example, to spinning rooms where younger (and older) women gathered together. Here, one could get to know each other under the supervision and control of mostly older community members. Something similar would happen at the end of the day as people gathered informally, or at the many church festivals where song and dance was the order of the day (Medick 1980). Contrary to what is often claimed, young men and women also worked quite closely together in the fields and in households, on farms, and in workshops. Female members of the family and hired maids were often employed in ancillary work, auxiliary services, and the commercial side of even trades mainly run and carried out by men. The suspicion that the sexes were getting too close in their labor and on all these occasions caused some concern to the morally strict city and church authorities in the sixteenth and seventeenth centuries. The sharpened social disciplining view of the matrimonial judges and their police assistants, as well as the verve of some neighbors, led to rising prosecutions of premarital *fornicatio* during this period. This could not have been based on a real increase in premarital intercourse among the poorer rural classes and dependent servants, however, because such contacts—if one takes the illegitimacy rates as an indicator—would seem to inexplicably decline between the late sixteenth and eighteenth centuries (Burghartz 2004: 88ff.).

The reformed courts of matrimony also dealt with the special circumstances in which the sexual partners met and—usually because a child was conceived—had not kept their promises, that is, the man didn't follow up on his marriage offer. If the women could not produce any witnesses, the proceedings usually did not turn out in their favor. In English courts in the seventeenth century, impregnated maids and maidservants argued that they were brought to sexual intercourse little by little through soft words, touching, and kissing. Not infrequently, the "seducers" had used their social supremacy, sometimes acting with force and violence, or luring people with money and marriage. The male repertoire also included the promise not to perform coitus to the end, but to be careful (Gowing 2003: 82ff.). Here, it becomes apparent that even in premarital contacts there was obviously a wide range of penetrative and probably also non-penetrative sexual acts taking place. If a marriage promise was in the air, chances increased of going to completion (Hitchcock 1996: 733ff.). According to the Prussian land regulations of 1577, the confessed perpetrator had to marry the "weakened" woman even in the case of a secret betrothal. If he had not promised marriage, monetary payments to the woman's guardian as well as church fines and shame or honor penalties were due. For the pregnant women, the order foresaw a difference between premature intercourse (between fiancées), frivolity, seduction, and whoring about:

> Should it come to pass that a virgin or a maid forces herself upon a man, pursues him, lies with him or another means of impregnation and has done this extensively or according to public opinion is a notorious person, then the offender shall not be obliged to marry her or pay her money, but must help to feed the child" (Eder 2009a: 65f.)

Here it becomes apparent that the sexual exchange between women and men took place under largely unequal conditions (Beck 1983: 135ff.; Burghartz 1999: 155ff.).

While the Western European marriage pattern was characterized by late marriages, a relatively high proportion of (lifelong) single people and frequent remarriages, early marriages, and almost continuous conjugal life continued to dominate in Eastern Europe and some areas of Southern Europe in the early modern period. Women usually entered into marriage there before the age of twenty-two, men were about two years older. Hardly 5 percent of the population remained unmarried for life. The average number of children born to a woman was correspondingly higher. In many regions, however, the higher mortality rate reduced the number of surviving offspring, so that the overall values did not significantly differ from the north and western parts of the continent. Similar patterns can be found in most southern parts of Spain and Portugal and some Italian regions, as well as in Ireland and parts of Finland (Livi Bacci 1999: 135f.; Ehmer 2011a: 146ff.).

Concrete sexual practices in premarital relationships are mostly only known indirectly or from normative and institutional sources for both Western and Eastern patterns. These types of text are difficult to interpret. The reports of accused persons in the files of the Basel Marital Court in the sixteenth and seventeenth centuries are influenced by the threat of punishment and, as such, tainted. Women usually presented themselves as sexually coerced, overwhelmed victims; whereas men blamed the female arts of seduction for their unchaste act. For all their critical distance, such sources nevertheless provide an impression of the possibilities for action of these men and women (Burghartz 1999: 237ff.). In most cases, premarital sexual interaction seems to have been mostly initiated by men. They usually tried to persuade women they had recently met or with whom they had a long working relationship. If this took place within the framework of a ritualized and standardized form of getting to know each other, the women usually agreed to an intimate meeting or even suggested it themselves. The defendants' stories in court were often similar: In the beginning men limited themselves to kissing and embraces in hidden places, later they lie in bed together—clothed—in the woman's chamber (Roberts and Groenendijk 2004: 145). Mutual contact needn't be of a sexual nature *per se* and therefore not necessarily lewd. The next step would be a public engagement or public promise of marriage (expressed in front of witnesses).

Frequently, cases came to court that did not follow this ritualized path, but arose from a "culture of overpowerment" (Becker 1992: 165). Men would force a woman against her will by means of harassment and coercion in such cases. But then, in front of the judge, they accused the woman of having incited them to this assault. If she failed to sufficiently resist, the men (and the court) interpreted this as consent. Although the roles and power relations were thus clear, there was a certain amount of female room for maneuver even in such predicaments. Women could give in to their oppressors or vehemently fight back (Eder 2009a: 46ff.). What is significant, however, is that the women often left the sexual and emotional aspects of their actions unsaid in court in order to conform to the pure and chaste image of women. Conversely, female honor or the (alleged) lewd behavior of women played a prominent role in male argumentation (Roper 1995b: 66ff.).

Relationships of authority, dependence, and service made it difficult to avoid assaults and overpowering for a long time to come, especially for younger women. The circumstances also played a significant role whether a deed was tolerated or overlooked in the social environment. A typical case concerned the parish priest Quirinus Müller of a Westphalian parish, Ruppichteroth, in the second half of the seventeenth century. As surveys of the parishioners revealed, the clergyman had sexual relations with his two housemaids Margaretha Jeandrer and Ursula Schmitz. The latter admitted that she was constantly being groped and touched by him and that he tried to seduce her by flirting, kissing, and tempting her into drinking alcohol together. Ultimately, she succumbed, "carnally mixing" with him "in the hay, on his chair, otherwise when and where" several times. By and by, she became pregnant. He had also had intercourse with the second maid and also impregnated her. Apart from the exploitation of the dependency relationship, this case also shows that priestly concubines were no longer a matter of wide acceptance (Flüchter 2006: 341).

Violence and Rape

From seduction it was often only a small step to rape, especially since the concept of consent—in the sense of a consensus, a negotiation between two legally and socially equal subjects—had little meaning in the early modern world. There are enough court cases from that time in which women claimed to have been "used" against their will, to assume rather porous boundaries to what we now call sexual assault. Until the eighteenth century (and beyond), women hardly ever wore underwear, so that there were enough cases in which a woman would accuse a man of having lifted her frock and fondled her genitals—and this was understood as a gesture of sexual possession, along with the accompanying loss of honor for the woman (Simons 2011: 45f.). While rape was still primarily regarded in medieval law as a property offence against another man (such as the father or husband), the focus was now on the sexual act and the participation of the woman concerned (Koch 2004: 42ff.). According to the *Constitutio Criminalis Carolina* (1532), anyone who "wrongs an undefamed spouse / widow or virgin / with violence and against her will / taking her virginity or honor" is guilty of rape. Now it was up to the victim to prove that penetration had taken place without her consent and by force. She had to show an attempt to resist. And she had to otherwise have an honorable reputation and led an impeccable moral life. Often, it was also a question of whether ejaculation had also occurred during vaginal penetration (by the perpetrator's penis). This high bar for facts and evidence was the reason that the punishment for rape was generally very harsh, including capital punishment, in the sixteenth and seventeenth centuries (Figure 15).

The perpetrator would lose their head in the Holy Roman Empire; in England, Wales, and Ireland he was to be hanged, and in France he was to be broken on the wheel or hanged. The severity of the offence was also underlined by the fact that in some countries agonizing corporal punishment led up to the execution. In Venice in the sixteenth century, the rapist would lose a hand, and often he was to be blinded. Where there was no prospect of a capital penalty, the punishment usually had the same effect in practice. In the Republic of the United Netherlands, the perpetrator was flogged, branded, and banished; in Spain, he was sentenced to life in a galley (Walker 2012: 432f.). In all these cases, however, detailed explanations as to what exactly was meant by the crime were missing. In contrast, the provisions concerning sexual violence against children were clearly not applicable. Whether there was consent or not, the abuse of girls under twelve years of age was punishable by execution if penetration occurred or could be substantiated by witnesses. The rape of a boy, on the other hand, fell under the sodomy law.

Particular cases involved the rape of girls under the age of consent and in prepubescence. In addition to sexual violence against a minor, these trials in seventeenth-century England focused on the loss of virginity and

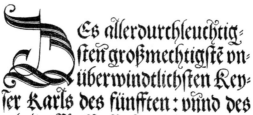

FIGURE 15 *Title and woodcut of the* Constitutio Criminalis Carolina, *1532.*

sometimes also infection with a venereal disease. Even if, in the opinion of the population, the girls were innocent, the sexual assault led to the destruction of their reputation and chastity. Her future was "ruined." The parents, therefore, tried to restore their daughter's reputation in court, to "righten it." The parents' objective was not to demand the execution of the rapist—that would have attracted public attention and damaged the reputation of the girl and her family—but to banish him (Toulalan 2017).

Even though secular laws provided for severe corporal punishment for sexual violence and rape, this did not have to be executed in the same way in judicial practice. For example, in Siena in 1558, the revision of the Florentine law was introduced, abolishing fines and imposing corporal punishment for those "who do violence to women and men to satisfy their sexual desire." Without visible physical harm, offenders were to be sent to the galleys for several years; if wounded, the offender was to be executed. Ten years after its introduction, however, cases were still treated with leniency toward the accused, despite evidence from victims and eyewitnesses. In cases of sexual violence against children, the perpetrators argued that the accusations were untrustworthy because of their age or that they were induced to lie by others (Brizio 2019). As the analysis of court records in Venice showed, there was already a relatively high level of awareness there in the sixteenth and seventeenth centuries, both in the hearings and among the population as a whole, regarding the protection of prepubescent children from sexual assault (Ferraro 2016).

In the cities of Delft and Rotterdam, only fourteen cases of attempted or actual rape of primarily young unmarried women could be proven throughout the whole seventeenth century (Heijden 2000: 624f.). The *Parlement de Paris*, a court of appeals that had jurisdiction over about half of the country, only heard a maximum of three such cases per year in the sixteenth and seventeenth centuries (Vigarello 2001: 54). In the northern parts of England, only two rapes a year were reported in the second half of the seventeenth century (Chaytor 1995: 378). In court, the women had to struggle with numerous adversities. In most cases, they could not bring physical proof of the deed, which led to a subsequent inspection of their virginity, for example, by a midwife. Witnesses who had seen the deed or could testify that the woman had fought back, like by screaming loudly, were rarely found. If the rape led to a pregnancy, this contradicted the facts—at least according to some medical experts—because fertilization could only be achieved by mutual orgasm and thus the woman must have experienced physical pleasure, that is, she hadn't shown sufficient resistance/had indeed been an honorable person, as this line of thinking went. If a woman waited too long to report the crime, this silence had its own set of consequences. In the Italian city of Ferrara, an accusation had to be made within forty days, otherwise the woman's reticence was interpreted as a form of consent (Brundage 1987: 484). In addition, respectability and innocence had to be proven, and the community member's moral upstanding had to be established.

It should not be underestimated, however, that until the eighteenth century male sexuality was considered fundamentally aggressive and taking in cases of rape; a judicial acquittal therefore did not automatically mean that the accused escaped guilt for their sinful actions (Walker 2013, 2017: 17). This was particularly evident in Russian court records: They trusted the statements of the women more than the accused men for exactly that reason: men were assumed to be takers (Kaiser 2002: 216). As the Russian example shows, the protection of the female body and its honor was dependent on one's position in a socially divided society and in the context of serfdom (Muravyeva 2016: 346ff.). In popular English pamphlets and ballads, which reflected the mentality of the broad population better than laws, medical treatises, and religious writings, rape was described as an appalling act and the lecherous and dirty men who committed such a crime—especially when it was directed against a girl or child—were threatened with the harshest punishments (Pallotti 2012).

Rape occurred mainly in relationships of dependence between men and women. Sexual assault and rape were inscribed in the relationship between slave owners and slaves that existed in the cities of the Mediterranean region in the sixteenth and seventeenth centuries. But such assaults also occurred with unfree persons, for example in 1610 in the Italian port city of Livorno, where enslaved female Jews from the northern Moroccan city of Tétouan were raped by Muslim slaves and Catholic forced laborers (Herzig 2022). Younger domestic servants were repeatedly the victims of assaults, as were maidservants who were taken by a farmhand or the farmer. In Zurich in 1599, Alban Sultzer was called before the judge because his seventeen-year-old maid accused him of rape. Sultzer counterattacked and said that the young woman had agreed to sexual intercourse, did not resist or scream and was probably no longer a virgin anyway. He maintained she had a bad reputation before. As a result of all this, the court did not condemn him for rape, but only for adultery (Loetz 2009: 577).

In Dijon in the fifteenth century, maids, daughters of poor manual laborers, younger widows, single women from marginal urban groups, and prostitutes became the victims of downright *gang rapes*. Groups of five or six youths, sons of citizens and journeymen—usually from the same neighborhood or from a specific trade—attacked women at night by gaining access to their dwellings (Rossiaud 1984: 109). Sexual violence against unprotected women by soldiers in towns and villages they captured was standard practice (Fairchilds 2007: 285; (Muravyeva 2014). Accordingly, the fear of such attacks could easily be functionalized for political purposes. This is what happened in the religious and political conflicts between the Netherlands and Spain in the early seventeenth century, in which Spanish soldiers were presented as brutal rapists. In the *Morghen-Wecker der vrye Nederlantsche provintien* (1610) by the Calvinist theologian Willem Baudartius (1565–1640), for example, it was said about the Duke of Alba (1507–1582) and his troops: They had "threatened, beaten, robbed, plundered [and] raped the women and young daughters." Furthermore, "many beautiful and rich women who had been taken away from their husbands . . . were handed over to his soldiers to satisfy their sexual desires and serve them as loot" (Pipkin 2009: 243, 2013: 236ff.). The horrors of rape revealed the reprehensibility of the Spaniards in a double sense: on the one hand, as an act of violence against Dutch women, and, on the other hand, as a property offence against Dutch men.

Court records of rape cases also contain passages describing the practices of sexual violence against women. Considering that such texts were produced institutionally and that such specific circumstances—such as the strategic speaking of the accused and the writing and transcription by court clerks—were brought to bear, some characteristics of these actions and of speaking about them can be observed. In more than 100 examined rape case records, which were heard before secular and ecclesiastical courts in seventeenth-century England, the focus was less on the sexual act than on the use of physical violence by the man. The penetration itself was usually expressed in the form of a standardized phrase (in court terminology). Male action was presented as willing and energetic and was attributed with terms such as "using," "occupying," and "knowing carnally." The raped women, on the other hand, adopted a passive attitude, they had "given in," "submitted," they were "used" and "known" (Walker 1998: 6ff.). How they reacted to the male violence, whether they resisted or submitted, usually remained between the lines. Only a few documents show (possible) options for female action—the most common was flight. For example, Katherine Ireish reported that in March 1670 John Holte

> tooke me by the necke . . . and held me soe fast that I was nott able to speake. And he did take up my Cotes and did Indeavour to Ravish me but I strugleing with him did get from him and was forced to leave the lanthorne I lighted him home by in the place where he did strugle with me. (Walker 1998: 11)

Sometimes, women were just able to escape, as Elizabeth Sansbury's 1614 accusation of Sir John Lawrence shows. He had knocked on her door during her husband's absence, and she had opened—not knowing who it was—her six-week-old son in her arms. Lawrence forced his way in, blocked the entrance, and followed her into the kitchen:

> [He] compelled me to lay downe my child, and he holdinge his sworde over my head did sweare terrible oathes that he would lye with me, and I thinking to escape from him did run upp a paire of staires in the howse to gett into a chamber and locke myself therein but [Sir John] followed me and before I could locke the chamber doore he did laye hold on me and he bowed my handes behinde me and thereupon I cried out but he stopped my mouth and there had carnal knowledge of me against my will and did then and there infect me with a burninge and fowle disease. (Walker 1998: 15)

Physical disadvantage left women with few options, yet—contrary to the dominant account given by the sources—there was room for female action to the extent that they protested forcible taking and forced sexual intercourse by means of strongly articulated rejection and energetic resistance. As the last example shows, there was also the fear of pregnancy and the threat of venereal infection.

The fact that sexual violence and rape also occurred within the marriage was shown in cases of mariticide. The motive for murdering one's husband was often his adulterous behavior (or accusations thereof) and jealousy, or refusal of coitus by the wife and the resulting outbreaks of violence, in addition to conflicts over money and property. As Jean de Marconville (c. 1520–1580) explained in *De l'heur el malheur de mariage* (1573), jealousy was considered a particularly charged emotion:

> But if such a grievance occurs and persists between a man and a woman who are married to each other, it would be better for both to die, for no suffering can be imagined in the world comparable to this, because out of jealousy quarrelling, complaining, conflict, hatred, enmity, beating and murder are born (Nolde 2003: 111ff.).

Conversely, women would also accuse their husbands of impotence and sterility, which in turn was one of the reasons for their outbreaks of violence.

Contraception and Abortion

In the case of non-marital sexual contacts and in later years of marriage, questions of contraception were also discussed. Although there are hardly any sources about concrete practices, the range of non-penetrative actions seems to have extended from coitus interruptus to the complete renunciation of sexual intercourse. As already mentioned, there are examples of conscious family planning among married people. Coitus interruptus was probably the most popular precautionary measure. In a 1650 Basel Marital Court protocol, this practice is openly addressed in a conflict between spouses. The husband explained that "when he mingled with her [his wife], she never really wanted to finish this, but both let the seed run out into the bed." He accused his wife of having counteracted conception by breaking off sexual intercourse: "At the moment he figured that his seed and hers had mixed together, they turned away and began to cry out" (Burghartz 1999: 247f.). A seamstress from Constance was certain that she was not impregnated by her master's son, because he "had completed the work but had not opened her body, but had left the seed between her feet before coming to the place" (Rublack 1998: 249). Condoms made from animal skins and bladders or textiles and pessaries were also used—all of them with very limited success and immoral odor, as they were more likely to be used by prostitutes. Breastfeeding for (several years) proved to be more effective, reducing the likelihood of successive conception. This method was usually not used by aristocratic and wealthy urban women, as they mostly engaged wet nurses. The church demanded at least a certain period of sexual abstinence after a birth, which should last thirty-six days for male offspring and fifty-six days for female children (Jütte 2008: 85).

Historical demography has shown that family planning was successfully practiced in the urban upper classes and among nobility at least from the seventeenth century. This was the case, for example, with the Zurich patriciate in the seventeenth century, several population groups in Geneva at the end of this century, and the French aristocracy around 1700—although this practice can be observed above all in the Protestant population. These groups had multiple reasons for targeted birth planning or contraception: On the one hand, maternal mortality in childbirth remained quite high, in rural areas of England at 1,250 to 2,940 women, in London at about 2,100 women per 100,000 births, which meant a mortality rate of up to 20 percent among twenty-five- to thirty-four-year-old women (Loudon 1992: 107ff.). On the other hand, the second wave of the Reformation spread a rather rational reproductive behavior that focused on fewer offspring. This attitude, however, only managed to establish itself in practice after the end of high infant and child mortality in the wake of the plague, famine, and wars of the period. Protestant parents also ensured that their surviving sons and daughters who had made it to adulthood were brought up in a manner appropriate to their status—and to this end they also extended the intervals between births. Coitus interruptus was the means of choice (Pfister 1985; Santow 1995; Jütte 2008: 57ff.; Ehmer 2011b: 24ff.). Conversely, a stable margin of sustenance and greater security of supply in farming regions—for example, in the course of the introduction of the high-yielding potato in the eighteenth century—tended to have the opposite effect, namely, higher fertility due to smaller birth intervals, as has been shown for the Valais mountain village of Törbel around 1750 (Pfister 1994: 35).

As the effectiveness of the contraceptive methods mentioned proved more or less unreliable, the next step in an unwanted pregnancy remained abortion. Even though abortion was banned by church and secular authorities, it continued to be practiced throughout Europe and in all social classes. However, the severity of the offence depended on how the generation and the state of the pregnancy was assessed (Christopoulos 2021: 250f.). Detailed knowledge thereof, which could also be found in the rediscovered ancient texts, was usually limited to a small group of people who had studied it—midwives and herbalists. These—mostly—women prescribed mainly abortive drinks and liquids, which could be regarded as medical measures. Strong smelling and spicy drinks such as aniseed water, marjoram stock, or vinegar were regarded as tried and tested household remedies. On the other hand, oils and decoctions from the poisonous sade tree, which could cause bleeding and miscarriages, as well as hellebore and mandrake and about twenty-five other plants mentioned in the medical literature proved to be effective. These were boiled out and the essence was drunk or inserted into the vagina or uterus using textiles and tampons (Leibrock-Plehn 1993: 71ff.).

A typical court case in 1606 concerned the maid Joan Michell, a native of Somerset. She came to London pregnant and in the sixth month she received from her mistress, the lady-in-waiting Anne Ellis, "a drink to purge her head which she took three mornings" and (apparently) led to a miscarriage

(Gowing 2012: 251). In court, women often said that they used these drugs merely to restore regular menstruation or to remove a blockage in the blood. They had been completely unaware that they'd been pregnant—this was the topos of one indictment—because they'd not felt any movements of the fetus (Rublack 1998: 248ff.). In the medical manuals, the absence of menstruation was by no means a (sure) indication of pregnancy, and the doctors and midwives often did not know until the third or fourth month whether the condition was caused by a *fetus* or a *mola*, a blood stagnation (Duden 2002: 41ff.; Jones 2011: 42).

The fact that abortion and knowledge about it were increasingly fought against since the late fifteenth century had nothing to do with an increase in abortions—as far as we know, there were no serious quantitative changes. Rather, it was seen as a gross violation of natural law and order and as murder, at least at the point of perceivable child movements. The authorities therefore moved to do more against abortion (Brannan Lewis 2020: 225ff.). Some cities enacted new pharmacist regulations in which the sale of abortive medicines was prohibited. Midwives who applied their knowledge of the "secrets of women" or even gave advice on how to do so faced heavy penalties. In Lyon in the seventeenth century, some men involved were recorded trying to find remedies for unintentionally pregnant women, be it herbal remedies or measures taken by surgeons (Hardwick 2015: 650). For "fallen" women—depending on the length of their aborted pregnancy—there were also severe, if not capital punishments. The penalties were rarely applied, however, as the crime could hardly be proven; the witnesses involved also had to expect penalties and therefore remained silent. This is also one of the reasons why historical research knows very little about the actual extent of abortions in the early modern period and demographic studies also have their limits in this regard (Jütte 2008: 51ff.; Wiesner-Hanks 2000: 83).

Adultery as Capital Crime

In the sixteenth and seventeenth centuries, adultery was an offence that was extremely strictly sanctioned by local and supra-regional orders and laws and was prosecuted accordingly by both Catholic and Protestant courts. *Adulterium* threatened not only the marriage relationship but also the social existence of a couple as a whole (Roper 1995b: 55). If both adulterers were married, they were threatened with a fifty-year ban in the United Provinces of the Netherlands at the end of the sixteenth century, and even execution in England in 1650. Spanish legislation covered yet another aspect: Infidelity might endanger the *limpieza de sangre* (purity of blood) of the children, which received great attention since the forced conversion of Muslims and Jews in the Iberian Peninsula. In the worst case, such an infamous act could even be passed down, the instance of adultery echoing through the following generations as an inherited sin

(Davidson 2011: 102). The *Carolina* also declared adultery a capital crime. However, the actual sentencing of the adulterers depended on their gender and social status as well as the associated public nuisance and material damages (Eder 2009a: 55). Although the *Carolina* sanctioned both sexes in cases of adultery, the proceedings revealed a clear asymmetry: The women involved were punished more severely and differently than men (with social equality) and had to endure above all public shame and corporal punishment as well as fines and banishment. Often, they also lost their dowry (if it had remained in their possession after the marriage) to their husband (Crawford 2007: 148ff.). In the second half of the sixteenth and the first half of the seventeenth century, marital disputes and petitions for annulment before Venetian courts revealed that in most cases it was not only the immediate actors who were affected by an escapade, but that events quickly affected families and neighbors, inciting them to take sides and intervene (Ferraro 2001).

So, it is not surprising that with *adulterium*, the deceived wives also sought to assert their rights or at least tried to protect their family from punishment of the husband and father. One possibility was not to report the unfaithful husband, but to take the punishment into her own hands—for example when he visited prostitutes, she could confront him in public, his humiliation playing to her favor. Josias Marda of the Hague was thusly disgraced by his wife and their children in 1724 when he had gone to a certain prostitute in the whorehouse in the city center for the second time. She called aloud: "My husband is here with you again, you keep my husband here, my children and I have nothing to eat and drink, he spends all his wages in your house and lets me and my children starve." A passing beadle (policeman) asked her why she did not report him, to which she replied: "I would have done so long ago, but my neighbors advise against it for fear of harming my husband." Such excitement not only cast the prostitutes in a bad light, it potentially also made the ashamed husband refrain from further adulterous actions (van de Pol 2006: 141).

The case of Susanna Mahl in Protestant Basel in 1687 shows that it was often not possible to distinguish clearly between adultery, promiscuity, exploitation of dependency relationships, and prostitution. The maidservant had sexual intercourse with several "honorable men" of the urban society, including her former employer. According to his testimony, she had seduced him into adultery with the following words:

> Why do you sleep alone and not with your wife? Could it be that you have little joy with your wife, does she not kiss you?" During an interrogation she gave information about where her adulterous meetings had taken place: He "had first taken her in his own house three years ago in the parlor in bed, when she served there, when on a Sunday

morning his wife was in church between the morning sermon, the other time in the wooden house standing up, the third time on the balcony at night when the wife was in the parlor, again standing up. (Burghartz 1999: 257)

The analysis of 136 criminal trials for adultery prosecuted in Calvinist Geneva between 1550 and 1700 revealed that almost half of those convicted were men. However, when the social status of the persons is taken into account, it becomes clear that mainly non-elite wives were convicted of this offence. As everywhere else in Europe, it was assumed that women who committed adultery were either victims or morally corrupt, even harlots. Therefore, they were usually punished more severely than men, for whom such a misstep was considered less dramatic and less consequential for the social order, the offspring, and the patriarchal family. The Geneva Consistory, a body of pastors and lay elders charged with policing morality and religious conformity, punished male adulterers with public humiliation, non-elite husbands were imprisoned and banished, and elite husbands had to pay a fine. For female adulterers, the punishment was much harsher; for those from the upper class it depended on whether the husband or the family continued to stand by her, for the others there was the threat of more violent torture and punishment, and in the worst case the death penalty (Beam 2020: 101ff.).

The *Carolina* also covered many forms of unchastity with close *gesipte freunde* (familial friends) such as brothers-in-law and step relatives, as well as the abduction of a spouse or virgin—whereby in the latter case it was the legal right of the husband, father, or guardian that had been violated. Each of these crimes was punishable by death according to the Reich law. Yet, the local and territorial orders and laws were usually applied in everyday court life. These were oriented to the living environment of the population. They provided for moderate honorary, monetary, and prison sentences for such cases. Only in the case of serious offences was the highest judicial authority called upon. No matter at what court level, the principle of retaliation was applied in trial, which is why the social situation of the defendants also played a role. Thus, in the case of a married woman, in addition to her chastity and faithfulness, her honor was also in question, as was the now uncertain descent of her offspring, called into question due to the extramarital sexual act. At the lower court level, more or less all forms of concubinage were now also pursued. The illegitimate mingling practiced was committed by persons "who are unmarried to each other, even those who, so far as they are of equal status, leave each other and sit with others in public adultery." Their behavior should "in no way be tolerated . . . but severely punished," according to the Bavarian State Order issued in 1530, for instance (Eder 2009a: 56ff. and 65).

Non-Christian Sexual Cultures

Heresy and Sexual Otherness

Since the Late Middle Ages, massive bias was directed against one group that crossed sexual boundaries: the sexual heretics. In addition to the sodomites, Jews and Muslims found themselves among the heretics. Since the Crusades and the successes of the Spanish *Reconquista*, they were seen as a fundamental threat not only to individual Christians but to the entire body of the church. The Dominican monk Vincent Ferrer (1350–1419), who preached in France and Spain, declared them to be the arch enemies of chaste Christian life (Ackerman Smoller 2018). He was particularly harsh when it came to persons who had relations with animals or anal intercourse (Nirenberg 1996: 142). Their actions were said to have caused the Black Death—as the great European plague pandemic between 1346 and 1353 was called—which tormented late medieval population. Preachers of his ilk contributed to why sexual outsiders regularly became victims of outbreaks of violence by an agitated population (Clark 2008: 67). At the end of the fourteenth century, Spain passed into law the death penalty for sexual contacts between Christians and Jews. The law was not in reaction to an increase in sexual relations across the obvious religio–cultural divide or between the white (i.e., Christian) and black ("Moorish" mixed) populations. The intention was rather to prevent sexual and racial mixing in the wake of the forced *mass conversion*. Thanks to their lighter appearance, pure Christian descendants were thought to be clearly recognizable, whereas the dark ones were assumed to be secret crypto-Muslims. As a consequence, children from mixed relationships with converts were also legally worse off and discriminated against (Nirenberg 2002).

In 1420, the Italian city of Padua called for the flogging of Jewish men who had had sexual intercourse with Christian prostitutes, and they were even threatened with death for sexual intercourse with a married Christian woman. From the thirteenth century, the Jewish population had already been forcibly relocated to special quarters and districts, partly to avoid these intimate contacts, and were obliged to wear distinguishable clothing and symbols (Richards 1990: 106ff.).

A Christian man, on the other hand, who had sexual intercourse with a heretic slave woman and fathered children with her went unpunished in fifteenth-century Italy if he brought his offspring up as Christians. Especially in the Mediterranean region, sexual contact between slaveholders and slave women remained common. In sixteenth-century Granada and Seville, black African female slaves worked primarily as domestic servants and wet nurses and took care of their master's children. Sometimes, they were also forced into prostitution. As a result of the sexual exploitation of female slaves by their masters, between 80 and 90 percent of mostly unmarried black women had one or two children (Fracchia 2017: 120f.).

The university-trained physicians also made their contributions to proposed characteristics typical of the foreign and strange sexual body. In the Late Middle Ages, some of them gathered to debate the new body images, which at the same time rested on the shoulders of the ancient authorities (Stolberg 2003). Until the sixteenth century, anatomy prevailed as the leading scientific discipline. Its representatives were highly fascinated by the "monstrous" deviations from the polar sexual system that could be observed in the hermaphrodite. What disturbed them most was the fact that the specimens exhibited both sexes and thus went beyond the established male–female dichotomy. In the Renaissance, these intersex creatures were monsters and wonders, to be feared and marveled at the same time. In practice, however, there seems to have been quite a true-to-life approach to the hermaphrodite, as can be seen from a report in the Constance city chronicle:

> In the year of our Lord 1388, to citizen of Rottweil, whose name is Hell, was born a daughter named Katharina; and as she grew up, she wore men's clothing and said she was a man and called herself Hans; and this selfsame Hans took a wife, who was a fine daughter, and both were of the age of 20 years; and Hans grew breasts and so did his wife. Therefore, the citizens of Rottweil send the married couple to Constance to appear before the Holy Court, to find out if this was permitted. Hans was thus inspected and it was found that he had both a "Zagel" (penis) and a "Fud" (vulva). And so, they were sent back home together. (Rolker 2013: 609)

After (probably) the church official in Constance had determined in the course of a physical examination that Hans (also) possessed a penis, nothing stood in the way of a continuation of the marriage.

By the sixteenth century, hermaphrodites were increasingly sexualized and at the same time pornographized (Cleminson and García 2013)—for example by Antonio Beccadelli (1394–1471), who published obscene epigrams under the title *Hermaphroditus*, irrespective of actually sexually ambiguous people, but rather concerned with male sexual practices (Daston and Parks 1995; Schleiner 2008). By the end of the seventeenth century at the latest, the unusual glow of the hermaphrodites had faded and the ambiguous creatures mutated into an anatomical anomaly of the two-gender model (Jacobs 2011: 89ff.; Gilbert 2002). If they were found to have a penis capable of erection and ejaculation, they were assigned to the penetrating male sexual role (Long 2006: 41ff.).

Irritations were also caused by those bodies that did not function in a way that corresponded to their gender physiology—for example, men who menstruated from the "loins" (from hemorrhoids). Their blood flow was explained as a humoral excess in analogy to the female humoral mechanism and, as long as they remained capable of reproduction, they were not accused of lacking masculinity (Pomata 2001). In Spain in the seventeenth century, it was believed that the bodies of Jews disposed of its surplus of impure blood in this way (Beusterien 1999).

The Sexual Power of Witches and "Savages"

In the sixteenth and seventeenth centuries, witches could also be held responsible for disturbances and problems in married love and sexual life. Already the scholastic authors of the twelfth to fifteenth centuries feared that demonic *incubi* and *succubi* either took possession of the male seed at night or would mate with a sleeping woman (Elliott 1999: 14ff.; Karras 2006a: 243ff.; Owens 2017). Contrary to what is often assumed, however, the main waves of witch hunts did not take place in the Middle Ages, but between 1450 and 1750, with a peak between 1550 and 1650. An estimated 60,000 of those accused of witchcraft in Europe were killed—more than 75 percent were women (Levack 2009: 35, 133). They were accused of a particularly sinister form of heresy. Witches had made a pact with the devil, which they sealed by sexual means, and gave themselves to the demons during the witches' sabbath and nightly orgies. However, the satanic paramour could also appear in the form of a husband or lover and differed from the latter only by his low body temperature—noticeable by his hard yet cold member. Alternatively, the witches had intercourse with animal representatives of Satan, such as the satyric goat. These *incubi* (male demons) appeared at night to ride their half-asleep, paralyzed victims (Stephens 2002: 32ff.). According to court and Inquisition records, especially older women had surrendered to the devil and were accused by their neighbors and acquaintances of *maleficia* and consorting with the powers of darkness. They had perverted the sexual conditions of the real world in doing so; the real word being that in which older women were mostly denied sexual lust and pleasure (Roper 2007: 172f.).

Witchcraft entered the canon of the church at the latest when Pope Innocent VIII (1432–1492) introduced the *Summis desiderantes affectibus* in the year 1484. This papal bull verified the existence of sexual intercourse with demons, and thus justified its persecution. The Dominican monk Heinrich Kramer declared in the *Hexenhammer* (*Malleus Maleficarum*, around 1486) that women were the ideal *Einfallstor* (gateway) for demons, as they were sexually insatiable, "bad by nature," and thus could hardly resist satanic attacks. Witches mutated into tools of evil and caused infertility, impotence, lovesickness, premature birth, abortion, and other deviations of sexual life, pregnancy, and birth (Pregesbauer 2009: 38ff.; Duni 2014; Opitz-Belakhal 2017: 58ff.). In view of this threat, it is not surprising that the priests blessed not only the spouses at the wedding but also the marriage bed and thus wanted to prevent a demon from being present during consummation and slipping into one of the newlyweds (Bohaumilitzky and Nägl 1989: 171). In the background of the madness around sorcery, there were fears and anxieties about women's fertility, animals breeding, and the vitality of the soil, all under apparent attack by supernatural, evil forces. The Roman and Spanish Inquisitions were particularly fond of such cases. The fact that charges of witchcraft often came down to denunciation and accusations is clear from certain court files of Augsburg. These show that such accusations often originated from one woman and concerned another—for example, when a young woman who had recently given birth accused an older midwife or nurse of having bewitched her newborn (Roper 1995b: 204ff.). Or they were women accused of crimes, such as having an illegitimate child or an abortion, that resulted from the unrestrained and insatiable lust of a witch. Mostly the power of language was at play—spells cast and curses uttered by the accused. As in Scotland in the seventeenth century, a woman who already had a bad reputation might also bring suspicion of witchcraft upon themselves if they made careless remarks (Dye 2012: 28ff.).

The flare-up of witch hunts had several causes, ranging from sectarian to social and economic. The sorcery paradigm offered contemporaries a supernatural explanation for crises of faith and church as well as crop failures and inflation or long wars and epidemics. Even marital and neighborly conflicts could be chalked up to the intervention of the devil. The witchcraft mania distinguished it from the high medieval love and fertility spells insofar as sexual magic and demon worship now coincided, and the illiterate popular belief entered the scholarly discourse (especially of clerics and lawyers) (Stephens 2011: 140ff.). Where the earlier heretics had already been suspected of sexual fornication, unnatural coitus was regarded as constitutive of a witch's behavior. There were questions as to whether sexual contact between a demon and a woman forcibly led to a pregnancy, however. What was certain was that the fruit had to be unnatural: While in ancient times heroic figures still grew out of relations between gods and humans, in early modern times only half demons arose from the seed of the devil. *Wechselbälger* (changelings) were among the potential offspring—insatiable babies who could drink the breasts of three to five wet nurses empty without gaining an ounce (Roper 2007: 146).

Clerics were also vexed by certain magical practices that, although not directly related to witchcraft, were definitely not associated with the Christian canon. In Sweden, this was revealed in a court case at the end of the sixteenth century involving the preacher Mårten Bäckman and Brita Sterne, the daughter of the mayor. The cleric had first arrived in his new community without his wife and had begun a relationship with Sterne. In the subsequent court case, letters came to light that showed that the two had used love magic to strengthen their bond. They gave each other rings of silk and later rings fashioned with locks of pubic hair. Sterne wrote to her lover a note with the gift:

> Guard well this ring, woven from the sweet, tender brown [a euphemism for the pudendum] none but you and I shall know (. . .). It is most dear

to me, for in it all our friendship abides. Bind yours in mine with the vow we made each other (Liliequist 2017: 222).

Pubic hair was said to have a strong magical binding power, and it seems that Bäckman even swallowed part of the ring and encouraged his lover to do the same. In the court case, the wife of the preacher announced that she had burned the remaining part of the ring, thus freeing her husband from the spell of love.

There were also rumors circulating in the Italian communes about the sexual otherness of the foreigners—especially blacks—who worked as slaves in the households of nobles and citizens. *Moors* and similarly "dark figures" were suspected of being sexually extremely potent and possessing an irresistible erotic charisma (Groebner 2007: 336f.). In the sixteenth century, the idea continued to spread that dark-skinned people had a wild, atavistic sexual desire that supposedly drove their every action, an idea that was to become entrenched for centuries. These images also quickly found their way into art and iconography (Kaplan 2021: 49ff.). Dark skin was now also considered an outward sign of female lustfulness in European science and medicine. Such stereotypes have regularly been resurrected and condensed into a characteristic of the black *raza* (race). In the late medieval and early modern discourse on this phenotype, however, it was primarily about the consequences of sexual relationships between members of supposedly incompatible social castes, classes, and strata, as well as about the mixing of free and unfree or Christians and heretics.

Sexual circumstances that stood in opposition to Christian natural law were also reported out of the colonies. The sexual stereotypes of the "savage" imported by the Spanish conquistadors stood in contradiction to European ideas of morality and respectability—and partly resulted from cultural practices being lost in translation due to the Christian-Eurocentric worldview of the *conquistadores* and missionaries (Sigal 2009: 1350; von Germeten 2021). The very first conquerors, already, had recognized young Mayan women as cultural mediators offering sexual gifts and mostly abused them as objects in accordance with their rape of the Southern American continent (Clark 2008: 87ff.). As with the racial exclusion of Jews and Muslims on the Iberian Peninsula, they saw the Aztecs and other American peoples primarily as infidels and savages—but this did not stop the soldiers from mixing with these "impure" women. A major misunderstanding came also from the Europeans not realizing that when the rulers of the Mexican Tlaxcaltecs offered their daughters (and female slaves) to the invaders in line with indigenous polygynous custom, they were seeking to establish blood alliances, as had traditionally been done between local kingdoms and sub-kingdoms (Carrasco 1997: 89ff.). For the Spaniards, however, the aristocratic Meso-American women were culturally beneath them, and they treated these women like slaves. Their martial superiority and possessive thinking legitimized them to take women and keep them for sexual purposes—a consequence of the macho masculinity that was widespread on the Iberian Peninsula, where low-ranked women were seen as objects of premarital or extramarital conquest (Poska 2008). What the Spaniards ignored or failed to see was that gender relations in the familial, social, and economic world of the indigenous population were valued very highly, and represented, so to speak, the glue between families, clans, and the rich (Gutierrez 1991: 17ff.).

The Christian missionaries, many of them Franciscans, criticized the sexual assaults of their Spanish and Portuguese compatriots, but at the same time tried to dissuade the pagans from their unnatural practices. Same-sex and promiscuous behavior was at the top of their list of sins and should be eradicated from the peoples of both Americas (Trexler 1995: 5; Horswell 2005: 220). The friars also considered it to be a reversal of the divine plan of creation when the Mexican Nahua created a confusion of sexes and sexualities in their cosmological fertility rites, which was also expressed in their social and warfare systems (Sigal 2011: 14f.). For the Mayas, arranged marriages were usually monogamous, but some couples separated after a few years and entered into a subsequent marriage without any great resistance from the community. Among the warrior upper classes, polygamy and concubinage were routine facts of life (Clark 2008: 97). For Christian Europeans, such conditions were seen as an indication that the natural order had been disrupted by evil or the devil, and that a global crusade was needed to save these souls. In the colonies, all necessary measures should therefore be taken to lead the savages down a Christian path, which meant them vowing to monogamous marriage and ending the (alleged) sexual and gender chaos. Iberian imperialism also reinforced and prolonged a racialization of sexuality (von Germeten 2021: 24).

Muslim Marriage and *Zina* in the Ottoman Empire

Those who looked toward the Ottoman Empire would also encounter a sexual culture that differed in many ways from Christian customs, but was partly based on the same traditions. The medical past was a shared cultural good. Here, until the eighteenth and nineteenth centuries, Galen's humoral system and its corresponding effects in the psychophysiology of men and women found resonance. Even though modifications were made by physicians like Ibn Sina (Lat. Avicenna, 980–1037), these basic constants were in agreement with the body image of the Christian Occident described above (Ze'evi 2006: 21 ff.). As in other Islamic cultures, however, the Ottomans also followed a body of knowledge that dealt with *'ilm al-bah* (the doctrine of sexual intercourse). The Ottoman scholar Ahmad ibn Mustafa Tashköprüzade (1494–1561) showed in his encyclopedia that several strands of tradition wove together to make up this knowledge base, namely erotic guides, medical compendia, and pornographic writings. In the first, readers were taught about the beauty of women, the use of perfumes, sexual positions, and techniques. In the medical *Bah* books, they learned about the physical functions and the optimal circumstances for coitus and its moderate use. Finally, there were books in circulation with titles such as *Dafi' al-ghumum wa-rafi' al-humum* (*The Defense Against Worries and the Expulsion of Troubles*) by the writer Deli Birader Gazali (1466–1535). Its detailed descriptions dealt with masturbation, adultery, and same-sex practices. Apart from the regent and a selected courtly audience, only very high-ranking and wealthy persons were considered readers of such literature (Franke 2012: 162ff.).

The differences to Christianity were clear at least in the area of religious sexual norms. Since the fifteenth century, the Ottoman Sultanate, which also included large parts of Southeastern Europe, had developed into a Sunni state. On the one hand, the religious and secular guidelines for sexual life were based on *şeriat* (the Turkish term for *scharī'a*—Sharia law). *Şeriat* was considered a God-given right, cemented in the Quran and the Sunna. The Islamic legal doctrine or science of the *fiqh* refers to the interpretation of *şeriat*. The legal scholars' task was to draft the decrees of the ruler and his administration in such a way that they did not contradict the *şeriat*. In cases of doubt, *kadis*, legal scholars, or judges delegated by the Sultan, then decided on the correct interpretation and the wording of arbitral rulings (Ze'evi 2001: 220 ff.).

When it came to the punishment of deviant sexual life and thus to offences such as premarital and extramarital sex, seduction, temptation and rape, sexual intercourse with slaves, same-sex acts, incest, sexual violence against children, and others, Ottomans had to operate within the framework of the divine law, which laid down some basic principles. According to the Sunni Hanafite school of constitutional law, the *şeriat* or *scharī'a* differentiated according to a person's gender, their marital status (married or not), age, religion (Muslim or not), and whether they were free or a slave. The Islamic jurisdiction focused on determining whether a person had violated divine principles through fornication or whether the definition and severity of his offense should be left to the secular courts. *Zina*, every form of fornication and especially adultery, was the focal point: For women, *zina* involved all sexual acts except with the husband or master/owner. For men, it meant all sexual contacts except with his one to four wives and his own female slaves. Accusations of sexual intercourse between men sparked heated discussions as to whether these were among the crimes against God and therefore to be severely punished, namely with death, or whether they were to be condemned but sanctioned by the jurists according to the social criteria mentioned above. For Sharia law, sexual contacts between women simply did not exist, so there was no threat of punishment. Interreligious contacts were problematic when a non-Muslim man consorted with a Muslim woman. As far as penalties were concerned, the free should be punished more severely than slaves, the elderly more severely than the young, and married people more severely than singles (Ze'evi 2001: 225 ff.).

Religious principles were adapted into practicable legal codes of law, such as the famous *Kanun-ı Osmani*, which Süleyman I (1494/96–1566) issued between 1534 and 1545. This codex was adopted and further adapted by the subsequent Ottoman rulers up into the seventeenth century (Semerdjian 2008: 58). Adultery of a Muslim man ranked first in the *zina* and was to be sanctioned with fines, depending on a man's riches. This was followed by single men, married women, widows, slaves, etc., with correspondingly graduated fines up to banishment and forced labor. Overall, the penalties in secular law were much less severe and ought to be adapted to local customary law. If the *şeriat* for adultery provided for stoning to death, the injured husband was offered the prospect of a compensation payment, and in return he could flexibly adapt his testimony to something more applicable (Semerdjian 2008: 30). The *kanun* (secular code) also allowed the husband to keep his unfaithful wife and reconcile with her. For consensual sexual acts among adults, the common code generally provided for fines, a sanction that does not appear at all in the Sharia. Repeat offenders, such as procurers, were to be flogged, while rape and kidnapping of a (young) woman risked castration, but the death penalty didn't apply for these offences. According to the *kanun*, as opposed to the *şeriat*, men and women faced the same penalties. Probably the most obvious difference to the Christian codes was the punishment of homosexual acts: According to Süleyman's *kanun*, offenders faced a monetary penalty and, depending on the circumstances, increasing corporal punishment, as in the case of adultery between a man and a woman. Islamic law did not call for capital punishment of same-sex intercourse (Ze'evi 2001: 231f.). In view of the predominance of fines, the Sultan's law opened up relatively wide discretionary powers pertaining to consensual sexual acts among adults. At the same time, it had a much broader judicial interpretation framework in regard to proving the crime and thus became an instrument of religious-state authorities for regulating and disciplining its subjects (Semerdjian 2008: 29ff.).

According to the Hanafi legal school, a woman could terminate her pregnancy up to four months after conception, as the fetus was not yet considered to be fully animated. This applied, however, only under very specific circumstances, such as when the pregnant woman would later be unable to breastfeed the baby herself and the family could not afford a wet nurse. It is striking that the fatwa collections before the seventeenth century did not contain any legal rulings on abortion issues. Later on, causing miscarriages, for example by the use of force, was sanctioned with reprimands and fines (so-called *diyet*, "blood money") or prison sentences of varying lengths. If a woman committed the act without the consent of her husband, she had to pay him additional damages (Demirci and Somel 2008: 383ff.).

Unlike in Catholic countries, marriages in the Ottoman Empire could be dissolved in a variety of ways: In *talâk*, the rejection, a man declared himself free from his wife in front of witnesses, with or without giving reason. After a waiting period of three months, during which no sexual intercourse was allowed, he would repeat the announcement; the dissolution of marriage usually went into effect with the payment of a corresponding alimony to the woman. She could also divorce him if he proved to be impotent, but only if she was not (financially) supported by her husband. She had to go to court to apply for a dissolution of the marriage. Or she found witnesses who testified that her husband had announced *talâk*. Finally, the spouses were able to reach a consensual agreement to dissolve the marriage. Usually this way, called *khul*, was connected with the settlement of an outstanding bridal gift to the wife. *Khul* also seems to have been the preferred form of divorce in the Ottoman territories of the Balkans (Davis 1986: 119ff.; Voorhoeve 2013). In some areas, their number was quite considerable: thus, the 69 marriage contracts documented in Herakleio from 1669 to 1673 can be contrasted with 18 divorces, that is, 21.9 percent; from 1673 to 1689, 19 divorces (12.4 percent) were recorded for 153 marriages.

A form of institutionalization of sexual relations that completely deviated from Christian norms was *mut'a*, the temporary marriage. This legal option allowed a man, for example a merchant who had just arrived, to contractually bind a woman to him for a certain period of time—usually a month, but also longer. Even if this usually amounted to legalizing prostitution, it represented a possibility for arranging and conducting a trial marriage. However, only women who could not find a regular husband, due to their low social status for the most part, bound themselves in this way, sometimes even sold themselves and hoped for a subsequent prolongation of the temporary marriage (Sariyannis 2008: 47f.). Prostitution was also tolerated in the Ottoman Empire because, for the Islamic legal scholars of the sixteenth to eighteenth centuries, it represented a form of purchase. The thinking went: If owners were allowed to use (purchased) slaves sexually, why shouldn't prostitution also be considered as a barter relationship, where a whore was temporarily acquired for sexual services? The opposite case—where a woman paid a man for sexual intercourse—was simply unthinkable on the basis of *şeriat* and *kanun* (Leiser 2017: ch. 5; Baldwin 2012: 125).

For Greek Orthodox and Armenian Apostolic Christians, as well as for Jews, a complex situation arose in the Ottoman Empire when it came to the application of the law to sexual offences. Since Mehmed II (1432–1481), these individual religious communities exercised their own jurisdiction (when their exercise did not affect Muslims). For example, Greek Orthodox Christians in Samos, Crete, and Chios were subject to the laws issued by the Patriarch of Constantinople. In practice, especially when there were differences between the Christian and Muslim provisions, they had three authorities to turn to: their own clerical (Christian) court, the court of the respective community, and, if necessary, a Muslim-Sunni court. In view of the relatively liberal divorce laws, Greek Orthodox women who wanted to separate from their husbands would, in the event of a conflict, appeal to a Muslim court because their own law prevented them from doing so. In order to prevent such a defection to a non-Christian jurisdiction, the Patriarch of Constantinople, Jeremiah III (*c.* 1650/1660–1735), decided that the city should be given a new jurisdiction. He decided in 1717 that the Christian members of the faith would also be allowed to dissolve their marriage by consensus. However, they had to reach agreement beforehand on all financial matters and ownership issues (Laiou 2007: 246).

Godless Brothels and the French Disease

In the late fifteenth and sixteenth centuries, many European cities began to close brothels and ban prostitution, which had been tolerated until then (Pluskota 2020). This was also reflected in a change in terminology: While in the early fifteenth century the term *freies Haus* (free house) was still used in the Austrian-South German area, in 1562 it was dubbed the *gottlose Hurenhaus* (godless whorehouse) (Rath 1986: 570f.). There were two main reasons for this shift: On the one hand, the moral rigor of the Reformers led to the discrediting of sexual double standards in those Central and Northern European regions where Protestants, Lutherans, Calvinists, Anglicans etc., found many followers. This was also reflected in the local chastity and morality regimes. On the other hand, in the countries of Southern Europe dominated by the Roman Catholic Church, in parts of the Habsburg Monarchy, and in France, the Counter-Reformation was intended to reform not only the sexual practices of the clergy but also those of the laity. Thus, male premarital and extramarital intercourse also faced criticism. The municipalities in any case should definitely no longer act as brothel operators and certainly not profit financially from this unchaste business.

For some historians, the rapid spread of the "French disease" (syphilis) from the late fifteenth century onward was also responsible for brothel closures. However, this argument is controversial, since the city ordinances and decrees hardly mentioned prostitution as the cause of the spread of the new venereal disease and, at least in the early stages, did not establish a direct venereal transmission route. Some municipalities even reacted with contrary measures and, like Nuremberg and Seville, opened municipal brothels with greater quality controls for the prostitutes and, if necessary, to take them out of circulation in case of infection (Stein 2003: 176f.; Mummey 2011: 179). In the contemporary discourse on the French disease, however, it was repeatedly demanded that social places such as brothels or bathing establishments should be closed, as they encouraged contact with foul fumes—even though initially there was no thought of transmission through sexual intercourse or penetration. The humanist Jakob Wimpfeling (1450–1528), for example, sent a petition to Emperor Maximilian I (1459–1519), in which he demanded the city brothel in Alsatian Schlettstadt be shuttered and pointed out the dangers of infection there: "He who sets foot in the women's house, has the other in the hospital" (Jütte 1996: 100).

The tightening of the city's moral codes and the prostitution regime began in some places as early as the second half of the fifteenth century and had to do with the increased appearance of "street girls." Due to the deterioration of women's employment opportunities and the displacement of women from traditional areas of commercial income, such as beer production and bar sales, but also from some craft enterprises, more and more women were forced into other, less respected jobs such as whoring themselves. As in York, Coventry, and Leicester, they worked alone or under the protection of a pimp on the street and thus fell into the sights of the city authorities and the morality police. In England, therefore, even before the Reformation and the emergence of the Anglican Church, there was cooperation between the congregation, the (morality) police, and church leaders, who together tried to raise the moral standard of the population (Goldberg 1999; Ingram 2017: 138ff.). They focused mainly on prostitutes and their clientele. In London's Southwark, for example, whores were forbidden to call out to potential clients from the brothel doorway. In Frankfurt, too, boarded women were forbidden to sit in front of the entrance to the brothel and encourage male passers-by to step inside (Wolfthal 2010: 87). In the Rhone Valley and in Burgundy in the 1490s, preachers raged against the generally increasing licentiousness, aiming their fury above all at the widespread brothels (Rossiaud 1988: 33ff.). In Florence, Girolamo Savonarola (1452–1498) preached against prostitution and incited the population against courtesans (Hatty and Hatty 1999:121ff.).

Reformation of Prostitution

Several reasons can be given for this vehement appearance of the Reformers: On the one hand, Luther, in contrast to Roman teaching, had already proclaimed a "natural sexual drive" to be undeniable, comparing it to food and drink, which likewise could not be put off for any great length of time. Therefore, early marriage would have to be introduced, which would keep the "foul, savage, disorderly nature" (Peters 1990: 244) of premarital intercourse in check and deprive street prostitution and whorehouses of their customers. In his *Tischreden* (*Table Talks*), he highlighted another aspect: "For a wife shall not be taken only for urgent want, but also because one must dwell and live together" (Luther 1846: 113). He saw the main reason for the flourishing fornication in the clerical and (urban) civil order, which denied young people access to marriage. To put an end to this deplorable state of affairs, among other things, the provisions on celibacy should be removed from the guild regulations and the purchase of children by monasteries should be prohibited. The priestly concubines entailed by celibacy were also conducive to immorality and had to be replaced by priestly marriage—even if the bishops lost income from the accruing fines from the clergy.

Luther also rejected commercial fornication because it disturbed the peace of marriage or the regulated marital intercourse. Brothels and clandestine prostitutes encouraged men not to be satisfied with the pleasures of the marriage bed, but to fall into the clutches of the devil. Here, he radically broke with Augustine's teaching, who saw prostitution as a necessary means to keep fornication out of marriage (Wiesner-Hanks 2000: 63). Luther's position left nothing to be desired in terms of clarity. In 1540, he wrote to fellow Reformer Hieronymus Weller (1499–1572) in Freiberg, where the city brothel had been closed in 1537 and was to be reopened in 1540:

> My dear Hieronymus, You should have nothing to do with nor be involved with those who want to reopen the public brothel. It would have been better and more tolerable not to have driven the devil out, than to let him in again and acknowledge him. Those who want to open such houses again have denied the name of Christ, and confessed that they are not Christians but heathens who know nothing of God. . . . How can one teach publicly against whoredom and punish this, if one praises the authorities that tolerate and allow it? . . . [My] answer: there is a good remedy for this from God's grace, that is, marriage or the hope of becoming married. Who would need the hope or remedy of marriage, if we let whoredom go unpunished? (Luther 1846: 112; Karant-Nunn and Wiesner-Hanks 2003: 159)

Luther also thought that the clergy should undergo this therapy. If forced celibacy were abolished, and with that priests' concubines could become wives, their shamelessness and the blurring of purity and impurity, both carnal and spiritual, would also come to an end. In the whoring clerics he suspected a work of the devil, which served to defile the pure souls. In one of his powerful rhetorical attacks, he even equated service in the papal church with prostitution itself:

> We too were formerly stuck in the behind of this hellish whore, this new church of the pope. We supported it in all earnestness, so that we regret having spent so much time and energy in that vile hole. But God may be praised and thanked that he rescued us from the scarlet whore (Roper 1994: 51).

In his attacks, the Catholic clergy appeared sweepingly as lewd men who plunged honorable women into sin and at best took them as their companions. He insulted the Pope's church as the "Whore of Babylon," who plunged the faithful into ruin—for which God had punished him with the *Sacco di Roma*, the plundering of Rome in 1527 by German as well as

FIGURE 16 Albrecht Dürer (1471–1528), The Whore of Babylon, woodcut, c. 1497.

Italian and Spanish mercenaries. All in all, he also figured that whores must wish to remain Catholic because they could atone for their sins by buying indulgences and thus go on to commit new ones (Figure 16).

John Calvin condemned prostitution much more vigorously and implemented the prosecution of whores and *fornicatio* (premarital sex) with verve. In 1562/63, for example, about 20 percent of the court cases in Geneva—at that time a city of 18,000 to 20,000 inhabitants in which he established his "divine state"—concerned sexual offences. Short prison sentences or fines were imposed for fornication. Stricter sanctions fell for adultery and homosexual acts. Singing vicious songs, indecent dancing, and drunkenness were also persecuted (Monter 1973). The Consistory (consisting of pastors of the Geneva churches as well as the twelve elders of the city councils) proved to be a useful instrument for the implementation of church discipline, which acted as a court of law, but also as a balancing authority in marital disputes. Before the Reformation, the whores of Geneva had been banished to a special district, as in other cities, they had to wear recognizable clothing and were only allowed to use the public bathrooms (where they found most of their customers) at certain times. During international fairs, they were met with brisk demand from foreign traders. The Calvinist Reformation, however, brought prostitution to an abrupt end. Some whores were even offered money to leave the city. From 1560 onward, whoredom, especially by married women, was condemned with capital punishment, namely drowning (Witte and Kingdon 2005: 72ff.).

A typical court case of a Geneva prostitute concerned Loise Mestre, who was sentenced to death for multiple adultery charges in 1566. Her confession, forced under torture, reveals the life story of a woman living promiscuously even as a prostitute during the Reformation. Even as a girl, Mestre had had sexual intercourse with three men in her father's house, two of whom were married. After her marriage to Jean-Jacques Bonivard, she ran a tavern and hostelry, convivial places that were often linked to the "profession." Just one year after the wedding, she confessed to have begun an affair with another married man. She was subsequently banned from the city for a year because of theft. After her return, she had sexual relations with four married men, which is why she was brought before the Consistory and admonished—and subsequently disappeared from the city again. For a few weeks, she lived in a village controlled by Bern, where she met women who had also fled Geneva from the terror of virtues. After the death of her first husband, she remarried, returned to the city, and still repeatedly consorted with other men. This was enough (with some minor offences) to condemn them to death in 1566 (Kingdon 1995: 135).

The Reformers' ideas and measures to abolish prostitution did not meet with universal understanding. For example, the Basel chronicler Wurstisen (1544–1588) reports that there were difficulties in closing the brothels because the men felt that it helped to avoid serious damage and maintain moral order:

> But the common man argued that one should let these houses stay to avoid adultery, virgin weakness and sins that shall not be named: yes, they were spoilt, as if they could not keep pious daughters or wives, one would then keep these common houses (Schuster 1995: 185).

In contrast to this, the Basel clergy had insisted quite vehemently on closure and the council did so in 1534. Here, a favorite argument of Reform-minded clerics was brought to bare:

> If a godly father wants that his son enters chaste into marriage, lives purity therein, sires children, who bring him joy, he must keep him clean and chaste with industry and labor; in particular he must keep him away from such unclean and unashamed women, who sell their bodies for a bit of money in "open houses"; so that he properly spurns such women, make a point of what shall befall him [if he does visit such a place]: the son will become unclean in body and spirit. (. . .) The spirit shall become so unclean that it may never be purified again; therefore, it will be inept

for marriage, for it will want to treat the body of the wife as it would the whore's. (Burghartz 1999: 252f.)

Whoever went to the *Maetzen* (whores) as a husband also defiled the physical and mental purity of the wives and transported fornication into marital intercourse. Worse still, the toleration of prostitution itself was a moral defilement of the community, because it gave the sons the idea of satisfying their sexual desires before marriage. In Basel, as in other cities, it became clear that the closure of the women's house was by no means the end of "free" prostitution; although some whores did disappear from the city, they offered their services in the surrounding villages and the clients simply visited them.

Shutdown and Control of Municipial Brothels

The Protestant campaign against prostitution and procuring resulted in the closure of brothels in almost all Protestant towns between 1520 and 1590 (Schuster 1992 and 1995: 450f.). For example, whorehouses closed in Wittenberg 1522, in Augsburg 1522, in Göttingen 1529, in Bern 1531, and in Hamburg 1532–40 (Roper 1989: 89ff.; Schuster 1995: 450f.). In Languedoc, the spread of Protestantism also went hand in hand with their abolition in the 1550s (Otis 1985: 43). A parallel development was marital and ecclesiastical courts having been established or the existing ones having been equipped with extended powers and appropriate institutions having been created to receive repentant sinners. In Amsterdam, the so-called *Werkhuis*, a workhouse to which women from brothels were admitted, opened in 1597. After its destruction by fire, the *Spinnhaus* (spinning house) was built on the same site in 1645, where dishonorable women were to be improved (and disciplined) through industrious spinning and sewing. In the 1681 travelogue *Het wonderlyk leeven van't Boullonnois Hondtie*, one finds a description of the conditions there which shocked the visitor. He had obviously expected to meet happy young women:

> This house [has] a reputation throughout the country for seeing miracles and being full of lovely maidens, but instead you often see only a group of smallpox-drawn creatures that give off such a bad smell that you have to hurry up the stairs to the workroom or hold your nose (van de Pol 2006: 113).

Amsterdam was a good example for how the abolition of brothels was handled. In the Late Middle Ages, brothels were tolerated there under the supervision of the police; in 1478 fornication was restricted to Pijlsteeg and Halssteeg and secret prostitution was clamped down more strictly. The clientele were apprentices; married men and clerics, on the other hand, were strictly forbidden and pursued. After the Calvinists had taken power in the city in 1578, prostitution was banned completely, and from 1580 a prostitution law passed for the United Provinces punished both whoredom and anything associated with it. The relevant persecution and jurisdiction were conducted by the city's mayor and aldermen, who sent beadles out to actively investigate. Even if the penalty was quite grave in theory, actually sanctioning whores and their hosts was initially limited to warnings, only followed by pillorying and fines, and if the offence were repeated, then public corporal punishment and banishment. If girls between the ages of fourteen and sixteen were picked up, they were returned to their parents and handed back into their guardianship. These vice squads, however, did not enjoy a good reputation. The agents' pay consisted of a small part of the fines imposed, which was meant to increase the low base salary of their wages as a sort of commission. But the result was that many of them took bribes on the spot. Instead of reporting and stopping the operation of a whorehouse, they could be bought off with the full price of the would-be fine (van de Pol 2006: 105ff.).

The operation of brothels repeatedly came to public attention and was the focus of protests and scandals, for example in London in 1668 in the context of the so-called *Bawdy House Riots* (Harris 1986). Already, the decades before had seen riots in the city, especially among apprentices, journeymen, and other young men, because the inmates of the brothels did not respect the silence during Lent but continued to solicit customers; similar things happened during the topsy-turvy world of carnival and Fastelavn. The violent protests during Easter week 1668 emanated from religious *dissidents*, however, radical Protestant groups who demanded stricter moral reform. This was in response to a royal proclamation banning private religious gatherings, which meanwhile did nothing about immoral gatherings in illegal establishments. Over a period of several days, hundreds and then thousands of men destroyed the brothels in the East End and other sinister areas of the city, attacking the operators as well as the prostitutes. In satirical pseudo-petitions, they called for the "poor whores" to receive more support and (ironically) proposed a law which called on parliament to tolerate the whorehouses but not to allow any religious assembly whatsoever (Mowry 2004: 89).

The rigid approach of the reformed communities also forced the Catholic cities into action. Their councils, however, usually took less rigorous measures, instead pursuing a dual strategy: Many municipalities maintained their licensed brothels under supervision but tried to register and control the free prostitutes and, if they didn't follow the rules, to punish them more severely. The well-known streetwalkers should only be active in the urban areas where they were permitted to work. As before, regulated prostitution was seen as a necessary evil to protect respectable women from fornication and immorality. Other Catholic cities tried to ban brothels, but were not very successful. Rome itself was significant, where three years after the Council of Trent (1545–1563), at which the Roman Catholic Church had determined its counter-reformatory course, Pope Pius V (1504–1572) called for the moral cleansing of the city. One measure was to order prostitutes to leave the city, which some of them obliged. The appeal was only partially successful, however, which is why Pope Clement VIII called for a new, more effective and more efficient policy (1536–1605). He issued a decree in 1592 threatening whores with banishment if they did not settle in a certain quarter or limit their activities to the "red light zone." The citizens intervened and ultimately all whoredom was assigned to the *Campo Marzia*, away from the city center. After that there was no more talk of an all-out ban on prostitution, rather an attempt was made to keep the women away from the respectable population. As a guarantee, they were appointed their own watchmen, called the *Birri* in Rome, who visited the taverns, collected taxes, and investigated whores (Storey 2008: 71ff.). Other Catholic monarchs and mayors that wanted to abolish brothels and with them prostitution altogether only managed similarly limited successes. Like Philip IV (1605–1665), who forbade brothels in Spain in 1623. The Edict of Blois (1560), which was to end prostitution in France (Norberg 2013: 395ff.), also had little effect.

Also in Central and Eastern Europe, for example in the Kingdom of Hungary, the cities in the sixteenth century tried to secure the public order more strongly with their municipal statutes and to regulate the lives of their inhabitants. This also included strict punishment for all kinds of extramarital liaisons. From the middle of the century onward, stricter action was taken against the previously tolerated and official municipal brothels and street prostitution. Convicted women were now increasingly banished from the city or sentenced to penalties of shame at the pillory and flogging, while the man would get off with a fine only. If prostitution and adultery went hand in hand, it could also lead to the death penalty (Szeghyová 2019).

Catholic as well as some Protestant cities tried to get the "fallen women" off the streets by building workhouses and introducing their own aforementioned Magdalene houses and to provide them with another source of income. These facilities were also open to women in danger of slipping into prostitution. Often built by reform-minded (Catholic) bishops, these asylums also took in people who were predicted to have a bawdy future—such as the daughters of prostitutes, raped women, and outcast wives. The houses were run like convents, their inmates had to submit to a strict labor regime as well as to the Catholic rules of the mass, prayer, and penance. Discipline and repentance were considered a necessary prerequisite for the successful conversion of former whores—which had rather little chance of success, since this usually meant prison and further punishment (Wiesner-Hanks 2000: 124f.). The institutions bore significant names such as *Santa Marta* (house for the reform of prostitution, Rome 1543 and Modena, Trapani, Agrigento, Messina, and Palermo 1546–1556), *Casa delle Malmaritate* (house for unhappily married women, Florence 1579), *Casa Pia das Convertidas* (pious house of the converted, Lisboa 1587), *Santa*

Maria Magdalena de la Penitencia (Magdalene house for penitents, Madrid 1619), and *Hôpital du refuge* (hospital of refuge, Marseille 1640) (Cohen 1992: 64ff.; Crawford 2007: 93; Rijo 2017: 131f.). If the prostitutes could not be persuaded to convert, coercive measures were taken: Philip III of Spain, for example, had a women's prison built in 1608, and in Dijon the *Maison du Bon Pasteur* was built in 1681 for unruly whores. The most famous was the *Hôpital de la Salpêtrière* in Paris, which was built in 1656 at the instigation of Louis XIV and took in the poor and beggars, but was also a contact point for prostitutes and those ridden with venereal disease. Some of the inmates entered the institution through a so-called *Lettre de cachet*, letters signed in advance by the king (and a minister), which was also used to arrest prostitutes off the street. But husbands could also use these to get rid of their unfaithful or unwelcome wives, often with flimsy accusations (Strayer 1992).

All this was part of a far-reaching denominationalization, in the course of which the secular and ecclesiastical rulers and institutions—whether Lutheran, Calvinist, Anglican, or Catholic—tried to control the morals and mores, religious attitudes, and sexual behavior of their subjects. To do so, marriage courts, consistories, and similar institutions were created or expanded—as well as marriage and chastity regulations on which they were based—and the public and private (sexual) life of the population was thoroughly monitored and sanctioned. The basic idea had medieval roots, which were to be found in the separation of private and public morality; the former was the responsibility of the priests and the confessional, the latter was the task of secular judges and courts. In the late fifteenth century and during the Reformation, these disciplinary attempts gained urgency and penetrating power. The population experienced the *reformatio vitae* through the closing of brothels, the sanctioning of premarital pregnancy, and that public drunkenness and boisterous dancing were evermore shunned (Roper 1995b: 147ff.).

Nightloopsters, Playhouses, and Courtesans

The structure of prostitution and the origin of the women changed relatively little between the late fifteenth and seventeenth centuries (McEnery and Baker 2017: 33ff.). There were also streetwalkers who worked more or less "professionally" out on the street, some of them under a pimp, and went about their business in their own accommodations, a rented room, a park, or a nearby forest. In Amsterdam in the seventeenth century, these women were called *nightloopsters* (night runners) because they were often out and about at a time when respectable women no longer went out on the streets alone. In Rome, this led to the practice around 1600 of whores dressing as men in order to move around the city after the Ave Maria, which was forbidden to women (Storey 2004: 96).

Brothel prostitutes, on the other hand, were, as before, bound by the orders of the procurers and madams. Whorehouses were usually small and comprised only two to four women, supplemented by "free" whores from the street if necessary. In Amsterdam, where running whorehouses was banned in 1578, women often ran the brothels and continued to run them as "playhouses" where you could eat and drink and listen to music—and meet a prostitute on the side. The smokescreen business as such could continue even if the women got arrested during a police raid, a major advantage for the owners (van de Pol 2006: 25ff.).

In addition, women who prostituted only occasionally—mostly recruited from the lower social groups—could be found in all major European cities. They often had come to the city on their own to fend for themselves or had come from poorer urban families. Others, also in poorer parts of the city, lived married lives or had been widowed and contributed to the family upkeep with their income. The courts usually imposed only minor punishments, as the women could point to their unfortunate living conditions—often with testimonials from neighbors—and thus give a good reason for their shameless activity. Their argument for practicing occasionally rested on the fact that if they joined a bordello, their social status would sink as official whores, and there was the danger of their situation becoming permanent. Additionally, official registration as a prostitute could result in financial burdens due to taxes and paying for medical checks (Ruggiero 2011: 161). *Prostitución clandestina* was therefore not only found in the city of Seville in the seventeenth century, but everywhere in Europe (Candau Chacón 2018).

Another type of prostitute flourished in the Renaissance cities: the elite courtesan. The ability to afford or keep an exceptionally beautiful lover who was desired by other men was associated with high social prestige. These women were at the top of the prostitution pyramid, so to speak. A courtesan could potentially take her own actions and make her own decisions. She could choose from among the admirers the one who promised her the best financial offer and a higher social status. Courtesans were not only physically attractive; their social performance and presentable manners were key. This included being able to engage in sophisticated conversation or possessing artistic skills such as singing and playacting. If their physical attraction faded with age, the "beloved" usually looked around for a new lover and the former was threatened with social decline.

The English term courtesan was borrowed from the French *courtisane*. This, in turn, stems from the Italian *cortigiana* and denoted the female form of the *cortigiano*, the courtier. The first women called this with this meaning appeared in Italy in the sixteenth century, and there again in Rome as the mistresses of the many unmarried clerics at the Holy See. Although the reputation and title of these women originally testified to an exceptional position, this designation quickly trickled down and was soon used for average whores (Storey 2008: 234ff.). The Venetian penal code no longer made a distinction between *cortigiana* (courtesans) and *meretrice* (whores).

In regulations dating from 1571, 1582, and 1613, both were forbidden to enter churches on feast days or to wear silk, jewels, gold, and silver. In the opinion of the urban *Signoria* in 1542, all women were considered prostitutes who, as unmarried persons, had contact and sexual intercourse (*commercia et practica*) with one or more men or, as married persons, did not live under the same roof as their husband and behaved thusly (Robin 2003: 38).

Respected courtesans in Rome around 1600 conveyed their value by their clothing. Bedecked with gold and silver, and wearing noble fabrics such as velvet, silk, and satin, they were often indistinguishable from the noble women. In doing so, however, they crossed the dividing line between social differences articulated in public through clothing and jewelry. The respectable city society therefore found their presentation extremely inappropriate. Conversely, the conspicuous fashions of the courtesans in particular was glitzy proof that their suitors could afford such an expensive lover and could support them in such extravagance (Storey 2004: 95ff.). In Rome, they went about their business relatively undisturbed in the later sixteenth century. They differed from the cheap streetwalkers in that they had no pimps and maintained quite personal and long-term relationships with their customers, which usually included visiting restaurants and attending the theater together. They were generally well integrated with their neighbors and surroundings. However, their social status could change quickly: Some saw her as a *donna*, others as a *cortigana*, and others as just an ordinary *putta* (Cohen 1991: 206; Budin 2021: 117ff.).

The fact that even such well-known courtesans as Veronica Franco (1546–1591), a woman from Venice who was a writer and ran her own artistic salon, were perceived as "public women" was revealed in 1565 by *Il Catalogo Di tutte le principale* and *Pi ù honorate cortigiane Di Venezia*. In these municipal prostitution registers, her name was also mentioned along with her address and price (Rosenthal 1992: 288). In her collection of letters *Lettere familiari a diversi* (1580), Franco made it unmistakably clear that the existence of a *cortigiana onesta*, a righteous courtesan, was usually glossed over and romanticized in poetry. In truth, her life was no picnic. What she found hardest to bear was that she was not in charge of her own body and that her life was determined by others:

> To give oneself over to many . . . to eat with the mouth of another, sleep with the eyes of another, move according to the wishes of another, always risking the shipwreck of one's faculties and life . . . Believe me: of all worldly tribulations, this is the worst (Ray 2009: 152).

Making Prostitution Invisible

Even though the harmful influence and appearance of prostitutes was a source of consternation in the Catholic cities, the "common" women never fully disappeared from the public eye. In Florence and Venice, they continued to stand provocatively in the entrances and woo clientele. On his walks through Rome in the early 1580s, Michel de Montaigne (1533–1592) observed how they addressed passing men from the windows:

> The commonest exercise of the Romans is to promenade through the streets. (. . .) To tell the truth, the greatest profit that is derived from this is to see the ladies at the window, and notably the courtesans, who show themselves at their Venetian blinds with such treacherous artfulness that I have often marveled how they tantalize our eyes as they do; and often, having got off my horse immediately and obtained admission, I wondered at how much more beautiful they appeared to be than they really were. They know how to present themselves by their most agreeable feature; they will show you only the upper part of the face, or the lower, or the side, and cover themselves or show themselves in such a way that not one single ugly one is seen at the window. All the men are there taking off their hats and making deep bows, and receiving an ogling glance or two as they pass. (Wolfthal 2010: 83)

Popular places to initiate business were also bathing establishments, taverns, and inns, mostly in areas of ill repute. In Italian cities, they acted their role in even better and busier parts of the city center. In Venice, prostitutes performed southwest of the Rialto Bridge and in Florence east of the Mercato Vecchio and southeast of the cathedral (Ruggiero 2011: 168; Weddle 2019). Even long after the Council of Trent, people here remained tolerant of prostitution because they feared an increase in sodomitic seductions of young men. It should not be underestimated that prostitution was also tolerated for its alleviating effects of the social and economic problems that come with a lack of unmarried (yet marriageable) young women. At the same time, mothers in Venice were banned in 1563 from sending their daughters into prostitution and collecting the profits for themselves. Public disgrace was the penalty. Condemned women had to sit on a platform in Piazza San Marco wearing a whore's crown. Standing next to them a herald announced the respective offence. They were then banned from the city for a period of two years (Rosenthal 1993: 116f.).

In Bologna at the end of the sixteenth and the beginning of the seventeenth century there were no containment rules and the prostitutes—as the annual registers from 1583 to 1630 show—lived across the city. As a result, Bolognese of all social classes were familiar with the sight of whores in their neighbourhood. The city administration saw them above all as an economic factor, as fee- and fine-paying workers they were administered by a civic magistracy, the *Ufficio delle Bollette* (Office of Receipts). The prostitutes were integrated into their neighbourhoods through family and work relationships, some living and working together, such as sisters or daughters with their mothers in rented rooms and small apartments, where they also pursued their activity. They found their clients in inns or in the few brothels in town, and some had stable relationships with men. However, this tolerant attitude toward prostitution repeatedly led to protests and measures by other urban groups. Neighbors complained about the noise and the sight of the business as gossip and visibility acted as advertisements. Also, whores were not supposed to walk the streets with men at night. Nuns and monks, in particular, felt indignant by their appearance, which is why they were banned from the vicinity of some religious institutions (McCarthy and Terpstra 2019).

In other Italian cities such as Genoa in the mid-sixteenth century, it was mainly the clergy who spoke out against the moral poisoning and pollution caused by prostitution. There, the friars of San Francesco di Castelletto voted to ensure sanctity and moral cleanliness in the city and to suppress public brothels. Their argumentation was indicative of the church's attitude toward prostitution:

> The brothel in the city then, is like the stable or latrine in the house. Because just as the city keeps itself clean by providing a separate place where filth and dung are gathered, so neither less nor more, acts the brothel; where the filth and ugliness of the flesh are gathered like the garbage and dung of the city. (Crawshaw 2017: 168)

When the city brothel in Toulouse, France, had to be relocated in the early sixteenth century, discussions about the place and nature of the establishment revealed all the problems: in order to make prostitution invisible and restrict it, and to preserve public and moral order, the brothel building should be surrounded by high walls, located in a hidden place on the city wall, placed near warehouses and foul-smelling markets, and have only one entrance. In this way, the prostitutes were to be isolated and moral contamination of the townspeople avoided. The newly established urban brothel *Château Vert* then lasted only a few decades and, like most brothels in the French kingdom, was closed in the 1550s. The authorities subsequently banned the venereal trade from the city altogether (Roby 2017).

In the English town of Deal (in the county of Kent), the Puritan Mayor Thomas Powell took action against whores by his own hand and made an example of one of them in 1703. He wrote in his diary of the incident:

> I took up a common prostitute, whose conduct was very offensive, brought her to the whipping-post—being about mid-market, where was present some hundreds of people—I caused her to have twelve lashes; and at every third lash I parleyed with her and bid her tell all the women of the like calling wheresoever she came that the Mayor of Deal would serve them as he had served her, if they came to Deal and committed such wicked deeds as she had done. (Dabhoiwala 2012: 55)

In morally strict England, the *societies for reformation of manners*, a movement that also spread to other European countries until the eighteenth century, were generally favored (Hunt 1999). Environments that fostered prostitution were also targeted with greater vigor. Especially male pimps and female procuresses, but also innkeepers were discredited as debaucherous beneficiaries of temptation. Also attacked were all who supplied women from the countryside and lured them into the city with the promise of work opportunities or marriage, whereafter they were led into prostitution.

Love Magic and Sexual Initiation

Another aspect of the history of prostitution recedes slightly into the background in view of the economic and regulatory aspects: From the fifteenth to the seventeenth centuries, prostitutes were also regarded as women who not only knew the language and practices of love but were also specialists in love magic. A case from a small Italian town in 1573 can be considered symptomatic: The abbot of Sumaga in Friuli, Alessandro Ruis, complained about his former concubine Cecilia Padovana, with whom he had lived for years in full knowledge of the community. However, she had also gotten involved with other men—as her mother later testified—because she received too little support from the abbot and no nice clothes. According to Ruis, the much younger woman cast a love spell on him, an accusation which also came to the attention of the Sant' Uffizio of Inquisition in Venice and led to investigations. In the abbot's case, she had allegedly rubbed her palms with holy oil and in bed she would grasp his "male member" and say: "For this is my body"—an allusion to the transformation of the "Holy Host" and at the same time a magical manifestation of sexual bonding. Her separation from him had broken and emasculated him, which is why he needed her to return.

Another Roman case shows that such magical practices did not require the presence of the victim. In 1559, in investigations against a courtesan called "Lucretia the Greek," a maid testified that she picked up a cloth with which she had wiped herself after intercourse. She then burned the cloth while mumbling a spell. With this ritual she wanted to make one of her suitors, a papal servant, fall in love with her. Another time, she had a servant sweep the dust off the door of other prostitutes and collect it in order to transfer their good luck to her house (Cohen and Cohen 2000: 182f.). Scenes like these explain why, in cases of conflict and separation of whores, courtesans, and concubines, men liked to invoke witchcraft and presented themselves as victims of supernatural powers. The women were accused of getting to a man's body and heart by means of magnets, animal hearts, body fluids, or other magical mediators and had bewitched him with sexual desire and lovesickness. In Spanish erotic literature and in many of the writings there about prostitutes, they were metaphorically referred to as bees, thus dehumanizing them and placing them in the category of beasts (Kuffner 2020). In court, the men thus secured their advantageous position, which was difficult to refute in times of witchcraft (Ruggiero 2007: 71ff.).

These examples also show that prostitutes often possessed knowledge and skills that the suitors did not know from their wives. For young, unmarried men, who were the main clientele, there was another aspect that is hardly mentioned but which was not insignificant: As a sexual teacher, the prostitute introduced ignorant male virgins to their role as an active man and thus carried out a kind of sexual socialization, this being a service of sophisticated prostitutes, because the mean business was rather quick and hardly "romantic." The unofficial age of protection was probably around fourteen years; some younger boys, for example, got expelled from the women's house by the Ulm council in 1527. In 1532, the Basel clergymen wrote to their council, pointing out that young people in particular, and here again the apprentices and journeymen, would be corrupted by contact with shameless prostitutes and that for this reason alone, fornication should be prohibited and abolished. In doing so, they also stood up against a long-standing form of youth culture and socialization in which prostitution was part of sociability and pleasure for unmarried young men and their peer groups. At least the sexual side should be renounced from here on out (Schuster 1995: 252f.). In the sixteenth century, too, craft guilds monitored the whoring of their apprentices and journeymen and classified such behavior as contrary to the Christian way of life, which was a prerequisite for the advancement to master craftsman (Wiesner-Hanks 2000: 85). The Vienna *Handwerksordnungsbuch* (*Handicrafts Code*) of 1439 contained regulations forbidding contact with women of ill repute and common women of low birth. Cobblers should pay a fine if they were caught in a brothel near St Martin's Hospital near Widmer-Tor (Lutter 2021: 285).

For many young men, peer pressure was the legitimation to lose their innocence with a prostitute. This also applied to the sociability forms of students, who formed the main clientele in university towns such as Leiden (Roberts and Groenendijk 2004: 146). The Cologne jurist and councilor Hermann von Weinsberg (1518–1597) had had this experience as a student:

> In 1537, I was seduced for the first time when I entered the company of frivolous people.
>
> For, as good as all my journeymen with whom I lived and studied, as skilled, diligent and learned as they were, they still talked about beautiful women. One tells this, the other that, without shame, ugly and bold. So fornication was committed by the students, one of whom says that he had intercourse with this [woman], lay with her, slept with her. Another, how he had done it outside and inside [of the house].
>
> It was a clergyman who lived in Im Dall Street who told me how he had fornicated with harlots over and again. He asked me many and many things I didn't know anything about and told me about many evil things.

I was simple-minded, and yet I heard so much that I thought about and was angered by.

My colleagues often went to a *Buhlschaft* [whore].

Finally Master Joseph Goldberg took me to a place in Schemmersgasse, where an old woman lived whom he knew [a little better], and had her send for two silk spinners. They came quite quickly. We had drunk quite a lot before and he sent for [more] wine, so we drank even more. It was on the Day of David after the holy days of Christmas [December 30, 1537].

Here I must confess my sin and confess with St. David that I am woefully sorry.

For as we sat and drank there, it happened that I lost my virginity with one of them, named Trine Hoestirne, when I just turned 20 years old.

This was my first accident, that I came into in such troublesome company. Such a life does not please me well, because I think it is a cruel, unseemly act to live with such whores.

After that, when I was drunk, I boarded four or five more times with whores, which the socializing and drinking had made me do.

But since French pox or Spanish disease [syphilis] was still prevalent at that time, causing misery and harm to many people, I have to thank God Almighty for protecting me and have protected myself from the careless women, whores, whore teachers [procuresses] so that I was not harmed. (von Seggern 2012: 157)

Whorers, wages, practices

In the chastity regulations, criticism of the married clients, who were mostly called "whorers" (*Hurer*) in the German-speaking countries, intensified. One reason was that married persons should fulfil their marital obligations and not engage in extramarital relations. In many places, they were strictly forbidden to visit brothels and prostitutes. Jews were also not allowed to frequent Christian whores; the women would realize at the latest whom they were dealing with when confronted by a circumcised penis (Bonfil 2012: 101ff.). During raids, the police paid particular attention to these two groups. But their silence to higher authorities could be bought with a bribe. Similarly, Christian whores in Spain were forbidden to accept Muslim clients and faced the most severe punishments. In Venice, a Jew named Simeon was accused in 1514 after having slept with a whore in the district around the church of Santa Maria Mater Domini. In the verdict, it was said that in this way he had also defiled the Christian neighborhood, which earned him a sentence of two years in prison and a fine of 500 ducats (Ortega 2009: 81). Conversely, in the Kingdom of Valencia, Muslim prostitutes were not to accept Christian clients. In practice, however, the consequences were milder in such cases (Meyerson 1991: 220ff.). Muslim merchants, who were able to trade again in the lagoon city after the peace treaty between Venice and the Ottoman Empire from 1575, also enjoyed a degree of leniency. Prostitution was permitted in Venice and whores and foreign merchants were constantly crossing paths around the Rialto Bridge; so, sexual intercourse with a Muslim man was not welcome, but seems to have been quite common (Ortega 2009: 80f.).

Young men on a grand tour, journeys taken by the noblemen for educational purposes, also frequently vied for courtesans in cities such as Venice, Rome, and Paris. Relevant travel guides of the time detailed the "flirtatious ladies'" dress codes and offered pick-up phrases in the local language. In the travel novels they read in preparation, on the other hand, they also came across frightening stories in which cavaliers died of syphilis after their return, due to too many and too careless love affairs. The travel companions of the aristocratic youths were at any rate advised to make sure that their protégés had gained sexual experience but had not lost their hearts in the process, let alone entered into a clandestine marriage, which would then block parental marriage machinations (Stannek 2001: 239ff.).

In trading towns, merchants were among the most popular clients; in smaller towns, on trade and market days, peasants from the surrounding area would also seek love for money. They were joined by the usual clientele—apprentices, journeymen, students, and soldiers. The latter were accompanied by a considerable number of *vivandières* or *cantinières* (food and canteen women), civilian women who took care of provisions for an army in the field. They were responsible for the supply of goods and services, essentially cooking and cleaning. In 1494, the 20,000 mercenaries of the French king were followed by about 25,000 of them. In the late seventeenth century, only 15 *vivandières* were allowed per 100 soldiers in the French armies. Many of them were also active as "baggage whores" (Lynn 2008: 12f.). The wives of soldiers were also a problem, either because they were prostitutes in the troop or because they were forced to engage in transitory prostitution during the absence of their husbands for lack of other means of earning a living (Andersson 2021: 171) (Figure 17).

In port cities it was mainly seamen who brought their wages to the prostitutes. In cities like Amsterdam, Rotterdam, and Southampton in the sixteenth and seventeenth century, many women lived without their temporarily absent husbands and worked as prostitutes in the face of chronic poverty and lack of other sources of income (Schmidt 2020: 123ff.; Butler 2017). A typical meeting between the sailors and whores was reported in 1644 by Peter Hansen (*c.* 1624–1672) from North Schleswig, who arrived by ship at the age of about twenty in Amsterdam, at that time the third largest city in Europe. In his journal, he tells (a few years later) about the first day of his stay and the visit to a hostel outside the city walls. This inn soon turned out to be a brothel and was also situated at the gates because, since 1578, inner-city prostitution had been prohibited:

> On the 27th of August, Sunday, at the stroke of 7, I and my comrade went to see the city of Amsterdam, since he had known all the ways, he

FIGURE 17 Urs Graf (c. 1485–1528), *Two mercenary soldiers, a prostitute and death*, woodcut, 1524.

also walked outside the Hellewegß gate; there he brought us into an inn, yet obviously a whorehouse. The lady pointed us into a pleasure garden, behind the house, where my comrade asked for a pint of wine, when we were brought in, a madam who was so beautifully dressed up that some might have thought her a noblewoman. But when she came to us with the wine, she sat down with my comrade and asked him how he was doing and how so long he had done; she said he had a long way yet to go, as she saw it, he had God to thank. Meanwhile she grabs into his trousers and asked further how it is down there, and then starts embracing and kissing him. I, upon seeing that, sat astounded; I did not know what to think, because I was then still young and inexperienced in the thing. But as she left, I to my comrade said: "What is this for a [place]? I think you have brought me to a whorehouse." There he answers me: "Do you think differently? Let us be merry by day, and let us be merry with these maidens! There will come another one, even more beautiful than she. That one shall be for you." I said: "No, I don't want to stay here!" So, the whore comes again, bringing, as she thought, me one too. They sit down with us, start kissing and grabbing. But as I sat still and was bothered, the whore asked me if I lacked anything. I said: "No!" Then she began to take me also in her arms, and because I had no use for such and did not believe her, I struck her by the head with one fist, so that she fell at the table on to the ground. My comrade was [too] enraged about this, saying: "You are not upright in beating this picture of a woman." I answer: "I have struck a frivolous whore; and she that is more despicable than I, I am no better than a wicked man. I'll never keep such company!" So, I paid for the wine and left. But as I entered the [Hellewegß] gate again, I could not find the way back to my lodgings, nor did know the name of my inn, nor the road; so, when I had spent a whole day in the city, I came to the old West Indian house for dinner and remembered so that I returned to my lodgings, but would not keep my comrade thereafter. (von Seggern 2014: 538)

It is irrelevant whether Hansen's records are authentic or fictional. They provide an insight into the customs of prostitution and its social and cultural embedding: the joint visit to the brothel, the associated strategies of justification—one is seduced into this milieu or had unknowingly been gotten into it—the fascination of the unusual beauty and special presentation of the ladies and the spatial marginalization of the scene (here beyond the city walls).

In the sources that have been handed down, there are also details of the average whore's wage, which usually neither the prostitutes nor the brothel owners got rich from, but were able to live on. In Amsterdam in the second half of the seventeenth century, the public prostitutes charged an average of one to two shillings (or 0.05 to 0.1 florins) for sex; the daily wage of a worker was about one florin, ten to twenty times that. A visit to a brothel was usually accompanied by expenses for food and drink, a room or bed allowance, and possibly tips. The streetwalkers cost the least. They had to balance their per capita income with a high turnover of clients. In a middle-priced whorehouse, an inmate would thus earn a weekly wage of about six to eight guilders, which was equivalent to that of a skilled worker and two to three times higher than the wage a woman could expect for honest work. However, the prostitutes had to hand over about half of this to the brothel operators for expenses, furnishings, lodging, or even debts (van de Pol 2006: 201ff.).

A confession by Ursula Belzenhofer from Constance in the seventeenth century reveals a mixture of money and wages in kind. It also describes the clients typical of urban prostitution. Belzenhofer had already started fornication at the age of fourteen, namely with a porter boy and another boy who had climbed into her chamber and promised her marriage. After her marriage, she was occasionally forced to sell her body due to poverty, among others with the following suitors: an old watch-master, the bailiff, the former city captain, a sulfur burner, students, journeymen, the brother of a grocer, and the well master, whereby she received just one kreutzer for a quick *standling*, from some clients three or, rarely, even nine kreutzer. From a married man she got a pound of pork instead of cash, and the old baker Johannes Waibel also paid in kind. He took Ursula to his back room on a carnival,

> and exposed her above and below, and pressed her on the *Lotlerbetl* [wiggling bed], and did so with unsparing touch and attack, until he poured out his seed in great quantity into the parlors, and promised her in return to waive her debts for flour and milk, and to wipe it (her debts) at the table (Rublack 1998: 219).

In order to be able to carry on their business regularly, prostitutes tried to avoid getting pregnant to the extent possible. The contraceptive measures and means known from earlier times changed little until the seventeenth century, and the borderline with abortion also remained fluid. Italian poet Pietro Aretino (1492–1556), in one of his plays, had a courtesan say about aphrodisiacs and contraception: "I experimented with as many herbs as would fill two meadows" (Riddle 1992: 156). Knowledge about herbal contraceptives and abortion was not only passed on orally but also through herbalists and midwifery books. In the German edition of Brunfels' *Kräuterbuch* (*Book of Herbs*), which appeared in Strasbourg from 1532 to 1537, for example, thirty-one plants with abortive effects were still mentioned (Leibrock-Plehn 1993: 77f.). It was not until the eighteenth century that this popular body of knowledge faded into the background due to the scientific-medical revolution.

In Cologne in 1629, a prostitute testified that she had used "savin juniper and other things to drive out the fruit" (Jütte 1989: 224). Among the abortive remedies, the savin juniper continued to occupy a prominent position. According to the Protestant preacher doctor Hieronymus Bock (1498–1554), it was used especially by "old witches" and whores. In his *Kreuter Buch* (1539) he reported: "In the end they seduce the young whores/ give them pulverized seven palms [savin juniper] powder/ or drink on top/ so that they may be corrupted by children" (Leibrock-Plehn 1993: 78). In addition to prostitutes, midwives acted as disseminators of knowledge and, where appropriate, introduced such practices to respectable women. Clients and suitors probably also spread ideas about the right way to perform sexual intercourse and possible sexual positions to avoid pregnancy. While primarily vaginal intercourse with prostitutes was still the most common way in early modern times, the common women did take active part in acts that decent wives considered indecent. Non-vaginal practices, however, such as oral stimulation and anal intercourse, were still considered unnatural, even by whores and called for a considerable extra charge.

Lyndal Roper and others have drawn attention to an important aspect of the Protestant approach to prostitution, which has also led to a change in the sexual perception of women. While prostitutes represented a separate type of dishonorable woman in urban society in the Late Middle Ages, the new chastity regime focused on the public as well as private moral conditions of *all* women, regardless. Whether premarital or extramarital coitus or sexual disorder in the conjugal bed, women who allowed or even initiated such lewd relationships were considered bawdy and shameless. In view of the strict paradigm of morality and sin, quite a few were paraded out and punished in public. Although the chastity regulations and penal laws also addressed and sanctioned the immoral behavior of men, women were regarded as the real temptresses and (main) culprits of sexual offences. This argumentation was heard in paternity suits as well as in premarital and extramarital sexual offences. In all these cases, the men liked to portray themselves as victims of female eroticism, against which they were as helpless as the sexual advances of a whore (Roper 1994: 40ff.; Burghartz 1992).

Prostitution in the Ottoman Empire

In the Ottoman Empire, the legal provisions on prostitution were also influenced by religion and patriarchal power relations. Islamic culture had a clear basic position: If a person committed *zina*, sexual intercourse outside marriage or concubinage, if he was free, a Muslim, and married, he should be stoned to death. Slaves, non-Muslims, or unmarried persons faced 100 lashes. This also applied to whores and their clientele. However, the circumstances under which such a severe or even capital punishment could be imposed for an act of *zina* were so specific that it was almost impossible to implement. The deed—that is, the penetration—had to have been observed by at least four male Muslim eyewitnesses with a good reputation or the accused had to repeat their confession at least four times without coercion, a high bar indeed: As far as is known, no prostitute was ever stoned for this reason (Yilmaz 2016: 256f.). This opened up considerable leeway for the courts. In most cases, prostitutes and men who fornicated with them were not punished according to the draconian rules, but only had to leave the neighborhood—which was often also responsible for making their deeds known—or face a fine or disgraceful punishment. This was possible because they were sanctioned according to the principle of *istihsan*, which allowed the doctrine to be adapted to customary law.

As in Christian Europe, it was assumed in the Ottoman Empire, too, that prostitution had to be tolerated, because only it could spare the respectable women from the lusty hunger of unmarried men (Leiser 2017: ch. 5). Islamic legal scholars of the sixteenth to eighteenth centuries also came up with argumentation that established an analogy between prostitution and legal forms of sexual intercourse, such as conjugal intercourse and coitus between a slave and her owner. The latter form was then also based on a financial exchange, the first by paying a bride price, the other by buying the slave. In both cases, the man purchased the right to sexual intercourse. Prostitution corresponded to this trade relationship, because here, too, sexual intercourse had to be paid for and a man temporarily acquired a woman for her sexual services (Baldwin 2012: 125).

Mut'a, a contractual temporary marriage, was also a way to legalize a relationship with a prostitute without giving her the status of a real wife for a time. Finally, female slaves were also hired out by their owners for sexual purposes. In the legal code laid down by Sulieman I (1494/96–1566), one such a scenario is found:

> Some slave traders, paying a somehow higher rent to innkeepers, bring dancers and other concubines and make them entertain the customers of the inn. (. . .) Sometimes a customer makes a nominal purchase of a concubine, who stays with him as long as he remains in the inn; when he is to go, the trader buys her back a few aspers [Ottoman coin] cheaper. (Sariyannis 2008: 59)

Evidence of tolerated fornication can also be found in some Ottoman cities where a whore tax was levied. In contrast to Christian Europe and especially the Catholic regions, however, there was no general regulation of prostitution, for example in the form of banishment to certain districts or barracking them in urban brothels (Semerdjian 2008: 101ff.; Sabev 2021: 25ff.). Sultan Selim II (1524–1574) issued a decree in 1567 in which he not only ordered the closure of the beer and wine taverns in Eyüp, a district of Constantinople, but also prohibited prostitution there. Three years later, he took action against laundresses who not only cleaned the clothes of unmarried men but also offered sexual services (Andrews and Kalpakli 2005: 281ff.). In Constantinople in the sixteenth century, prostitution was forbidden only during Ramadan, the month of fasting. Some other cities took a stricter stance against fornication and wanted to force the Muslim culture upon territories they had conquered. The Ottoman historian Evliya Çelebi (1611–1683), for example, reports of Melek Ahmed Pasha (1588–1662), the governor of Rumelia (the part of the Ottoman Empire located on the Balkan Peninsula), that he had banished all prostitutes from Sofia in 1652. In order to emphasize his decree, some women were hung, as chandeliers in the silk market to "reform the world." After Çelebi, the dignitaries of the city thanked him for the peace and quiet that followed, while the "rogues and brigands" thought that the city's resources for their carnal pleasures were now running out and that a venereal epidemic was imminent (Kia 2011: 205).

When prostitution was practiced on a large scale or commercially, the Ottoman Empire usually threatened harsh punishments, as the inquiry to a *mufti* in the seventeenth century and his subsequent *fatwa* revealed:

> If a group, travelling from village to village, makes a habit of inducing their wives and daughters and slave girls to commit zinā', what is necessary according to the sharī'a?

Answer: After they have all been beaten severely they should be imprisoned until such time as their uprightness has become apparent. Any of the wives proven to have committed zinā' should be stoned. (Baldwin 2012: 131)

The legal sources also call for a relatively strict approach to pimping, procuring, and the criminal environment of prostitution. Potential perpetrators were often tavern owners, brothel operators, and repeat "infidels," that is, Jews and Christians, who were allegedly increasingly involved in the fornication business. In practice the brothels were often run by madams. A popular workplace for whores was also the *hammam*, where visitors could meet interested women or were referred to them (Sariyannis 2008: 55ff.). Meanwhile, respectable bathhouses paid attention to a strict separation of the sexes (Ze'evi 2006: 112). If one believes the (often exaggerated) descriptions in European traveler's journals, up to 4,000 privately run brothels were reported in Constantinople at the beginning of the seventeenth century, despite the prohibition. This number is probably too high but nevertheless testifies to the mass occurrence of this institution. Some neighborhoods, such as in Constantinople Beyoğlu, Galata and Cihangir, stood out for their particular accumulation and had problems separating respectable women and whores. If they were not distinguishable by their clothing, the latter could usually be recognized by the fact that they drew attention to themselves through cosmetic tricks and signaled to men through their active presence and exchange of glances that they were interested in sexual contact (Boyar 2016: 210ff.).

Cases of judicial prosecution of fornication are found relatively rarely in the archives, because the parties involved were not interested in accusing each other of such an offence in view of the threatened penalties, and the legal evidence was scant. In the case of charges which nevertheless ended up in court, the vice police was usually informed by the neighborhood, who had caught the whores in *(crimen) flagrante*. Even in these cases, there was a tendency toward fines, which went so far that the cities regarded the income and taxes from prostitution as a *zina* levy to be paid in advance and made their amount dependent on the financial situation of the woman (Sariyannis 2008: 40). In addition to monetary punishments, shaming was also imposed; whores would be pilloried or tied onto the back of a donkey with the neighborhood looking on, gloating. They were then banned from the quarter or town for a certain period of time.

The spectrum of clientele proved to be diverse in the cities of the Ottoman Empire: An important group were the Janissaries, elite soldiers, who were allowed to marry from 1566 onward, but remained single for many years of their lives and therefore visited prostitutes. Since the middle of the fifteenth century, these well-trained soldiers were recruited (or kidnapped) as boys in large numbers in the subjugated Christian areas of the Balkans, Islamized, and trained for years, then forced to live in barracks and prepare for war. Some who additionally spent their pay on prostitutes were the normal soldiers, who joined the army troop only during campaigns. In port cities, the whores sought clients among the sailors, at the Golden Horn, for example, in the city of Galata opposite Constantinople on the European side. According to the historian Çelebi, in the 1630s there was a proper amusement district with a range of offers for all tastes:

> Along the edge of the sea and at Ortahisar are two hundred multi-storied taverns for the dissolute. Each one caters to five or six hundred depraved people devoted to pleasure and drinking. There is such a tumult with singing and music that it defies description (Leiser 2017: 230).

Just to the north, in Ortaköy, also located on the Bosporus, *hammams* specialized in "public women," either addressing them as bathing visitors or to serve as a contact exchange. As everywhere in ports, not only sailors but also widely traveled merchants showed up there. In addition, there were the usual mix of craftsmen, students, and married men in all the towns.

Syphilis, a New Venereal Disease?

Throughout Europe, prostitutes in the sixteenth century also fell into disrepute because they spread the new French disease and thus endangered the health of the community. Even before the appearance of this very serious and usually fatal disease, brothels had been closed during plague outbreaks to avoid any form of overcrowding and contact with foul vapors. It was soon suspected that the French disease was transmitted during sexual intercourse—however, it was not clear for a long time whether this was only due to physical proximity or direct genital contact. Infected persons were easily identifiable due to ulcers, which contributed to their public stigmatization. Albrecht Dürer gave a depiction of one such pockmarked person in 1496, already, and associated his pitiful condition with a particular constellation of stars. This was in line with the common opinion of many scholars that a certain planetary position—on the command of God—had led to foul miasms (vapors from the ground, which are spread with the air) and that these in turn disturbed the complexion of the humors of the human body. The humanist Ulrich von Hutten (1488–1523), who himself fell ill with the French disease, saw one of the main causes in the polluted and rotten air, which he thought had been caused by a special star constellation in tandem with a solar eclipse (Stein 2003: 49f.; Walter 2003).

Until recently, it was assumed that syphilis—in today's bacteriological model, the disease caused by *Treponema pallidum*—first appeared in Europe in 1493 (Arrizabalaga 2005: 8 et seq.; Harper et al. 2011). However, genetic and anthropological studies in recent years have shown that this strain or a similar one existed in Europe before that (Baker et al. 2020; Majander

2020). If these findings are confirmed, the symptoms of the disease were in any case assigned differently in the Middle Ages or even in antiquity (especially to leprosy) or the bacterium caused a much weaker clinical picture. One of the explanations for the syphilis epidemic of the following decades assumes that the bacterium mutated into an aggressive variant at the end of the fifteenth century. Another explanation is that the bacterium was brought to Europe from the west coast of Africa by seafarers in the course of the fifteenth century and also mutated here. Even before the gene analyses, archeopathological examinations of bones from medieval graves showed typical signs of degeneration of late syphilis (Crosby 2003: 123ff.; Harper et al. 2011; Armelagos, Zuckerman and Harper 2012; Lopez 2017).

In any case, it is a fact that at the end of the fifteenth century, syphilis symptoms appeared frequently and were diagnosed. Rodrigo Ruiz Diaz de Isla (1462–1542) observed the symptoms as early as 1493 among the crew of one of the ships that accompanied Columbus on his second voyage to America. In this sense, the disease came to Europe from the New World as part of the widespread Columbian Exchange. Upon their first return to Spain, the debarking sailors imported it to the Mediterranean ports. In February 1495, the mercenary army of the French King Charles VIII (1470–1498)—some 20,000 men, including 8,000 Swiss—came into contact with the disease when it took and occupied Naples. When the troops were billeted there for months, lively sexual contacts with prostitutes resulted in the first major outbreak of syphilis (Quétel 1990: 9ff.). In July 1495, after the battle of Fornovo south of Parma, Italian doctors diagnosed typical painful pustules under the foreskin of Charles' soldiers; in addition, those affected complained of pains in the arms and legs, followed by larger ulcers on the skin (Poirier 2005: 157).

From then, the symptoms were called French or Neapolitan or Italian disease. The respective ascriptions changed according to origin, which is why the English and Germans spoke of the former, the French of the latter (Cady 2005). From Italy, syphilis spread northwards through the mercenaries' countries of origin. In the summer of 1496, it was registered in numerous German towns (Jütte 1996: 97). Syphilis spread rapidly across Europe and beyond along trade and pilgrimage routes and shipping lanes, becoming the first globalized infectious disease (Webb 2015: 54f.). As archaeological bone findings in the Augustinian monastery of Skriðuklaustur in eastern Iceland prove, it reached even the most remote regions of Europe between 1496 and 1554 (Kristjánsdóttir 2011); for European Russia, the disease is documented for the middle of the sixteenth century (Buzhilova 1999). Along with it also wandered the narrative that the French disease was God's punishment for the allegedly increasing immorality and sinfulness. As the physician and astrologer Joseph Grünpeck (c. 1473–c. 1530) put it in his writing *Ein Hübscher Tractat von dem Ursprung des Bösen Franzos* (*A neat treatise on the French evil*) (1496): "Three major sins are from which all other sins originate. So there are three tortures for punishing man. The three sins are.

Pride. Greed. Unchastity. But the punishments are. Pestilence. Bloodshed. and hunger" (Boehrer 1990: 202).

Initially, around 1500, no direct connection between sexual intercourse and an infection was suspected. Only in the 1520s did this cause come to the fore (Arrizabalaga 2005: 34). In the French translation of a medical-surgical work by Giovanni da Vigo (*c.* 1450–1525), it was first stated in 1525 that the disease was "fundamentally contagious through association with a vile and impure woman or, in contrast, an impure man with a woman who exercises the pleasures of Venus; and it arises primarily in the private members of man and woman" (Poirier 2005: 159). *Morbus Venereus* (disease of Venus) or *Lues Venera* (disease of Venus) was first mentioned by the physician Jacques de Béthencourt in 1527 (Walter 2003: 171). The Italian physician Girolamo Fracastoro (1476/1478–1553) then gave the disease its modern name in 1530 with his teaching poem *Syphilis sive Morbus gallicus* (*Syphilis or the French disease [Gallic Death]*) (Vons and Gourevitch 2012). The poem's first stanza aptly describes the spread of the illness:

Within the purple womb of night, a slave,
The strangest plague returned to sear the world.
Infecting Europe's breast, the scourge was hurled
From Lybian cities to the Black Sea's wave.
When warring France would march on Italy,
It took her name. I consecrate my rhymes
To this unbidden guest of twenty climes,
Although unwelcomed, and eternally.

(Fracastoro 1934)

In this poem, he had the Greek shepherd Syphilis appear as the first to be punished with this disease by Apollo for having offended him. The term syphilis did not become generally accepted, however, until the second half of the eighteenth century. Until then, the French disease, the *Great Pox*, or the generally referred to venereal disease was still on people's tongues. In any case, the vagueness of these terms is an indication that it was often a rather colorful complex of symptoms—consisting of other venereal illnesses as well—and that, on the basis of the descriptions in the sources, it is not always certain whether authors were actually describing syphilis caused by the bacterium *Treponema pallidum* (Siena 2012: 464; Arrizabalaga, Henderson and French 1997: 1ff.).

Fracastoro was also the first to postulate an infection by *seminaria morbi* (sick germs), thus deviating somewhat from the miasm theory put forward by Hippocrates of Kos (around 460–375 BCE). The majority of scholars, however, continued to adhere to the latter. The causes of the disease were therefore manifold: As so often in the Galenic humoral teachings, disease vectors were sought in wrong, too little, or too much food, as well as in the disruption of the bodily complexion through direct or indirect contact with the bodily fluids of a sick person, through poisonous sweat, for instance, or saliva, semen, and urine, which also settled in clothing or bedding. Poisoning through bad evaporation could also occur through dishes and cutlery or through food shared with the sick person. In bathing parlors, the miasmas must penetrate the victims particularly easily via the humid, heated air. Newborns could also supposedly get the vapors at birth from their mother. Finally, sexual comingling was suspected, since the body heated up intensely during intercourse and thus the poisons could penetrate unhindered via the open skin pores (Stein 2003: 64f.).

Jacques de Béthencourt had the idea that the male and female seed degenerated in the uterus into a dangerous poison, in the case of the *pox*, by mixing in unequal proportions or when the male seed comes into contact with menstrual blood, which also had fatal consequences. Another contemporary theory said that syphilis had originated in Naples because menstruating whores comingled there with lepers, and leprous Neapolitan women comingled with French mercenaries, and evil developed in their wombs (Foa 1990: 39). Because prostitutes had evil bodily and humoral substances, they were considered an incubator for a variety of diseases, including ulcers, fistulas, smallpox, and, of course, syphilis. The Italian physician Aurelius Minadoi said in 1596 that the French disease occurred in whores because the sperm from several men mixed in their uterus, resulting in poisoning (Siena 2012: 466). For the Lutheran preacher Andreas Hoppenrod (?–1584), prostitutes even committed murder by poisoning, which the devil would have selected them for by spreading syphilis. In his writing *Wider den Huren Teufel* (*Against the whores' devil*) (1565), he demanded "that one good company should warn the other, for such a French whore . . . can poison the children of good people and is therefore to be counted as a murderer much more eagerly than a poisoner" (Walter 2003: 171). For the most part, the illness was understood as God's punishment for an unchaste life at the very least and as a call for a complete moral reversal.

In view of the multitude of projections associated with the French disease, non-Christians, heretics and foreign people also came into play: Sephardic Jews were accused of having brought syphilis from Spain when they were expelled in 1492. The real source of the disease was rumored to be their country of origin, because of their unChristian activities. Others thought of the horror stories about the sexual misconduct of *Native Americans*, who (allegedly) practiced polygamy, incest, and gender blurring—all circumstances that could be considered the cause of semen spoilage and low resistance to pathogenic fumes. A further factor was that the "Indians" were supposedly on a lower level of humanity and were closer to the animals, which is why a human–animal mixture developed among them and from this the monstrous epidemic developed (Siena 2012: 465). In France, syphilis became the hot potato of religious disputes, as both Catholics and Protestants used the syphilis narrative and the presumed origin of the disease from the savages and cannibals to accuse the other side of lacking sexual self-control, which endangered the divine order (Losse 2015).

The horrors of syphilis were also at the center of a fictional conversation about "The Unequal Marriage," which appeared in the *Colloquia* of Erasmus of Rotterdam in 1518/19. The story is about the "leprous and purulent" wedding of an older man with a young beautiful woman. The bridegroom suffered from "the Mange, which has no proper Name to it, tho' indeed it has a great many . . . A very proud Distemper, that won't strike Sail to the Leprosy, the Elephantine Leprosy, Tetters, the Gout, or Ringworm, if there was to be an Engagement between them." The syphilitic's appearance was described as follows:

> In the mean Time out comes our blessed Bridegroom with his Snub-Nose, dragging one Leg after him, but not so cleverly neither as the Switzers do; itchy Hands, a stinking Breath, heavy Eyes, his Head bound up with a Forehead-Piece, and a Running at his Nose and Ears . . . for his Breath is rank Poison, what he speaks is Pestilence, and what he touches mortifies. . . . This Pox is more infectious and destructive than the worst of Leprosies: It invades on a sudden, goes off, and rallies again, and frequently kills at last; while the Leprosy will sometimes let a Man live, even to extreme old Age. (Erasmus 1878: 157; Trog 2016: 31ff.)

Erasmus paints the figure in a sinister light, associating French disease with social fringe groups: "he's a great Gamester, he'll drink down any Body, a vile Whoremaster, the greatest Artist in the World at bantering and lying, a notable Cheat, pays no Body, revels prodigally; and in short, whereas there are but seven liberal Sciences taught in the Schools, he's Master of more than ten liberal ones."

Finally, he made suggestions as to what should be done with such sick people so that their evil would not spread further. As for women with the disease: "I'd padlock them up [with a chastity belt]. That's one Way, indeed, to prevent us from having more of the Breed." For the men, he recommended castration as the best preventive measure, possibly combined with seclusion or even execution, for

> [e]ven those that are castrated, have an itching Desire upon them; nor is the Infection convey'd by one Way only, but by a Kiss, by Discourse, by a Touch, or by drinking with an infected Party. And we find also, that there is a certain malicious Disposition of doing Mischief peculiar to this Distemper, that whosoever has it, takes a Delight to propagate it to as many as he can, tho' it does him no good. Now if they be only separated, they may flee to other Places, and may either by Night impose upon Persons, or on them that do not know them. But there can be no Danger from the Dead. (Erasmus 1878: 163; Trog 2016: 38)

Mercury Cure and Pox Houses

The treatment of syphilis fell under several responsibilities, mainly those of doctors, surgeons, and apothecaries. In addition to the usual measures for restoring physical homeostasis, the use of mercury salts by means of pastes and sweating baths lasting for days were the remedies of choice (Stein 2003; Gienow 2006: 119ff.; Henderson 2021: 32ff.). Alternatively, a decoction was administered from the expensive guaiac wood (the so-called French or pock wood). The Spaniards had learned about this medication from the Maya culture and brought it back with them to Europe. The Augsburg Fuggers subsequently made an excellent business out of importing this wood. Since such cures were very expensive, the poorer patients had no choice but to ask for admission to one of the *Blatternhäuser* (pox houses), where, as in Augsburg, treatment was free or very cheap. The patients of these institutions were not allowed to leave during the course of the therapy in order to avoid spreading harmful miasms among the people, and it would be a long time yet before people figured out that the disease was spread through sexual intercourse.

Marketplaces also offered all kinds of self-medications—which people learned about by word of mouth or in collections of home remedies. One prescription concocted by the city physician of Eschwege, Georg Freund (*c.* 1523–1593), for example, provided for a potion that "drives the French disease out from within, without smears [topical pastes], smoke or soaking, and betakes [away] the yellow color from their faces" (Jütte 2013: 46f.). One cure, obviously fatal from what we know now, was the hope some men had to get rid of syphilis by way of counteracting its very means of infection: coitus with a healthy woman. The logic was that if they got it from a whore, they could get rid of it with a pure virgin, or a black woman, Ethiopians being particularly popular. The idea was that the disease or the disease-causing vapors and humors were then transferred to her (Terpstra 2010: 164ff.).

The efforts and agonies that a syphilitic person had to go through in the sixteenth century for treatment are illustrated by the case of Francesco Maria Marconi, who appeared before the medical tribunal of the city of Mantua on March 1, 1581, with the following complaint: He had suffered from severe headaches and typical syphilis symptoms during the winter and had come across a leaflet posted in the town apothecary, which a friend had read to him. There the medical practitioner Guiseppe dell'Isola promised that he could treat all ailments, especially the pain of the *morbus gallico*. Marconi went to see the doctor in a room in town and paid two gold scudi (a very considerable sum) in advance for the treatment. In return, he received pills and three sachets of powder, which he had to take on various occasions, and three different syrups to drink over a period of about thirty days. Dell'Isola performed a bloodletting on his left arm and left foot, which caused him considerable weakness. Afterward, Marconi wanted his money back because he hadn't seen any improvement. Instead, he was further prescribed cupping glasses on his left breast—on the ulcers—and a mixture of herbs was prescribed three times. In the end, he felt "as death" and broke off treatment because he was afraid of completely ruining his health (Gentilcore 2005: 57).

Ulrich van Hutten (1488–1523), the famous humanist who died of the illness, also suffered through a mercury cure himself and studied its effects:

> After they were smeared with the mercury cream, the sick were taken to a 'hot room', which was heated continuously and very strongly, some for twenty days, others for thirty days; some even longer. No sooner was the sick man lying in the grease than he began to feel weak in a strange way. The ointment was of such power that it drove the sick from the furthest part of the body into the mouth and from there upwards to the brain. Therefore, the disease flowed out through the throat and mouth with such a great and enormous damage that the teeth which were not sitting firmly in the mouth fell out. Everyone's throat, tongue and palate swelled, the gums swelled, the teeth wobbled, saliva flowed out of the mouth incessantly, from the very beginning terribly smelly and so infectious that it immediately contaminated and sullied everything. Therefore, the lips wetted with it also became ulcerous and the inside of the cheeks sore. The whole dwelling stank, and this kind of cure was so hard that most people would rather die than be cured in this way. Many were attacked in the brain in such a way that they got dizzy, others became raving mad. Then not only the hands trembled, but also the feet and the whole body, the speech became stammering, for some it was no longer curable. I have seen many perished in the middle of the cure. . . . Only a few have ever recovered, and even these only through this risk, this bitterness and this suffering. (Gienow 2006: 120f.)

With the limited success of the therapies, the cities took drastic measures to isolate and care for the sick: Frankfurt, Augsburg, and other imperial cities ordered the sick to be sealed off and for others to avoid contact with them. The taverns and restaurants were forbidden to serve guests with signs of the illness. Bathing establishments had to exercise extreme care. Some of the wicked institutions were closed, in others more emphasis was placed on cleanliness and sick people were denied entry. In the public brothels of Valencia, two doctors were tasked with examining the women weekly for venereal diseases. In 1512, a special room was set up in the hospital there to investigate cases (Berco 2011: 789). Hospitals already existed for the care and custody of leprosy and other epidemic patients. These were located away from other settlements and were mostly financed by the cities. These ultimately opened their doors to French patients as well. Individual benefactors, such as the Strasbourg preacher Geiler von Kaysersberg (1445–

1510), also made sure more pox houses were established (Jütte 1996: 105). These operations were financed through grants, foundations, and fees paid by sick people, as well as by benefactors and subsidies from the city council. Even the general hospitals opened special departments, and church institutions and religious brotherhoods took care of patients. In Venice, women's convents and brothels were converted into infection prevention facilities. Arrested prostitutes would be admitted, alongside many who decided to go to an institution themselves. New facilities for this were placed on the island of Giudecca to keep them away from the city, and to save costs (McGough 2010: 112ff.). Ecclesiastical and municipal institutions emerged from the Christian Caritas organizations for the poor, the needy, and the sick, but were also intended as disciplinary measures to sanction immoral population groups, like prostitutes and their clients, and to encourage them to repent.

Syphilis as an Endemic Plague

For the purpose of prevention, the Italian anatomist and surgeon Gabriele Falloppio (1523–1562) suggested in *De morbo Gallico* that when visiting a prostitute suffering from venereal disease, clients should tie a small linen bag soaked in a special ointment around their penis and thus avoid direct physical contact. In addition, they would have to wash their genitals after coitus in order to cleanse them of harmful vapors (Gentilcore 2005: 60f.). In the sixteenth and seventeenth centuries, dried animal intestines (from sheep, for example) were recommended for intercourse with a prostitute, which were moistened to soften them before use. The poet James Boswell (1740–1795) called his condom his "machine" and *armour* and even soaked it in the pond of St James' Park in London before use (Jütte 2008: 98f.). In 1600, the doctor and surgeon Pedro de Torres prescribed in his popular book that after intercourse with a sick prostitute one should not only clean the genitals but also urinate properly so as to prevent the French disease. Women practiced self-care by inserting a piece of cotton fabric dipped in hot water into the vagina after coitus with a syphilitic man (Berco 2016: 116f.).

The medical and cultural treatment of the French disease changed over the course of the sixteenth century. In the beginning, the doctors had been helpless in the face of the new epidemic coming from outside, but after a while they had a proven treatment with mercury and *guaiacum* (guaiac wood), and thought that they could cure or at least alleviate syphilis. By the seventeenth century, a standard procedure existed for treatment. In the two London hospitals of St Bartholomew and St Thomas, those treated for a venereal disease, such as syphilis, gonorrhea, etc., accounted for about 20 percent of patients between 1622 and 1666. They were treated with mercury paste in separate "foul camps" for an average stay of forty days. For sick people who could not be cured or whose symptoms reappeared—in the tertiary stage after three to five years—infirmaries were built in which they died (Siena 2004: 69ff.).

Moreover, from the second half of the sixteenth century, it was believed that *gallicus disease* had mutated into an old and attenuated disease that could be controlled medically. This did not mean that the majority of cases treated at the pox house in Strasbourg in the 1550s didn't nevertheless end in death—not infrequently due to the painful and dangerous "smear cure" (Jütte 1996: 112). From that time, syphilis was considered an endemic venereal disease that could be domesticated and kept under control with medical and moral policing measures. Therefore, doctors blamed patients for the incurable cases. In the public eye, ulcers and scars continued to be considered a symptomatic stigma of promiscuous women and unrestrained men (McGough 2010: 4ff.).

Another problem was the large number of young unmarried sick men who wanted to marry after treatment or (temporary) healing and thus infected their future spouses. This also applied to aristocratic women who were infected by their husbands, who in turn came into contact with syphilis through courtesans and prostitutes. As paleopathological studies on bone lesions have shown, there is probably a larger number of unreported cases among women who, like Maria Salviati (1499–1543), the wife of Giovanni de' Medici, may have died as a result of the "secret illness" (Fornaciari et al. 2020).

For the inmates of the Hospital de Santiago in Toledo, Spain, who were suffering from the French disease, there are data on the civil status of the persons for the years 1654 to 1665 which allow certain conclusions to be drawn. Among the 953 patients from the city, about 70 percent were men and 30 percent women, of whom about 50 percent and 34 percent were single. Thus, among the urban men, single as well as married and widowed (mainly) prostitutes were infected. Among the women, however, infection by the husband dominated—although the proportion of married prostitutes remains unclear. Among the 3,006 patients from outside the country, men dominated with 80 percent, 64 percent of whom were single. Of the out-of-town women admitted to the hospital, the proportion of single women (41 percent) was significantly higher than among those living in the city. Both are an indication that premarital relationships continued to be widespread in the countryside even after the reform efforts of the Council of Trent, and that young women also became infected during premarital intercourse. In Toledo, a bishop's see and Inquisition headquarters, however, the moral guidelines of the church and the corresponding efforts of the priests had a heightened effect. Single men who suffered from the French disease and were undergoing treatment had much worse prospects on the marriage market. The proportion of those who remained unmarried for life was disproportionately high. Of those who nevertheless stepped up to the altar, many were found to have high social prestige and above-average economic backgrounds (Berco 2016: 105ff.).

One stigma of the French disease was that at a late stage it caused deformities in the face. It was characteristic that the nose fell in, the eyes and lips were eaten up, and the teeth fell out—some of this was also a result of the mercury cure. In order to cover up the particularly conspicuous deformation of the nose, artificial noses were crafted that could be worn, some being quite decorative. The Italian surgeon and anatomist Gaspare Tagliacozzi (1546–1599) proposed a plastic surgery operation as early as 1597, in which a nose could be reconstructed from a flap of skin on the upper arm within five months (Pitts-Taylor 2008: 372). Images of these horrors soon echoed in painting and graphic art. The deterrent body images symbolized the danger of sexual intercourse with prostitutes. Thus, the aforementioned man disfigured by the French disease, whom Albrecht Dürer immortalized in 1496 on a woodcut, also had a deterrent effect. Rembrandt portrayed the Dutch painter Gerard de Lairesse (1641–1711) around 1665–67, whose deformed facial features were apparently caused by inherited syphilis (Haverkamp-Begemann 1998).

The Erotic Regime of Art and Literature

Culture of the Erotic Gaze

While such graphic depictions were primarily tried to paint the negative consequences of lewd sexual life as a deterrent, Renaissance art and literature for the most part were more interested in the eroticization and sexualization of the visual language and the naked human form. In the fifteenth and sixteenth centuries, one had to walk a fine line between acceptable allusions and metaphors and lewd motifs and scenes. Indeed, censorship was increasingly practiced on unchaste writings and illustrations in the strict regime of the Reformers. With the *Index auctorum et librorum prohibitorum*, also known as the Roman Index, a papal body was empowered to take action against heretical literature as well as (possibly) unchaste texts and images from 1559 onward (Green and Karolides 2005: 258). The Council of Trent (1545–1563) defined the borderlines:

> Books which self-avowedly treat, tell or teach frivolous or lewd things are forbidden completely, since not only faith but also morals which are thoughtlessly corrupted by the reading of books of this kind are to be taken into consideration. Those who possess them are to be severely punished by the bishops. Yet the old books written by pagans are permitted for the elegance and beauty of their presentation, but should not be used in the teaching of naves. (Hütt 1990: 10)

Medical and religious representations as well as those that met the criteria of classical Greek-Roman aesthetics were thus spared the ban. The (semi-) naked gods and the women seduced by them could still be depicted as these belonged to the mythological motives of that ancient aesthetic. Nevertheless, the censorship offices ceaselessly tried to stop all distribution of lewd and unchaste publications and prints. Their avidity was necessary in so far as erotic writings and pictures could be reproduced quite easily in Europe due to the invention of moveable type letterpress printing by goldsmith Johannes Gutenberg (c. 1400–1468) in Mainz, Germany. Now erotic works were no longer available only to the courtly elite and wealthy patricians; a somewhat broader section of the population could get their hands on such things, too (Findlen 1994: 49ff.; Robin 2003).

In order to ensure that the population adhered to the prescribed conventions of viewing and the prohibition of possession, the Jesuit "Brotherhood of the Blessed Virgin" in Antwerp, for example, announced in a confessional manual of 1615 that no one was allowed to own indecent pictures. Repentant sinners would also have to self-diagnose whether they had "indecent thoughts when they looked at or touched these pictures for a long time and felt lust and pleasure" (Thøfner 2004: 5). Should contemplation of a naked woman or her image indeed trigger sexual desire, the sinner was breaking the sixth commandment "Thou shalt not commit adultery!" These fears were not unfounded, since Leonardo da Vinci (1452–1519) had already recognized the persuasive power of imagery in his painting treatise: "This beauty (. . .) will awaken love in you and will awaken the desire for possession not only with the eye but with all the senses" (Hammer-Tugendhat 2009: 43).

So, people started to hide intimate body parts in pictures and on statues in public spaces and especially in churches, pre-empting such enticements. The painter Daniele da Volterra (1509–1566) was mocked because he was commissioned by Pope Pius IV (1499–1565) to paint over the all too visible sexual characteristics in Michelangelo's Sistine Chapel masterwork. *Braghettone* (trouser painter) was his nickname forever after. A typical example was also the fresco *Expulsion from Paradise* (1425) painted by Masaccio (1401–428) on the wall of the Brancacci side chapel in the Church of Maria del Carmine in Florence. In the realistic, lifelike original, Adam and Eve were naked. Adam covers his face with his hands in desperation, thereby uncovering his genitals, and Eve hides part of her breasts and vulva in the style of ancient *Venus pudica*. With this gesture, she expressed her shame that was inherent in the woman after the temptation of Adam and the Fall. However, it was not until the end of the seventeenth century that the sight of genitalia in the church was no longer tolerated and penis and vulva gained their famous fig leaves (Clifton 1999) (Figure 18).

However, naked bodies and their constellations did not always have to have a primarily erotic or sexual frame of meaning. As in the Netherlands in the sixteenth century, this could morally determine the evoked associations and connotations. In paintings by Hieronymus Bosch (c. 1450–1516), the staging of the landscape colored the message, as in *The Garden of Earthly*

FIGURE 18 *Sandro Botticelli (1445–1510), Venus pudica, c. 1490.*

Delights (c. 1495–1505). If, for example, the background depicted a *hortus conclusus* (enclosed garden), this was meant as a powerful emblem of purity and the love and union between Christ and the Church, which led to a moralization of the naked figures (Pearson 2019: 5ff.).

Faced with this gaze regime, the artists of the Renaissance and Baroque periods proved themselves to be true masters of staging naked bodies ambiguously, packaging them into mythological figures and scenes and seemingly innocuous situations. For example, women appear doing their toilette with partially uncovered breasts or were the focal point of boudoir scenes that were en vogue at the French court in Fontainebleau around the middle of the sixteenth century. Subjects were also scantily clad ladies, often mistresses of princes and regents, who seductively combed their hair in the morning or prepared themselves for bed in the evening. In the second half of the seventeenth century, some rich English husbands also commissioned erotic portraits of their wives (usually in their early years of marriage), on which they could be seen with open hair and low neckline or even bare breasts, so men could be in the company of their wives on long (merchant) voyages—in pictorial form. The stimulation strategy often consisted of positioning the spouses in such a way that not only their physical advantages were emphasized, but they also appeared more in the role of lovers and seducers than prudish wives.

The Arnolfini Wedding by the Flemish painter Jan van Eyck (*c.* 1390–1441), painted in Bruges in 1434, shows the clothed couple Giovanni Arnolfini and Giovanna Cenami. At first glance, nothing suspicious. The woman has a distinct curvature of the belly. The objective gestures and posture of the Italian merchant and his wife, who comes from a wealthy family, refer to their marital relationship and the love that unites them. However, the conspicuous furnishings also allow a further, sexual reading. At the lower left edge of the picture two fragile wooden slippers can be seen. These had erotic significance: The slippers, askew, look as if they've been hastily kicked off, perhaps because the two of them had hurried into bed inflamed with sexual passion? The lone burning candle on the chandelier can be understood as a reference to the wedding candle that newlyweds took with them into their bedroom and left burning throughout the night. The fruit on and under the window sill symbolize (marital) fertility. The small dog in the foreground—an animal that shamelessly copulates in public—also stands for carnality. In the traditional reading, however, it was considered a symbol of marital fidelity. The conspicuous (marriage) bed to the right of the woman sets the mood in this intimate setting. The scene would have connoted the couple's marital obligations and fertility as well as the joys associated with them (Harbison 1990; Pearson 2019: 10ff.). A further interpretation could also take a look at the sociocultural context, namely, the excitement raging around the sodomites in Florence and Siena in those years. In this context, Italian merchants were also portrayed in a bad light, as they were primarily in male company and (allegedly) indulged in same-sex seduction. Perhaps Arnolfini also wanted to use this painting to communicate that he had found his rightful place in marriage with his wife and was a pious and honorable businessman (Wolfthal 2010: 37ff.) (Figure 19).

The mythological frescoes with which the papal banker Agostino Chigi (1465–1520) had the walls of his Villa Farnesina painted served for private but also semi-public consumption where it was built in the Roman district of Trastevere on the western bank of the Tiber. For Chigi and his mistress or courtesan and later wife Francesca Ordeaschi, the magnificently furnished building primarily offered retreat from daily business and obligations. It was also used for extravagant banquets and theater. Contemporary visitors saw it as a place where Cupid and Venus were worshipped in a sensual and physical way (Günther 2001: 161ff.). The pupils of Raphael, Giulio Romano (*c.* 1499–1546), Giovanni Francesco Penni (*c.* 1488–*c.* 1530), and Giovanni da Udine (1487–1564), decorated the garden loggia with frescoes of "Amor and Psyche" from the "Golden Ass" by the ancient poet Apuleius (*c.* 123–*c.* 170). Numerous sensual nudes, predominantly female, populate the mythological image repertoire of this place. In the garlands of fruit between the pictures, the artists incorporated sexual interpretation aids: Composed

FIGURE 19 *Jan van Eyck (c. 1390–1441), The Arnolfini wedding, 1434.*

of a zucchini or cucumber and an aubergine, an erect penis emerges, adding a carnal reading to the religious-philosophical, but above all Platonic interpretation of this story—it is about human curiosity, beauty, and god-human relationships. Chigi's villa is full of erotically charged imagery. For example, in the bedroom on Giovanni Antonio Bazzi's (1477–1549) fresco *The Marriage of Alexander the Great with Roxane*, the princess reclines naked on the marriage bed. In the garden, visitors can expect a sculpture that also shows Cupid and Psyche closely entwined as well as a satyr that is in the process of seducing a youthful boy (Wolk-Simon 2008: 43ff.; Saslow 2019: 192).

Renaissance and Baroque painters often toyed with the adamantly censored as well as avidly shameless gaze in their erotic offerings. The prototype is Giulio Romano's *Due Amati* (*Two Lovers, c.* 1524), in which a nude couple embrace each other on a (marriage) bed and the young woman is just lifting a sheet under which her lover's genitals are hidden. Their sexual intent is evoked by the context: Carved into one of the bedposts is a satyr, the mythological figure driven by uncontrollable lust, not letting himself be deterred from his favorite activity: penetration. Meanwhile, an old woman watches the love scene. She apparently has a key for the locked bedroom and is obviously enjoying the sight of the two lovers, from her undiscovered, voyeuristic view from behind the door. Here, too, an obscene reading is quite appropriate, because *chiavare* (unlock) was used in Italian as a vulgar expression that roughly equates to *fuck*. Just as important is the fact that the old woman represents a third person in the picture, who—like the viewer outside the picture—takes part visually in what is going on and anticipates his gaze. The *Due Amati* addresses yet another aspect: The voyeur's face is filled with melancholy and envy, probably a sign of the memories of earlier sexual experiences. This is in keeping with the vision of older women, especially widows, from earlier years as being the lustiest having gained carnal knowledge they may no longer fulfil. In another way, her twisted grin reflects the emotions of the viewers, who also long to experience such a love scene themselves yet perhaps must leave such tender moments to their imagination (Zorach 2011: 269ff.).

Intimate Pictures or Visual Violence?

Probably the most famous intimate portrait of the seventeenth century is *Het Pelsken* (*The Little Fur*) (1635–1640) by Peter Paul Rubens (1577–1640). It portrays Helena Fourment (1614–1673), the artist's second wife, largely nude and only covered by a fur coat (probably her husband's). This depiction is unusual, if only because during this period it wasn't typically the wife or mistress of an artist who served as a model but rather a prostitute or a woman with a questionable reputation (Hammer-Tugendhat 2009: 27). For a long time, art history overlooked the fact that the woman portrayed—the daughter of an Antwerp silk merchant—had first owned this painting herself, and that it was indeed created within their conjugal intimacy. Seen in this light, his highly erotic language of signs—fur was considered a symbol of untamed nature and wild sexual desire (Lurati 2017)—calls forth sexual pleasures not only for the artist (as a traditional male observer and voyeur) himself but also the wife (as both poser and observer). For the much older Rubens, the erotic association was obvious, since he had chosen his second wife mainly for sexual reasons:

> I decided to marry [as I am] not yet finding myself fit for the abstinence of the celibate, and, if we must give first place to mortification, we may enjoy licit pleasures with thankfulness etc., and I have taken a young wife of modest but citizen family (Thøfner 2004: 2f.).

Whether the visual signs offered were interpreted sexually or whether they were understood more as a declaration of love and a promise of loyalty (Goffen 1994) was left to the discretion of the viewers of that time (and of today). Whatever the reading, such ambivalence was provided by many an image made for the members of the upper classes. Especially polysemous were scenes around the marriage bed. In most cases, the bed itself didn't stand for marital duties alone—which, according to the Christian credo, were to be fulfilled in chastity and under avoidance of too much carnal lust—it was considered a refuge of sensual pleasure at the same time, a place of mutual physical satisfaction (Wolfthal 2010: 58ff.).

Artists such as Titian (*c.* 1488–1576), Tintoretto (1518–1594), and Rembrandt van Rijn (1606–1669) used a visual language that had the capacity to express female desire in a positive way. At the same time, some addressed the male gaze regime inscribed in patriarchal gender relations. Tintoretto's *Susanna and the Elders* (*c.* 1555–1556) as well as Rembrandt's (1636) showed in an exemplary way how the erotic and simultaneously violent male gaze could be problematized. The Susanna motif comes from the Old Testament and is about the chaste wife of a rich man named Joakim. Two lecherous elder judges pursue her, catch her bathing, and conspire to force her to adultery. She steadfastly resists their blackmail attempt, and in court their conflicting stories lead to justice being served. In contrast to medieval iconography, in which Susanna appeared as the prototype of female chastity and willingness to make sacrifices, the Renaissance gave her an erotic touch. Because now she was (also) painted as a Venus figure, a desirable nude, at best covering her pubis and breasts with arm and hand. Tintoretto's Susanna seems unaware of the voyeurs and absorbed in her beauty, almost a Narcissus figure; Rembrandt's seems terrified, and yet others depict the steadfast irritation on her face at being looked at. Visual guidance is provided by the male figures in the picture as they approach the naked female figure with violence in their eyes. As a representative of femininity, Susanna alternated back and forth between seduction and chastity. Tintoretto's version shows two true male voyeurs who, as yet undiscovered by the female gaze, demonstrate the male dominance of the gaze. Her eyes direct the viewer's attention to those parts of the female body that should not be seen on a woman whom one does not know. Rembrandt, on the other hand, shows Susanna alone in the picture and at the very moment she becomes aware of the viewer. She is startled and chastely covers her nakedness with a cloth and her hand. Her dismissive gestures and facial expression show that she does not want to be looked at in any way and did not want to serve as an erotic object. Rembrandt thus problematizes the sublimating and at the same time actively taking gaze of the male (image) viewer and the violence inscribed in such an erotic gaze order. He also exposes what for most contemporary artists was simply unthinking, standard practice: male protagonists offered the place of "the observing subject in front of the picture" (Hammer-Tugendhat 2009: 42ff., 55), the depicted women functioned as passive objects of their desire.

Coital representations also made it onto the canvas in metaphorical form. In many cases this happened without the male figure appearing in human form. Ancient mythology offered a huge reservoir of motifs and narratives. Especially popular were the *Metamorphoses* of Ovid. Zeus (Jupiter) mutated into a swan for Leda (Michelangelo's *Leda*, 1529/1530), into a bull to kidnap Europa (Titian's *Rape of Europa*, around 1560), into a satyr with Antiope (Correggio's *Jupiter and Antiope*, around 1528), and into a billowing cloud for Io (Correggio's *Jupiter and Io*, around 1530) (Martin 2014: 83ff.). In each case, the ancient myth made it clear what was meant and where the narrative was heading: The respective materialization of Zeus served only the seduction of an earthly woman. The rain of gold, for example, had a visually stimulating potential, in the form of Zeus falling on the naked Danaë in Titian's painting of the same name (1544–1546). In the six versions produced by Titian and his workshop, the gold pieces can be understood as payment for sexual intercourse and can be associated with purchasable love; the coins also represent male semen and fertility; finally, Danaë's hand position (between the legs) indicates that such a work was also a model as well as an instigation to masturbation (Santore 1991; Griffey 2010). Henrick Goltzius' (1558–1616/7) *The Sleeping Danaë* (1603) goes one step further and leaves no doubt about the prostitutive interpretation. Here, the slumbering woman, who chastely covers her pubis, is offered a tin filled with gold pieces by an old maid. One of the floating putti carries a purse whose shape is reminiscent of an erect penis with huge testicles (Sluijter 2006: 227ff.).

In Rembrandt's *Danaë* (1636 and 1643–1649) these ambiguous readings fade into the background. He shows a woman who is expecting her lover. The realistic posture and fullness of her body, the representation of the skin and the lighting is practically a tactile experience. With outstretched hand, she invites him to her. This female figure no longer symbolizes either chastity or greed. Hers are individual sensual and erotic desires that cannot be interpreted in a moralizing or negative way. Zeus appears here not as an easily misunderstood shower of money but as a ray of light and/or as an absent person that first has to be projected into the picture. The desire and eroticism felt for the man is no longer directly addressed but shifted to the (male) viewer of the painting (Hammer-Tugendhat 2009: 139ff.).

Since the Renaissance, the male voyeur has been made to face himself again and again in the visual arts. Albrecht Dürer (1471–1528), for example, in his pen-and-ink drawing *The Women's Bath* (1498) not only shows the bare bodies of women of all ages but also has two of them directing their gaze outward at the external observer. Viewing Dürer's drawing, the observer loses his secret position and thus also his intimate shamefacedness. To further emphasize this, a voyeur peers into the room from an opening in the background; he could be looking at the ladies, but his penetrating eyes seem to look into the viewer's own. The situation is similar with Titian's (1490–1576) *Venus of Urbino* (1538) and Diego Velazquez's (1599–1660) *Venus with the Mirror* (*c*. 1644–1648). Both show women naked on a bed, fixing the viewer with their eyes and making him recognize that his gaze is not devoted to their faces but rather primarily to other physical facts. As in this case, other artists also played with the guided gaze of the naked female body and the visual transgression of moral norms when viewing it (Böhme 2011: 444ff.). By means of a pendulum, the painter and engraver Agostino

Carracci (1557–1602) has a beastly satyr stand in for a (more or less) erect man gazing down directly at the genitals of a sleeping nymph, thus building a visual bridge for the unveiling eye of the beholder of his *Satyr Mason* (1578). The part that is veiled by the mason's skimpy apron is a not so subtle jab at the censors' attempts (Simons 2011: 19, 36).

Erotic and Pornographic Graphics

Direct representations of sexual intercourse are mainly to be found in engravings instead of paintings. Even though engravings, too, were made by well-known artists, little is known about their distribution until the later seventeenth century. The numbers of copies necessary for the mass market were not available until the eighteenth century, as printing costs came down and, above all, censorship loosened up. Marcantonio Raimondi (c. 1475–c. 1534) provided *the* model for coitus representations with his sixteen copper engravings *I modi* (1524), which he had based on drawings by Giulio Romano (Talvacchia 1999: 161ff.). Other artists used Raimondi's "modes" as inspiration to produce many coitus scenes. Zoan Andrea's copperplate engraving *Lovers*—the actual engraver was Giovanni Antonio da Brescia, active between 1490 and 1519—makes obvious why the two figures hold each other in their arms. Giulio Bonasones' (c. 1498–c. 1574) copperplate engraving *A man overpowers a woman* (1556) outlines the way there (Schlieker 2001: 58, 88f.). Rembrandt's etching *Ledikant* (*The French Bed*, 1646) is even clearer. It shows a man and a woman on a canopied bed, the curtains drawn apart, where—although mostly dressed in their sleeping garments—they are unmistakably copulating. As is so often the case, the man is de-individualized and only shown in a view of his back, while the woman's sexual arousal can be read in her face (Hammer-Tugendhat 2009: 156) (Figure 20).

A special group of erotic prints and paintings includes brothel scenes, which were particularly popular in the Netherlands in the sixteenth and seventeenth centuries. These *Bordeeltjes* depict how such establishments work, often combined with the motif of the lost son. Made by well-known painters and engravers such as Lucas van Leyden (1494–1533), Jan van Hemessen (1500–before 1566), and Dirck van Baburen (1595–1624), they have a wide scope of interpretation. One interpretation says, these are mainly about women in suggestive poses and with exposed breasts. The scenes illustrate how the stories unfold; they are about seduction, the negotiation of the whore's wage, and the subsequent coitus being paid for. In view of the narrative tradition, the *Bordeeltjes* could be interpreted both as a condemnation of the depravity of some women and of brothels on the whole. In contrast to this is a reading that sees these women as actors capable of making decisions and doing business. These ambivalent connotations made it possible to use such images in private settings as well as in taverns and

FIGURE 20 *Marcantonio Raimondi (c. 1475–c. 1534) engraving to Pietro Aretino's (1492–1556) Sonetti lussuriosi (I modi), 1524.*

inns—and they make up part of the pictorial inventory of brothels (Solomon 2000: 145ff.; Thompson 1977: 176ff.).

Erotic graphics are also found in anatomical works, where illustrations, legends, prefaces, and headings sometimes try to thwart erotic ideas, sometimes stimulate this kind of reading (Heyam 2019); for example, in Charles Estiennes' (1504–1564) *De dissectione partium corporis humani* (1545). His anatomical treatise is peppered with artistic woodcuts that show the naked human body in a domestic context, only the figures' parts are opened up to show the innards and provided with Latin explanations and text references. The female figures are depicted in stimulating positions, with their legs spread on beds or reclining on cushioned couches. In doing so, they demonstrate what is carnally hidden in and behind their vulva. The facial expressions of the figures prove to be quite ambivalent. Most of them are asleep or half-awake with still closed eyes. This way one can—without being irritated by the women's gaze—intensively observe the female sexual anatomy. Some of the women depicted also give the impression that they are expecting a lover and have fallen asleep while waiting. Anyone who knew Marcantonio Raimondi's (c. 1475–c. 1534) copperplate engravings *I modi* (1524) or those of his successors could not have been so naive as to see these later images to merely be imparting anatomical knowledge (Talvacchia 1999: 161ff.). Already in Raimondi's sixteen copper engravings the classical mythological background might be looked for, but in vain. His copulating couples show only the sexual intercourse itself and the feelings associated with it. Raimondi also showed little shame toward his viewers, because on his plates one could admire the male and female actors equally.

The anatomical view and the visual-tactile illumination of the beauty and ugliness of the corporeal body was accompanied by anthropological self-reflection (Böhme 2011: 440). The fact that the artistic depiction of the genitals also changed in the process becomes visible in Albrecht Dürer's (1471–1528) *Self-portrait as a naked man* (after 1514). Whereas Renaissance penises were depicted in keeping with the ancient Greek practice of minimization to reflect sexual self-control and modesty, Dürer portrayed his genitals in full here, in all their carnality, which for contemporaries must have seemed downright obscene and piqued their sense of shame. Even the genitals of the Christ Child came into the visual focus of art in the fifteenth and sixteenth centuries. However the *ostentatio genitalium*, the conscious showing of Jesus' genitals, is interpreted, here too the progress of naturalization since the Late Middle Ages tended, consequently, to emphasize the sexuality of the Son of God and thus the sexual principle of creation. This also applied to the feminization of Mary, in which the breasts became visually significant and thus semiotically loaded with her motherliness (Lindquist 2012: 10f.).

These frescoes, paintings, and graphics led to the Italian humanist Lodovico Castelvetro (c. 1505–1571), in his commentary on Aristotle (1567), pointing out a problem associated with the blunt depiction of sexual organs and the showing of erotic or sexual scenes. Their effect depended on whether they were viewed alone and unobserved or in the presence of others:

> To the fourth and last kind of pleasant things that provoke laughter belong all things that are connected with carnal pleasure, such as the pubic parts, the lecherous unions, the reminders and the parables for them. It should be noted, however, that these things do not make us laugh if they are presented openly to the eyes or imagination while we are in the company of other people—then they create shame and make us blush. (Pfisterer 2012: 211)

This also applied to depictions of unnatural sexuality by witches, both young and old. Even established Renaissance artists were so fascinated by their bodies that they contributed immensely to their iconography. Albrecht Dürer and Hans Baldung Grien (c. 1484–1545), for example, used their serious representations of witches as an occasion to depict the threat to the moral order posed by vice and sorcery, but also to visualize sexual debauchery and naked women's bodies—or their aging and decay (Sullivan 2000; Venjakob 2012) (Figure 21).

The Origins of Pornographic Literature?

Descriptions of sexual events can also be found in literature, whether addressed directly or through innuendo. The beginnings of modern pornographic literature are mostly attributed to Pietro Aretino's (1492–1556) poems to

FIGURE 21 *Hans Baldung Grien (1484–1485), The witches' Sabbath, woodcut, 1510.*

accompany Raimondi's rather egalitarian *I modi* (1524). These are sonnets called *Sonetti lussuriosi* (pleasure sonnets). The poems and the engravings were conceived together as the world's first pornographic bestseller. While Aretino intended to contribute to the sexual arousal that resulted from the engravings, he created "a world that was ordered according to the logic of the gaze" for a primarily male target audience (Findlen 1994: 62) and anticipated the active actions of men. Sonnet 11 calls for imitation and appropriation in the following way:

> Open your thighs so I can look straight
> At your beautiful ass·and cunt in my face,
> An ass equal to paradise in its enjoyment,
> A cunt that melts hearts through the kidneys.
>
> While I compare these things,
> Suddenly I long to kiss you,
> And I seem to myself more handsome than Narcissus
> In the mirror that keeps my prick erect.

(Findlen 1993: 69)

Aretino's pornographic poetics were also so successful because he created a printed work in which image and text complemented each other and new contexts and associations emerged from this synthesis. Printed together on one sheet, they could be offered on a mass scale (Waddington 2003: 41ff.). Distributed through publishing houses and sold in bookstores as well as in peddlers' and street shops, these prints brought to light an event that was supposed to remain private and secret. Meanwhile, Titian's (c. 1488–1576) erotic paintings were created for private viewing and for a selected public, such as with the *Venus of Urbino* (1534) for Ippolito de' Medici (1511–1535) and the *Danaë* (1553/54) for Philip II (1527–1598), erotic and obscene prints were available under the table for any paying clientele (Findlen 1994: 50). Even if still for a rather limited, namely, wealthy audience, these erotic-pornographic picture-text arrangements now made visible actions that were partly unknown or attributed to lewd and common women.

The fact that these pictures were viewed in private was a major break from previous image regimes, a pioneering new way forward for the visual medium. Even literature produced primarily for the courts, such as the Spanish sentimental *novelas*, were also translated into other European languages and were no longer intended for reading aloud but for meditative silent reading, bringing "the irruption of desire in a courtly setting, with its trail of sexual violence, erotica and parody" (Duché 2021: 189). But it was precisely this possibility of solitary stimulation and satisfaction that seemed particularly dangerous to the censors; viewers of pornography and readers of erotic and obscene texts could now surrender themselves to their own imagination, well beyond any social control. The secret circumstances of consumption were another reason why the Reformers vehemently opposed the sale and possession of such prints and why the Catholic censors also pursued them with verve (Talvacchia 1999: 80ff.). In a letter, Aretino appealed in vain against this puritanical pursuit of the gaze:

> I renounce the bad judgment and dirty habit which forbid the eyes to see what pleases them most (. . .). It seems to me that the you-know- what given us by nature for the preservation of the species should be worn as a pendant round our necks or as a badge in our caps, since it is the spring that pours out the flood of humanity. (Hunt 1993: 25)

In the *Ragionamenti* (*Reasonable Discussions*), a work published between 1534 and 1536, Aretino has women of the lower class—courtesans and madams—engage dialogues about their life experiences (Moulton 2010, 2019). In the tradition of Lucian's *hetairikoi dialogoi* (whore dialogues) (Rosellini 2020: 63ff.), which first appeared in print in 1494, Aretino describes sexual acts from a female perspective. He blames the men for the fact that their wives experienced no or too little sexual pleasure. In so doing, he parodies the contemporary boom in courtesy books, such as

Baldassare Castiglione's (1478–1529) *Il Libro del Cortegiano* (*The Book of the Courtier*, 1528), which were aimed at the clerical and aristocratic public as an ethical and socially compliant guide to manners. In contrast to the male and female figures idealized in those prudish works, Nanna and Antonia, the protagonists of Aretino's first part, *Ragionamento della Nanna e della Antonia* (1534), give an account of life in the streets of Rome (Ray 2009: 130ff.). Pippa, Nanna's daughter, has only three realistic options: nun, wife, or prostitute. Antonia advises to take the latter route:

> I am of the opinion that you should let your Pippa become a whore, because the nun betrays her holy vows, and the wife deals the deathblow to the sacrament of marriage; but the whore does not harm the convent or the husband, but does it like a soldier who is paid to make mischief. And she can't be blamed for the evil she does, because that which is in her shop simply is what gets sold. When a barkeep opens a new pub, he does not need to put up a sign, because right on the first day one knows that his is a place where people drink, eat, play, whore, curse and cheat. And whoever goes there to pray or fast, would find neither altar nor fasting. The gardeners sell herbs, the spice merchants sell spices, and the brothels sell curses, lies, slander, scandal, disgrace, racketeering, swindle, hatred, cruelty, murder, French disease, ambush, bad reputation and poverty. But with the confessor it's similar to the doctor: He heals the evil faster if it is shown to him on the flat of his hand than if it is hidden from him. Therefore, do not let Pippa take the detour, let her become a whore *forthwith*, for with the help of a little repentance, together with two drops of holy water, her soul will be free of all whorishness; furthermore, if I have understood you correctly, all vices in a whore are to be regarded as virtues. Besides, it is a beautiful thing to be called a "madam" even by gracious gentlemen, to always dress and eat like a signora, and to always live in bliss and pleasure, as you yourself, who have told me so much about them, know much better than I do. It is also no small thing to be able to satisfy every whim and to please everyone whom one pleases. For Rome has always been and always will be . . . I will not say the whore's city, lest I should have to confess the expression. (Aretino 2017: 159f.)

Aretino also demonstrates the linguistic characteristics of pornographic or obscene literature. It is characterized by a more or less direct representation of sexual behavior and sometimes also by a (artificially) low linguistic register (Frei and Labère 2021). Instead of continuing to speak (only) metaphorically—as one sees in literature—Antonia asks her interlocutor in the *Ragionamenti* to call a spade a spade:

> Antonia: I've wanted to tell you something for a long time, but I kept forgetting. Speak freely and say: cu, ca, po and fo [meaning the Italian words *culo*, *cazzo*, *potta* and *fottere*; translatable into English as(s),

co(ck), cu(nt) and fu(ck)]. Otherwise, at most the Sapienza Capranica [the University of Rome] will understand you with your: hose in the ring, obelisk in the Coliseo, turnip in the garden, bolt in the hole, key in the lock, stamp in the mortar, nightingale in the nest, stake in the ditch, bellows in the stove hole, rapier in the sheath, and with the stake, the shawm, the carrot, the mimi, the little bit, the little one, the backside bitter orange, the missal leaves, the verbigratia, the thing, the story, the stem, the arrow, the root, the radish and the filth, you would like to get it—I don't want to put words in your mouth, because otherwise you wouldn't be able to tell what you saw when you tiptoed through the cloister. Why don't you call the yes "yes" and the no "no" or keep it to yourself? (Aretino 2017: 37)

Political Aims of Obscene Texts

From Aretino, the censors and judges began taking a very strong stand against obscene literature because it usually had a political thrust. With their satirical and distorted portrayal of sexual life, writers shattered the social and moral conventions of their time. Aretino denounced the depravity and corruption at the court of Pope Clement VII and the Roman elites. Antonio Vignali (1500–1559) found a particularly creative form of criticism in *La Cazzaria* (1525–1526). He disavowed the phallocracy of Siena by portraying the population as patrician cocks and cunts, aristocratic testicles, and plebeian butts, and staged a revolution with them that could easily be deciphered as the overthrow of feudal rule in 1524 (Findlen 1994: 82ff.).

It is not surprising that these works were banned and burned. Sodomites also typically appeared in obscene literature alongside prostitutes—as knowledgeable observers of the nobility, the patricians, and the clergy—revealing to readers the true morals of their socially high-ranked bedfellows. The clergy got off the worst of it. Many preached water and drank wine, so that their sermons and appeals to morals appeared to be highly hypocritical. In the ethics of obscene literature, whore morals ranked above courtly honor—more importantly, they genuinely did correspond to social reality. By means of satirical social criticism and (pseudo-)philosophical treatises, the authors shook the foundations of the courtly and ecclesiastical system. Despite censorship, confiscation, and destruction, these writings spread rapidly and were translated into other languages. This often happened in cities such as Amsterdam or Grenoble, where such products were also observed with suspicious eyes, but the censorship was less rigid. In any case, the repression of obscene works in the second half of the sixteenth and seventeenth centuries was not exclusively because they exceeded moral boundaries, but because they contained explosive political power (DeJean 2002: 4ff.).

The *Ragionamenti* found numerous imitators, such as Lorenzo Veniero's (1510–1550) *La puttana errante* (*The Wandering Whore*) from the 1530s or in 1642 Ferrante Pallavicino's (1615–1644) *La retorica delle puttanne* (*The Rhetoric of a Whore*)—both also burlesques in which prostitutes denounced the social conditions and derisively presented the authorities. What they had in common was that although they were written by men, they depicted the obscene world from a female perspective. In later English and French writings, the protagonists mostly came from the aristocracy and upper citizens. The authors also employed a didactic gesture of older, experienced women explaining the (heterosexual) world to younger ones. Homosexual desires of men came off rather badly, as did masturbation. Sexual acts between women—if they were even discussed at all—were regarded merely as a first step toward heterosexual actualization, therefore disregarded as a sexual variant on its own terms. This also applied to the fixation on vaginal penetration, which was considered the ultimate goal of every preparatory practice, such as clitoral stimulation (Moulton 2013: 214).

Margaret de Navarre's (1492–1549) *Heptaméron* contains yet another aspect of erotic literature. This collection of novellas, begun in 1542 and published posthumously in 1559 by Margaret's daughter Jeanne d'Albret, takes a critical look at Boccaccio's *Decameron* (*c.* 1350) (Ferguson and McKinley 2013; Bertrand 2005). It is framed as a panel of ten people debating the morality of the stories, which were mainly about conflicts between the sexes (Classen 2008a: 53ff.). For example, deceitful seducers and men who force women to intercourse and consider these disgraceful acts to be legitimate. Navarre portrays Franciscan monks just as badly as men who abuse their social position to overpower women. The eleventh tale deals with the *Facetious sayings of a Franciscan friar in his sermons* and the seductive power of his words:

> Not far from the small town of Bleré in Touraine, there is a village of Saint-Martin-le-Beau, where a Franciscan from his monastery in Tours was called to preach there during Advent and Lent. He was more verbose than learned, and since he sometimes did not know how to fill the prescribed hour, he told many a story that did not seem too edifying to his congregation. One Maundy Thursday, he was talking about the Pascal Lamb and how it must be eaten at night. Then he saw some young, beautiful ladies newly arrived from Amboise, wanting to spend Easter in the village. He wished to surpass himself and asked the female listeners if they knew the pleasures of eating raw meat at night, and then continued: "If not, I will tell you, ladies." The young men of Amboise, who had come accompanied by their wives or their sisters and nieces, and who were not acquainted with the pilgrim's humor, began to be scandalized; By and by, their shock turned to laughter as they listened and learned that to eat the Pascal Lamb, one would have to gird the loins, have one's feet in one's shoes, and a hand on one's staff. Now that the Franciscan saw them laughing and knew quite well why, he hastily corrected: "Well, indeed, shoes on one's feet and a staff in one's hand. Is a hen plucked not a

plucked hen?" Whether they laughed, I'm sure you don't doubt. Even the ladies could not suppress it, especially since he addressed other edifying advice to them. And when the hour was through, he could not leave the ladies unsatisfied, he spoke to them: "Perhaps, ladies, you will now go gossiping and clasp your hands and ask, What kind of noble friar is that, who speaks so boldly? He's some fine company? I will tell you, ladies, I will tell you, don't mind, no, if I speak boldly, for I come from Anjou, at your service."

In the ensuing discussion, the narrators warn against clerics who take advantage of their position to seduce female parishioners and rely on the pull of such erotic stories:

"But don't you see", Oisille says excitedly, "how audacious he is, who twists the text as he pleases, thinking he is dealing with beasts like himself, and, in so doing, shamelessly tries to suborn the poor creatures to have them to eat raw flesh at night?"—"You forget", replied Simontault, "that he saw those young ladies before him in whose. . . Pot he would have liked to wash his—Dare I say? No, but you hear me well: and have them a fresh taste, not roasted, but wriggling frisky. . ."—"Enough! Quiet Enough, my dear Simontault," said Parlamente; "you forget yourself. . . Where's your usually reserved modesty?"—"Pardon, for this shameless monk has led me astray. To get back to our topic, I pray Nomerfide, who is the cause of my misguidance, will give the floor to another, who may make us forget our mistakes." (Navarra 2022: 11th Tale)

Margaret of Navarre pointed out a dilemma that could hardly be avoided in the early modern discussion about unchastity: Anyone who condemns the lack of morality of their contemporaries inevitably entered a terrain where he, himself or she, herself contributed to the dissemination of arousing narratives and fantasies. Once set in the world, these stories developed their own dynamics and could hardly be wiped away.

After its first heyday in Renaissance Italy, the production of pornography—like trade and wealth accumulation in general—migrated north and found a new home in France, England, and the Netherlands, and in a second wave all over Europe. In the English publications of that time, a specific feature is evident which clearly distinguishes them from modern works: Many stories are not just about sexual pleasures but guides on how to increase fecundity. These writings therefore tend to be didactic and advise sexual practices that are conducive to reproduction. Moreover, they were meant to appeal not only to male but also female readers. For the most part, however, the stories and pictures give life to a possessive view of the female sexual object. At the same time, they emphasize the central role that women play in coitus and procreation. In contrast, same-sex sexual practices are viewed negatively, as they contribute nothing to reproduction (Toulalan 2007: 62ff.). The figures of obscenity differ even according to religious denomination: If, for example, the lascivious nun appears in Protestant countries merely as a popular stereotype, in Catholic areas she is considered a scandalous figure of pure provocation (Moulton 2013: 211).

In late seventeenth century England, obscene literature was increasingly used for propaganda purposes and to disavow political opponents—especially in conflicts between Royalists and Republicans. The preferred figure was the prostitute, who (allegedly) used the easy seductability of men to enrich herself. While the social and economic origins of whoredom was the hot topic in the beginning, for the Royalists these common women later represented the lower classes generally or *the* woman as such. They were characterized as depraved beings who looked exclusively after their personal and above all financial advantages in these obscene polemics (Mowry 2004). The wide distribution of writings such as *The Whore's Rhetorick* (1683) and *The Politick Whore* (1683–84) also shows that in urban centers, like London, it was possible to obtain printed copies of such works toward the end of the seventeenth century. Not only booksellers and publishers sold them, but street vendors and simple shops and taverns also had them on hand (Mudge 2000: 227).

Female Authors and Readers

Only a few women had much success in erotic or obscene literature in the sixteenth and seventeenth centuries, but the already mentioned Veronica Franco (1546–1591), a Venetian courtesan and active writer, became quite famous. In her *Lettere familiari a diversi* (1580), she pulled back the curtain on upper-class prostitution. She was the daughter of a *cortigiana*, a courtesan, and made it clear in her literary works that even sophisticated prostitutes—like women who wrote poetry—were dependent on the patronage of male customers or suitors. It took great skill in both aspects to be successful. In her epistolary literature, she attempts the difficult balancing act between reflective self-portrayal and advertising for her profession, between individual experiences as a courtesan and erotic social gossip. In one of the letters, written in the 1570s, she talks about the dangers of prostitution and warns the mother of a mature girl:

> "You know how many times I have begged and warned you to protect her virginity; and because this world is so dangerous and frail and the homes of poor mothers are not immune to the temptations of the lusty youth, I showed you how you can shelter her from the dangers and assist her in settling her life decently and in such a way that you will be able to marry her honestly." But often girls are simply "taken" by force without their mothers being able to protect them from it or, perhaps worse in Franco's eyes, pushed into it like Aretino's poor Pippa: "It is noted in this

city there has been a great increase in the vice of raping young girls who have not yet reached the age of consent and who are often prostituted and practically sold by their relatives owing to a lust for money." (Rosenthal 1992: 128ff.)

Franco's writings are now part of the canon of classical pornographic literature, partly because her works were circulated in print and thus found their way into estates, archives, and libraries. Much less is known about all those ephemeral writings and images that did not make it down this path.

So, it took some time until the erotic sonnets of Madeleine de l'Aubéspine (1546–1596) made it to the presses. An obscene riddle is to be found in a collection of the manuscripts:

As the sweetest diversion that I could ever choose,
Frequently, after dinner, for fear of getting bored,
I take his neck in hand, I touch him, and I stroke,
Till he's in such a state as to give me delight.

I fall upon my bed and, without letting go,
I grasp him in my arms, I press him to my breast,
And moving hard and fast, all ravished with pleasure,
Amidst a thousand delights I fulfill my desire.

If he sometimes unfortunately happens to slacken,
I erect him with my hand, and right away I strive
To enjoy the delight of such a tender stroking.

Thus my beloved, so long as I pull on his sinew,
Contents and pleases me. Then away from me, softly,
Tired and not sated, I finally withdraw him.

[Answer:] A lute!

(l'Aubespine 2007: 57; Klosowska 2008: 190)

As a member of the French court, l'Aubéspine wrote the text to read in the literary salons. The point of such sonnets was to direct the imagination in a clear direction and express *Honi soit qui mal y pense* ("shamed be the person that thinks evil of it," the motto of the English Order of the Garter). Manuscripts like this one circulated in aristocratic circles and also came into the hands of women. Perhaps they motivated the ladies to read with ambivalence. The frequently used image of the flute did not only refer to the penis, the absence of a male actor also made one think of a sex toy that women used alone or together with their partner (Kłosowska 2008: 194f.). In view of texts like this, it can be assumed that, at least in aristocratic circles, women at least came into contact with erotic and pornographic literature (Moulton 2000: 56).

Crude Farces, Comedies, Fables, and Shadow Plays

The situation is better with lower literary forms such as farces, comedies, fables, and romances, in which the everyday life of the sexes is presented—usually as caricatures—and their sexual roles get discussed. Here, the figures, albeit humorous, often act much more realistically than in the normative marriage tracts and *Ehespiegeln* (didactic writings in Reformation Germany). As Martin Montanus (after 1537–after 1566) formulated in his *Schwankbücher* (Books of Farce) (1557–1566), it was necessary to learn "how one maintained false love, deprive one another of honor, live whorishly and commit adultery" (Bachorski 1991: 528). In contrast to high literature, the actions and motives were presented without didactic seriousness but rather wit and situational comedy. By means of pictorial language—an enormous repertoire of metaphors, homologies, ambiguities, parables, allegories, etc.—the authors also got straight to the point (Gowing 2012: 247f.; Williams 1997). The German farce poet Michael Lindener (c. 1520–1562) found in his *Rastbüchlein* (*Little Booklet of Repos* 1558) no less than nineteen synonyms for sexual intercourse, among which were

> *stropurtzlen* (falling in the hay), *ficken* (fucking), *nobisen* (nobbing), *raudi-maudi* (onomatopoeia), *schirimiri* (onomatopoeia), *nullen* (nothin'ing), *menscheln* (peopling), *zuosammenschrauben* (screwing together), *pirimini* (onomatopoeia), *leuß im peltz* (lause in the pelt), *pampeln* (flailing about), *strampeln* (kicking about), *federziehen* (feather-pulling), *auff dem hackpret schlahen* (striking on the chopping board), *pfefferstossen* (pounding pepper), *immbereiben* (rubbing), *fleyschlen* (fleshing), *holtzhawen* (hacking wood) and *scheiterklüben* (splitting wood billets). (Bachorski 1991: 529)

What the *Rastbüchlein* was about is made abundantly clear from the titles of each story:

> "A student asks a miller for the hostel she failed to give him because she was already bedding the pastor."

> "A pastor lays with a peasant woman, but the woman let him know was a woman and her natural sister."

> "To fine journeymen, one who sleeps with the other's wife." (Lindener 1883).

In François Rabelais' (c. 1494–1553) five-volume cycle of novels *Gargantua and Pantagruel* (1532–1564), one encounters an inverted world which features the grotesque bodies of giants with rampant carnal needs, including eating, drinking, shitting, and sexual pleasure. The explicit subject matter is put to vivid prose—for example, in a scene in which the mother of Gargantua rubs his father's ham (Clark 2008). Rabelais was also one of those poets who no longer slavishly imitated ancient philosophers, physicians, and poets, but instead supplemented, if not replaced, their epistemology with observation and experience. As a (male) author, however, when it came to the female body and the emotions and affects of women, he reached the limits of what can be experienced. The female genitals were therefore not only imagined as places of lust and fulfilment, but also as an open wound or a gaping hole that made men afraid—and then made them tell obscene stories (Broomhall 1998; Rees 2013: 196f.; Szabari 2021)). Rabelais used this image in a chapter in which he sent Panurge, one of the men from Pantagruel's troops, with others to Sybille of Panzoust, an old sorceress, to obtain advice and a prophecy from her regarding his imminent marriage. She writes her answer with a spindle on eight leaves fallen from a tree, then

> [n]o sooner had she done thus speaking than she did withdraw herself unto her lurking-hole, where on the upper seat of the porch she tucked up her gown, her coats, and smock, as high as her armpits, and gave them a full inspection of the nockandroe; which being perceived by Panurge, he said to Epistemon, "God's bodikins, I see the sibyl's hole!" She suddenly then bolted the gate behind her, and was never since seen any more. They jointly ran in haste after the fallen and dispersed leaves, and gathered them at last, though not without great labour and toil, for the wind had scattered them amongst the thorn-bushes of the valley. When they had ranged them each after other in their due places, they found out their sentence, as it is metrified in this octastich:
>
> Thy fame upheld
> Even so, so:
> And she with child
> Of thee: No.
> Thy good end
> Suck she shall,
> And flay thee, friend,
> But not all.
>
> (Rabelais 1894: ch. 3, XVII)

Panurge describes his expectations of a future wife to a guest named Triboullet of Blois as follows:

> For you may be assured that my humour is much better satisfied and contented with the pretty, frolic, rural, dishevelled shepherdesses, whose bums through their coarse canvas smocks smell of the clover grass of the field, than with those great ladies in magnific courts, with their flandan top-knots and sultanas, their polvil, pastillos, and cosmetics... He gave me a lusty rapping thwack on my back,—what then? ... He flirted me on

the nose. In that there is no harm; for it importeth nothing else but that betwixt my wife and me there will occur some toyish wanton tricks which usually happen to all new-married folks. (Rablais 1894: ch. 3, XLVI)

Dutch comedies and farces in the seventeenth century also contained such crude stories, full of obscenities and obscene allusions. Their authors took everyday offences of morality as an occasion to talk about them obscenely and thus legitimize the subordination of women (Leuker 1992). Thus, while comedy poets did criticize the reigning marriage and sexual morals, in the end they restored the patriarchal gender order. However, we do encounter a few female figures who actively and self-determinedly implemented their own sexual desires. This was reason enough for the Dutch Calvinists to condemn such theatrical and prose plays altogether with a total ban (Hammer-Tugendhat 2009: 40).

The medical advice literature of the fifteenth to seventeenth centuries also dealt with the "secrets of reproduction" and the sexual questions and problems associated with it. Here, too, lusty topics got the attention of the censors. This is what happened in the case of the *Traité de l'essence et guérison de l'amour ou de la melancholie erotique* (*Treatise on the essence and healing of love or erotic melancholy*) (1610) by the French physician Jacques Ferrand (1575–c. 1630). In it, he not only popularized medical knowledge, he also addressed delicate astrological issues and gave tips for love potions and recipes that awakened and enhanced the sexual desire of men and women. This was to prevent the spread of lovesickness or erotic melancholy. But the real scandal was that Ferrand wrote about it in common French for the first version of his book. Chapter 23 offers the following recipe for maintaining sexual attraction between spouses:

> take only one ounce of nutmeg powder and one ounce of laudanum (if she does not want to risk of the falling of uterus), make a pessary, [put both on it] and put it in the labyrinth of love, and if the lack of pleasure derives from the fact that her wicket is too split and the tunnel is too stretched, or the door to Alibec's inferno is too wide so that Rustic gets no thrill out of running his devil, let her make use of the following remedy which the Italian courtesans use in order to sell themselves as virgins. Take two drams of stone alum, half a handful of red roses with half a dram of English galingale. Boil them all in water in which a piece of hot iron has been quenched. Let the third part of it be red wine. The woman then dips into it a sponge in the form of a pessary and puts it into the Venus's pig sty. (Beecher 1989: 44f.)

The figures mentioned are all protagonists from Boccaccio's *Decameron* (1349–1353), in which the simple-minded virgin Alibec wanted to get closer to God by going into the desert as a hermit and ending up in the bed of the sex-starved hermit Rustic. He used religious talk to get her to drive out his carnal devil. In view of such Rabelais-styled passages, Ferrand came under the scrutiny of the Inquisition and was indicted in Toulouse a full decade after the publication of his work. In addition to the accusation of blasphemy and working with evil and sorcery, he was also accused of endangering public morals and chastity. In revised and significantly toned-down new editions, he therefore kept the spicy passages in Latin, a strategy of the scientification of sexual narratives that proved its worth well into the twentieth century (Altbauer-Rudnik 2006; Beecher 1989).

In Spanish and Italian Renaissance literature, texts in which erotic puns and double meanings played an important role were popular and widespread. Apples, figs, keys, locks, and the like had a still familiar sexual connotation that could be decoded by the audience. In the Poetry of Garcilaso de la Vega (c. 1501–1536), for example, this was done by referring to Ovid's text about lovesickness (Frantz 1989: 38). Words such as *esperança* (hope), *remedio* (remedy), *galardón* (reward), *desseo* (desire), *voluntad* (will), *servicio* (service), and *morir* (die) could also be read in a possible sexual context (Eriksen 2020: 65ff.).

In the poem *The Choise of Valentines*, the English playwright and poet Thomas Nashe (1567–c. 1601) even treated premature ejaculation pornographically and satirically at the same time. The text, first written for circulation in an aristocratic circle and only later printed, is about a young man named Tomalin who visits a brothel where his mistress Mistris Francis works. Highly aroused by her naked body, he ejaculates before sexual intercourse can occur and therefore a dildo is used instead of his penis. In addition to the problem of the impotent man, the compensatory and regressive function of the sexual-textual fantasy was thematized here:

> Oh, who is able to abstaine so long? / I com, I com (. . .)
> I pennd this storie onelie for myself,
> Who giuing suck unto a childish Elfe,
> And quitte discourag'd in my nurserie
> Since all my store seemes to hir, penurie.
>
> (Jones 2013: 91ff.)

In the Ottoman Empire, erotic and pornographic scenes also reached the stage in the form of *Karagöz* (shadow plays). Since the sixteenth century, such humorous performances were mainly shown during the month of Ramadan and at circumcision celebrations. Their repertoire of figures included *Karagöz*, a simple but cunning representative of the people, and his neighbor and adversary *Hacivat*, who represented the urban, educated classes. Together with the standard secondary characters, they also get into erotic situations, which are underlaid with one- and two-sided expressions, some of them in the everyday vernacular. The shadow figures sometimes took up positions whose sexual intentions could not be denied. Religious scholars had their hands full with such earthly profane theater—as, for example, a fatwa issued by the Hanafi legal scholar Mehmed Ebüssuud Efendi (1490–1574) shows:

> Question: One night a shadow play was brought to a gathering, and Zeyd, *imam* and *hatib* [preacher], stayed at that gathering. Would it be in accordance with [*shari'a*] law, if he saw the play until the end, to dismiss him from his position as *imam* and *hatib*?
>
> Answer: If he watched the play to learn its moral lesson and thought about it with a tame mind, it is forbidden [to dismiss him]. (Ze'evi 2006: 130)

In contrast to the morally normative literature of the theological scholars, secular legislators, and spiritual Sufis, in which men appear as the (more) virtuous sex and women as driven by the sexual and insatiable, in shadow plays both appeared as libidinous and promiscuous where appropriate. Even homoerotic cravings (of both men and women) were addressed by means of innuendo, but usually only in the form of salacious jokes and crude language. This also included crossing the gender divide, for example, men dressed as women. It should be borne in mind here that respectable Muslim women usually wore a veil in public, and so the humorous effect was all the greater when a man hidden underneath got unmasked (Ze'evi 2006: 239 ff.).

Erotic, Obscene, or Pornographic works?

The question of whether media forms such as the *Karagöz* or other textual and pictorial representations presented here can be considered erotic or obscene or go so far as to be pornographic has repeatedly occupied historiography in recent decades. Is this pornography in the modern sense of the word, which only came into use in the early nineteenth century? With the classical demarcation of *pornographos* as whore stories, it is no longer possible to do justice to the literature and images of the sixteenth and seventeenth centuries. In contemporary terminology, these works have been described in English as *bawdy* and *lewd* (etymologically "bold" and "common"), in French and German they have also been attributed as being *aretine*, from Aretino's works (Moulton 2000: 158ff.). The true definitional difficulties, however, lay in the almost indefinable term "pornography" itself (Toulalan 2007: 1ff.), because in the relevant research this term is understood to include texts and images in which sexual acts are usually depicted by explicitly naming or viewing the genitals. Pornographic works lead to sexual arousal, because they stimulate the imagination of the recipients and urge them to continue the sexual story and even to act on their own (which was not the actual purpose of medical materials, for example).

Here, however, the edges of the conceptual field begin to fray. It has often been and still often is cited as a further characteristic of pornography that it comes into conflict with the prevailing social norms and moral concepts, because it clearly exceeds the given limits. It follows from this that the classification of literary or pictorial representations as pornography also greatly depends on the extent to which they have been banned and censored. Another attraction of the incriminated writings and pictures was that they had to be produced, distributed, sold, and usually also consumed in secret (Hunt 1993; Mowry 2004). Another definitional fuzziness around it concerns the political focus of pornography. Since the social satires of Aretino through the libertine literature of the seventeenth century, the violation of sexual taboos has also been a reference to the two-faced morality of the upper classes and especially of the clergy (Turner 2002, 2003). Finally, the definition of pornography also encompasses its potential to denounce the power and violence relations between the sexes—or to stabilize and prolong them without reflection (Mantioni 2019). After all, many of the writings and imagery were also about where the borderlines between antisocial lust and pro-social love could be drawn (Thauvette 2012).

Although pornographic writings of the fifteenth to seventeenth centuries often dominate vulgar language and address sexual acts directly, it is the indirect and ambiguous linguistic strategies (such as metaphor, symbol, and allusion) that often do not so much cover up what is actually meant as bring it to the fore. Read with contemporary eyes, many a passage in an obstetrics book then appears just as exciting as relevant scenes in villainy stories or in guidebooks for married couples and betrayed spouses. Even popular songs and poems as well as classical Greco-Roman literature could stimulate the sexual fantasy and thus came under suspicion of promoting fornication. The reception and adaptation of Lucretius' epic poem *De rerum natura* (On the Nature of Things; around 50 BCE) was one of the ways in which sixteenth- and seventeenth-century poets could treat sexual themes under a classical guise (Hock 2021). More shamefaced audiences found enough passages in philosophical, medical, and pedagogical writings, as well as in fine literature, to make them blush (Turner 2003). Thus, the approximately 250 manuscript collections that have survived for England from 1560 to 1660 are interspersed with erotic poems that demand a certain amount of fantasy but stimulate the sexual imagination (Moulton 2017: 66f.). This also applied to any kind of pictures that were drawn or painted in a manner that was ambiguous and open to interpretation. In most cases, it was enough for mythological figures such as Mars and Venus to be placed next to each other (sometimes naked) in one of the paintings to convey the sexual narrative (Toulalan 2007: 17f.). William Shakespeare's (1564–1616) poem *Venus and Adonis* (1593) may therefore seem to today's recipients to be harmless love games and only offer a few lyrically framed kisses, but for contemporary readers it was driven by a deeply erotic impulse (Thauvette 2012; Maurette 2017). Seen and read with sensitive eyes, even the chaste Occident possessed a highly developed *ars erotica* from the fifteenth to the seventeenth century, which drew from popular and scientific knowledge and sign systems as well as from *scientia sexualis* and the socio-sexual experience of readers and viewers (Foucault 1977: 90ff.).

Another strategy of erotic and pornographic texts and images was, as in the Late Middle Ages, the description of foreign cultures. In the sixteenth and seventeenth centuries, this ethnopornography concerned in particular the eroticization of Ottoman culture and its homoeroticism. In travelogues and fictional descriptions of countries, erotic slave girls and harem ladies appeared as sexual playmates of sultans and viziers, wealthy Turkish men could afford several wives and concubines, and boys acted as "beloved" and sexual servants of their masters. All this was conveyed in a language rich in metaphors. These narratives and images were European projections with which the sexual imagination of European readers could be stimulated by means of the fictitious Orient and, at the same time, Christian-Occidental moral concepts could be transported. In this way, it was possible to expose sexual forms that were forbidden in Europe and hidden for many, and to use them for erotic, obscene, and pornographic purposes. The reporters were exonerated by simultaneously pointing out the immorality and sinfulness of Ottoman customs and traditions. In the guise of boyhood love, even sodomy mutated into a legitimate and serious topic for the wider readership (Boone 2020: 181f.).

In travel narratives about religious rites and everyday practices in the colonies, Christian monks were also able to create sexual imaginaries in European readers. Among them were Franciscan ethnographers in the sixteenth century who told about the people of New Spain and used a voyeuristic gaze to recode these acts of sex and violence (Sigal 2020). West African women and black women in general, on the other hand, appeared to be particularly gripped by their sexuality. At the heart of the stories, however, was the fantasy that white, racially superior men have uninhibited access to black women's bodies. Peppered with such sexual interracial stories, this publication sold even better. One of the most widely read books was *A New and Accurate Description of the Coast of Guinea* (1704/5) by the merchant and Chief Factor for the Dutch William Bosman, in which he also told about prostitution on the Gold Coast. In the book, one could also find an initiation scene between an enslaved woman with a young boy in the marketplace, which simulated sexual intercourse and prepared her for prostitution—a scene that had to be simultaneously repulsive and arousing for the European readers:

> The Novice is smeared all over with Earth, and several Offerings offered for her success in her future Occupation. This over, a little Boy, yet immature for Love Affairs, makes a feint or representation of lying with her before all the People; by which 'tis hinted to her that from this time forwards, she is obliged to receive all Persons indistinguishable who offer themselves to her, not excepting little Boys. (Ipsen 2020: 211)

Prosecution and Culture of Same-Sex Sexual Acts

Sodomites at the Stake and in Court

Between the fifteenth and the early seventeenth century, same-sex sexual acts were punished ever more severely throughout Europe, often by execution. In addition, people started to agitate against sodomites and disavow them for populist purposes, as can be seen in the example of Girolamo Savonarola (1452–1498) in Florence. In 1494, he asked the municipal Signoria to pass a law according to which "such persons should be stoned and burned without mercy." The sodomites had made Florence famous throughout Europe as the capital of "unnatural fornication" in that not only young unmarried men were being tempted, but their political networking was supposedly a threat to community order. The subsequent municipal ordinance stipulated that these offences were not sanctioned with fines as before, but that shameful, corporal, and capital punishments were imposed. Delinquents over the age of eighteen were bound to the column of shame for one hour upon the first offence. Repeat violators were paraded through the city tied up, and then branded on their foreheads; after that they were no longer allowed to hold public office. After the third conviction they were burned alive (Weinstein 2011: 154f.; Chitty 2020: 43ff.).

In the *Carolina* in 1532, it was stipulated under *vnkeusch, so wider die natur beschicht* (unchastity, thus against nature's way): "In that such a man with a beast, man with man, woman with woman, to be unchaste, they also have ruined life, and they shall be judged from life to death according to the custom" (*Die Peinliche Gerichtsordnung*: Art. 116; Roth 2008: 91ff.; Eder 2009: 54ff.; Graupner 1997). In England, Henry VIII (1491–1547) in his fight against the papacy in 1533 issued the secular *buggery statute*, in which sodomy is defined as a sexual act against nature and against the will of God (Johnson and Vanderbeck 2014: 34). Even the English clergy were now subject to secular law (Godbeer 2002: 112). In the event of a conviction, the delinquents were to be beheaded, their property became the state's. During the approximately two and a half centuries in which this paragraph was valid, however, only a few persons were executed, since the penetration (including ejaculation in the anus) had to be proven beyond doubt and by two witnesses, which was hardly feasible (Moran 1996: 33ff.; Norton 2011: 62).

In Sweden, in 1608, the secular Supplementary Law included a clear proscription against homosexuals for the first time, but this only applied to men: "You shall not lie close to a man in the same manner as you lie close to a women; if you do, you are both condemned to death and your blood shall be shed." However, the paragraph was very rarely applied, so that no more than twenty cases are recorded in Sweden until 1750 (Österberg 2010:

169f.). The Norwegian Penal Code was only amended in 1687 to include a paragraph punishing sodomites with death by fire. So far, however, only one case is known to have been charged under this paragraph, but it never came to court (Teige 2020).

Spanish and Portuguese Inquisitions were characterized by a particular zeal in the persecution of sodomites and their frequent executions. Yet, the ecclesiastical authorities tended to be even milder in their judgment than the secular authorities (Crompton 2003: 291ff.; Berco 2005: 334ff.). As in other European countries, the judicial approach to this depended on the social status of the defendants and their families (Martín Romera 2018; Peakman 2020). Some of the trials grew into absolute scandals and spread the view that the sodomites not only acted against the divine order but also caused enormous damage to the Christian community and spread their "rotten seed" into politics (Monter 1990; Hamilton 2021). The decisive factor was that the (homo-)sexual constellations were described in court in a light unfavorable to the defendants and their entourage. Their actions were associated with coercion and dependency or even rape and overpowering, blackmail and prostitution. This occurred in a number of Spanish cities, for which acts of Inquisition have been studied in detail. Between 1540 and 1700, the Inquisition Tribunal in Valencia heard 380 cases of sodomy, 791 trials are documented for Zaragoza and 453 for Barcelona. In Valencia, thirty-seven people were burned at the stake during this period, most of them in the first half of the seventeenth century (Carvajal 2003: 71).

But even this flood of trials could not bring same-sex life and sexual contacts to a standstill. Among the persons recorded in the court files, as in Italy, there are representatives of very different urban classes. In Valencia, slaves, domestic servants, itinerants (such as soldiers, sailors, vagabonds), and clerics were disproportionately often brought before the tribunal for the *pecado nefando* (nefarious sin) (Carrasco 1992: 53f.). The Inquisition cases under the Aragonese Crown concerned two age groups, namely youths and adult respectively older men. Insofar as these sources can be regarded as representative, same-sex relations were mostly structured along age and power relations and sometimes gender-analogously. In the same-sex sexual culture of men, it was a matter of penetrative masculinity, in which the older, active partner appeared as the victorious dominator, while the younger, passive partner appeared as effeminate and submissive (Berco 2007: 9). It is striking that in Spain even the young men were severely punished so as to destroy the sexual objects of the older men. Long-term sexual relationships between men are unlikely to have occurred very often. Some delinquents did not, however, feel that their homosexual experiences were merely a substitute for sexual intercourse with women; these few preferred male partners generally. In the late sixteenth century, the acts of the Seville Inquisition recorded groups of men who met regularly in certain places and in pubs for sexual exchanges (Perry 1990: 126). In the late seventeenth century, the sodomites in Spain were less and less frequently punished by execution. Instead, harsh corporal punishment and imprisonment as well as banishment and forced labor prevailed—if the latter lasted more than several years in the galleys, though, it was pretty much tantamount to a death sentence.

In 110 sodomy appeal cases handled by the so-called *Parlement of Paris* between 1540 and 1680, where information on the age of the passive person is recorded, forty-three persons in the passive position were referred to as "children," "young children," or "boys" (or "choirboys") (Hamilton 2020: 323ff.). Witnesses often stated that older men sexually assaulted minors. The accused were mainly clergies, nobles, officeholders, schoolmasters, but also artisans, laborers, servants, and merchants—a list that shows that men who had authority over children and young people were clearly overrepresented. The structure in the age ratio of the persons and their authority ratio was, however, also related to the fact that primarily the most scandalous cases, often those of sexual abuse, were heard before the appeals chamber.

For the prosecution of sodomites in European countries, many examples can be cited for the early modern period, with Spain and Portugal, England, France, Germany, the Netherlands, Denmark, and Sweden having had the most thorough historical investigations (Crompton 2003: 291ff.; Hergemöller 1999: 82ff.). The range extends from waves of persecution with hundreds of trials in the Netherlands to a few cases here and there in England (Gerard/Hekma 1989: 207ff.). In Frankfurt, only two men were convicted of sodomy between 1562 and 1696 (Boes 2013: 184).

Non-Heterosexual Relations and Foreign Cultures

Age-structured relationships between men and youths were also at the center of those erotic works that explicitly dealt with same-sex contacts in the seventeenth century. In 1652, the satirical dialogue *L'Alcibiade fanciullo a scola* (*Alkibiades the Schoolboy*) was published. It had been written in 1630 by the rhetoric professor and libertine Antonio Rocco (1586–1653) on the occasion of carnival (Salazar 2001: 441ff.). It caricatures the principles of Socratic dialogue in a conversation between the teacher, Philotimos and his pupil Alkibiades (who, according to Plato's *Symposium*, tried to get Socrates to seduce him). Instead of bringing the young man to the truth through rhetorical guidance—as was customary in contemporary didactic manuals—he is seduced into sexual intercourse through pseudo-philosophical talk. Instead of Socratic insemination of words and ideas, oral and anal penetration takes place. Widespread fears and apprehensions also came to the fore, according to which skillful older men could lead innocent young men into perdition through verbal seduction (and through material promises) (Fasoli 2010: 30).

Such suspicions also appeared in patronage networks such as those that existed at the court of James I (1566–1625), King of England and Scotland

(Young 1999). He surrounded himself with young men like Robert Carr, Earl of Somerset (c. 1587–1645), with whom he apparently fell in love at a tournament. George Villiers, the Duke of Buckingham (1592–1628), who captivated James during a hunt and was awarded court offices, later served as his advisor and representative. Whether the king and the attractive men were involved through classical pedagogical *eros* with the ruler educating and protecting the young men in this sense, or whether it came to the sexual realization of his or their desires, cannot be determined, however. The letters the king wrote to them allow for both interpretations (Bergeron 1999: 28ff.). For the public, at any rate, the line between homosexual constellation on the one hand and erotic-sexual practices on the other was quickly crossed in such alliances, which is why there were also sodomy accusations against James and he was compared with the sexually licentious Roman Emperor Tiberius (Asch 2005: 90ff.).

Non-heterosexual sexual forms in the colonies also bewildered Europeans in the sixteenth and seventeenth centuries. For old world eyes, these forms were difficult to impossible to read or see past, and were therefore eagerly reported back to the motherlands. In the two Americas and in Africa, the Europeans encountered gender and sexual types that seemed altogether alien to the mostly clerical chroniclers (Murray 1995; Beemyn 2007: 145ff.): On the one hand, there were beings who opposed the dual-gender order and formed a third or even fourth sex. Europeans encountered such multiple models, for example among the indigenous societies of Peru, where some boys grew up as girls and were sexually used by the tribal leaders during religious ceremonies (Sigal 2003: 1ff.). In North American tribal societies, such people referred in sources as *berdache* or "two-spirits" located between the familiar sexes were considered to be a separate gender, closer to the spiritual and divine than ordinary men and women, and therefore functioned as healers, shamans, or religious-spiritual functionaries. These representatives of the third sex usually dressed as women, could be married or live with a partner (who was not himself a *berdache*) whom they practiced sexual intercourse with (Herdt 1991; Dynes/Donaldson 1992a: viiff.; Gutiérrez 2007). In some places, *berdache* were also regarded as part of the power games of the indigenous upper class—for example, the forced effemination of the sons of others strengthened one's own social position through regulating the offspring of competing men (Trexler 2003: 70ff.). To Europeans, these figures appeared to be hermaphrodites, who in the case of the Timucua Indians in present-day Florida had a rather male body, yet dressed like women and carried out their work (such as caring for the sick and gathering instead of hunting) (Roscoe 1998: 12).

Overseas, the missionaries encountered age-oriented sexual relationships that were more in keeping with the ancient pederast type. With indigenous peoples, they usually played a role in initiation rites with which masculinized warrior societies marked the transition from boy to man. According to European observers, the initiate took a passive position toward an older, active, or powerful man who symbolically transferred knowledge, skills, and power to them. Significantly, the penetrators usually had heterosexual intercourse in addition to ritual same-sex contacts and were often married. Characteristically, we are informed about such sexual relations and contacts either from ecclesiastical sources or from court records, and these were entirely dedicated to the paradigm of sodomy. Moreover, many of the judicial statements were designed as a defense or came about as a result of torture (Tortorici 2018: 57ff.).

No matter which sexual form one came across, in the colonial view of the Europeans it seemed significant that such counter-natural relations predominated among the "savages." By all means its spread to Christianity had to be prevented. For the conquistadors, the transgressive figures also contradicted their own martial ethics. These were based on machist dominance, upholding categories such as honor and sexual potency. To maintain this male dominance, a female counterpart was needed—weak women in need of conquering. An effeminate man was regarded as the quintessential antithesis of the warrior type—which is why in colonial discourse the savages were also portrayed as effeminate and generally unmanly (Trexler 1995; Lewis 2007: 132ff.). In practice, sexual contacts with the soft indigenous men occurred despite or because of this. Exercising possession by sodomizing the savage was often a demonstration of political power. Here, it became apparent that sexual violence and domination in colonial and slave-owning societies was not only widespread in heterosexual but also in same-sex constellations (Block 2006).

In Mexico and Brazil, the colonial authorities feared a possible spread of the sodomitic plague among young people and soldiers (Sigal 2003: 7). Exotic sexual and gender forms, which blurred the boundaries of the polar gender logic, seemed to indicate that diabolical forces were at work and that the possessed had to be opened to Christian missionary zeal—and if this did not help, they had to be consigned to death by fire. To prevent sodomy from spreading further in the colonies, missionaries and clerics called for silence about this sin. However, this did not prevent the transatlantic narratives about these confusing gender and sexual phenomena from being disseminated in Europe in the most colorful ways. In the storied voyages, many a sailor, explorer, and conqueror had a shameful preference for young men and even formed real male couples on the long journeys (Aldrich 2003; Bleys 1996). Although sexual contact between men in homosocial institutions such as the navy and the crews of merchant ships has always occurred, only very few cases have survived, e.g., for the East India Company (Massarella 2017).

Everyday Same-Sex Constellations

In contrast to such sexual forms, the files of Catholic and Protestant courts in Germany and Switzerland in the sixteenth century often contain relatively routine sexual interactions between men. Contacts were established because, for example, peasant laborers had to sleep in the same bed, or an exciting situation arose at an inn, or the cooperation between a master craftsman and his apprentice took an awkward turn. One such case is of a Swiss man, Werner Steiner, a former Catholic priest, later a follower of Zwingli and a wealthy married citizen of Zurich. He was arrested in 1541 and accused of repeated same-sex sexual relations. In earlier years, he had allegedly slept in the same bed with an itinerant laborer and taught him—with the promise of money and clothing gifts—the joys of mutual masturbation. Similarly, he'd also enticed a bath attendant into joint pleasuring. Steiner confessed that he had long practiced this form of same-sex act but had never committed the *vicium sodomiticum*, anal penetration. As a punishment he was sentenced to lifelong house arrest, and he promptly left the city (Puff 2008: 25ff.). Cases such as these show that homoerotic and sexual acts were closely related, and same-sex sexual contacts did not automatically entail a lifelong and exclusive sexual orientation. Often, they shifted with age or marital status and were mixed with heterosexual experiences—but this did not exclude that there were plenty of men with a dominant or exclusively homosexual preference.

Such unspectacular cases often only garnered the attention of the public because in certain court cases the accused had wanted to exonerate themselves from another charge and such stories came out although sodomy hadn't been the trial focus (in the first place) (Puff 2003: 77). In Augsburg, a wholesale sexual network between members of different urban strata was uncovered this way. The participants continued to cultivate the same-sex connections even after marriage (Hergemöller 2000). Lyndal Roper points out that in the court records an almost "domesticated, domestic homosexuality comes to light" (Roper 1995a: 218). Such constellations were promoted by the fact that in the Late Middle Ages and early modern times physical closeness among men had an important social function. The language of friendship was even shaded in homosocial and homoerotic hues, without immediately raising general suspicion of (secret) sexual acts (Phillips and Reay 2011: 73ff.; Stewart 1997). One court case against the pâté baker Ludwig Boudin in Frankfurt in 1598 revealed that for more than twenty years there had been gossip about his same-sex preferences (in the city of less than 20,000 inhabitants) and that some people knew about his homosexual contacts. It was met with tolerance for such a long time because the baker was very popular throughout the surrounding area and his goods were highly appreciated. It was equally unusual that the accused dared to confess his love for one of the young men at trial, which was to his disadvantage in view of the impending punishment (Boes 2013: 186ff.).

In addition to these clandestine contact possibilities, there were also more visible forms of public initiation and homosexual prostitution in urban centers. In the Italian Renaissance cities both seem to have flourished. In Florence, the red light area for boys coalesced around the cathedral, the

Ponte Vecchio, and the streets of Via dei Pelliccai (Ruggiero 2007: 165). Niccolò Machiavelli (1469–1527) reported on it in 1514 to his friend and patron Francesco Vettori (1474–1539), who at that time was ambassador of the city to the Holy See, in a humorous hunting yarn. Their mutual friend Giuliano Brancacci, a well-known sodomite, had gone on a bird hunt there:

> He crossed the bridge of the Carraia and went along the street of the Canto de' Mozzi which leads to Santa Trinita, (. . .) and entering Borgo Santo Apostolo, he wandered about a bit through those narrow alleys that are in between. Not finding any birds waiting for him, (. . .) he moved on past the headquarters of the Guelph party, through the Mercato Nuovo and, going along the street of the Calimala, he came to the Tetto de' Pisani where, looking carefully through all those hiding places, he found a little thrush. (Ruggiero 2010: 1)

Not only Machiavelli's correspondence partner understood which bird their friend was looking for. What was special about this incident was that Brancacci did not meet a "cheap hustler," but Michele, the son of an important Florentine official, who demanded payment for his sexual services. Brancacci allowed himself to be served, but put off paying the boy until the next day by giving him a false name. But, since Michele did not receive any payment at the stated location, he exposed Brancacci's identity and the shameful deed—which made the story a parable of deception and counter-deception and cast a bad light on the already badly maligned scene (Reinhard 2012: 245f.).

In Rome, a special case was uncovered involving a wedding ceremony between two men. In July 1578, a Portuguese man, Marco Pinto, had planned a wedding in the church of San Giovanni a Porta Latina between two members of a group of men, who also otherwise met there for sexual contacts with each other. The plan failed, the group was accused, and eight of them—besides the Portuguese, six Spaniards (possibly *marranos*, that is, converted Jews) and one Venetian Albanian—were burned at the stake. In addition to the classical active–passive and old–young roles, the many sources that have been handed down also show that some of these men had a longer same-sex orientation and that their lives were shaped by it (Ferguson 2016: 157). This is also because they moved in a kind of same-sex subculture. Taken together, all this indicates that there may have been social fields already by the sixteenth century that had a sexual identity-forming effect.

In the Scandinavian countries, there was no anti-sodomite panic until the first half of the eighteenth century, and accordingly no waves of police or judicial persecution. If same-sex relationships became known, people tried to sweep them under the carpet. Most of the documented sexual contacts took place in the context of the household and in homosocial environments such as prisons and the military, and were often characterized by hierarchical relationships of authority and dependence. In court, sodomy was then primarily dealt with through metaphors. The defendants argued that their behavior was sinful and shameful, but that they were not aware of the criminal relevance. In addition to witness testimony, it also had to be proven that ejaculation had occurred in addition to anal penetration—all of which made a conviction, including execution, more difficult. The number of court cases and convictions only increased in the second half of the eighteenth century with the urbanization and the associated emergence of relevant subcultures (Teige 2020; Liliequist 1998).

Violence, "Unspeakable Sin," and Identity

Little is known about same-sex sexual violence against boys and men in the early modern period, as the number of charges is low and there was hardly any visible and therefore evident damage. Moreover, the courts would have assumed that there had been some kind of consent in such contacts and that the victims could hardly give reasons to excuse this crime against nature. As a result, boys and men who had been raped did not turn to the courts. In Spain's machist culture, rapists argued before the Inquisition tribunal that it was a natural expression of their masculinity to have taken a boy, even if he resisted. From today's perspective, it is all the more striking that even in such cases the rape victims were convicted, at least in part, as complicit and punished with exile or corporal punishment (Berco 2008: 261ff.). The accusation of non-consensual sodomitic rape, however, could also be used for political purposes. Pier Luigi Farnese (1503–1547), Duke of Castro, Parma, and Piacenza, was accused of raping the young Bishop Cosimo Gheri (1513–1537) while passing through Fano in Italy in 1537. The bishop died forty days later. This was a welcome occasion for Protestant critics to point to the spread of violent sodomy in the higher Catholic echelons and polemically defame the "rape of Fano" as a novel form of holy martyrdom (Dall'Orio 2001: 187f.).

Martin Luther also exposed sinful male relationships (Puff 2017). In his opinion, papal Rome itself was a stronghold of sodomy. Roman Christianity had not broken with the tradition of ancient sin, according to him. His campaign against the *peccatum contra naturam* (sin against nature) was directed above all against the moral depravity of the clergy, which he said flourished because the clergy could not officially enter into marriage. Since even men of the church could not escape their sexual drive, they would therefore turn to prostitution, concubinage, and even sodomy. Luther thought marriage, heterosexuality, and procreation were the will of God; same-sex acts, on the other hand, were an expression of diabolical powers. Those who practiced them not only indulged their (carnal) desires but were incapable of escaping the devil's temptations and maintaining self-control (Puff 2003: 124ff.). At the same time, the Reformers demanded that the "unspeakable sin" or "unmentionable vice" be hushed up in public to prevent it from spreading. Not just in Protestant areas, delinquents had to swear, after serving their sentence, to tell nothing of their deeds and not to draw anyone else into the circle of heretical sin. Accusations of sodomy thus represented a powerful weapon for defaming religious and political opponents. This happened, for example, in the early modern Low Countries, where, contrary to the imposed ban on silence, polemical songs about sodomy were sung to promote the Reformation, in order to spread images of mortal sin—e.g., in the form of burning cities—among the faithful and to disavow the opponents (Roelens 2018, 2019).

Sodomy trials, however, dealt with only a very small sample of the actual man-to-man sexual relationships and practices that took place (Puff 2003: 75ff.). Some of the incriminated cases make it clear that the accused knew that they were acting unchastely, but not that they had committed a capital crime. An innocent attitude seemed quite legitimate to them, since their immorality had been tolerated for a long time before and they had never faced any serious consequences apart from rumor-mongering and malicious talk. Furthermore, little attention was paid to the question of activity and passivity during sexual acts or penetration, according to Swiss court records. Either way, it was "unnatural fornication." But it is also a fact that anal intercourse was punished most severely by the judges as it represented a reversal of the heterosexual and procreative world. In view of the dominant paradigm of sodomy, Helmut Puff has advocated that we not underestimate the plurality of same-sex sexual relationships as a whole. Even before 1700, in addition to the predominant age- and socio-relational sexual relationships among men, there was also a great variety of constellations—including those that were of the same age, at the same social level, and anchored in a long-term relationship (Puff 2003: 91f., 2011: 60).

A number of studies also assume that same-sex characters and early forms of subjectivity and identity developed as early as the sixteenth century (and possibly earlier) (Borris 2008: 4f.). Same-sex sexual desire was therefore often defined as an inner peculiarity, a kind of constitutional quirk or illness that made the persons concerned spiritually unable to direct their often excessive sexual desire in the right direction. Such a disposition made it all the more dangerous for Christian society. In connection with the ancient medical tradition, the scientification of same-sex sex also progressed. In medical treatises, their type was determined by certain physical characteristics. Like their ancient predecessors, early modern authors also tended to incarnate psychological characteristics (Salih 2002: 125). Around 1600, comments on classical antique and Arabic writings indicated that a *cinaedus* had a phlegmatic female temperament (being cold and wet) and, for the purpose of masculinization, should better live in a warm, harsh, and dry environment. In the wake of Hippocratic, Aristotelian, and Galenic teachings on reproduction and the body, it was also assumed that *tribades* and sodomites suffered from a disorder in sexual imprinting during procreation and pregnancy, which led to an aberration of sexual desire. Physiological and physiognomic peculiarities could also be perceived in these persons, for example, characteristic signs on the face or in the creases of the hands (Borris 2008: 14ff.).

Muslim Homosocial Culture and Sexuality

In the Ottoman Empire and in Muslim culture there was a comparatively tolerant attitude toward same-sex practices during this period. Even if they were punished in the Quran and *şeriat* or Sharia—depending on the severity with payment of money, flogging, imprisonment, or death—erotic attraction was considered a natural emotion, especially among men, and no particular feelings of shame or guilt were associated with it (Ben-Naeh 2005: 81; Engin and Özbarlas 2021: 220ff.). In the spirituality of the Sufis and their religious practices, young beardless men were even regarded as the epitome of holy beauty and as one of the manifestations of divine love, which could be found in everything on earth—a belief that earned them harsh criticism from orthodox Sunnis (Ze'evi 2006: 89 ff.). There are also scenes in erotic art and literature in which male youths and their desirable bodies are aestheticized. However, it would be far from true to speak of a complete or even extensive acceptance of homosexual relationships regardless of social status. As with opposite-sex contacts, same-sex contacts were structured along the active–passive role, the position taken in terms of penetration, social status, and gender. A man who let himself be penetrated put himself in a passive, submissive, and humiliating position. For free, respectable Muslim men this was unthinkable (Rafeq 1990: 187). However, boys and prepubescent or beardless youths were assumed to have a more feminine nature, and it was therefore quite legitimate for them to be desired by men (El-Rouayheb 2005).

The "abducted boys," who were often poetically dressed up as beloved boys by Ottoman writers, represented a special figure in this context. In historical reality, however, the trope of the "beloved" could conceal very different relationships of dependency, depending on their class, age, ethnicity, and religion. The boys could be students or hamam boys, prostituting boys from the urban fringes or even young Janissaries. Abducted and enslaved boys made up a special "category," as their erotic and sexual image could be transformed according to the ideas of their owners in the urban or imperial hierarchy (Arvas 2021: 40f.).

Male prostitution seems to have been relatively widespread in the large cities of the Ottoman Empire. As court records and decrees from the sixteenth century show, boys and young men were active in the social life of Constantinople as apprentices and workers, for example in coffee houses, beer and wine taverns, and bathhouses, where they were often staged as erotic attractions. Some of them also sold themselves as catamites. The historian Mustapha Ali (1541–1600) describes how these boys and adolescents were prepared for the customers: They had to don "colorful dresses that enchant even kings" and were "extraordinary boys, with a silvery face and neck [shining] like camphor candles and golden rings" (Andrews and Kalpakli 2005: 284). How many of these *şehr oğlanları* (city boys) actually prostituted themselves or entered into long-term relationships cannot be said, however, on the basis of the sources evaluated so far (Sariyannis 2005: 4ff.). Entertainers and dancers were also often accused of prostitution in Constantinople (public dance performances by women were not common). Finally, young slaves could even be rented for sexual use (Faroqhi 2002: 253f.). A frequent place to make same-sex contacts were *hammams*, in which the usually clear separation of the sexes brought people interested in same sex together. Young masseurs and barbers were also among those accused of prostitution (Sariyannis 2008: 51). Vani Mehmed Efendi, a famous preacher from Constantinople who reformed Sunni Islam and tried to bring the everyday life of the Ottomans closer to Sharia law, also accused the Janissaries of taking boys on campaigns for sexual pleasure.

To Christian observers, a homosocial and same-sex culture this tolerant seemed to be the epitome of heretic or pagan depravity (Lavenia 2020). In England, accusations of sodomy against the Turks were heard only from the second half of the sixteenth century, in the German Lutheran discourse even before. In a newssheet from Vienna, for example, one could read in 1566, that "they [the Turks] use such Sodomish abhomination and tyranny as may not the shame be knowen, nor without harty sorrow be declared" against their prisoners (Shamgunova 2021: 71f.; Falkner 2004). Reports on the sodomitic practices of the Ottomans came primarily from European travel accounts (Boone 2020). In their tropes and stereotypes, homoeroticism was described as a sophisticated affection for younger men by older men. It was linked to specific sites such as bathhouses and coffee houses and to upper social classes or certain Sufi orders. Some authors argued that homoeroticism was promoted by Islam, others that it was even opposed to it. Mostly, the sodomite culture of the Turks was presented as customs and learned (sinful) behaviors and not as a specific human essence or racial specificity. "Renegades" (converts to Islam) were therefore accused of a particular moral turpitude and sodomite tendencies (Malcolm 2022: 8ff.).

Paul Rycaut (1629–1700), who lived as consul in the port city of Smyrna (present-day Izmir), reports in his *History of the Ottoman Empire* about the sodomitic conditions in the city:

[The men] burn in lust one towards another, (. . .) they call it a passion very laudable and virtuous, and a step to that perfect love of God (. . .) this is the colour of virtue they paint over the deformity of their depraved inclinations, but in reality this love is nothing but libidinous each to another (. . .) and this passion hath boiled sometimes to that heat that jealousies and rivalries have broken forth in their Chambers (. . .) Nor is this passion only amongst the young men each to other, but persons of eminent degree in the Seraglio become enveigled in this sort of love. (...) The Grand Signiors themselves have also been slaves to this inordinate passion. (Ben-Naeh 2005: 85)

These descriptions must be taken with a grain of salt, however, as they were aimed at a European readership, for whom the author wanted to emphasize the moral superiority of the Christian Occident.

Homosexual relationships between people of different faiths were also more or less tolerated—as long as they did not cross the lines to mingle with the Islamic population. There is evidence of Jewish boys who prostituted themselves in the sixteenth century. Here too, erotic contacts were made at dance performances, in bathhouses, and in taverns. In trial proceedings, the focus was then on the respective sexual and social position of the parties involved (Murray 1997: 21). Although same-sex intercourse between men was regarded as a serious transgression in the *halakha*, the legal interpretation of the written Torah, and the authorities of the Jewish communities took action against it, such homosexual relationships were as much a part of social practice as in the Muslim majority society (Ben-Naeh 2005: 90ff.). In the border regions of present-day Bosnia and Herzegovina, sexual contacts between Christian and Muslim men have also been documented. There seems to have been a less strict policy against same-sex acts under Ottoman influence. *Pobratimstvo*, the ritual brotherhood across religious boundaries, however, had nothing to do with homosexual relationships in the modern sense of the word, even though the sources spoke of love and kisses between men. The practice of sworn brothers served primarily to master religiously and legally impossible relations between the Christian-Orthodox and Muslim populations (Bracewell 2016: 343).

Same-Sex Relations among Women

The history of same-sex sexual relations among women continues to be a research desideratum for the early Ottoman Empire. For earlier historiography, Ottoman culture was the breeding ground of oriental eroticism and it was not uncommon to imagine that same-sex sexual practices found their way through the High Gate into Renaissance Italy and from there to the rest of Europe. Thanks to the research of recent decades, such romantic stories have proved to be a mirage that travelers of the eighteenth and nineteenth centuries projected onto their surroundings. And historians had been willing to entertain them for a long time (Andrews and Kalpakli 2005: 129ff.). A closer examination of the sources revealed that even in literary works hardly any reference was made to erotic, let alone sexual, relationships between women. Exceptions such as Deli Birader Gazali (1466–1535), a Sharia scholar and writer who compiled a compilation of erotic and pornographic stories of Turkish, Arab, and Persian provenance, offered a male-phallic view of it:

In big cities, there are famous *dildo women*. They put on manly clothes, they ride cavalry horses, and they also ride *kochis* (covered wagons) for fun. Rich and noble women invite them to their houses and offer them nice shirts and clothing. These women tie dildos on their waists and grease them with almond oil and then start the job, of dildoing the cunt (Arvas 2014: 157).

For contemporaries, a satisfying sexual life among women seemed almost unthinkable and could only be realized in phallic-penetrative actions, which is why such deeds were not addressed in legal documents (Andrews and Kalpakli 2005: 172). An alternative view is provided by the works of a few female poets. One such writer, Mihri Hatun (1460–1506) was known as "Sappho of the Ottomans" and clearly preferred women in her poetry. However, it was one of the peculiarities of Turkish grammar that expressions of love and erotic fantasies were usually formulated without gender classification and that the (imagined) addressees could only be delimited by means of female attributes such as the veil (Arvas 2014: 158f.).

In other parts of Europe, same-sex sexual acts among women came up for discussion again in the middle of the sixteenth century. The anatomists Realdo Colombo and Gabriele Falloppio gave a reason for this with their dispute about the discovery of the clitoris (Laqueur 1992: 81ff.; Park 1997). Was this part of the body used for pleasurable rubbing and tickling during sexual contact, or could a woman of appropriate size possibly use it for vaginal penetration? Did an oversized clitoris represent a metamorphosis of the penis, and did intercourse between women represent the equivalent of vaginal or anal penetration by and between men? Must this crime then be punished just as severely? How was the use of a dildo to be classified and sanctioned? The centuries-old confusion about *tribades* and hermaphrodites now appeared in a new light (Roelens 2014: 19f.; Martín Romera 2018: 17ff.): *Tribades* were no longer seen as potential hermaphrodites (as female men with an underdeveloped penis) but as genuine women with an oversized clitoris. Such an unnatural development pointed to pathological sexual desire. The anatomist Caspar Berthelsen Bartholin (the elder) (1585–1629) called them *confricatrices* because of their sexual practice (Andreadis 2001: 43).

The *Zimmern Chronicle* (1540/1558–1566), which was written in Baden-Württemberg, showed that the distinction between hermaphrodites and women desiring women was already part of general knowledge by the middle of the sixteenth century. In it, Froben Christoph von Zimmern (1519–1566) reported about a maid nicknamed Greta of the market:

So was the time when a poor servant was at Mösskirch, serviced now and then, and was called Greta of the market. She wanted to take (. . .) no man or young apprentice to her, but loved the young daughters, followed them and rummaged around, she even had gestures and manners, as if she had a male affect. She has been suspected several times for being a hermaphrodite or androgen, which was not a fabrication, then she has been visited by mad and courageous people and seen as a true, quite female. (Rolker 2015)

The Body of the *Tribades*

Until the seventeenth and eighteenth centuries, many physicians, philosophers, and clerics believed, in accordance with the complementary gender model, that the female body was to be understood as the opposite pole of the male and that the female sexual organ was an inward-facing counterpart of the penis. Vagina and uterus should correspond to the penis, the fallopian tubes to the testicles. The (re)discovered clitoris, however, led to the problem that there were now two homologies to the penis. As already mentioned, Thomas Laqueur even spoke in this context of a "one-sex model" that was intended to legitimize female inferiority—and was heavily criticized for it, among other things, because he left out many early modern voices that assumed two genders (Laqueur 1992; Park and Nye 1991; Hergemöller 1999: 57ff.; Mathes 2001: 49ff.; Pomata 2001; Schnell 2002: 67ff.). Following studies have shown that as early as the fifteenth and sixteenth centuries, leading physicians insisted on the specific characteristics of the female (and male) body, and in particular the genitals, and formed a corresponding opinion of them. It was precisely the anatomical and physiological differences between the two sexes that formed an essential basis for the construction and justification of gender characters—and has done so since ancient times (Stolberg 2003; King 2013). Regardless of the gender model toward which one inclined, the hermaphrodites were in any case located in the middle of the spectrum and should bare characteristics of both sides (Laqueur 1992: 156ff.).

Despite the theoretical confusion, after the anatomical "discovery" of the clitoris—of which the ancient doctors and writers were already aware—women desiring same sex were no longer considered anatomically disguised men or (pseudo-)hermaphrodites transforming themselves into men, but rather women with an overdeveloped sexual organ and drive. Due to this physical peculiarity, as well as due to an unusual seed production or lack of heterosexual satisfaction, these *tribades* were forced into their sexual preference by their bodies and thus represented a perversion of the female body (Traub 2002: 188ff., 2007: 128). Helkiah Crooke (1576–1648), the English court physician, in his *Description of the Body of Man* (1631) established a direct connection between female anatomy and sexual practices among women:

> Sometimes [the clitoris] grows to such a length that it hangs outside the slit like a man's penis, especially when it is irritated by contact with cloth,

and becomes stiff and hard like a man's penis. And this part is abused by vicious women called tribade (often mentioned by many authors and rightly punished in some states) for their mutual and unnatural lust. (Traub 2003: 306)

It is not surprising then that in the sixteenth and early seventeenth centuries there were considerations to surgically remove the clitoris of these women. According to the 1573 work *Des monstres et des prodiges* by the French surgeon Ambroise Paré (*c.* 1510–1590), figuring out whether someone was a hermaphrodite or a woman with an overdeveloped clitoris was impossible in most cases. It nevertheless seemed necessary in view of the essential gender polarity of early modern society.

Erotic and Sexual Practices among Women

From early modern court records we can also learn a lot about the lived practice of the "shameful passions" among women (Roelens 2014). Well-known are Benedetta Carlini (1590–1661), the abbesses of the Theatine Sisters of Pescia (1619–1623) (Puff 1999; Brown 1988; Benkov 2001; Simons 2019). Some women were banned or exiled because of sodomy, for example: Catalina de Belunçe from the Basque Country in 1503; Agatha Dietschi from Freiburg in 1547; Françoise Morel from Geneva in 1568; Esperanza de Rojas from Valencia in 1597 (Roelens 2015: 8). The records make it clear that contemporary rhetoric and perception tended to ignore non-phallic aspects of their same-sex lives and that there was no separate criminal category for the offence of a "silent sin" among women—although the term *tribade* (a woman rubbing herself against another woman) came into use again at the turn of the fifteenth and sixteenth centuries (Bonnet 1997). In the case of Benedetta Carlinis, it became conversely clear that an emancipatory reading of such (here church) records also went too far. Critically regarded, the passions of the abbess turned out to be a hardly comprehensible web of ecstatic visions, spirituality, mysticism, charity, and (alleged) sexual acts with her nuns—but one can hardly speak of a lesbian nun in today's sense (Matter 1989/90; Simons 2019).

The use of dildos between women is also reported by other sources, with the imitation of penetration (by a man) and the assumption of the male role by a woman usually being quite problematic. In England, this was punished severely, while mutual masturbation, rubbing genitals, and caressing breasts were exempt from punishment (Traub 2003: 309ff.). The word dildo was first used in Thomas Nashe's (1567 to around 1601) poem *The Choice of Valentines or the Merie Ballad of Nash his Dildo* (around 1593). It was actually a nonsense term that was supposed to sound Italian, because the shameful habit of using artificial objects instead of a real penis supposedly came from regions that spoke Italian. According to the widely travelled Pierre de Bourdeille, Seigneur de Brantôme (*c.* 1540–1614), one would encounter its use in many European countries, such as France, Italy, Spain, and the Ottoman Empire. Italy was preferred as the origin of this instrument because in Aretino's *Ragionamenti* (1534–1536) there were *pastinaca muranese* (parsnips from Murano), which were allegedly made in the glassworks of Murano for orgies between monks and nuns (Simons 2010: 77f.). Mostly, however, dildos played a role in a satirical context: They were used to make fun of those men who failed to satisfy their wives and drove them into the hands of female sexual partners who then used pseudo-penises.

The *Portrait of Gabrielle d'Estrée and One of Her Sisters* (anonymous, *c*. 1594) is one of the pictures that deals with erotic relationships between women. It shows (probably) Gabrielle d'Estrées (*c*. 1570–1599), Duchesse de Beaufort et Verneuil, the long-time mistress of the French King Henry IV, with whom she had three children. She stands naked in a wash tub together with her sister. Both have nude torsos. One of the women pinches the other's nipple with her index finger and thumb; the latter holds a ring out to the viewer in a similar gesture. The picture belongs to the many portraits of mistresses from the school of Fontainebleau. Thus, on the one hand, it can be interpreted as an allegory of fertility and pregnancy, as a symbolic marriage and possession, or as an erotic animation for the addressee, in this case the king. This interpretation is supported by two figures that can be seen in the background: a clothed seamstress and a partially unclothed female lower body on a bed (a picture within the picture). If one follows that latest interpretative offer, this painting is a typical example of contemporary heterosexual pornography. On the other hand, the image animates the viewer to adopt actor positions geared toward same-sex desire under another gaze regime. As in many depictions of naked women who wrap their legs around each other or touch their vulva with their hands, there is always the arousing possibility of women teasing and satisfying each other in this way (Zorach 2001: 196). Such representations can also be found in the (semi-)public sphere, for example in a ceiling fresco that Parmigianino (1503–1540) had painted in 1523/24 in the Rocca Sanvitale Palace in Fontanellato, Italy. In it, naked nymphs embrace each other with an intimate gaze and animate the viewer to spin the erotic story further. Two depictions of virtue designed by Hendrick Goltzius (1558–1616/17) also show naked female couples kissing and embracing each other in an erotic atmosphere (Guth 2012: 321f.).

Erotic depictions of female couples as well as literary accounts of love and desire between them offered a wide range of interpretations from the fifteenth through the seventeenth century. However, whether this was an explicit or even ambiguous problematization of tribadian feelings and homoerotic, even homosexual acts among women remains controversial. The respective historical interpretation depends on the understanding of the modern term "lesbian": While one side primarily refers to sexual desire and behavior of women, which is (exclusively) directed at their own sex, the other side aims at rather diffuse forms of love and erotic attraction.

The manner in which the everyday practice of same-sex erotic and sexual contacts and relationships actually took place, and whether these women had a lesbian identity, is not mentioned in the available sources—despite queer reading. It seems more fruitful to examine, for example, fictional literature for those positions that opened up a positive framework for same-sex love and eroticism and made possible sexual activity (Traub 2016b: 122). For example, the works of the English author Katherine Philips (1631/2–1664), who adapted Neoplatonic ideas to reflect on Sappho, to write poems about her, and to join her in a poetic and erotic series (Andreadis 2001: 55ff., 2008: 258ff.). In rare cases—such as that of Mayken and Magdaleene in early seventeenth-century Bruges (Roelens 2014: 26f.)—it can even be read from court records that some same-sex desiring women were aware of their sexual and erotic preference and that they also knew that they were not the only ones with these feelings. In the world of ideas of the time, however, their romance still seemed like evil forces at work.

7

Coda

The present volume is the first of a two-volume publication on the history of sexuality in Europe from antiquity to the present. The second volume will deal with the emergence and assertion of "sexuality"—in the modern sense of the word—from the seventeenth and eighteenth centuries onward and follow it up to the beginning of the twenty-first century. It thus deals with a period that some historians understand as a sequence of sexual revolutions; the first of which took place—depending on the author pinpointing it—in the seventeenth, eighteenth, and nineteenth centuries, in the interwar period or in the 1960s and 1970s (Godbeer 2002; Cook 2004; Carleton 2004; Dabhoiwala 2012; Hekma and Giami 2014; Bänziger et al. 2015). According to Foucault's famous dictum, "king sex" was enthroned during this century (Foucault 1978b: 185). This implementation of sexuality is critically pursued on the basis of the construction of illegitimate, enlightened, and romantic desires from the seventeenth to the early nineteenth century, the separation of sexuality and reproduction from the nineteenth century to the Second World War, and the pluralization and normalization of sexualities from 1945 to the present. In continuation of the social and cultural-historical perspective, the focus will be on the formation of sexual subjects, the change in bodily reference, and self- and heteronomous determination under the sign of sexuality, the scientification, medicalization, and medialization as well as the commercialization and commodification of sexual life. Finally, Volume 2 provides a condensed overview of the lines of development in the history of sexuality in Europe from antiquity to the present.

BIBLIOGRAPHY

Abbott, Elizabeth (2001), *A History of Celibacy*, Cambridge
Abbott, Elizabeth (2010), *Mistresses: A History of the Other Woman*, London
Aberth, John (2019), No Sex Please, We're Medieval: Sexuality in the Middle Ages, in: Aberth, John (ed), *Contesting the Middle Ages: Debates That Are Changing our Narrative of Medieval History*, London, pp. 141–178
Abraham, Erin V. (2017), *Anticipating Sin in Medieval Society: Childhood, Sexuality, and Violence in the Early Penitentials*, Amsterdam
Ackerman Smoller, Laura (2018), Dominicans and Demons: Possession, Temptation, and Reform in the Cult of Vincent Ferrer, in: *Speculum* 93, 4, pp. 1010–1047
Adair, Richard (1996), *Courtship, Illegitimacy and Marriage in Early Modern England*, Manchester/New York
Adam, Birgit (2001), *Die Strafe der Venus. Eine Kulturgeschichte der Geschlechtskrankheiten*, München
Adam, Hans Christian (1991), Die erotische Daguerreotypie, in: Köhler, Michael/Barche, Gisela (eds), *Das Aktfoto. Ansichten vom Körper im fotografischen Zeitalter. Ästhetik, Geschichte, Ideologie*, München, pp. 56–61
Adams, James N. (1982), *The Latin Sexual Vocabulary*, London
Ahern, Eoghan (2018), The Sin of Sodom in Late Antiquity, in: *Journal of the History of Sexuality* 27, 2, pp. 209–233
Ajootian, Aileen (2003), The Only Happy Couple: Hermaphrodites and Gender, in: Koloski-Ostrow, Ann Olga/Lyons, Claire L. (eds), *Naked Truths. Women, Sexuality, and Gender in Classical Art and Archaeology*, New York, pp. 220–242
Akashe-Böhme, Farideh (2006), *Sexualität und Körperpraxis im Islam*, Frankfurt a. M.
Akkermann, Antke/Betzelt, Sigrid/Daniel, Gabriele (1990), Nackte Tatsachen. Teil 1 und 2, in: *Zeitschrift für Sexualforschung* 3, pp. 1–24, 140
Albers, Irene (2010), Das Erröten der Princesse de Clèves. Körper - Macht - Emotion, in: Kasten, Ingrid (ed), *Machtvolle Gefühle*, Berlin, pp. 263–296
Albertson, Fred C. (2007), Constantine, in: Howell, James W. (ed), *The Greenwood Encyclopedia of Love, Courtship, and Sexuality through History, Vol. 1: The Ancient World*, Westport, pp. 95–102
Aldrich, Robert F. (1993), *The Seduction of the Mediterranean: Writing, Art and Homosexual Fantasy*, London/New York
Aldrich, Robert F. (2003), *Colonialism and Homosexuality*, London et al.
Aldrich, Robert F./Wotherspoon, Garry (eds) (2001), *Who's Who in Contemporary Gay and Lesbian History: From World War II to the Present Day*, New York/London

Allen, Robert H. (2006), *The Classical Origins of Modern Homophobia*, Jefferson
Allen, Robert C. (2011), *Global Economic History: A Very Short Introduction*, Oxford et al., p. 170
Allyn, David (2000), *Make Love, Not War: The Sexual Revolution: An Unfettered History*, Boston
Altbauer-Rudnik, Michael (2006), Love, Madness and Social Order: Love Melancholy in France and England in the Late Sixteenth and Early Seventeenth Centuries, in: *Gesnerus* 63, pp. 33–45
Alter, George/Clark, Gregory (2010), The Demographic Transition and Human Capital, in: O'Rourke, Kevin H./Broadberry, S. N. (eds), *The Cambridge Economic History of Modern Europe: Vol. 1, 1700–1870*, Cambridge, pp. 43–69
Alvar, Jaime (2008), *Romanising Oriental Gods: Myth, Salvation, and Ethics in the Cults of Cybele, Isis and Mithras*, Leiden
Álvarez, Lourdes (2005), The Mystical Language of Daily Life. Vernacular Sufi Poetry and the Songs of Abu Al-Hasan-Al-Shushtari, in: *Exemplaria: A Journal of Theory in Medieval and Renaissance Studies* 27, 1, pp. 1–32
Amer, Sahar (2008), *Crossing Borders. Love Between Women in Medieval French and Arabic Literatures*, Philadelphia
Amer, Sahar (2009), Medieval Arab Lesbians and Lesbian-Like Women, in: *Journal of the History of Sexuality* 18, 2, pp. 215–236
Amt, Emilie (ed) (1993), *Women's Lives in Medieval Europe: A Sourcebook*, New York
Anderson, Roberta/Bellenger, Dominic Aidan (eds) (2003), *Medieval Worlds: A Sourcebook*, London/New York
Anderson, Wendy Love (2020), The Goy of Sex: A Short Historical Tour of Relations between Jews and Non-Jews, in: Ruttenberg, Danya (ed), *The Passionate Torah: Sex and Judaism*, New York, pp. 136–151
Andersson, Martin (2021), How Soldiers' Women Built Early Modern States, in: Dørum, Knut/Hallenberg, Mats/Katajala, Kimmo (eds), *Bringing the People Back In: State Building from Below in the Nordic Countries Ca. 1500–1800*, Milton, pp. 162–180
Andreadis, Harriette (2001), *Sappho in Early Modern England: Female Same-Sex Literary Erotics, 1550–1714*, Chicago
Andreadis, Harriette (2008), Erotics versus Sexualities: Current Science and Reading Early Modern Female Same-Sex Relations, in: Borris, Kenneth/Rousseau, George (eds), *The Sciences of Homosexuality in Early Modern Europe*, London/New York, pp. 254–267
Andrews, Walter G./Kalpakli, Mehmet (2005), *The Age of Beloveds: Love and the Beloved in Early Modern Ottoman and European Culture and Society*, Durham
Angelides, Steven (2001), *A History of Bisexuality*, Chicago
Angenendt, Arnold (1990), *Das Frühmittelalter: Die abendländische Christenheit von 400 bis 900*, Stuttgart, 3rd edn
Angenendt, Arnold (2015), *Ehe, Liebe und Sexualität im Christentum: Von den Anfängen bis heute*, Münster
Aretino, Pietro (2017), *Kurtisanengespräche (Ragionamenti) (übers. von Heinrich Conrad)*, Berlin
Ariès, Philippe (1992), Die unauflösliche Ehe, in: Ariès, Philippe/Béjin, André/Foucault, Michel (eds), *Die Masken des Begehrens und die*

Metamorphosen der Sinnlichkeit. Zur Geschichte der Sexualität im Abendland, Frankfurt a. M., pp. 176–197
Arieti, James A. (2002), Rape and Livy's View of Roman History, in: Deacy, Susan/Pierce, Karen F. (eds), *Rape in Antiquity: Sexual Violence in the Greek and Roman Worlds*, London, pp. 209–229
Aristophanes (2004), *Clouds: A Dual Language Edition*, trans. Ian Johnston, Oxford
Armelagos, George J./Zuckerman, Molly K./Harper, Kristin N. (2012), The Science behind Pre-Columbian Evidence of Syphilis in Europe: Research by Documentary, in: *Evolutionary Anthropology* 21, 2, pp. 50–57
Armstrong, Elizabeth A. (2003), *Forging Gay Identities: Organizing Sexuality in San Francisco, 1950–1994*, Chicago
Armstrong, Rebecca (2004), Retiring Apollo: Ovid on the Politics and Poetics of Self-Sufficiency, in: *Classical Quarterly* 54, 2, pp. 528–550
Armstrong-Partida, Michelle (2013), Priestly Wives: The Role and Acceptance of Clerics' Concubines in the Parishes of Late Medieval Catalunya, in: *Speculum* 88, 1, pp. 166–214
Armstrong‐Partida, Michelle (2019), Concubinage, Illegitimacy and Fatherhood: Urban Masculinity in Late‐medieval Barcelona, in: *Gender & History* 31, 1, pp. 195–219
Arnórsdóttir, Agnes (2018), Marriage Regulations in Denmark and Iceland 1550–1650: With a Special Focus on Change in the Practice of Marital Gift Giving and the Ideal of Motherhood, in: Holm, Bo Kristian/Koefoed, Nina J. (eds), *Lutheran Theology and the Shaping of Society: The Danish Monarchy as Example*, Göttingen, pp. 283–301
Arrizabalaga, Jon (2005), Medical Responses to the "French Disease" in Europe at the Turn of the Sixteenth Century, in: Siena, Kevin Patrick (ed), *Sins of the Flesh: Responding to Sexual Disease in Early Modern Europe*, Toronto, pp. 33–56
Arrizabalaga, Jon/Henderson, John/French, Roger Kenneth (1997), *The Great Pox: The French Disease in Renaissance Europe*, New Haven et al.
Artman-Partock, Tali (2021), The Tale Type of the Repenting Prostitute: Between Rabbis and Church Fathers, in: *AJS Review* 42, 1, pp. 1–20
Arvas, Abdulhamit (2014), From the Pervert, Back to the Beloved: Homosexuality and Ottoman Literary History, 1453–1923, in: McCallum, E. L./Tuhkanen, Mikko (eds), *The Cambridge History of Gay and Lesbian Literature*, New York, pp. 145–163
Arvas, Abdulhamit (2021), Leander in the Ottoman Mediterranean: The Homoerotics of Abduction in the Global Renaissance, in: *English Literary Renaissance* 51, 1, pp. 31–62
Asch, Ronald (2005), *Jakob I. (1567–1625): König von England und Schottland. Herrscher des Friedens im Zeitalter der Religionskriege*, Stuttgart
Astbury, Lea (2020), When a Woman Hates Her Husband: Love, Sex and Fruitful Marriages in Early Modern England, in: *Gender & History (Special Issue: Gender and Reproduction)* 32, 3, pp. 523–541
Augart, Julia (2006), *Eine romantische Liebe in Briefen. Zur Liebeskonzeption im Briefwechsel von Sophie Mereau und Clemens Brentano*, Würzburg
Augustine (2013), *The Confessions of St. Augustine. St. Augustine, Bishop of Hippo (345–430)*, trans. Edward Pusey, Four Oaks

Auhagen, Ulrike (2009), *Die Hetäre in der griechischen und römischen Komödie*, München
Babbi, Anna Maria (2021), Aspetti della marginalità sessuale in alcuni romanzi medievali/Aspects of sexual marginality in some medieval novels, in: Benjamins, John (ed), *Biografies Invisibles: Invisible Biographies*, Amsterdam, pp. 225–232
Bachorski, Hans-Jürgen (1991), Diskursfeld Ehe. Schreibweisen und thematische Setzungen, in: Bachorski, Hans-Jürgen (ed), *Ordnung und Lust. Bilder von Liebe, Ehe und Sexualität in Spätmittelalter und Früher Neuzeit*, Trier, pp. 511–545
Baechle, Sarah/Harris, Carissa M./Strakhov, Elizaveta (eds) (2022), *Rape Culture and Female Resistance in Late Medieval Literature: With an Edition of Middle English and Middle Scots Pastourelles*, University Park
Baer, Brian James (2005), The New Visibility. Representing Sexual Minorities in the Popular Culture of Post-Soviet Russia, in: Stulhofer, Aleksandar/Sandfort, Theo (eds), *Sexuality and Gender in Postcommunist Eastern Europe and Russia*, New York, pp. 193–208
Bagerius, Henric/Ekholst, Christine (2016), The Unruly Queen: Blanche of Namur and Dysfunctional Rulership in Medieval Sweden, in: Rohr, Zita Eva/Benz, Lisa (eds), *Queenship, Gender, and Reputation in the Medieval and Early Modern West, 1060–1600*, Cham, pp. 99–118
Bagerius, Henric/Ekholst, Christine (2017), Kings and Favourites: Politics and Sexuality in Late Medieval Europe, in: *Journal of Medieval History* 43, 3, pp. 298–319
Bairoch, Paul/Goertz, Gary (1986), Factors of Urbanisation in the Nineteenth Century Developed Countries: A Descriptive and Econometric Analysis, in: *Urban Studies* 23, pp. 285–305
Bake, Rita/Kiupel, Birgit (1996), *Unordentliche Begierden. Liebe, Sexualität und Ehe im 18. Jahrhundert*, Hamburg
Baker, Brenda J. et al. (2020), Advancing the Understanding of Treponemal Disease in the Past and Present, in: *Yearbook of Physical Anthropology* 171, pp. 5–41
Baldwin, James E. (2012), Prostitution, Islamic Law and Ottoman Societies, in: *Journal of the Economic and Social History of the Orient* 55, pp. 117–152
Ballhaus, Alexander (2009), *Liebe und Sex im Mittelalter*, Bergisch Gladbach
Bannert, Herbert (2005), Herr Wirt, die Rechnung! Ein Grabstein aus Aesernia (CIL IX 2689) und einige Bemerkungen zur Interpretation von Text und Bild, in: Beutler, Franziska/Hameter, Wolfgang (eds), *Eine ganz normale Inschrift ... und Ähnliches zum Geburtstag von Ekkehard Weber*, Wien, pp. 203–213
Bänziger, Perter-Paul/Beljan, Magdalena/Eder, Franz X./Eitler, Pascal (eds) (2015), *Sexuelle Revolution? Zur Geschichte der Sexualität im deutschsprachigen Raum seit den 1960er Jahren*, Bielefeld
Barbezat, Michael D. (2016), Bodies of Spirit and Bodies of Flesh: The Significance of the Sexual Practices Attributed to Heretics from the Eleventh to the Fourteenth Century, in: *Journal of the History of Sexuality* 25, 3, pp. 387–419
Barbin, Herculine/Foucault, Michel (1998), *Über Hermaphrodismus*, Frankfurt a. M.
Bardsley, Sandy (2007), *Women's Roles in the Middle Ages*, Westport
Barker-Benfield, Graham John (1992), *The Culture of Sensibility. Sex and Society in Eighteenth-Century Britain*, Chicago

Barnes, Corey (2010), Thomas Aquinas on the Body and Bodily Passions, in: Kamitsuka, Margaret D. (ed), *The Embrace of Eros: Bodies, Desires, and Sexuality in Christianity*, Minneapolis, pp. 83–98

Barnes-Karol, Gwendolyn/Spadaccini, Nicholas (2002), Sexuality, Marriage, Power in Medieval and Early Modern Iberia, in: Lanz, Eukene Lacarra (ed), *Marriage and Sexuality in Medieval and Early Modern Iberia*, London/New York, pp. 233–246

Barret-Ducrocq, Francoise (1989), *L'amour sous Victoria. Sexualité et classes populaires à Londres au XIX siècle*, Paris

Barton, Simon (2015), *Conquerors, Brides, and Concubines: Interfaith Relations and Social Power in Medieval Iberia*, Philadelphia

Barton, Ulrich (2009), Was wir do machen, das ist schimpf. Zum Selbstverständnis des Nürnberger Fastnachtspiels, in: Ridder, Klaus (ed), *Fastnachtspiele: Weltliches Schauspiel in literarischen und kulturellen Kontexten*, Tübingen, pp. 167–185

Bartsch, Shadi (2005), Eros and the Roman Philosopher, in: Bartsch, Shadi/Bartscherer, Thomas (eds), *Erotikon: Essays on Eros, Ancient and Modern*, Chicago, pp. 59–84

Baskin, Judith (2003), Marriage, in: Roth, Norman (ed), *Medieval Jewish Civilization: An Encyclopedia*, New York, pp. 424–429

Baskin, Judith R. (2002), *Midrashic Women: Formations of the Feminine in Rabbinic Literature*, Hannover

Baskin, Judith R./Ruttenberg, Danya (2020), Prostitution: Not a Job for a Nice Jewish Girl, in: Ruttenberg, Danya (ed), *The Passionate Torah: Sex and Judaism*, New York, pp. 24–35

Bauer, Heike (2011), Sex, Popular Beliefs and Culture, in: Peakman, Julie (ed), *A Cultural History of Sexuality in the Enlightenment (=A Cultural History of Sexuality Vol. 4)*, Oxford/New York, pp. 159–182

Bauer, Ingrid/Hämmerle, Christa/Hauch, Gabriella (2005), Liebe widerständig erforschen: Eine Einleitung, in: Bauer, Ingrid/Hämmerle, Christa/Hauch, Gabriella (eds), *Liebe und Widerstand. Ambivalenzen historischer Geschlechterbeziehungen*, Wien/Köln/Weinar, pp. 9–35

Bayer, Ronald (1981), *Homosexuality and American Psychiatry: The Politics of Diagnosis*, New York

Beam, Sara (2020), Gender and the Prosecution of Adultery in Geneva, 1550–1700, in: van der Heijden, Manon et al. (eds), *Women's Criminality in Europe, 1600–1914*, Cambridge, pp. 91–113

Beard, Mary (1994), The Roman and the Foreign: The Cult of the "Great Mother" in Imperial Rome, in: Thomas, Nicholas/Humphrey, Caroline (eds), *Shamanism, History, and the State*, Ann Arbor, pp. 164–190

Beard, Mary/North, John/Price, Simon (1998), *Religions of Rome: A History. Vol. 2: A Sourcebook*, Cambridge

Beccalossi, Chiara (2011), Sex, Medicine and Disease: From Reproduction to Sexuality, in: Beccalossi, Chiara/Crozier, Ivan (eds), *A Cultural History of Sexuality in the Age of Empire (=A Cultural History of Sexuality Vol. 5)*, Oxford/New York, pp. 101–122

Beck, Rainer (1983), Illegitimität und vorehelihe Sexualität auf dem Land. Unterfinning, 1661–1770, in: Dülmen, Richard van (ed), *Kultur der einfachen Leute. Bayerisches Volksleben vom 16. bis zum 19. Jahrhundert*, München, pp. 112–150

Becker, Peter (1990), *Leben und Lieben in einem kalten Land. Sexualität im Spannungsfeld von Ökonomie und Demographie. Das Beispiel St. Lamprecht 1600–1850*, Frankfurt a. M.
Becker, Peter (1992), Ich bin halt immer liederlich gewest und habe zu wenig gebetet. Illegitimität und Herrschaft im Ancien Régime. St. Lambrecht 1600–1850, in: Vierhaus, Rudolf (ed), *Frühe Neuzeit—Frühe Moderne? Forschungen zur Vielschichtigkeit von Übergangsprozessen*, Göttingen, pp. 157–179
Beecher, D. A. (1989), Erotic Love and the Inquisition: Jacques Ferrand and the Tribunal of Toulouse, 1620, in: *The Sixteenth Century Journal* 20, 1, pp. 41–53
Beemyn, Brett Genny (2007), Nord- und Südamerika. Von der Kolonialzeit bis zum 20. Jahrhundert, in: Aldrich, Robert (ed), *Gleich und anders. Eine globale Geschichte der Homosexualität*, Hamburg, pp. 145–165
Behrend-Martínez, Edward (2012), Taming Don Juan: Limiting Masculine Sexuality in Counter-Reformation Spain, in: *Gender & History* 24, 2, pp. 333–352
Behrisch, Lars (2007), Protestantische Sittenzucht und katholisches Ehegericht: Die Stadt Görlitz und das Bautzner Domkapitel im 16. Jahrhundert, in: Isaiasz, Vera et al. (eds), *Stadt und Religion in der frühen Neuzeit. Soziale Ordnungen und ihre Repräsentationen*, Frankfurt a. M., pp. 33–66
Bei, Neda (2001), Die sozial schädliche Verbrecherin. Frauen und der § 129 I b StG, in: Förster, Wolfgang/Natter, Tobias G./Rieder, Ines (eds), *Der andere Blick. Lesbischwules Leben in Österreich*, Wien, pp. 163–171
Bei, Neda/Förster, Wolfgang/Hacker, Hanna/Lang, Manfred (eds) (1986), *Das lila Wien um 1900. Zur Ästhetik der Homosexualitäten*, Wien
Bein, Thomas (2003), *Liebe und Erotik im Mittelalter*, Graz
Bejosa Gould, Deborah (2009), *Moving Politics: Emotion and ACT UP's Fight against AIDS*, Chicago/London
Belemann-Smit, Anja (2003), *Wenn schnöde Wollust dich erfüllt... Geschlechtsspezifische Aspekte in der Anti-Onanie-Debatte des 18. Jahrhunderts*, Frankfurt a. M. et al.
Bell, Alan P./Weinberg, Martin S. (1978), *Homosexualities: A Study of Diversity among Men and Women*, New York
Bell, Jacob (2023), Ok lá þar at óvilja hennar: A Reconsideration of Sexual Violence in the Old Norse World, in: *Journal of Family History* 48, 1, pp. 3–29
Bellinger, Gerhard J. (1993), *Im Himmel wie auf Erden. Sexualität in den Religionen der Welt*, München
Belting, Hans (2001), *Bild-Anthropologie. Entwürfe für eine Bildwissenschaft*, Müchen
Benhabib, Seyla et al. (eds) (1993), *Der Streit um Differenz. Feminismus und Postmoderne in der Gegenwart*, Frankfurt a. M.
Benito Julià, Roger (2018), *La prostitució a la Barcelona Baixmedieval (segles XIV-XV)*, Barcelona
Benkel, Thorsten (2012), Elemente einer Sexualtheorie der Praxis, in: *Zeitschrift für Sexualforschung* 25, 4, pp. 356–372
Benkov, Edith (2001), The Erased Lesbian. Sodomy and the Legal Tradition in Medieval Europe, in: Sautman, Francesca Canadé/Sheingorn, Pamela (eds), *Same-Sex Love and Desire among Women in the Middle Ages*, New York, pp. 101–122

Ben-Naeh, Yaron (2005), Moshko the Jew and His Gay Friends: Same-Sex Sexual Relations in Ottoman Jewish Society, in: *Journal of Early Modern History* 9, 1, pp. 79–108

Bennett, Judith M. (2000), Lesbian-Like and the Social History of Lesbianisms, in: *Journal of the History of Sexuality* 9, 1/2, pp. 1–24

Bennett, Judith M. (2019), Wretched Girls, Wretched Boys and the European Marriage Pattern in England (c. 1250–1350), in: *Continuity and Change* 34, pp. 315–347

Berco, Christian (2005), Social Control and Its Limits: Sodomy, Local Sexual Economies, and Inquisitors during Spain's Golden Age, in: *Sixteenth Century Journal* 36, pp. 331–358

Berco, Christian (2007), *Sexual Hierarchies, Public Status. Men, Sodomy, and Society in Spains Golden Age*, Toronto

Berco, Cristian (2008), Producing Patriarchy: Male Sodomy and Gender in Early Modern Spain, in: *Journal of the History of Sexuality* 17, 3, pp. 335–350

Berco, Christian (2011), Textiles as Social Texts: Syphilis, Material Culture and Gender in Golden Age Spain, in: *Journal of Social History* 44, 3, pp. 785–810

Berco, Christian (2016), *From Body to Community: Venereal Disease and Society in Baroque Spain*, Toronto

Berger, Ruth (2003), *Sexualität, Ehe und Familienleben in der jüdischen Moralliteratur, 900-1900*, Wiesbaden

Bergeron, David M. (1999), *King James and Letters of Homoerotic Desire*, Iowa City

Berkowitz, Eric (2012), *Sex and Punishment: Four Thousand Years of Judging Desire*, Berkeley

Bernos, Marcel et al. (1985), *Le fruit défendu. Les chrétiens et la sexualité de l'antiquité à nos jours*, Paris

Bertrand, Dominique (ed) (2005), *Lire l'Heptaméron de Marguerite de Navarre*, Clermont-Ferrand

Bérubé, Allan (1990), *Coming Out under Fire: The History of Gay Men and Lesbians in World War Two*, New York

Bérubé, Allan (2003), The History of Gay Bathhouses, in: Woods, William J./Binson, Diane (eds), *Gay Bathhouses and Public Health Policy*, New York, pp. 33–55

Besant, Annie (1887): *The Law of Population: Its Consequences, and Its Yearing upon Human Conduct and Morals*, London

Betancourt, Roland (2020), *Byzantine Intersectionality: Sexuality, Gender, and Race in the Middle Ages*, Princeton/Oxford

Beukes, Johann (2020), Intervroulike seksualiteit in die latere middeleeue: 'n ideëhistoriese oorsig, in: *Verbum et Ecclesia* 41, 1, pp. 1–13

Beukes, Johann (2021), Augustinus en vroulike homoërotiek in die vroeë Middeleeue: 'n Foucaultiaanse ideëhistoriese interpretasie, in: *Hervormde teologiese studies*, 77, 4, pp. 1–12

Beusterien, John L. (1999), Jewish Male Menstruation in Seventeenth-Century Spain, in: *Bulletin of the History of Medicine* 73, 3, pp. 447–456

Beutin, Wolfgang (2004), Das nerrisch tut vii manig man, / der sich des schamt ein ander zeit: Zur Problematik des Obszönen im Mittelalter, in: Winkelman, Johan H./Wolf, Gerhard (eds), *Erotik, aus dem Dreck gezogen*, Amsterdam/New York, pp. 21–36

Biale, David (1992), *Eros and the Jews: From Biblical Israel to Contemporary America*, New York
Bickart, Noah Benjamin (2016), Overturning the "Table": The Hidden Meaning of a Talmudic Metaphor for Coitus, in: *Journal of the History of Sexuality* 25, 3, pp. 489–507
Biller, Peter (2016), Goodbye to Catharism?, in: Sennis, Antonio (ed), *Cathars in Question*, York, pp. 274–313
Biller, Peter A. (1998), Birth Control in the Medieval West, in: Biller, Peter/Minnis, Alastair J. (eds), *Handling Sin: Confession in the Middle Ages*, Woodbridge/Rochester, pp. 165–184
Biller, Peter A. (2005), Black Women in Medieval Scientific Thought, in: Brero, Thalia (ed), *La Pelle Umana/The Human Skin (=Micrologus 13)*, Florenz, pp. 165–184
Billing, Valerie (2017), Sexuality and Queerness on the Early Modern Stage, in: Kinney, Arthur F./Hopper, Thomas Warren (eds), *A New Companion to Renaissance Drama*, Hoboken, pp. 441–455
Binhammer, Katherine (2009), *The Seduction Narrative in Britain, 1747–1800*, Cambridge
Bitel, Lisa M. (2002), *Women in Early Medieval Europe 400–1100*, Cambridge
Blank, Hanne (2007), *Virgin: The Untouched History*, New York
Blanshard, Alastair J. L. (2010), *Sex: Vice and Love from Antiquity to Modernity*, Malden/Oxford
Blaschitz, Gertrud (2008), Das Freudenhaus im Mittelalter. In der stat was gesessen ain unrainer pulian, in: Classen, Albrecht (ed), *Sexuality in the Middle Ages and the Early Modern Times: New Approaches to a Fundamental Cultural-Historical and Literary-Anthropological Theme*, Berlin/New York, pp. 715–750
Blasius, Mark/Phelan, Shane (eds) (1997), *We Are Everywhere: A Historical Sourcebook in Gay and Lesbian Politics*, New York
Bleibtreu-Ehrenberg, Gisela (1978), *Tabu Homosexualität. Die Geschichte eines Vorurteils*, Frankfurt a. M.
Bleys, Rudi C. (1996), *The Geography of Perversion: Male-to-Male Sexual Behaviour Outside the West and the Ethnographic Imagination, 1750–1918*, New York/London
Block, Sharon (2006), *Rape and Sexual Power in Early America*, Chapel Hill
Blondell, Ruby (2008), Introduction, in: *Helios* 35, 2, pp. 113–118
Blondell, Ruby/Ormand, Kirk (eds) (2015), *Ancient Sex: New Essays: Classical Memories, Modern Identities*, Columbus
Blud, Victoria (2017), *The Unspeakable, Gender and Sexuality in Medieval Literature, 1000–1400*, Cambridge
Blundell, Sue (2002), Amazons, from Women in Ancient Greece, in: Burg, Barry Richard (ed), *Gay Warriors: A Documentary History from the Ancient World to the Present*, New York et al., pp. 28–34
Bochow, Michael et al. (1994), Sexual Behavior of Gay Men in Eight European Countries, in: *AIDS Care* 6, 5, pp. 533–549
Boehrer, Bruce Thomas (1990), Early Modern Syphilis, in: *Journal of the History of Sexuality* 1, 2, pp. 197–214
Boehringer, Sandra (2007), *L'homosexualité féminine dans l'Antiquité grecque et romaine*, Paris

Boehringer, Sandra (2014), Female Homoeroticism, in: Hubbard, Thomas K. (ed), *A Companion to Greek and Roman Sexualities*, New York, pp. 1283–1308

Boes, Maria R. (2013), *Crime and Punishment in Early Modern Germany: Courts and Adjudicatory Practices in Frankfurt am Main, 1562–1696*, Farnham

Bof, Ricardo/Leyser, Conrad (2016), Divorce and Remarriage between Late Antiquity and the Early Middle Ages: Canon Law and Conflict Resolution, in: Cooper, Kate/Leyser, Conrad (eds), *Making Early Medieval Societies: Conflict and Belonging in the Latin West, 300–1200*, Cambridge, pp. 155–180

Bohaumilitzky, Peter/Nägl, Isolde (1989), Sexualität und Volksfrömmigkeit in Europa, in: Ehalt, Hubert Ch. (ed), *Volksfrömmigkeit. Von der Antike bis zum 18. Jahrhundert*, Wien/Köln, pp. 143–189

Böhme, Hartmut (2011), Nacktheit und Scham in der Anatomie der Frühen Neuzeit, in: Gvozdeva, Katja/Velten, Hans Rudolf (eds), *Scham und Schamlosigkeit. Grenzverletzungen in Literatur und Kultur der Vormoderne*, Berlin/Boston, pp. 434–471

Boiadjiev, Tzotcho (2003), *Die Nacht im Mittelalter*, Würzburg

Bokody, Péter (2021), Images of Wartime Sexual Violence in the Chronicles of Giovanni Villani and Giovanni Sercambi, in: *Renaissance Studies* 36, 4, pp. 565–589

Bolder-Boos, Marion (2015), Der Krieg und die Liebe. Untersuchungen zur römischen Venus, in: *Klio* 97, pp. 81–134

Bologne, Jean Claude (2001), *Nacktheit und Prüderie. Eine Geschichte des Schamgefühls*, Weimar

Bonfil, Robert (2012), Jews, Christians, and Sex in Renaissance Italy: A Historiographical Problem, in: *Jewish History* 26, 1/2, pp. 101–111

Bonnard, Jean-Baptiste (2013), Male and Female Bodies according to Ancient Greek Physicians, in: *Clio. Women, Gender, History* 37, pp. 19–37

Bonnet, Anne-Marie (1981), *Un Choix sans équivoque. Techerches historiques sur les relations amoureuses entre les femmes XVIe-(Krafft-Ebing, Richard v. 1912) e siècle*, Paris

Bonnet, Anne-Marie (1997), Sappho, or the Importance of Culture in the Language of Love: Tribade, Lesbienne, Homosexuelle, in: Livia, Anna/Hall, Kira (eds), *Queerly Phrased: Language, Gender and Sexuality*, New York/Oxford, pp. 147–166

Boone, Joseph Allen (2020), European Travelogues and Ottoman Sexuality: Sodomitical Crossings Abroad, 1550–1850, in: Sigal, Peter H./Tortorici, Zeb/Whitehead, Neil L. (eds), *Ethnopornography: Sexuality, Colonialism, and Archival Knowledge*, Durham/London, pp. 169–204

Boone, Marc (1996), State Power and Illicit Sexuality: The Persecution of Sodomy in Late Medieval Bruges, in: *Journal of Medieval History* 22, pp. 135–153

Borg, Barbara (2001), Eunomia oder: Vom Eros der Hellenen, in: von den Hoff, Ralf/Schmidt, Stefan (eds), Konstruktionen von Wirklichkeit. Bilder im Griechenland des 5. und 4. Jahrhunderts v, Chr., Stuttgart, pp. 299–314

Borris, Kenneth (2008), Introduction: The Prehistory of Homosexuality in the Early Modern Sciences, in: Borris, Kenneth/Rousseau, George (eds), *The Sciences of Homosexuality in Early Modern Europe*, London/New York, pp. 1–40

Borris, Kenneth (ed) (2004), *Same-Sex Desire in English Renaissance: A Sourcebook of Texts, 1470–1650*, New York/London

Borscheid, Peter (1986), Romantic Love or Material Interest: Choosing Partners in Nineteenth-Century Germany, in: *Journal of Family History* 11, 2, pp. 157–168

Borsje, Jacqueline (2017), The Power of Words: Sacred and Forbidden Love Magic in Medieval Ireland, in: Berlis, Angela/Korte, Anna-Marie J. A. C. M./Biezeveld, Kune (eds), *Everyday Life and the Sacred: Re/configuring Gender Studies in Religion*, Leiden/Boston, pp. 218–248

Bossong, Georg (2008), *Die Sepharden: Geschichte und Kultur der spanischen Juden*, München

Bossong, Georg (2010), *Das maurische Spanien. Geschichte und Kultur*, München

Boswell, John (1980), *Christianity, Social Tolerance and Homosexuality. Gay People in Western Europe from the Beginning of the Christian Era to the Fourteenth Century*, Chicago/London

Boswell, John (1994), *Same-Sex Unions in Premodern Europe*, New York

Boureau, Alain (1996), *Das Recht der Ersten Nacht. Zur Geschichte einer Fiktion*, Düsseldorf/Zürich

Bowers, Tony (2000), Collusive Resistance. Sexual Agency and Partisan Politics in Love in Excess, in: Saxton, Kirsten T./Bocchicchio, Rebecca P. (eds), *The Passionate Fictions of Eliza Haywood: Essays on Her Life and Work*, Lexington, pp. 48–68

Boyar, Ebru (2016), An Imagined Moral Community: Ottoman Female Public Presence, Honour and Morality, in: Boyar, Ebru/Fleet, Kate (eds), *Ottoman Women in Public Space*, Leiden, pp. 187–229

Boyarin, Daniel (1995), *Carnal Israel: Reading Sex in Talmudic Culture*, Berkeley/Los Angeles/London

Boyarin, Daniel (2003), On the History of the Early Phallus, in: Farmer, Sharon A./Pasternack, Carol Braun (eds), *Gender and Difference in the Middle Ages*, Minneapolis, pp. 3–44

Boyarin, Daniel/Castelli, Elizabeth A. (2001), Introduction: Foucault's History of Sexuality – The Fourth Volume, or, a Field Left Fallow for Others to Till, in: *Journal of the History of Sexuality* 10, 3/4 (Special Issue: Sexuality in Late Antiquity), pp. 357–374

Bracewell, Wendy (2016), Ritual Brotherhood across Frontiers in the Eastern Adriatic Hinterland, Sixteenth to Eighteenth Centuries, in: *History and Anthropology* 27, 3, pp. 338–358

Brady, Sean (2011), Homosexuality: European and Colonial Encounters, in: Beccalossi, Chiara/Crozier, Ivan (eds), *A Cultural History of Sexuality in the Age of Empire (=A Cultural History of Sexuality Vol. 5)*, Oxford/New York, pp. 43–62

Brakke, David (2001), Ethiopian Demons. Male Sexuality, the Black-Skinned Other, and the Monastic Self, in: *Journal of the History of Sexuality* 10, 3/4 (Special Issue: Sexuality in Late Antiquity), pp. 501–535

Brändström, Anders (1998), Illegitimacy and Lone-Parenthood in XlXth Century Sweden, in: *Annales de démographie historique* 2, pp. 93–113

Brannan Lewis, Margaret (2020), Corpses and Confessions: Forensic Investigation and Infanticide in Early Modern Germany, in: de Ceglia, Francesco Paolo (ed), *The Body of Evidence: Corpses and Proofs in Early Modern European Medicine*, Boston, pp. 224–244

Braun, Rudolf (1979), *Industrialisierung und Volksleben. Veränderungen der Lebensformen unter Einwirkung der verlagsindustriellen Heimarbeit in einem ländlichen Industriegebiet (Zürcher Oberland) vor 1800*, Göttingen, 2nd edn

Bray, Alan (1982), *Homosexuality in Renaissance England*, London

Bredbeck, Gregory W. (1991), *Sodomy and Interpretation: Marlowe to Milton*, Ithaca/London
Bredekamp, Horst (2011), Von der Schamlosigkeit zur großen Form, in: Gvozdeva, Katja/Velten, Hans Rudolf (eds), *Scham und Schamlosigkeit. Grenzverletzungen in Literatur und Kultur der Vormoderne*, Berlin/Boston, pp. 223–263
Breit, Stefan (1991), *Leichtfertigkeit und ländliche Gesellschaft. Voreheliche Sexualität in der frühen Neuzeit*, München
Breitbach, Udo (1998), *Die Vollmacht der Kirche Jesu Christi über die Ehen der Getauften. Zzur Gesetzesunterworfenheit der Ehen nichtkatholischer Christen*, Rome
Brenner, Athalya (1996), *A Feminist Companion to the Hebrew Bible in the New Testament*, Shefflied
Breul, Wolfgang (2014), Celibacy – Marriage – Unmarriage: The Controversy over Celibacy and Clerical Marriage in the Early Reformation, in: Luebke, David/Lindemann, Mary (eds), *Transgressive Unions in Germany from the Reformation to the Enlightenment*, Oxford/New York, pp. 31–44
Brieler, Ulrich (1998), *Die Unerbittlichkeit der Historizität. Foucault als Historiker*, Köln/Wien
Brinkschröder, Michael (2006), *Sodom als Symptom. Gleichgeschlechtliche Sexualität im christlich Imaginären - Eine religionsgeschichtliche Anamnese*, Berlin/New York
Brisson, Luc (2002), *Sexual Ambivalence: Androgyny and Hermaphroditism in Graeco-Roman Antiquity*, Berkeley/Los Angeles/London
Brisson, Luc/Renaut, Olivier (eds) (2017), *Érotique et politique chez Platon: Erôs, genre et sexualité dans la cité platonicienne*, Sankt Augustin
Brizio, Elena (2019), Sexual Violence in the Sienese State before and after the Fall of the Republik, in: Murray, Jacqueline/Terpstra, Nicholas (eds), *Sex, Gender and Sexuality in Renaissance Italy*, London, pp. 35–52
Bromley, James M./Stockton, Will (eds) (2013), *Sex before Sex: Figuring the Act in Early Modern England*, Minneapolis
Brooten, Bernadette J. (1996), *Love between Women: Early Christian Responses to Female Homoeroticism*, Chicago/London
Brown, Judith C. (1988), *Schändliche Leidenschaften. Das Leben einer lesbischen Nonne in Italien zur Zeit der Renaissance*, Stuttgart
Brown, Peter (1988), *The Body and the Society: Men, Women and Sexual Renunciation in Early Christianity*, New York
Brożyna, Martha A. (ed) (2005), *Gender and Sexuality in the Middle Ages: A Medieval Source Documents Reader*, Jefferson
Brugger, E. Christian (2017), *The Indissolubility of Marriage and the Council of Trent*, Washington
Brundage, James A. (1982), Rape and Seduction in the Medieval Canon Law, in: Bullough, Vern L./Brundage, James A. (eds), *Sexual Practices and the Medieval Church*, Chicago, pp. 141–148
Brundage, James A. (1984), Let Me Count the Ways: Canonists and Theologians Contemplate Coital Positions, in: *Journal of Medieval History* 10, pp. 81–93
Brundage, James A. (1987), *Law, Sex and Christian Society in Medieval Europe*, Chicago
Brundage, James A. (1996), Sex and Canon Law, in: Bullough, Vern L./Brundage, James A. (eds), *Handbook of Medival Sexuality*, New York/London, pp. 33–50

Brunner, Andreas/Rieder, Ines/Schefzig, Nadja/Sulzenbacher, Hannes/Wahl, Niko (eds) (2005), *Geheimsache:Leben. Schwule und Lesben in Wien im 20. Jahrhundert (Ausstellungskatalog)*, Wien

Brunner, Karl (1998), Geluste und gelange. Anmerkungen zur Sexualität im ersten Mittelalter, in: Tuczay, Christa et al. (eds), *Ir sult sprechen willekommen. Grenzenlose Mediävistik. Festschrift für Helmut Birkhan*, Bern et al., pp. 245–287

Bruns, Claudia (2005), Skandale im Beraterkreis um Kaiser Wilhelm II. Die homoerotische „Verbündelung" der „Liebenberger Tafelrunde" als Politikum, in: zur Nieden, Susanne (ed), *Homosexualität und Staatsräson. Männlichkeit, Homophobie und Politik in Deutschland 1900–1945*, Frankfurt a. M./New York, pp. 52–80

Bruns, Claudia (2008), *Politik des Eros. Der Männerbund in Wissenschaft, Politik und Jugendkultur (1880–1934)*, Köln/Wien

Bruns, Volker (1997), Education homophile in Klein-Paris. Die sechziger Jahre in Düsseldorf, in: Kraushaar, Elmar (ed), *Hundert Jahre schwul. Eine Revue*, Berlin, pp. 85–103

Budin, Stephanie Lynn (2008), *The Myth of Sacred Prostitution in Antiquity*, Cambridge/New York

Budin, Stephanie Lynn (2021), *Freewomen, Patriarchal Authority, and the Accusation of Prostitution*, London

Buffière, Félix (1980), *Eros adolescent. La pédérastie dans la Grèce antique*, Paris

Buffington, Robert Marshall (2014), Introduction, in: Buffington, Robert Marshall/Luibheid, Eithne/Guy, Donna (eds), *A Global History of Sexuality: The Modern Era*, London, pp. 1–15

Bullough, Bonnie (1994), Abortion, in: Bullough, Vern L./Bullough, Bonnie (eds), *Human Sexuality: An Encyclopedia*, New York/London, pp. 4–8

Bullough, Vern L. et al. (eds) (2001), *Encyclopedia of Birth Control*, Santa Barbara

Bullough, Vern L./Bullough, Bonnie (1987), *Women and Prostitution: A Social History*, Buffalo

Bulst, Neithard (1994), Illegitime Kinder – Viele oder wenige? Quantitative Aspekte der Illegitimität im spätmittelalterlichen Europa, in: Schmugge, Ludwig (ed), *Illegitimität im Spätmittelalter*, München, pp. 21–40

Bunzl, Matti (2001), Die Regenbogen-Parade als kulturelles Phänomen, in: Förster, Wolfgang/Natter, Tobias G./Rieder, Ines (eds), *Der andere Blick. Lesbischwules Leben in Österreich*, Wien, pp. 261–265

Burch, Karen (2019), Love and Marriage: Emotion and Sexuality in the Early Medici Family, in: *Carte Italiane* 12, 1, pp. 17–34

Burger, Glenn/Kruger, Stephen (eds) (2001), *Queering the Middle Ages*, Minneapolis

Burger, Glenn D. (2018), *Conduct Becoming: Good Wives and Husbands in the Later Middle Ages*, Philadelphia

Burghartz, Susanna (1992), Jungfräulichkeit oder Reinheit? Zur Änderung von Argumentationsmustern vor dem Baseler Ehegericht im 16. und 17. Jahrhundert, in: Dülmen, Richard van (ed), *Dynamik der Tradition*, Frankfurt a. M., pp. 13–40

Burghartz, Susanna (1999), *Zeiten der Reinheit. Orte des Unzucht. Ehe und Sexualität in Basel während der Frühen Neuzeit*, Paderborn

Burghartz, Susanna (2004), Ordering Discourse and Society. Moral Politics, Marriage and Fornication during the Reformation and the Confessionalisation Process in Germany and Switzerland, in: Roodenburg, Herman/Spierenburg, Pieter (eds), *Social Control in Europe, 1500–1800*, Vol. 1, Columbus, pp. 78–98

Burghartz, Susanna (2016), Competing Logics of Public Order: Matrimony and the Fight against Illicit Sexuality in Germany and Switzerland from the Sixteenth to the Eighteenth Century, in: *Marriage in Europe 1400–1800*, pp. 176–200

Burgwinkle, William E. (2004), *Sodomy, Masculinity, and Law in Medieval Literature: France and England, 1050–1230*, Cambridge

Burmann, Henriette (2000), *Die kalkulierte Emotion der Geschlechterinszenierung. Galanterierituale nach deutschen Etikette-Büchern in soziohistorischer Perspektive*, Konstanz

Burrus, Virginia (2004), *The Sex Lives of Saints: An Erotics of Ancient Hagiography*, Philadelphia

Busch, Nathanael (2019), Höfische Obszönitäten? Ein "Rosendorn"-Fund und seine Folgen, in: *Zeitschrift für deutsches Altertum und deutsche Literatur* 148, 3, pp. 331–347

Busch, Stephan (1999), *Versus balnearum. Die antike Dichtung über Bäder und Baden im römischen Reich*, Stuttgart

Bush, M. L. (1998), *What Is Love? Richard Carlile's Philosophy of Sex*, London/New York

Butler, Cheryl (2017), Incontinent of Her Body: Women, Society and Morality in Tudor Southampton, in: *The Local Historian* 47, 2, pp. 96–110

Butler, Judith (1991), *Das Unbehagen der Geschlechter*, Frankfurt a. M.

Butler, Sara M. (2005), Abortion by Assault: Violence against Pregnant Women in Thirteenth- and Fourteenth-Century England, in: *Journal of Women's History* 17, 4, pp. 9–31

Butler, Shane (2019), The Youth of Antiquity: Reception, Homosexuality, Alterity, in: *Classical Receptions Journal* 11, 4, pp. 373–406

Butrica, James L. (2006), Some Myths and Anomalies in the Study of Roman Sexuality, in: Verstraete, Beert C./Provencal, Vernon L. (eds), *Same-Sex Desire and Love in Greco-Roman Antiquity and in the Classical Tradition of the West*, New York/Binghamton, pp. 209–270

Buzhilova, Alexandra (1999), Medieval Examples of Syphilis from European Russia, in: *International Journal of Osteoarchaeology* 9, 5, pp. 271–276

Bynum, Caroline W. (1991), *Fragmentation and Redemption: Essays on Gender and the Human Body in Medieval Religion*, New York

Cadden, Joan (1993), *Meanings of Sex Difference in the Middle Ages: Medicine, Science and Culture*, Cambridge

Cadden, Joan (1996), Western Medicine and Natural Philosophy, in: Bullough, Vern L./Brundage, James A. (eds), *Handbook of Medieval Sexuality*, New York/London, pp. 51–80

Cadden, Joan (2013), *Nothing Natural Is Shameful: Sodomy and Science in Late Medieval Europe*, Philadelphia

Cady, Diane (2005), Linguistic Dis-Ease: Foreign Language as Sexual Disease in Early Modern England, in: Siena, Kevin Patrick (ed), *Sins of the Flesh. Responding to Sexual Disease in Early Modern Europe*, Toronto, pp. 159–186

Cady, Diane (2006), Medieval Prostitution, in: Hope Ditmore, Melissa (ed), *Encyclopedia of Prostitution and Sex Work*, Vol. I, Connecticut/London, pp. 299–301

Cady, Joseph (1992), Masculine Love: Renaissance Writing, and the "New Invention of Homosexuality", in: Summers, Claude J. (ed), *Homosexuality in Renaissance and Enlightenment England: Literary Representation in Historical Context*, New York, pp. 9–40

Caldwell, Lauren (2014), *Roman Girlhood and the Fashioning of Femininity*, Cambridge

Callis, April S. (2009), Playing with Butler and Foucault: Bisexuality and Queer Theory, in: *Journal of Bisexuality* 9, 3–4, pp. 213–233

Camille, Michael (1998), Obscenity under Erasure: Censorship in Medieval Illuminated Manuscripts, in: Ziolkowski, Jan M. (ed), *Obscenity: Social Control and Artistic Creation in the European Middle Ages*, Leiden, pp. 139–154

Campanile, Domitilla (2017), The Patrician, the General and the Emperor in Women's Clothes: Examples of Cross-Dressing in Late Republican and Early Imperial Rome, in: Campanile, Domitilla et al. (eds), *TransAntiquity: Cross-dressing and Transgender Dynamics in the Ancient World*, London, pp. 52–64

Candau Chacón, María Luisa (2018), Transgresión, miseria y desenvoltura: La prostitución clandestina en la Sevilla moderna, in: *Tiempos modernos* 36, 1, pp. 454–475

Cantarella, Eva (1992), *Bisexuality in the Ancient World*, New Haven

Cantarella, Eva (ed) (1999), *Pompeji. Liebe und Erotik in einer römischen Stadt*, Stuttgart

Carleton, Gregory (2004), *Sexual Revolution in Bolshevik Russia*, Pittsburgh

Carrasco, Pedro (1997), Indian Spanish Marriages in the First Century of the Colony, in: Schroeder, Susan/Wood, Stephanie/Haskett, Robert (eds), *Indian Women of Early Mexico*, Norman, pp. 87–104

Carrasco, Rafael (1992), Sodomiten und Inquisitoren im Spanien des sechzehnten und siebzehnten Jahrhunderts, in: Corbin, Alain (ed), *Die sexuelle Gewalt in der Geschichte*, Berlin, pp. 45–58

Carter, David (2004), *Stonewall: The Riots That Sparked the Gay Revolution*, New York

Carvajal Garza, Federico (2003), *Butterflies Will Burn: Prosecuting Sodomites in Early Modern Spain and Mexico*, Austin

Cassidy, Tanya (2007), People, Place, and Performance. Theoretically Revisiting Mother Clap's Molly House, in: Mounsey, Chris/Gonda, Caroline (eds), *Queer People: Negotiations and Expressions of Homosexuality, 1700–1800*, Lewisburg, pp. 99–113

Castuera, Ignacio (2017), A Social History of Christian Thought on Abortion: Ambiguity vs. Certainty in Moral Debate, in: *The American Journal of Economics and Sociology* 76, 1, pp. 121–227

Catlos, Brian A. (2014), Ethno-Religious Minorities, in: Horden, Peregrine/Kinoshita, Sharon (eds), *A Companion to Mediterranean History*, London, pp. 361–377

Catullus (2015), *The Poems of Catullus: An Annotated Translation by Jeannine Diddle Uzzi and Jeffrey Thomson*, Cambridge

Caviness, Madeline H. (2011), A Son's Gaze on Noah: Case or Cause of Viriliphobia?, in: Lindquist, Sherry C. M. (ed), *The Meanings of Nudity in Medieval Art*, Farnham et al., pp. 103–148

Chakrabarty, Dipesh (2000), *Provincializing Europe: Postcolonial Thought and Historical Difference*, Princeton
Chasin, Alexandra (2000), *Selling Out: The Gay and Lesbian Movement Goes to Market*, New York
Chauncey, George Jr. (1994), *Gay New York: Gender, Urban Culture and the Making of the Gay Male World, 1890–1940*, New York
Chauncey, George Jr./Duberman, Martin/Vicinus, Martha (1989), Introduction, in: Chauncey, George Jr./Duberman, Martin/Vicinus, Martha (eds), *Hidden from History: Reclaiming the Gay and Lesbian Past*, New York, pp. 1–16
Chaytor, Miranda (1995), Husband(ry): Narratives of Rape in the Seventeenth Century, in: *Gender and History* 7, pp. 378–407
Cheek, Pamela (2003), *Sexual Antipodes: Enlightenment, Globalization, and the Placing of Sex*, Stanford
Chitty, Christopher (2020), *Sexual Hegemony: Statecraft, Sodomy, and Capital in the Rise of the World System*, Durham/London
Christ-von Wedel, Christine (2017), *Erasmus von Rotterdam. Ein Porträt*, Basel, 2nd edn
Christensen, Birgit (2000), Gleichwertigkeit des Verschiedenen. Zum Verhältnis der Geschlechter bei Julien Offray de La Mettrie, in: Opitz, Claudia et al. (eds), *Tugend, Vernunft und Gefühl. Geschlechterdiskurse der Aufklärung und weibliche Lebenswelten*, Münster, pp. 195–208
Christopoulos, John (2021), *Abortion in Early Modern Italy*, Cambridge
Cicero, Marcus Tullius (2018), *Cicero' Orations*, trans. Charles Duke Yonge, Mineola
Clancy-Smith, Julia (2004), Exemplary Women and Sacred Journeys: Women and Gender in Judaism, Christianity, and Islam from Late Antiquity to the Eve of Modernity, in: Smith, Bonnie G. (ed), *Women's History in Global Perspective*, Vol. 1, Urbana, pp. 92–144
Clark, Anna (1995), *The Struggle for the Breeches: Gender and the Making of the British Working Class*, Berkeley et al.
Clark, Anna (2008), *Desire: A History of European Sexuality*, New York/London
Clark, Anna (2011), Heterosexuality: Europe and North America, in: Peakman, Julie (ed), *A Cultural History of Sexuality in the Enlightenment (=A Cultural History of Sexuality Vol. 4)*, Oxford/New York, pp. 33–57
Clark, Anna (2019), *Desire: A History of European Sexuality*, New York/London, 2nd ed
Clark, David (2009), *Between Medieval Men: Male Friendship and Desire in Early Medieval English Literature*, Oxford/New York
Clark, David (2017), Discourses of Masturbation: The (Non)solitary Pleasures of the (Medieval) Text, in: *Men and Masculinities* 20, 4, pp. 453–481
Clark, Elizabeth A. (1986), Adam's Only Companion: Augustine and the Early Christian Debate on Marriage, in: *Recherches Augustiniennes* 21, 139–162
Clark, Elizabeth A. (1988), Foucault, the Fathers and Sex, in: *Journal of the American Academy of Religion* 56, 4, pp. 619–641
Clark, Elizabeth A. (1995), Antifamilial Tendencies in Ancient Christianity, in: *Journal of the History of Sexuality* 5, 3, pp. 356–380
Clark, Elizabeth A. (1999), *Reading Renunciation: Asceticism and Scripture in Early Christianity*, Princeton
Clarke, John R. (1998), *Looking at Lovemaking. Constructions of Sexuality in Roman Art, 100 B. C.–A. D. 250*, Berkeley

Clarke, John R. (2002), Men and Women Viewers in the Apodyterium of the Suburban Bath of Pompeii, in: Fredrick, David (ed), *The Roman Gaze: Vision, Power, and the Body*, Baltimore/London, pp. 149–181

Clarke, John R. (2005), Representations of the Cinaedus in Roman Art. Evidence of ‚Gay' Subculture?, in: *Journal of Homosexuality* 49, 3–4, pp. 271–299

Clarke, John R. (2006), Same-Sex Desire and Love in Greek-Roman Antiquity, in: Verstraete, Beert C./Provencal, Vernon L. (eds), *Same-Sex Desire and Love in Greco-Roman Antiquity and in the Classical Tradition of the West*, New York/Binghamton, pp. 271–298

Clarke, John R. (2009), *Ars erotica. Sexualität und ihre Bilder im antiken Rom*, Darmstadt

Clarke, John R. (2011), Visual Representation of Greek and Roman Sexual Culture, in: Golden, Mark/Toohey, Peter (eds), *A Cultural History of Sexuality in the Classical World (=A Cultural History of Sexuality Vol. 1)*, Oxford/New York, pp. 169–190

Clarke, John R. (2013), Before Pornography: Sexual Representation in Ancient Rome, in: Hans Maes (ed), *Pornographic Art and the Aesthetics of Pornography*, New York, pp. 141–161

Clarke, John R. (2014), Sexuality and Visual Representation, in: Hubbard, Thomas K. (ed), *A Companion to Greek and Roman Sexualities*, New York, pp. 509–533

Clarke, Paula C. (2015), The Business of Prostitution in Early Renaissance Venice, in: *Renaissance Quarterly* 68, 2, pp. 419–464

Classen, Albrecht (2007), *The Medieval Chastity Belt: A Myth-Making Process*, Houndmills/Basingstoke/Hampshire/New York

Classen, Albrecht (2008a), Introduction. The Cultural Significance of Sexuality in the Middle Ages, the Renaissance, and Beyond. A Secret Continuous Undercurrent or a Dominant Phenomenon of the Premodern World? Or: The Irrepressibility of Sex Yesterday and Today, in: Classen, Albrecht (ed), *Sexuality in the Middle Ages and the Early Modern Times: New Approaches to a Fundamental Cultural-Historical and Literary-Anthropological Theme*, Berlin/New York, pp. 1–142

Classen, Albrecht (2008b), Naked Men in Medieval German Literature and Art: Anthropological, Cultural Historical, and Mental. Historical Investigations, in: Classen, Albrecht (ed), *Sexuality in the Middle Ages and the Early Modern Times: New Approaches to a Fundamental Cultural-Historical and Literary-Anthropological Theme*, Berlin/New York, pp. 143–170

Classen, Albrecht (2010), The Ultimate Transgression of the Courtly World: Peasants on the Courtly Stage and Their Grotesque Quests for Sexual Pleasures. The Poetry by the Thirteenth-Century Austrian-Bavarian Neidhart, in: *Medievalia et Humanistica* 36, pp. 1–24

Classen, Albrecht (2011a), *Sex im Mittelalter: Die andere Seite einer idealisierten Vergangenheit. Literatur und Sexualität*, Badenweiler

Classen, Albrecht (2011b), *Sexual Violence and Rape in the Middle Ages: A Critical Discourse in Premodern German and European Literature*, Berlin/Boston

Classen, Albrecht (2018a), Sexuality in Medieval and Early Modern Art: From the Corbels and Misericords to Late Medieval Manuscript Illustrations, in: *International Journal of History and Cultural Studies* 4, 4, pp. 1–19

Classen, Albrecht (2018b), Erotik und Sexualität im Märe des Spätmittelalters. Sprachwitz, Intelligenz, Spiel und sexuelle Erfüllung, in: Classen, Albrecht (ed), *Eros und Logos: Literarische Formen des sinnlichen Begehrens in der (deutschsprachigen) Literatur vom Mittelalter bis zur Gegenwart*, Tübingen, pp. 47–69

Classen, Albrecht (2019), *Prostitution in Medieval and Early Modern Literature: The Dark Side of Sex and Love in the Premodern Era*, Lanham

Classen, Albrecht (2022), The Kiss in Medieval Literature: Erotic Communication, with an Emphasis on Roman de Silence, in: *Journal of Humanities, Arts and Social Science* 6, p. 2

Clement, Ulrich (1986), Zur Sozialpsychologie des "Safer Sex", in: Frings, Matthias (ed), *Dimensionen einer Krankheit - AIDS*, Reinbek, pp. 227–238

Cleminson, Richard/García, F. Vázquez (2013), *Sex, Identity and Hermaphrodites in Iberia, 1500–1800*, London

Clifton, James (1999), Gender and Shame in Masaccio's Expulsion from the Garden of Eden, in: *Art History* 22, 5, pp. 637–655

Coale, Ansley J./Treadway, Roy (1986), A Summary of the Changing Distribution of Overall Fertility, Marital Fertility and the Proportion Married in the Provinces of Europe, in: Coale, Ansley J./Watkins, Susan Cotts (eds), *The Decline of Fertility in Europe: The Revised Proceedings of a Conference on the Princeton European Fertility Project*, Princeton, pp. 31–79

Cobb, L. Stephanie (2008), *Dying to Be Men: Gender and Language in Early Christian Martyr Texts*, New York

Cocks, Harry G./Houlbrook, Matt (2006), Introduction, in: Cocks, Harry G./Houlbrook, Matt (eds), *Palgrave Advances in the Modern History of Sexuality*, Basingstoke et al., pp. 1–18

Cohen, David (1991), *Law, Sexuality, and Society: The Enforcement of Morals in Classical Athens*, Cambridge

Cohen, David (1993), Consent and Sexual Relations in Classical Athens, in: Laiou, Angeliki E. (ed), *Consent and Coercion to Sex and Marriage in Ancient and Medieval Societies*, Washington, DC, pp. 5–16

Cohen, David (2004), Law, Society and Homosexuality in Ancient Greece, in: Osborne, Robin (ed), *Studies in Ancient Greek and Roman Society*, Cambridge, pp. 61–77

Cohen, David/Saller, Richard (1994), Foucault on Sexuality in Greco-Roman Antiquity, in: Goldstein, Jan (ed), *Foucault and the Writing of History*, Oxford, pp. 35–59

Cohen, Edward E. (2006), Free and Unfree Sexual Work. An Economic Analysis of Athenian Prostitution, in: Faraone, Christopher A./McClure, Laura K. (eds), *Prostitutes and Courtesans in the Ancient Worlds*, Madison, pp. 95–124

Cohen, Edward E. (2014), Sexual Abuse and Sexual Rights: Slaves' Erotic Experience at Athens and Rome, in: Hubbard, Thomas K. (ed), *A Companion to Greek and Roman Sexualities*, New York, pp. 184–198

Cohen, Edward E. (2015), *Athenian Prostitution: The Business of Sex*, Oxford/New York

Cohen, Elizabeth S. (1991), "Courtesans" and "Whores": Words and Behavior in Roman Streets, in: *Women's Studies* 19, pp. 201–208

Cohen, Elizabeth S. (1992), Honor and Gender in the Streets of Early Modern Rome, in: *The Journal of Interdisciplinary History* 22, 4, pp. 597–625

Cohen, Sherrill (1992), *The Evolution of Women's Asylums since 1500: From Refuges for Ex-Prostitutes to Shelters for Battered Women*, New York/Oxford
Cohen, Thomas V./Cohen, Elizabeth S. (2000), *Words and Deeds in Renaissance Rome: Trials Before the Papal Magistrates*, Toronto, 2nd edn
Collier, Aine (2007), *The Humble Little Condom: A History*, Amherst
Connell, Sophia M. (2000), Aristotle and Galen on Sex Difference and Reproduction: A New Approach to an Ancient Rivalry, in: *Studies in History and Philosophy of Science Teil A*, Band 31, Nr. 3, Sept. 2000, pp. 405–427
Constable, Olivia Remie (ed) (2012), *Medieval Iberia: Readings from Christian, Muslim, and Jewish Sources*, Philadelphia, 2nd edn
Cook, Hera (2004), *The Long Sexual Revolution: Women, Sex, and Contraception in England 1800–1975*, Oxford
Cooper, Kate (2007), *The Fall of the Roman Household*, Cambridge
Copley, Antony (1989), *Sexual Moralities in France, 1780–1980: New Ideas on the Family, Divorce and Homosexuality*, London/New York
Cornelius, Michael G. (2016), *Edward II and a Literature of Same-Sex Love: The Gay King in Fiction, 1590–1640*, Lanham et al.
Cossar, Roisin (2001), Clerical "Concubines" in Northern Italy During the Fourteenth Century, in: *Journal of Women's History* 23, 1, pp. 110–131
Cossar, Roisin (2011), Clerical "Concubines" in Northern Italy during the Fourteenth Century, in: *Journal of Women's History* 23, 1, pp. 110–131
Costlow, Jane T./Sandler, Stephanie/Vowles, Judith (1993), Introduction, in: Costlow, Jane T./Sandler, Stephanie/Vowles, Judith (eds), *Sexuality and the Body in Russian Culture*, Stanford, pp. 1–40
Cotter-Lynch, Margaret (2020), The Gender Genealogy of St. Mary of Egypt, in: Rogers, Will/Roman, Christopher Michael (eds), *Medieval Futurity: Essays for the Future of a Queer Medieval Studies*, Kalamazoo, pp. 131–151
Coudert, Allison P. (2008), From the Clitoris to the Breast: The Eclipse of the Female Libido in Early Modern Art, Literature and Philosophy, in: Classen, Albrecht (ed), *Sexuality in the Middle Ages and the Early Modern Times: New Approaches to a Fundamental Cultural-Historical and Literary-Anthropological Theme*, Berlin/New York, pp. 837–878
Crawford, Katherine (2007), *European Sexualities, 1400–1800*, Cambridge et al.
Crawford, Katherine (2010), *The Sexual Culture of the French Renaissance*, Cambridge
Crawford, Katherine (2011), Erotica: Representing Sex in the Eighteenth Century, in: Peakman, Julie (ed), *A Cultural History of Sexuality in the Enlightenment (=A Cultural History of Sexuality Vol. 4)*, Oxford/New York, pp. 203–222
Crawford, Katherine (2012), The Good, the Bad, and the Textual. Approaches to the Study of the Body and Sexuality, 1500–1750, in: Fisher, Kate/Toulalan, Sarah (eds), *The Routledge History of Sex and the Body, 1500 to the Present*, Oxford et al., pp. 23–37
Crawford, Patricia (1994), Sexual Knowledge in England 1500–1750, in: Porter, Roy/Teich, Mikuláš (eds), *Sexual Knowledge, Sexual Science: The History of Attitudes to Sexuality*, Cambridge, pp. 82–106
Crawshaw, Jane L. Stevens (2017), Cleaning up the Renaissance City: The Symbolic and Physical Place of the Genoese Brothel in Urban Society, in: Spicer, Andrew/Crawshaw, Jane L. Stevens (eds), *The Place of the Social Margins, 1350–1750*, New York/Abingdon, pp. 155–180

Crompton, Louis (1981), The Myth of Lesbian Impunity: Capital Laws from 1270 to 1791, in: Licata, Salvatore J./Petersen, Robert P. (eds.), *Historical Perspectives on Homosexuality*, New York, pp. 11–25

Crompton, Louis (2003), *Homosexuality and Civilization*, Cambridge/London

Crosby, Alfred W. (2003), *The Columbian Exchange: Biological and Cultural Consequences of 1492. The 30th Anniversary Edition*, New York

Cryle, Peter/O'Connell, Lisa (2004), Sex, Liberty and Licence in the Eighteenth Century, in: Cryle, Peter/O'Connell, Lisa (eds), *Libertine Enlightenment: Sex, Liberty and Licence in the Eighteenth Century*, Houndsmills/New York, pp. 1–14

Cullum, Pat (2013), Give Me Chastity: Masculinity and Attitudes to Chastity and Celibacy in the Middle Ages, in: *Gender & History* 25, 3, 621–636

D'Ambra, Eve (2007), *Roman Women*, Cambridge

D'Emilio, John/Freedman, Estelle B. (1988), *Intimate Matters: A History of Sexuality in America*, New York

Dabhoiwala, Faramerz (2012), *The Origins of Sex: A History of the First Sexual Revolution*, London/New York

Dall'Orio, Giovanni (2001), Farnese, Pier Luigi, in: Aldrich, Robert F./Wotherspoon, Garry (eds), *Who's Who in Gay and Lesbian History: From Antiquity to World War II*, London, pp. 187–188

Dallai, Ahmad (2009), Sexualities: Scientific Discourses, Premodern, in: Joseph, Suad (ed), *Encyclopedia of Women and Islamic Cultures*, Vol. 3, Leiden, pp. 401–407

Danna, Daniela (2011), Sex, Religion, and the Law, in: Hekma, Gert (ed), *A Cultural History of Sexuality in the Modern Age World (=A Cultural History of Sexuality Vol. 6)*, Oxford/New York, pp. 105–125

Dannecker, Martin (1991), *Der homosexuelle Mann im Zeichen von Aids*, Hamburg

Dannecker, Martin (1997), Der unstillbare Wunsch nach Anerkennung. Homosexuellenpolitik in den fünfziger und sechziger Jahren, in: Grumbach, Detlef (ed), *Was heißt hier schwul? Politik und Identitäten im Wandel*, Hamburg, pp. 27–44

Dannecker, Martin (2000), Der „gewöhnliche Homosexuelle" an der Jahrtausendwende, in: Setz, Wolfram (ed), *Die Geschichte der Homosexualitäten und die schwule Identität an der Jahrtausendwende. Eine Vortragsreihe aus Anlaß des 175. Geburtstags von K.H. Ulrichs*, Berlin, pp. 177–195

Dannecker, Martin/Reiche, Reimut (1974), *Der gewöhnliche Homosexuelle. Eine soziologische Untersuchung über männliche Homosexuelle in der Bundesrepublik*, Frankfurt a. M.

Dannenberg, Lars-Arne (2008), *Das Recht der Religiosen in der Kanonistik des 12. und 13. Jahrhunderts*, Berlin/Münster

Darnton, Robert (1996a), Denkende Wollust. Oder die sexuelle Aufklärung der Aufklärung, in: Darnton, Robert (ed), *Denkende Wollust*, Frankfurt a. M., pp. 7–44

Darnton, Robert (1996b), *The Forbidden Best-Sellers of Pre-Revolutionary France*, London

Daston, Lorraine/Parks, Katharine (1995), The Hermaphrodite and the Orders of Nature. Sexual Ambiguity in Early Modern France, in: *GLQ: A Journal of Lesbian and Gay Studies* 1, 1, pp. 419–438

Davenport-Hines, Richard P. T. (=Treadwell, Richard Peter) (1990), *Sex, Death and Punishment: Attitudes to Sex and Sexuality in Britain since the Renaissance*, London

Davidson, Arnold I. (2001), *The Emergence of Sexuality: Historical Epistemology and the Formation of Concepts*, Cambridge et al.
Davidson, James N. (1997), *Courtesans and Fishcakes: The Consuming Passions of Classical Athens*, New York
Davidson, James N. (2007), *The Greeks and Greek Love: A Radical Reappraisal of Homosexuality in Ancient Greece*, London
Davidson, Nicholas C. (1994), Theology, Nature, and the Law Sexual Sin and Sexual Crime in Italy from the Fourteenth to the Seventeenth Century, in: Dean, Trevor/Lowe, K. J. P. (eds), *Crime, Society, and the Law in Renaissance Italy*, Cambridge, pp. 74–98
Davidson, Nicholas C. (2011), Sex, Religion, and the Law: Disciplining Desire, in: Talvacchia, Bette (ed), *A Cultural History of Sexuality in the Renaissance (=A Cultural History of Sexuality Vol. 3)*, Oxford/New York, pp. 95–112
Davies, Anthony (1991), Sexual Behaviour in Later Anglo-Saxon England, in: Kooper, Erik (ed), *This Noble Craft: Proceedings of the Xth Research Symposium of the Dutch and Belgian University Teachers of Old and Middle English and Historical Linguistics*, Amsterdam, pp. 83–105
Davies, Glenn (2006), The Exeter Book Ridles and Place of Sexual Idiom in Old English Literature, in: McDonald, Nicola (ed), *Medieval Obscenities*, Woodbridge, pp. 39–54
Davis, Fanny (1986), *The Ottoman Lady: A Social History from 1718 to 1918*, New York
Deane, Jennifer Kolpacoff (2010), *A History of Medieval Heresy and Inquisition*, Lanham
de Angelis, Francesco (2008), Pliny the Elder and the Identity of Roman Art, in: *Res: Anthropology and Aesthetics* 53/54, Spring/Autumn, pp. 79–92
de Jongh, Eddy (2000), A Bird's-Eye View of Erotica: Double Entendre in a Series of Seventeenth-Century Genre Scenes, in: de Jongh, Eddy/Hoyle, Michael (eds), *Questions of Meaning: Theme and Motif in Dutch Seventeenth-Century Painting*, Leiden, pp. 21–58
de Troyes, Chrétien (2006), *Arthurian Romances*, trans. W. W. Comfort, Mineola/New York
Deacy, Susan/Pierce, Karen F. (eds) (2002), *Rape in Antiquity: Sexual Violence in the Greek and Roman Worlds*, London
Dean, Carolyn J. (2000), *The Frail Social Body: Pornography, Homosexuality and Other Fantasies in Interwar France*, Berkeley
Dean, Trevor (2001), *Crime in Medieval Europe, 1200–1550*. London
Dean, Trevor (2004), Gender and Insult in an Italian City: Bologna in the Later Middle Ages, in: *Social History* 29, 2, pp. 217–231
Dean, Trevor (2017), Sodomy in Renaissance Bologna, in: *Renaissance Studies* 31, 3, pp. 426–443
Dean, Trevor/Lowe, Kate (1998), Introduction: Issues in the History of Marriage, in: Dean, Trevor/Lowe, Kate (eds), *Marriage in Italy, 1300–1650*, Cambridge/New York, pp. 1–24
Dean-Jones, Lesley (1992a), The Politics of Pleasure: Female Sexual Appetite in the Hippocratic Corpus, in: Stanton, Domna C. (ed), *Discourses of Sexuality: From Aristotle to AIDS*, Ann Arbor, pp. 48–77
Dean-Jones, Lesley (1992b), *Women's Body in Classical Greek*, Oxford

Dean-Jones, Lesley (1994), Medicine: The "Proof" of Anatomy, in: Fantham, Elaine et al. (eds), *Women in the Classical World*, New York/Oxford, pp. 183–206
DeJean, Joan (1994), Politische Aspekte der Pornographie: L'Ecole des Filles, in: Hunt, Lynn (ed), *Die Erfindung der Pornographie. Obszönität und die Ursprünge der Moderne*, Frankfurt a. M., pp. 115–131
DeJean, Joan (2002), *The Reinvention of Obscenity: Sex, Lies, and Tabloids in Early Modern France*, Chicago et al.
Dekker, Rudolf M./Pol, Lotte van de (1990), *Frauen in Männerkleidern. Weibliche Transvestiten und ihre Geschichte*, Berlin
Demandt, Alexander (2007), *Das Privatleben der römischen Kaiser*, München
Deming, Will (2004), *Paul on Marriage and Celibacy. The Hellenistic Background of 1 Corinthians 7*, Cambridge/New York, 2nd edn
Demirci, Tuba/Somel, Selçuk Akşin (2008), Women's Bodies, Demography, and Public Health: Abortion Policy and Perspectives in the Ottoman Empire of the Nineteenth Century, in: *Journal of the History of Sexuality* 17 (2008), 3, pp. 335–350
Den Hartog, Marlisa (2021), Women on Top: Coital Positions and Gender Hierarchies in Renaissance Italy, in: *Renaissance Studies* 35, 4, pp. 638–657
Denzler, Georg (1988), *Die verbotene Lust. 2000 Jahre christliche Sexualmoral*, München
Derks, Paul (1990), *Die Schande der heiligen Päderastie. Homosexualität und Öffentlichkeit in der deutschen Literatur, 1750–1850*, Berlin
DeRusha, Michelle (2016), *Katharina and Martin Luther: The Radical Marriage of a Runaway Nun and a Renegade Monk*, Grande Rapids
Desan, Suzanne (2009), Making and Breaking Marriage: An Overview of Old Regime Marriages as a Social Practice, in: Desan, Suzanne/Merrick, Jeffrey (eds), *Family, Gender, and Law in Early Modern France*, University Park, pp. 1–35
Descharmes, Bernadette (2015), Von Bürgern und Bärten. Körper, Männlichkeit und Politik im klassischen Athen, in: *Historische Anthropologie* 23, 2, pp. 254–272
Deschner, Karlheinz (1989), *Das Kreuz mit der Kirche. Eine Sexualgeschichte des Christentums*, Düsseldorf
Deslauriers, Marguerite (2021), *Aristotle on Sexual Difference: Metaphysics, Biology and Politics*, Oxford
Desmond, Marilynn (2006), *Ovid's Art and the Wife of Bath: The Ethics of Erotic Violence*, Ithaca/London
Detel, Wolfgang (1998), *Macht, Moral, Wissen. Foucault und die klassische Antike*, Frankfurt a. M.
Deutsche Encyclopädie (1780), *Oder Allgemeines Real-Wörterbuch aller Künste und Wissenschaften, Bd. 3*, Frankfurt a. M.
Die Bibel in der Einheitsübersetzung (http://www.uibk.ac.at/theol/leseraum/bibel/)
Die Peinliche Gerichtsordnung Kaiser Karls V. von 1532 (1980), *hg. und erläutert von Gastav Radbruch*, Stuttgart, 5th edn
Diem, Albrecht (2001), Organisierte Keuschheit. Sexualprävention im Mönchtum der Spätantike und des frühen Mittelalters, in: Fachverband Homosexualität und Geschichte (ed), Invertito. Jahrbuch für die Geschichte der Homosexualitäten 3 (2001) (Special Issue: Homosexualitäten und Crossdressing im Mittelalter), pp. 8–37

Diem, Albrecht (2005), *Das monastische Experiment. Die Rolle der Keuschheit bei der Entstehung des westlichen Klosterwesens*, Münster
Diem, Albrecht (2013), Die Wüste im Kopf. Askese und Sexualität in Spätantike und Frühmittelalter, in: Ammicht Quinn, Regina (ed), *Guter Sex: Moral, Moderne und die katholische Kirche*, Paderborn, pp. 31–42
Diem, Albrecht (2016), Teaching Sodomy in Carolingian Monastery: A Study of Walahfrid Strabo's and Heito's Visio Wettini, in: *German History* 34, 3, pp. 385–401
DiGangi, Mario (1997), *The Homoerotics of Early Modern Drama*, Cambridge/NewYork
DiGangi, Mario (2020), Rethinking Early Modern Sexuality through Race, in: *English Literary Renaissance* 50, 1, pp. 25–31
Dillon, John M. (2004), *Morality and Custom in Ancient Greece*, Bloomington
Dinges, Martin (1995), Sexualitätsdiskurse in der Frühen Neuzeit, in: *SOWI: Sozialwissenschaftliche Informationen* 24, 1, 12–20
Dinshaw, Carolyn (1999), *Getting Medieval: Sexualities and Communities, Pre- and Postmodern*, Durham
Dinshaw, Carolyn (2001), Got Medieval?, in: *Journal of the History of Sexuality* 10, 2, pp. 202–212
Dinzelbacher, Peter (1993), Sexualität/Liebe. Mittelalter, in: Dinzelbacher, Peter (ed), *Europäische Mentalitätsgeschichte. Hauptthemen in Einzeldarstellungen*, Stuttgart, pp. 70–89
Dinzelbacher, Peter (2007), *Körper und Frömmigkeit in der mittelalterlichen Mentalitätsgeschichte*, Paderborn et al.
Dinzelbacher, Peter (2008), Gruppensex im Untergrund. Chaotische Ketzer und kirchliche Keuschheit im Mittelalter, in: Classen, Albrecht (ed), *Sexuality in the Middle Ages and the Early Modern Times: New Approaches to a Fundamental Cultural-Historical and Literary-Anthropological Theme*, Berlin/New York, pp. 405–428
Dixon, Suzanne (2003), Sex and the Married Woman in Ancient Rome, in: Balch, David L./Osiek, Carolyn (eds), *Early Christian Families in Context: An Interdisciplinary Dialogue*, Grand Rapids, pp. 111–129
Doller, Carolin (2007), Bürgerliche Gattinnen. Standesungleiche Verbindungen im Hause Anhalt-Bernburg, in: Labouvie, Eva (ed), *Adel in Sachsen-Anhalt. Höfische Kultur zwischen Repräsentation, Unternehmertum und Familie*, Köln/Weimar/Wien, pp. 17–48
Donaghy, Paige (2020), Before Onanism: Women's Masturbation in Seventeenth-Century England, in: *Journal of the History of Sexuality* 29, 2, pp. 187–221
Donahue, Charles Jr. (2016), The Legal Background: European Marriage Law from the Sixteenth to the Nineteenth Century, in: Seidel Menchi, Silvana (ed), *Marriage in Europe 1400–1800*, Toronto, pp. 33–60
Doniger, Wendy (2000), *The Bedtrick: Tales of Sex and Masquerade*, Chicago
Donoghue, Emma (1993), *Passions between Women: British Lesbian Culture, 1668–1801*, London
Döpp, Hans-Jürgen/Thomas, Joe A./Charles, Victoria (eds) (2012), *1000 Erotische Meisterwerke*, New York
Dorion, Louis-André (2017), Xénophon, Socrate et l'homosexualité, in: Brisson, Luc/Renaut, Olivier (ed), *Érotique et politique chez Platon: Erôs, genre et sexualité dans la cité platonicienne*, Sankt Augustin, pp. 99–125

Dose, Ralf (1990), Der Paragraph 175 in der Bundesrepublik Deutschland, 1949 bis heute, in: Freunde eines Schwulen-Museums in Berlin e.V. (eds), *Die Geschichte des § 175. Strafrecht gegen Homosexuelle. Ausstellungskatalog*, Berlin, pp. 122–143

Dover, Kenneth J. (1978), *Greek Homosexuality*, Cambridge.

Dover, Kenneth J. (2002), Classical Greek Attitudes to Sexual Behaviour, in: McClure, Laura K. (ed), *Sexuality and Gender in the Classical World: Readings and Sources*, Oxford, pp. 19–33

Downham Moore, Alison (2020), Foucault's Scholarly Virtues and Sexuality Historiography, in: *History: The Journal of the Historical Association* 105 (July 2020), pp. 446–469

Downham Moore, Alison M. (2020), Foucault, Early Christian Ideas of Genitalia, and the History of Sexuality, in: *Journal of the History of Sexuality* 29, 1, pp. 28–50

Drake, Susanna (2013), *Slandering the Jew: Sexuality and Difference in Early Christian Texts*, Philadelphia

Dreger, Alice Domurat (1998), *Hermaphrodites and the Medical Invention of Sex*, Cambridge

Dreyer, Mechthild (2014), Die Ausrichtung des Menschen auf das Gute. Gefühl und Sittlichkeit nach Thomas von Aquin, in: Kann, Christoph (ed), *Emotionen in Mittelalter und Renaissance*, Düsseldorf, pp. 57–67

Drife, James Owen (2010), Historical Perspective on Induced Abortion through the Ages and Its Links with Maternal Mortality, in: *Best Practice & Research Clinical Obstetrics and Gynaecology* 24, pp. 431–441

Drysdale, George (anonym erschienen) (1871), *Die Grundzüge der Gesellschaftswissenschaft; oder Physische, Geschlechtliche und Natürliche Religion*, Berlin

Duben, Alan/Behar, Cem (1991), *Istanbul Households: Marriage, Family and Fertility 1880–1940*, Cambridge

Duché, Véronique (2021), Sentimental Obscenity, in: Frei, Peter/Labère, Nelly (eds), *Obscene Means in Early Modern French and European Print Culture and Literature*, Milton, pp. 179–192

Duden, Barbara (2002), Zwischen "wahrem Wissen" und Prophetie. Geschichte des Ungeborenen, in: Duden, Barbara/Schlumbohm, Jürgen/Veit, Patrice (eds), *Geschichte des Ungeborenen. Zur Erfahrungs- und Wissenschaftsgeschichte der Schwangerschaft, 17. - 20. Jahrhundert*, Göttingen, 2nd edn, pp. 11–48

Duerr, Hans Peter (1988), *Nacktheit und Scham. Der Mythos vom Zivilisationsprozess, Bd. 1*, Frankfurt a. M.

Duhamelle, Christophe/Schlumbohm, Jürgen (2003), Einleitung. Vom "europäischen Heiratsmuster" zu Strategien der Eheschließung?, in: Duhamelle, Christophe/Schlumbohm, Jürgen (eds), *Eheschliessungen im Europa des 18. und 19. Jahrhunderts. Muster und Strategien*, Göttingen, pp. 11–24

Duncan, Derek (2006), *Reading and Writing Italian Homosexuality: A Case of Possible Difference*, Aldershot/Hampshire/Burlington

Duni, Matteo (2014), Impotence, Witchcraft and Politics: A Renaissance Case, in: Matthews-Grieco, Sara F. (ed), *Cuckoldry, Impotence and Adultery in Europe (15th–17th century)*, Farnham, pp. 85–102

Dunn, Caroline (2013), *Stolen Women in Medieval England: Rape, Abduction, and Adultery, 1100–1500*, Cambridge

Dunning, Benjamin H. (2009), What Sort of Thing Is This Luminous Woman? Thinking Sexual Difference in On the Origin of the World, in: *Journal of Early Christian Studies* 17, 1, pp. 55–84

Dupont, Florence/Éloi, Thierry (2001), *L'érotisme masculin dans la Rome antique*, Paris

Dupras, André (2007), L'apport du Dr Nicolas Venette à l'éducation à la sexualité au XVIIe siècle, in: *Sexologies* 16, 3, pp. 171–179

Dür, Wolfgang/Haas, Sabine/Till, Wolfgang (1993), Homosexuelle Lebenszusammenhänge und AIDS, in: *Österreichische Zeitschrift für Soziologie* 17, pp. 35–48

Durães, Margarida et al. (2009), Introduction: Historicizing Well-Being from a Gender Perspective, in: Durães, Margarida et al. (ed), *The Transmission of Well-Being: Gendered Marriage Strategies and Inheritance Systems in Europe (17th–20th Centuries)*, Bern et al., pp. 1–52

Dye, Sierra Rose (2012), To Converse with the Devil? Speech, Sexuality, and Witchcraft in Early Modern Scotland, in: *International Review of Scottish Studies* 37, pp. 9–40

Dyer, Abigail (2003), Seduction by Promise of Marriage: Law, Sex, and Culture in Seventeenth-Century Spain, in: *Sixteenth-Century Journal* 34, pp. 439–455

Dynes, Wayne R./Donaldson, Stephen (1992a), Introduction, in: Dynes, Wayne R./Donaldson, Stephen (eds), *Ethnographic Studies of Homosexuality (=Studies in Homosexuality II)*, New York, pp. vii–xv

Dynes, Wayne R./Donaldson, Stephen (eds) (1992b), *Ethnographic Studies of Homosexuality (=Studies in Homosexuality II)*, New York

Earp, Brian D./Chambers, Clare/Watson, Lori (eds) (2022), *The Routledge Handbook of Philosophy of Sex and Sexuality*, New York

Ebner, Martin (2012), *Die Stadt als Lebensraum der ersten Christen*, Göttingen

Ebner, Michael (2004), The Persecution of Homosexual Men under Fascism, in: Willson, Perry (ed), *Gender, Family and Sexuality: The Private Sphere in Italy, 1860–1945*, Basingstoke, New York, pp. 139–156

Eder, Franz X. (1990), *Geschlechterproportion und Arbeitsorganisation im Land Salzburg (17.-19. Jahrhundert)*, Wien

Eder, Franz X. (1994), Sexualunterdrückung oder Sexualisierung? Zu den theoretischen Ansätzen der Sexualitätsgeschichte, in: Erlach, Daniela/Reisenleitner, Markus/Vocelka, Karl (eds), *Privatisierung der Triebe. Sexualität in der frühen Neuzeit*, Frankfurt a. M., pp. 7–29

Eder, Franz X. (1996), Sexualized Subjects: Medical Discourses on Sexuality in German-Speaking Countries in the Late 18th and in the 19th Century, in: Forrai, Judit (ed), *Civilization, Sexuality and Sozial Life in Historical Context: The Hidden Face of Urban Life*, Budapest, pp. 17–29

Eder, Franz X. (1999), Sexual Cultures in Germany and Austria, 1700–2000, in: Eder, Franz X./Hall, Lesley A./Hekma, Gert (eds), *Sexual Cultures in Europe: National Histories*, Manchester/New York, pp. 138–172

Eder, Franz X. (2000), Sexuelle Kulturen in Deutschland und Österreich, 18.-20. Jahrhundert, in: Eder, Franz X./Frühstück, Sabine (eds), *Neue Geschichten der Sexualität. Beispiele aus Ostasien und Zentraleuropa 1700–2000*, Wien, pp. 41–68

Eder, Franz X. (2001), Degeneration, Konstitution oder Erwerbung? Die Konstruktion der Homosexualität bei Richard von Krafft-Ebing und Sigmund

Freud, in: Förster, Wolfgang/Natter, Tobias G./Rieder, Ines (eds), *Der andere Blick. Lesbischwules Leben in Österreich*, Wien, pp. 155–162
Eder, Franz X. (2003), Diskurs und Sexualpädagogik: Diskurs und Sexualpädagogik. Der deutschsprachige Onanie-Diskurs des späten 18. Jahrhunderts, in: *Paedagogica historica* 39, 6, pp. 719–735
Eder, Franz X. (2004), Discourse and Sexual Desire: German-Language Discourse on Masturbation in the Late Eighteenth Century, in: *Journal of the History of Sexuality* 13, 4, pp. 428–445
Eder, Franz X. (2005), Die „Sexuelle Revolution" - Befreiung und/oder Repression?, in: Bauer, Ingrid/Hämmerle, Christa/Hauch, Gabriella (eds), *Liebe und Widerstand. Ambivalenzen historischer Geschlechterbeziehungen*, Wien/Köln/Weinar, pp. 397–416
Eder, Franz X. (2008), Auf die "gesunde Sinnlichkeit" der Nationalsozialisten folgte der Einfluss der Amerikaner. Sexualität und Medien vom Nationalsozialismus bis zur Sexuellen Revolution, in: Orland, Barbara (ed), *Sexualität und Fortpflanzung in den Medien des 20. Jahrhunderts (=zeitenblicke 7, 3)* (http://www.zeitenblicke.de/2008/3/eder/)
Eder, Franz X. (2009a), *Kultur der Begierde. Eine Geschichte der Sexualität*, München, 2nd edn
Eder, Franz X. (2009b), Pornographie, in: Jaeger, Friedrich (ed), *Enzyklopädie der Neuzeit. Bd. 10*, Stuttgart/Weimar, pp. 214–220
Eder, Franz X. (2010), Das Sexuelle beschreiben, zeigen und aufführen. Mediale Strategien im deutschsprachigen Sexualdiskurs von 1945 bis Anfang der siebziger Jahre, in: Bänziger, Peter-Paul/Duttweiler, Stefanie/Sarasin, Philipp/Wellmann, Annika (eds), *Fragen Sie Dr. Sex! Ratgeberkommunikation und die mediale Konstruktion des Sexuellen*, Frankfurt a. M., pp. 94–123
Eder, Franz X. (2011a), *Homosexualitäten. Diskurse und Lebenswelten 1870–1970*, Wien/Weitra
Eder, Franz X. (2011b), Sex, Popular Beliefs, and Culture, in: Hekma, Gert (ed), *A Cultural History of Sexuality in the Modern Age (=A Cultural History of Sexuality Vol. 6)*, Oxford/New York, pp. 149–175 and 243–246
Eder, Franz X. (2014), Homo- und andere gleichgeschlechtliche Sexualitäten in Geschichte und Gegenwart, in: Mildenberger, Florian/Evans, Jennifer/Lautmann, Rüdiger/Pastötter, Jakob (eds), *Was ist Homosexualität? Forschungsgeschichte, gesellschaftliche Entwicklungen und Perspektiven*, Hamburg, pp. 17–40
Eder, Franz X. (2016), Michel Foucault, der Rattenfänger der Sexualitätsgeschichte?, in: *Zeitschrift für Sexualforschung* 29, 4, pp. 323–326
Eder, Franz X./Hall, Lesley A./Hekma, Gert (eds) (1999), *Sexual Cultures in Europe: Vol. 1: National Histories; Vol. 2: Themes in Sexuality*, Manchester/New York
Edsall, Nicholas C. (2003), *Toward Stonewall: Homosexuality and Society in the Modern Western World*, Charlottesville/London
Edwards, Catherine (1996), Unspeakable Professions: Public Performance and Prostitution in Ancient Rome, in: Hallett, Judith P./Skinner, Marilyn B. (eds), *Roman Sexualities*, Princeton, pp. 66–95
Edwards, Clive (2004), *Turning Houses into Homes: A History of the Retailing and Consumption of Domestic Furnishings*, Aldershot
Ehmer, Josef (1991), *Heiratsverhalten, Sozialstruktur, ökonomischer Wandel. England und Mitteleuropa in der Formationsperiode des Kapitalismus*, Göttingen

Ehmer, Josef (2004), *Bevölkerungsgeschichte und historische Demographie, 1800–2000*, München
Ehmer, Josef (2011a), Bevölkerung und historische Demographie, in: Cerman, Markus/Eder, Franz X./Eigner, Peter/Komlosy, Andrea/Landsteiner, Erich (eds), *Wirtschaft und Gesellschaft, Europa 1000–2000*, Wien, pp. 134–160
Ehmer, Josef (2011b), The Significance of Looking Back: Fertility Before the "Fertility Decline", in: Ehmer, Josef/Ehrhardt, Jens/Kohli, Martin (eds), *Fertility in the 20th Century: Trends, Theories, Politics, Discourses (= Historical Social Research/Historische Sozialforschung* 136, 2, pp. 11–34
van Eickels, Klaus (2007), Die Konstruktion des Anderen. (Homo)sexuelles Verhalten als Element des Sarazenenbildes zur Zeit der Kreuzzüge und die Beschlüsse des Konzils von Nablus 1120 (mit lat./dt. Textanhang: Die Beschlüsse des Konzils von Nablus 1120), in: Limbeck, Sven/Thoma, Lev Mordechai (eds), *Die Sünde, der sich der Tiuvel Schamet in der Helle. Homosexualität in der Kultur des Mittelalters und der frühen Neuzeit*, Ostfildern, pp. 43–68
Eidinow, Esther (2011), Sex, Religion, and the Law, in: Golden, Mark/Toohey, Peter (eds), *A Cultural History of Sexuality in the Classical World (=A Cultural History of Sexuality Vol. 1)*, Oxford/New York, pp. 87–106
Eisenberg, Daniel (2003), Homosexuality, in: Gerli, Michael (ed), *Encyclopedia of Medieval Iberia*, New York, pp. 398–399
Eisenring, Gabriela (2002), *Die römische Ehe als Rechtsverhältnis*, Wien/Köln/Weimar
Ekholst, Christine (2014), *A Punishment for Each Criminal: Gender and Crime in Swedish Medieval Law*, Leiden/Boston
El Rouayheb, Khaled (2005), *Before Homosexuality in the Arab-Islamic World 1500–1800*, Chicago
Eldorado (1984), *Homosexuelle Frauen und Männer in Berlin, 1850–1950: Geschichte, Alltag und Kultur (Ausstellungskatalog)*, Berlin
Elias, Norbert (1976), *Über den Prozeß der Zivilisation. Soziogenetische und psychogenetische Untersuchungen. 2 Bde.*, Frankfurt a. M.
Elliott, Dyan (1993), *Spiritual Marriage: Sexual Abstinence in Medieval Wedlock*, Princeton
Elliott, Dyan (1999), *Fallen Bodies: Pollution, Sexuality and Demonology in the Middle Ages*, Philadelphia
Elliott, Dyan (2008), Tertullian, the Angelic Life, and the Bride of Christ, in: Bitel, Lisa M./Lifshitz, Felice (eds), *Gender and Christianity in Medieval Europe: New Perspectives*, Philadelphia, pp. 16–33
Elliott, Dyan (2020), *The Corrupter of Boys: Sodomy, Scandal, and the Medieval Clergy*, Philadelphia
Ellis, Havelock (1897), *Sexual Inversion (=Studies in the Psychology of Sex 2)*, London
Engin, Ceylan/Özbarlas, Zeynep (2021), Tracing the Reverse History of Homosexuality from the Ottoman Empire to Contemporary Turkey: From Tolerance to Discrimination, in: Jongerden, Joost (eds), *The Routledge Handbook on Contemporary Turkey*, Milton, pp. 219–229
Ennen, Edith (1999), *Frauen im Mittelalter*, München, 6th edn
Epperlein, Siegfried (2003), *Bäuerliches Leben im Mittelalter: Schriftquellen und Bildzeugnisse*, Köln
Erasmus, Desiderius (1878), *The Colloquies*, Vol. 2 [1518], London

Erdelyi, Gabriella (2009), Tales of Immoral Friars: Morality and Religion in an Early Sixteenth-Century Hungarian Town, in: *Social History* 34, 2, pp. 184–203

Eriksen, Casey R. (2020), Renaissance Erotica and Intertextuality: New Ovidian Approximations and Cancionero Word Games in the Poetry of Garcilaso de la Vega, in: Jones, Nicholas R./Leahy, Chad (eds), *Pornographic Sensibilities: Imagining Sex and the Visceral in Premodern and Early Modern Spanish Cultural Production*, London, pp. 56–74

Erlach, Daniela/Reisenleitner, Markus/Vocelka, Karl (eds) (1994), *Privatisierung der Triebe? Sexualität in der frühen Neuzeit*, Frankfurt a. M.

Eros oder Wörterbuch über die Physiologie und über die Natur- und Cultur-Geschichte des Menschen in Hinsicht auf seine Sexualität. 2 Bde. (1823), Berlin

Escoffier, Jeffrey (ed) (2003), *Sexual Revolution*, New York

Esmyol, Andrea (2002), *Geliebte oder Ehefrau? Konkubinen im frühen Mittelalter*, Köln/Weimar/Wien

Espach, Verena (2017), Formen sexueller Gewalt gegen männliche Kindersklaven in der griechischen und römischen Antike, in: *Österreichische Zeitschrift für Geschichtswissenschaften* 28, 3, pp. 183–195

Evans, Jennifer V. (2014), *Aphrodisiacs, Fertility and Medicine in Early Modern England*, Woodbridge

Evans, Ruth (2011), Introduction: What Was Sexuality in the Middle Ages?, in: Evans, Ruth (ed), *A Cultural History of Sexuality in the Middle Ages (=A Cultural History of Sexuality Vol. 2)*, Oxford/New York, pp. 1–36

Evans Grubbs, Judith (2002), *Woman and the Law in the Roman Empire: A Sourcebook on Marriage, Divorce and Widowhood*, London et al.

Fachverband Homosexualität und Geschichte (ed) (2002), *Denunziert, verfolgt, ermordet. Homosexuelle Männer und Frauen in der NS-Zeit (=Invertito. Jahrbuch für die Geschichte der Homosexualitäten)* 4, Hamburg

Faderman, Lillian (1991), *Odd Girls and Twilight Lovers: A History of Lesbian Life in Twentieth-Century America*, New York

Faerman, Marina et al. (1998), Determining the Sex of Infanticide Victims from the Late Roman Era through Ancient DNA Analysis, in: *Journal of Archaeological Science* 25 (September 1998), 9, pp. 861–865

Fairchilds, Cissie C. (2007), *Women in Early Modern Europe, 1500–1700*, Harlow

Falkner, Silke R. (2004), Having it Off with Fish, Camels, and Lads: Sodomitic Pleasures in German-Language "Turcica", in: *Journal of the History of Sexuality* 13, 4, pp. 401–428

Fantham, Elaine (2011), *Roman Readings: Roman Response to Greek Literature from Plautus to Statius and Quintilian*, Berlin/New York

Faraone, Christopher A. (2001), *Ancient Greek Love Magic*, Harvard

Farley, Margaret A. (2006), *Just Love: A Framework for Christian Sexual Ethics*, New York/London

Farmer, Sharon A./Pasternack, Carol Braun (eds) (2003), *Gender and Difference in the Middle Ages*, Minneapolis/London

Faroqhi, Suraiya (2002), *Stories of Ottoman Men and Women: Establishing Status, Establishing Control*, Istanbul

Fasoli, Paolo (2010), Body Language: Sex-Manual Literature from Pietro Aretino's Sixteen Positions to Antonio Rocco's Invitation to Sodomy, in: Levy, Allison (ed), *Sex Acts in Early Modern Italy: Practice, Performance, Perversion, Punishment*, Farnham, pp. 27–42

Fauve-Chamoux, Antoinette (1995), The Stem Family, Demography and Inheritance, in: Rudolf, Richard L. (ed), *The European Peasant Family and Society*, Liverpool, pp. 86–113

Feld, Helmut (2001), *Franziskus von Assisi*, München

Feldman, David M. (1974), *Marital Relations, Birth Control, and Abortion in Jewish Law*, Wiesbaden

Fenster, Thelma S./Lees Clare E. (eds) (2002), *Gender in Debate From the Early Middle Ages to the Renaissance*, New York/Houndsmill

Ferguson, Gary (2008), *Queer (Re)Readings in the French Renaissance: Homosexuality, Gender, Culture*, Aldershot et al.

Ferguson, Gary (2016), *Same-Sex Marriage in Renaissance Rome: Sexuality, Identity, and Community in Early Modern Europe*, Ithaca

Ferguson, Gary/McKinley, Mary B. (2013), Heptaméron. Word, Spirit, World, in: Ferguson, Gary/McKinley, Mary B. (eds), *A Companion to Marguerite de Navarre*, Leiden/Boston, pp. 323–371

Fernández-Morera, Darío (2015), *The Myth of the Andalusian Paradise: Muslims, Christians, and Jews under Islamic Rule in Medieval Spain*, Wilmington

Ferragud, Carmel/Roca, Guillem (2020), El cos de la dona maltractada sota l'escrutini mèdic: Els casos de València i Lleida en la baixa edat mitjana/The body of the abused woman under medical Examination: The Cases of Valencia and Lleida in the Late Middle Ages, in: *Scripta: Revista internacional de literatura i cultura medieval i moderna* 16, pp. 320–342

Ferrand, Jacques (1994), *A Treatise On Lovesickness*, ed. Beecher, Donald A./Ciavolella, Massimo, Syracuse

Ferraro, Joanne Marie (2001), *Marriage Wars in Late Renaissance Venice*, New York

Ferraro, Joanne Marie (2007), One Community's Secret: Incest and Infanticide in the Late Sixteenth-Century Veneto, in: *Acta Histriae* 15, 2, pp. 441–452

Ferraro, Joanne Marie (2016), Youth in Peril in Early Modern Venice, in: *Journal of Social History* 49, 4, pp. 761–783

Fetner, Tina (2008), *How the Religious Right Shaped Lesbian and Gay Activism*, Minneapolis

Fichte, Johann Gottlieb (1796/7), *Werke. Auswahl in 6 Bänden, hrsg. u. eingel. von Fritz Medicus, Bd. 2: Grundlage des Naturrechts. Das System der Sittenlehre*, Leipzig

Findlen, Paula (1993), Humanism, Politics and Pornography in Renaissance Italy, in: Hunt, Lynn (ed), *The Invention of Pornography: Obscenity and the Origins of Modernity, 1500–1800*, New York, pp. 49–108

Findlen, Paula (1994), Humanismus, Politik und Pornographie im Italien der Renaissance, in: Hunt, Lynn (ed), *Die Erfindung der Pornographie. Obszönität und die Ursprünge der Moderne*, Frankfurt a. M., pp. 44–114

Finley, M. I. (2002), The Silent Women of Rome, in: McClure, Laura K. (ed), *Sexuality and Gender in the Classical World: Readings and Sources*, Oxford, pp. 147–156

Fisher, Kate/Toulalan, Sarah (eds) (2012), *The Routledge History of Sex and the Body, 1500 to the Present*, Oxford et al.

Fisher, Nick (2014), Athletics and Sexuality, in: Hubbard, Thomas K. (ed), *A Companion to Greek and Roman Sexualities*, New York, pp. 244–264

Fisher, Nick R. E. (1998), Violence, Masculinity and the Law in Classical Athens, in: Foxhall, Lin/Salmon, John (eds), *When Men Were Men: Masculinity, Power and Identity in Classical Antiquity*, London/New York, pp. 68–97

Fittock, Matthew G. (2020), More Than Just Love and Sex: Venus Figurines in Roman Britain, in: Ivleva, Tatiana/Collins, Rob (eds), *Un-Roman Sex: Gender, Sexuality, and Lovemaking in the Roman Provinces and Frontiers*, Milton, pp. 54–89

Flandrin, Jean-Louis (1981), *Le sexe et l'occident. Évolution des attitudes et des comportements*, Paris

Flandrin, Jean-Louis (1983), *Un temps pour embrasser. Aux origines de la morale sexuelle occidentale, VIe-XIe siècle*, Paris

Flandrin, Jean-Louis (1992), Das Geschlechtsleben der Eheleute in der alten Gesellschaft. Von der kirchlichen Lehre zum realen Verhalten, in: Ariès, Philippe/Béjin, André/Foucault, Michel (eds), *Die Masken des Begehrens und die Metamorphosen der Sinnlichkeit. Zur Geschichte der Sexualität im Abendland*, Frankfurt a. M., pp. 147–164

Flemming, Rebecca (2000), *Medicine and the Making of Roman Women: Gender, Nature, and Authority from Celsus to Galen*, Oxford/New York

Flemming, Rebecca (2018), Galen's Generations of Seeds, in: Hopwood, Nick et al. (eds), *Reproduction: Antiquity to the Present Day*, Cambridge, pp. 95–108

Flemming, Rebecca (2019), (The Wrong Kind of) Gonorrhea in Antiquity, in: Szreter, Simon (ed), *The Hidden Affliction: Sexually Transmitted Infections and Infertility in History*, Rochester, pp. 43–67

Fleßenkämper, Iris (2014), Von ehelicher Zusage, fleischlicher Vermischung und heimlicher Verlöbnis. Normen und Praktiken der Eheschließung in der frühneuzeitlichen Grafschaft Lippe, in: *Frühneuzeit-Info* 25, pp. 199–212

Floßmann, Ursula/Kriz, Elisabeth (1988), Die geschichtliche Entwicklung des Sexualstrafrechts. Dargestellt an zwei Beispielen: Abtreibung und Vergewaltigung, in: Floßmann, Ursula (ed), *Frau im Recht. Geschichte, Praxis, Politik*, 27–59

Flüchter, Antje (2006), *Der Zölibat zwischen Devianz und Norm. Kirchenpolitik und Gemeindealltag in den Herzogtümern Jülich und Berg im 16. und 17. Jahrhundert*, Köln/Weimar/Wien

Flüchter, Antje (2008), Lust und Moral: Zur Alltagsgeschichte der Sexualität seit der Frühen Neuzeit, in: Pethes, Nicolas/Schicktanz, Silke (eds), *Identität, Lust, Reproduktion zwischen Science und Fiction*, New York, pp. 156–171

Foa, Anna (1990), The New and the Old: The Spread of Syphilis 1494–1530, in: Ruggiero, Guido/Muir, Edward (eds), *Sex and Gender in Historical Perspective*, Baltimore, pp. 26–45

Fone, Byrne R. S. (2000), *Homophobia: A History*, New York

Fonrobert, Charlotte Elisheva (2000), *Menstrual Purity: Rabbinic and Christian Reconstructions of Biblical Gender*, Stanford

Foreman-Peck, James (2011), The Western European Marriage Pattern and Economic Development, in: *Explorations in Economic History* 48, 2, pp. 292–309

Fornaciari, Antonio et al. (2020), Syphilis in Maria Salviati (1499–1543), Wife of Giovanni de' Medici of the Black Bands, in: *Emerging Infectious Diseases* 26, 6, pp. 1274–1283

Foskett, Mary F. (2002), *A Virgin Conceived: Mary and Classical Representations of Virginity*, Bloomington

Foucault, Michel (1977), *Der Wille zum Wissen. Sexualität und Wahrheit. Bd. 1*, Frankfurt a. M.

Foucault, Michel (1978a), Ein Spiel um die Psychoanalyse. Gespräch mit Angehörigen des Département des Psychoanalyse der Universität Paris VIII in Vincennes, in: Foucault, Michel (ed), *Dispositive der Macht. Über Sexualität, Wissen und Wahrheit*, Berlin, pp. 118–175

Foucault, Michel (1978b), Nein zum König Sex. Ein Gespräch mit Bernard-Henri Lévy, in: Foucault, Michel (ed), *Dispositive der Macht. Über Sexualität, Wissen und Wahrheit*, Berlin, pp. 176–198

Foucault, Michel (1986), The Care of the Self: The History of Sexuality, Vol. 3, trans. Robert Hurley, New Yorkw

Foucault, Michel (1989a), *Der Gebrauch der Lüste. Sexualität und Wahrheit. Bd. 2*, Frankfurt a. M.

Foucault, Michel (1989b), *Die Sorge um sich. Sexualität und Wahrheit. Bd. 3*, Frankfurt a. M.

Foucault, Michel (1992), Der Kampf um die Keuschheit, in: Ariès, Philippe/Béjin, André/Foucault, Michel (eds), *Die Masken des Begehrens und die Metamorphosen der Sinnlichkeit. Zur Geschichte der Sexualität im Abendland*, Frankfurt a. M., pp. 25–39

Foucault, Michel (2005a), Omnes et singulatim. Zu einer Kritik der politischen Vernunft, in: Defert, Daniel/Ewald, François (eds), *Michel Foucault. Dits et Ecrits. Schriften. 4. Bd. 1980–1988*, Frankfurt a. M., pp. 165–198

Foucault, Michel (2005b), Technologien des Selbst, in: Defert, Daniel/Ewald, François (eds), *Michel Foucault. Dits et Ecrits. Schriften. 4. Bd. 1980–1988*, Frankfurt a. M., pp. 966–999

Foucault, Michel (2018), Les aveux de la chair (=Histoire de la sexualité vol. 4), Paris.

Fountoulakis, Andreas (2022), Silencing Female Intimacies: Sexual Practices, Silence and Cultural Assumptions in Lucian, Dial. Meretr. 5, in: Serafim, Andreas/Kazantzidis, George/Demetriou, Kyriakos (Hg.), *Sex and the Ancient City: Sex and Sexual Practices in Greco-Roman Antiquity*, Berlin/Boston, pp. 111–139

Fout, John C. (1990), A Note from the Editor, in: *Journal of the History of Sexuality* 1, 1, pp. 1–2

Fouz-Hernández, Santiago (2011), Queer in Spain: Identity without Limits, in: Downing, Lisa/Gillet, Robert (eds), *Queer in Europe: Contemporary Case Studies*, Farnham/Burlington, pp. 189–202

Fracastoro, Girolamo (1934), *The Sinister Shepherd: A Translation of Girolamo Fracastoro's "Syphilidis Sive de Morbo Gallico Libri Tres" by William Van Wyck (1883–1956)*, Los Angeles

Fracchia, Carmen (2017), The Place of African Slaves in Early Modern Spain, in: Spicer, Andrew/Crawshaw, Jane L. Stevens (eds), *The Place of the Social Margins, 1350–1750*, New York/Abingdon, pp. 117–134

Fradenburg, Louise/Freccero, Carla (eds) (1996), *Premodern Sexualities*, London/New York

Franke, Patrick (2012), Before Scientia Sexualis in Islamic Culture: 'Ilm al-bāh Between Erotology, Medicine and Pornography, in: *Social Identities* 18, 2, pp. 161–173

Frantz, David O. (1989), *Festum Voluptatis: A Study of Renaissance Erotica*, Columbus

Freccero, Carla (2006), *Queer/Early/Modern*, Durham

Frei, Peter/Labère, Nelly (2021), Introduction: The Obscenity of Books: The Politics of the Obscene in Early Modern Print Cultur, in: Frei, Peter/Labère, Nelly (eds), *Obscene Means in Early Modern French and European Print Culture and Literature*, Milton, pp. 1–28

Freitag, Barbara (2004), *Sheela-na-gigs: Unravelling an Enigma*, London/New York

Frenken, Ralph (2002), *Kindheit und Mystik im Mittelalter*, Frankfurt a. M.

Freud, Sigmund (1940–1955), Eine Schwierigkeit der Psychoanalyse (1917), in: Freud, Sigmund (ed), *Gesammelte Werke. Bd. 12*, London, pp. 1–12

Freud, Sigmund (1960), *Briefe 1873–1939*, Frankfurt a. M.

Freud, Sigmund (1964), Anxiety and Instinctual Life (= New Introductory Lectures on Psych-Analysis (1933 [1932])), in: *The Standard Edition of the Complete Psychological Works of Sigmund Freud*, Vol. XXII (1932–1936); translated from the German under the General Editorship of James Strachey, London, pp. 81–101

Freud, Sigmund (1982), Drei Abhandlungen zur Sexualtheorie (1905), in: Mitscherlich Alexander (ed), *Studienausgabe Bd. 5: Sexualleben*, Frankfurt a. M, pp. 37–145

Frevert, Ute (2009), Was haben Gefühle in der Geschichte zu suchen?, in: *Geschichte und Gesellschaft* 35, 2 (Themenheft "Geschichte der Gefühle"), pp. 183–208

Frey, Winfried/Raitz, Walter/Seitz, Dieter (1982), *Einführung in die deutsche Literatur des 12. bis 16. Jahrhunderts: Patriziat und Landesherrschaft - 13.-15. Jahrhundert*, Opladen

Friedeburg, Ludwig V. (1953), *Die Umfrage in der Intimsphäre*, Stuttgart

Friedl, Raimund (1996), *Der Konkubinat im kaiserzeitlichen Rom. Von Augustus bis Septimius Severus*, Stuttgart

Friedman, Mordechai A. (1989), Marriage as an Institution: Jewry under Islam, in: Kraemer, David (ed), *The Jewish Family: Metaphor and Memory*, New York/Oxford, pp. 31–45

Fritz, Gerhard (2016), *Geschichte der Sexualität. Von den Anfängen bis zur Gegenwart - Südwestdeutschland und seine Nachbargebiete*, Heidelberg

Frost, Ginger S. (1995), *Promises Broken: Courtship, Class and Gender in Victorian England*, Charlottesville

Fuchs, Esther (2020), Intermarriage, Gender, and Nation in the Hebrew Bible, in: Ruttenberg, Danya (ed), *The Passionate Torah: Sex and Judaism*, New York, pp. 73–92

Fuchs, Rachel (1992), *Poor and Pregnant in Paris: Strategies for Survival in the Nineteenth Century*, New Brunswick

Fuchs, Rachel Ginnis (1984), *Abandoned Children: Foundlings and Child Welfare in Nineteenth Century France*, Albany

Fuente, María Jesús (2009), Christians, Muslims and Jewish Women in Late Medieval Iberia, in: Corfis, Ivy A. (ed), *Al-Andalus, Sepharad and Medieval Iberia: Cultural Contact and Diffusion*, Leiden, pp. 163–180

Gaca, Kathy L. (2003), *The Making of Fornication: Eros, Ethics, and Political Reform in Greek Philosophy and Early Christianity*, Berkeley

Gaca, Kathy L. (2014a), Early Christian Sexuality, in: Hubbard, Thomas K. (ed), *A Companion to Greek and Roman Sexualities*, New York, pp. 549–564

Gaca, Kathy L. (2014b), Martial Rape, Pulsating Fear, and the Sexual Maltreatment of Girls (paides), Virgins (parthenoi), and Women (gynaikes) in Antiquity, in: *American Journal of Philology* 135, pp. 303–357

Gaca, Kathy L. (2018), The Martial Rape of Girls and Women in Antiquity and Modernity, in: Haynes, Dina/Aoláin, Fionnuala Ni/Valji, Nahla/Cahn, Naomi (eds), *The Oxford Handbook of Gender and Conflict*, New York, pp. 305–315

Gane, Mike (1993), *Harmless Lovers? Gender, Theory and Personal Relationships*, London/New York

Garber, Marjorie (2000), *Die Vielfalt des Begehrens. Bisexualität von der Antike bis heute*, Frankfurt a. M.

Garrison, John S. (2014), *Friendship and Queer Theory in the Renaissance: Gender and Sexuality in Early Modern England*, London

Garton, Stephen (2004), *Histories of Sexuality: Antiquity to Sexual Revolution*, London

Gay, Peter (1986), *Erziehung der Sinne. Sexualität im bürgerlichen Zeitalter*, München

Gentilcore, David (2005), Charlatans, the Regulated Marketplace and the Treatment of Venereal Disease in Italy, in: Siena, Kevin Patrick (ed), *Sins of the Flesh: Responding to Sexual Disease in Early Modern Europe*, Toronto, pp. 57–80

Gerard, Kent/Hekma, Gert (eds) (1989), *The Pursuit of Sodomy: Male Homosexuality in Renaissance and Enlightenment Europe*, New York

Geremek, Bronislaw (1991), *The Margins of Society in Late Medieval Paris*, Cambridge

Gestrich, Andreas (2004), After Dark: Girls' Leisure, Work and Sexuality in 18th and 19th Century Rural Southwest Germany, in: Maynes, Mary Jo/Søland, Birgitte/Benninghaus, Christina (eds), *Secret Gardens, Satanic Mills: Placing Girls in European History, 1750–1960*, Bloomington, pp. 54–68

Ghirardo, Dianne Yvonne (2001), The Topography of Prostitution in Renaissance Ferrara, in: *Journal of the Society of Architectural Historians* 60, 4, pp. 402–431

Giddens, Anthony (1993), *Wandel der Intimität. Sexualität, Liebe und Erotik in modernen Gesellschaften*, Frankfurt a. M.

Gienow, Peter (2006), *Die miasmatische Therapie der Syphilinie*, Buchendorf

Gil, Daniel Juan (2006), *Before Intimacy: Asocial Sexuality in Early Modern England*, Minnesota

Gilbert, Ruth (2002), *Early Modern Hermaphrodites: Sex and Other Stories*, Basingstoke/New York

Gilhuly, Kate (2015), Lesbians Are Not from Lesbos, in: Blondell, Ruby/Ormand, Kirk (eds), *Ancient Sex: New Essays: Classical Memories, Modern Identities*, Columbus, pp. 143–176

Gilhuly, Kate (2017), *Erotic Geographies in Ancient Greek Literature and Culture*, London

Given, James Buchanan (2001), *Inquisition and Medieval Society. Power, Discipline, and Resistance in Languedoc*, Ithaca

Gladfelder, Hal (2007), In Search of Lost Texts: Thomas Cannon's Ancient and Modern Pederasty Investigated and Exemplify'd, in: *Eighteenth-Century Life* 31, pp. 22–38

Glancy, Jennifer A. (2002), *Slavery in Early Christianity*, Oxford
Glazebrook, Allison (2009), Cosmetics and Sôphrosunê: Ischomachos' Wife in Xenophon's Oikonomikos, Bodies, Households and Landscapes: Sex and Gender in the Greco-Roman World, in: *Classical World* 102, 3, pp. 231–246
Glazebrook, Allison (2011a), Prostitution, in: Golden, Mark/Toohey, Peter (eds), *A Cultural History of Sexuality in the Classical World (=A Cultural History of Sexuality Vol. 1)*, Oxford/New York, pp. 145–168
Glazebrook, Allison (2011b), Porneion: Prostitution in Athenian Civic Space, in: Glazebrook, Allison/Henry, Madeleine M. (eds), *Greek Prostitutes in the Ancient Mediterranean, 800 BCE to 200 CE*, Madison, pp. 34–59
Glazebrook, Allison (2016), Is There an Archaeology of Prostitution?, in: Glazebrook, Allison/Tsakirgis, Barbara (eds), *Houses of Ill Repute: The Archaeology of Brothels, Houses, and Taverns in the Greek World*, Philadelphia, pp. 169–196
Glazebrook, Allison (2022), *Sexual Labor in the Athenian Courts*, Austin
Glazebrook, Allison/Olson, Kelly (2014), Greek and Roman Marriage, in: Hubbard, Thomas K. (ed), *A Companion to Greek and Roman Sexualities*, New York, pp. 69–82
Glazebrook, Allison/Tsakirgis, Barbara (2016), Introduction, in: Glazebrook, Allison/Tsakirgis, Barbara (eds), *Houses of Ill Repute: The Archaeology of Brothels, Houses, and Taverns in the Greek World*, Philadelphia, pp. 1–12
Gleason, Maud (1995), *Making Men: Sophists and Self-Presentation in Ancient Rome*, Princeton
Gleixner, Ulrike (1994), *Das Mensch und der Kerl. Die Konstruktion von Geschlecht in Unzuchtsverfahren der Frühen Neuzeit, 1700–1760*, Frankfurt a. M./New York
Gleixner, Ulrike (2005), *Pietismus und Bürgertum: Eine Historische Anthropologie der Frömmigkeit, Württemberg 17. - 19. Jahrhundert*, Göttingen
Godbeer, Richard (2002), *Sexual Revolution in Early America*, Baltimore/London
Goetz, Hans-Werner (2002), *Leben im Mittelalter. Vom 7. bis zum 13. Jahrhundert*, München, 7th edn
Goetz, Hans-Werner (2016), *Gott und die Welt. Religiöse Vorstellungen des frühen und hohen Mittelalters. Teil I, Band 3: IV. Die Geschöpfe: Engel, Teufel, Menschen*, Göttingen
Goez, Werner (2008), *Kirchenreform und Investiturstreit 910–1122*, Stuttgart, 2nd edn
Goffen, Rona (1994), The Problematic Patronage of Titian's Venus of Urbino, in: *The Journal of Medieval and Renaissance Studies* 24, 2, pp. 301–321
Goldberg, Jonathan (1992), *Sodometries: Renaissance Texts, Modern Sexualities*, Stanford
Goldberg, Jonathan (ed) (1994), *Queering the Renaissance*, Durham
Goldberg, Peter J. P. (1999), Pigs and Prostitutes: Streetwalking in Comparative Perspective, in: Lewis, Katherine J. et al. (eds), *Young Medieval Women*, Stroud, pp. 172–193
Goldberg, Peter J. P. (2008), *Communal Discord, Child Abduction, and Rape in the Later Middle Ages*, New York
Goldberg, Peter J. P. (ed) (1995), *Women in England, c. 1275–1525: Documentary Sources*, Manchester
Golden, Mark (1992), Slavery and Homosexuality in Athens, in: Dynes, Wayne R./Donaldson, Stephen (eds), *Homosexuality in the Ancient World (=Studies in Homosexuality I)*, New York/London, pp. 162–178

Golden, Mark/Toohey, Peter (2011), Introduction, in: Golden, Mark/Toohey, Peter (eds), *A Cultural History of Sexuality in the Classical World (=A Cultural History of Sexuality Vol. 1)*, Oxford/New York, pp. 1–16

Goldhill, Simon (1995), *Foucault's Virginity: Ancient Erotic Fiction and the History of Sexuality*, Cambridge/New York

Goldhill, Simon (2014), Is There a History of Prostitution?, in: Masterson, Mark/Sorkin Rabinowitz, Nancy/Robson, James (eds), *Sex in Antiquity: Exploring Gender and Sexuality in the Ancient World*, London/New York, pp. 179–197

Gollner, Günther (1974), *Homosexualität. Ideologiekritik und Entmythologisierung einer Gesetzgebung*, Berlin

Gordon, Pamela (2002), Some Unseen Monsters: Rereading Lucretius on Sex, in: Fredrick, David (ed), *The Roman Gaze: Vision, Power, and the Body*, Baltimore, pp. 86–109

Götsch, Silke (2001), Körpererfahrung und soziale Schicht, in: Münch, Paul (ed), *Erfahrung als Kategorie der Frühneuzeitgeschichte*, München, pp. 107–113

Gowing, Laura (2003), *Common Bodies: Women, Touch, and Power in Seventeenth Century England*, New Haven

Gowing, Laura (2007), Lesbierinnen und ihre „Halbschwestern" im Europa der frühen Neuzeit, 1500–1800, in: Aldrich, Robert (ed), *Gleich und anders. Eine globale Geschichte der Homosexualität*, Hamburg, pp. 125–143

Gowing, Laura (2012), Knowledge and Experience, C. 1500–1750, in: Fisher, Kate/Toulalan, Sarah (eds), *The Routledge History of Sex and the Body, 1500 to the Present*, Oxford et al., pp. 239–275

Grahn-Wilder, Malin (2018), *Gender and Sexuality in Stoic Philosophy*, Cham

Grassi, Umberto (2007), L'offitia sopra l'onestà: La repressione della sodomia nella Lucca del cinquecento (1551–1580), in: *Studi storici* 48, pp. 127–159

Grau, Günter (1993), *Homosexualität in der NS-Zeit. Dokumente einer Diskriminierung und Verfolgung*, Frankfurt a. M.

Grau, Günter (1995), Sozialistische Moral und Homosexualität. Die Politik der SED und das Homosexuellenstrafrecht 1945 bis 1989—Ein Rückblick, in: Grumbach, Detlev (Hg), *Die Linke und das Laster. Schwule Emanzipation und die Linke*, Hamburg, pp. 85–141

Grau, Günter (2002), Unschuldige Täter. Mediziner als Vollstrecker der nationalsozialistischen Homosexuellenpolitik, in: Jellonnek, Burkhard/Lautmann, Rüdiger (eds), *Nationalsozialistischer Terror gegen Homosexuelle. Verdrängt und ungesühnt*, Paderborn et al., pp. 209–235

Grau, Günter (2003), Schmerzhafte Erinnerungen, in: *Dijk, Lutz van (unter Mitarbeit von Günter Grau), Einsam war ich nie. Schwule unter dem Hakenkreuz, 1933–1945*, Berlin, pp. 142–158

Graupner, Helmut (1997), Von „Widernatürlicher Unzucht" zu „Sexueller Orientierung". Homosexualität und Recht, in: Hey, Barbara/Pallier, Ronald/Roth, Roswitha (eds), *Que(e)rdenken. Weibliche, männliche Homosexualität und Wissenschaft*, Innsbruck/Wien, pp. 198–253

Gravdal, Kathryn (1991), *Ravishing Maidens. Writing Rape in Medieval French Literature and Law*, Philadelphia

Green, Jonathon/Karolides, Nicholas J. (2005), *The Encyclopedia of Censorship*, New York, 2nd edn

Green, Monica H. (2008), Conversing with the Minority: Relations among Christian, Jewish, and Muslim Women in the High Middle Ages, in: *Journal of Medieval History* 34, pp. 105–118

Greenberg, David F. (1988), *The Construction of Homosexuality*, Chicago

Greene, Ellen (1996), Apostrophe and Women's Erotics in the Poetry of Sappho, in: Greene, Ellen (ed), *Reading Sappho: Contemporary Approaches*, Berkeley, pp. 233–247

Greene, Ellen (2002), Subjects, Objects, and Erotic Symmetry in Sappho's Fragments, in: Rabinowitz, Nancy Sorkin/Auanger, Lisa (eds), *Among Women: From the Homosocial to the Homoerotic in the Ancient World*, Austin, pp. 82–105

Grieser, Heike (2018), Was ist πορνεία? Frühchristliche Positionen zu sexuellen Beziehungen zwischen Freien und ihren Sklavinnen, in: Fischer, Irmtraud/Feichtinger, Daniela (eds), *Sexualität und Sklaverei*, Münster, pp. 83–105

Griffey, Erin (2010), Currency and Conquest, or Love for Sale in Titian's Danaë, in: Levy, Allison (ed), *Sex Acts in Early Modern Italy: Practice, Performance, Perversion, Punishment*, Farnham et al., pp. 137–149

Grimm, Matthias (ed) (1990), *Die Geschichte des § 175. Strafrecht gegen Homosexuelle. Ausstellungskatalog*, Frankfurt a. M.

Grmek, Mirko D. (1990), *History of AIDS: Emergence and Origin of a Modern Pandemic*, Princeton

Grmek, Mirko D. (1991), *Diseases in the Ancient Greek World*, Baltimore/London

Groebner, Valentin (2000), Flüssige Gaben und die Hände der Stadt. Städtische Geschenke, städtische Korruption und politische Sprache am Vorabend der Reformation, in: Schreiner, Klaus/Signori, Gabriela (eds), *Bilder, Texte, Rituale. Wirklichkeitsbezug und Wirklichkeitskonstruktion politisch-rechtlicher Kommunikationsmedien in Stadt- und Adelsgesellschaften des späten Mittelalters*, Berlin, pp. 17–34

Groebner, Valentin (2007), Mit dem Feind schlafen. Nachdenken über Hautfarben, Sex und "Rasse" im spätmittelalterlichen Europa, in: *Historische Anthropologie. Kultur, Gesellschaft, Alltag* 15, 3, pp. 327–338

Grove, Jen (2015), The Role of Roman Artefacts in E. P. Warren's "Paederastic Evangel", in: Ingleheart, Jennifer (ed), *Ancient Rome and the Construction of Modern Homosexual Identities*, Oxford, pp. 214–231

Gruber, Franjo/Lipozenčić, Jasna/Kehler, Tatjana (2015), History of Venereal Diseases from Antiquity to the Renaissance, in: *Acta Dermatovenerol Croat* 23, 1, pp. 1–11

Grulich, Josef (2010), Heiratsstrategien der Dorfbevölkerung. Die Herrschaft Trebon/Wittingau 1792–1836, in: Schmidt-Voges, Inken (ed), *Ehe, Haus, Familie: Soziale Institutionen im Wandel 1750–1850*, Köln/Weimar/Wien, pp. 143–178

Guénette, Maryse (1987), Errances et solitude féminines à Manosque (1314–1358), in: Hébert, Michel (ed), *Vie privée et ordre publique à la fin du Moyen-Âge. Études sur Manosque, la Provence et le Piémont (1250–1450)*, Aix-en-Provence, pp. 23–43

Günther, Bettina (2000), Sittlichkeitsdelikte in den Policeyordnungen der Reichsstädte Frankfurt am Main und Nürnberg (15.-17. Jahrhundert), in:

Härter, Karl (ed), *Policey und frühneuzeitliche Gesellschaft*, Frankfurt a. M., pp. 121–148

Günther, Hubertus (2001), Amor und Psyche. Raffaels Freskenzyklus in der Gartenloggia der Villa des Agostino Chigi und die Fabel von Amor und Psyche in der Malerei der italienischen Renaissance, in: *Artibus et Historiae* 22, 44, pp. 149–166

Gust, Geoffrey W. (2018), *Chaucerotics: Uncloaking the Language of Sex in The Canterbury Tales and Troilus and Criseyde*, Cham

Guth, Doris (2012), Das Bildnis Gabrielle d'Estrees und ihre Schwester. Kunsthistorische Forschung zur Homoerotik zwischen Frauen, in: Guth, Doris/Priedl, Elisabeth (eds), *Bilder der Liebe. Liebe, Begehren und Geschlechterverhältnisse in der Kunst der Frühen Neuzeit*, Bielefeld, pp. 301–332

Gutierrez, Ramón A. (1991), *When Jesus Came, the Corn Mothers Went Away: Marriage, Sexuality and Power in New Mexico 1500–1846*, Stanford

Gutiérrez, Ramón A. (2007), Warfare, Homosexuality, and Gender Status among American Indian Men in the Southwest, in: Foster, Thomas A. (ed), *Long Before Stonewall: Histories of Same-Sex Sexuality in Early America*, New York et al., pp. 19–31

Gutmann, Hans-Martin (1991), *Über Liebe und Herrschaft: Luthers Verständnis von Intimität und Autorität im Kontext des Zivilisationsprozesses*, Göttingen

Gvozdeva, Katja/Velten, Hans Rudolf (2011), Einleitung, in: Gvozdeva, Katja/Velten, Hans Rudolf (eds), *Scham und Schamlosigkeit. Grenzverletzungen in Literatur und Kultur der Vormoderne*, Berlin/Boston, pp. 1–26

Haage, Bernhard D. (1990), Amor hereos. als medizinischer Terminus technicus in der Antke und im Mittelalter, in: Stemmler, Theo (ed), *Liebe als Krankheit: 3. Kolloquium der Forschungsstelle für Europäische Lyrik des Mittelalters*, Tübingen, pp. 31–73

Habinek, Thomas N. (1997), The Invention of Sexuality in the World-City of Rome, in: Habinek, Thomas N./Schiesaro, Alessandro (eds), *The Roman Cultural Revolution*, Cambridge, pp. 23–43

Hacke, Daniela (2004), *Women, Sex, and Marriage in Early Modern Venice*, Aldershot

Hacker, Hanna (1987), *Frauen und Freundinnen. Studien zur "weiblichen Homosexualität" am Beispiel Österreich, 1870–1938*, Weinheim/Basel

Hacker, Hanna (1993), Männliche Autoren der Sexualwissenschaft über weibliche Homosexualität, 1870–1930, in: Lautmann, Rüdiger (ed), *Homosexualität. Handbuch der Theorie- und Forschungsgeschichte*, Frankfurt a. M., pp. 134–140

Haeberle, Erwin J. (1994), Bisexualitäten – Geschichte und Dimensionen eines modernen wissenschaftlichen Phänomens, in: Gindorf, Rolf/Haeberle, Erwin (eds), *Bisexualitäten. Ideologie und Praxis des Sexualkontaktes mit beiden Geschlechtern*, Stuttgart/Jena/New York, pp. 1–40

Haemers, Jelle (2021), Women and Stews: The Social and Material History of Prostitution in the Late Medieval Southern Low Countries, in: *History Workshop Journal* 92, 1, pp. 29–50

Hagemann, Karen (1990), *Frauenalltag und Männerpolitik. Alltagsleben und gesellschaftliches Handeln von Arbeiterfrauen in der Weimarer Republik*, Bonn

Haggerty, George E. (ed) (2000), *The Encyclopedia of Gay Histories and Cultures*, New York

Hagner, Michael (1995), Vom Naturalienkabinett zur Embryologie. Wandlungen des Monströsen und die Ordnung des Lebens, in: Hagner, Michael (ed), *Der falsche Körper. Beiträge zu einer Geschichte der Monstrositäten*, Göttingen, pp. 73–107

Hain, Kathryn A. (2020), The Prestige Makers: Greek Slave Women in Ancient India, in: *Journal of World History* 31, 2, pp. 265–294

Haks, Donald (1988), Libertinisme en Nederlands verhalend Prosa 1650–1700, in: Hekma, Gert/Roodenburg, Herman (eds), *Soete minne en helsche boosheit. Seksuele voorstellingen in Nederland, 1300–1850*, Nijmegen, pp. 85–107

Haldemann, Arno (2015), Das gerügte Haus: Rügerituale am Haus in der Ehrgesellschaft der Frühen Neuzeit, in: Eibach, Joachim/Schmidt-Voges, Inken (eds), *Das Haus in der Geschichte Europas: Ein Handbuch*, Berlin/München/Boston, pp. 433–448

Haliczer, Stephen (1996), *Sexuality in the Confessional: A Sacrament Profaned*, New York/Oxford

Hall, Lesley A. (1998), *The Other in the Mirror: Sex, Victorians and Historians* (http://www.lesleyahall.net/sexvict.htm)

Hall, Lesley A. (2000), *Sex, Gender and Social Change in Britain since 1880*, Houndmills/London

Hall, Lesley A. (2013), *Victorian Sex Factoids* (http://www.lesleyahall.net/factoids.htm#thinking)

Hallett, Judith P. (1996), Sappho and Her Social Context: Sense and Sensuality, in: Greene, Ellen (ed), *Reading Sappho: Contemporary Approaches*, Berkeley et al., pp. 125–142

Hallett, Judith P./Skinner, Marilyn B. (eds) (1997), *Roman Sexualities*, Princeton

Halperin, David M. (1990), *One Hundred Years of Homosexuality and Other Essays on Greek Love*, New York/London

Halperin, David M. (2000a), Forgetting Foucault: Acts, Identities, and the History of Sexuality, in: Nussbaum, Martha/Sihvola, Juha (eds), *The Sleep of Reason: Erotic Experience and Sexual Ethics in Ancient Greece and Rome*, Chicago, pp. 21–54

Halperin, David M. (2000b), The First Homosexuality?, in: Nussbaum, Martha/Sihvola, Juha (eds), *The Sleep of Reason: Erotic Experience and Sexual Ethics in Ancient Greece and Rome*, Chicago, pp. 229–268

Halperin, David M. (2002), *How to Do the History of Homosexuality*, Chicago et al.

Halperin, David M. (2003a), Ein Wegweiser zur Geschichtsschreibung der männlichen Homosexualität, in: Kraß, Andreas (ed), *Queer Denken: Queer Studies*, Frankfurt a. M., pp. 171–220

Halperin, David M. (2003b), Introduction: Among Men – History, Sexuality, and the Return of the Affect, in: O'Donnell, Katherine/O'Rourke, Michael (eds), *Love, Sex, Intimacy and Friendship between Men, 1550–1800*, Basingstoke/New York, pp. 1–11

Halperin, David M. (2017), L'erôs platonicien et ce qu'on appelle "amour", in: Brisson, Luc/Renaut, Olivier (ed), *Érotique et politique chez Platon: Erôs, genre et sexualité dans la cité platonicienne*, Sankt Augustin, pp. 19–70

Halperin, David M./Winkler, John J./Zeitlin, Froma I. (eds) (1990), *Before Sexuality: The Construction of Erotic Experience in the Ancient Greek World*, Princeton

Hamel, Debra (2003), *Trying Neaira: The True Story of a Courtesan's Scandalous Life in Ancient Greece*, New Haven
Hamilton, Tom (2020), Sodomy and Criminal Justice in the Parlement of Paris, ca. 1540 - ca.1700, in: *Journal of the History of Sexuality* 29, 3, pp. 303–334
Hamilton, Tom (2021), A Sodomy Scandal on the Eve of the French Wars of Religion, in: *Historical Journal* 64, 4, pp. 844–864
Hammer, Michael M. (2018), Das Frauenhaus in Bozen: Ein Fallbeispiel für das spätmittelalterliche Bordellwesen, in: *Storia e Regione* 27, 1, pp. 155–171
Hammer, Michael M. (2019), *Gemeine Dirnen und gute Fräulein: Frauenhäuser im spätmittelalterlichen Österreich*, Berlin
Hammer-Tugendhat, Daniela (2009), *Das Sichtbare und das Unsichtbare: Zur holländischen Malerei des 17. Jahrhunderts*, Köln/Wien
Hanson, Ann Ellis (1990), The Medical Writers' Woman, in: Halperin, David M./Winkler, John J./Zeitlin, Froma I. (eds), *Before Sexuality: The Construction of Erotic Experience in the Ancient World*, Princeton, pp. 309–338
Harbison, Craig (1990), Sexuality and Social Standing in Jan van Eyck's Arnolfini Double Portrait, in: *Renaissance Quarterly* 43, 2, pp. 249–291
Hardach-Pinke, Irene (2005), Managing Girls' Sexuality among German Upper Classes, in: Maynes, Mary Jo/Soland, Brigitte/Benninghaus, Christine (eds), *Secret Gardens, Satanic Mills: Placing Girls in European History, 1750–1960*, Bloomington, pp. 101–114
Hardwick, Julie (2015), Policing Paternity: Historicising Masculinity and Sexuality in Early-Modern France, in: *European Review of History* 22, 4, pp. 643–657
Harlow, Mary/Laurence, Ray (2002), *Growing Up and Growing Old in Ancient Rome: A Life Course Approach*, London
Harms-Ziegler, Beate (1997), Außereheliche Mutterschaft in Preußen im 18. und 19. Jahrhundert, in: Gerhard, Ute (ed), *Frauen in der Geschichte des Rechts. Von der Frühen Neuzeit bis in die Gegenwart*, München, pp. 324–344
Harnisch, Wolfgang (1994), *Christusbindung oder Weltbezug? Sachkritische Erwägungen zur paulinischen Argumentation in 1Kor7*, München
Harper, April/Proctor, Caroline (eds) (2008), *Medieval Sexuality: A Casebook*, New York
Harper, Kristin N. et al. (2011), The Origin and Antiquity of Syphilis Revisited: An Appraisal of Old World Pre-Columbian Evidence for Treponemal Infection, in: *Yearbook of Physical Anthropology* 54, pp. 99–133
Harper, Kyle (2011), *Slavery in the Late Roman Mediterranean, AD 275–425*, Cambridge
Harper, Kyle (2013), *From Shame to Sin: The Christian Transformation of Sexual Morality in Late Antiquity*, Cambridge
Harper, Kyle (2016), Freedom, Slavery, and Female Sexual Honor in Antiquity, in: Bodel, John/Scheidel, Walter (eds), *On Human Bondage: After Slavery and Social Death*, Chichester/Malden, pp. 109–121
Harrington, Joel F. (1995), *Reordering Marriage and Society in Reformation Germany*, Cambridge/New York
Harrington, Joel F. (2009), *The Unwanted Child: The Fate of Foundlings, Orphans, and Juvenile Criminals in Early Modern Germany*, Chicago/London
Harris, Carissa M. (2016), Rape Narratives, Courtly Critique, and the Pedagogy of Sexual Negotiation in the Middle English Pastourelle, in: *Journal of Medieval & Early Modern Studies* 46, 2, pp. 263–287

Harris, Carissa M. (2018), *Obscene Pedagogies: Transgressive Talk and Sexual Education in Late Medieval Britain*, Ithaca/London

Harris, Edward M. (2014), "Yes" and "No" in Women's Desire, in: Masterson, Mark/Sorkin Rabinowitz, Nancy/Robson, James (eds), *Sex in Antiquity: Exploring Gender and Sexuality in the Ancient World*, London/New York, pp. 298–314

Harris, Lydia Michelle (2017), *Evacuating the Womb: Abortion and Contraception in the High Middle Ages, circa 1050–1300*. Dissertation, Durham

Harris, Tim (1986), The Bawdy House Riots of 1668, in: *The Historical Journal* 29, 3, pp. 537–556

Harris, Victoria (2010), Sex on the Margins: New Directions in the Historiography of Sexuality and Gender, in: *The Historical Journal* 53, 4, pp. 1085–1104

Hartmann, Elke (2002), *Heirat, Hetärentum und Konkubinat im klassischen Athen*, Frankfurt a. M.

Hartmann, Elke (2006), Hetären bei Lukian, in: Ulf, Christoph/Rollinger, Robert (eds), *Frauen und Geschlechter. Bilder—Rollen—Realitäten in den Texten antiker Autoren der römischen Kaiserzeit*, Wien, pp. 339–354

Hartmann, Elke (2007), *Frauen in der Antike: Weibliche Lebenswelten von Sappho bis Theodora*, München

Hartmann, Elke (2015), Zur Semantik des Seitensprungs. Ehebruch als politische Waffe in der späten römischen Republik, in: *Historische Anthropologie* 23, 2, pp. 229–252

Hartmann, Martin (2010), *Gefühle. Wie die Wissenschaften sie erklären*, Frankfurt a. M./New York, 2nd edn

Hartney, Aideen (1999), Manly Women and Womanly Men: The Subintroductae and John Chrysostom, in: James, Liz (ed), *Desire and Denial in Byzantium: Papers from the 31st Spring Symposium of Byzantine Studies, University of Sussex, Brighton, March 1997*, London/New York, pp. 41–48

Harvey, Katherine (2017), Episcopal Virginity in Medieval England, in: *Journal of the History of Sexuality* 26, 2, pp. 273–293

Haseldine, Julian (1999), Love, Separation and Male Friendship: Words and Actions in Saint Anselm's Letters to his Friends, in: Hadley, Dawn N. (ed), *Masculinity in Medieval Europe*, London, pp. 238–255

Hatfield, Elaine/Luckhursta, Cherie/Rapsona, Richard L. (2012), A Brief History of Attempts to Measure Sexual Motives, in: *Interpersona: An International Journal on Personal Relationships* 6, 2, pp. 138–154

Hatty, Suzanne E./Hatty, James (1999), *The Disordered Body: Epidemic Disease and Cultural Transformation*, New York

Haug, Walter (2004), *Die höfische Liebe im Horizont der erotischen Diskurse des Mittelalters und der Frühen Neuzeit*, Berlin

Hausner, Sondra L. (2016), *The Spirits of Crossbones Graveyard: Time, Ritual, and Sexual Commerce in London*, Bloomington

Haverkamp-Begemann, Egbert (1998), Rembrandt van Rijn, Portrait of Gerard de Lairesse, in: Sterling, Charles et al. (eds), *Fifteenth- to Eighteenth-Century European Paintings: France, Central Europe, The Netherlands, Spain, and Great Britain*, Princeton, pp. 139–147

Hawkes, Gail (2004), *Sex and Pleasure in Western Culture*, Cambridge/Malden

Healey, Dan (2001), *Homosexual Desire in Revolutionary Russia: The Regulation of Sexual and Gender Dissent*, Chicago

Heebøll-Holm, Thomas K. (2021), Piratical Slave-Raiding: The Demise of a Viking Practice in High Medieval Denmark, in: *Scandinavian Journal of History* 46, 4, pp. 431–454

Hegel, Georg Friedrich Wilhelm (1970/71), *Enzyklopädie der philosophischen Wissenschaften, in: Georg Friedrich Wilhelm Hegel, Werke, Bd. 9*, Frankfurt a. M.

Heid, Stefan (1997), *Zölibat in der frühen Kirche. Die Anfänge einer Enthaltsamkeitspflicht in für Kleriker in Ost und West*, Paderborn/Wien

Heijden, Manon van der (2000), Women as Victims of Sexual and Domestic Violence in Seventeenth-Century Holland: Criminal Cases of Rape, Incest, and Maltreatment in Rotterdam and Delft, in: *Journal of Social History* 33, pp. 623–644

Heijden, Manon van der (2004), Punishment versus Reconciliation: Marriage Control in Sixteenth- und Seventeenth Century Holland, in: Roodenburg, Hermann/Spierenburg, Pieter (eds), *Social Control in Europe. Vol. 1: 1500– 1800*, Columbus, pp. 55–77

Heine, Alexander (ed) (1992), *Germanen und Germanien in griechischen Quellen*, Essen

Heinig, Paul-Joachim (2006), Fürstenkonkubinat um 1500 zwischen Usus und Devianz, in: Tacke, Andreas (ed), *Wir wollen der Liebe Raum geben. Konkubinate geistlicher und weltlicher Fürsten um 1500*, Göttingen, pp. 11–37

Heiss, Gernot (1989), Konfessionsbildung. Kirchenzucht und frühmoderner Staat, in: Ehalt, Hubert Ch. (ed), *Volksfrömmigkeit. Glaubensvorstellungen und Wirklichkeitsbewältigung im Wandel*, Wien/Köln, pp. 191–220

Hekma, Gert (1989), Sodomites, Platonic Lovers, Contrary Lovers. The Backgrounds of the Modern Homosexual, in: Kent, Gerard/Hekma, Gert (eds), *The Pursuit of Sodomy: Male Homosexuality in Renaissance and Enlightenment Europe*, New York, pp. 433–456

Hekma, Gert (1998), Die Verfolgung der Männer. Gleichgeschlechtliche Begierden und Praktiken in der europäischen Geschichte, in: *Österreichische Zeitschrift für Geschichtswissenschaften* 9, 3, pp. 311–341

Hekma, Gert (1999), Amsterdam, in: Higgs, David (ed), *Queer Sites: Gay Urban Histories Since 1600*, London, pp. 61–88

Hekma, Gert (2004), *Homoseksualiteit in Nederland van 1730 tot de moderne tijd*, Amsterdam

Hekma, Gert (2007), Die schwul-lesbische Welt. 1980 bis zur Gegenwart, in: Aldrich, Robert (ed), *Gleich und anders. Eine globale Geschichte der Homosexualität*, Hamburg, pp. 333–363

Hekma, Gert/Giami, Alain (eds) (2014), *Sexual Revolutions*, Basingstoke et al.

Hekma, Gert/Oosterhuis, Harry/Steakley, James D. (1995), Leftist Sexual Politics and Homosexuality. An Historical Overview, in: Hekma, Gert/Oosterhuis, Harry/Steakley, James D. (eds), *Gay Men and the Sexual History of the Political Left*, London/New York, pp. 1–40

Heller, Erdmute/Mosbahi, Hassouna (1993), *Hinter den Schleiern des Islam. Erotik und Sexualität in der arabischen Kultur*, München

Hemmie, Dagmar (2007), *Ungeordnete Unzucht. Prostitution im Hanseraum (12.- 16. Jahrhundert)*. Lübeck, Bergen, Helsingør, Wien/Köln/Weimar

Henderson, John (2021), Die bildliche Darstellung der Franzosenkrankheit im frühneuzeitlichen Italien. Patienten, Krankheitsbild und Behandlung, in:

Stolberg, Michael (ed), *Körper-Bilder in der Frühen Neuzeit: Kunst-, Medizin- und Mediengeschichtliche Perspektiven*, Berlin/München/Boston, pp. 15–37

Hendrix, Scott H. (2008), Masculinity and Patriarchy in Reformation Germany, in: Hendrix, Scott H./Karant-Nunn, Susan C. (eds), *Masculinity in the Reformation Era*, Kirksville, pp. 71–91

Heng, Geraldine (2018), *The Invention of Race in the European Middle Ages*, Cambridge/New York

Herbers, Klaus (2006), *Geschichte Spaniens im Mittelalter. Vom Westgotenreich bis zum Ende des 15. Jahrhunderts*, Stuttgart

Herdt, Gilbert H. (1991), Representations of Homosexuality: An Essay on Cultural Ontology and Historical Comparison, in: *Journal of the History of Sexuality* 1, 3 and 4, pp. 481–504 and 603–632

Hergemöller, Bernd-Ulrich (1990), Sodomiter. Schuldzuschreibungen und Repressionsformen im Mittelalter, in: Hergemöller, Bernd-Ulrich (ed), *Randgruppen der spätmittelalterlichen Gesellschaft. Ein Hand- und Studienbuch*, Warendorf, pp. 316–356

Hergemöller, Bernd-Ulrich (1998), *Sodom und Gomorrha. Zur Alltagswirklichkeit und Verfolgung Homosexueller im Mittelalter*, Hamburg

Hergemöller, Bernd-Ulrich (1999), *Einführung in die Historiographie der Homosexualitäten*, Tübingen

Hergemöller, Bernd-Ulrich (2000), *Männer, „die mit Männer handeln", in der Augsburger Reformationszeit*, München

Hergemöller, Bernd-Ulrich (2007), Das Mittelalter, in: Aldrich, Robert (ed), *Gleich und anders. Eine globale Geschichte der Homosexualität*, Hamburg, pp. 57–78

Hermans, Lex (1995), *Bewust van andere lusten. Homoseksualiteit in het Romeinse keizerrijk*, Amsterdam

Hersch, Karen K. (2010), *The Roman Wedding: Ritual and Meaning in Antiquity*, Oxford

Herzer, Manfred (1990), Deutsches Schwulenstrafrecht vor der Gründung des zweiten Kaiserreichs, 1795–1870, in: *Die Geschichte des § 175. Strafrecht gegen Homosexuelle. Ausstellungskatalog*, Frankfurt a. M., pp. 30–41

Herzer, Manfred (1992), *Magnus Hirschfeld. Leben und Werk eines jüdischen, schwulen und sozialistischen Sexologen*, Frankfurt a. M.

Herzer, Manfred (2000), Kertbenys Leben und Sexualitätsstudien, in: Herzer, Manfred (ed), *Karl Maria Kertbeny. Schriften zur Homosexualitätsforschung*, Berlin, pp. 7–61

Herzig, Tamar (2017), The Prosecution of Jews and the Repression of Sodomy in Fifteenth-Century Italy, in: Schutte, Anne Jacobson/Del Col, Andrea (eds), *L'Inquisizione Romana, i giudici e gli eretici: Studi in onore di John Tedeschi*, Rome, pp. 59–74

Herzig, Tamar (2022), Slavery and Interethnic Sexual Violence: A Multiple Perpetrator Rape in Seventeenth-Century Livorno, in: *The American Historical Review* 127, 1, pp. 194–222

Herzog, Dagmar (2009), Syncopated Sex: Transforming European Sexual Cultures, in: *The American Historical Review* 114, 5, pp. 1287–1308

Herzog, Dagmar (2011), *Sexuality in Europe: A Twentieth-Century History*, Cambridge

Heyam, Kit (2019), Paratexts and Pornographic Potential in Seventeenth-Century Anatomy Books, in: *Seventeenth Century* 34, 5, pp. 615–647

Higgs, David (ed) (1999), *Queer Sites: Urban Histories since 1600*, New York/London
Hin, Saskia (2013), *The Demography of Roman Italy: Population Dynamics in an Ancient Conquest Society 201 BCE - 14 CE*, Cambridge
Hirschfeld, Magnus (1924), *Sexualität und Kriminalität. Überblick über Verbrechen geschlechtlichen Ursprungs*, Wien/Berlin
Hitchcock, Tim (1996), Redefining Sex in Eighteenth-Century England, in: *History Workshop Journal* 41, pp. 73–90
Hitchcock, Tim (1997), *English Sexualities, 1700–1800*, Basingstoke
Hoche, Gerrit (2010), *Utopische Liebesentwürfe der Moderne: Zur narrativen Produktion und Reflexion von Geschlechterdifferenzen in Friedrich Schlegels Lucinde und Ingeborg Bachmanns Malina*, Frankfurt a. M.
Hock, Jessie (2021), *The Erotics of Materialism: Lucretius and Early Modern Poetics Pornographic Sensibilities*, Philadelphia
Hocquenghem, Guy (1974), *Das homosexuelle Verlangen*, München
Hoffschildt, Rainer (2001), Rosa-Winkel-Häftlinge im KZ Mauthausen, in: *Aus dem Leben. Begleitpublikation zur Ausstellung über die nationalsozialistische Verfolgung der Homosexuellen in Wien 1938–45 (=Sonderheft der Lambda-Nachrichten. Zeitschrift der Homosexuellen Initiative Wien (Juni 2001))*, pp. 38–41
Hollander, Anne (1995), *Anzug und Eros. Eine Geschichte der modernen Kleidung*, Berlin
Holtzendorff, Franz von (1874), *Handbuch des deutschen Strafrechts in Einzelbeiträgen, Bd. 3: Die lehre von den Verbrechensarten*, Berlin
Holy, Michael (1998), Lang hieß es, Homosexualität sei gegen die Ordnung. Die westdeutsche Schwulenbewegung, 1969–1980, in: Herzer, Manfred (ed), *100 Jahre Schwulenbewegung. Dokumentation einer Vortragsreihe in der Akademie der Künste*, Berlin, pp. 83–110
Honegger, Claudia (1991), *Die Ordnung der Geschlechter. Die Wissenschaften vom Menschen und das Weib*, Frankfurt a. M./New York
Hope Ditmore, Melissa (2006), Introduction, in: Hope Ditmore, Melissa (ed), *Encyclopedia of Prostitution and Sex Work, Vol. I*, Connecticut/London, pp. 25–32
Hopkins, Amanda/Rushton, Cory (2007), Introduction: The Revel, the Melodye and the Bisynesse of Solas, in: Hopkins, Amanda/Rushton, Cory (eds), *The Erotic in the Literature of Medieval Britain*, Suffolk, pp. 1–17
Horley, James/Clarke, Jan (2016), Constructing Sexuality: A Theory of Stability and Fluidity, in: *Sexuality & Culture* 20, 4, pp. 906–922
Horswell, Michael J. (2005), *Decolonizing the Sodomite: Queer Tropes of Sexuality in Colonial Andean Culture*, Austin
Hosang, Boddens (2014), Attraction and Hatred: Relations between Jews and Christians in the Early Church, in: Geljon, Albert/Roukema, Riemer (eds), *Violence in Ancient Christianity: Victims and Perpetrators*, Leiden, pp. 90–107
Höschele, Regina (2012), Priapea (Carmina Priapea), in: *Brill's New Pauly Supplements I - Volume 5: The Reception of Classical Literature*, English edition by Matthijs H. Wibier (https://referenceworks-brillonline-com.uaccess.univie.ac.at/entries/brill-s-new-pauly-supplements-i-5/*-e1008240).
Houlbrook, Matt (2005), *Queer London: Perils and Pleasures in the Sexual Metropolis, 1918–1957*, Chicago

Howell, James W. et al. (eds) (2008), *The Greenwood Encyclopedia of Love, Courtship, and Sexuality through History*. 6 Vols, Westport
Hubbard, Thomas K. (2002), Pindar, Theoxenus, and the Homoerotic Eye, in: *Arethusa* 35, pp. 255–296
Hubbard, Thomas K. (2014), Peer Homosexuality, in: Hubbard, Thomas K. (ed), *A Companion to Greek and Roman Sexualities*, New York, pp. 128–149
Hubbard, Thomas K. (ed) (2003), *Homosexuality in Greece and Rome: A Sourcebook of Basic Documents*, Berkeley/Los Angeles
Hubbard, Thomas K./Doerfler, Maria (2014), From Ascesis to Sexual Renunciation, in: Hubbard, Thomas K. (ed), *A Companion to Greek and Roman Sexualities*, New York, pp. 164–183
Hull, Isabel V. (1996), *Sexuality, State, and Civil Society in Germany, 1700–1815*, Ithaca/London
Hull, Isabel V. (1997), Sexualstrafrecht und geschlechtsspezifische Normen in den deutschen Staaten des 17. und 18. Jahrhunderts, in: Gerhard, Ute (ed), *Frauen in der Geschichte des Rechts. Von der Frühen Neuzeit bis in die Gegenwart*, München, pp. 221–234
Humbert, Pierre/Palazzolo, Jérôme (2009), *Petite histoire de la masturbation*, Paris
Humfress, Caroline (2020), Cherchez la femme! Heresy and Law in Late Antiquity, in: *Studies in Church History* 56, pp. 36–59
Hunt, Alan (1999), *Governing Morals: A Social History of Moral Regulation*, Cambridge
Hunt, Emily J. (2003), *Christianity in the Second Century: The Case of Tatian*, London/New York
Hunt, Lynn (1993), Introduction: Obscenity and the Origins of Modernity, 1500–1800, Hunt, Lynn (ed), *The Invention of Pornography: Obscenity and the Origins of Modernity, 1500–1800*, New York, pp. 9–48
Hunt, Lynn (ed) (1994a), *Die Erfindung der Pornographie. Obszönität und die Ursprünge der Moderne*, Frankfurt a. M.
Hunt, Lynn (1994b), Obszönität und die Ursprünge der Moderne, in: Hunt, Lynn (ed), *Die Erfindung der Pornographie. Obszönität und die Ursprünge der Moderne*, Frankfurt a. M., pp. 7–34
Hunter, David G. (2005), Rereading the Jovinianist Controversy. Asceticism and Clercical Authority in Late Ancient Christianity, in: Martin, Dale B./Miller, Patricia Cox (eds), *The Cultural Turn in Late Ancient Studies: Gender, Asceticism, and Historiography*, Durham, pp. 119–135
Hunter, David G. (2007), *Marriage, Celibacy, and Heresy in Ancient Christianity: The Jovinianist Controversy*, Oxford/New York
Hunter, Matthew (2018), Talk That Talk: Shakespeare's Venus and Adonis and the Seductions of a Form, in: *Representations* 148, 1, pp. 1–29
Huot, Sylvia (2000), Bodily Peril: Sexuality and the Subversion of Order in Jean de Meun's Roman de la Rose, in: *Modern Language Review* 95, pp. 41–61
Hupperts, Charles (2007), Homosexualität in der Antike, in: Aldrich, Robert (ed), *Gleich und anders. Eine globale Geschichte der Homosexualität*, Hamburg, pp. 29–56
Hutcheson, Gregory S. (2021), Spain's Pecado Sodomítico and Its Mediterranean Intertextualities, in: Hutcheson, Gregory S. (ed), *Queering the Medieval Mediterranean: Transcultural Sea of Sex, Gender, Identity, and Culture*, Leiden, pp. 191–219

Hutchison, Emily J. (2020), Sex, Knowledge and "Women of Sin" in the Registre Criminel du Châtelet de Paris (1389–92), in: *Gender & History* 32, 1, pp. 131–148

Hütt, Wolfgang (ed) (1990), *Hintergrund. Mit den Unzüchtigkeits- und Gotteslästerungsparagraphen des Strafgesetzbuches gegen Kunst und Künstler, 1900–1933*, Berlin

Hutter, Jörg (1992), Die Entstehung des Paragraphen 175 im Strafgesetzbuch und die Geburt der deutschen Sexualwissenschaft, in: Lautmann, Rüdiger/Taeger, Angela (eds), *Männerliebe im alten Deutschland. Sozialgeschichtliche Abhandlungen*, Berlin, pp. 187–238

Hutter, Jörg (2000), Von der Sodomie zu Queer-Identitäten. Ein Beitrag zur Geschichte der homosexuellen Identitätsentwicklung, in: Setz, Wolfram (ed), *Die Geschichte der Homosexualitäten und die schwule Identität an der Jahrtausendwende. Eine Vortragsreihe aus Anlaß des 175. Geburtstags von K.H. Ulrichs*, Berlin, pp. 141–175

Ibn Ḥazm, 'Alī ibn Aḥmad Ibn Ḥazm (1994), *The Ring of the Dove: A Treatise on the Art and Practice of Arab Love*, trans. Arthur John Arberry, London

Ihm, Sibylle (2004), *Eros und Distanz. Untersuchungen zu Asklepiades und seinem Kreis*, München/Leipzig

Illich, Ivan (2006), *In den Flüssen nördlich der Zukunft. Letzte Gespräche über Religion und Gesellschaft mit David Caley*, München

Ingraham, Chrys (ed) (2005), *Thinking Straight: The Promise, the Power and Paradox of Heterosexuality*, New York/London

Ingram, Martin (1987), Spousals Litigation in the English Ecclestical Courts, c. 1350–c. 1640, in: Outwaite, R. B. (ed), *Marriage and Society: Studies in the Social History of Marriage*, Cambridge, pp. 35–57

Ingram, Martin (2012), Courtship and Marriage, c. 1500–1750, in: Fisher, Kate/Toulalan, Sarah (eds), *The Routledge History of Sex and the Body, 1500 to the Present*, Oxford et al., pp. 313–327

Ingram, Martin (2017), *Carnal Knowledge: Regulating Sex in England, 1470–1600*, Cambridge

Ipsen, Pernille (2020), Sexualizing the Other: From Ethnopornography to Interracial Pornography in European Travel Writing about West African Women, in: Sigal, Peter H./Tortorici, Zeb/Whitehead, Neil L. (eds), *Ethnopornography: Sexuality, Colonialism, and Archival Knowledge*, Durham/London, pp. 205–224

Irsigler, Franz/Lassotta, Arnold (1996), *Bettler und Gaukler, Dirnen und Henker. Außenseiter in einer mittelalterlichen Stadt. Köln 1300–1600*, München, 7th edn

Isherwood, Lisa (2006), *The Power of Erotic Celibacy: Queering Heteropatriarchy*, London/New York

Isler-Kerényi, Cornelia (2007), *Dionysos in Archaic Greece: An Understanding through Images*, Leiden et al.

Ivleva, Tatiana (2020), Coming Out of the Provincial Closet: Masculinity, Sexuality, and Same-Sex Sexual Relations amongst Roman Soldiers in the European North-West, First–Third Centuries A.D., in: Ivleva, Tatiana/Collins, Rob (eds), *Un-Roman Sex: Gender, Sexuality, and Lovemaking in the Roman Provinces and Frontiers*, Milton, pp. 241–273

Jackson, Louise A. (2011), Sex, Religion, and the Law: Regulation of Sexual Behaviours, 1820–1920, in: Beccalossi, Chiara/Crozier, Ivan (eds), *A Cultural*

History of Sexuality in the Age of Empire (=A Cultural History of Sexuality Vol. 5), Oxford/New York, pp. 83–100

Jackson, Mark (1996), *New-Born Child Murder: Women, Illegitimacy and the Courts in Eighteenth-Century England*, Manchester

Jacobs, Frederika (2011), Sexual Variations: Playing with (Dis)similitude, in: Talvacchia, Bette (ed), *A Cultural History of Sexuality in the Renaissance (=A Cultural History of Sexuality Vol. 3)*, Oxford/New York, pp. 73–93

Jacquart, Daniel/Thomasset, Claude (1988), *Sexuality and Medicine in the Middle Ages*, Cambridge

Jagose, Annamarie (2001), *Queer Theory: Eine Einführung*, Berlin

James, Christopher (1996), Denying Complexity: The Dismissal and Appropriation of Bisexuality in Queer, Lesbian, and Gay Theory, in: Beemyn, Brett/Eliason Michele J. (eds), *Queer Studies: A Lesbian, Gay, Bisexual, & Transgender Anthology*, New York, pp. 217–240

James, Sharon L. (2006), A Courtesan's Choreography: Female Liberty and Male Anxiety at the Roman Dinner Party, in: Faraone, Christopher A./McClure, Laura K. (eds), *Prostitutes and Courtesans in the Ancient Worlds*, Madison, pp. 224–251

Janan, Micaela (1994), *When the Lamp Is Shattered: Desire and Narrative in Catullus*, Carbondale

Jankrift, Kay Peter (2008), *Henker, Huren, Handelsherren. Alltag in einer mittelalterlichen Stadt*, Stuttgart

Jarzebowski, Claudia (2006), *Verwandtschaft und Sexualität im 18. Jahrhundert*, Köln/Weimar/Wien

Jean-Jacques Rousseau (1993), *Emil oder Über die Erziehung*, Paderborn et al., 11th edn

Jellonnek, Burkhard (2002), Staatspolizeiliche Fahndungs- und Ermittlungsmethoden gegen Homosexuelle, in: Jellonnek, Burkhard/Lautmann, Rüdiger (eds), *Nationalsozialistischer Terror gegen Homosexuelle. Verdrängt und ungesühnt*, Paderborn et al., pp. 149–161

Jellonnek, Burkhard/Lautmann, Rüdiger (eds) (2002), *Nationalsozialistischer Terror gegen Homosexuelle. Verdrängt und ungesühnt*, Paderborn et al.

Jennings, Rebecca (2007), *Tomboys and Bachelor Girls: A Lesbian History of Post-War Britain, 1945–71*, Manchester

Jensen, David H. (2010), Bible and Sex, in: Kamitsuka, Margaret D. (ed), *The Embrace of Eros: Bodies, Desires, and Sexuality in Christianity*, Minneapolis, pp. 15–32

Jerouschek, Günter (1990), *Diabolus habitat in eis*. Wo der Teufel zu Hause ist. Geschlechtlichkeit im rechtstheoretischen Diskurs des ausgehenden Mittelalters und der frühen Neuzeit, in: *Rechtshistorisches Journal 9*, pp. 301–329

Jerouschek, Günter (1993), Mittelalter. Antikes Erbe, weltliche Gesetzgebung und Kanonisches Recht, in: Jütte, Robert (ed), *Geschichte der Abtreibung. Von der Antike bis zur Gegenwart*, München, pp. 44–67

Johansen, Hanne Marie (2005), Marriage or Money? Legal Actions for Enforcement of Marriage Contracts in Norway, in: Ågren, Maria/Erickson, Amy Louise (eds), *The Marital Economy in Scandinavia and Britain, 1400–1900*, Aldershot/Burlington, pp. 23–38

Johansson, Warren/Percy, William A. (1990), Law, Germanic, in: Wayne R. Dynes (ed), *Encyclopedia of Homosexuality*, Vol. 1, Oxford/New York, pp. 687–689

Johansson, Warren/Percy, William A. (1996), Homosexuality, in: Bullough, Vern L./Brundage, James A. (eds), *Handbook of Medieval Sexuality*, New York/London, pp. 155–190

Johnson, David K. (2004), *The Lavender Scare: The Cold War Persecution of Gays and Lesbians in the Federal Government*, Chicago

Johnson, Marguerite/Ryan, Terry (2005), *Sexuality in Greek and Roman Literature and Society: A Sourcebook*, London/New York

Johnson, Paul/Vanderbeck, Robert (2014), *Law, Religion and Homosexuality*, Abingdon

Johnson, William Stacy (2010), New Testament, Empire, and Homoeroticism, in: Kamitsuka, Margaret D. (ed), *The Embrace of Eros: Bodies, Desires, and Sexuality in Christianity*, Minneapolis, pp. 51–66

Jones, Ann Rosalind (2011), Heterosexuality: A Beast with Many Backs, in: Talvacchia, Bette (ed), *A Cultural History of Sexuality in the Renaissance (=A Cultural History of Sexuality Vol. 3)*, Oxford/New York, pp. 35–50

Jones, Malcolm (1994), Sex and Sexuality in Late Medieval and Early Modern Art, in: Erlach, Daniela/Reisenleitner, Markus/Vocelka, Karl (eds), *Privatisierung der Triebe? Sexualität in der frühen Neuzeit*, Frankfurt a. M. et al., pp. 187–304

Jones, Malcolm (2011), Sex, Popular Beliefs, and Culture, in: Evans, Ruth (ed), *A Cultural History of Sexuality in the Middle Ages (=A Cultural History of Sexuality Vol. 2)*, Oxford/New York, pp. 139–164

Jones, Melissa J. (2013), Spectacular Impotence: Or, Things That Hardly Ever Happen in the Critical History of Pornography, in: Bromley, James M./Stockton, Will (eds), *Sex Before Sex: Figuring the Act in Early Modern England*, Minneapolis, pp. 89–110

Jones, Nicholas R./Leahy, Chad (eds) (2020), *Pornographic Sensibilities: Imagining Sex and the Visceral in Premodern and Early Modern Spanish Cultural Production*, Milton

Jope, James (2014), Platonic and Roman Influence on Stoic and Epicurean Sexual Ethics, in: Hubbard, Thomas K. (ed), *A Companion to Greek and Roman Sexualities*, New York, pp. 417–430

Jordan, Mark D. (1997a), Homosexuality, Luxuria, and Textual Abuse, in: Lochrie, Karma/McCracken, Peggy/Schultz, James A. (eds), *Constructing Medieval Sexuality*, Minneapolis/London, pp. 24–39

Jordan, Mark D. (1997b), *The Invention of Sodomy in Christian Theology*, Chicago/London

Jordan, Mark D. (2000), *The Silence of Sodom: Homosexuality in Modern Catholicism*, Chicago

Jordanova, Ludmilla (1995), Sex and Gender, in: Fox, Christopher/Porter, Roy/Wokler, Robert (eds), *Inventing Human Science: Eighteenth-Century Domains*, Berkeley/Los Angeles, pp. 152–183

Jørgensen, Torstein (2008), Illegal Sexual Behavior in Late Medieval Norway as Testified in Supplications to the Pope, in: *Journal of the History of Sexuality* 17, 3, pp. 335–350

Joshel, Sandra R. (1997), Female Desire and the Discourse of Empire: Tacitus' Messalina, in: Hallett, Judith P./Skinner, Marilyn B. (eds), *Roman Sexualities*, Princeton, pp. 221–254

Jussen, Bernhard (2014), *Die Franken: Geschichte, Gesellschaft, Kultur*, München

Just, Roger (1989), *Women in Athenian Law and Life*, London/New York
Jütte, Robert (1989), Die Persistenz des Verhütungswissens in der Volkskultur. Sozial- und medizinhistorische Anmerkungen zur These von der "Vernichtung der weisen Frauen", in: *Medizinhistorisches Journal* 24, 3/4, pp. 214–231
Jütte, Robert (1993), Griechenland und Rom. Bevölkerungspolitik, Hippokratischer Eid und antikes Recht, in: Jütte, Robert (ed), *Geschichte der Abtreibung. Von der Antike bis zur Gegenwart*, München, pp. 27–42
Jütte, Robert (1996), Syphilis and Confinement. Early Modern German Hospitals for Syphilitics, in: Finzsch, Norbert/Jütte, Robert (eds), *Institutions of Confinement. Hospitals, Asylums and Prisons in Western Europe and North America, 1500–1950*, Cambridge, pp. 97–116
Jütte, Robert (2008), *Contraception: A History*, Cambridge/Malden
Jütte, Robert (2013), *Krankheit und Gesundheit in der Frühen Neuzeit*, Stuttgart
Jütte, Robert (ed) (1993), *Geschichte der Abtreibung. Von der Antike bis zur Gegenwart*, München
Kaimio, Maarit (2002), Erotic Experience in the Conjugal Bed: Good Wives in Greek Tragedy, in: Nussbaum, Martha Craven/Sihvola, Juha (eds), *The Sleep of Reason: Erotic Experience and Sexual Ethics in Ancient Greece and Rome*, Chicago, pp. 95–119
Kaiser, Daniel H. (2002), He Said, She Said: Rape and Gender Discourse in Early Modern Russia, in: *Kritika: Explorations in Russian and Eurasian History* 3, 2, pp. 197–216
Kallander, Amy (2021), Women, Gender, and Sexuality in the Middle East, in: Meade, Teresa A./Wiesner-Hanks, Merry E. (eds), *A Companion to Global Gender History*, Newark, 2nd edn, pp. 335–349
Kaltenstadler, Wilhelm (1999), *Das Haberfeldtreiben. Theorie, Entwicklung, Sexualität und Moral, sozialer Wandel und soziale Konflikte, staatliche Bürokratie, Niedergang, Organisation*, München
Kamen, Deborah/Levin-Richardson, Sarah (2014), Revisiting Roman Sexuality: Agency and the Conceptualization of Penetrated Males, in: Masterson, Mark/Sorkin Rabinowitz, Nancy/Robson, James (eds), *Sex in Antiquity: Exploring Gender and Sexuality in the Ancient World*, London/New York, pp. 449–460
Kamen, Deborah/Levin-Richardson, Sarah (2015), Lusty Ladies in the Roman Imaginary, in: Blondell, Ruby/Ormand, Kirk (eds), *Ancient Sex: New Essays: Classical Memories, Modern Identities*, Columbus, pp. 231–252
Kane, Bronach C. (2022), Men and Women in Love: Courtship, Marriage and Gender in Late Medieval England, in: Brooks, Ann (ed), *The Routledge Companion to Romantic Love*, Oxon/New York, pp. 36–47
Kaplan, Paul H. D. (2021), Black Women in Early Modern European Art and Culture, in: Hobson, Janell (eds), *The Routledge Companion to Black Women's Cultural Histories*, London/New York, pp. 44–56
Kapparis, Konstantinos (2002), *Abortion in the Ancient World*, London
Kapparis, Konstantinos A. (2018a), *Athenian Law and Society*, London
Kapparis, Konstantinos A. (2018b), *Prostitution in the Ancient Greek World*, Berlin/Boston
Kapparis, Konstantinos A. (2022), Dover's "Pseudo-sexuality" and the Athenian Laws on Male Prostitutes in Politics, in: Serafim, Andreas/Kazantzidis,

George/Demetriou, Kyriakos (eds), *Sex and the Ancient City: Sex and Sexual Practices in Greco-Roman Antiquity*, Berlin/Boston, pp. 21–42

Karant-Nunn, Susan C./Wiesner-Hanks, Merry E. (2003) (eds and trans), *Luther on Women: A Sourcebook*, Cambridge

Karbić, Marija (2019), Prostitutes and Urban Communities of Medieval Slavonia: Examples from Gradec, in: Mielke, Christopher/Znorovsky, Andrea-Bianka (eds), *Same Bodies, Different Women: "Other" Women in the Middle Ages and the Early Modern Period*, Budapest, pp. 83–96

Karras, Ruth Mazo (1990), Holy Harlots: Prostitute Saints in Medieval Legend, in: *Journal of the History of Sexuality* 1, 1, pp. 3–32

Karras, Ruth Mazo (1996), *Common Women: Prostitution and Sexuality in Medieval England*, New York

Karras, Ruth Mazo (1999), Prostitution and the Question of Sexual Identity in Medieval Europe, in: *Journal of Women's History* 11, 2, pp. 159–177

Karras, Ruth Mazo (2000), Active/Passive, Acts/Passions. Greek and Roman Sexualities, in: *American Historical Review* 105, 4, pp. 1250–1265

Karras, Ruth Mazo (2001), Sexuality in the Middle Ages, in: Linehan, Peter/Nelson, Janet Laughland (eds), *The Medieval World*, Vol. 10, London/New York, pp. 279–293

Karras, Ruth Mazo (2003), *From Boys to Men: Formations of Masculinity in Late Medieval Europa*, Philadelphia

Karras, Ruth Mazo (2005), *Sexualität im Mittelalter*, Düsseldorf

Karras, Ruth Mazo (2006), The History of Marriage and the Myth of Friedelehe, in: *Early Medieval Europe* 14 (2006), pp. 119–151

Karras, Ruth Mazo (2008), Thomas Aquina's Chastity Belt. Clergical Masculinity in Medieval Europe, in: Bitel, Lisa M./Lifshitz, Felice (eds), *Gender and Christianity in Medieval Europe. New Perspectives, Philadelphia*, pp. 52–67

Karras, Ruth Mazo (2011), The Regulation of Sexuality in the Late Middle Ages: England and France, in: *Speculum* 86, 4, pp. 1010–1039

Karras, Ruth Mazo (2012a), *Sexuality in Medieval Europe: Doing Unto Others*, London/New York, 2nd edn

Karras, Ruth Mazo (2012b), *Unmarriages: Women, Men, and Sexual Unions in the Middle Ages*, Philadelphia

Karras, Ruth Mazo (2020), The Regulation of "Sodomy" in the Latin East and West, in: *Speculum* 95, 4, pp. 969–986

Karras, Ruth Mazo/Boyd, David Lorenzo (1996), Ut cum muliere: A Male Transvestite Prostitute in Fourteenth-Century London, in: Fradenburg, Louise/Freccero, Carla (eds), *Premodern Sexualities*, New York, pp. 99–116

Karsch, Ferdinand (1996), Heinrich Hössli, 1784–1864, in: Heinrich, Hössli (ed), *Eros. Die Männerliebe der Griechen. Ihre Beziehungen zur Geschichte, Erziehung, Literatur und Gesetzgebung aller Zeiten Bd. 3*, Berlin, pp. 35–142

Kaser, Karl (2000), *Macht und Erbe. Männerherrschaft, Besitz und Familie im östlichen Europa (1500 - 1900)*, Wien et al.

Kasten, Ingrid (2002), Emotionalität und der Prozeß männlicher Sozialisation. Auf den Spuren der Psycho-Logik eines mittelalterlichen Textes, in: *Querelles* 7, pp. 52–71

Katz, Jonathan Ned (1995), *The Invention of Heterosexuality*, New York

Keilson-Lauritz, Marita (2005), Tanten, Kerle und Skandale. Die Geburt des "modernen Homosexuellen" aus den Flügelkämpfen der Emanzipation, in:

zur Nieden, Susanne (ed), *Homosexualität und Staatsräson. Männlichkeit, Homophobie und Politik in Deutschland 1900–1945*, Frankfurt a. M./New York, pp. 81–99
Keller, Achim (1988), *Die Abortiva in der römischen Kaiserzeit*, Stuttgart
Kelly, Henry Ansgar (2003), Law and Nonmarital Sex in the Middle Ages, in: Brown, Warren/Górecki, Piotr (eds), *Conflict in Medieval Europe. Changing Perspectives on Society and Culture*, Aldershot et al., pp. 175–194
Kelly, Kathleen Coyne (2000), *Performing Virginity and Testing Chastity in the Middle Ages*, London et al.
Kelly, Kathleen Coyne/Leslie, Marina (1999), Introduction: The Epistemology of Virginity, in: Kelly, Kathleen Coyne/Leslie, Marina (eds), *Menacing Virgins: Representing Virginity in the Middle Ages and Renaissance*, Newark, pp. 15–30
Kelly, Kathleen Coyne/Leslie, Marina (eds) (1999), *Menacing Virgins: Representing Virginity in the Middle Ages and Renaissance*, Newark
Kenaan, Vered Lev (2020), Love, Sex, and Sexuality: Marriage: The Myth of Intimate Strangers, in: Klaiber-Hersch, Karen (ed), *A Cultural History of Marriage in Antiquity*, London/New York, pp. 97–112
Kennedy, Elizabeth Lapovsky/Davis, Madeline D. (1993), *Boots of Leather, Slippers of Gold. The History of a Lesbian Community*, New York/London
Keyser, Linda Migl (2008), The Medieval Chastity Belt Unbuckled, in: Harris, Stephen/Grigsby, Bryon L. (eds), *Misconceptions about the Middle Ages*, New York, pp. 254–261
Kia, Mehrdad (2011), *Daily Life in the Ottoman Empire*, Santa Barbara
Kieckhefer, Richard (1991), Erotic Magic in Medieval Europe, in: Salisbury, Joyce E. (ed), *Sex in the Middle Ages. A Book of Essays*, New York/London, pp. 30–55
Kiel, Yishai (2016), *Sexuality in the Babylonian Talmud: Christian and Sasanian Contexts in Late Antiquity*, New York
Kilmer, Martin F. (1993), *Greek Erotica on Attic Red-Figure Vases*, Duckworth
Kimmel, Michael S. (ed) (2007), *The Sexual Self: The Construction of Sexual Scripts*, Nashville
King, Helen (1998), *Hippocrates' Woman. Reading the Female Body in Ancient Greece*, London
King, Helen (2005), The Mathematics of Sex. One to Two, or Two to One?, in: Soergel, Philip M. (ed), *Sexuality and Culture in Medieval and Renaissance Europe*, New York, pp. 47–58
King, Helen (2011), Sex, Medicine, and Disease, in: Golden, Mark/Toohey, Peter (eds), *A Cultural History of Sexuality in the Classical World (=A Cultural History of Sexuality Vol. 1)*, Oxford/New York, pp. 107–124
King, Helen (2013), *The One-Sex Body on Trial: The Classical and Early Modern Evidence*, Farnham
King, Helen (2018), Women and Doctors in Ancient Greece, in: Hopwood, Nick et al. (eds), *Reproduction: Antiquity to the Present Day*, Cambridge, pp. 39–52
Kingdon, Robert M. (1995), *Adultery and Divorce in Calvin's Geneva*, Cambridge (MA)/London
Kinsey, Alfred C./Pomeroy, Wardell B./Martin, Clyde E. (1948), *Sexual Behavior in the Human Male*, Philadelphia
Kinsey, Alfred C./Pomeroy, Wardell B./Martin, Clyde E. (1953), *Sexual Behavior in the Human Female*, Philadelphia

Kirchhöfer, Dieter (2009), *Kinderarbeit? Ein pädagogisches Fragezeichen! Ein subjekttheoretischer Ansatz*, Frankfurt a. M.

Kistler, Erich (2012), Bilder des Exzesses und Pornographie als visuelle Vehikel der Skandalisierung im frühdemokratischen Athen (510–470 v. Chr.), in: Müller, Florian M./Sossau, Veronika (eds), *Gefährtinnen. Vom Umgang mit Prostitution in der griechischen Antike und heute*, Innsbruck, pp. 37–54

Klapisch-Zuber, Christiane (1992a), Famille, religion et sexualité à Florence au moyen age, in: *Revue de l'histoire des religions* 209, 4, pp. 381–392

Klapisch-Zuber, Christiane (1992b), Family and Social Strategies, in: Klapisch-Zuber, Christiane (ed), *A History of Women in the West: Silences of the Middle Ages*, Cambridge (MA), pp. 159–169

Klein, Michele (2000), *A Time to Be Born. Customs and Folklore of Jewish Birth*, Philadelphia

Klein, Stacy S. (2021), Queer Intimacies in Goscelin of St. Bertin's Liber confortatorius (ca. 1080–1082), in: *Journal of the History of Sexuality* 30, 2, pp. 279–309

Klestinec, Cynthia (2011), Sex, Medicine, and Disease: Welcoming Wombs and Vernacular Anatomies, in: Talvacchia, Bette (ed), *A Cultural History of Sexuality in the Renaissance (=A Cultural History of Sexuality Vol. 3)*, Oxford/New York, pp. 113–136

Kłosowska, Anna (2005), *Queer Love in the Middle Ages*, New York

Kłosowska, Anna (2008), Erotica and Women in Early Modern France. Madeleine de l'Aubespine's Queer Poems, in: *Journal of the History of Sexuality* 17, 2, pp. 190–215

Klotter, Christoph (1999), Abendländische Liebesvorstellungen, in: Klotter, Christoph (ed), *Liebesvorstellungen im 20. Jahrhundert. Die Individualisierung der Liebe*, Gießen, pp. 11–82

Knefelkamp, Ulrich (1996), Diskriminierung durch Prostitution. Dirnen, Huren und städtische Gesellschaft in Mitteleuropa vom 14.-16. Jahrhundert, in: Joerden, Jan C. (ed), *Diskriminierung - Antidiskriminierung*, Berlin et al., pp. 39–66

Knirk, James E. (2017), Love and Eroticism in Medieval Norwegian Runic Inscriptions, in: Krüger, Jana et al. (eds), *Die Faszination des Verborgenen und seine Entschlüsselung – Rādi sār kunni: Beiträge zur Runologie, skandinavistischen Mediävistik und germanischen Sprachwissenschaft*, Berlin/Boston, pp. 217–232

Knust, Jennifer Wright (2006), *Abandoned to Lust. Sexual Slander and Ancient Christianity*, New York/Chichester

Koch, Angela (2004), Die Verletzung der Gemeinschaft. Zur Relation der Wort- und Ideengeschichte von "Vergewaltigung", in: *Österreichische Zeitschrift für Geschichtswissenschaften* 15, 1, pp. 37–56

Koldeweij, Jos (2004), Shameless and Naked Images: Obscene Badges as Parodies of Popular Devotion, in: Blick, Sarah/Tekippe, Rita (eds), *Art and Architecture of Late Medieval Pilgrimage in Northern Europe and the British Isles*, Leiden, pp. 493–510

Köllner, Erhard (2001), *Homosexualität als anthropologische Herausforderung. Konzeption einer homosexuellen Anthropologie*, Bad Heilbrunn

Koltun-Fromm, Naomi (2010), *Hermeneutics of Holiness: Ancient Jewish and Christian Notions of Sexuality and Religious Community*, New York

Kon, Igor S. (2004), Russia, in: Francoeur, Robert T./Noonan, Raymond J. (eds), *The Continuum Complete International Encyclopedia of Sexuality*, New York, pp. 888–908

Koos, Leonard R. (2001), Making Angels: Abortion Literature in Turn-of-the-Century France, in: Grossman, Kathryn M. (ed), *Confrontations. Politics and Aesthetics in Nineteenth Century France. Selected Proceedings of the Twenty-Fourth Annual Colloquium in Nineteenth Century French Studies 1998*, Amsterdam, pp. 259–273

Korpiola, Mia (2009), *Between Betrothal and Bedding. Marriage Formation in Sweden 1200–1600*, Leiden/Boston

Koschorke, Albrecht (1999), *Körperströme und Schriftverkehr. Mediologie des 18. Jahrhunderts*, München

Kössler, Simon (2012), Die Rolle der ehrbaren Frau in der Gesellschaft des antiken Griechenland, in: Müller, Florian M./Sossau, Veronika (eds), *Gefährtinnen. Vom Umgang mit Prostitution in der griechischen Antike und heute*, Innsbruck, pp. 107–120

Kostick, Conor (2008), *The Social Structure of the First Crusade*, Leiden

Kotis, India (2020), She Is a Boy, or if Not a Boy, Then a Boy Resembles Her: Cross-Dressing: Homosexuality and Enslaved Sex and Gender in Umayyad Iberia, in: *The Macksey Journal* 1, 1, pp. 1–23

Kotrosits, Maia (2018), Penetration and Its Discontents: Greco-Roman Sexuality, the Acts of Paul and Thecla, and Theorizing Eros without the Wound, in: *Journal of the History of Sexuality* 27, 3, pp. 343–366

Kouamenan, Djro Bilestone Roméo (2020), The Reproach of Sodomy in the Deposition of Edward II of England and Its Repercussions in the Historiography of the Middle Ages to the Twentieth Century, in: Domeier, Norman/Mühling, Christian (eds), *Homosexualität am Hof: Praktiken und Diskurse vom Mittelalter bis heute*, Frankfurt a. Main, pp. 151–178

Koutsopetrou-Møller, Sotiria Rita (2021), Rape Culture in Classical Athens?, in: *Clara: Classical Art and Archaeology* 7, pp. 1–32

Kowaleski, Maryanne (1999), Singlewomen in Medieval and Early Modern Europe. The Demographic Perspective, in: Bennett, Judith M./Froide, Amy M. (eds), *Singlewomen in the European past, 1250–1800*, Philadelphia, pp. 38–81

Kraakman, Dorelies (1999), Pornography in Western European Culture, in: Eder, Franz X./Hall, Lesley A./Hekma, Gert (eds), *Sexual Cultures in Europe. Themes in Sexuality*, Manchester/New York, pp. 104–120

Krafft-Ebing, Richard v. (1912), *Psychopathia sexualis. Mit besonderer Berücksichtigung der konträren Sexualempfindung. Eine medizinisch-gerichtliche Studie für Ärzte und Juristen*, Stuttgart

Kraß, Andreas (2007), Sprechen von der stummen Sünde. Das Dispositiv der Sodomie in der deutschen Literatur des 13. Jahrhunderts (Berthold von Regensburg, Der Stricker), in: Limbeck, Sven/Thoma, Lev Mordechai (eds), *Die Sünde, der sich der Tiuvel Schamet in der Helle. Homosexualität in der Kultur des Mittelalters und der frühen Neuzeit*, Ostfildern, pp. 123–136

Kraß, Andreas (2016), *Ein Herz und eine Seele: Geschichte der Männerfreundschaft*, Frankfurt a. M.

Kraß, Andreas (2020), Verdrängtes Begehren. Homosexualität in der höfischen Dichtung des deutschen Mittelalters, in: Domeier, Norman/Mühling, Christian (eds), *Homosexualität am Hof: Praktiken und Diskurse vom Mittelalter bis heute*, Frankfurt a. Main, pp. 233–245

Kraus, Karl (1970), *Sittlichkeit und Kriminalität*, München (Erstausg. Wien 1908)

Krell, David Farell (1998), *Contagion. Sexuality, Disease and Death in German Idealism and Romanticism*, Bloomington

Krenkel, Werner (2006), *Naturalia non turpia. Sex and Gender in Ancient Greece and Rome. Schriften zur antiken Kultur- und Sexualwissenschaft*, Hildesheim

Kristjánsdóttir, Steinunn (2011), The Poisoned Arrows of Amor: Cases of Syphilis from 16th-Century Iceland, in: *Scandinavian Journal of History* 36, 44, pp. 406–418

Kršljanin, Nina (2021), Legal Regulation of Sex Crimes in Medieval Serbia and the Mediterranean Communes Under its Rule, in: Zanetti Domingues, Lidia L./Caravaggi, Lorenzo/Paoletti, Giulia M. (eds), *Women and Violence in the Late Medieval Mediterranean, ca. 1100-1500*, Milton, pp. 101–120

Kruger, Steven (1997), Conversion and Medieval Sexual, Religious, and Racial Categories, in: Lochrie, Karma/McCracken, Peggy/Schultz, James A. (eds), *Constructing Medieval Sexuality*, Minneapolis/London, pp. 158–179

Kruse, Britta-Juliane (1996), *Verborgene Heilkünste: Geschichte der Frauenmedizin im Spätmittelalter*, Berlin

Kruse, Britta-Juliane (1999), *Die Arznei ist Goldes wert. Mittelalterliche Frauenrezepte*, Berlin/New York

Küchler Williams, Christiane (2004), *Erotische Paradiese: Zur europäischen Südseerezeption im 18. Jahrhundert*, Göttingen

Kuefler, Mathew (ed) (2007), *The History of Sexuality Sourcebook*, Orchard Park

Kuefler, Mathew S. (2001), *The Manly Eunuch. Masculinity, Gender Ambiguity, and Christian Ideology in Late Antiquity*, Chicago

Kuefler, Mathew S. (2006), The Boswell Thesis, in: Kuefler, Mathew S. (ed), *The Boswell Thesis. Essays on Christianity, Social Tolerance, and Homosexuality*, Chicago, pp. 1–31

Kuefler, Mathew S. (2017), Physical and Symbolic Castration and the Holy Eunuch in Late Antiquity, Third to Sixth centuries ce 1, in: Höfert, Almut/Mesley, Matthew M./Tolino, Serena (eds), *Celibate and Childless Men in Power: Ruling Eunuchs and Bishops in the Pre-Modern World*, Florence, pp. 177–191

Kuefler, Mathew S. (2018), Homoeroticism in Antiquity and the Middle Ages: Acts, Identities, Cultures Christianity, Social Tolerance, and Homosexuality: Gay People in Western Europe from the Beginning of the Christian Era to the Fourteenth Century, by John Boswell, in: *American Historical Review* 123, 4, pp. 1246–1266

Kuffner, Emily (2020), Eros in the Apiary: Bees and Beehives in Early Modern Spanish Erotic Literature, in: *Revista Canadiense de Estudios Hispánicos* 44, 3, pp. 641–665

Kuhn, Bärbel (2000), *Familienstand: Ledig. Ehelose Frauen und Männer im Bürgertum (1850 - 1914)*, Köln

Kühnel, Harry (1986), Normen und Sanktionen, in: Kühnel, Harry (ed), *Alltag im Spätmittelalter, Graz/Wien/Köln*, 2nd edn, pp. 17–48

Kümper, Hiram (2012), Sexualität - Gewalt - Humor, in: Kuhn, Christian/Bießenecker, Stefan (eds), *Valenzen des Lachens in der Vormoderne (1250–1750)*, Bamberg, pp. 437–461

Kuster, Thomas (2003), *Aufstieg und Fall der Mätresse im Europa des 18. Jahrhunderts. Versuch einer Darstellung anhand ausgewählter Persönlichkeiten*, Nordhausen

l'Aubespine, Madeleine de (2007), *Selected Poems and Translations: A Bilingual Edition*, ed. and trans. by Anna Kłosowska, Chicago/London

Labouvie, Eva (1999), *Beistand in Kindsnöten. Hebammen und weibliche Kultur auf dem Land (1550-1910)*, Frankfurt a. M.

Lacarra Lanz, Eukene (2002), Changing Boundaries of Licit and Illicit Unions. Concubinage and Prostitution, in: Lanz, Eukene Lacarra (ed), *Marriage and Sexuality in Medieval and Early Modern Iberia*, New York, pp. 158–196

Lachiri, Nadia (2002), Anadalusi Proverbs on Women, in: Marín, Manuela/Deguilhem, Randi (eds), *Writing the Feminine. Women in Arab Sources*, London, pp. 41–48

Laes, Christian (2010), When Classicists Need to Speak Up: Antiquity and Present Day Pedophilia - Pederasty, in: Association of Classical Philologists - ANTIKA (ed), *Aeternitas Antiquitatis. Proceedings of the Symposium Held in Skopje*, August 28, 2009, Skopje, pp. 30–59

Laes, Christian (2012), *Children in the Roman Empire. Outsiders Within*, Cambridge et al.

Laes, Christian (2019) "Stay Away from My Children!" Educators and the Accusation of Sexual Abuse in Roman Antiquity, in: Flynn, Shawn W. (ed), *Children in the Bible and the Ancient World: Comparative and Historical Methods in Reading Ancient Children*, London, pp. 115–134

Laes, Christian (2021), The Loneliness of a Marriage with Age Difference in Graeco-Roman Antiquity. Exploring the (Im)possibility of Writing Emotional History, in: Matuszewski, Rafał (ed), *Being Alone in Antiquity: Greco-Roman Ideas and Experiences of Misanthropy, Isolation and Solitude*, Berlin/Boston, pp. 319–348

Laiou, Angeliki (1993), Sex, Consent, and Coercion in Byzantium, in: Laiou, Angeliki (ed), *Consent and Coercion to Sex and Marriage in Ancient and Medieval Societies*, Washington, pp. 109–221

Laiou, Sophia (2007), Christian Women in an Ottoman World: Interpersonal and Family Cases Brought Before the Shari'a Courts During the Seventeenth and Eighteenth Centuries (Cases Involving the Greek Community), in: Buturović, Amila/Schick, İrvin C. (eds), *Women in the Ottoman Balkans. Gender, Culture and History*, London/New York, pp. 243–271

Lane Fox, Robin (1987), *Pagans and Christians*, New York

Langlands, Rebecca (2006), *Sexual Morality in Ancient Rome*, Cambridge

Lansing, Carol (2003), Concubines, Lovers, Prostitutes: Infamy and Female Identity in Medieval Bologna, in: Findlein, Paula/Fontaine, Michelle M./Osheim, Duane J. (eds), *Beyond Florence: The Contours of Medieval and Early Modern Italy*, Stanford, pp. 85–100

Lansing, Carol (2005), Donna con Donna? A 1295 Inquest into Female Sodomy, in: Soergel, Philip M. (ed), *Studies in Medieval and Renaissance History: Sexuality and Culture in Medieval and Renaissance Europe* (3rd Series, Vol. 2), New York, pp. 110–122

Lansing, Carol (2021), Opportunities to Charge Rape in Thirteenth-Century Bologna, in: Zanetti Domingues, Lidia L./Caravaggi, Lorenzo/Paoletti, Giulia M.

(eds), *Women and Violence in the Late Medieval Mediterranean, ca. 1100–1500*, Milton, pp. 83–100

Lape, Susan (2004), *Reproducing Athens. Menander's Comedy, Democratic Culture, and the Hellenistic City*, Princeton/Oxford

Lape, Susan (2011), Heterosexuality, in: Golden, Mark/Toohey, Peter (eds), *A Cultural History of Sexuality in the Classical World (=A Cultural History of Sexuality Vol. 1)*, Oxford/New York, pp. 17–36

Laqueur, Thomas (2009), Sexuality and the Transformation of Culture: The Longue Duree, in: *Sexualities* 12, 4, pp. 418–436

Laqueur, Thomas W. (1986), Female Orgasm, Generation and the Politics of Reproductive Biology, in: *Representations* 14, pp. 1–82

Laqueur, Thomas W. (1992), *Auf den Leib geschrieben. Die Inszenierung der Geschlechter von der Antike bis Freud*, Frankfurt a. M./New York

Laqueur, Thomas W. (2008), *Die einsame Lust. Eine Kulturgeschichte der Selbstbefriedigung*, Berlin

Laragy, Georgina (2012), Stories of Care and Coercion: Narratives of Poverty and Suffering among Patients with Veneral Disease in Sweden 1860–1920, in: Gestrich, Andreas/Hurren, Elizabeth/King, Steven (eds), *Poverty and Sickness in Modern Europe. Narratives of the Sick Poor, 1780–1938*, London/New York, pp. 161–180

Lardinois, André (1991), Lesbian Sappho and Sappho of Lesbos, in: Bremmer, Jan (ed), *From Sappho to de Sade. Moments in the History of Sexuality*, London/New York, pp. 15–35

Larmour, David H. J./Miller, Paul Allen/Platter, Charles (1998), Introduction. Situating the History of Sexuality, in: dies. (eds), *Rethinking Sexuality. Foucault and Classical Antiquity*, Princeton, pp. 3–41

Larson, Jennifer (2012), *Greek and Roman Sexualities. A Sourcebook*, London

Larson, Jennifer (2014), Sexuality in Greek and Roman Religion, in: Hubbard, Thomas K. (ed), *A Companion to Greek and Roman Sexualities*, New York, pp. 214–229

Latour, Bruno (2010), *Das Parlament der Dinge*, Frankfurt a. M.

Launderville, Dale (2010), *Celibacy in the Ancient World. Its Ideal and Practice in Pre-Hellenistic Israel, Mesopotamia, and Greece*, Collegeville

Laurence, Ray (2006), *Roman Pompeii: Space and Society*, London

Laurin, Joseph R, (2005), *Homosexuality in Ancient Athens*, Victoria

Lauriola, Rosanna (2022), *Brill's Companion to Episodes of "Heroic" Rape/Abduction in Classical Antiquity and Their Reception*, Boston

Lauritsen, John (2003), Homosexuality, Intolerance, and Christianity. A Critical Examination of John Boswell's Work (http://www.pinktriangle.org.uk/lib/hic/lauritsen.html)

Lautmann, Rüdiger (2002a), Geschichte und Politik. Paradigmen der nationalsozialistischen Homosexuellenverfolgung, in: Jellonnek, Burkhard/Lautmann, Rüdiger (eds), *Nationalsozialistischer Terror gegen Homosexuelle. Verdrängt und ungesühnt*, Paderborn et al., S. 41–54

Lautmann, Rüdiger (2002b), *Soziologie der Sexualität. Erotischer Körper, intimes Handeln und Sexualkultur*, Weinheim/München

Lavenia, Vincenzo (2020), Between Heresy and Crimes against Nature: Sexuality, Islamophobia and the Inquisition in Early Modern Europe, in: Grassi, Umberto (ed), *Mediterranean Crossings: Sexual Transgressions in Islam and Christianity (10th–18th Centuries)*, Roma, pp. 65–88

Lazda-Cazers, Rasma (2008), Oral Sex in Oswald von Wolkenstein's "Es seusst dort her von orient" (Kl. 20), in: Classen, Albrecht (ed), *Sexuality in the Middle Ages and the Early Modern Times. New Approaches to a Fundamental Cultural-Historical and Literary-Anthropological Theme*, Berlin/New York, pp. 579–598

Le Goff, Jacques/Troung, Nicolas (2007), *Die Geschichte des Körpers im Mittelalter*, Stuttgart

Le Roy Ladurie, Emmanuel (1980), *Montaillou. Ein Dorf vor dem Inquisitor 1294 bis 1324*, Frankfurt a. M.

Lear, Andrew (2014), Ancient Pederasty. An Introduction, in: Hubbard, Thomas K. (ed), *A Companion to Greek and Roman Sexualities*, New York, pp. 102–127

Lear, Andrew/Cantarella, Eva (2008), *Images of Ancient Greek Pederasty. Boys Were Their Gods*, London

Lechtermann, Christina (2005), *Berührt werden. Narrative Strategien der Präsenz in der höfischen Literatur um 1200*, Berlin

Leibbrand, Annemarie/Leibbrand, Werner (1972): *Formen des Eros. Kultur- und Geistesgeschichte der Liebe*, 2 Bde., Freiburg

Leibrock-Plehn, Larissa (1992), *Hexenkräuter oder Arznei. Die Abtreibungsmittel im 16. und 17. Jahrhundert*, Stuttgart

Leibrock-Plehn, Larissa (1993), Frühe Neuzeit. Hebammen, Kräutermedizin und weltliche Justiz, in: Jütte, Robert (ed), *Geschichte der Abtreibung. Von der Antike bis zur Gegenwart*, München, pp. 68–90

Leiser, Gary (2017), *Prostitution in the Eastern Mediterranean World: The Economics of Sex in the Late Antique and Medieval Middle East*, London/New York

Leitao, David (2000), The Legend of the Sacred Band, in: Nussbaum, Martha/Sihvola, Juha (eds), *The Sleep of Reason. Erotic Experience and Sexual Ethics in Ancient Greece and Rome*, Chicago, pp. 143–169

Leitao, David D. (2014), Sexuality in Greek and Roman Military Contexts, in: Hubbard, Thomas K. (ed), *A Companion to Greek and Roman Sexualities*, New York, pp. 231–243

Leppin, Volker (2012), *Geschichte des mittelalterlichen Christentums*, Tübingen

Lett, Didier (2017), Sexuelle Gewalt und Gender in den Gerichtsakten von Bologna im 15. Jahrhundert, in: *Österreichische Zeitschrift für Geschichtswissenschaften* 28, 3, pp. 88–105

Leuker, Maria-Theresia (1992), *De last van't huys, de wil des mans ... Frauenbilder und Ehekonzepte im niederländischen Lustspiel des 17. Jahrhunderts*, Münster

Levack, Brian P. (2009), *Hexenjagd: Die Geschichte der Hexenverfolgung in Europa*, München, 4th edn

Levin, Eve (1989), *Sex and Society in the World of the Orthodox Slavs, 900–1700*, Ithaca

Levin, Eve (1993), Sexual Vocabulary in Medieval Russia, in: Costlow, Jane T./Sandler, Stephanie/Vowles, Judith (eds), *Sexuality and the Body in Russian Culture*, Stanford, pp. 41–52

Levin, Eve (1996), Eastern Orthodox Christianity, in: Bullough, Vern L./Brundage, James A. (eds), *Handbook of Medieval Sexuality*, New York/London, pp. 329–344

Levin-Richardson, Sarah (2019), *The Brothel of Pompeii: Sex, Class, and Gender at the Margins of Roman Society*, Cambridge

Levin-Richardson, Sarah (2020), Roman and Un-Roman Sex, in: Ivleva, Tatiana/Collins, Rob (eds), *Un-Roman Sex: Gender, Sexuality, and Lovemaking in the Roman Provinces and Frontiers*, Milton, pp. 346–359

Lewis, Laura A. (2007), From Sodomy to Superstition: The Active Pathic and Bodily Transgressions in New Spain, in: *Ethnohistory* 54, 1, pp. 139–157

Liebertz-Grün, Ursula (2000), Ambivalenz, poetologische Selbstreflexion und inszenierte Sexualität: Die Tagelieder Reinmars des Alten, Walthers von der Vogelweide und Wolframs von Eschenbach, in: Stemmler, Theo/Horlacher, Stephan (eds), *Sexualität im Gedicht. 11. Kolloquium der Forschungsstelle für europäische Lyrik*, Mannheim, pp. 11–49

Liliequist, Jonas (1998), State Policy, Popular Discourse, and the Silence on Homosexual Acts in Early Modern Sweden, in: *Journal of Homosexuality* 35 (1998), 3/4, pp. 15–52

Liliequist, Jonas (2017), Between Passion and Lust. Framing Male Desire in Early Modern Sweden, in: Lidman, Satu et al. (eds), *Framing Premodern Desires. Sexual Ideas, Attitudes, and Practices in Europe*, Amsterdam, pp. 211–232

Liliequist, Jonas (ed) (2016), *A History of Emotions, 1200–1800*, Milton Park/New York

Limbeck, Sven/Thoma, Lev Mordechai (eds) (2007), *„die Sünde, der sich der Tiuvel Schamet in der Helle". Homosexualität in der Kultur des Mittelalters und der frühen Neuzeit*, Ostfildern

Lindener, Michael (1883), *Rastbüchlein und Katzipori* (hrsg. von Franz Lichtenstein), Tübingen

Lindquist, Sherry C. M. (2012), The Meanings of Nudity in Medieval Art. An Introduction, in: Lindquist, Sherry C. M. (ed), *The Meanings of Nudity in Medieval Art*, Farnham/Burlington, pp. 1–46

Linkinen, Tom (2015), *Same-Sex Sexuality in Later Medieval English Culture*, Amsterdam

Lischke, Ralph-Jürgen/Michel, Harald (2001), Zur Entwicklung der Bevölkerungswissenschaft im deutschsprachigen Raum von den Anfängen bis 1945, in: *Statistische Monatsschrift* 3 (2001), pp. 110–120

Littlewood, A. R. (2006), Education, in: Wilson, Nigel (ed), *Encyclopedia of Ancient Greece*, New York, pp. 251–253

Livi-Bacci, Massimo (1986), Social-Group Forerunners of Fertility Control in Europe, in: Coale, Ansley J./Watkins, Susan Cotts (eds), *The Decline of Fertility in Europe. The Revised Proceedings of a Conference on the Princeton European Fertility Project*, Princeton, pp. 182–200

Livi-Bacci, Massimo (1999), *Europa und seine Menschen. Eine Bevölkerungsgeschichte*, München

Loader, William R. G. (2012), *The New Testament on Sexuality*, Grand Rapids

Lochrie, Karma (1999), *Covert Operations. The Medieval Uses of Secrecy*, Philadelphia

Lochrie, Karma (2005), *Heterosyncrasies. Female Sexuality When Normal Wasn't*, Minneapolis

Lochrie, Karma (2011), Heterosexuality, in: Evans, Ruth (ed), *A Cultural History of Sexuality in the Middle Ages (=A Cultural History of Sexuality Vol. 2)*, Oxford/New York, pp. 37–56

Lochrie, Karma/McCracken, Peggy/Schultz, James A. (eds) (1997), *Constructing Medieval Sexuality*, Minneapolis/London
Loetz, Francisca (2009), Sexualisierte Gewalt in Europa 1520–1850. Zur Historisierung von "Vergewaltigung" und "Missbrauch", in: *Geschichte und Gesellschaft* 3, 4, pp. 561–602
Loetz, Francisca (2021), Them Too? Überlegungen zur Erforschung sexualisierter Gewalt im frühneuzeitlichen Europa, in: Homme: Zeitschrift für Feministische Geschichtswissenschaft 32, 2, pp. 117–125
Loewen, Peter v./Waugh, Robin (2014), Introduction. Where Sacred Meets Secular. The many Conflicted Roles of Mary Magdalene, in: Loewen, Peter v./Waugh, Robin (eds), *Mary Magdalene in Medieval Culture: Conflicted Roles*, New York, pp. 1–32
Löfström, Jan (1997), Sexuality and the Performance of Manliness. Sketching the Historical Trajectory of Male Fear, in: *Ethnologia Scandinavica* 27, pp. 21–40
Lömker-Schlögell, Annette (1990), Prostituierte—"umb vermeydung willen merers übels in der christenhait", in: Hergemöller, Bernd-Ulrich (ed), *Randgruppen der spätmittelalterlichen Gesellschaft. Ein Hand- und Studienbuch*, Warendorf, pp. 52–85
Long, Kathleen P. (2006), *Hermaphrodites in Renaissance Europe*, Aldershot
Lopez, Belén et al. (2017), Treponemal Disease in the Old World? Integrated Palaeopathological Assessment of a 9th–11th Century Skeleton from North-Central Spain, in: *Anthropological Science* 125, 2, pp. 101–114
Lorenzo-Rodríguez, Abel (2021), Concubare sine mea volumtate: Indictments and Rape Trials in North-Western Iberia (8th–12th Centuries), in: *Studia historica. Ha. Medieval* 39, 2, pp. 103–130
Losert, Kerstin (2001), Kleider machen Männer. Mittelalterliche Geschlechterkonstruktion und die Legende der Hildegund von Schönau, in: Fachverband Homosexualität und Geschichte (ed), *Homosexualitäten und Crossdressing im Mittelalter* (=Invertito. Jahrbuch für die Geschichte der Homosexualitäten 3 (2001)), pp. 68–93
Losse, Deborah N. (2015), *Syphilis: Medicine, Metaphor, and Religious Conflict in Early Modern France*, Columbus
Loudon, Irvine (1992), *Death in Childbirth. An International Study of Maternal Care and Maternal Mortality, 1800–1950*, Oxford
Lucretius (1864) *Titi Lucreti Cari De Rerum Natura Libri Sex. Liber Quartus. With a Translation and Notes by H. A. J. Munro*, Cambridge
Ludwig, Paul W. (2002), *Eros and Polis. Desire and Community in Greek Political Theory*, Cambridge
Luhmann, Niklas (1982), *Love as Passion: The Codification of Intimacy*, Cambridge
Lurati, Patricia (2017), To Dust the Pelisse: The Erotic Side of Fur in Italian Renaissance Art, in: *Renaissance Studies* 31, 2, pp. 240–260
Luther, Martin (1846), *Sämmtliche Schriften, Bd. 22: Die Colloquia oder Tischreden. Hg. v. Karl Eduard Förstemann*, Leipzig
Luther, Martin (1983), Von der babylonischen Gefangenschaft der Kirche (1520), in: Martin Luther, *Die reformatorischen Grundschriften. Neu übertr. und komm. Ausgabe hrsg. von Horst Beinntker*, München, Bd. 3, pp. 9–131
Luther, Martin (1995), *Der Große Katechismus (1529)*, Gütersloh
Lutter, Christina (2008), Mulieres fortes, Sünderinnen und Bräute Christi. Geschlecht als Markierung in religiösen Symbolen und kulturellen Mustern des

12. Jahrhunderts, in: Mommertz, Monika/Opitz-Belakhal, Claudia (eds), *Das Geschlecht des Glaubens. Religiöse Kulturen Europas zwischen Mittelalter und Moderne*, Frankfurt a. M./New York, pp. 49–70

Lutter, Christina (2021), Ways of Belonging to Medieval Vienna, in: Zapke, Susana/Gruber, Elisabeth (eds), *Companion to Medieval Vienna*, Leiden/Boston, pp. 267–311

Lutterbach, Hubertus (1999), *Sexualität im Mittelalter. Eine Kulturstudie anhand von Bußbüchern des 6. bis 12. Jahrhunderts*, Köln

Lynch, Kathryn L. (1999), Diana's "Bowe Ybroke": Impotence, Desire, and Virginity in Chaucer's Parliament of Fowls, in: Kelly, Kathleen Coyne/Leslie, Marina (eds), *Menacing Virgins. Representing Virginity in the Middle Ages and Renaissance*, Newark, pp. 83–96

Lynn, John A. (2008), *Women, Armies, and Warfare in Early Modern Europe*, Cambridge

Maasen, Sabine (1998), *Genealogie der Unmoral. Zur Therapeutisierung sexueller Selbste*, Frankfurt a. M.

Macfarlane, Alan (1979), The Family, Sex and Marriage in England, 1500–1800. By Lawrence Stone. New York, 1977, in: *History and Theory. Studies in the Philosophy of History* 18, 1, pp. 103–126

Macfarlane, Alan (1986), *Marriage and Love in England. Modes of Reproduction, 1300–1840*, Oxford

Magnúsdóttir, Auður G. (2008), Women and Sexual Politics, in: Brink, Stefan/Price, Neil (Hg.), *The Viking World*, London, pp. 40–48

Maier, Gideon (2005), *Amtsträger und Herrscher in der Romania Gothica. Vergleichende Untersuchungen zu den Institutionen der ostgermanischen Völkerwanderungsreiche*, Stuttgart

Majander, Kerttu (2020), Ancient Bacterial Genomes Reveal a High Diversity of Treponema pallidum Strains in Early Modern Europe, in: *Current Biology* 30, pp. 3788–3803

Makowsky, Elizabeth M. (1977), The Conjugal Dept and Medieval Canon Law, in: *Journal of Medieval History* 3, pp. 99–114

Malcolm, Noel (2022), Forbidden Love in Istanbul: Patterns of Male–Male Sexual Relations in the Early-Modern Mediterranean World, in: *Past & Present* 257, 1, pp. 55–88

Mantioni, Susanna (2019), Pornografia, violenza sessuale e «mandato di mascolinità» in alcune fonti di età moderna, in: *Genesis* 18, 2, pp. 17–37

Marín, Manuela (2002), Marriage and Sexuality in Al-Andalus, in: Lanz, Eukene Lacarra (ed), *Marriage and Sexuality in Medieval and Early Modern Iberia*, New York, pp. 3–38

Markus, Georg (1984), *Der Fall Redl. Mit unveröffentlichten Geheimdokumenten zur folgenschwersten Spionage-Affäre des Jahrhunderts*, Wien

Markus, Robert Austin (1997), *The End of Ancient Christianity*, Cambridge

Martel, Frédèric (1996), *Le Rose et le Noir. Les homosexueles en France depuis 1968*, Paris

Martial (1987), *Epigramms of Martial*. Englished by Diverse Hands, ed. by J. P. Sullivan and Peter Wigham, Berkeley/Los Angeles

Martin, Dale B. (2006), The Queer History of Galatians 3:28: No Male and Female, in: Dale B. Martin (ed), *Sex and the Single Savior. Gender and Sexuality in Biblical Interpretation*, Louisville, pp. 77–90

Martin, Thomas (2014), Bestial Desire: About the Silent Sin against Nature. Sodomia and Bestiality in Early Modern Art, in: Nakas, Kassan/Ullrich, Jessica (eds), *Scenes of the Obscene: The Non-Representable in Art and Visual Culture, Middle Ages to Today*, Weimar, pp. 81–96

Martín Romera, María Ángeles (2018), Contra el oficio y contra natura. Parcialidad, sodomía y self-fashioning en los procesos contra Fernando de Vera y Vargas, corregidor de Murcia (1594–1595), in: *Cuadernos de Historia Moderna* 43, 1, pp. 157–181

Martschukat, Jürgen/Stieglitz, Olaf (2008), *Geschichte der Männlichkeiten*, Frankfurt a. M.

Mascher, Konstantin (2003), Homosexualität unter Männern und die Bedrohung durch AIDS, in: Funk, Heide/Lenz, Karl (eds), *Sexualitäten. Diskurse und Handlungsmuster im Wandel*, Weinheim/München, pp. 161–174

Massarella, Derek (2017), "& Thus Ended the Buisinisse": A Buggery Trial on the East India Company Ship *Mary* in 1636, in: *Mariner's Mirror* 103, 4, pp. 417–430

Masterson, Mark (2006), Impossible Translation. Antony and Paul the Simple in the Historia Monachorum, in: Kuefler, Matthew (ed), *The Boswell Thesis. Essays on Christianity, Social Tolerance, and Homosexuality*, Chicago, pp. 215–235

Masterson, Mark (2014a), *Man to Man: Desire, Homosociality, and Authority in Late-Roman Manhood*, Columbus

Masterson, Mark (2014b), Studies of Ancient Masculinity, in: Hubbard, Thomas K. (ed), *A Companion to Greek and Roman Sexualities*, New York, pp. 17–30

Masterson, Mark (2022), *Between Byzantine Men: Desire, Homosociality, and Brotherhood in the Medieval Empire*, Milton

Masterson, Mark/Sorkin Rabinowitz, Nancy/Robson, James (eds) (2014), *Sex in Antiquity. Exploring Gender and Sexuality in the Ancient World*, London/New York

Mathes, Bettina (2001), *Verhandlungen mit Faust. Geschlechterverhältnisse in der Kultur der Frühen Neuzeit*, Königstein/Ts.

Matter, E. Ann (1989/90), Discourses of Desire. Sexuality and Christian Women's Visionary Narratives, in: *Journal of Homosexuality* 18, 3/4, pp. 119–131

Matuszewski, Rafal (2021), Same-Sex Relations between Free and Slave in Democratic Athens, in: Kamen, Deborah/Marshall, C. W. (eds), *Slavery and Sexuality in Classical Antiquity*, Madison/London, pp. 104–123

Mauf, Pascal/Sladeczek, Martin (2012/2013), Straßennamen des städtischen Randes, in: Namenkundliche Informationen / NI 101/102, pp. 332–351

Maurette, Pablo (2017), Shakespeare's Venus and Adonis and Sixteenth-Century Kiss Poetry, in: *English Literary Renaissance* 47, 3, pp. 355–379

Mayhew, Robert J. (2014), *Malthus. The Life and Legacies of an Untimely Prophet*, Cambridge, MA.

Mayor, Adrienne (2014), *The Amazons. Lives and Legends of Warrior Women across the Ancient World*, Princeton/Oxford

Mazzi, Maria Serena (2020), *A Life of Ill Repute: Public Prostitution in the Middle Ages*, Montreal/London/Chicago

McCann, Hannah/Monaghan, Whitney (2020), *Queer Theory Now: From Foundations to Futures*, London

Mccarthy, Conor (2004), Introduction, in: Mccarthy, Conor (ed), *Love, Sex and Marriage in the Middle Ages. A Sourcebook*, London/New York, pp. 1–24

McCarthy, Vanessa/Terpstra, Nicholas (2019), In the Neighborhood: Residence, Community, and the Sex Trade in Early Modern Bologna, in: Murray, Jacqueline/Terpstra, Nicholas (eds), *Sex, Gender and Sexuality in Renaissance Italy*, London, pp. 53–74

McClive, Cathy (2015), *Menstruation and Procreation in Early Modern France*, Farnham

McClure, Laura K. (2003), *Courtesans at Table. Gender and Greek Literary Culture in Athenaeus*, New York

McClure, Laura K. (2006), Introduction, in: Faraone, Christopher A./McClure, Laura K. (eds), *Prostitutes and Courtesans in the Ancient Worlds*, Madison, pp. 3–20

McClure, Laura K. (2019), *Women in Classical Antiquity: From Birth to Death*, Hoboken

McCormick, Ian (ed) (1997), *Secret Sexualities. A Sourcebook of 17th and 18th Century Writing*, London/New York

McDonough, Susan (2022), Moving beyond Sex: Prostitutes, Migration and Knowledge in Late Medieval Mediterranean Port Cities, in: *Gender & History* 34, 2, pp. 401–419

McDougall, Sara (2014), The Opposite of the Double Standard: Gender, Marriage, and Adultery Prosecution in Late Medieval France, in: *Journal of the History of Sexuality* 23, 2, pp. 206–225

McDougall, Sara (2017), *Royal Bastards: The Birth of Illegitimacy, 800–1230*, Oxford

McDougall, Sara (2019), Bastard Priests: Illegitimacy and Ordination in Medieval Europe, in: *Speculum* 94, 1, pp. 138–172

McEnery, Anthony/Baker, Helen (2017), *Corpus Linguistics and 17th-Century Prostitution: Computational Linguistics and History*, London

McGinn, Thomas (2006), Zoning Shame in the Roman City, in: Faraone, Christopher A./McClure, Laura K. (eds), *Prostitutes and Courtesans in the Ancient Worlds*, Madison, pp. 161–176

McGinn, Thomas A. (1998), *Prostitution, Sexuality, and the Law in Ancient Rome*, Oxford

McGinn, Thomas A. (2004), *The Economy of Prostitution in the Roman World. A Study of Social History and the Brothel*, Ann Arbor

McGinn, Thomas A. J, (2014), Prostitution, in: Hubbard, Thomas K. (ed), *A Companion to Greek and Roman Sexualities*, New York, pp. 83–101

McGough, Laura J. (2010), *Gender, Sexuality, and Syphilis in Early Modern Venice: The Disease That Came to Stay*, Basingstoke/New York

McInerney, Jeremy (2022), Hephaistos among the Satyrs: Semen, Ejaculation and Autochthony in Greek Culture, in: Serafim, Andreas/Kazantzidis, George/Demetriou, Kyriakos (eds), *Sex and the Ancient City: Sex and Sexual Practices in Greco-Roman Antiquity*, Berlin/Boston, pp. 287–306

McLaren, Angus (1984), *Reproductive Rituals. The Perception of Fertility in England from the Sixteenth to the Nineteenth Century*, London/New York

McLaren, Angus (1990), *A History of Contraception from Antiquity to the Present Day*, Oxford/Cambridge

McLaren, Angus (1999), *Twentieth-Century Sexuality. A History*, Oxford/Malden

McLaren, Angus (2002), *Sexual Blackmail. A Modern History*, Cambridge, MA.

McLaren, Angus (2007), *Impotence. A Cultural History*, Chicago

McLaughlin, Megan (2010), The Bishop in the Bedroom: Witnessing Episcopal Sexuality in an Age of Reform, in: *Journal of the History of Sexuality* 19, 1 (Special issue on Desire and Eroticism in Medieval Europe, Eleventh to Fifteenth Centuries: Sex Without Sex; Guest Editor Sally N. Vaughn and Christina Christoforatou), pp. 17–34

McMahon, Joanne/Roberts, Jack (2001), *The Sheela-Na-Gigs of Ireland & Britain. The Divine Hag of the Christian Celts. An Illustrated Guide*, Cork et al.

McSheffrey, Shannon (2006), *Marriage, Sex, and Civic Culture in Late Medieval London*, Philadelphia

Meade, Teresa A./Wiesner-Hanks, Merry E. (eds) (2021), *A Companion to Global Gender History*, Newark, 2nd edn.

Medick, Hans (1980), Spinnstuben auf dem Dorf. Jugendliche Sexualkultur und Feierabendbräuche in der ländlichen Gesellschaft der frühen Neuzeit, in: Huck, Gerhard (ed), *Sozialgeschichte der Freizeit. Untersuchungen zum Wandel der Alltagskultur in Deutschland*, Wuppertal, pp. 19–49

Meer, Theo van der (1994), Sodomy and the Pursuit of a Third Sex in the Early Modern Period, in: Herdt, Gilbert (ed), *Third Sex, Third Gender. Beyond Sexual Dimorphism in Culture and History*, New York, pp. 137–212

Mees, Ulrich (2006), Zum Forschungsstand der Emotionspsychologie - eine Skizze, in: Schützeichel, Rainer (ed), *Emotionen und Sozialtheorie*, Frankfurt a. M., pp. 104–123

Mehlmann, Sabine (2006), *Unzuverlässige Körper. Zur Diskursgeschichte des Konzepts geschlechtlicher Identität*, Königstein/Taunus

Mencacci, Francesca (1999), Päderastie und lesbische Liebe. Die Ursprünge zweier sexueller Verhaltensweisen und der Unterschied der Geschlechter in Rom, in: Vogt-Spira, Gregor/Rommel, Bettina/Musäus, Immanuel (eds), *Rezeption und Identität: Die kulturelle Auseinandersetzung Roms mit Griechenland als europäisches Paradigma*, Stuttgart, pp. 238–262

Mengel, David C. (2004), From Venice to Jerusalem and Beyond: Milíč of Kroměříž and the Topography of Prostitution in Fourteenth-Century Prague, in: *Speculum* 79, 2, pp. 407–442

Merrick, Jeffrey (2002), Nocturnal Birds in the Champs-Elysées. Police and Pederasty in Pre-Revolutionary Paris, in: *GLQ. A Journal of Lesbian and Gay Studies* 8, pp. 425–432

Messis, Charis/Nilsson, Ingela (2018), Eros as Passion, Affection and Nature: Gendered Perceptions of Erotic Emotion in Byzantium, in: Messis, Charis/Nilsson, Ingela (eds), *Emotions and Gender in Byzantine Culture. New Approaches to Byzantine History and Culture*, Cham, pp. 159–190

Mette-Dittmann, Angelika (1991), *Die Ehegesetze des Augustus. Eine Untersuchung im Rahmen der Gesellschaftspolitik des Princeps*, Stuttgart

Metzler, Irina (2011), Sex, Religion, and the Law, in: Evans, Ruth (ed), *A Cultural History of Sexuality in the Middle Ages (=A Cultural History of Sexuality Vol. 2)*, Oxford/New York, pp. 101–118

Meyerson, Mark D. (1991), *The Muslims of Valencia in the Age of Fernando and Isabel Between Coexistence and Crusade*, Berkeley

Meyer-Zwiffelhoffer, Eckhard (1995), *Im Zeichen des Phallus. Die Ordnung des Geschlechtslebens im antiken Rom*, Frankfurt a. M./New York

Micheler, Stefan (1999), Heteronormativität, Homophobie und Sexualdenunziation in der deutschen Studierendenbewegung, in: Fachverband Homosexualität und

Geschichte (ed), *Homosexualitäten in der Bundesrepublik Deutschland 1949 bis 1972* (=Invertito. Jahrbuch für die Geschichte der Homosexualitäten 1 (1999)), Hamburg, pp. 70–101

Micheler, Stefan (2005), *Selbstbilder und Fremdbilder der "Anderen". Männer begehrende Männer in der Weimarer Republik und der NS-Zeit*, Konstanz

Micheler, Stefan/Müller, Jürgen K./Pretzel, Andreas (2002), Die Verfolgung homosexueller Männer in der NS-Zeit und ihre Kontinuität. Gemeinsamkeiten und Unterschiede in den Großstädten Berlin, Hamburg und Köln, in: Fachverband Homosexualität und Geschichte (ed), *Denunziert, verfolgt, ermordet. Homosexuelle Männer und Frauen in der NS-Zeit* (=Invertito. Jahrbuch für die Geschichte der Homosexualitäten 4 (2002)), Hamburg, pp. 8–51

Micheler, Stefan/Schader, Heike (2004), Gleichberechtigung als Ideal? Partnerschaftsmodelle und Beziehungen Männer begehrender Männer und Frauen begehrender Frauen in der Weimarer Republik, in: *Invertito. Jahrbuch zur Geschichte der Homosexualitäten* 6, pp. 49–95

Michelsen, Jakob (1996), Von Kaufleuten, Waisenknaben und Frauen in Männerkleidern. Sodomie im Hamburg des 18. Jahrhunderts, in: *Zeitschrift für Sexualforschung* 9, 3, pp. 205–237

Mildenberger, Florian Georg (2002), *In der Richtung der Homosexualität verdorben. Psychiater, Kriminalpsychologen und Gerichtsmediziner über männliche Homosexualität, 1850–1970*, Hamburg

Mildenberger, Florian Georg (2020), *Sexualgeschichte: Überblick - Problemfelder - Entwicklungen*, Wiesbaden

Mills, Robert (2010), Acts, Orientations and the Sodomites of San Gimignano, in: Levy, Allison (ed), *Sex Acts in Early Modern Italy: Practice, Performance, Perversion, Punishment*, Ashgate, pp. 196–208

Mills, Robert (2011), Homosexuality. Specters of Sodom, in: Evans, Ruth (ed), *A Cultural History of Sexuality in the Middle Ages* (=A Cultural History of Sexuality Vol. 2), Oxford/New York, pp. 57–79

Mills, Robert (2015), *Seeing Sodomy in the Middle Ages*, Chicago/London

Mistry, Zubin (2011), Alienated from the Womb. Abortion in the Early Medieval West, c.500-900. PhD Thesis, University College, London

Mistry, Zubin (2015), *Abortion in the Early Middle Ages, c.500-900*, Woodbridge

Mitchell, W. J. T. (2008), *Das Leben der Bilder. Eine Theorie der visuellen Kultur. Mit einem Vorwort von Hans Belting*, München

Mitterauer, Michael (1977), Der Mythos von der vorindustriellen Großfamilie, in: Mitterauer, Michael/Sieder, Reinhard, *Vom Patriarchat zur Partnerschaft. Zum Strukturwandel der Familie*, München, pp. 38–65

Mitterauer, Michael (1983), *Ledige Mütter. Zur Geschichte illegitimer Geburten in Europa*, München

Mitterauer, Michael (2003), *Warum Europa? Mittelalterliche Grundlagen eines Sonderwegs*, München

Mitterauer, Michael (2011), Kontrastierende Heiratsregeln. Traditionen des Orients und Europas im interkutlurellen Vergleich, in: *Historische Sozialkunde. Geschichte - Fachdidaktik - Politische Bildung* 41, 2, pp. 4–16

Mohr, Andreas (2009), *Eheleute, Männerbünde, Kulttransvestiten. Zur Geschlechtergeschichte germanischsprachiger gentes des ersten bis siebten Jahrhunderts*, Franktfurt a. M. et al.

Monter, E. William (1973), Crime and Punishment in Calvin's Geneva, 1562, in: *Archiv für Reformationsgeschichte - Archive for Reformation History* 64, pp. 281–287

Monter, William E. (1990), *Frontiers of Heresy. The Spanish Inquisition from the Basque Lands to Sicily*, Cambridge

Moore, K. R. (ed) (2022), *The Routledge Companion to the Reception of Ancient Greek and Roman Gender*, Milton

Moore, Patrick (2004), *Beyond Shame. Reclaiming the Abandoned History of Radical Gay Sexuality*, Boston

Moos, Peter von (2005), *Abaelard und Heloise (=Gesammelte Studien zum Mittelalter Bd. 1)*, Berlin et al.

Moran, Leslie J. (1996), *The Homosexual(ity) of Law*, London/New York

Moritz, Verena/Leidinger, Hannes (2012), *Oberst Redl. Der Spionagefall, der Skandal, die Fakten*, Wien

Morris, Stephen (2016), *When Brothers Dwell in Unity: Byzantine Christianity and Homosexuality*, Jefferson

Morton, Robert S. (1977), *Gonorrhoea*, London

Moshövel, Andrea (2009), *Wîplîche man. Formen und Funktionen von "Effemination" in deutschsprachigen Erzähltexten des 13. Jahrhunderts*, Göttingen

Moulton, Ian Frederick (2000), *Before Pornography. Erotic Writing in Early Modern England*, Oxford et al.

Moulton, Ian Frederick (2010), Whores as Shopkeepers: Money and Sexuality in Aretino's Ragionamenti, in: Wolfthal, Diane/Vitullo, Juliann (eds), *Money, Morality, and Culture in Late Medieval and Early Modern Europe*, London, pp. 71–86

Moulton, Ian Frederick (2013), Erotic Representations, in: Toulalan, Sarah/Fisher, Kate (eds), *The Routledge History of Sex and the Body: 1500 to the Present*, London, pp. 207–222

Moulton, Ian Frederick (2017), The Manuscript Circulation of Erotic Poetry in Early Modern England, in: Mudge, Bradford K. (ed), *The Cambridge Companion to Erotic Literature*, Cambridge, pp. 64–84

Moulton, Ian Frederick (2019), Vagina Dialogues: Piccolomini's Raffaella and Aretino's Ragionamenti, in: Murray, Jacqueline/Terpstra, Nicholas (eds), *Sex, Gender and Sexuality in Renaissance Italy*, London, pp. 211–226

Mowry, Melissa M. (2004), *The Bawdy Politic in Stuart England 1660–1714. Political Pornography and Prostitution*, Aldershot

Moxnes, Halvor (2003), *Putting Jesus in His Place. A Radical Vision of Household and Kingdom*, Louisville

Muchembled, Robert (2008), *Die Verwandlung der Lust. Eine Geschichte der abendländischen Sexualität*, München

Mudge, Bradford K. (2000), *The Whore's Story. Women, Pornography, and the British Novel, 1684–1830*, Oxford

Mueller-Vollmer, Tristan/Wolf, Kirsten (2022), *Vikings: An Encyclopedia of Conflict, Invasions, and Raids*, Santa Barbara

Müller, Jan-Dirk (2007), Gebrauchszusammenhang und ästhetische Dimension mittelalterlicher Texte.. Nebst Überlegungen zu Walthers "Lindenlied" (1,39,11), in: Braun, Manuel/Young, Christopher John (eds), *Das fremde Schöne: Dimensionen des Ästhetischen in der Literatur des Mittelalters*, Berlin, pp. 281–308

Müller, Johannes (1988), *Schwert und Scheide. Der sexuelle und skatologische Wortschatz im Nürnberger Fastnachtspiel des 15. Jahrhunderts*, Bern

Müller, Klaus (1991), *Aber in meinem Herzen sprach eine Stimme so laut. Homosexuelle Autobiographien und medizinische Pathographien im 19. Jahrhundert*, Berlin

Müller, Klaus (1993), Johann Ludwig Casper, in: Lautmann, Rüdiger (ed), *Homosexualität. Handbuch der Theorie- und Forschungsgeschichte*, Frankfurt a. M., pp. 29–31

Müller, Klaus (2002), Totgeschlagen, totgeschwiegen? Das autobiographische Zeugnis homosexueller Überlebender, in: Jellonnek, Burkhard/Lautmann, Rüdiger (eds), *Nationalsozialistischer Terror gegen Homosexuelle. Verdrängt und ungesühnt*, Paderborn et al., pp. 397–418

Müller, Ulrich (1994), Zur Lachkultur in der deutschen Literatur des Mittelalters. Neidhart und Neidhart Fuchs, in: Jäkel, Siegfried/Timonen, Asko (eds), *Laughter Down the Centuries*, Vol. 1, Turku, pp. 161–181

Müller, Wolfgang P. (2000), *Die Abtreibung. Anfänge der Kriminalisierung 1140–1650*, Köln et al.

Mummey, Kevin (2011), Prostitution. The Moral Economy of Medieval Prostitution, in: Evans, Ruth (ed), *A Cultural History of Sexuality in the Middle Ages (=A Cultural History of Sexuality Vol. 2)*, Oxford/New York, pp. 165–180

Mummey, Kevin/Reyerson, Kathryn (2011), Whose City Is This? Hucksters, Domestic Servants, Wet-Nurses, Prostitutes, and Slaves in Late Medieval Western Mediterranean Urban Society, in: *History Compass* 9/12, pp. 910–922

Muravyeva, Marianna (2014), Ni pillage ni viol sans ordre préalable. Codifier la guerre dans l'Europe moderne, in: *Clio: Women, Gender, History* 39, pp. 55–81

Muravyeva, Marianna (2016), Abduction of Women in Early Modern Russia: Modernizing the Empire, in: *Russian History* 43, 3/4, pp. 338–371

Murphy, Patrick J. (2011), *Unriddling the Exeter Riddles*, University Park, PA.

Murray, Jacqueline (1996), Twice Marginal and Twice Invisible. Lesbians in the Middle Ages, in: Bullough, Vern L./Brundage, James A. (eds), *Handbook of Medieval Sexuality*, New York/London, pp. 191–222

Murray, Jacqueline (2019), The Battle for Chastity: Miraculous Castration and the Quelling of Desire in the Middle Ages, in: *Journal of the History of Sexuality* 28, 1, pp. 96–116

Murray, Jacqueline/Eisenbichler, Konrad (eds) (1996), *Desire and Discipline. Sex and Sexuality in the Premodern West*, Toronto

Murray, James M. (2004), *Bruges, Cradle of Capitalism, 1280–1390*, Cambridge

Murray, Stephen O. (1997), The Will Not to Know: Islamic Accommodations of Male Homosexuality, in: Murray, Stephen O./Roscoe, Will (eds), *Islamic Homosexualities: Culture, History, and Literature*, New York, pp. 14–54

Murray, Stephen O. (ed) (1995), *Latin American Male Homosexualities*, Albuquerque

Muurling, Sanne/Kamp, Jeannette/Schmidt, Ariadne (2021), Unwed Mothers, Urban Institutions and Female Agency in Early Modern Dutch, German and Italian Towns, in: *The History of the Family* 26, 1, pp. 11–28

Myerowitz, Molly (1992), The Domestication of Desire. Ovid' Parva Tabella and the Theater of Love, in: Richlin, Amy (ed), *Pornography and Representation in Greece and Rome*, Oxford, pp. 131–157

Myrne, Pernilla (2020), *Female Sexuality in the Early Medieval Islamic World: Gender and Sex in the Arabic Literature*, London et al.

Naphy, William G. (2002), *Sex Crimes. From Renaissance to Enlightenment*, London

Navarra, Margarete von (2022), *Das Heptameron*, Stockholm

Navarre, Marguerite de (1823), *The Heptameron of Margaret, Queen of Navarre*. trans. by Walter K. Kelly, London

Neal, Derek G. (2008), *The Masculine Self in Late Medieval England*, Chicago

Nehlsen, Hermann (2005), Die Sklaverei bei den germanischen Stämmen, in: Scholler, Heinrich/Tellenbach, Silvia (eds), *Faktoren der Entstehung und Überwindung unfreier Arbeit in Europa und in den afrikanischen Kolonien*, Münster, pp. 31–56

Neill, James (2009), *The Origins and Role of Same-Sex Relations in Human Societies*, Jefferson et al.

Neumeyer, Harald (2001), Ich bin einer von denjenigen Unglückseligen (...). Rückkopplungen und Autoreferenzen. Zur Onaniedebatte im 18. Jahrhundert, in: Bergengruen, Maximilian/Borgards, Roland/Lehmann, Johannes Friedrich (eds), *Die Grenzen des Menschen. Anthropologie und Ästhetik um 1800*, Würzburg, pp. 65–95

Neureiter, Livia (2010), Zwischen Enthaltsamkeit und Begehren. Formen des Zusammenlebens von Männern und Frauen im frühen Christentum, in: Fischer, Irmtraud/Heil, Christoph (eds), *Sexualität und Macht. Lebensformen in der Zeit des frühen Christentums*, Wien et al., pp. 211–229

Niiranen, Susanna (2015), Sexual Incapacity in Medieval Materia Medica, in: Krötzl, Christian/Mustakallio, Katariina/Kuuliala, Jenni (eds), *Infirmity in Antiquity and the Middle Ages: Social and Cultural Approaches to Health, Weakness and Care*, Farnham, pp. 223–240

Nirenberg, David (1996), *Communities of Violence. Persecution of Minorities in the Middle Ages*, Princeton

Nirenberg, David (2002), Conversion, Sex and Segregation. Jews and Christians in Medieval Spain, in: *The American Historical Review* 107, pp. 1065–1093

Nirenberg, David (2004), Love between Muslim and Jew in Medieval Spain. A Triangular Affair, in: Hames, Harvey J. (ed), *Jews, Muslims, and Christians in and Around the Crown of Aragon. Essays in Honour of Professor Elena Lourie*, Leiden, pp. 127–156

Nolde, Dorothea (2003), *Gattenmord. Macht und Gewalt in der frühneuzeitlichen Ehe*, Köln et al.

Nolde, Dorothea (2020), Les violences sexuelles faites aux enfants. Un état des recherches, in: *Clio. Women, Gender, History* 52, 2, pp. 137–161

Norberg, Kathryn (2013), The Body of the Prostitute. Medieval to Modern, in: Toulalan, Sarah/Fisher, Kate (eds), *The Routledge History of Sex and the Body: 1500 to the Present*, London, pp. 393–408

Norton, Rictor C. (2006), *Mother Clap's Molly House. The Gay Subculture in England 1700–1830* (revised and enlarged edition), Stroud/Glos., 2nd edn

Norton, Rictor C. (2011), Homosexuality, in: Peakman, Julie (ed), *A Cultural History of Sexuality in Enligthenment* (=A Cultural History of Sexuality Vol. 4), Oxford/New York, pp. 57–83

Núñez Roldán, Francisco (1995), *Mujeres públicas. Historia de la prostitución en Espana*, Madrid
Nussbaum, Felicity (2003), *The Limits of the Human. Fictions of Anomaly, Race and Gender in the Long Eighteenth Century*, Cambridge/New York
Nussbaum, Martha (2000a), Eros and Ethical Norms. Philosophers Respond to a Cultural Dilemma, in: Nussbaum, Martha/Sihvola, Juha (eds), *The Sleep of Reason. Erotic Experience and Sexual Ethics in Ancient Greece and Rome*, Chicago, pp. 55–94
Nussbaum, Martha (2000b), The Incomplete Feminism of Musonius Rufus, Platonist, Stoic, and Roman, in: Nussbaum, Martha/Sihvola, Juha (eds), *The Sleep of Reason. Erotic Experience and Sexual Ethics in Ancient Greece and Rome*, Chicago, pp. 283–326
Nye, Robert A. (1999), Sex and Sexuality in France since 1800, in: Eder, Franz X./Hall, Lesley A./Hekma, Gert (eds), *Sexual Cultures in Europe. National Histories*, Manchester/New York, pp. 91–113
O'Donnell, Katherine/O'Rourke, Michael (eds) (2003), *Love, Sex, Intimacy and Friendship Between Men, 1550–1800*, Basingstoke/New York
O'Donnell, Katherine/O'Rourke, Michael (eds) (2006), *Queer Masculinities. Siting Same-Sex Desire in the Early Modern World*, Basingstoke/New York
Obermayer, Hans P. (1998), *Martial und der Diskurs über männliche "Homosexualität" in der Literatur der frühen Kaiserzeit*, Tübingen
Offen, Karen (1984), Depopulation, Nationalism and Feminism in Fin-de-siècle France, in: *American Historical Review* 89 (1984), pp. 648–667
Ogden, Daniel (1995), Women and Bastardy in Ancient Greece and the Hellenistic World, in: Powell, Anton (ed), *The Greek World*, Oxford/New York, pp. 219–244
Ogden, Daniel (2011), Homosexuality, in: Golden, Mark/Toohey, Peter (eds), *A Cultural History of Sexuality in the Classical World (=A Cultural History of Sexuality Vol. 1)*, Oxford/New York, pp. 37–54
Ojakangas, Mika (2016), *On the Greek Origins of Biopolitics: A Reinterpretation of the History of Biopower*, London/New York
Olechowski, Thomas (2010), *Rechtsgeschichte: Einführung in die historischen Grundlagen des Rechts*, Wien, 3rd edn
Olson, Kelly (2006), Matrona and Whore. Clothing and Definition in Roman Antiquity, in: Faraone, Christopher A./McClure, Laura K. (eds), *Prostitutes and Courtesans in the Ancient World*, Madison, pp. 186–204
Olson, Kelly (2012), *Dress and the Roman Woman. Self-Presentation and Society*, Hoboken
Olson, Kelly (2017), *Masculinity and Dress in Roman Antiquity*, London
Omitowoju, Rosanna (2002), *Rape and the Politics of Consent in Classical Athens*, Cambridge
Online Etymology Dictionary, https://www.etymonline.com/
Onlywomen Press Collective (ed) (1981), *Love Your Enemy? The Debate between Heterosexual Feminism and Political Lesbianism*, London
Oosterhuis, Harry (1998), Plato war doch gewiß kein Schweinehund. Richard von Krafft-Ebing und die homosexuelle Identität, in: *Österreichische Zeitschrift für Geschichtswissenschaften* 9, 3, pp. 358–383
Oosterhuis, Harry (2000), *Stepchildren of Nature. Krafft-Ebing, Psychiatry and the Making of Sexual Identity*, Chicago/London

Opitz-Belakhal, Claudia (2017), *Böse Weiber: Wissen und Geschlecht in der Dämonologie der frühen Neuzeit*, Sulzbach
Opper, Thorsten (2008), *Hadrian. Empire and Conflict*, Cambridge, MA
Oriel, J. David (2013), *The Scars of Venus. A History of Venerology*, London
Orlin, Lena Cowen (2000), Chronicles of Private Life, in: Kinney, Arthur F. (ed), *The Cambridge Companion to English Literature, 1500–1600*, Cambridge, pp. 241–264
Ormand, Kirk (2009), *Controlling Desires. Sexuality in Ancient Greece and Rome*, Westport et al.
Ormand, Kirk (2014), Foucault's History of Sexuality and the Discipline of Classics, in: Hubbard, Thomas K. (ed), *A Companion to Greek and Roman Sexualities*, Malden, pp. 54–68
Ornitowoju, Rosanna (2002), Regulating Rape. Soap Operas and Self Interest in the Athenian Courts, in: Deacy, Susan/Pierce, Karen F. (eds), *Rape in Antiquity. Sexual Violence in the Greek and Roman Worlds*, London, pp. 1–24
Ortega, Stephen (2009), Across Religious and Ethnic Boundaries: Ottoman Networks and Spaces in Early Modern Venice, in: *Mediterranean Studies* 18 (2009), pp. 66–89
Osborne, Robin (2011), *The History Written on the Classical Greek Body*, Cambridge
Osiek, Carolyn (2003), Female Slaves, Porneia, and the Limits of Obedience, in: Balch, David L./Osiek, Carolyn (eds), *Early Christian Families in Context: An Interdisciplinary Dialogue*, Grand Rapids, pp. 255–276
Österberg, Eva (2010), *Friendship and Love, Ethics and Politics: Studies in Mediaeval and Early Modern History*, Budapest/New York
Otis-Cour, Leah Lydia (1985), *Prostitution in Medieval Society. The History of an Urban Institution in Languedoc*, Chicago/London
Owens, Yvonne (2017), Pollution and Desire in Hans Baldung Grien: The Abject, Erotic Spell of the Witch and Dragon, in: Pollali, Angeliki (ed), *Images of Sex and Desire in Renaissance Art and Modern Historiography*, New York/London, pp. 181–208
Pabst, Esther Suzanne (2007), *Die Erfindung der weiblichen Tugend. Kulturelle Sinngebung und Selbstreflexion im französischen Briefroman des 18. Jahrhunderts*, Göttingen
Page, Jamie (2019), Masculinity and Prostitution in Late Medieval German Literature, in: *Speculum* 94, 3, pp. 739–773
Page, Jamie (2021), *Prostitution and Subjectivity in Late Medieval Germany*, Oxford
Page, Jamie (2022), No Way to Run a Brothel? Prostitution and Policey in the Late Medieval Holy Roman Empire, in: *German History* 40 (2022), 1, pp. 1–21
Pallaver, Günther (1987), *Das Ende der schamlosen Zeit. Die Verdrängung der Sexualität in der frühen Neuzeit am Beispiel Tirols*, Wien
Paolella, Christopher (2020), *Human Trafficking in Medieval Europe. Slavery, Sexual Exploitation, and Prostitution*, Oldenbourg
Pallotti, Donatella (2012), A Most Detestable Crime. Representations of Rape in the Popular Press of Early Modern England, in: *LEA - Lingue e letterature d'Oriente e d'Occidente* 1, 1, pp. 287–302
Parish, Helen L. (2010), *Clerical Celibacy in the West, c.1100-1700*, Farnham

Parisot, Jeannette (1987), *Dein Kondom, das unbekannte Wesen. Eine Geschichte der Pariser*, Hamburg
Park, Katherine (1997), The Rediscovery of the Clitoris. French Medicine and the Tribade, 1570-1620, in: Hillman, David/Mazzio, Carla (eds), *The Body in Parts. Fantasies of Corporeality in Early Modern Europe*, New York, pp. 171–193
Park, Katherine (2006), *Secrets of Women. Gender, Generation, and the Origins of Human Dissection*, New York
Park, Katherine/Nye, Robert A. (1991), Destiny is Anatomy, in: *The New Republic* 204, 7, pp. 53–57
Parker, Holt (2007), Free Women and Male Slaves, or Mandingo Meets the Roman Empire, in: Serghidou, Anastasia (ed), *Fear of Slaves, Fear of Enslavement in the Ancient Mediterranean*, Besançon, pp. 281–298
Parker, Holt (ed) (2010), *Antonio Beccadelli "The Hermaphrodite"*, Harvard
Parker, Holt N. (1992), Love's Body Antomized. The Ancient Erotic Handbooks and the Rhetoric of Sexuality, in: Richlin, Amy (ed), *Pornography and Representation in Greece and Rome*, Oxford, pp. 90–107
Parker, Holt N. (1997), The Tetratogenic Grid, in: Hallett, Judith P./Skinner, Marilyn B. (eds), *Roman Sexualities*, Princeton, pp. 47–65
Parker, Holt N. (2011), Sex, Popular Beliefs, and Culture, in: Golden, Mark/Toohey, Peter (eds), A *Cultural History of Sexuality in the Classical World (=A Cultural History of Sexuality Vol. 1)*, Oxford/New York, pp. 125–133
Parodi, Karime (2020), From Seduction to Sexual Assault: Consent and Heterosexual Interaction in the Libro de buen amor, in: *La corónica: A Journal of Medieval Hispanic Languages, Literatures, and Cultures* 49, 1, pp. 45–72
Pasco, Allan H. (2009), *Revolutionary Love in Eighteenth- And Early Nineteenth-Century France*, Farnham/Burlington
Patton, Pamela Anne (ed) (2016), *Envisioning Others: Race, Color, and the Visual in Iberia and Latin America*, Leiden
Paul, Axel T. (2011), Die Gewalt der Scham. Elias, Duerr und das Problem der Historizität menschlicher Gefühle, in: Bauks, Michaela/Meyer, Martin F. (eds), *Zur Kulturgeschichte der Scham*, Hamburg, pp. 195–216
Pawlowsky, Verena (2001), *Mutter ledig - Vater Staat. Das Gebär- und Findelhaus in Wien 1784–1910*, Innsbruck/Wien/München
Payer, Pierre J. (1984), *Sex and the Penitentials. The Development of a Sexual Code, 550–1150*, Toronto
Payer, Pierre J. (1993), *The Bridling of Desire. Views of Sex in the Later Middle Ages*, Toronto
Payer, Pierre J. (1996), Confession and the Study of Sex in the Middle Ages, in: Bullough, Vern L./Brundage, James A. (eds), *Handbook of Medieval Sexuality*, New York/London, pp. 3–32
Peakman, Julie (2003), *Mighty Lewd Books. The Development of Pornography in Eighteenth-Century England*, Basingstoke et al.
Peakman, Julie (2009), Sexual Perversions in History. An Introduction, in: Peakman, Julie (ed), *Sexual Perversions, 1670–1890*, London, pp. 1–49
Peakman, Julie (2013), *The Pleasure's All Mine. A History of Perverse Sex*, London
Peakman, Julie (2020), Male Homosexuality at the English Royal Court, in: Domeier, Norman/Mühling, Christian (eds), *Homosexualität am Hof: Praktiken und Diskurse vom Mittelalter bis heute*, Frankfurt/New York, pp. 119–132

Peakman, Julie (ed) (2011), *A Cultural History of Sexuality*, 6 Vols., Oxford/New York
Pearson, Andrea (2019), *Gardens of Love and the Limits of Morality in Early Netherlandish Art*, Leiden/Boston
Pechriggl, Alice (2009), *Eros*, Wien
Peirce, Leslie P. (2009), Writing Histories of Sexuality in the Middle East, in: *The American Historical Review* 114, 5, pp. 1325–1339
Peña, E. J. Hernández (2016), Reclaiming Alterity: Strangeness and the Queering of Islam in Medieval and Early Modern Spain, in: *Theology & Sexuality* 22, 1–2, pp. 42–56
Penn, Michael Philip (2005), *Kissing Christians: Ritual and Community in the Late Ancient Church*, Philadelphia
Pepe, Laura (2014), Abortion in Ancient Greece, in: Gagarin, Michael/Lanni, Adriaan (eds), *Symposion 2013: Österreichische Akademie der Wissenschaften, Philosophisch-Historische Klasse, Documenta Antiqua - Antike Rechtsgeschichte*, Wien, pp. 1–26
Percy, William A. (1996), *Pederasty and Pedagogy in Archaic Greece*, Champaign-Urbana
Percy, William A. (2006), Reconsiderations about Greek Homosexualities, in: Verstraete, Beert C./Provencal, Vernon L. (eds), *Same-Sex Desire and Love in Greco-Roman Antiquity and in the Classical Tradition of the West*, New York/Binghamton, pp. 13–62
Perrin, Faustine (2021), On the Origins of the Demographic Transition: Rethinking the European Marriage Pattern, in: *Cliometrica* 16, pp. 431–475
Perry, Mary E. (1978), Lost Women in Early Modern Seville. The Politics of Prostitution, in: *Feminist Studies* 4, 1, pp. 195–214
Perry, Mary E. (1990), *Gender and Disorder in Early Modern Seville*, Princeton
Perry, Matthew J. (2014), *Gender, Manumission, and the Roman Freedwoman*, New York
Perry, Matthew J. (2020), State and Law, in: Klaiber-Hersch, Karen (ed), *A Cultural History of Marriage in Antiquity*, London/New York, pp. 59–76
Perry, Matthew J. (2021), Control of Roman Slave Sexuality Authority, Profit, and Resistance, in: Kamen, Deborah/Marshall, C. W. (eds), *Slavery and Sexuality in Classical Antiquity*, Madison/London, pp. 254–269
Persisanifi, Maroula (2017), Was There a Marital Debt in Byzantium?, in: *Journal of Ecclesiastical History* 68, 3, pp. 510–528
Pesendorfer, Philipp (2018), Ne serva prostituatur: Sklavinnen als Prostituierte im Römischen Recht, in: Fischer, Irmtraud/Feichtinger, Daniela (eds), *Sexualität und Sklaverei*, Münster, pp. 45–62
Peters, Albrecht (ed) (1990), *Kommentar zu Luthers Katechismen. 1. Die Zehn Gebote, Luthers Vorreden*, Göttingen
Petherbridge, Deanna (1998), Art and Anatomy. The Meeting of Text and Image, in: Petherbridge, Deanna/Jordanova, Ludmilla (eds), *The Quick and the Dead. Artists and Anatomy*, Berkeley/Los Angeles/London, pp. 7–32
Petrey, Taylor (2016), *Resurrecting Parts: Early Christians on Desire, Reproduction, and Sexual Difference*, London
Peukert, Rüdiger (2008), *Familienformen im sozialen Wandel*, Opladen, 7th edn
Pfister, Christian (1994), *Bevölkerungsgeschichte und historische Demographie 1500–1800*, München

Pfister, Ulrich (1985), *Die Anfänge der Geburtenbeschränkung. Eine Fallstudie ausgewählter Zürcher Familien im 17. und 18. Jahrhundert*, Bern

Pfisterer, Ulrich (2012), Bildbegehren und Texterotik. Ambivalente Lektüren weiblicher Aktdarstellungen in der Frühen Neuzeit, in: Guth, Doris/Priedl, Elisabeth (eds), *Bilder der Liebe. Liebe, Begehren und Geschlechterverhältnisse in der Kunst der Frühen Neuzeit*, Bielefeld, pp. 191–217

Phang, Sara Elise (2001), *The Marriage of Roman Soldiers (13 B.C. - A.D. 235). Law and Family in the Imperial Army*, Leiden/Boston

Phang, Sara Elise (2008), *Roman Military Service: Ideologies of Discipline in the Late Republic and Early Principate*, Cambridge

Phillips, Kim M. (2018), The Breasts of Virgins: Sexual Reputation and Young Women's Bodies in Medieval Culture and Society, in: *Cultural & Social History* 15, 1, pp. 1–19

Phillips, Kim M./Reay, Barry (2011), *Sex before Sexuality. A Premodern History*, Cambridge/Malden

Phipps, William E. (2004), *Clerical Celibacy. The Heritage*, New York

Pichler, Dietlind (2003), *Bürgertum und Protestantismus. Die Geschichte der Familie Ludwig in Wien und Oberösterreich (1860 - 1900)*, Wien

Pigg, Daniel F. (2017), Bald's Leebook and the Construction of Male Health in Anglo-Saxon England, in: Classen, Albrecht (ed), *Bodily and Spiritual Hygiene in Medieval and Early Modern Literature. Exploration of Textural Presentations of Filth and Water*, Berlin, pp. 114–128

Piller, Gudrun (2006), *Private Körper. Spuren des Leibes in Selbstzeugnissen des 18. Jahrhunderts*, Wien/Köln/Weimar

Pinto-Correia, Clara (1997), *The Ovary of Eve. Egg and Sperm and Preformation*, Chicago

Pipkin, Amanda (2009), They Were Not Humans, but Devils in Human Bodies: Depictions of Sexual Violence and Spanish Tyranny as a Means of Fostering Identity in the Dutch Republic, in: *Journal of Early Modern History* 13, 4, pp. 229–264

Pipkin, Amanda (2013), *Rape in the Republic, 1609–1725: Formulating Dutch Identity*, Leiden/Boston

Piquero, Álvaro (2020), Cuando te tocares, niña: An Approach to Images of Masturbation in Medieval and Early Modern Spanish Poetry, in: Jones, Nicholas R./Leahy, Chad (eds), *Pornographic Sensibilities: Imagining Sex and the Visceral in Premodern and Early Modern Spanish Cultural Production*, Milton, pp. 201–218

Pitts-Taylor, Victoria (ed) (2008), *Cultural Encyclopedia of the Body*, 2 Vols., Westport

Plamper, Jan (2012), *Geschichte und Gefühl. Grundlagen der Emotionsgeschichte*, München

Plato (2001), *Selected Dialogues of Plato. The Benjamin Jowett Translation. Revised and with an Introduction by Haydn Pelliccia*, New York

Plöchl, Willibald M. (1962), *Geschichte des Kirchenrechts. Bd. 2: Das Kirchrecht der abendländischen Christenheit 1055 bis 1517*, Wien/München, 2nd edn

Plummer, Majorie Elizabeth (2014), Nothing More than Common Whores and Knaves: Married Nuns and Monks in the Early German Reformation, in: Luebke, David/Lindemann, Mary (eds), *Transgressive Unions in Germany from the Reformation to the Enlightenment*, Oxford/New York, pp. 45–62

Pluskota, Marion (2020), Governing Sexuality: Regulating Prostitution in Early Modern Europe, in: Gunn, Simon/Hulme, Tom (eds), *New Approaches to Governance and Rule in Urban Europe Since 1500*, Milton, pp. 87–109
Poirier, Guy (2005), A Contagion at the Source of Discourse on Sexuality. Syphilis during the French Renaissance, in: Carlin, Claire (ed), *Imagining Contagion in Early Modern Europe*, Basingstoke, pp. 157–176
Pollini, John (2003), Slave-Boys for Sexual and Religious Service: Images of Pleasure and Devotion, in: Boyle, Anthony/Dominik, William J. (ed), *Flavian Rome: Culture, Image, Text*, Leiden/Boston, pp. 149–166
Pollis, Carol A. (1987), The Apparatus of Sexuality. Reflections on Foucault's Contributions to the Study of Sex in History, in: *Journal of Sex Research* 23, pp. 401–408
Poly, Jean-Pierre (2003), *Le chemin des amours barbares. Genèse médiévale de la sexualité européenne*, Paris
Pomata, Gianna (1995), Vollkommen oder verdorben? Der männliche Samen im frühneuzeitlichen Europa, in: *L'homme. Zeitschrift für feministische Geschichtswissenschaft* 6, 2, pp. 59–85
Pomata, Gianna (2001), Menstruating Men. Similarity and Difference of the Sexes in Early Modern Medicine, in: Finucci, Valeria/Brownlee, Kevin (eds), *Generation and Degeneration. Tropes of Reproduction in Literature and History from Antiquity to Early Modern Europe*, Durham/London, pp. 109–152
Pomata, Gianna (2018), Innate Heat, Radical Moisture and Generation, in: Hopwood, Nick et al. (eds), *Reproduction: Antiquity to the Present Day*, Cambridge, pp. 195–208
Porter, Jason Douglas (2021), The Sexual Agency of Slaves in Classical Athens, in: Kamen, Deborah/Marshall, C. W. (eds), *Slavery and Sexuality in Classical Antiquity*, Madison/London, pp. 89–103
Porter, John R. (2018) Funeral Monument of L. Calidius Eroticus and Fannia Voluptas (CIL IX.2689) (https://www.academia.edu/36829697/Funeral_Monument_of_L._Calidius_Eroticus_and_Fannia_Voluptas_CIL_IX.2689_)
Porter, Roy (1994), The Literature of Sexual Advice before 1800, in: Porter, Roy/Teich, Mikuláš (eds), *Sexual Knowledge, Sexual Science. The History of Attitudes to Sexuality*, Cambridge, pp. 134–157
Porter, Roy/Hall, Lesley (1995), *The Facts of Life. The Creation of Sexual Knowledge in Britain, 1650–1950*, New Haven/London
Posch, Caroline (2012), Nur Frauen? Männliche Prostitution im klassischen Athen, in: Müller, Florian M./Sossau, Veronika (eds), *Gefährtinnen. Vom Umgang mit Prostitution in der griechischen Antike und heute*, Innsbruck, pp. 71–88
Poska, Allyson M. (2008), A Married Man Is a Woman. Negotiating Masculinity in Early Modern Northwestern Spain, in: Hendrix, Scott H./Karant-Nunn, Susan C. (eds), *Masculinity in the Reformation Era*, Kirksville, pp. 3–20
Prange, Peter (1990), *Das Paradies im Boudoir. Glanz und Elend der erotischen Libertinage im Zeitalter der Aufklärung*, Marburg
Pregesbauer, Helga (2009), *Irreale Sexualitäten. Zur Geschichte von Sexualität, Körper und Gender in der europäischen Hexenverfolgung*, Wien
Pretzel, Andreas (2002), Aufbruch und Resignation. Zur Geschichte der Berliner "Gesellschaft für Reform des Sexualstrafrechts e. V." 1948-1960, in: *NS-Opfer unter Vorbehalt. Homosexuelle Männer in Berlin nach 1945*, pp. 287–344

Priapus Poems (1999), *The Priapus Poems: Erotic Epigrams from Ancient Rome*, trans. Richard W. Hooper, Urbana
Probert, Rebecca (2009), *Marriage Law and Practice in the Long Eighteenth Century: A Reassessment*, Cambridge
Prono, Luca (2008), *Encyclopedia of Gay and Lesbian Popular Culture*, Westport
Puff, Helmut (1994), Die Sünde und ihre Metaphern. Zum Liber Gomorrhianus des Petrus Damiani, in: *Forum Homosexualität und Literatur* 21, pp. 45–77
Puff, Helmut (1998), Überlegungen zu einer Rhetorik der "unsprechlichen Sünde". Ein Basler Verhörprotokoll aus dem Jahr 1416, in: *Österreichische Zeitschrift für Geschichtswissenschaften* 9, 3, pp. 342–357
Puff, Helmut (1999), Weibliche Sodomie. Der Prozeß gegen Katharina Hetzeldorfer und die Rhetorik des Unaussprechlichen an der Wende vom Mittelalter zur frühen Neuzeit, in: *Historische Anthropologie* 7, 3, pp. 364–380
Puff, Helmut (2003), *Sodomy in Reformation Germany and Switzerland, 1400–1600*, Chicago
Puff, Helmut (2007), Die frühe Neuzeit in Europa, 1400-1700, in: Aldrich, Robert (ed), *Gleich und anders. Eine globale Geschichte der Homosexualität*, Hamburg, pp. 79–102
Puff, Helmut (2008), The Reform of Masculinities in Sixteenth-Century Switzerland: A Case Study, in: Hendrix, Scott H./Karant-Nunn, Susan C. (eds), *Masculinity in the Reformation Era*, Kirksville, pp. 21–44
Puff, Helmut (2011), Homosexuality: Homosociabilities in Renaissance Nuremberg, in: Talvacchia, Bette (ed), *A Cultural History of Sexuality in the Renaissance (=A Cultural History of Sexuality Vol. 3)*, Oxford/New York, pp. 51–72
Puff, Helmut (2013), Same-Sex Possibilities, in: Bennett, Judith M./Karras, Ruth Mazo (Hg.), *The Oxford Handbook of Women and Gender in Medieval Europe*, Oxford, 379–395
Puff, Helmut (2017), Martin Luther, the Sexual Reformation, and Same-Sex Sexuality, in: Melloni, Alberto (ed), *Martin Luther: A Christian between Reforms and Modernity (1517–2017)*, Berlin, pp. 663–678
Pullan, Brian (2016), *Tolerance, Regulation and Rescue: Dishonoured Women and Abandoned Children in Italy, 1300–1800*, Manchester
Pushkareva, N. L. (1991), Women in the Medieval Russian Family of the Tenth through Fifteenth Centuries, in: Evans Clement, Barbara/Engel, Alpern Barbara (eds), *Russia's Women. Accomodation, Resistance, Transformation*, Berkley, pp. 29–43
Pushkareva, N. L. (1997), *Women in Russian History: From the Tenth to the Twentieth Century*, London/New York
Quétel, Claude (1990), *The History of Syphilis*, Oxford
Rabelais, François (1894), *Gargantua und Pantagruel*, trans. by Sir Thomas Urquhart and Peter Antony Motteux, Derby
Rabin, Dana (2003), Beyond "Lewd Women" and "Wanton Wenches". Infanticide and and Child-Murder in the Long Eighteenth Century, in: Thorn, Jennifer (ed), *Writing British Infanticide. Child-Murder, Gender, and Print, 1722–1859*, Newark, pp. 45–69
Rabinowitz, Nancy S. (2002), Excavating Women's Homoeroticism in Ancient Greece. The Evidence from Attic Vase Paintings, in: Rabinowitz,

Nancy S./Auanger, Lisa (eds), *Among Women. From the Homosocial to the Homoerotic in the Ancient World*, Austin, pp. 106–166

Radle, Gabriel (2018), Bishops Blessing the Bridal Bedchamber in the Early Middle Ages: Reconsidering the Western Evidence, in: *Medium aevum* 87, 2, pp. 219–238

Rafeq, Abdul-Karim (1990–92), Public Morality in 18th Century Ottoman Damascus, in: *Revue du monde Musulman et de la Méditerranée* 55–56, pp. 180–196

Raffield, Ben/Price, Neil/Collard, Mark (2017), Polygyny, Concubinage, and the Social Lives of Women in Viking-Age Scandinavia, in: *Viking and Medieval Scandinavia* 13, pp. 165–209

Rakoczy, Thomas (1996), *Böser Blick, Macht des Auges und Neid der Götter. Eine Untersuchung zur Kraft des Blickes in der griechischen Literatur*, Tübingen

Ramazanoglou, Caroline (ed) (2009), *Up Against Foucault. Explorations of Some Tensions Between Foucault and Feminism*, London u. New York, 2nd edn

Ranke-Heinemann, Uta (1999), *Eunuchen für das Himmelreich. Katholische Kirche und Sexualität*, München

Rapp, Claudia (2016), *Brother-Making in Late Antiquity and Byzantium: Monks, Laymen, and Christian Ritual*, New York

Rasmussen, Ann Marie (2014), Moving Beyond Sexuality in Medieval Sexual Badges, in: Grafetstätter, Andrea (ed), *Nahrung, Notdurft und Obszönität in Mittelalter und Früher Neuzeit: Akten der Tagung Bamberg 2011*, Bamberg, pp. 125–154

Rath, Brigitte (1986), Prostitution und spätmittelalterliche Gesellschaft im österreich-süddeutschen Raum, in: *Appelt, Heinrich (e), Frau und spätmittelalterlicher Alltag*, Wien, pp. 553–571

Rauh, Nicholas K. (2011), Prostitutes, Pimps, and Political Conspiracies during the Late Roman Republic, in: Glazebrook, Allison/Henry, Madeleine M. (eds), *Greek Prostitutes in the Ancient Mediterranean, 800 BCE to 200 CE*, Madison, pp. 197–221

Raveh, Inbar (2014), *Feminist Rereadings of Rabbinic Literature*, Waltham

Ray, Meredith K. (2009), *Writing Gender in Women's Letter Collections of the Italian Renaissance*, Toronto

Rayside, David M. (1998), *On the Fringe. Gays and Lesbians in Politics*, Ithaca/New York

Read, Sara (2015), *Maids, Wives, Widows. Exploring Early Modern Women's Lives 1540–1714*, Barnsley

Reckwitz, Andreas (2014), Die Materialisierung der Kultur, in: Friederike Elias et al. (eds), *Praxeologie. Beiträge zur interdisziplinären Reichweite praxistheoretischer Ansätze in den Geistes- und Sozialwissenschaften*, Berlin/Boston, pp. 13–25

Reddy, William M. (2012), *The Making of Romantic Love. Longing and Sexuality in Europe, South Asia, and Japan, 900–1200 CE*, Chicago/London

Rees, Emma L. E. (2013), *The Vagina: A Literary and Cultural History*, New York

Reeser, Todd W. (2016), *Setting Plato Straight: Translating Ancient Sexuality in the Renaissance*, Chicago/London

Reher, David Sven (1990), *Town and Country in Pre-Industrial Spain: Cuenca 1550–1870*, Cambridge/New York

Reinhardt, Volker (2012), *Machiavelli oder Die Kunst der Macht. Eine Biographie*, München
Reinhard, Wolfgang (2006), Lebensformen Europas: Eine historische Kulturanthropologie, München
Reinholdt, Katharina (2012), *Ein Leib in Christo werden: Ehe und Sexualität im Täufertum der Frühen Neuzeit*, Göttingen
Reinle, Christiane (2007), Das mittelalterliche Sodomiedelikt im Spannungsfeld von rechtlicher Norm, theologischer Deutung und gesellschaftlicher Praxis, in: Limbeck, Sven/Thoma, Lev Mordechai (eds), *Die Sünde, der sich der Tiuvel Schamet in der Helle. Homosexualität in der Kultur des Mittelalters und der frühen Neuzeit*, Ostfildern, pp. 13–42
Reinsberg, Carola (1989), *Ehe, Hetärentum und Knabenliebe im antiken Griechenland*, München,
Reiss, Ben (2017), Pious Phalluses and Holy Vulvas: The Religious Importance of Some Sexual Body-Part Badges in Late-Medieval Europe, in: *Peregrinations: Journal of Medieval Art and Architecture* 6, 1, pp. 151–176
Renaut, Olivier (2017), Introduction, in: Brisson, Luc/Renaut, Olivier (ed), *Érotique et politique chez Platon: Erôs, genre et sexualité dans la cité platonicienne*, Sankt Augustin, pp. 7–16
Rennie, Neil (2003), The Point Venus "Scene". Tahiti, 14 May 1769, in: Nussbaum, Felicity (ed), *The Global Eighteenth Century*, Baltimore, pp. 239–250
Resnick, Irven M. (2012), *Marks of Distinctions: Christian Perceptions of Jews in the High Middle Ages*, Washington
Rey, Michel (1989), Police and Sodomy in Eighteenth-Century Paris. From Sin to Disorder, in: Gerard, Kent/Hekma, Gert (eds), *The Pursuit of Sodomy. Male Homosexuality in Renaissance and Enlightenment Europe*, New York/London, pp. 129–146
Reyerson, Kathryn (2016), *Women's Networks in Medieval France. Gender and Community in Montpellier, 1300–1350*, London
Reynolds, Dwight F. (2017), The Qiyan of al-Andalus, in: Gordon, Matthew S./Hain, Kathryn A. (eds), *Concubines and Courtesans: Women and Slavery in Islamic History*, New York, pp. 100–123
Rheinberger, Hans-Jörg (2006*), Experimentalsysteme und epistemische Dinge. Eine Geschichte der Proteinsynthese im Reagenzglas*, Frankfurt a. M.
Rhodes, Elizabeth (2020), Indecent Theology: Sex and Female Heresy in Counter-Reformation Spain, in: *Renaissance Quarterly* 73, 3, pp. 866–896
Rich, Adrienne (1991), Zwangsheterosexualität und lesbische Existenz, in: Schulz, Dagmar (ed), *Macht und Sinnlichkeit. Ausgewählte Texte von Audrey Lorde und Adrienne Rich*, Berlin, 2nd edn, pp. 136–169
Richards, Jeffrey (1990), *Sex, Dissidence, and Damnation. Minority Groups in the Middle Ages*, London/New York
Richlin, Amy (1991), Zeus and Metis. Foucault, Feminism, Classics, in: *Helios* 18, 2, pp. 160–180
Richlin, Amy (1992), *The Garden of Priapus. Sexuality and Aggression in Roman Humor*, Revised edn, New York
Richlin, Amy (1993), Not Before Homosexuality. The Materiality of the Cinaedus and the Roman Law against Love Between Men, in: *Journal of History of Sexuality* 3, 4, pp. 523–573

Richlin, Amy (1998), Foucault's History of Sexuality. A Useful Theory for Women?, in: Larmour, David H. J./Miller, Paul Allen/Platter, Charles (eds), *Rethinking Sexuality. Foucault and Classical Antiquity*, Princeton, pp. 138–170

Richlin, Amy (2006), Sexuality in the Roman Empire, in: Potter, David Stone (ed), *A Companion to the Roman Empire*, Malden, pp. 327–353

Richlin, Amy (ed) (1991), *Pornography and Representation in Greece and Rome*, Oxford

Riddle, John M. (1992), *Contraception and Abortion from the Ancient World to the Renaissance*, Cambridge (MA)/London

Riddle, John M. (1996), Contraception and Early Abortion in the Middle Ages, in: Bullough, Vern L./Brundage, James A. (eds), *Handbook of Medieval Sexuality*, New York/London, pp. 261–278

Riddle, John M. (1997), *Eve's Herbs. A History of Contraception and Abortion in the West*, Cambridge, MA

Rider, Catherine (2006), *Magic and Impotence in the Middle Ages*, Oxford/New York

Rider, Catherine (2016), Men and Infertility in Late Medieval English Medicine, in: *Social History of Medicine* 29, 2, pp. 245–266

Riechers, Burckhardt (1999), Freundschaft und Anständigkeit. Leitbilder im Selbstverständnis männlicher Homosexueller in der frühen Bundesrepublik, in: Fachverband Homosexualität und Geschichte (ed), *Homosexualitäten in der Bundesrepublik Deutschland 1949 bis 1972* (=Invertito. Jahrbuch für die Geschichte der Homosexualitäten 1 (1999)), Hamburg, pp. 12–46

Riisøy, Anne Irene (2009), *Sexuality, Law and Legal Practice and the Reformation in Norway*, Leiden/Boston

Rijo, Delminda Miguéns (2017), Memórias da Casa Pia das Convertidas. Instituição, Espaços e Agentes face ao Problema da Prostituição em Lisboa (Séculos XVI-XX), in: *Revista de História da Sociedade e da Cultura* 17, pp. 129–153

Rimmerman, Craig A. (2002), *From Identity to Politics. The Lesbian and Gay Movements in the United States*, Philadelphia

Ringdal, Nils Johan (1997), *Verdens vanskeligste yrke. De prostituertes verdenshistorie*, Oslo

Rizzo, Domenico (2007), Öffentlichkeit und Schwulenpolitik seit dem Zweiten Weltkrieg, in: Aldrich, Robert (ed), *Gleich und anders. Eine globale Geschichte der Homosexualität*, Hamburg, pp. 197–221

Robb, Graham (2005), *Strangers. Homosexual Love in the Nineteenth Century*, New York

Roberts, Benjamin B./Groenendijk, Leendert F. (2004), Wearing Out a Pair of Fool's Shoes. Sexual Advice for Youth in Holland's Golden Age, in: *Journal of the History of Sexuality* 13, 2, pp. 139–157

Robin, Diana (2003), Courtesans, Celebrity and Print Culture in Venice. Tullia d'Aragona, Gaspara Stampa, and Veronica Franco, in: Smarr, Janet (ed), *Italian Women and the City*, Cranbury, pp. 38–59

Robinson, David M. (2006), *Closeted Writing and Lesbian and Gay Literature. Dlassical, Early Modern, Eighteenth-Century*, Aldershot

Robson, James (2013), *Sex and Sexuality in Classical Athens*, Edinburgh

Roby, Agathe (2017), De la Grande Abbaye au Château Vert: L'installation d'un nouveau bordel municipal à Toulouse au XVIe siècle, in: *Histoire urbaine* 49, 2, pp. 17–35

Rocke, Michael (2002), Gender and Sexual Culture in Renaissance Italy, in: Martin, John Jeffries (ed), *The Renaissance: Italy and Abroad*, New York, pp. 139–158
Rocke, Michael J. (1996), *Forbidden Friendships. Homosexuality and Male Culture in Renaissance Florence*, Oxford/New York
Rodríguez García, Magaly/Heerma van Voss, Lex/van Nederveen Meerkerk, Elise (eds) (2017), *Selling Sex in the City. A Global History of Prostitution, 1600s-2000s*, Leiden/Boston
Roelens, Jonas (2014), A Woman Like Any Other: Female Sodomy, Hermaphroditism and Witchcraft in Seventeenth-Century Bruges, in: *Journal of Women's History* 29, 4, pp. 11–34
Roelens, Jonas (2015), Visible Women: Female Sodomy in the Late Medieval and Early Modern Southern Netherlands (1400–1550), in: *Bijdragen en mededelingen betreffende de geschiedenis der Nederlanden* 130, 3, pp. 3–24
Roelens, Jonas (2018), Gossip, Defamation and Sodomy in the Early Modern Southern Netherlands, in: *Renaissance Studies* 32, 2, pp. 236–252
Roelens, Jonas (2019), Songs of Sodom: Singing about the Unmentionable Vice in the Early Modern Low Countries, in: *Journal of homosexuality* 66, 8, pp. 1126–1147
Rogers, Jack (2009), *Jesus, the Bible, and Homosexuality. Explode the Myths, Heal The Church*, Louisville
Roisman, Joseph (2014), Greek and Roman Ethnosexuality, in: Hubbard, Thomas K. (ed), *A Companion to Greek and Roman Sexualities*, New York, pp. 398–416
Rolker, Christof (2013), Der Hermaphrodit und seine Frau. Körper, Sexualität und Geschlecht im Spätmittelalter, in: *Historische Zeitschrift* 297, 3, pp. 593–620
Rolker, Christof (2015), Als ob sie ain mannlichen affect het: Hermaphroditismus in der Zimmer'schen Chronik, in: *Männlich-weiblich-zwischen*, September 13, 2015 (= http://intersex.hypotheses.org/676)
Rollo, David (2022), *Medieval Writings on Sex between Men: Peter Damian's Book of Gomorrah and Alain de Lille's The Plaint of Nature*, Leiden/Boston
Rollo-Koster, Joëlle (2002), From Prostitutes to Brides of Christ: The Avignonese Repenties in the Late Middle Ages, in: *Journal of Medieval & Early Modern Studies* 32, 1, pp. 110–144
Roper, Lyndal (1985), Discipline and Respectability. Prostitution and Reformation in Augsburg, in: *History Workshop Journal* 19, pp. 3–28
Roper, Lyndal (1989), *The Holy Household. Women and Morals in Reformation Augsburg*, Oxford
Roper, Lyndal (1991), Sexualutopien in der deutschen Reformation, in: Bachorski, Hans-Jürgen (ed), *Ordnung und Lust. Bilder von Liebe, Ehe und Sexualität in Spätmittelalter und Früher Neuzeit*, Trier, pp. 307–336
Roper, Lyndal (1994), *Oedipus and the Devil. Witchcraft, Sexuality and Religion in Early Modern Europe*, London/New York
Roper, Lyndal (1995a), *Das fromme Haus. Frauen und Moral in der Reformation*, Frankfurt a. M. et al.
Roper, Lyndal (1995b), *Ödipus und der Teufel. Körper und Psyche in der Frühen Neuzeit*, Frankfurt a. M.
Roper, Lyndal (2007), *Hexenwahn. Geschichte einer Verfolgung*, München
Roper, Lyndal (2016), *Der Mensch Martin Luther. Die Biographie*, Frankfurt a. M.

Rosario, Vernon A. (1997a), *The Erotic Imagination. French Histories of Perversity*, New York

Rosario, Vernon A. (ed) (1997b), *Science and Homosexualities*, New York/London

Roscoe, Will (1998), *Changing Ones. Third and Fourth Genders in Native North America*, New York

Rose, Melody (2008), *Abortion: A Documentary and Reference Guide*, Westport

Rosellini, Michèle (2020), Prose satirique / discours satyrique: l'intertexte de Lucien dans les dialogues français d'éducation érotique au XVIIe siècle, in: *Dans Dix-septième siècle* 286, 1, pp. 63–85

Rosenberg, Michael (2018), *Signs of Virginity: Testing Virgins and Making Men in Late Antiquity*, Oxford

Rosenkranz, Bernhard/Lorenz, Gottfried (2005), *Hamburg auf anderen Wegen. Die Geschichte des schwulen Lebens in der Hansestadt*, Hamburg

Rosenthal, Margaret F. (1992), *The Honest Courtesan: Veronica Franco, Citizen and Writer in Sixteenth-Century Venice*, Chicago

Rosenthal, Margaret F. (1993), Venetian Women Writers and Their Discontents, in: Turner, James Grantham (ed), *Sexuality and Gender in Early Modern Europe. Institutions, Texts, Images*, Cambridge, pp. 107–132

Rossiaud, Jacques (1984), Prostitution, Sexualität und Gesellschaft in den französischen Städten des 15. Jahrhunderts, in: Ariès, Philippe/Béjin, André/Foucault, Michel (eds), *Die Masken des Begehrens und die Metamorphosen der Sinnlichkeit. Zur Geschichte der Sexualität im Abendland*, Frankfurt a. M., pp. 97–120

Rossiaud, Jacques (1988), *Medieval Prostitution*, Oxford

Roth, Andreas (2008), Crimen Contra Naturam, in: Daston, Lorraine/Stolleis, Michael (ed), *Natural Law and Laws of Nature in Early Modern Europe: Jurisprudence, Theology, Moral and Natural Philosophy*, Aldershot, pp. 89–104

Roth, Carla (2017), Obscene Humour, Gender, and Sociability in Sixteenth-Century St Gallen, in: *Past and Present* 234, 1, pp. 39–70

Roth, Norman (1996), A Note on Research into Jewish Sexuality in the Medieval Period, in: Bullough, Vern L./Brundage, James A. (eds), *Handbook of Medieval Sexuality*, New York/London, pp. 309–318

Roth, Norman (2005), *Daily Life of the Jews in the Middle Ages*, Westport

Rouche, Michel (ed) (2000), *Mariage et sexualité au Moyen Age. Accord ou crise? Colloque international de Conques*, Paris

Rouillard, Linda Marie (2020), *Medieval Considerations of Incest, Marriage, and Penance*, Cham

Rousseau, George (2011), Sex, Medicine and Disease, in: Peakman, Julie (ed), *A Cultural History of Sexuality in the Enlightenment (=A Cultural History of Sexuality Vol. 4)*, Oxford/New York, pp. 133–158

Rousseau, Jean-Jacques (1905), *Die Bekenntnisse*, Berlin

Rousselle, Aline (1988), *Porneia. On Desire and the Body in Antiquity*, Oxford

RSV Revised Standard Version of the Bible (https://www.bible.com/versions/2020-rsv-revised-standard-version)

Rubin, Israel Netanel (2021), The Eunuch and the Baldhead: Sexuality in early Jewish-Christian Polemic, in: *The Review of Rabbinic Judaism: Ancient, Medieval and Modern* 24, 2, pp. 197–206

Rublack, Ulinka (1995), Viehisch, frech vnd onverschämpt. Inzest in Südwestdeutschland, ca. 1530–1700, in: Ulbricht, Otto (ed), *Von Huren und*

Rabenmüttern. Weibliche Kriminalität in der frühen Neuzeit, Köln/Weimar/Wien, pp. 171–213

Rublack, Ulinka (1998), *Magd, Metz' oder Mörderin. Frauen vor frühneuzeitlichen Gerichten*, Frankfurt a. M

Rublack, Ulinka (2012), Interior States and Sexuality in Early Modern Germany, in: Spector, Scott/Puff, Helmut/Herzog, Dagmar (eds), *After the History of Sexuality. German Genealogies With and Beyond Foucault*, Oxford/New York, pp. 43–62

Rüdiger, Jan (2020), *All the King's Women. Polygyny and Politics in Europe, 900–1250*, Leiden/Boston

Ruggiero, Guido (1985), *The Boundaries of Eros. Sex, Crime and Sexuality in Renaissance Venice*, New York

Ruggiero, Guido (2007), *Machiavelli in Love. Sex, Self, and Society in the Italian Renaissance*, Baltimore

Ruggiero, Guido (2010), Introduction. Hunting for Birds in the Italian Renaissance, in: Matthews-Grieco, Sara F. (ed), *Erotic Cultures of Renaissance Italy*, London/New York, pp. 1–16

Ruggiero, Guido (2011), Prostitution: Looking for Love, in: Talvacchia, Bette (ed), *A Cultural History of Sexuality in the Renaissance (=A Cultural History of Sexuality Vol. 3)*, Oxford/New York, pp. 137–156

Ründal, Erik O. (2002), Über Männlichkeit, Sexualität und Potenz in der Frühen Neuzeit, in: Jacobi, Günther H. (ed), *Praxis der Männergesundheit. Prävention, schulmedizinische Fakten, ganzheitlicher Zugang*, Stuttgart, pp. 46–52

Rupp, Leila J. (2007), Liebende Frauen in der Welt von heute, in: Aldrich, Robert (ed), *Gleich und anders. Eine globale Geschichte der Homosexualität*, Hamburg, pp. 223–247

Rupp, Leila J. (2009), *Sapphistries. A Global History of Love Between Women*, New York/London

Rushton, Cory James (2011), Sexual Variations, in: Evans, Ruth (ed), *A Cultural History of Sexuality in the Middle Ages (=A Cultural History of Sexuality Vol. 2)*, Oxford/New York, pp. 81–100

Rust, Paula C. (2001), Two Many and Not Enough. The Meanings of Bisexual Identities, in: *Journal of Bisexuality* 1, 1, pp. 31–69

Rydström, Jens (2003), *Sinners and Citizens. Bestiality and Homosexuality in Sweden, 1880–1950*, Chicago

Saar, Stefan Chr. (2002), *Ehe, Scheidung, Wiederheirat. Zur Geschichte des Ehe- und des Ehescheidungsrechts im Frühmittelalter (6. - 10. Jahrhundert)*, Münster et al.

Sabean, David Warren (1982), Unehelichkeit. Ein Aspekt sozialer Reproduktion kleinbäuerlicher Produzenten. Zur Analyse dörflicher Quellen um 1800, in: Berdahl, Robert et al. (eds), *Klassen und Kultur. Sozialanthropologische Perspektiven in der Geschichtsschreibung*, Frankfurt a. M., pp. 54–76

Sabean, David Warren (1998), *Kinship in Neckarhausen, 1700–1870*, Cambridge

Sabev, Orlin (2021), How to Manage the Unmanageable: Inconsistent Ottoman Strategies to Prevent Prostitution, in: *Turkish Historical Review* 12, 1, pp. 19–46

Said, Edward (1978), *Orientalism*, London

Salazar, Philippe-Joseph (2001), Rocco, Antonio, in: Aldrich, Robert F./Wotherspoon, Garry (eds), *Who's Who in Gay and Lesbian History. From Antiquity to World War II*, London, pp. 441–444

Salih, Sarah (2002), Sexual Identities. A Medieval Perspective, in: Betteridge, Tom (ed), *Sodomy in Early Modern Europe*, Manchester et al., pp. 112–130

Salih, Sarah (2011), Erotica, in: Evans, Ruth (ed), *A Cultural History of Sexuality in the Middle Ages (=A Cultural History of Sexuality Vol. 2)*, Oxford/New York, pp. 181–212

Salisbury, Joyce E. (1992), *Church Fathers, Independent Virgins*, London/New York

Salisbury, Joyce E. (2001), *Encyclopedia of Women in the Ancient World*, Santa Barbara

Salisbury, Joyce E. (2008), When Sex Stopped Being a Social Disease. Sex and the Dessert Fathers and Mothers, in: Harper, April/Proctor, Caroline (eds), *Medieval Sexuality. A Casebook*, New York, pp. 47–58

Salomon, Nanette (1997), Making a World of Difference. Gender Asymmetry, and the Greek Nude, in: Koloski-Ostrow, Olga/L. Lyons, Claire (eds), *Naked Truths. Women, Sexuality, and Gender in Classical Art and Archaeology*, London/New York, pp. 197–219

Salomon, Nanette (2000), Early Netherlandish Bordeeltjes and the Construction of Social „Realities", in: Wheelock, Arthur K./Seeff, Adele (eds), *The Public and Private in Dutch Culture of the Golden Age*, Newark, pp. 141–163

Salzmann, Christian G. (1785), *Ueber die heimlichen Sünden der Jugend*, Leipzig

Sansone, David (1988), *Greek Athletics and the Genesis of Sport*, Berkeley

Santore, Cathy (1991), Danaë: The Renaissance Courtesan's Alter Ego, in: *Zeitschrift für Kunstgeschichte* 54, 3, pp. 412–427

Santow, Gigi (1995), Coitus Interruptus and the Control of Natural Fertility, in: *Population Studies* 49, pp. 19–43

Sapsford, Tom (2022), *Performing the Kinaidos: Unmanly Men in Ancient Mediterranean Cultures*, Oxford

Sarasin, Philipp (2001), *Reizbare Maschinen. Eine Geschichte des Körpers, 1765–1914*, Frankfurt a. Main

Sariyannis, Marinos (2005), "Mob", "Scamps" and Rebels in 17th Century Istanbul: Some Remarks on Ottoman Social Vocabulary, in: *International Journal of Turkish Studies* 11, 1–2, pp. 1–15

Sariyannis, Marinos (2008), Prostitution in Ottoman Istanbul, Late Sixteenth–Early Eighteenth Century, in: *Turcica* 40, pp. 37–65

Sartorius, Michael (1994), Wider Gutmachung. Die versäumte Entschädigung der schwulen Opfer des Nationalsozialismus, in: Schulz, Christian/Sartorius, Michael (eds), *Paragraph 175. (abgewickelt). Homosexualität und Strafrecht im Nachkriegsdeutschland. Rechtsprechung, juristische Diskussionen und Reformen seit 1945*, Hamburg, pp. 88–128

Saslow, James M. (1986), *Ganymede in the Renaissance. Homosexuality in Art and Society*, New Haven/London

Saslow, James M. (1999), *Pictures and Passions. A History of Homosexuality in the Visual Arts*, New York

Saslow, James M. (2019), Gianantonio Bazzi, Called "Il Sodoma": Homosexuality in Art, Life, and History, in: Murray, Jacqueline/Terpstra, Nicholas (eds), *Sex, Gender and Sexuality in Renaissance Italy*, London, pp. 183–210

Satjukow, Silke/Gries, Rainer (2015), *Bankerte! Besatzungskinder in Deutschland nach 1945*, Frankfurt a. M./New York

Satlow, Michael (1995), *Tasting the Dish: Rabbinic Rhetorics of Sexuality*, Atlanta

Satlow, Michael L. (2001), *Jewish Marriage in Antiquity*, Princeton

Saunders, Corinne J. (2001), *Rape and Ravishment in the Literature of Medieval England*, Suffolk
Saunders, Corinne J. (2002), Classical Paradigms of Rape in the Middle Ages. Chaucer's Lucretia and Philomena, in: Deacy, Susan/Pierce, Karen F. (eds), *Rape in Antiquity. Sexual Violence in the Greek and Roman Worlds*, London, pp. 243–266
Saurer, Edith (1997), Geschlechterbeziehungen, Ehe und Illegitimität in der Habsburgermonarchie. Venetien, Niederösterreich und Böhmen im frühen 19. Jahrhundert, in: Ehmer, Josef/Hareven, Tamara K./Wall, Richard (eds), *Historische Familienforschung. Ergebnisse und Kontroversen. Michael Mitterauer zum 60. Geburtstag*, Frankfurt a. M./New York, pp. 123–156
Sautman, Francesca Canadé/Sheingor, Pamela (2001), Introduction. Charting the Field, in: Sautman, Francesca Canadé/Sheingorn, Pamela (eds), *Same-Sex Love and Desire among Women in the Middle Ages*, New York, pp. 1–48
Sawyer, Erin (1995), Celibate Pleasures. Masculinity, Desire, and Asceticism in Augustine, in: *Journal of the History of Sexuality* 6, 1, pp. 1–29
Scanlon, Thomas F. (2005), The Dispersion of Pederasty and the Athletic Revolution in Sixth-Century BC Greece, in: *Journal of Homosexuality* 49, 3–4, pp. 63–85
Schader, Heike (2004), *Virile, Vamps und wilde Veilchen. Sexualität, Begehren und Erotik in den Zeitschriften homosexueller Frauen in Berlin der 1920er Jahre*, Königstein i. Taunus
Scheer, Tanja S. (2009), Einführung, in: Scheer, Tanja S. (ed), *Tempelprostitution im Altertum. Fakten und Fiktionen*, Berlin, pp. 9–22
Scheidel, Walter (2007), *Epigraphy and Demography: Birth, Marriage, Family, and Death (=Princeton/Stanford Working Papers in Classics)*, Stanford
Schelling, Friedrich Wilhelm J. von (1799), *Erster Entwurf eines Systems der Naturphilosophie*, Jena/Leipzig
Schiefelbein, Dieter (1995), Wiederbeginn der juristischen Verfolgung homosexueller Männer in der Bundesrepublik Deutschland. Die Homosexuellenprozesse in Frankfurt a. M. 1950/1, in: *Zeitschrift für Sexualforschung* 5, H. 1, pp. 59–73
Schilling, Heinz (1994), Die Kirchenzucht im frühneuzeitlichen Europa in interkonfessionell vergleichender und interdisziplinärer Perspektive - Eine Zwischenbilanz, in: Schilling, Heinz (ed), *Kirchenzucht und Sozialdisziplinierung im frühneuzeitlichen Europa (=Beiheft 16 der Zeitschrift für Historische Forschung)*, Berlin, pp. 11–40
Schilling, Heinz (ed) (2002), *Kirchenzucht und Sozialdisziplinierung im frühneuzeitlichen Europa (Zeitschrift für historische Forschung, Beiheft 16)*, Berlin
Schipperges, Heinrich (2001), *Hildegard von Bingen*, München, 4th edn
Schleiner, Winfried (2008), Intrigues of Hermaphrodites and the Intercourse of Science with Erotica, in: Borris, Kenneth/Rousseau, George (eds), *The Sciences of Homosexuality in Early Modern Europe*, London/New York, pp. 247–267
Schlesier, Renate (1990), *Konstruktionen der Weiblichkeit bei Sigmund Freud. Zum Problem von Entmythologisierung und Remythologisierung in der psychoanalytischen Theorie*, Frankfurt a. M.
Schlicht, Alfred (2006), *Die Araber und Europa. 2000 Jahre gemeinsamer Geschichte*, Stuttgart
Schlieker, Lieselotte (2001), Humoristische Erotik in der italienischen Graphik des 16. Jahrhunderts. Die Götterliebschaften von Gian Jacopo Caraglio und Giulio Bonasone, Dissertation University Kiel

Schlierkamp, Petra (1984), Die Garconne, in: Eldorado. *Homosexuelle Frauen und Männer in Berlin, 1850–1950. Geschichte, Alltag und Kultur (Ausstellungskatalog)*, Berlin, pp. 169–179

Schlotheuber, Eva (2001), Nullum regimen difficulius et periculosius est regimine feminarum. Die Begegnung des Beichtvaters Frederik van Heilo mit den Nonnen in der Devotio moderna, in: Hamm, Berndt/Lentes, Thomas (eds), *Spätmittelalterliche Frömmigkeit zwischen Ideal und Praxis*, Tübingen, pp. 45–84

Schmale, Wolfgang (2003), *Geschichte der Männlichkeit in Europa (1450–2000)*, Wien

Schmidt, Ariadne (2020), *Prosecuting Women: A Comparative Perspective on Crime and Gender Before the Dutch Criminal Courts, c.1600-1810*, Leiden/Boston

Schmidt, Gunter (2004), Zur Sozialgeschichte jugendlichen Sexualverhaltens in der zweiten Hälfte des 20. Jahrhunderts, in: Claudia Bruns/Tilmann Walter (eds), *Von Lust und Schmerz. Eine Historische Anthropologie der Sexualität*, Köln, Weimar u. Wien, pp. 313–326

Schmidt, Gunter/Dekker, Arne/Matthiesen, Silja (2000), Sexualverhalten, in: Schmidt, Gunter (ed), *Kinder der sexuellen Revolution. Kontinuität und Wandel studentischer Sexualität 1966-1996. Eine empirische Untersuchung*, Giessen, pp. 39–67

Schmidt, Ondřej (2019), *John of Moravia between the Czech Lands and the Patriarchate of Aquileia (ca. 1345–1394)*, Boston

Schmieder, Carsten (2008), Martial und die "lasciva nomismata": Eine Bestandsaufnahme, in: *Hermes. Zeitschrift für klassische Philologie* 138, H. 2, pp. 250–254

Schmitt, Arno (2001–2002), Liwāṭ im Fiqh. Männliche Homosexualität?, in: *Journal of Arabic and Islamic Studies* 4, pp. 49–110

Schmitz, Winfried (2007), *Haus und Familie im antiken Griechenland*, München

Schnell, Rüdiger (1998), Geschlechtergeschichte, Diskursgeschichte und Literaturgeschichte. Eine Studie zu konkurrierenden Männerbildern in Mittelalter und Früher Neuzeit, in: Keller, Hagen/Meier, Christel (eds), *Frühmittelalterliche Studien. Jahrbuch des Instituts für Frühmittelalterforschung der Universität München Bd. 32*, Berlin/New York, 307–364

Schnell, Rüdiger (1999), Seelsorge und kanonistische Norm. Eine schwierige Vermittlung. Das Fallbeispiel "Ehefrau mit unehelichem Kind", in: Brinker-von der Heyde, Claudia/Largier, Niklaus (eds), *Homo medietas. Aufsätze zur Religiosität, Literatur und Denkformen des Menschen vom Mittelalter bis in die Neuzeit. Festschrift für Alois Maria Haas*, Bern et al., pp. 117–138

Schnell, Rüdiger (2002), *Sexualität und Emotionalität in der vormodernen Ehe*, Köln/Weimar/Wien

Schnell, Rüdiger (2013), Der queer turn in der Mediävistik. Ein kritisches Resümee, in: *Archiv für Kulturgeschichte 95*, pp. 31–68

Schnell, Rüdiger (2015), *Haben Gefühle eine Geschichte? Aporien einer "History of emotions"*, Göttingen

Schnell, Rüdiger (2017), Geschlechtscharaktere in Mittelalter und Moderne. Interdisziplinäre Überlegungen zur Natur/Kultur-Debatte, in: *Frühmittelalterliche Studien. Jahrbuch des Instituts für Frühmittelalterforschung der Universität Münster* 51, pp. 325–388

Schnitzler, Norbert (2009), Contra naturam. Sexuelle Devianz und christlich-jüdische Koexistenz im Mittelalter, in: Grenzmann, Ludger et al. (ed),

Wechselseitige Wahrnehmung der Religionen im Spätmittelalter und in der Frühen Neuzeit. Bd. 4, Berlin/Boston, pp. 251–291

Schnyder, Mirreille (2005), Erzählte Gewalt und die Gewalt des Erzählens. Gewalt im deutschen höfischen Roman, in: Braun, Manuel/Herberichs, Cornelia (eds), *Gewalt im Mittelalter. Realitäten - Imaginationen*, München, pp. 365–380

Schochow, Maximilian (2009), *Die Ordnung der Hermaphroditen-Geschlechter: Eine Genealogie des Geschlechtsbegriffs*, Berlin

Schofield, R. S./Wrigley, E. A. (1981), *The Population History of England 1541–1871. A Reconstruction*, Cambridge

Schoppmann, Claudia (1999), *Verbotene Verhältnisse. Frauenliebe, 1938–1945*, Berlin

Schorn-Schütte, Luise (1991), Gefährtin und Mitregentin. Zur Sozialgeschichte der evangelischen Pfarrfrau in der Frühen Neuzeit, in: Wunder, Heide/Vanja, Christina (eds), *Wandel der Geschlechterbeziehungen zu Beginn der Neuzeit*, Frankfurt a. M., pp. 109–153

Schröter, Michael (1981), Staatsbildung und Triebkontrolle. Zur gesellschaftlichen Regulierung des Sexualverhaltens vom 13. bis 16. Jahrhundert, in: *Amsterdams sociologisch tijdschrift* 8, 1, pp. 48–89

Schuller, Wolfgang (2008), *Die Welt der Hetären. Berühmte Frauen zwischen Legende und Wirklichkeit*, Stuttgart

Schultz, James A. (2006a), *Courtly Love, the Love of Courtliness, and the History of Sexuality*, Chicago

Schultz, James A. (2006b), Heterosexuality as a Threat to Medieval Studies, in: *Journal of the History of Sexuality* 15, 1, pp. 14–29

Schulz, Hans/Basler, Otto (1995), *Deutsches Fremdwörterbuch*, Berlin/New York, 2nd edn

Schuster, Beate (1995), *Die freien Frauen. Dirnen und Frauenhäuser im 15. und 16. Jahrhundert*, Frankfurt a. M.

Schuster, Peter (1992), *Das Frauenhaus. Städtische Bordelle in Deutschland 1350–1600*, Paderborn

Schuyf, Judith/Krouwel, Andre (1999), The Dutch Gay and Lesbian Movements. The Politics of Accommodation, in: Adam, Barry D./Duyvendak, Jan Willem/Krouwel, André (eds), *The Global Emergence of Gay and Lesbian Politics. National Imprints of a Worldwide Movement*, Philadelphia, pp. 158–183

Schwaibold, Matthias (1988), Mittelalterliche Bußbücher und sexuelle Normalität, in: *Ius Commune. Zeitschrift für Europäische Rechtsgeschichte* 15, pp. 107–133

Schwanitz, Dietrich (1995), Exklusion, Temporalisierung, Selbstreferenz. Soziokulturelle Aspekte der Entstehung von Individualität in systemtheoretischer Sicht, in: Bachorski, Jans-Jürgen/Röcke, Werner (eds), *Weltbildwandel. Selbstdeutung und Fremderfahrung im Epochenübergang vom Spätmittelalter zur Frühen Neuzeit*, Trier, pp. 179–202.

Sears, James T. (ed) (2005), *Youth, Education, and Sexualities. An International Encyclopedia*, Westport.

Seccombe, Wally (1993), *Weathering the Storm. Working-Class Families from the Industrial Revolution to the Fertility Decline*, London/New York

Sedgwick, Eve Kosofsky (1990), *Epistemology of the Closet*, Berkeley

Seidel Menchi, Silvana (2001), The Girl and the Hourglass: Periodization of Women's Lives in Western Preindustrial Societies, in: Schutte, Anne Jacobson (ed), *Time, Space, and Women's Lives in Early Modern Europe*, Kirksville, pp. 41–76

Seidel Menchi, Silvana (2016), Conjugal Experiments in Europe 1400–1800, in: Seidel Menchi, Silvana (ed), *Marriage in Europe 1400-1800*, Toronto, pp. 318–332

Seidler, Eduard (1993), 19. Jahrhundert. Zur Vorgeschichte des Paragraphen 218, in: Jütte, Robert (ed), *Geschichte der Abtreibung. Von der Antike bis zur Gegenwart*, München, pp. 120–139

Seidman, Steven (1997), *Difference Troubles. Queering Social Theory and Sexual Politics*, Cambridge

Seifert, Lewis C. (2001), Masculinity and Satires of "Sodomites" in France, 1600-1715, in: Merrick, Jeffrey/Sibalis, Michael (eds), *Homosexuality in French History and Culture* (=Journal of Homosexuality 41 (2001), 3/4), New York, pp. 37–52

Semerdjian, Elyse (2008), *Off the Straight Path: Illicit Sex, Law and Community in Ottoman Aleppo*, Syracuse

Sennis, Antonio (ed) (2016), *Cathars in Question*, York

Sergent, Bernard (1986), *L'Homosexualite initiatique dans l'Europe ancienne*, Paris

Shakespeare, William (2005), Venus and Adonis, in: William Shakespeare, *The Complete Works*, ed. by Stanley Wells et al., Oxford, 2nd edn

Shamgunova, Nailya (2021), Sodomy and Human Difference: Anglophone Conceptualisations of Ottoman Male Same-Sex Activity, c.1590–1700. Dissertation, Cambridge

Sharrock, Alison (2002), Ovid and the Diskurses of Love. The Amatory Works, in: Hardie, Philip R. (ed), *The Cambridge Companion to Ovid*, Cambridge, pp. 150–162

Shaw, Teresa M. (1998), *The Burden of the Flesh. Fasting and Sexuality in Early Christianity*, Minneapolis

Shoemaker, Stephen J. (2016), *Mary in Early Christian Faith and Devotion*, New Haven/London

Shorter, Edward (1975), *The Making of the Modern Family*, New York

Shorter, Edward (1980), Illegitimacy, Sexual Revolution, and Social Change in Modern Europe, in: Rotberg, Robert I./Rabb, Theodore K. (eds), *Marriage and Fertility. Studies in Interdisciplinary History*, Princeton, pp. 85–120

Shorter, Edward (1997), *Women's Bodies: A Social History of Women's Encounter With Health, Ill-Health, and Medicine*, New Brunswick/London, 2nd edn

Shorter, Edward (2005), *Written in the Flesh. A History of Desire*, Toronto

Shusterman, Richard (2021), *Ars Erotica: Sex and Somaesthetics in the Classical Arts of Love*, Cambridge

Sibalis, Michael (2007), Die männliche Homosexualität im Zeitalter der Aufklärung und Französischen Revolution, 1680-1850, in: Aldrich, Robert (ed), *Gleich und anders. Eine globale Geschichte der Homosexualität*, Hamburg, pp. 103–124

Sibalis, Michael D. (1996), The Regulation of Male Homosexuality in Revolutionary and Napoleonic France, 1789-1815, in: Merrick, Jeffrey/Ragan, Bryant T. Jr. (eds), *Homosexuality in Modern France*, New York/Oxford, pp. 80–101

Sibalis, Michael D. (2002), Homophobia, Vichy France, and the "Crime of Homosexuality" The Origins of the Ordinance of 6 August 1942, in: *GLQ: A Journal of Lesbian and Gay Studies* 8, 3, pp. 301–318

Sidhu, Nicole Nolan (2016), *Indecent Exposure: Gender, Politics, and Obscene Comedy in Middle English Literature*, Philadelphia
Siebenhüner, Kim (2006), *Bigamie und Inquisition in Italien 1600–1750*, Paderborn
Sieber, Andrea (2008), *Medeas Rache: Liebesverrat und Geschlechterkonflikte in Romanen des Mittelalters*, Köln/Wien
Siena, Kevin (2012), The Venereal Disease, 1500-1800, in: Fisher, Kate/Toulalan, Sarah (eds), *The Routledge History of Sex and the Body, 1500 to the Present*, Oxford et al., pp. 463–478
Siena, Kevin P. (2004), *Venereal Disease, Hospitals and the Urban Poor. London's "Foul Wards", 1600–1800*, Rochester
Sigal, Pete (2003), (Homo)Sexual Desire and Masculine Power in Colonial Latin America. Notes Toward an Integrated Analysis, in: Sigal, Pete (ed), *Infamous Desire. Male Homosexuality in Colonial Latin America*, Chicago, pp. 1–24
Sigal, Pete (2009), Latin America and the Challenge of Globalizing the History of Sexuality, in: *American Historical Review* 11, 4/5, pp. 1340–1353
Sigal, Pete (2011), Imagining Cihuacoatl. Masculine Rituals, Nahua Goddesses and the Texts of the Tlacuilos, in: Murphy, Kevin P./Spear, Jennifer M. (eds), *Historicising Gender and Sexuality*, Malden/Oxford, pp. 12–37
Sigal, Pete (2020), Franciscan Voyeurism in Sixteenth-Century New Spain, in: Sigal, Peter H./Tortorici, Zeb/Whitehead, Neil L. (eds), *Ethnopornography: Sexuality, Colonialism, and Archival Knowledge*, Durham/London, pp. 139–168
Signori, Gabriela (2011), *Von der Paradiesehe zur Gütergemeinschaft. Die Ehe in der mittelalterlichen Lebens- und Vorstellungswelt*, Frankfurt a. M.
Sigusch, Volkmar (2000), Uranität als Existenzweise. Karl Heinrich Ulrichs als Präzeptor der Homosexuellen- und Schwulenbewegung, in: Setz, Wolfram (ed), *Die Geschichte der Homosexualitäten und die schwule Identität an der Jahrtausendwende. Eine Vortragsreihe aus Anlaß des 175. Geburtstags von K.H. Ulrichs*, Berlin, pp. 65–92
Sigusch, Volkmar (2005), *Neosexualitäten. Über den kulturellen Wandel von Liebe und Perversion*, Frankfurt a. M./New York
Sigusch, Volkmar (2008), *Geschichte der Sexualwissenschaft*, Frankfurt a. M./New York
Sigusch, Volkmar (2013), *Sexualitäten. Eine kritische Theorie in 99 Fragmenten*, Franzfurt a. M./New York
Sillge, Ursula (1991), *Un-Sichtbare Frauen. Lesben und ihre Emanzipation in der DDR*, Berlin
Silver, Morris (2018), *Slave-Wives, Single Women and "Bastards" in the Ancient Greek World. Law and Economics Perspectives*, Oxford/Philadelphia
Silver, Morris (2019), *Sacred Prostitution in the Ancient Greek World: From Aphrodite to Baubo to Cassandra and Beyond*, Münster
Simon, Eckehard (1998), Carnival Obscenities in German Towns, in: Ziolkowski, Jan M. (ed), *Obscenity. Social Control and Artistic Creation in the European Middle Ages*, Leiden, pp. 193–213
Simon, William/Gagnon, John H. (2003), Sexual Scripts. Origins, Influences and Changes, in: *Qualitative Sociology* 26, 4, pp. 491–497
Simons, Patricia (2010), The Cultural History of Seigneur Dildo, in: Levy, Allison M. (ed), *Sex Acts in Early Modern Italy. Practice, Performance, Perversion, Punishment*, Farnham, pp. 77–91

Simons, Patricia (2011), *The Sex of Men in Premodern Europe: A Cultural History*, Cambridge/New York

Simons, Patricia (2019), Bodily Things and Brides of Christ: The Case of the Early Seventeenth-Century "Lesbian Nun" Benedetta Carlini, in: Murray, Jacqueline/Terpstra, Nicholas (eds), *Sex, Gender and Sexuality in Renaissance Italy*, London, pp. 97–124

Sinfield, Alan (1994), *The Wilde Century. Effeminacy, Oscar Wilde and the Queer Moment*, New York

Sissa, Giulia (2014), Phusis and Sensuality. Knowing the Body in Greek Erotic Culture, in: Hubbard, Thomas K. (ed), *A Companion to Greek and Roman Sexualities*, New York, pp. 265–281

Skinner, Marilyn B. (2005), *Sexuality in Greek and Roman Culture*, Oxford

Skinner, Marilyn B. (2014), Feminist Theory, in: Hubbard, Thomas K. (ed), *A Companion to Greek and Roman Sexualities*, New York, pp. 1–16

Sluijter, Eric Jan (2006), *Rembrandt and the Female Nude*, Amsterdam

Smith, Merril D. (2011), Sex, Religion, and the Law, in: Peakman, Julie (ed), *A Cultural History of Sexuality in the Enlightenment (=A Cultural History of Sexuality Vol. 4)*, Oxford/New York, pp. 107–132

Smith-Rosenberg, Caroll (1975), The Female World of Love and Ritual. Relations between Women in the Nineteenth-Century America, in: *Signs. Journal of Women in Culture and Society* 1, pp. 1–29

Smythe, Dion C. (1999), In Denial: Same-Sex Desire in Byzantium, in: James, Liz (ed), *Desire and Denial in Byzantium. Papers from the 31st Spring Symposium of Byzantine Studies, University of Sussex, Brighton, March 1997*, London/New York, pp. 139–148

Snyder, Jane M. (1997), *Lesbian Desire in the Lyrics of Sappho*, New York

Soble, Alan (ed) (2005), *Sex from Plato to Paglia. A Philosophical Encyclopedia*, 2 Bde., Westport

Soble, Alan (2009), A History of Erotic Philosophy, in: *Journal of Sex Research* 46 (2009), pp. 104–120

Soergel, Philip M. (ed) (2005), *Sexuality and Culture in Medieval and Renaissance Europe*, New York

Sogner, Sølvi (2003), Abortion, Birth Control, and Contraception: Fertility Decline in Norway, in: *The Journal of Interdisciplinary History* 34, 2 (Special Issue: Before the Pill: Preventing Fertility in Western Europe and Quebec), pp. 209–234

Solomon-Godeau, Abigail (1996), The Other Side of Venus. The Visual Economy of Feminine Display, in: de Grazia, Victoria/with Ellen Furlough (eds), *The Sex of Things. Gender and Consumption in Historical Perspective*, Berkeley/Los Angeles/London, pp. 113–149

Solórzano-Telechea, Jesús Ángel (2022), Sedom's Subjects: Sodomy and Urban Politics in the Late Medieval Kingdom of Castile, in: *The Medieval History Journal* 25, 1, pp. 60–92

Somerville, Siobhan (1994), Scientific Racism and the Emergence of the Homosexual Body, in: *Journal of the History of Sexuality* 5, 2, pp. 243–266

Søndergaard, Leif (2002), Combat between the Genders. Farce and Farcical Elements in the German Fastnachtspiel, in: Hüsken, Wim N. M./Schoell, Konrad/Søndergaard, Leif (eds), *Farce and Farcical Elements*, Amsterdam/New York, pp. 169–187

Sossau, Veronika (2012), "Dirnen" und "Gefährtinnen". Prostitution in der giechischen Antike, in: Müller, Florian M./Sossau, Veronika (eds), *Gefährtinnen. Vom Umgang mit Prostitution in der griechischen Antike und heute*, Innsbruck, pp. 9–36

Soyer, François (2012), *Ambiguous Gender in Early Modern Spain and Portugal: Inquisitors, Doctors and the Transgression of Gender Norms*, Leiden

Spanakis, Manolis (2022), "Fell in Love with an Anus": Sexual Fantasies for Young Male Bodies and the Pederastic Gaze in Rhianus' Epigrams, in: Serafim, Andreas/Kazantzidis, George/Demetriou, Kyriakos (eds), *Sex and the Ancient City: Sex and Sexual Practices in Greco-Roman Antiquity*, Berlin/Boston, pp. 89–109

Spearing, A. C. (1993), *The Medieval Poet as Voyeur. Looking and Listening in Medieval Love-Narratives*, Cambridge

Speitkamp, Winfried (1998), *Jugend in der Neuzeit: Deutschland vom 16. bis zum 20. Jahrhundert*, Göttingen

Spreitzer, Brigitte (1988), *Die stumme Sünde. Homosexualität im Mittelalter. Mit einem Textanhang*, Göppingen

Spurlin, William J. (2008), *Lost Intimacies. Rethinking Homosexuality under National Socialism*, New York et al.

Stafford, Emma (2022), Olive Oil, Dildos and Sandals: Greek Sex Toys Reassessed, in: Serafim, Andreas/Kazantzidis, George/Demetriou, Kyriakos (eds), *Sex and the Ancient City: Sex and Sexual Practices in Greco-Roman Antiquity*, Berlin/Boston, pp. 221–243

Stahl, Michael (2003), *Gesellschaft und Staat bei den Griechen. Archaische Zeit*, Paderborn/Wien

Stähli, Adrian (2001), Der Körper, das Begehren, die Bilder. Visuelle Strategien der Konstruktion einer homosexuellen Männlichkeit, in: von den Hoff, Ralf/Schmidt, Stefan (eds), *Konstruktionen von Wirklichkeit. Bilder im Griechenland des 5. und 4. Jahrhunderts v. Chr.*, Stuttgart, pp. 197–210

Stähli, Adrian (2006), Nacktheit und Körperinszenierung in Bildern der griechischen Antike, in: Schroer, Silvia (ed), *Images and Gender. Contributions to the Hermeneutics of Reading Ancient Art*, Freiburg i.Ü./Göttingen, pp. 209–227

Stahlmann, Ines (1997), *Der gefesselte Sexus. Weibliche Keuschheit und Askese im Westen des Römischen Reiches*, Berlin

Stannek, Antje (2001), *Telemachs Brüder. Die höfische Bildungsreise des 17. Jahrhunderts*, Frankfurt a. M.

Staples, Ariadne (2004), *From Good Goddess to Vestal Virgins: Sex and Category in Roman Religion*, London/New York, 2nd edn

Stayer, James M. (1980), Vielweiberei als "innerweltliche Askese". Neue Eheauffassungen in der Reformationszeit, in: *Mennonitische Geschichtsblätter NF* 32, pp. 24–41

Steakley, James (2007), *Anders als die Andern. Ein Film und seine Geschichte*, Hamburg

Steakley, James D. (2002), Selbstkritische Gedanken zur Mythologisierung der Homosexuellenverfolgung im Dritten Reich, in: Jellonnek, Burkhard/Lautmann, Rüdiger (eds), *Nationalsozialistischer Terror gegen Homosexuelle. Verdrängt und ungesühnt*, Paderborn et al., pp. 55–68

Stearns, Peter N. (2009), *Sexuality in World History*, New York

Steenblock, Maike (2013), *Sexualmoral und politische Stabilität. Zum Vorstellungszusammenhang in der römischen Literatur von Lucilius bis Ovid*, Berlin

Steidele, Angela (2004), *In Männerkleidern. Das verwegene Leben der Catharina Margaretha Linck alias Anastasius Rosenstengel, hingerichtet 1721. Biografie und Dokumentation*, Wien

Steigerwald, Jörn (2004), Encyclopédie der Sexualpathologie, in: Zaun, Stefanie/Watzke, Daniela/Steigerwald, Jörn (eds), *Imagination und Sexualität. Pathologien der Einbildungskraft im medizinischen Diskurs der frühen Neuzeit*, Frankfurt a. M., pp. 137–164

Stein, Claudia (2003), *Die Behandlung der Franzosenkrankheit in der Frühen Neuzeit am Beispiel Augsburgs*, Stuttgart

Steinberg, Sylvie (2020), Reading and Interpreting Accounts of Rape in the Criminal Archives (Early Modern Europe), in: *Clio. Women, Gender, History* 52, 2, pp. 163–193

Stephens, Walter (2002), *Demon Lovers. Witchcraft, Sex, and the Crisis of Belief*, Chicago

Stephens, Walter (2011), Sex, Popular Beliefs, and Culture: "In the Waie of Lecherie", in: Talvacchia, Bette (ed), *A Cultural History of Sexuality in the Renaissance (=A Cultural History of Sexuality Vol. 3)*, Oxford/New York, pp. 137–156

Sternke, René (2012), Juno die Schwanzsaugerin. Karl August Böttigers erotisch-antiquarische Studien, in: Sternke, René (ed), *Böttiger-Lektüren. Die Antike als Schlüssel zur Moderne. Mit Karl August Böttigers antiquarisch-erotischen Papieren im Anhang*, Berlin, pp. 209–338

Sternweiler, Andreas (1993), *Die Lust der Götter. Homosexualität in der italienischen Kunst. Von Donatello zu Caravaggio*, Berlin

Sternweiler, Andreas (1997), Die Freundschaftsbünde - Eine Massenbewegung, in: Schwules Museum Berlin (ed), *Goodbye to Berlin? 100 Jahre Schwulenbewegung. Eine Ausstellung des Schwulen Museums und der Akademie der Künste*, Berlin, pp. 95–104

Stewart, Alan (1997), *Close Readers. Humanism and Sodomy in Early Modern England*, Princeton

Stewart, Chuck (ed) (2010), *The Greenwood Encyclopedia of Lgbt Issues Worldwide*, 2 Bde., Westport

Stockhorst, Stefanie (2004), Offene Obszönität. Bedeutungsangebote der Geschlechtsdarstellungen profaner Tragezeichen im kulturellen Kontext, in: Winkelman, Johan H./Wolf, Gerhard (eds), *Erotik, aus dem Dreck gezogen*, Amsterdam/New York, pp. 215–235

Stofferahn, Steven A. (2017), Lucky Bastards: Illegitimacy and Opportunity in Carolingian Europe, in: *The Heroic Age: A Journal of Early Medieval Northwestern* 17

Stolberg, Michael (2000), An Unmanly Vice. Self-Pollution, Anxiety, and the Body in the Eighteenth Century, in: *Social History of Medicine* 13, 1, pp. 1–21

Stolberg, Michael (2001), Menstruation and Sexual Difference in Early Modern Medicine, in: Howie, Gillian/Shail, Andrew (eds), *Menstruation: A Cultural History*, München, pp. 90–101

Stolberg, Michael (2003a), A Woman Down to Her Bones. The Anatomy of Sexual Difference in the Sixteenth and Early Seventeenth Centuries, in: *Isis* 94, pp. 274–299

Stolberg, Michael (2003b), The Crime of Onan and the Laws of Nature. Religious and Medical Discourses on Masturbation in the Late Seventeenth and Early Eighteenth centuries, in: *Paedagogica Historica* 39, 6, pp. 701–717

Stoler, Ann Laura (2002), *Carnal Knowledge and Imperial Power. Race and the Intimate in Colonial Rule*, Berkeley
Stolte, Bernard (1999), Desires Denied: Marriage, Adultery and Divorce in Early Byzantine Law, in: James, Liz (ed), *Desire and Denial in Byzantium. Papers from the 31st Spring Symposium of Byzantine Studies, University of Sussex, Brighton, March 1997*, London/New York, pp. 77–86
Stone, Ken (2001), Lovers and Raisin Cakes. Food, Sex, and Divine Insecurity in Hosea, in: Stone, Ken (ed), *Queer Commentary and the Hebrew Bible*, London/New York, pp. 116–139
Stone, Lawrence (1977), *The Family, Sex and Marriage in England, 1500–1800*, London
Storey, Tessa (2004), Clothing Courtesans: Fabrics, Signals and Experiences, in: Richardson, Catherine (ed), *Clothing Culture, 1350–1650*, Burlington, pp. 95–108
Storey, Tessa (2008), *Carnal Commerce in Counter-Reformation Rome*, Cambridge
Stow, Kenneth R. (1992), *Alienated Minority. The Jews of Medieval Latin Europe*, Cambridge/Harvard
Strayer, Brian E. (1992), *Lettres de Cachet and Social Control in the Ancien Regime, 1659–1789*, New York et al.
Strickland, Debra Higgs (2003), *Saracens, Demons, & Jews: Making Monsters in Medieval Art*, Princeton
Stroh, Wilfried (2000), Sexualität und Obszönität in römischer „Lyrik", in: Stemmler, Theo/Horlacher, Stephan (eds), *Sexualität im Gedicht. 11. Kolloquium der Forschungsstelle für europäische Lyrik*, Mannheim, pp. 11–49
Strong, Anise K. (2007), Clodia, in: Howell, James W. (ed), *The Greenwood Encyclopedia of Love, Courtship, and Sexuality through History, Vol. 1: The Ancient World*, Westport, pp. 94–95
Strong, Anise K. (2016), *Prostitutes and Matrons in the Roman World*, New York
Stukenbrock, Karin (1993), Das Zeitalter der Aufklärung. Kindsmord, Fruchtabtreibung und medizinische Policey, in: Jütte, Robert (ed), *Geschichte der Abtreibung. Von der Antike bis zur Gegenwart*, München, pp. 91–119
Stumpp, Bettina Eva (2001), *Prostitution in der römischen Antike*, Berlin
Sturma, Michael (2002), *South Sea Maidens. Western Fantasy and Sexual Politics in the South Pacific*, Westport/London
Suárez Müller, Fernando (2004), *Skepsis und Geschichte: das Werk Michel Foucaults im Lichte des absoluten Idealismus*, Würzburg
Suetonius (2009), *The Twelve Ceasars*, trans. by Alexander Thomson, ed. by T. Forester
Sullivan, Margaret A. (2000), The Witches of Dürer and Hans Baldung Grien, in: *Renaissance Quarterly* 53, pp. 332–401
Surtees, Allison/Dyer, Jennifer (2020), Introduction: Queer Classics, in: Surtees, Allison/Dyer, Jennifer (eds), *Exploring Gender Diversity in the Ancient World*, Edinburgh, pp. 1–25
Sutton, Robert F. (1992), Pornography and Persuasion in Attic Pottery, in: Richlin, Amy (ed), *Pornography and Representation in Greece and Rome*, Oxford, pp. 3–35
Swancutt, Diana M. (2004), Sexy Stoics and the Rereading of Romans 1.18-2.16, in: Levine, Amy-Jill (ed), *A Feminist Companion to Paul*, London, pp. 42–73
Swancutt, Diana M. (2006), Sexing the Pauline Body of Christ. Scriptural "Sex" in the Context of the American Christian Culture War, in: Burrus, Virginia/Keller,

Catherine (eds), *Toward a Theology of Eros. Transfiguring Passion at the Limits of Discipline*, New York, pp. 65–98

Swancutt, Diana M. (2007), Still Before Sexuality. "Greek" Androgyny, the Roman Imperial Politics of Masculinity and the Roman Invention of the Tribas, in: Penner, Todd C./Vander, Caroline (eds), *Mapping Gender in Ancient Religious Discourses*, Leiden, pp. 11–61

Symonds, John Addington (1901), *A Problem in Greek Ethics. Being an Inquiry into the Phenomenon of Sexual Inversion*, London

Szabari, Antónia (2021), From Panurge to Pan: Rabelais's Fictions of Undiplomatic Diplomacy and the Ambassador's Pleasure, in: Frei, Peter/Labère, Nelly (eds), *Obscene Means in Early Modern French and European Print Culture and Literature*, Milton, pp. 161–178

Szeghyová, Blanka (2019), Fornicatrices, Scortatrices et Meretrices Diabolares: Disciplining Women in Early Modern Hungarian Towns, in: Mielke, Christopher/Znorovsky, Andrea-Bianka (eds), *Same Bodies, Different Women: "Other" Women in the Middle Ages and the Early Modern Period*, Budapest, pp. 169–194

Szöllösi-Janze, Margit (1997), Notdurft - Bedürfnis. Historische Dimensionen eines Begriffswandels, in: *Geschichte in Wissenschaft und Unterricht* 48, pp. 653–673

Szreter, Simon (1999), Falling Fertility and Changing Sexualities in Europe since c. 1850. A Comparative Survey of National Demographic, in: Eder, Franz X./Hall, Lesley A./Hekma, Gert (eds), *Sexual Cultures in Europe. Themes in Sexuality*, Manchester/New York, pp. 159–194

Tacitus (1906), *The Anales of Tacitus. Book I to VI*, trans. by Aubrey V. Symonds, London

Taeger, Angela (1998), Die Karriere von Sodomiten in Paris während des 18. Jahrhunderts, in: Schmale, Wolfgang (ed), *MannBilder. Ein Lese- und Quellenbuch zur historischen Männerforschung*, Berlin, pp. 113–130

Taeger, Angela (1999), *Intime Machtverhältnisse. Moralstrafrecht und administrative Kontrolle der Sexualität im ausgehenden Ancien régime*, München

Talvacchia, Bette (1999), *Taking Positions. On the Erotic of Renaissance Culture*, Princeton

Talvacchia, Bette (2011a), Introduction: The Look and Sound of Sexuality in the Renaissance, in: Talvacchia, Bette (ed), *A Cultural History of Sexuality in the Renaissance (=A Cultural History of Sexuality Vol. 3)*, Oxford/New York, pp. 1–34

Tamagne, Florence (2006), *A History of Homosexuality in Europe. Vol. I&II: Berlin, London, Paris 1919–1939*, New York

Tamagne, Florence (2007), Das homosexuelle Zeitalter, 1870-1940, in: Aldrich, Robert (ed), *Gleich und anders. Eine globale Geschichte der Homosexualität*, Hamburg, pp. 167–195

Tamagne, Florence (2011), Homosexuality, in: Hekma, Gert (ed), *A Cultural History of Sexuality in the Modern Age (=A Cultural History of Sexuality Vol. 6)*, Oxford/New York, pp. 49–78

Tanner, Ralph (2005), *Sex, Sünde, Seelenheil. Die Figur des Pfaffen in der Märenliteratur und ihr historischer Hintergrund (1200 - 1600)*, Würzburg

Tartakoff, Paola (2015), Testing Boundaries: Jewish Conversion and Cultural Fluidity in Medieval Europe, c. 1200-1391, in: *Speculum* 90, 3, pp. 728–762

Tasioulas, Jacqueline A. (2011), Sex, Medicine and Disease, in: Evans, Ruth (ed), *A Cultural History of Sexuality in the Middle Ages (=A Cultural History of Sexuality Vol. 2)*, Oxford/New York, pp. 119–138

Taube, Christine (2013), Literarische Amazonenbilder der Antike, in: Schubert, Charlotte/Weiß, Alexander (eds), *Amazonen zwischen Griechen und Skythen. Gegenbilder in Mythos und Geschichte*, Berlin/Boston, pp. 39–56

Taylor, Chloe (ed) (2016), *The Routledge Guidebook to Foucault's The History of Sexuality*, London

Taylor, Rabun (1997), Two Pathic Subcultures in Ancient Rome, in: *Journal of the History of Sexuality* 7, 3, pp. 319–371

Teige, Ola (2020), En unevnelig synd: Rettssaken mot Aron Åsulsen i 1693 og rettsforfølgelsen av homoseksuelle handlinger i Norge i tidlig nytid, in: *Historisk tidsskrift* 99, 4, pp. 266–285

Tentler, Thomas N. (1977), *Sin and Confession on the Eve of the Reformation*, Princeton

Terpstra, Nicholas (2010), *Lost Girls: Sex and Death in Renaissance Florence*, Baltimore

Thauvette, Chantelle (2012), Defining Early Modern Pornography: The Case of Venus and Adonis, in: *Journal for Early Modern Cultural Studies* 12, 1, pp. 26–48

Thauvette, Chantelle (2016), Sexual Education and Erotica in the Popular Midwifery Manuals of Thomas Raynalde and Nicholas Culpeper, in: Moulton, Ian Frederick (ed), *Eroticism in the Middle Ages and the Renaissance: Magic, Marriage, and Midwifery*, Turnhout, pp. 151–168

Théry-Astruc, Julien (2016), The Heretical Dissidence of the "Good Men" in the Albigeois (1276–1329): Localism and Resistance to Roman Clericalism, in: Sennis, Antonio (ed), *Cathars in Question*, York, pp. 79–111

Thiel, John E. (2010), Augustine on Eros, Desire, and Sexuality, in: Kamitsuka, Margaret D. (ed), *The Embrace of Eros. Bodies, Desires, and Sexuality in Christianity*, Minneapolis, pp. 67–82

Thøfner, Margit (2004), Helena Fourment's Het Pelsken, in: *Art History* 27, 1, pp. 1–33

Thomas, Keith (1978), The Puritans and Adultery. The Act of 1650 Reconsidered, in: *Puritans and Revolutionaries: Essays in Seventeenth-Century History Presented to Christopher Hill*, New York, pp. 257–281

Thommen, Lukas (2007), *Antike Körpergeschichte*, Zürich

Thompson, Roger (1977), *Unfit for Modest Ears. A Study of Pornographic, Obscene and Bawdy Works Written or Published in England in the Second Half of the Seventeenth Century*, London

Thompson, Victoria (1996), Creating Boundaries. Homosexuality and the Changing Social Order in France, 1830-1870, in: Merrick, Jeffrey/Ragan, Bryant T. Jr. (eds), *Homosexuality in Modern France*, New York/Oxford, pp. 102–127

Thornton, Bruce S. (1997), *Eros. The Myth of Ancient Greek Sexuality*, Boulder

Thorp, John (1992), The Social Construction of Homosexuality, in: *Phoenix* 46, pp. 54–61

Thumiger, Chiara (2022), Clitoridectomy in Ancient Greco-Roman Medicine and the Definition of Sexual Intercourse, in: Serafim, Andreas/Kazantzidis, George/Demetriou, Kyriakos (eds), *Sex and the Ancient City: Sex and Sexual Practices in Greco-Roman Antiquity*, Berlin/Boston, pp. 143–171

Tiersch, Claudia (2013), Von den Gründen, eine Amazone zu besiegen. Bezähmung des gefahrvoll Weiblichen?, in: Schubert, Charlotte/Weiß, Alexander (eds), *Amazonen zwischen Griechen und Skythen. Gegenbilder in Mythos und Geschichte*, Berlin/Boston, pp. 39–56

Tinagli, Paola (1997), *Women in Italian Renaissance Art: Gender, Representation, Identity*, Frankfurt a. M.

Tissot, Samuel August D. (1760), *Versuch von denen Krankheiten, welche aus der Selbstbefleckung entstehen*, Frankfurt/Leipzig

Tobin, Robert D. (2006), Faust's Transgressions. Male-Male Desire in Early Modern Germany, in: O'Donnell, Katherine/O'Rourke, Michael (eds), *Queer Masculinities. Siting Same-Sex Desire in the Early Modern World*, Basingstoke/New York, pp. 17–36

Tommasi, Chiara O. (2017), Cross-Dressing as Discourse and Symbol in Late Antique Religion and Literature, in: Campanile, Domitilla et al. (eds), *TransAntiquity: Cross-dressing and Transgender Dynamics in the Ancient World*, London, pp. 121–133

Tortorici, Zeb (2018), *Sins against Nature: Sex and Archives in Colonial New Spain*, Durham

Tougher, Shaun (2021), *The Roman Castrati. Eunuchs in the Roman Empire*, London/New York

Toulalan, Sarah (2007), *Imagining Sex. Pornography and Bodies in Seventeenth-Century England*, Oxford et al.

Toulalan, Sarah (2012), Age to Great, or to Little, Doeth Let Conception. Bodies, Sex and Life Cycle, 1500-1750, in: Fisher, Kate/Toulalan, Sarah (eds), *The Routledge History of Sex and the Body, 1500 to the Present*, Oxford et al., pp. 279–295

Toulalan, Sarah (2014), Is He a Licentious Lewd Sort of a Person? Constructing the Child Rapist in Early Modern England, in: *Journal of the History of Sexuality* 23, 1, pp. 21–52

Toulalan, Sarah (2017), Child Victims of Rape and Sexual Assault: Compromised Chastity, Marginalized Lives?, in: Spicer, Andrew/Crawshaw, Jane L. Stevens (eds), *The Place of the Social Margins, 1350–1750*, New York/Abingdon, pp. 181–202

Tracy, David (2005), The Divided Consciousness of Augustine on Eros, in: Bartsch, Shadi/Bartscherer, Thomas (eds), *Erotikon. Essays on Eros, Ancient and Modern*, Chicago, pp. 91–106

Trapp, Wilhelm (2003), *Der schöne Mann: Zur Ästhetik eines unmöglichen Körpers*, Berlin

Traub, Valerie (2002), *The Renaissance of Lesbianism in Early Modern England*, Cambridge et al.

Traub, Valerie (2003), Die (In)Signifikanz von "lesbischem" Begehren im England der frühen Neuzeit, in: Kraß, Andreas (ed), *Queer Denken. Queer Studies*, Frankfurt a. M., pp. 298–323

Traub, Valerie (2007), The Present Future of Lesbian Historiography, in: Haggerty, George/McGarry, Molly (eds), *A Companion to Lesbian, Gay, Bisexual, Transgender, and Queer Studies*, Maiden, pp. 124–145

Traub, Valerie (2008), The Past Is a Foreign Country? The Times and Spaces of Islamicate Sexuality Studies, in: Babayan, Kathryn/Najmabadi, Afsaneh (eds), *Islamicate Sexualities. Translations Across Temporal Geographies of Desire*, Harvard, pp. 1–40

Traub, Valerie (2016a), History in the Present Tense: Feminist Theories, Spatialized Epistemologies, and Early Modern Embodiment, in: Wiesner, Merry E. (ed), *Mapping Gendered Routes and Spaces in the Early Modern World*, London/ New York, pp. 15–53

Traub, Valerie (2016b), *Thinking Sex with the Early Moderns*, Philadelphia

Treggiari, Susan (1991), *Roman Marriage. Iusti coniuges from the Time of Cicero to the Time of Ulpian*, Oxford

Trepp, Anne-Charlott (1996), *Sanfte Männlichkeit und selbständige Weiblichkeit. Frauen und Männer im Hamburger Bürgertum zwischen 1770 und 1840*, Göttingen

Trepp, Anne-Charlott (2000), Emotion und bürgerliche Sinnstiftung oder die Metaphysik des Gefühls: Liebe am Beginn des bürgerlichen Zeitalters, in: Hettling, Manfred/Hoffmann, Stefan-Ludwig (eds), *Der bürgerliche Wertehimmel. Innenansichten des 19. Jahrhunderts*, Göttingen, pp. 23–56

Trepp, Anne-Charlott (2001), Liebe - Erlebte Emotion und gesellschaftliche Wertsetzung. Geschlechterbeziehungen im 18. und beginnenden 19. Jahrhundert, in: *Sozialwissenschaftliche Informationen* 30, 3, pp. 14–22

Trepp, Anne-Charlott (2002), Gefühl oder kulturelle Konstruktion? Überlegungen zur Geschichte der Emotionen, in: *Kulturen der Gefühle in Mittelalter und Früher Neuzeit* (=Querelles Jahrbuch 7 (2002)), Stuttgart et al., pp. 86–103

Trepp, Anne-Charlott (2014), Luther 1525. Vom "feisten Doktor", von brünstigen Jungfrauen und toten Bauern, in: Jendorff, Alexander/Pühringer, Andrea (eds), *Pars pro toto. Historische Miniaturen zum 75. Geburtstag von Heide Wunder*, Neustadt an der Aisch, pp. 299–310

Trexler, Richard C. (1981), La prostitution florentine au XVe siècle. Patronages et clientèle, in: *Annales E.S.C.* 36, pp. 983–1015

Trexler, Richard C. (1995), *Sex and Conquest. Gendered Violence, Political Order and the European Conquest of the Americas*, Cambridge

Trexler, Richard C. (2003), Gender Subordination and Political Hierarchy in Pre-Hispanic America, in: Sigal, Pete (ed), *Infamous Desire. Male Homosexuality in Colonial Latin America*, Chicago, pp. 70–101

Trinks, Stefan (2013), Sheela-na-gig Again. The Birth of a New Style from the Spirit of Pornography, in: Maes Hans (ed), *Pornographic Art and the Aesthetics of Pornography*, New York, pp. 161–182

Trog, Hans (ed) (2016), *Desiderius Erasmus von Rotterdam. Gespräche des Erasmus (Ausgewählt, übersetzt und eingeleitet von Hans Trog)*, Berlin

Trovesi, Andrea (2020), Warm, Blue and Bulgarian: The Development and Diffusion of Three Expressions to Denote a "Male Homosexual" in Central and Eastern European Languages, in: Zavrl, Andrej/Sosič, Alojzija Zupan (eds), *Go East!: LGBTQ+ Literature in Eastern Europe / Zbornik prispevkov s konference: Na vzhod! LGBTQ+ književnost v vzhodni Evropi*, Ljubljana, pp. 121–128

Trumbach, Randolph (1998), *Sex and the Gender Revolution. Heterosexuality and the Third Gender in Enlightenment London*, Chicago

Trumbach, Randolph/Hekma, Gert/Oosterhuis, Harry (1998), Die Entstehung der Homo- und der Heterosexuellen. Ein Gespräch, in: *Österreichische Zeitschrift für Geschichtswissenschaften* 9, 3, pp. 425–436

Tsoumpra, Natalia (2020), More Than a Sex-Strike: A Case of Medical Pathology in Aristophanes' Lysistrata, in: *Classical Journal* 116, 1, pp. 1–20

Tuchen, Birgit (2003), *Öffentliche Badhäuser in Deutschland und der Schweiz im Mittelalter und der frühen Neuzeit*, Petersberg

Turcan, Robert (2001), *The Gods of Ancient Rome: Religion in Everyday Life from Archaic to Imperial Times*, New York/London

Turner, David M. (2004), *Fashioning Adultery: Gender, Sex and Civility in England, 1660–1740*, Cambridge

Turner, James G. (2002), *Libertines and Radicals in Early Modern London. Sexuality, Politics, and Literary Culture, 1630–1685*, New York

Turner, James G. (2003), *Schooling Sex. Libertine Literature and Erotic Education in Italy, France, and England, 1534–1685*, Oxford

Turner, Wendy J. (2018), The Leper and the Prostitute: Forensic Examination of Rape in Medieval England, in: Turner, Wendy J./Lee, Christina (eds), *Trauma in Medieval Society*, Boston, pp. 122–147

Ulbricht, Otto (1990), *Kindsmord und Aufklärung in Deutschland*, München

Undheim, Sissel (2018), *Borderline Virginities: Sacred and Secular Virgins in Late Antiquity*, London

Ussel, Jos van (1970), *Sexualunterdrückung. Geschichte der Sexualfeindschaft*, Reinbek bei Hamburg

Välimäki, Mari (2020), Agency of Sons, Mothers and Fathers. Family Response to Son's Fornication in Seventeenth-Century Sweden, in: *Ennen ja Nyt: Historian Tietosanomat* 20, 3, pp. 24–42

Valverde Castro, Rosario (2020), La condena legal de la homosexualidad masculina en el reino visigodo de Toledo, in: *Studia historica. Ha. Antiqua* (Ediciones Universidad de Salamanca) 38, pp. 273–307

Van Arsdall, Anne (2002), *Medieval Herbal Remedies: The Old English Herbarium and Anglo-Saxon Medicine*, New York/London

van Bavel, Jan (2001), Family Control, Bridal Pregnancy, and Illegitimacy. An Event History Analysis in Leuven, Belgium, 1846-1856, in: *Social Science History* 25, 3, pp. 449–479

van de Pol, Lotte (2006), *Der Bürger und die Hure. Das sündige Gewerbe im Amsterdam der Frühen Neuzeit*, Frankfurt a. M. et al.

van der Heijden, Manon/Schmidt, Ariadne/Vermeesch, Griet (2021), Illegitimate Parenthood in Early Modern Europe, in: *The History of the Family* 26, 1, pp. 1–10

van der Meer, Theo (1999), Medieval Prostitution and the Case of a (Mistaken?) Sexual Identity, in: *Journal of Women's History* 11, 2, pp. 178–185

van Eickels, Klaus (2003), Kuss und Kinngriff, Umarmung und verschränkte Hände. Zeichen personaler Bindung und ihre Funktion in der symbolischen Kommunikation des Mittelalters, in: Martschukat, Jürgen/Patzold, Steffen (eds), *Geschichtswissenschaft und "performative turn"*, Köln/Wien, pp. 133–159

van Eickels, Klaus (2004), Tender Comrades. Gesten männlicher Freundschaft und die Sprache der Liebe im Mittelalter, in: *Invertito. Jahrbuch zur Geschichte der Homosexualitäten* 6, pp. 9–49

van Houts, Elisabeth (2019), *Married Life in the Middle Ages, 900–1300*, Oxford

Van Tine, R. Jarrett (2018), Castration for the Kingdom and Avoiding the αἰτία of Adultery (Matthew 19:10–12), in: *Journal of Biblical Literature* 137, 2, pp. 399–418

van Zanden, Jan Luiten/De Moor, Tine/Carmichael, Sarah (2019), *Capital Women: The European Marriage Pattern, Female Empowerment and Economic Development in Eastern Europe 1300–1800*, Oxford

Varone, Antonio (2002), *Erotica Pompeiana. Love Inscriptions on the Walls of Pompeii*, Rom, 2nd edn
Vattuone, Riccardo (2004), *Il mostro e il sapiente. Studi sull' erotica greca*, Bologna
Venette, Nicoulai (1738), *Abhandlung von Erzeugung des Menschen*, Königsberg/Leipzig
Venjakob, Judith (2012), Albrecht Dürers "Die Hexe", um 1500, in: *@KIH-eSkript. Interdisziplinäre Hexenforschung Online* 4, 4, pp. 46–78
Verdon, Jean (1996), *Le plaisir au Moyen Âge*, Paris
Verhaeghe, Paul (2003), *Liebe in Zeiten der Einsamkeit. Drei Essays über Begehren und Trieb*, Wien
Versluis, Arthur (2008), *The Secret History of Western Sexual Mysticism, Sacred Practices and Spiritual Marriage*, Rochester
Verstraete, Beert C./Provencal, Vernon L. (2006), Introduction, in: Verstraete, Beert C./Provencal, Vernon L. (eds), *Same-Sex Desire and Love in Greco-Roman Antiquity and in the Classical Tradition of the West*, New York/Binghamton, 1–12
Viazzo, Pier Paolo (1989), *Upland Communities. Environment, Population and Social Structure in the Alps since the 16th Century*, Cambridge
Vicinus, Martha (2004), *Intimate Friends. Women Who Loved Women, 1778–1928*, Chicago
Vidal, Fernando (2004), Nymphomania and the Gendering of the Imagination in the Eighteenth Century, in: Zaun, Stefanie/Watzke, Daniela/Steigerwald, Jörn (eds), *Imagination und Sexualität. Pathologien der Einbildungskraft im medizinischen Diskurs der frühen Neuzeit*, Frankfurt a. M., pp. 165–192
Vigarello, Georges (2001), *A History of Rape. Sexual Violence in France from the 16th to the 20th Century*, Cambridge
Vihervalli, Ulriika (2022), Wartime Rape in Late Antiquity: Consecrated Virgins and Victim Bias in the Fifth-Century West, in: *Early Medieval Europe* 30, 1, pp. 3–19
Villa, Paula-Irene (2006), *Sexy Bodies. Eine soziologische Reise durch den Geschlechtskörper*, Opladen, 3nd edn
Villa, Paula-Irene/Alkemeyer, Thomas (2010), Somatischer Eigensinn? Kritische Anmerkungen zu Diskurs- und Gouvernementalitätsforschung aus subjektivationstheoretischer und praxeologischer Perspektive, in: Angermüller, Johannes/van Dyk, Silke (eds), *Diskursanalyse meets Gouvernementalitätsforschung. Perspektiven auf das Verhältnis von Subjekt, Sprache, Macht und Wissen*, Frankfurt a. M./New York, pp. 315–336
Vocelka, Karl (1994), Überlegungen zum Phänomen der "Sozialdisziplinierung" in der Habsburgermonarchie, in: Erlach, Daniela/Reisenleitner, Markus/Vocelka, Karl (eds), *Privatisierung der Triebe. Sexualität in der frühen Neuzeit*, Frankfurt a. M. et al., pp. 31–45
Vogel, Samuel Gottlieb (1786), *Unterricht für Eltern, Erzieher und Kinderaufseher, wie das unglaublich gemeine Laster der zerstörenden Selbstbefleckung am sichersten zu entdecken, zu verhüten und zu heilen sei*, Stendal
von Germeten, Nicole (2021), Old Empires, New Perspectives: Sexuality in the Spanish and Portuguese Americas, in: Schields, Chelsea/Herzog, Dagmar (eds), *The Routledge Companion to Sexuality and Colonialism*, London, pp. 21–29
von Seggern, Harm (2012), Männer, Trinken, Sex. Der Kölner Hermann Weinsberg (1518–1597) über seine Bordellbesuche, in: Seggern, Harm von/Zeilinger, Gabriel (eds), *Es geht um die Menschen. Beiträge zur Wirtschafts- und*

Sozialgeschichte des Mittelalters für Gerhard Fouquet zum 60. Geburtstag, Frankfurt a. M. et al., pp. 149–165

von Seggern, Harm (2014), Ein kleiner Junge vom Land in der großen Stadt. Feter Hansen aus Hajstrup bei Tondern über sein Bordellerlebnis in Amsterdam (1644), in: Hundt, Michael/Lokers, Jan (eds), *Hanse und Stadt. Akteure, Strukturen und Entwicklungen im regionalen und europäischen Raum. Festschrift für Rolf Hammel-Kiesow zum 65. Geburtstag*, Lübeck, pp. 533–544

Vons, Jacqueline/Gourevitch, Danielle (2012), Où s'arrête l'histoire des noms de la syphilis? Décrire ou dissimuler une maladie honteuse?, in: *Histoire des Sciences médicales* 46, 3, pp. 219–224

Voorhoeve, Maaike (2013), Divorce: Historical Practice, in: DeLong-Bas, Natana J. (ed), *The Oxford Encyclopedia of Islam and Women*, Oxford

Voß, Heinz-Jürgen (2009), Konstituierung von "Geschlecht" in westlichen modernen biologisch-medizinischen Wissenschaften - Ausgangspunkt Hermaphroditismus, in: *Invertito. Jahrbuch für die Geschichte der Homosexualitäten* 11, pp. 49–75

Voß, Heinz-Jürgen (2010), *Making Sex Revisited. Dekonstruktion des Geschelchts aus biologisch-medizinischer Perspektive*, Bielefeld

Vout, Caroline (2007), *Power and Eroticism in Imperial Rome*, Cambridge/New York

Vout, Caroline (2013), *Sex on Show. Seeing the Erotic in Greece and Rome*, London

Vout, Caroline (2014), Biography, in: Hubbard, Thomas K. (ed), *A Companion to Greek and Roman Sexualities*, New York, pp. 446–462

Waddams, S. M. (2000), *Sexual Slander in Nineteenth-Century England: Defamation in the Ecclesiastical Courts, 1815–1855*, Toronto

Waddington, Raymond B. (2003), *Aretino's Satyr. Sexuality, Satire, and Self-Projection in Sixteenth-Century Literature and Art*, Toronto

Wade, Erik (2020), The Beast with Two Backs: Bestiality, Sex between Men, and Byzantine Theology in the Paenitentiale Theodori, in: *Journal of Medieval Worlds* 2, 1–2, pp. 11–26

Wahl, Elizabeth Susan (1999), *Invisible Relations. Representations of Female Intimacy in the Age of Enlightenment*, Stanford

Walker, Garthine (1998), Rereading Rape and Sexual Violence in Early Modern England, in: *Gender and History* 10, pp. 1–25

Walker, Garthine (2012), Sexual Violence and Rape in Europe, 1500-1750, in: Fisher, Kate/Toulalan, Sarah (eds), *The Routledge History of Sex and the Body, 1500 to the Present*, Oxford et al., pp. 429–443

Walker, Garthine (2013), Rape, Acquittal and Culpability in Popular Crime Reports in England, c. 1670-c. 1750, in: *Past & Present* 220, pp. 115–142

Walker, Garthine (2017), Framing Premodern Desires Between Sexuality, Sin, and Crime. An Introduction, in: Lidman, Satu et al. (ed), *Framing Premodern Desires. Sexual Ideas, Attitudes, and Practices in Europe*, Amsterdam, pp. 9–26

Walkowitz, Judith R. (1980), *Prostitution and Victorian Society. Women, Class and the State*, New York/Cambridge

Wall, Alison D. (ed) (1983*), Two Elizabethan Women: Correspondence of Joan and Maria Thynne 1575–1611*, Devizes

Wallace, Lee (2007), Zur Entdeckung der Homosexualität. Interkulturelle Vergleiche und die Geschichte der Sexualität, in: Aldrich, Robert (ed), *Gleich und anders. Eine globale Geschichte der Homosexualität*, Hamburg, pp. 249–269

Wallace, Mark I. (2010), Early Christian Contempt for the Flesh and the Woman Who Loved Too Muchin the Gospel of Luke, in: Kamitsuka, Margaret D. (ed), *The Embrace of Eros. Bodies, Desires, and Sexuality in Christianity*, Minneapolis, pp. 33–50

Walle, Etienne van de (1980), Illegitimacy in France during the Nineteenth Century, in: Laslett, Peter/Oosterveen, Karla/Smith, Richard M. (eds), *Bastardy and its Comparative History. Studies in the History of Illegitimacy and Marital Nonconformism in Britain, France, Germany, Sweden, North Amerika, Jamaica and Japan*, London, pp. 264–277

Wallraff, Martin (2011), Die antipaganen Maßnahmen Konstantins in der Darstellung des Euseb von Kaisareia, in: Hahn, Johannes (ed), *Spätantiker Staat und religiöser Konflikt. Imperiale und lokale Verwaltung und die Gewalt gegen Heiligtümer*, Berlin/New York, pp. 7–18

Walsh, Jerome T. (2001), Leviticus 18:22 and 20:13. Who Is Doing What to Whom, in: *Journal of Biblical Literature* 120, 2, pp. 201–209

Walter, Tilmann (1998), *Unkeuschheit und Werk der Liebe. Diskurse über Sexualität am Beginn der Neuzeit in Deutschland*, Berlin/New York

Walter, Tilmann (2003), Die Syphilis als astrologische Katastrophe. Frühe medizinische Fachtexte zur "Franzosenkrankheit", in: Groh, Dieter/Kempe, Michael/Mauelshagen, Franz (eds), *Naturkatastrophen. Beiträge zu ihrer Deutung, Wahrnehmung und... in der Geschichte des Menschen*, Tübingen, pp. 165–187

Walter, Tilmann (2004), Begrenzung und Entgrenzung. Zur Genealogie wissenschaftlicher Debatten über Sexualität, in: Bruns, Claudia/Walter, Tilmann (eds), *Von Lust und Schmerz. Eine Historische Anthropologie der Sexualität*, Köln/Weimar/Wien, pp. 129–174

Walters, Jonathan (1997), Invading the Roman Body. Manliness and Impenetrability in Roman Thought, in: Hallett, Judith P./Skinner, Marilyn B. (eds), *Roman Sexualities*, Princeton, pp. 29–44

Waqas, Syed (2022), Sex before Stigma: Making Sense of the Absence of Stigmatization in the Spiritual Aspect of Sacred Prostitution in the Ethical Systems of the Ancient World, in: *Athens Journal of Mediterranean Studies* 8, 3, pp. 167–182

Ward, Peter W. (2005), The Welfare of Female Servants. Five Case Studies (Bologna, Boston, Edinburgh, Utrecht, Vienna), in: Pasleau, Suzanne/Pasleau/Schopp, Isabelle/Sarti, Raffaella (eds), *Proceedings of the Servant Project/Actes de Servant Project: Vol. 5: The Modernization of Domestic Service*, Liège, pp. 91–106

Wasdin, Katherine (2020), Courtship and Ritual, in: Klaiber-Hersch, Karen (ed), *A Cultural History of Marriage in Antiquity*, London/New York, pp. 23–36

Webb, Eleanor (2018), Femmina masculo e masculo femmina: Androgynous Beauty and Ambiguous Sexualities in the Italian Renaissance, in: *Comitatus* 49, 1, pp. 103–135

Webb, Jr., James l. A. (2015), Globalization of Disease, 1300 to 1900, in: Bentley, Jerry H./Subrahmanyam, Sanjay/Wiesner-Hanks, Merry E. (eds), *The Cambridge World History: Vol. 6: The Construction of a Global World, 1400–1800 CE, Part 1: Foundation*, Cambridge, pp. 54–75

Webb, Melanie (2017), Augustine, Rape, and the Hermeneutics of Love, in: Gasper, Giles E. M./Watson, Francis/Crawford, Matthew R. (eds), *Producing*

Christian Culture: Medieval Exegesis and Its Interpretative Genres, London, pp. 11–43
Weber, Philippe (2008), *Der Trieb zum Erzählen. Sexualpathologie und Homosexualität, 1852–1914*, Bielefeld
Weddle, Saundra (2019), Mobility and Prostitution in Early Modern Venice, in: Early Modern Women 14, 1, pp. 95–108
Weeks, Jeffrey (1977), *Coming Out. Homosexual Politics in Britain, from the Nineteenth Century to the Present*, London
Weeks, Jeffrey (1990), *Coming Out. Homosexual Politics in Britain, from the Nineteenth Century to the Present*, London, 2nd edn
Weeks, Jeffrey (2000), *Making Sexual History*, Cambridge/Oxford/Molden
Weeks, Jeffrey (2010), Making the Human Gesture: History, Sexuality and Social Justice, in: History Workshop Journal 70, pp. 5–20
Weeks, Jeffrey (2016), *What Is Sexual History?*, Cambridge/Malden
Weigl, Andreas (2003), Frühneuzeitliches Bevölkerungswachstum, in: Vocelka, Karl/Traninger, Anita (eds), *Wien. Bd. 2: Die frühneuzeitliche Residenz (16. bis 18. Jahrhundert)*, Wien, pp. 109–132
Weikard, Melchior Adam (1799), *Der philosophische Arzt. Bd. 3: Philosophische Arzeneykunst oder von Erbrechen der Sensationen, des Verstandes, und des Willens*, Frankfurt am Main
Weikert, Katherine/Woodacre, Elena (eds) (2021), *Medieval Intersections: Gender and Status in Europe in the Middle Ages* (= Special Issue of Historical Reflection/Réflexions Historiques 42 (2016), 1), New York
Weiler, Ingomar (2018), Antike Sklaverei und Sexualität in der vergleichenden Geschichtswissenschaft, in: Fischer, Irmtraud/Feichtinger, Daniela (eds), *Sexualität und Sklaverei*, Münster, pp. 3–44
Weinstein, Donald (2011), *Savonarola*, Yale
Weir, Anthony/Jerman, James (1986), *Images of Lust. Sexual Carvings on Medieval Churches*, London
Weisbrod, Andrea (2001), Geliebte Freundin. Madam de Pompadour oder: Von der Freundschaft als Strategie des Machterhalts, in: *Werkstatt Geschichte* 28, pp. 61–70
Wemple, Suzanne F. (1993), Censent and Dissence to Sexual Intercourse in Germanic Societies from the Fifth to the Tenth Century, in: Laiou, Angeliki E. (ed), *Consent and Coercion to Sex and Marriage in Ancient and Medieval Societies*, Washington, DC, pp. 227–244
Wenzel, Horst (2009), *Spiegelungen. Zur Kultur der Visualität im Mittelalter*, Berlin
Wertheimer, Laura (2006), Children of Disorder. Clerical Parentage, Illegitimacy, and Reform in the Middle Ages, in: *Journal of the History of Sexuality* 15, 3, pp. 382–407
West, David (2005), *Reason and Sexuality in Western Thought*, Cambridge/Malden, MA
Wettlaufer, Jörg (1999), *Das Herrenrecht der ersten Nacht. Hochzeit, Herrschaft und Heiratszins im Mittelalter und in der frühen Neuzeit*, Frankfurt a. M./New York
Wheeler-Reed, David (2017), *Regulating Sex in the Roman Empire: Ideology, the Bible, and the Early Christians*, New Haven
Wheeler-Reed, David/Knust, Jennifer Wright/Martin, Dale B, (2018), Can a man commit πορνεια with his wife?, in: *Journal of Biblical Literature* 137, 2, pp. 383–398

Whitaker, Cord J. (2019), *Black Metaphors: How Modern Racism Emerged from Medieval Race-Thinking*, Philadelphia

White, Luise (1990), *The Comforts of Home. Prostitution in Colonial Nairobi*, Chicago

Widmer, Peter (1997), *Subversion des Begehrens. Eine Einführung in Jacques Lacans Werk*, Frankfurt a. M.

Wiesner, Merry E. (2000), *Women and Gender in Early Modern Europe*, New York, 2nd edn

Wiesner-Hanks, Merry (2012), Sexual Identity and Other Aspects of "Modern" Sexuality: New Chronologies, Same Old Problem?, in: Spector, Scott/Puff, Helmut/Herzog, Dagmar (eds), *After the History of Sexuality. German Genealogies With and Beyond Foucault*, Oxford/New York, pp. 31–42

Wiesner-Hanks, Merry E. (2000), *Christianity and Sexuality in the Early Modern World. Regulating Desire, Reforming Practice*, London/New York

Wiesner-Hanks, Merry E. (2005), Lustful Luther. Male Libido and the Writings of the Reformer, in: Soergel, Philip M. (ed), *Sexuality and Culture in Medieval and Renaissance Europe*, New York, pp. 123–147

Wiesner-Hanks, Merry E. (2020), *Christianity and Sexuality in the Early Modern World. Regulating Desire, Reforming Practice*, London/New York, 3rd edn

Wiethaus, Ulrike (1991), Sexuality, Gender and the Body in Late Medieval Spirituality. Cases from Germany and the Netherlands, in: *Journal of Feminist Studies in Religion 7*, 1, pp. 35–52

Wiethaus, Ulrike (2003), Female Homoerotic Discourse and Religion in Medieval German Culture, in: Farmer, Sharon A./Pasternack, Carol Braun (eds), *Gender and Difference in the Middle Ages*, Minneapolis, pp. 288–320

Wiethaus, Ulrike (2003), Sexuality, Gender and the Body in Late Medieval Spirituality. Cases from Germany and the Netherlands, in: *Journal of Feminist Studies in Religion 7*, 1, pp. 35–52

Wilke, Carsten L. (2016), Jewish Erotic Encounters with Christians and Muslims in Late Medieval Iberia: Testing Ibn Verga's Hypothesis, in: Shoham-Shṭainer, Efrayim (ed), *Intricate Interfaith Networks in the Middle Ages: Quotidian Jewish-Christian Contacts*, Turnhout, pp. 193–230

Williams, Craig (2014), Sexual Themes in Greek and Latin Graffiti, in: Hubbard, Thomas K. (ed), *A Companion to Greek and Roman Sexualities*, New York, pp. 493–508

Williams, Craig A. (1999), *Roman Homosexuality. Ideologies of Masculinity in Classical Antiquity*, New York

Williams, Gordon (1997), *A Glossary of Shakespeare's Sexual Language*, London

Williams, Graig (2014), The Language of Gender. Lexical Semantics and the Latin Vocabulary of Unmanly Men, in: Masterson, Mark/Sorkin Rabinowitz, Nancy/Robson, James (eds), *Sex in Antiquity. Exploring Gender and Sexuality in the Ancient World*, London/New York, pp. 461–481

Winkle, Stefan (2005), Geisseln der Menschheit. Kulturgeschichte der Seuchen, Düsseldorf, 3rd edn

Winkler, John J. (1990), *The Constraints of Desire: The Anthropology of Sex and Gender in Ancient Greece*, New York

Winkler, John J. (1997), *Der gefesselte Eros. Sexualität und Geschlechterverhältnis im antiken Griechenland*, Marburg

Winter, Thomas Nelson (1973), *Catullus Purified: A brief history of Carmen 16.* Faculty Publications, Classics and Religious Studies Department 2 (https://digitalcommons.unl.edu/classicsfacpub/2)

Winterer, Angelika (2005), *Verkehrte Sexualität—ein umstrittenes Pauluswort. Eine exegetische Studie zu Röm 1,26f. in der Argumentationsstruktur des Römerbriefes und im kulturhistorisch-sozialgeschichtlichen Kontext*, Frankfurt am Main

Witte, John/Kingdon, Robert M. (2005), *Sex, Marriage, and Family in John Calvin's Geneva. Courtship, Engagement and Marriage*, Grand Rapids

Wohl, Victoria (2002), *Love among the Ruins: The Erotics of Democracy in Classical Athens*, Princeton/Oxford

Wolf, Gerhard (1991), Spiel und Norm. Zur Thematisierung der Sexualität in Liebeslyrik und Ehelehre des späten Mittelalters, in: Bachorski, Hans-Jürgen (ed), *Ordnung und Lust. Bilder von Liebe, Ehe und Sexualität in Spätmittelalter und Früher Neuzeit*, Trier, pp. 477–509

Wolf, Gerhard (2004), Phallus am Grillspieß und Vulva auf Stelzen. Überlegungen zur kommunikativen Funktion erotischer und obszöner Tragezeichen aus den Niederlanden, in: *Amsterdamer Beiträge zur älteren Germanistik* 59, 1, pp. 285–330

Wolfthal, Diane (2010), *In and Out of the Marital Bed. Seeing Sex in Renaissance Europe*, New Haven

Wolicki, Aleksander (2007), Moicheia. Adultery or Something More?, in: *Palamedes: A Journal of Ancient History* 2, pp. 131–142

Wolk-Simon, Linda (2008), Rapture to the Greedy Eyes. Profane Love in the Renaissance, in: Metropolitan Museum of Art (ed), *Art and Love in Renaissance Italy*, New York, pp. 42–58

Woycke, James (1988), *Birth Control in Germany, 1871–1933*, London/New York

Wrenhaven, Kelly L. (2011), *Reconstructing the Slave. The Image of the Slave in Ancient Greece*, London

Wunder, Heide (1992), *Er ist die Sonn, sie ist der Mond. Frauen in der Frühen Neuzeit*, München

Wunder, Heide (2016), Marriage in the Holy Roman Empire of German Nation from the Fifteenth to the Eighteenth Century: Moral, Legal and Political Order, in: Menchi, Silvana Seidel (ed) *Marriage in Europe 1400-1800*, Toronto, pp. 61–93

Wurm, Achim (2008), *Platonicus amor. Lesarten der Liebe bei Platon, Plotin und Ficino*, Berlin

Wyatt, David (2009), *Slaves and Warriors in Medieval Britain and Ireland, 800 –1200*, Leiden/Boston

Xenophon (1994), *Memorabilia* (trans. Amy L. Bonnette), Ithaca/London

Yalom, Marilyn (2001), *A History of the Wife*, New York

Yilmaz, Fikret (2016), The Line Between Fornication and Prostitution: The Prostitute versus the Subaşı (Police Chief), in: *Acta Orientalia Academiae Scientiarum Hungaricae* 69, 3, pp. 249–264

Young, Michael B. (1999), *King James and the History of Homosexuality*, New York

Young, Paul J. (2008), *Seducing the Eighteenth-Century French Reader: Reading, Writing, and the Question of Pleasure*, Aldershot et al.

Younger, John G. (2005), *Sex in the Ancient World from A to Z*, London/New York

Younger, John G. (2011), Sexual Variations: Sexual Peculiarities of the Ancient Greeks and Romans, in: Golden, Mark/Toohey, Peter (eds), *A Cultural History of Sexuality in the Classical World (=A Cultural History of Sexuality Vol. 1)*, Oxford/New York, pp. 55–86

Youssef, Olfa (2017), *The Perplexity of a Muslim Woman: Over Inheritance, Marriage, and Homosexuality*, Lanham et al.

Zanetti Domingues, Lidia L./Caravaggi, Lorenzo/Paoletti, Giulia M. (eds) (2021), *Women and Violence in the Late Medieval Mediterranean, ca. 1100–1500*, Milton

Zanghellini, Aleardo (2015), *The Sexual Constitution of Political Authority. The "Trials" of Same-Sex Desire*, Oxon/New York

Zarri, Gabriela (2001), Die tridentinische Ehe, in: Prodi, Paolo/Reinhard, Wolfgang (eds), *Das Konzil von Trient und die Moderne*, Berlin, pp. 343–379

Ze'evi, Dror (2001), Changes in Legal-Sexual Discourses. Sex Crimes in the Ottoman Empire, in: *Continuity and Change* 16, 2, pp. 219–243

Ze'evi, Dror (2006), *Producing Desire. Changing Sexual Discourse in the Ottoman Middle East, 1500–1900*, Berkeley

Zieman, Katherine (2019), Minding the Rod: Sodomy and Clerical Masculinity in Fifteenth‑Century Leicester, in: *Gender & History* 31, 1, pp. 60–77

Zika, Charles (2003), *Exorcizing Our Demons: Magic, Witchcraft and Visual Culture in Early Modern Europe*, Leiden

Zimmermann, Ruben (2001), *Geschlechtermetaphorik und Gottesverhältnis. Traditionsgeschichte und Theologie eines Bildfelds in Urchristentum und antiker Umwelt*, Tübingen

Zimmermann, Ruben (2011), Marriage, Sexuality, and Holiness: Aspects of Marital Ethics in the Corpus Paulinum, in: *Acta Theologica* 31, 2, pp. 363–393

Ziolkowski, Jan M. (1998), Introduction, in: Ziolkowski, Jan M. (ed), *Obscenity. Social Control and Artistic Creation in the European Middle Ages*, Leiden, pp. 3–18

Žižek, Slavoj (2008), *Lacan: Eine Einführung*, Frankfurt a. M.

Zomeño, Amalia (2002), Abandoned Wives and Their Possibilities for Divorce in al-Andalus. The Evidence of the Wathā'iq Works, in: Marín, Manuela/Deguilhem, Randi (eds), *Writing the Feminine. Women in Arab Sources*, London, pp. 111–126

Zorach, Rebecca (2001), Desiring Things, in: *Art History* 24, 2, pp. 195–212

Zorach, Rebecca (2011), Triangular Passions and the Aemulatio of Point of View, in: Müller, Jan-Dirk/Pfisterer, Ulrich/Bleuler, Anna Kathrin/Jonietz, Fabian (eds), *Aemulatio. Kulturen des Wettstreits in Text und Bild (1450–1620)*, Berlin/Boston, pp. 249–276

Zunshine, Lisa (2005), *Bastards and Foundlings. Illegitimacy in Eighteenth-Century England*, Columbus

zur Nieden, Susanne (2005), Aufstieg und Fall des virilen Männerhelden. Der Skandal um Ernst Röhm und seine Ermordung, in: zur Nieden, Susanne (ed), *Homosexualität und Staatsräson. Männlichkeit, Homophobie und Politik in Deutschland 1900–1945*, Frankfurt a. M./New York, pp. 147–192

Zweig, Stefan (1970), *Die Welt von Gestern. Erinnerungen eines Europäers*, Frankfurt a. M.BibliographyBibliography

INDEX

abduction 30, 126, 148, 156, 180, 191, 319
abortion/abortifacients 6, 32, 41–2, 71–2, 129, 140, 149, 185–8, 230, 271, 295, 298, 316–17, 322, 323, 327, 348
Adam and Eve 109, 113, 120, 128–9, 215, 242, 362
adultery 1, 26, 29, 32, 39, 65, 68, 71–3, 75, 78, 85–6, 91, 100, 108, 112, 115, 126, 127, 129–30, 134, 138–9, 141–2, 148, 170, 177, 188–91, 198–9, 205, 209, 234, 238, 245, 262, 269–70, 272, 289, 292, 294, 295, 298, 300, 313, 315, 317–19, 326, 327, 332, 333, 336, 362, 367, 380
  Västgöta law for 190
Aeschines 54–5
age-oriented sexual relationships 15, 27–8, 55–8, 62–3, 137, 156, 182, 194, 207, 257–8, 304, 310, 388–90
Ahmed Pasha, Melek 350
Alcibiades 53–4
Alhambra Edict of 1492 207
Amazons 44–6
Ambrose 127–8
anal intercourse/penetration 2, 6, 8, 32, 40, 42, 46, 51–3, 55, 57, 58, 70, 73, 82, 83, 87, 88, 98, 99, 101, 103, 119, 121, 133, 134, 148, 185, 195, 233, 248, 250, 251, 254, 258, 270, 320, 348, 387, 389, 392, 394, 395, 399. *See also* penetration

Al-Andalus
  Muslim, Christian, and Jewish cultures 200–6, 250
  Muslim men and women 202–6
Anglicans 287, 289, 329, 330, 337
The Antipodes (1638, Brome) 276–7
Antony, Mark 94
Aphrodite 19, 20, 25, 27, 33, 45, 46, 60, 79, 96, 119, 135, 138–40. *See also* Venus
Apostolic Constitutions 136
apprentices 5, 15, 219, 224, 233, 234, 270, 334, 335, 343, 345, 392, 396, 399
Aquinas, Thomas 177–8, 185, 219, 252
Aretino, Pietro 348, 370–5, 378, 384, 385, 402
aristocrats/nobles 27, 47, 55, 73, 76, 77, 87, 103, 132, 154, 156, 171, 172, 174, 179, 183, 187, 189, 190, 196, 201, 233, 244, 254, 259, 260, 269, 273, 290, 304, 315, 316, 324, 339, 345, 346, 360, 374–7, 379, 383, 389, 399
Aristophanes 2, 31, 32, 49, 59
Aristotle 23, 26, 39, 42, 49, 53, 57, 68, 160, 161, 163, 177, 187, 255, 279, 371
  body theory 26–7
  seed theory 163
arkteia 27
The Arnolfini Wedding (van Eyck) 364
arranged marriages 27, 154, 166, 179, 258, 325, 340

ars erotica 46–7
 pornográphos and 46–8
 public shame and 80–2
Artemidorus of Daldis 67
asceticism 25, 72, 106, 107, 110, 114, 117, 119–21, 123–6, 128, 129, 135, 143, 147, 148, 152, 169, 175, 176, 195, 199, 203, 210, 285, 295, 301. *See also* celibacy; virginity/virgins
Athenaeus 35, 36, 45, 46
Athenian prostitution 38–41
Augsburg City Law of 1276 220
Augustine 128–31, 135–6, 141, 143, 170, 177, 182, 186, 214–16, 231, 236, 289, 331
Augustus 88, 89, 91
 marriage laws 65, 72–3, 85
Avicenna. *See* Ibn Sina

bastards 184, 270
bath/bathhouses 47, 163, 222, 225, 227, 230, 246, 272–4, 368, 392, 396
Baudartius, Willem 313
Bavarian laws (*Lex Baiuariorum*) 180
beauty and eroticism 22, 35, 48–9, 54, 253, 282–3
Benedictine reform 152
Benedict of Nursia 135
Béthencourt, Jacques de 355
bigamy/double marriage 290–1, 297–8
birth/childbirth 42, 63, 72–3, 167, 184, 200, 270–1, 306, 316. *See also* fertility
 control/planning 186, 305–6, 315
 rates 5, 63, 65, 72–3, 230, 257, 271, 304
Bishops, sexual mores and advices of 117, 123, 126–8, 136, 140, 149, 159, 165–9, 187, 188, 201, 210, 214, 217, 218, 235, 249, 250, 269, 286–9, 297–300, 360, 361, 396
black women 163, 212, 320, 357, 386
Bock, Hieronymus 348

body
 female 23–7, 48–9, 68–70, 77, 95, 111, 115–16, 122–4, 127, 138, 140–1, 152, 158, 160–3, 176, 203–6, 212, 277–82, 321, 342, 355, 395, 400–1
 male 23, 48–9, 51, 68–70, 77, 98, 111, 115, 152, 160, 176, 301, 321, 342, 355, 358, 395
Boniface 187
Bordeeltjes 369
Borg, Barbara 24
Borgarucci, Prospero 279
Bosman, William 386
Boswell, John 102, 106, 132, 133, 136–7
boy love. *See* pederasty
Bray, Alan 259
breast 49, 237
breastfeeding 163, 209
Brome, Richard 276
Brooten, Bernadette J. 132–3
brothels 15, 38–41, 85–7, 89–91, 93, 140–1, 213, 216, 219–28, 230, 273, 329–31, 334–7, 341, 347, 350–2, 369–70. *See also* prostitutes; prostitution
 abolition/closure/shutdown of 220–1, 329, 333–7
 actual number of 227
 in Bruges 224–5
 control of 333–7
 and French disease 329–30
 in Genoa 341
 institutionalization in 219–21
 Italian 223
 Ottoman Empire 351
 at outside of the city 224
Brown, Peter 124
Brundage, James 146
Budin, Stephanie Lynn 45–6
Butler, Judith 13
Byzantine/Byzantium
 male same-sex acts 249
 marriage and celibacy in 197–200
 rapes in 193

Cady, Joseph 260
Calvin, John 291, 292, 294, 332

Calvinists   287, 297, 298, 300, 313, 319, 329, 333–5, 337, 381, 382
canonical law   124, 148–50, 165–7, 182–3, 187–8, 208, 218–19, 251, 270–2, 286–7, 289–90, 292–3, 302, 322
Cantiga de escarnio y maldezir   245
Capellanus, Andreas   236
capital punishment   5, 56, 78, 134, 195, 201, 250, 265, 298, 310, 317, 318, 327, 333, 349, 387, 395
Carlini, Benedetta   401
carnal desires. *See* sexual desire
carnal knowledge   7, 159, 366
carnival   181–2, 213, 224, 240, 243, 245, 247, 274–5, 309, 335, 348, 389
Carolina (Constitutio Criminalis Carolina of 1532)   190, 270, 290, 310, 311, 318, 319, 387
Cartusianus, Dionysius   281
Castelvetro, Lodovico   371
castration   44, 73, 97–8, 101, 113, 120–1, 123, 126, 128–9, 204, 238, 244, 249, 327, 356
Cathars   175, 254
Catullus   66, 83–4, 92
Çelebi, Evliya   350, 352
celibacy   106–7, 116, 119, 123–4, 126, 135, 167–9, 199, 203, 285–7, 295, 301, 330–1
  bishops   169
  opposition of church to   285–7
Celsus   87
cenobitic monasticism   124
Cerealia   74
Chakrabarty, Dipesh   17–18
chancroid   43
Charles V   188
chastity   31, 67–8, 116–18, 120, 122, 124–7, 130–1, 135, 140–3, 149–51, 162, 169, 178, 199, 214, 264, 272–4, 288, 291–2, 309, 319, 361, 367–8
chastity belt   190–1, 356
Chigi, Agostino   364–5
chlamydia   42

The Choise of Valentines (Nashe)   383
Chrétien de Troyes   171
Christendom, sexual division of   124–5
Christian marriage   164, 166, 196, 207, 210, 220
  and sexual morals   129
Christopher's law   185
Chrysostom, John   115, 126–7, 136, 141, 197–8, 249
church/ecclesiastical courts   170, 192, 196, 235, 256, 270, 286, 294–5, 299–302, 307–10, 315, 317–18, 322–4, 328, 333–4, 337, 388, 391–2
Church Fathers   106, 107, 119, 123, 127, 131, 135, 138, 139, 141, 175, 216, 218, 289
  virginity and everyday life   127–30
Cicero, Marcus Tullius   61, 80, 92–4
cinaedus   77, 83, 95, 98–9, 102, 103, 137, 395
Clarke, John R.   82, 102
classes
  lower   5, 23, 35, 64, 73, 89, 140, 141, 153, 165, 183, 192, 194, 213, 218, 223, 225, 226, 229, 281, 299, 304, 306, 307, 313, 335, 337, 338, 357, 359, 378, 399
  middle   16, 67, 81, 91, 184, 269
  upper   3, 5, 17, 25, 34, 36, 48, 62–5, 67, 72, 73, 77, 81, 86, 90, 91, 100, 101, 103, 131, 140, 155, 156, 170, 181, 184, 202, 210, 250, 258, 281, 315, 319, 325, 366, 376, 378, 385, 390
Clement of Alexandria   119–20
clergy, marriage for   288–9
clients for prostitutes   37–41, 48, 83, 85, 87–90, 94, 138, 215, 218, 222, 225–7, 231–5, 250, 330, 334, 340, 343–5, 347–9, 351–2, 359
clitoris   95–6, 161, 262–3, 277–80, 376, 399–401
Cluniac monastic reforms. *See* Benedictine reform
Codex Theodosianus   126

Códido de las costumbres escritas de Tortosa 201
coitus/sexual intercourse 3–4, 7, 15, 25–6, 32, 48, 71–2, 88, 108, 119, 122, 130, 148–50, 158, 160–1, 163–4, 185–6, 213, 232, 278, 293, 302, 308, 315, 323, 357, 359, 361
   conjugal/marital 3, 24, 65, 77–8, 110, 116, 120, 129, 149, 152, 154, 162, 166, 177, 180, 198, 200, 208, 280, 290, 301, 331, 334
   positions 32, 48–51, 53, 55, 66, 71, 81, 89, 98, 110, 148, 149, 163, 175, 180, 237, 248, 249, 269, 278, 280, 325, 348, 370, 389, 390, 396
coitus interruptus 44, 72, 147, 186, 204–5, 231, 315–16
Colombo, Realdo 280
comedies 19, 24, 31, 32, 35, 36, 41, 48, 49, 54, 57, 59, 88, 91, 380, 382
concubinatus 64, 74
concubines/concubinages 17, 24, 34, 37–8, 43, 64, 74, 91–2, 103, 109, 126, 129, 145, 156–7, 164–5, 184, 196, 201, 204, 206–8, 223, 286, 289–90, 298, 319, 325, 342, 349–50, 386
   of priests 126, 129, 164–5, 167–8, 252, 270, 286, 289, 296, 309, 330–1
concupiscence 6, 128–30, 142–3, 170, 197, 231, 236
condoms 186, 315, 359
confession 146–8, 150, 265, 272, 285, 292, 293, 298, 299, 362
Confessiones (Augustine) 143
Constantine the African 160–1, 231
Constantine the Great 90, 126
Constitutio Criminalis Carolina of 1532. See Carolina
contraception 17, 32, 42, 71–2, 86, 89, 129, 140, 166, 185–6, 208–9, 216, 230, 299, 315–16, 348. *See also* abortion/abortifacients

contraceptives 42, 185–6, 208–9, 216, 316, 348
conubium 62
corporal punishment 147, 189, 191, 193–4, 209, 256, 298, 299, 310–11, 318, 327, 335, 387, 389, 394
Corpus Hippocraticum 26
Corrozet, Gilles 282
Council of Trent 296, 298
courtesans 34, 37, 91–3, 127, 330, 338–40, 342, 345, 348, 364, 373, 378, 382
courtly love/romance 171, 174, 196
craft/craftmen 39, 157, 181, 197, 225–6, 230, 259, 270, 295, 300, 330, 343, 352, 392
criminal sexual law 29, 33–4, 38, 42, 56, 65, 72–3, 85–6, 100, 126, 138, 142, 146, 165, 177, 180, 182, 185, 187–8, 190, 192–5, 201, 205–7, 216–20, 248–51, 260–1, 269–71, 299–303, 310–12, 317, 320, 326–9, 335, 349, 387, 397
Crooke, Helkiah 278
cross-dressing
   men 98, 233, 384, 390
   women 262, 264, 274–5, 337
The Crowned Hippolytus (Euripides) 25
cultic/sacred prostitution 45–6
cunnilingus 40, 59, 82, 96, 118
Cybele, the "Great Mother" 97–8

Daléchamps, Jacques 279–80
Damiani, Peter 169, 235, 251, 252
Danaë (Rembrandt) 368, 373
Davidson, James 59
debitum conjugale (marital debt) 6, 116, 149, 159, 177–8, 196, 198, 204–6, 262, 281
Decretum Gratiani (Gratian) 148, 187, 219, 251
Decretum Tametsi 296
De dissectione partium corporis humani (Estiennes) 370
defilement 79, 98, 118, 138, 198, 215, 251, 252, 285, 301, 331, 334, 344

Demeter 21
De rerum natura (On the Nature of Things) (Lucretius) 385
desecration 45, 78–9, 86, 189
de Vidas, Elijahu 301
Digenes Akritas 198
dildos 47, 71, 95–6, 245, 262–4, 277, 383, 399, 401–2
Diodorus 77
Diogenes of Sinope 29, 42
Dionysus 20, 21, 25, 40, 62, 100
divorce/dissolution of marriage 28, 64–5, 68, 72, 109, 112, 122, 126–7, 129, 158, 170, 177, 189, 195, 199, 205, 209–10, 245, 289, 294, 297–8, 302, 327–9. See also marriage
  prohibition of 169–70
Doniger, Wendy 9
double marriage. See bigamy/double marriage
Dover, Kenneth J. 103
dress codes 63, 85–6, 98, 168, 182, 218, 224, 228–9, 232, 235, 238, 256, 260, 264, 274–5, 296, 337, 345–6, 369, 374, 397
dual-seed theory 23, 68–9, 159–61, 205, 231, 278–9, 355
Due Amati (Romano) 365–6
Dürer, Albrecht 368, 371

Ebüssuud Efendi, Mehmed 384
Ecloga 193
effeminate/effemination 44, 49, 51, 57, 70–1, 93, 97–8, 103–4, 133, 248, 252–5, 260, 263, 388, 390–1
ejaculation 26, 32, 147, 162, 301, 306, 310, 394
emotions 9, 10
endogamy 108, 119, 210. See also exogamy
Epicureanism 180–2
Epicurus 26
Erasmus of Rotterdam 286, 287, 356
erastes 51–3, 55
Erec et Enide (Chrétien) 171
eromenos 51, 52, 54

eros 2, 19–26, 29–31, 48, 50, 52–6, 60, 66, 120, 121, 126, 129, 198, 282
  educational 52–6
  social regulation of 29–31
Essenes communities 119
Estiennes, Charles 370
Ethiopians 212, 357
ethnopornography 386
Étienne de Fougères 159
eunuch 98, 103, 112–13, 199, 204
Euripides 25
European marriage pattern 303–5, 308
Eusebius, Karl 278
Eusebius of Caesarea 124, 139
Exeter Book 152
exogamy 108
extramarital sexual intercourse. See adultery; premarital sex

fallen women 138, 189, 213, 216, 219, 336
Fall of Adam 4, 113, 115, 123, 128–30
Falloppio, Gabriele 280, 359, 399, 400
familia (household community) 62, 112, 119, 155
family planning. See birth/childbirth, control/planning
farces 247, 382. See also comedies
farmers. See peasants
Fastnachtsspiele 244
fellatio 40, 67, 73, 82, 88, 98, 103–4, 110, 117–18, 251, 255, 258
fellatrices 88
female same-sex sexuality 6–7, 13–14, 50, 58–60, 95–6, 202, 233, 260–7, 398–403. See also homosexual/homosexuality; same-sex sexuality
Ferrand, Jacques 382
Ferrer, Vincent 320
fertility 20–1, 27, 63, 65, 72, 181, 305–6. See also birth/childbirth, rates
  rituals 74, 127, 146
  signs and idols 63, 239–41, 364

Ficino, Marsilio   282
forced prostitution   34, 85, 141, 142, 215–17, 226, 227, 298, 320, 330, 345, 347. *See also* prostitutes
Fornicatio   292–3
fornication   4, 111–12, 116, 126, 129, 142, 153, 165, 199, 204, 210, 223, 248, 253–4, 258, 262, 281–2, 289, 292–3, 295, 299, 302. *See also* premarital sex
Foucault, Michel   19, 25, 50, 77, 264–6
  history of sexuality   12–14
  subjectivation   146–7
Fourment, Helena   366
Fourth Lateran Council (1215)   148, 150, 166, 170, 207
Fracastoro, Girolamo   354
Francis of Assisi   152
Franco, Veronica   339, 378–9
Frauenzucht (The breding of wives, Sibote)   174
Frederick of Heilo   285
free citizen/freeborn   22–3, 28–9, 34, 36–9, 50–3, 56, 63–5, 67, 70, 76, 78, 94–5, 98–101, 141, 144, 156, 186, 202–4
French disease. *See* syphilis
Freund, Georg   357
Friedelehe   155
Frouwen Minne, violence and romance in   173–4
Fulbert of Chartres   169

Galenus (Galen)   69, 77, 87, 279, 280, 325
gang rapes   313
Garcilaso de la Vega   383
Gargantua and Pantagruel (Rabelais)   380–2
gay   50, 102, 137, 265, 277
gaze   48–9, 51–2, 81, 139–40, 142–3, 202, 236–40, 282, 361–73, 386, 402
genital kissing/stimulation. *See* cunnilingus; fellatio; masturbation

genitals   9, 21, 33, 42, 46, 58, 67, 69, 80–2, 85, 87, 97, 125, 161, 176, 231, 238, 240–1, 245, 250, 262, 273, 278, 279, 281, 306, 310, 352, 359, 362, 365, 369, 371, 372, 375, 381, 384, 399–401. *See also* clitoris; penis; vagina/vaginal; vulva
Gerson, Jean   240, 255
al-Ghazzali, Muhammad   205
Gnosticism   120
Goldhill, Simon   33
Goltzius, Henrick   368
gonorrhea/gonnorhoea   42–3, 54, 87, 231, 359
Gratian   148, 159, 219
Greco-Roman culture   105, 109, 111, 112
Greek gymnasium practices   80
Greene, Ellen   59

Hadrian   101, 102
Halperin, David M.   57, 103
hamam. *See* bath/bathhouses
Hansen, Peter   345, 347
Ḥazm, Alí Ibn   203, 250
hedonism   26, 105
hegemonic masculinity   113, 132, 259
Heng, Geraldine   211
Heptaméron (Navarre)   376–7
herbal contraceptives/abortives   42, 185–6, 208–9, 230, 316–17, 348. *See also* abortion/abortifacients; contraception
heresy/heretics   117, 121, 124, 149, 153, 175, 207, 211–12, 235, 253–5, 267, 270, 298, 320–4, 397
heretical movements   174–5
Hergemöller, Bernd-Ulrich   256
hermaphrodite love   58–60
hermaphrodites   60, 103, 257, 280, 321, 390, 399–401
hermaphroditus   60, 96–7
Herodotus   31, 44, 45
Herzog Ernst   243
hetaeras   25, 35, 83, 91

hetairai 5, 24, 30, 31, 33–7, 43, 47, 55–6
  Neaira 37
  social ranks 35
  in vase paintings 34–5
hetairikoi dialogoi (whore dialogues, Lucian) 35, 83, 373
hetairistria 59
heterosexuality 6–7, 266
Het Pelsken (*The Little Fur*, Rubens) 366
Hildegard von Bingen 175, 186, 230
Hippocratic
  body 26, 29, 32, 42, 69, 72, 395
  doctrine of semen 160
  Oath 42, 72
  theory of humors 23, 162
Histoire de la sexualité (Foucault) 12–14
Histories (Herodotus) 44, 45
historiography of sexuality 12–14
homoerotic/homoeroticism 60, 101, 135–6, 212, 247, 250, 258, 260, 264–5, 282–3, 384, 386, 392, 397, 402
homophobic Christianity 248–9
homosexual/homosexuality 6–7, 13, 50–60, 93–104, 248–67, 387–403
  identities 57, 102–4, 260, 264–7
homosocial/homosociality 250, 253, 258–60, 396–8
humoral theory 23–7, 57, 69, 161–2, 164, 204–5, 278–80, 282, 321–2, 325, 352, 355, 366–7, 369
hybris 29, 39–40, 43

Ibn Sina 161, 162, 205, 252, 279, 325
identity/subjectivity 7, 12–17, 57, 102–3, 151, 228–9, 232–3, 251, 264–6, 285, 393, 395, 403
illegitimate births/children 39, 108, 154–5, 168, 183–4, 189, 192, 214, 270–1, 293, 307, 319, 323
I modi (Raimondi) 369, 370, 372

impudicitia 144
impurity 108, 110, 113, 114, 133, 142, 148, 149, 200, 203, 209, 252, 272, 301, 322, 324, 331, 354
incest 25, 44, 67, 92, 108, 118–20, 126, 148, 149, 169, 185, 199, 210, 238, 270–2, 292, 326, 355
infamia 67, 86, 94, 144
infant and child mortality 181, 305–6, 308, 316
infanticide 86–7
institutionalization, of brothels 219–21
intercrural sex 49, 52, 53
intersection of prostitution 43–5
intimate pictures 366–9
Italian brothels 223

Jacques de Vitry 168
Jeremiah III 329
Jerome 128, 141
Jesus of Nazareth 112–14, 116, 121, 123
Jews 61, 77, 105–12, 115, 117, 119, 121, 122, 124–6, 132–6, 138, 147, 153, 166, 195, 196, 201–10, 215, 223, 228, 235, 254, 301, 313, 317, 320, 322, 324, 328, 344, 351, 355, 393, 398
  in Al-Andalus 200–2
  law, marriage as a contract in 206–8
  marriage 206–8, 210
  prostitution and 138
  same-sex sexuality 132–4
Josephite marriage 129, 166, 199
journeymen 5, 15, 219, 233, 234, 270, 304, 313, 335, 343, 345, 347, 392
Judaism 109–11, 119, 123, 133, 209–10, 301
Julius Caesar, Gaius 75

Kanun-ý Osmani 327, 328
Karras, Ruth Mazo 158, 232
khul 328
kidnapping 30, 52, 79, 179

kinaidos (catamite) 57–8, 136
al-Kindi 263
kissing 117–18, 172, 253, 398
knights 65, 88, 172–4, 179, 183, 190, 191, 197, 243, 254, 260, 267, 287
Kuefler, Mathew S. 103
Kyeser, Konrad 190
kyrioi 23
kyrios 22, 29, 31, 44, 65

laborers 22, 141, 157, 213, 227, 305, 347, 396
Lacan, Jacques 8
Laqueur, Thomas W. 69, 400
lasciviousness 12, 84, 103
l'Aubéspine, Madeleine de 379
leprosy 231–2
lesbian 14, 50, 92, 103, 137, 261–5, 402–3
Lettere familiari a diversi (Franco) 339, 378
lex Iulia de adulteriis coercendis (Augustus) 72–3, 79, 85, 100
Lex Salica (507–511) 186
Lex Scantinia (149 BCE) 100
Lex Visigothorum (653/4) 186
Lindener, Michael 380
Liudprand of Cremona 244
Livius, Titus 79, 100, 131
Livre de manières (Book of Customs, Étienne) 159
liwāṭ 249–50, 253
Lombard legal code 180
love 1–2, 8–9, 20–1, 25, 32–3, 65–6, 82–3, 101–2, 120, 170–3, 195–7, 256, 260, 282–4, 289, 342, 364–5
  magic 146, 323, 342
  marriages 76–7, 195–7, 283–4
lovesickness 164, 322, 342, 382–3
Lucian of Samosata 35, 83, 373
Lucretia (rape victim) 131
Lucretia the Greek 342
Lucretius 69–71, 88
ludi florae 74
Luhmann, Niklas 8
lupanar 89–90

Lupercalia 74
lust. *See* sexual desire
Luther, Martin 287–93, 300, 330, 331, 394
Lutheran 287, 292–4, 297, 329, 337, 355, 397
Lysias 29, 32
Lysistrata (Aristophanes) 31, 32

Macfarlane, Alan 283
Machiavelli, Niccolò 393
Magdalene, Mary 138, 216, 218, 232
Magdalene houses 216, 229, 336
Maimonides, Moses 209
male body. *See* body
male same-sex 6–7, 13–14, 49–58, 93–5, 98–104, 106, 108, 132–7, 175, 212, 233, 247–60, 264–7, 281, 325–7, 377, 387–98. *See also* homosexual/homosexuality; same-sex sexuality
Manual of a Christian Knight (Erasmus) 287
Marconville, Jean de 315
marital debt/duties. *See debitum conjugale*
marriage 2–5, 11, 15, 22, 25, 38, 61–6, 101, 106–12, 116–17, 119–22, 125–30, 137, 140, 145, 148–50, 154–7, 164–7, 170–1, 177–80, 183–5, 192–3, 195–200, 203–4, 207–10, 283–93, 297–9, 303–8, 327–8, 360
  age for 27, 48, 52, 62–3, 109, 138, 156, 164, 182, 303–4
  annulment of 65, 158, 162, 169–70, 199, 208, 289, 318
  arranged 27, 154, 166, 179, 258, 325, 340
  vs. ascetic life 119–21
  Augustan laws 65, 72–3, 91
  and celibacy in Byzantine 197–200
  clandestine 297, 345
  for clergy 288–9

European marriage pattern 303–5, 308
forms of 64–5, 74, 154–6, 328
Foucault's assessment of marriage 76
holiness of 119–21
Josephite 129, 166, 199
laws and practices for Tribal, Roman, and Christian 155–8
marriage as a contract in Jewish law 206–8
moral demands of 290–3
for Muslims in Ottoman Empire 327–8
nieces 126
and cousins 108, 119
priests 167, 286, 288
prohibitions 149
prostitutes 219
reform of church laws 286–7
Roman 61–5
sacramental 61, 129, 165, 166, 170, 178, 195, 289, 296, 297, 374
as seedbed of the state 61–5
slaves/free/freed persons 64, 102
spiritual 128, 291
Württemberg regulations 293
marriage ban 5, 15, 86
marriage bed 127, 180, 198
purity of 198
sexual pleasure of 31–3
Martial 92, 96, 99, 117
Mary of Egypt 216
masculinity 63–4, 100, 113, 115, 131–2, 137
Masterson, Mark 58
masturbation 28, 29, 52, 67, 111, 119, 147, 149, 162, 203, 209, 255, 262, 277, 293, 301, 368, 376, 392, 401
maternal mortality 158, 316
matrona 73, 85, 90, 96
Matthew 112, 113, 138–9
menarche 279, 304
menstruation 23, 27, 83, 108–10, 120, 149, 161, 162, 185, 199, 202, 231–2, 262, 278, 279, 317, 321, 355

merchants 183, 190, 197, 212, 219, 224, 225, 233–5, 255, 259, 276, 288, 328, 344, 345, 352, 363, 364, 366, 374, 386, 389, 391
meretrix 85–6, 91, 92, 213, 214
military/warrior/soldiers 27, 28, 30, 42, 44, 51, 52, 56, 59, 63–5, 68, 71, 74, 79, 80, 89, 91, 99, 100, 111, 117, 124, 131, 132, 143, 183, 191, 195, 201, 213, 233, 248, 250, 304, 313, 324, 325, 345, 346, 351–3, 374, 388, 390, 391, 393
Minnelyrik 171
missionaries 114, 115, 324, 325, 390, 391
Mitchell, W. J. T. 8
moicheia 29
mokh 209
mollis 98, 104
Mongols 154, 200, 212
monks 5, 124, 125, 135, 146–8, 150, 151, 178, 195, 197, 199, 210, 238, 241, 247, 251, 279, 281, 285, 287, 288, 296, 320, 341, 376, 377, 386, 402
monogamy/monogamous 109, 112, 140, 141, 149, 166, 170, 206, 207, 215, 300, 325
Montaigne, Michel de 340
Montanus, Martin 380
Montbaston, Jeanne de 241
moral policy 301–3
municipal brothels
institutionalization in 219–21
shutdown and control of 333–7
Muntehe 155
Murray, Jacqueline 261
Muslims 18, 200–8, 211, 215, 228, 235, 237, 249–50, 253, 263, 267, 313, 317, 320, 324–9, 344, 345, 349, 350, 384, 396–8
homosocial culture and sexuality 396–8
marital obligations 204–6

marriages in Ottoman Empire 327–8
sexual contacts 203–4
sexual culture in Al-Andalus 200–2
Musonius Rufus, Gaius 78
Mut'a (temporary marriage) 328, 350

naked body/nakedness 33, 34, 47, 52, 67, 74, 80–1, 101, 108, 125, 127, 212, 236–42, 273, 306, 361–71, 402
Nashe, Thomas 383
Navarre, Margaret de 376–7
Neaira 37
Neidhart 172–3, 243
neo-Platonism 281–2
Nero 101–2
A New and Accurate Description of the Coast of Guinea (Bosman) 386
New Testament 105, 112–17
nightloopsters (night runners) 337
Noah's genitals 238
nobles. *See* aristocrats/nobles
nubit 136
nude images 236, 237, 240
nudity. *See* naked body/nakedness
nuns 5, 122, 124, 131, 146, 148, 150–2, 161, 168, 180, 187, 191, 195, 199, 210, 241, 245, 262, 264, 274, 288, 291, 341, 378, 401, 402
nuns, spiritual love of Christ 150–1

obscaenus 84
obscene/obscenity 46, 48, 74, 84, 181–2, 236, 240
  badges 240–1, 274
  jokes 276
  pictures/prints 241, 371, 373–4
  texts 152–3, 242–3, 246, 257, 276, 321, 366, 373, 378–9, 381, 384, 386
    erotic and 82–5
    political aims of 375–8
Odo of Cluny 152
oíkos 22, 28, 29, 38, 42, 57, 112

Old Testament 108–10, 115, 133, 134, 137–8
  male-male sexuality 133–4
  prostitution as dishonorable 137–8
  sexual offence with close relatives 108
one-sex model 69, 161, 400
orgasm 9, 26, 32, 46, 68–9, 111, 130, 160–3, 205, 209, 231, 263, 306, 312
Origen Adamantius 115
original sin 126–7, 129, 130, 178, 200, 215, 217
Orthodox Christians 193, 199, 200, 328, 398
Oswald von Wolkenstein 246
Ottoman Empire 325–9
  Christian marriages 329
  erotics and pornography 383–4, 386
  homosocial culture and sexuality 396–9
  marriages in 327–8
  prostitution in 328, 349–52
  şeriat (*scharī'a*-Sharia law) 326–8
  talâk 327–8
  Zina 326, 327, 349–51
Ovid 80–2, 91, 97, 367, 383

Pachomios the Elder 135
Page, Jamie 232–3
paiderastia 50–7, 59, 100–1, 135
pallakai 38, 43
pallake 38
pathicus 98
patria potestas 73, 74, 92
patriarchy 28, 31, 43–4, 51, 68, 73, 77, 91, 110–11, 113, 122, 142, 155, 179, 181, 195, 197, 220, 269, 300, 319, 349, 367, 382
Paul of Tarsus 114–17, 122, 128, 134–5, 138, 140
peasants 157, 172, 173, 179, 181, 183, 184, 191, 197, 203, 208, 219, 225, 271, 299, 301, 307, 313, 316, 345, 380, 392
pederasty 50–5, 59, 65, 78, 100–2, 137, 249, 251, 252, 257, 260, 390
pedicatus 99

penance/penalty/punishment 65, 73, 78, 79, 126, 135–7, 144, 146, 148–50, 178–80, 187, 190–3, 199, 201, 206, 209, 218, 226, 235, 248–51, 255–9, 262, 265, 270, 290, 292–3, 295, 297, 300, 302, 308, 310, 317, 319–20, 327, 335–6, 338, 340, 388
penetration 2, 6, 23, 25, 32, 38, 40, 45, 46, 49, 50, 52, 55, 57–8, 67, 70–1, 76, 77, 81–3, 88, 95–6, 98–9, 101, 103, 123, 133, 134, 136, 146, 149, 161, 180, 181, 194, 205, 231, 232, 245, 251, 254, 258, 261, 262, 278, 280, 308, 310, 314, 321, 349, 355, 365, 376, 387, 389, 391, 392, 394–6, 399, 401
penis 2, 8, 21, 24, 40, 41, 47, 49, 51, 58, 70, 71, 82, 85, 88–9, 95, 96, 107, 113, 146, 162, 170, 180, 183, 203, 212, 239–41, 246, 252, 274, 278, 279, 310, 321, 344, 359, 362, 365, 368, 371, 379, 383, 399–402
penitential books (*libri poenitentiales*) 147, 149, 150, 153, 248, 262
Persephone/Kore cult 21
phallus cult/symbols 21–2, 73–4, 113, 150, 240
Philo of Alexandria 110, 133
pimps 39, 43, 86, 87, 89, 94, 140, 142, 215, 216, 218, 219, 221, 226, 330, 337, 339, 342, 351
Pindar 45, 58
Plato 2, 21–2, 26, 42, 51, 53, 59, 106, 282, 283
Plautus 91, 99
playhouses 338
Pliny the Elder 80
Plutarch 51, 65, 100
poetry, erotic and obscene texts in 36, 41, 50, 53, 55, 57, 59, 66, 67, 75, 82–5, 91, 92, 99, 117, 172, 227, 243, 246, 253, 265, 267, 339, 348, 359, 364, 371–3, 381–3, 385, 396, 399, 401, 403

police/vice officers 87, 93, 99, 221, 223, 256, 257, 269, 270, 273, 302, 307, 318, 321, 330, 334, 338, 340, 344, 351
polis, prostitutes in 33–4
polygamy/polygyny 33, 44, 109, 112, 156, 164, 203, 206–8, 211, 212, 289–91, 324, 325, 355. *See also* bigamy/double marriage
pornai 47
porneia 41, 137–8, 142, 143
pornoboskoi 39, 43
pornographic/pornography 46–8, 80–5, 236–48, 384–5
  graphics/pictures 81–2, 93, 101, 118, 239–42, 362–71, 373, 385, 402
  literature/poetics 36, 41, 50, 53, 55, 57, 59, 66, 67, 75, 82–5, 91, 92, 99, 117, 172, 227, 243, 246, 253, 265, 267, 339, 348, 359, 364, 371–3, 381–3, 385, 396, 399, 401, 403
pornoi 38–40, 43, 55
Portrait of Gabrielle d'Estrée and One of Her Sisters 402
Powell, Thomas 341
premarital pregnancies 23, 27, 42, 69, 72, 86, 89, 149, 154, 161–3, 182, 183, 186–7, 192, 193, 202, 205, 206, 208, 230, 231, 271, 272, 275, 278, 294, 295, 304, 307, 308, 312, 315–17, 323, 327, 337, 348, 395, 402
premarital sex 63, 67, 119, 130, 138, 148, 152, 154, 158, 171, 179, 182–5, 192, 205, 217, 267, 270, 271, 281, 292–4, 297, 300, 302, 306–9, 322, 325, 326, 329, 332, 349, 360. *See also* fornication
  law for and punishment 130, 148, 149, 165, 182, 185, 192, 199, 204, 210, 217, 248, 269, 272, 292–5, 307, 308, 326, 332, 350, 351

priests/clerics   25, 45, 74, 86, 98,
        110, 113, 118, 120, 124,
        127–8, 144, 147, 148,
        150–1, 165–8, 184, 197,
        199, 202, 203, 233, 235,
        248, 249, 253, 254, 267,
        270, 286–8, 322, 323, 331,
        334, 338, 377, 388, 391. *See
        also* monks; nuns
    celibacy   68, 86, 124, 126, 167–8,
        295–6 (*see also* celibacy)
    concubinages of   167–9, 286,
        309, 330–1, 338 (*see also*
        concubines/concubinages)
    marriage   167, 286–8
procreation   27, 31, 44, 107, 110–11,
        121, 128–9, 133, 147, 154,
        163, 171, 175, 177, 181,
        185, 196, 205, 208, 209,
        240, 241, 266, 275, 277,
        278, 281, 288, 290, 297,
        301, 305, 306, 377, 394,
        395. *See also* birth/childbirth;
        fertility
promiscuity   27, 33, 37, 44, 75,
        86, 92, 109, 112, 120, 211,
        213–14, 216, 218, 219,
        272, 300, 318, 325, 333,
        360, 384
prostitutes   33–41, 54–8, 85–95,
        111, 115, 137–44, 214–15,
        329–52. *See also* courtesans;
        hetaeras
    abortion   41–2, 230, 348
    in Bologna   340–1
    Christians thought of   138–44,
        214–16, 229–34, 281, 292
    clients for   24, 28, 31, 39, 67, 87,
        89–90, 233–5, 318, 334,
        344–7, 351–2
    codes/colors of   73, 85, 220–5,
        228–30, 232, 275, 339
    contraception   42, 86, 89, 230,
        231, 315, 348
    exclusion from religious rites   86
    in Greek *polis*   33–4
    identity/subjectivity   232–3
    in literature/pictures   46, 48, 90,
        243, 374–6, 378–9

    love magic and sexual
        initiation   342–3
    marriage   50, 87–8, 219, 298
    mut'a (temporary marriage)   328,
        350
    as necessary evil   142, 214
    number of   227, 234
    pimps for   37, 39, 86, 87, 89 (*see
        also* pimps)
    pornographiae   236
    prices/wages/daily tax on   39, 41,
        88, 90, 92, 220, 223, 243,
        338, 347–8
    reasons to engage in sex work   37,
        214–15, 225–7
    recruitment and spread of   225–8
    Reformation   229–34, 334
    reformed or converted
        sinners   216–17, 336–7
    sexually transmitted diseases/
        venereal diseases   42–3, 54,
        87, 231, 329–30, 352, 353,
        355, 359–60
    sexual services/knowledge of   40,
        71, 72, 87–9, 343
prostitution   33–41, 54–8, 85–95,
        111, 137–44, 213, 329–52.
        See also brothels
    Athenian   38–41
    in Bologna   340–1
    in city of York   220–1
    clandestine   221, 226–9, 233–4,
        331, 338
    court cases of Geneva   332, 333
    cultic/sacred   45–6
    definition of/terms   33–4, 43, 85,
        213–14, 227
    districts/places of   34, 39, 41, 48, 86,
        87, 89–91, 206, 213, 220–5,
        227, 330, 335–42, 352, 393
    forced   142, 215, 226, 227, 320
    intersection of   43–5
    invisible/visible   48, 80–1, 220–5,
        339–42
    laws against/on/penance   38, 65,
        78, 86, 92, 142, 149, 165,
        189, 216–18, 220–5, 235,
        270, 273, 328, 329, 334–6,
        340–2, 349–51

male same-sex   54–8, 93–5, 101, 111, 250, 255–8, 265, 281, 396–8
  in military   91
  in Ottoman Empire   328, 349–52
  in Pompeii   87–90
  Porneia as the evil of   137–8
  registration   87–8
  of slaves   38–41, 43, 45, 63, 86, 89, 111, 131, 202, 204, 215, 228
protestant/s   18, 238, 271, 276, 287, 289–93, 295, 297, 299, 300, 302, 303, 316–18, 329, 334–6, 348, 355, 378, 391, 394, 395
pudicitia   67, 78, 100, 144
pueri   99
Puff, Helmut   395
Pythagoras   24, 26, 42

rabbis   110–11, 206, 208–10, 301
Rabelais, François   380–2
race, and sexuality   163, 211–12, 320, 324, 357, 386
Ragionamenti (Reasonable Discussions, Aretino)   373–5, 402
Ragionamento della Nanna e della Antonia (Aretino)   374
Raimondi, Marcantonio   369, 370, 372
Ranke-Heinemann, Uta   130–1
rape   30–1, 69, 73, 78–80, 86, 91, 126, 131, 157, 159–60, 183, 191–5, 207, 227, 271, 310–15, 394
  in Byzantium   193
  court cases/records   192, 194, 312–14
  gang   313
  law   78–9, 86, 100, 126, 141, 148, 179, 192–3, 270, 294, 310–11
  military   91, 100, 131, 157, 227, 250
  penalties/punishment for   69, 191–5, 310–11, 327
  pregnant   69, 162–3

Rastbüchlein (Lindener)   380
red light district   41, 42, 47, 56, 93, 221, 224, 229, 336, 392. See also prostitution, districts/places of
Reiss, Ben   242
Rembrandt   367–9
Richlin, Amy   69, 103
Roelens, Jonas   261
Roman d'Eneas   247–8
Romano, Giulio   365
Roper, Lyndal   348, 392
Rubens, Peter Paul   366
Rufus of Ephesus   77
Russia   200
Rütiner, Johannes   276
Rycaut, Paul   397
Rykener, John   233

sacramental marriage   61, 129, 165, 166, 170, 178, 195, 289, 296, 297, 374
sacred prostitution   45–6
Said, Edward   17
sailors   225, 345, 352, 388, 391
same-sex sexuality   6–7, 13, 50–60, 93–104, 132–7, 248–67, 387–403. See also homosexual/homosexuality
Same-Sex Unions (1994, Boswell)   136–7
Sapphic love   58–60
Sapsford, Tom   58
Saracens   211–12
savages   324–5, 356, 391
Savonarola, Girolamo   281, 387
Schaydung ains eevolks   245
Schnell, Rüdiger   151
scholasticism   177–8, 195, 292, 322
scrota   85, 89
Second Lateran Council (1139)   170
seduction   16, 20, 27, 29, 30, 32, 33, 36, 48, 51, 55, 79, 80, 91, 110, 115, 130, 133, 138, 142, 151, 158, 167, 183, 191, 209, 212, 217, 236, 247, 249, 263, 282, 291, 308–10, 326, 340, 361, 364, 367, 368, 376, 378, 401

seed   23, 26, 29, 32, 68, 69, 71, 72,
    87, 89, 97, 109, 133, 146,
    159–63, 175, 176, 178, 198,
    205, 208, 231, 252, 254,
    278–80, 290, 301, 315, 322,
    323, 348, 355, 388, 400
self-pleasure. *See* masturbation
Self-portrait as a naked man
    (Dürer)   371
Selim II, Sultan   350
sellarii   93
Seneca the Elder   86, 95
Seneca the Younger   66, 77, 93
Sercambi, Giovanni   195
şeriat (*scharī'a*-Sharia law)   326–8,
    396
servants   35, 56, 62, 95, 136, 157,
    180, 192, 194, 225–7, 235,
    240, 259, 270, 271, 291, 294,
    295, 304, 306, 307, 313, 318,
    320, 342, 386, 388, 389, 399
sexual desire   2, 7–9, 26, 69–70, 76–7,
    81, 106, 109–16, 121, 123,
    125, 129–34, 138, 139, 143,
    159–64, 177, 178, 205, 208,
    210–12, 217, 236, 237, 241,
    261, 263, 265, 282–3, 290–1,
    300, 301, 362, 366–7, 383,
    395, 402
sexual differences, in Jews and
    Christian   209–10
sexual division, of Christendom   124–5
sexual intercourse. *See* coitus/sexual
    intercourse
sexual lust. *See* sexual desire
sexually transmitted diseases   42–3,
    54, 87, 219, 231, 329–30,
    344, 345, 352–61
shadow plays (*Karagöz*)   383–4
Shakespeare, William   2, 385
shame/shameless   9, 29, 31, 48, 58, 67,
    73, 79–82, 92, 105, 127, 131,
    133, 134, 142–4, 148, 158,
    176, 180–2, 189, 195, 236–41,
    255, 276, 280, 290, 331, 349,
    362, 364, 365, 370, 371, 385,
    387, 391, 393, 396, 401
  penalties of   201, 255, 271,
    298–300, 308, 318, 336

sheela-na-gig figures   239
Shorter, Edward   283
Sibote   174
silphium   42
Silver, Morris   45
sin   114–17, 127–30, 136, 140–1,
    144, 146–8, 152, 159,
    167, 177–8, 185, 187, 196,
    198, 200, 203, 205, 215,
    217, 219, 236, 239, 248,
    251–7, 261–7, 281, 290,
    292, 297, 302, 318, 331,
    349, 353–4, 388, 391,
    394–5, 401
  against nature/*sodomia*/sodomy
    136, 181, 251–6, 261–7, 391,
    394–5, 401
  original sin   127, 129, 130, 178,
    200, 215, 217
Skinner, Marilyn B.   58
slaves   22, 25, 30, 34–8, 41, 43, 55,
    64, 67, 73, 74, 87–9, 95,
    96, 98–101, 137, 140, 141,
    144, 155, 157, 179, 186,
    193, 201–4, 215, 218, 220,
    228, 229, 262, 313, 320,
    324, 326, 349, 350, 354,
    386, 391
  female   41, 67, 96, 202–4,
    215, 220, 228, 320, 324,
    350
  marriage   64, 102
  prostitution of   38–41, 43, 45, 63,
    86, 89, 111, 131, 202, 204,
    215, 228
Slavic laws   199
The Sleeping Danaë (Goltzius)   368
social construction of sexuality   3–6
social discipline measures   299–300
Socrates   53–4
sodomia (sodomy)   132–7, 149, 207,
    212, 216, 221, 233, 250–61,
    263, 265–7, 269, 272, 310,
    340, 364, 387, 389–95,
    397, 401. *See also* same-sex
    sexuality
  as sin   136, 181, 251–6, 261–7,
    391, 394–5, 401
Turks   397

INDEX

sodomites 6, 83, 181, 194, 207, 212, 216, 221, 233, 250–61, 266, 375, 387
   court cases 388–90
   identifying 255–8
   Norwegian Penal Code 388
   Sweden's Supplementary Law 387
soldiers. *See* military/warrior/soldiers
Sommerlieder (Summer Songs, Neidhart) 172, 243–4
Sonetti lussuriosi (pleasure sonnets, Aretino) 372–3
Soranus of Ephesus 27, 42, 68, 72
sperm. *See* seed
Spiegel des Sünders (*Sinner's Mirror*) 272
spintriae 93
spiritual impurity 200, 203, 252. *See also* impurity
spiritual marriages 128, 291
sponsa Christi 122
Statues of Aphrodite 33
Statute of Westminister 192
Stoicism 75–6
Stone, Lawrence 283
Strabo 45, 52
street prostitution. *See* prostitution, districts/places of
students 55, 56, 223, 233, 234, 304, 343, 345, 347, 380, 396
subjectivation. *See* identity/subjectivity
Süleyman I 327
Susanna and the Elders (Tintoretto) 367
Symonds, John Addington 58–9
Symposium (Plato) 2, 21–2, 53–4
Synod of Elvira 126, 135
syphilis 219, 329, 344, 345, 352–61
   as endemic plague 359–61
   mercury cure 357–61
   pox houses 357–60

Tacitus 87–8, 93
talâk 327–8
Taranta, Valescus de 278
Tertullian 121–3, 138, 142–3
Theodosian Code 137
Theopompus of Chios 44
Thomas of Chobhams 213, 214

Thorp, John 57
Timaeus of Tauromenium 48
Timarchus 54–5
Tintoretto 367
Titian 367, 368, 373
Traub, Valerie 261
Treponema pallidum 352, 354
triba
   costums and rites 44, 51, 206, 390
   laws 155–6, 186
tribas/*tribades* 59, 77, 95–6, 98, 395, 399–402. *See also* female same-sex sexuality

Ulpianus, Domitius 86
(un)chastity. *See* chastity
Under der linden (von der Vogelweide) 172
unión de barraganía (non-marital concubinage) 165
unnatural fornication 253, 254, 258, 262, 282, 292, 387, 395
unspeakable sin 136, 181, 394–5
uterus 26, 42, 69, 71–2, 161, 163, 176, 179, 186, 231, 232, 263, 278–80, 306, 316, 355, 382, 400

vagina/vaginal 2, 6, 8, 32, 40, 42, 49, 70, 72, 88, 170, 180, 200, 209, 232, 233, 258, 288, 310, 316, 348, 359, 376, 399. *See also* penetration
Valla, Lorenzo 281
van Eyck, Jan 364
vase paintings 24, 34–5, 40, 47–50, 53
Västgöta laws 185, 190
Västmanna law 193
Velazquez, Diego 368
venereal diseases. *See* sexually transmitted diseases
Venus 2, 8, 69–71, 75, 79, 81, 86, 136, 236, 242, 362–4, 367, 368, 373, 385. *See also* Aphrodite
Venus and Adonis (Shakespeare) 2, 385
Venus figurines/pictures 75, 81, 363, 367, 368, 373

Venus of Urbino (Titian) 373
Vesalius, Andreas 279
Vincent of Beauvais 161
violence 5, 31, 32, 38–40, 46, 52, 56, 70, 73, 79–80, 100, 113, 131, 133, 136, 157, 159, 173–4, 179, 180, 183, 190–4, 205, 207, 214, 232, 234, 243, 272, 283, 308, 310–15, 319, 326, 366–7, 373, 385, 386, 391, 394. *See also* rape
virginity/virgins 25, 27, 63, 67–8, 70, 100, 109, 114, 119, 121–8, 131, 135, 138, 142–3, 148, 153, 156, 161, 169, 178–82, 189, 192–4, 199, 205, 208, 210, 248, 264, 271, 274, 276, 296, 308, 310, 312, 319, 333, 343, 357, 378, 382
  Church Fathers 127–30
Virgin Mary 113–14, 122, 127, 128, 138, 159, 178, 193, 200, 241, 242, 296, 371
virility 23, 49, 51, 64, 70, 75–7, 98, 100, 113, 116, 121, 131, 182
virtue (*virtus*) 11, 21, 26, 54, 63, 65, 67, 74, 78, 93, 130, 282, 285, 333, 374, 402
von der Vogelweide, Walther 172
vulva 8, 212, 239, 240, 274, 321, 362, 370, 402

Warren Cup 101
Weinsberg, Hermann von 343
whores. *See* prostitutes
widows 22, 29, 35, 38, 68, 92, 100, 128, 140, 147, 160, 165, 204, 206, 226, 248, 284, 306, 310, 313, 327, 338, 360, 366
William of Conches 159
Williams, Graig 103
Winkler, John J. 31, 57
witchcraft/witches 239, 263, 264, 322–3, 342–3, 348, 371–2
Wollust 291
The Women's Bath (Dürer) 368
workers. *See* laborers
Württemberg marriage regulations 293, 302
Wyatt, David 220
Wyclif, John 254

Xenarchus 41
Xenophon 28, 32, 53

yetzer hara 109–11

Zimmern, Froben Christoph von 399
Zimmern Chronicle (Zimmern) 399–400
zina 204, 326–7, 349–51
Zwingli, Ulrich 292, 294, 392
Zwinglians 287, 392

Printed in the USA
CPSIA information can be obtained
at www.ICGtesting.com
LVHW020805171024
794058LV00003B/80